The Internationalization
of Equity Markets

A National Bureau
of Economic Research
Project Report

The Internationalization of Equity Markets

Edited by Jeffrey A. Frankel

The University of Chicago Press

Chicago and London

JEFFREY A. FRANKEL is professor of economics at the University of
California, Berkeley, and a research associate of and director for
international finance and macroeconomics at the National Bureau of
Economic Research.

The University of Chicago Press, Chicago 60637
The University of Chicago Press, Ltd., London

Library of Congress Cataloging-in-Publication Data

The internationalization of equity markets / edited by Jeffrey A.
   Frankel.
       p.   cm.—(A National Bureau of Economic Research project
report)
   "The papers were originally presented at a conference held in San
Francisco on October 1–2, 1993"—Pref.
   Includes bibliographical references and index.
   1. Securities—Congresses.   2. International finance—Congresses.
3. Stock-exchange—Congresses.   4. Portfolio management—Congresses.
5. Investments, Foreign—Congresses.   I. Frankel, Jeffrey A.
II. Series.
HG4508.I57   1994
332.63'2—dc20   94-25987
                                                                CIP

⊗ The paper used in this publication meets the minimum requirements of
the American National Standard for Information Sciences—Permanence
of Paper for Printed Library Materials, ANSI Z39.48-1984.

Relation of the Directors to the
Work and Publications of the
National Bureau of Economic Research

1. The object of the National Bureau of Economic Research is to ascertain and to present to the public important economic facts and their interpretation in a scientific and impartial manner. The Board of Directors is charged with the responsibility of ensuring that the work of the National Bureau is carried on in strict conformity with this object.

2. The President of the National Bureau shall submit to the Board of Directors, or to its Executive Committee, for their formal adoption all specific proposals for research to be instituted.

3. No research report shall be published by the National Bureau until the President has sent each member of the Board a notice that a manuscript is recommended for publication and that in the President's opinion it is suitable for publication in accordance with the principles of the National Bureau. Such notification will include an abstract or summary of the manuscript's content and a response form for use by those Directors who desire a copy of the manuscript for review. Each manuscript shall contain a summary drawing attention to the nature and treatment of the problem studied, the character of the data and their utilization in the report, and the main conclusions reached.

4. For each manuscript so submitted, a special committee of the Directors (including Directors Emeriti) shall be appointed by majority agreement of the President and Vice Presidents (or by the Executive Committee in case of inability to decide on the part of the President and Vice Presidents), consisting of three Directors selected as nearly as may be one from each general division of the Board. The names of the special manuscript committee shall be stated to each Director when notice of the proposed publication is submitted to him. It shall be the duty of each member of the special manuscript committee to read the manuscript. If each member of the manuscript committee signifies his approval within thirty days of the transmittal of the manuscript, the report may be published. If at the end of that period any member of the manuscript committee withholds his approval, the President shall then notify each member of the Board, requesting approval or disapproval of publication, and thirty days additional shall be granted for this purpose. The manuscript shall then not be published unless at least a majority of the entire Board who shall have voted on the proposal within the time fixed for the receipt of votes shall have approved.

5. No manuscript may be published, though approved by each member of the special manuscript committee, until forty-five days have elapsed from the transmittal of the report in manuscript form. The interval is allowed for the receipt of any memorandum of dissent or reservation, together with a brief statement of his reasons, that any member may wish to express; and such memorandum of dissent or reservation shall be published with the manuscript if he so desires. Publication does not, however, imply that each member of the Board has read the manuscript, or that either members of the Board in general or the special committee have passed on its validity in every detail.

6. Publications of the National Bureau issued for informational purposes concerning the work of the Bureau and its staff, or issued to inform the public of activities of Bureau staff, and volumes issued as a result of various conferences involving the National Bureau shall contain a specific disclaimer noting that such publication has not passed through the normal review procedures required in this resolution. The Executive Committee of the Board is charged with review of all such publications from time to time to ensure that they do not take on the character of formal research reports of the National Bureau, requiring formal Board approval.

7. Unless otherwise determined by the Board or exempted by the terms of paragraph 6, a copy of this resolution shall be printed in each National Bureau publication.

(Resolution adopted October 25, 1926, as revised through September 30, 1974)

Contents

Preface

This volume contains eight papers examining the world's increasingly integrated equity markets, and the corresponding discussants' comments. The papers were originally presented at a conference held in San Francisco, California, on October 1–2, 1993. A preconference, held in Cambridge, Massachusetts, in July 1993, helped to keep everyone on track.

On behalf of the National Bureau of Economic Research, I would like to thank the Ford Foundation for its financial support of this project. I would also like to thank Martin Feldstein for asking me to undertake the project, Rob Shannon and Kirsten Foss Davis for their usual efficient help, and the participants for obeying a rigorous time schedule that allowed speedy publication of the volume.

Introduction

Jeffrey A. Frankel

The internationalization of equity markets encompasses the intersection of three important trends. The first trend is relevant even to the United States, where, as in the United Kingdom, equity markets have long been a dominant part of the financial system. Here the trend is increasing *integration* with the rest of the world, as American investors look abroad, foreign investors buy U.S. equities, and prices on the New York Stock Exchange become increasingly linked with those in London, Tokyo, and around the world. By 1993, for example, American holdings of foreign stocks had reached $210 billion, more than double the level of 1990.

The second trend is particularly relevant to countries such as Japan, Germany, and France, where equity markets have not in the past been as developed or active. It is *securitization,* defined as increased reliance of the financial system on markets in equities and bonds at the expense of banks and other financial intermediaries. In 1989, the capitalization of the stock market in Japan, for example, surpassed that of the U.S. market.[1] World stock market capitalization for developed countries exceeded $10 trillion in 1991, quadruple the nominal level of ten years earlier.

The third trend is particularly relevant to newly industrializing countries, though it, like the first two trends, can also be identified with other sorts of countries. It is the *opening* of national financial systems to international finan-

Jeffrey A. Frankel is professor of economics at the University of California, Berkeley, and a research associate of and director for international finance and macroeconomics for the National Bureau of Economic Research.

The author thanks Stijn Claessens, Charles Engel, Wayne Ferson, Gikas Hardouvelis, Campbell Harvey, and other conference participants for comments on the introduction, and the Ford Foundation for research support under its Initiative in International Economics and Development.

1. The crossover appears to have occurred earlier, if one does not adjust the Japanese stock market for cross-holdings. Using either basis of comparison, the U.S. market regained the lead soon thereafter.

cial flows and institutions, as governments remove capital controls and other barriers. Foreign holdings of equities in emerging markets have been estimated to have risen as high as $160 billion by the end of 1993, compared to only $2 billion seven years earlier. Part of this phenomenal rate of growth is attributable to large increases in market prices. New purchases of equities from developing countries are still smaller than the volume of gross flows among industrialized countries. They are bound, however, to play an increasingly important role in the financial development of the recipient countries.[2]

An increasingly integrated, securitized, and open world financial system suggests important questions, and offers a rich set of data with which to attempt to answer them. Some of these questions are new ones raised by the international environment itself. What are the gains to international diversification, for example, from the viewpoint of a U.S. investor? To what extent are markets in fact now integrated across countries? Do investors still exhibit an unexplained home-country bias, despite the degree of globalization that has taken place? What is the role of the specific times and locations around the world at which stocks are traded?

Other questions are versions of questions of longstanding interest in the context of domestic equity markets. Are the markets efficient? Are expected returns determined in world markets by variances, covariances, and the price of risk as suggested by the capital asset pricing model (CAPM)? If not, what is the correct alternative model? To answer these questions we will also have to ask, What is the appropriate international version of the CAPM, or of other models of asset pricing that have been developed in the domestic context?

Most less-developed countries have previously been "financially repressed" and partially closed off from world financial markets. What are the effects when such countries liberalize and open up to foreign investors? Do the theoretical gains from trade across time and across states of nature in fact show up in the data? How can one disentangle the extent to which fundamental shocks in such economies are independent of those in industrialized economies (offering a valuable opportunity for diversification) and the extent to which barriers continue to segment the markets? Have country funds offered an effective first wedge into markets where barriers still prevent foreign investors from entering freely?

These are some of the questions this volume seeks to address. Many of them have until recently been underexplored, sufficiently so that it is possible to make relatively tangible progress.

---

2. Claessens and Rhee (chap. 5 in this volume) give some figures for 1989–1992. A third of the flow over the four-year period took place via country funds.

Part I: Asset Pricing and Home-Country Bias in Internationally Integrated Markets

Limitations of the Existing Literature

Models of equity pricing have been the centerpiece of the finance field over the last twenty-five years. The literature has continued to develop rapidly in a technical sense. Such innovations as allowing variation over time in first and second moments of returns (that is, in expected rates of return, variances, and covariances) are very important if one hopes to be able to capture a world of changing realities. In other respects, however, the research has not entirely kept pace with some of the major phenomena in world markets that need to be addressed.

Two shortcomings of standard tests of asset-pricing models have been known for a long time, but have become even more important as equity markets have become internationalized. More than fifteen years ago, Richard Roll (1977) emphasized the importance in tests of the CAPM of using as comprehensive a set of assets as possible. Today, a majority of tests conducted by American researchers leave out other countries' assets entirely. Other tests conducted by international financial economists often commit the symmetric sin of concentrating on a sample of countries' bonds, either omitting equities entirely or else simply adding a single equity index such as the Standard and Poor's 500 to the list of assets. Both approaches blithely omit categories of assets that are some of the most important in world markets.

A second shortcoming of the standard tests is that they usually measure all returns in terms of dollars. The implicit assumption is that any asset whose return is fixed in terms of dollars, such as U.S. deposits, is completely safe, and that the risk of other assets can be measured by their correlation with the market basket return expressed in dollars. If U.S. investors were the only ones whose behavior mattered, this assumption would not be too bad at short horizons. Because monthly variability in the U.S. consumer price index is so low—compared to the variability in the prices of stocks, bonds, and foreign exchange—the real value of dollar deposits is almost certain at a horizon of one month or less, from the viewpoint of American investors.

U.S. investors, however, are not the only ones in the market, either the market for U.S. stocks or the market for foreign stocks. Just as American investors find dollar assets less risky than deutsche mark or yen assets, so do Japanese investors find yen assets less risky and German residents find mark assets less risky. If major stock markets are integrated, then the behavior of each nationality of investors who participate in this integrated global market is relevant. More precisely, in market equilibrium, each investor nationality should be weighted by the size of its total portfolio. The weight has been shifting away from U.S. investors. Because U.S. assets abroad are now exceeded by foreigners' assets in the United States, it would be more correct to oversimplify by assuming that the representative global investor in world markets is a foreign resident, than to continue with the old oversimplification of assuming that the representative investor is an American. There is no need, however, for either sort of oversimplification.

If purchasing power parity (PPP) held among currencies, the proper test would be a simple matter of identifying the price index of the appropriate international basket of goods consumed by investors, and measuring asset returns in terms of it.[3] PPP does not hold in the short run, however, not even approximately. Thus, using a single composite international price index is not much better than using a dollar price index. There is little way around letting investors of different countries behave differently. We will use the phrase "preferred local habitat" to refer to the implication that follows from this failure of PPP: the proposition that investors who live in different countries will use different reference currencies to evaluate what is a safe asset and what is a risky asset.

More than fifteen years after these points were first emphasized,[4] very few modern tests of international asset pricing seriously address them. This refusal by most researchers to allow investors to live in whatever country they choose seems rather intolerant.

Other kinds of heterogeneity of investors across countries are possible as well. One can allow investors to have different degrees of risk aversion, as in Charles Engel's contribution to this volume (chap. 3), or to have different expectations regarding stock market performance, as in French and Poterba (1991). These extensions are probably of a lower priority, however, than allowing for differences in the consumption basket.

International Factors and Rates of Return

The state-of-the-art work of Campbell Harvey (1989, 1991, 1993), alone and together with Wayne Ferson (1993, 1994), addresses some serious shortcomings of the previous literature. It allows expected returns to vary over time by conditioning them on a set of observable instrumental variables, such as dividend yields. It also allows variances to vary over time, for example, by means of the famous ARCH process introduced by Robert Engle and developed in subsequent elaborations, such as Bollerslev, Engle, and Wooldridge (1988). In the technique of Harvey (1991), variances and covariances are also allowed to vary in a general way (somewhat analogously to the way first moments are allowed to vary in a completely unrestricted way in the method used by Charles Engel).

---

3. A classic reference that follows this approach is Grauer, Litzenberger, and Stehle (1976).
4. Solnik (1977) first modeled investors in each country as caring only about returns expressed in their own country's terms, because they consume no foreign goods, and domestic goods prices are nonstochastic. The more general framework in which investors have a home-country bias based on consuption patterns (the "preferred local habitat" model) was developed by Kouri and de Macedo (1978), Dornbusch (1983), and Frankel (1982) in the economics literature, and Stulz (1981a) and Adler and Dumas (1983), a classic survey, in the finance literature.

Many researchers have sought refuge from the mundane realities of CAPM tests—such as the aforementioned difficulty of measuring all assets—by assuming a world of representative agents, each of whom maximizes an (identical) intertemporal expected utility function. The solution is more apparent than real, however, as the theoretical constructs in such models are often even more difficult to measure empirically. Moreover, a representative agent model is clearly inappropriate for addressing our second concern, explained above, heterogeneity of investors across countries. Dumas (1993) has considered the prospects for reconciling this model, which he calls the "orthodox general equilibrium approach," with some of the stylized facts of international finance that concern us in this volume: PPP deviations, home bias in equity preferences, and differences in expected returns across countries. He concludes that the CAPM, which he calls the "heterodox partial-equilibrium approach," is more likely to accommodate these stylized facts.

In recent work, Dumas and Solnik (1993) use instrumental variables similar to Harvey's to condition expected returns, but at the same time seek to move beyond the assumption that all investors live in the United States, to address the issue of preferred local habitats. Their technique for choosing between the international and classical versions of the CAPM allows the data to suggest whether the return on a country's equities is determined by putting weight on correlations with individual currencies, or solely by the correlation with the aggregate market portfolio. In chapter 1 of this volume, Bernard Dumas extends this approach in the direction of addressing what I will call the Summers ketchup critique.

Larry Summers (1985) registered a complaint with research in finance: that it spends all its energies testing, essentially, whether the price of one-quart ketchup bottles bears the hypothesized relationship to the price of one-pint ketchup bottles. Summers was referring to the habit of testing the relationship between the first moment of stock returns and the second moment of stock returns, with no other data beyond stock prices entering the analysis. (One might add that the practice of using lagged stock returns as instrumental variables does little to reduce the circularity.) In a study of the ketchup market, one would hope to explain the price of ketchup in terms of such factors as wages, the price of tomatoes, the income of consumers, the price of hamburgers, the price of mustard, and so on. Similarly, argues Summers, one would hope to be able to explain stock returns in terms of fundamental economic variables.

The Dumas study appearing here dispenses with the variables internal to the financial markets, such as dividend/price ratios, that others have relied on to predict returns. Instead, indicators of real economic activity are used as instrumental variables: for example, housing-start authorizations, increases in manufacturing inventories, the percentage of companies reporting slower deliveries, and other variables found by Stock and Watson (1992) to be important in predicting real activity. Viewed in the light of the Summers ketchup critique of the circularity of the standard approach, the Dumas study is a commendable attempt to relate international equity returns to real economic variables. This line of inquiry is useful even if the real economic variables do not predict returns as well as the financial variables do, although one is reassured to see that these instruments have at least some statistical power. Dumas then tests the international conditional CAPM against the classic conditional CAPM and statistically does not reject the former. He also tests the classic conditional CAPM (against an unspecified alternative), and *does* reject it; so the reader's prior beliefs regarding the CAPM will affect the way he or she wishes to interpret the findings.

Chapter 2 in this volume consists of Wayne Ferson and Campbell Harvey's latest contribution to tests of international asset pricing. They seek to bridge the gap between state-of-the-art finance and practitioners who engage in "asset allocation" based on whatever observable variables seem to be useful for picking stocks.

Like Adler and Dumas (1983) and Dumas and Solnik (1993), they assume that returns on individual assets will be related not only to the return on a world market portfolio (the Morgan Stanley Capital International index),[5] but also to the return on holding a portfolio of G10 currencies. Ferson and Harvey interpret the two coefficients as betas, one on the world stock market portfolio and one on the currency portfolio, and let them vary over time as functions of certain attributes of the national equity markets. The idea is that attributes of the national markets should predict the cross section of future returns only to the extent that differences in the attributes across countries measure differences in the betas. Ferson and Harvey model the betas as functions of three groups of attributes: (*a*) valuation ratios, such as price-to-book value and price-to-cash-flow, (*b*) industrial structure, and (*c*) economic performance measures, such as relative gross national product (GNP) growth and relative inflation.

They test whether these betas are statistically related to expected returns on the assets in question, against a number of ad hoc alternative hypotheses. They do not, however, focus explicitly on second moments to test whether a higher level of risk on an asset requires a higher expected return to induce investors to willingly hold that asset—as in classic tests of the CAPM. The proposition that predictable components of returns must be risk premia is assumed rather than tested.[6] This approach has become the norm in models of risk.[7] As Bruce Lehmann notes, yesterday's "anomalies" of predictability have become today's risk premiums. (Possible alternative interpretations of predictability are considered below, in part II.)

5. They cite Stulz (1984) for the conditions under which a single-beta CAPM based on a world market portfolio holds.
6. Harvey (1989) tests the proposition.
7. Many researchers follow the strategy of, first, developing a complete intertemporal optimization theory, and then—when it comes time to test, and the empirical counterparts of the theoretical "state variables" are nowhere to be found—adopting convenient observable variables as proxies.

There is always a concern that a test of the CAPM is not meaningful because one cannot actually measure the correct benchmark portfolio. The concern has given rise to a tradition of adding in whatever additional factors the researcher thinks might be useful in explaining returns. Ferson and Harvey (1993, 1994) have found oil prices, industrial-country industrial production, and industrial-country inflation rates useful in past work, but do not get very far with them here. The coefficients in cross-sectional regressions of returns on lagged attributes, which should be the factor premia if the attributes measure betas, are only weakly related to premiums for these global risk factors. Ferson and Harvey's tests do suggest that the attributes may be useful for modeling the world equity market and the currency portfolio. Findings that returns on some countries' stocks are related to observable economic factors will always be of interest to practitioners.

Tests of the International CAPM and Home-Country Bias

The contribution to this volume by Engel (and that by Linda Tesar and Ingrid Werner [chap. 4]) tests the international CAPM with a technique that addresses many of the limitations of the existing literature.[8] Like the state-of-the-art finance tests, Engel's test in chapter 3 allows conditional expected returns to vary over time. Unlike these tests, however, the CASE method (Constrained Asset Share Estimation) does not require that the information set upon which investors condition their expectations be limited to a handful of variables observed by the econometrician. Rather, investors' expectations, regardless of what they are based on, can be inferred from their observed asset holdings. Asset stock measures do not have to be introduced extraneously; they are already implicitly present in the standard CAPM measure of the return on the overall market portfolio that everyone uses, as the weights that are used to aggregate individual assets' returns.

The downside of the technique, as Engel admits, is that the second moments must be modeled in an ad hoc way reminiscent of how other studies model the first moments. Variances and covariances must be assumed either to follow some sort of ARCH or GARCH process or to be related to lagged values of observable economic variables, if they are not assumed constant altogether.[9] Of course the same is true of other tests.

8. Some of these attractions were also claimed by the tests in Frankel (1982, 1983, and 1985) and Frankel and Engel (1984). But the technique has in the past included only a limited set of assets—thus being subject to the Roll critique. Furthermore, the four papers cited also required that the variances and covariances be constant over time.

9. The GARCH version of the CASE method has also been tested by Engel and Rodrigues (1989), and Engel, Frankel, Froot, and Rodrigues (1994). The application of the technique by Giovannini and Jorion (1989) added the U.S. stock market to the set of international bonds considered in the earlier papers, and conditioned variances on the level of interest rates. Like the earlier papers, it rejected the CAPM hypothesis. Engel and Rodrigues (1993) included a range of countries' stock markets, and conditioned variances on a set of economic variables like some of the instrumental variables used in the Dumas (chap. 1) and Ferson-Harvey (chap. 2) contributions to the present volume.

A second advantage of the CASE method is that the null hypothesis of the international conditional CAPM is tested against interesting explicit alternative hypotheses. Most notably, it affords a natural test of the CAPM against the Tobin model in which investors balance their portfolios across assets as general functions of expected returns, without necessarily diversifying optimally. One must conclude that this particular alternative hypothesis is of more interest to economists than to finance specialists, however, given the gulf that appears between the two strands in the literature. Other alternative hypotheses that one could imagine, and that are considered by other contributors to this volume, include market segmentation, noise trading, and the possibility that ex ante returns cannot in finite samples reliably be inferred from ex post realizations. Tests are always more interesting with an alternative hypothesis.

A third important advantage is that Engel allows his investors to live in whatever country they choose, like Dumas and Solnik (1993) but unlike most tests. In other words, residents of each country are allowed to have their own asset preferences, and their asset demands are then added up to arrive at the overall market equilibrium. This trick is accomplished by using cumulated data on countries' current account positions, measuring their net investment positions vis-à-vis each other. For example, Japan's wealth increases at the expense of America's when the former runs a current account surplus and the latter a current account deficit.

One of the nested hypotheses tested by Engel, his Model 3, seeks to dispense with the data on national wealths by assuming them constant and allowing their levels to be estimated endogenously. His Model 3 is in fact somewhat like the famous equation (14) of Adler and Dumas (1983), as tested, for example, by Dumas and Solnik (1993) or reproduced here as equation (1) in Dumas's paper. (The main difference is that Dumas estimates betas in the traditional first step of a two-step method, while Engel imposes the CASE constraint in a single estimation procedure. This is a constraint of proportionality between the coefficients in the expected return equation, on the one hand, and the variance-covariance matrix of the error term in the same equation, on the other hand.) Engel finds that his Model 3 performs the worst of all the models he tests. Evidently it is necessary to allow for the fact that countries' shares of world wealth do in fact change over time.

Engel's results offer some relatively clear verdicts on some hypotheses that have been widely pondered. First, he does not reject the hypothesis that the coefficient of risk aversion is equal across countries (Model 2 in section 3.4 of chap. 3). The estimated coefficient of relative risk aversion is approximately 4.0. Second, the special case of ARCH is rejected against the more general GARCH.

Especially noteworthy are the verdicts on some of the hypotheses that are central to the goals of this volume. There is weak evidence (that is, at approximately the 10 percent significance level; see section 3.5 of chap. 3) that the international CAPM has some ability to predict expected returns.[10] Investor heterogeneity appears to be key to the relative success of several versions of the model.[11] Ultimately, however, Engel again rejects the CAPM, because the heterogeneity observed in the data is not quite of the right sort.

Previous results have sounded negative for the international CAPM, but they have been on less firm ground than Engel's. A failure to reject the hypothesis that expected returns are equalized internationally, within the CAPM framework, sounds like bad news for the model; but a failure to reject does not allow one to claim a positive finding. A rejection of CAPM against the more general Tobin alternative also sounds like bad news, but again is somewhat less compelling if the Tobin alternative itself has no explanatory power for expected returns. By paying due attention to a full international array of assets and countries of residence, Engel has been able to reject the constraints of the international CAPM *in favor of a more general alternative that has a particular claim on our interest.* That alternative, the portfolio balance model with an allowance for preferred local habitats, has a particular claim on our interest because it seems to be the only model that has predictive power for asset returns *empirically,* and at the same time follows from a widely used *theory.*[12]

Tesar and Werner in chapter 4 have a more direct way of addressing the failure of the standard tests of the CAPM to allow diversity of investor residence. They work with data on purchases of assets from the balance of payments capital accounts of major countries. Previous researchers have virtually ignored these data. Large measurement errors in the balance of payments data are part of the explanation. Nevertheless there is much to be learned from the data, even with its imperfections, and the authors are to be commended for undertaking this line of research. A good example of the issues that are difficult to analyze without the balance of payments data is precisely the hypothesis of optimal diversification by investors of differing nationalities.

After exploring various patterns in the data, Tesar and Werner use the same technique as Engel to test the CAPM. Instead of aggregating across investors

10. A great many researchers have found an ability to predict expected return differentials using ad hoc predictors. *Within the constraints of the CAPM,* however, previous tests such as Frankel (1982) and Giovannini and Jorion (1989) have been unable to reject the hypothesis that expected returns are equalized across countries. Engel suggests that this may be due to the failure to consider a full set of bonds and equities, or to allow the variances to vary.

11. Thomas and Wickens (1993) apply the CASE method to a portfolio of four countries' bonds and equities. They obtain a rejection of the CAPM, like the earlier studes cited in notes 6 and 7 and other applications of the technique. Their study has all the advantages of Engel's—a reasonably complete international set of assets, time-varying variances, conditional expected returns that can vary freely, an explicit test of the CAPM against an alternative hypothesis—except that it is missing investor heterogeneity.

12. Once again, the portfolio-balance theory has traditionally been of greater interest to economists than to finance specialists. Branson and Henderson (1985) is one survey of the portfolio balance model, with emphasis on the finance perspective. A recent example is Brainard and Tobin (1992).

in different countries of residence, however, they make use of their balance of payments data to examine the behavior of individual nationalities. In the last section of this paper, they concentrate on the asset demands of U.S. investors, due to greater data availability than for other countries. Their test is necessarily only a test of mean-variance efficiency of the portfolios held by American residents, rather than a test of the interntional CAPM hypothesis; but since the latter hypothesis amounts to the proposition that all important investors in the marketplace hold portfolios characterized by mean-variance efficiency, a test of Americans' behavior is certainly a useful piece of information. Like Engel, they are able to reject conditional mean-variance efficiency, against the more general Tobin alternative.

A major motivation for the volume, and especially for Tesar and Werner, is a puzzle that also seems likely to be connected with the statistical rejection of the international CAPM. Investors who reside in different countries are thought to exhibit a bias toward holding home assets. French and Poterba (1991), Golub (1991), and Tesar and Werner (1992) find that there is such a bias in portfolios actually held, notwithstanding the widely noted progress already made in recent years toward the globalization of equity markets. (The data used by Tesar and Werner [1992] for this purpose are the same sort that they use in their contribution to the present volume.) In 1989, U.S. investors reportedly held 94 percent of their stock-market wealth in domestic stocks, Japanese investors held 98 percent, and U.K. investors held 82 percent. In 1990, pension funds in G-7 countries continued to hold more than 90 percent of their assets domestically.[13] Why does not each hold more of the others' equities?[14]

One can readily explain a substantial home-country bias in investors' holdings of short-term bonds, as opposed to equities. The explanation is rational preferences for local currency habitats. Assume a simple model of investors' portfolio allocations based on one-period mean-variance optimization (which is the CAPM). Assume further that goods prices are predetermined in the currency of the country where the good is produced, over a horizon as long as the maturity of the bond. Calculating the optimal portfolio for a given investor, even approximately, is difficult because of sensitivity to expected rates of return, which are difficult to measure precisely. Calculating the *difference* between optimal portfolios held by domestic and foreign residents is much easier, however, assuming that both share the same expectations (and, for simplicity, the same coefficient of risk aversion, as in Engel's results). The reason is that the expectations component of the optimal portfolio share drops out of the difference.

13. Jorion, comment on chapter 4 in this volume.
14. Recent surveys by Dumas (1993) and Obstfeld (1994) each devote sections to this observed bias and its possible explanations.

Let x_A be the share of their portfolio that Americans allocate to U.S. assets and x_G the share of their portfolios that Germans allocate to U.S. assets. Then it can be shown that

$$x_A - x_G = [a_A - a_G]/[1 - 1/\rho],$$

where a_A and a_G are the shares of their consumption that optimally diversified American and German residents, respectively, allocate to U.S. goods, and ρ is the coefficient of relative risk aversion.[15] Intuitively, to the extent that investors are relatively risk-averse ($\rho > 1$), they differ in their portfolio preferences in simple proportion to how they differ in their consumption preferences. The term representing the home-country bias in consumption, $a_A - a_G$, is certainly large in practice. Assume for simplicity that it takes its maximum value of $1 - 0 = 1$. Let us try a value for the coefficient of risk aversion that emerges from Engel's estimates: 4. It follows that the measure of home country bias is relatively large: $x_A - x_G = .75$. If residents of each country in fact hold a mere 10 or 15 percent of their portfolios in foreign bonds, that is fully consistent with optimal diversification ($.85 - .15 = .70 < .75$)! At first glance, home-country bias poses no puzzle.

The puzzle arises in a portfolio that includes equities. To a first approximation, the return on equities is determined as a random draw in the currency of the home country. In other words, in practice this return has a surprisingly low correlation with the exchange rate. There is a substantial correlation of equity returns across countries; Wen-Ling Lui and Takatoshi Ito's contribution to this volume (chap. 7) constitutes the latest piece of evidence on how stock market movements are transmitted from one country to another. The correlation is far from 1, however, which is of course the reason why international equity investment offers a valuable opportunity to diversify.

The key point is that exchange-rate risk is not an impediment to holding foreign equities in the way that it is an impediment to holding foreign bonds. Once investors have given vent to the home-country bias that optimally follows from differences in consumption patterns, in the form of bond portfolios that are relatively undiversified, there is little reason for their equity portfolios to exhibit the same home-country bias. Rather, in theory, American investors should take advantage of the opportunity to diversify by holding approximately the same amount of German equities as German residents hold. They can easily eliminate the gratuitous exchange risk by reducing their holdings of German bonds correspondingly or, equivalently, by selling marks on the forward market. (The prescription to hold foreign equities but hedge the exchange risk has been recommended to portfolio managers as a "free lunch."[16])

---

15. One of many possible examples is Frankel (1983), equations (1) and (3).
16. Perold and Schulman (1988). This prescription, and many of the other conclusions that follow from the one-period mean-variance model, change if investors are obliged to take into consideration longer horizons. See Froot (1993).

Clearly, investors' equity portfolios are in fact less diversified than this. In a framework that allows investors of each country to diversify among countries' stocks and bonds as they will, rejection of the CAPM constraint might be attributed to its implication that investors should exhibit home-country bias only in their bonds, not in their stocks.[17] Tesar and Werner, certainly, infer that there is a significant home-country bias puzzle—which cannot be explained by transactions costs—from their evidence that investors trade a lot on the small fraction of the portfolio that they dedicate to foreign assets. They find that gross transactions volumes are very large compared to the magnitude of the corresponding net transactions volume.

Part II: Emerging Markets, Trading Volume, Location, Taxes, Controls, and Other Imperfections

We have seen that the tests, even those that make full allowance for the range of international assets to be held and the range of countries where investors live, seem consistently to reject the international CAPM hypothesis. Why? One possibility is that investors are sophisticated and markets are efficient, but the CAPM does not hold because the assumptions upon which the simple one-period mean-variance framework depends are not justified. The alternative possibility is that international equity markets fall short, in one way or another, of the ideal of a perfectly integrated efficient market where rationally expected returns correctly price risk and investors are able to optimize fully. There are (at least) three ways that markets could fall short of the ideal, all involving an extra degree of heterogeneity arising from such factors as imperfect information. Investor heterogeneity must always be with us; otherwise it would be difficult to explain the high volume of transactions in the equities markets. But it arises more forcefully in a global context than in the domestic context. I have in mind an extra degree of heterogeneity beyond the mere fact of different national consumption baskets considered above.

First, integration may still be far from perfect, due to remaining taxes, regulations, legal differences, and imperfect transmittal of information across countries, segmenting some countries' markets from the world market. Such barriers may be the explanation for observed home-country bias. Second, because markets are not perfectly liquid, there may be a relevant dichotomy between "liquidity traders" and "informed traders." Third, in a world of imperfect information, some investors may make worse use of the available information than others. So-called noise traders may undergo waves of optimism or pessi-

17. Engel tests the version of the international CAPM that does not allow any home-country bias in equities whatsoever, which is a particularly extreme version of the model, the Solnik form, in which investors are assumed to consider the home currency completely safe, because they are assumed to consume no foreign goods whatsoever. There is room for generalization of the test here to allow for some uncertainty in the investor's home-currency consumer price index, but a different result seems unlikely.

mism regarding investments in particular countries. Each of these three possibilities would be a departure from the Efficient Markets Hypothesis. They each play a role in the second half of the volume.

Segmentation and Emerging Markets

Imperfect integration, as a deviation from the Efficient Markets Hypothesis, is a possibility even in the case of industrialized countries.[18] Japan, for example, had heavy restrictions on foreign stock ownership as recently as 1979, and legal and information differences may still be disinducements to cross-border investment.

Imperfect integration is most evident, however, in the case of less-developed countries (LDCs). Many LDCs have undergone financial liberalization in recent years, spurring a boom in emerging markets. As these countries remove explicit barriers to cross-border investment, they incidentally provide us with convenient experimental data on which to try out tests of segmentation versus integration. This underexplored area promises much exciting research.[19]

Studies of the extent of segmentation have been challenged by the difficulty of disentangling the implications of barriers to integration from the implications of independent economic shocks across countries. While the extent of independence of shocks provides an important *incentive* for cross-border investments and the extent of barriers provides an important *obstacle,* both can show up empirically in the same way: as a relatively low correlation between emerging markets and markets in industrialized countries. One approach is to divide countries into subsamples, according to whether their markets are known to be open at a particular time. Usually, however, liberalization is more of a gradual continuous process, rather than a one-time complete event.

Stijn Claessens and Moon-Whoan Rhee, in chapter 5, study the process of opening by less-developed countries by making use of some interesting new indexes on the degree of foreign "investability" computed by the International Finance Corporation (IFC). They build on a standard test of segmentation in which returns on a countries' equities could either obey the CAPM vis-à-vis the world market portfolio (if the markets are integrated) or vis-à-vis the domestic portfolio alone (if markets are segmented). They reject the hypothesis of complete integration for ten out of sixteen countries. For most of the countries they are not able to reject the opposite polar case of complete segmentation. On the other hand, their results are favorable to integration for more countries than has been the case in past studies on pre-1988 data sets, suggesting that the degree of integration has increased over time.

They then test an equation in which individual returns are determined by the world market beta plus the extra local portfolio beta *interacted* with the IFC

18. Stulz (1981b) and Errunza and Losq (1985) are examples of the theory and testing, respectively, of segmented equity markets.
19. Many of the authors working on this subject have recently been brought together by Claessens and Gooptu (1993).

investability index (which runs on a scale from 0 to 1). This seems like a test well specified to distinguish the effects of segmentation from the inherent correlation of countres' economic disturbances. Yet the results are poor. Only when they look for an effect of the investability index on the *level* of price/earnings ratios, as opposed to the *rate of return,* do they find statistically significant effects: the higher a country's degree of investability, the greater the effective demand for its stocks and the higher their prices.

Claessens and Rhee suspect that the source of their difficulty in finding meaningful effects on rates of return is that ex post price changes are a very noisy indicator of ex ante expectations. Specifically, if a country starts off with some degree of segmentation, and then liberalizes during the sample period, its equity prices should rise at the same time. Investors in this country will have experienced capital gains during the sample period, as compared to another country that retains a high level of capital controls throughout. The first country shows a higher return during the sample, even though the ex ante required rate of return should in theory be higher in the second country. The lesson is that small-sample statistical tests that are implicitly based on an assumption of stationary structure are likely to go awry if used to study a period of structural change. This is an example of a failure of the rational expectations methodology, as distinct from the hypothesis of rational expectations or efficient markets *per se,* that plagues much empirical work throughout the finance field.

The Location and Volume of Trading

Usually in the study of equity markets, we abstract from issues regarding the volume of trading and the location of the trading. It is interesting to reflect, however, that the volume of the day's equity transactions in London, New York, or Tokyo is the economic statistic that the audience of the CNN network and other information outlets apparently finds one of the most important. (Most reported is the day's change in the stock market price index.)

What determines whether a given trade takes place in one financial center or another? The location of the financial industry is not deeply rooted in fundamentals of comparative advantage. In chapter 6, John Campbell and Kenneth Froot study the role of taxes on securities transactions. They examine two kinds of taxes: one in effect in Sweden, which is essentially a tax on domestic brokerage services, and another in effect in the United Kingdom, which is a tax on the legal transfer of ownership of U.K. equities. They find that both kinds of taxes lead to significant responses in the form of a fall in domestic trading. The response can involve either a shift of the same transactions offshore (though this is not an option in the U.K. case), a substitution into other similar (but untaxed) assets, or a decline in trading altogether.

Such research naturally has important implications for the securities industry itself, and potentially for public policy as well. The motivation of countries with securities transactions taxes is usually simply to raise revenue. The Swedish tax might be judged successful if its goal were to reduce the "excessive income" of securities traders. The U.K. tax might be judged successful if its goal were to reduce the volume of trading in particular U.K. assets, for example, under the theory that "excessive trading" leads to "excessive volatility." Campbell and Froot conclude, however, that proposals to tax securities transactions as a source of tax revenue are less likely to be successful, unless perhaps the taxes can be imposed worldwide so as to prevent traders from shifting offshore.

The transactions tax experiment shows that relatively large shifts in the location of trading can result from relatively small changes in the cost of trading. (Similar implications presumably follow from other elements of trader costs, such as rents, telecommunications costs, and salaries of lawyers and translators.) The conclusion does not rule out the possibility, however, that the location and volume of trading are irrelevant to the determination of securities prices, beyond the epsilon-width band of arbitrage created by such costs. If location and trading volume are to have broader implications for securities prices, it is likely that imperfect information will have to play a role. It is considered below.

Timing around the globe—for example, the closing of New York markets at 4:00 P.M. (EST) and the opening of Tokyo markets approximately three or four hours later (9:30 A.M. Japan time)—offers a natural experiment to help answer a number of questions. Several researchers have noted the strengthened links between foreign markets and the U.S. market, particularly in the October 1987 crash and subsequently.[20] In chapter 7, Lin and Ito focus on the interrelation of price movements, volatility clusters, and trading volumes, between the New York and Tokyo markets. They consider trading volume a possible proxy for heterogeneous beliefs, since investors would not trade if all were identical. This study makes a contribution to the literature on correlation across markets, by testing under what circumstances the correlation is higher than others. It also makes a contribution to the literature on trading volumes, by testing the effects from one market to the next.

Lin and Ito consider two competing hypotheses regarding correlation across markets. The first is that markets are imperfectly liquid, so that when a "liquidity trader" wishes to sell a stock in a hurry, he or she is obliged to give up a bit of return, which goes to the other class of traders ("informed traders") as compensation. A testable implication of this hypothesis is attributed to Campbell, Grossman, and Wang (1993): that a temporary upsurge in trading volume should cause a temporary decrease in returns, followed by a rebound in the subsequent period (i.e., negative autocorrelation). Lin and Ito, however, after looking in vain for evidence that trading volume in New York has a negative

---

20. For example, Eun and Shim (1989), King and Wadhwani (1990), and von Furstenberg and Jeon (1989). Shiller, Kon-ya, and Tsutsui (1991) conclude from a systematic study of questionnaires that Japanese traders in the crash were responding in an immediate sense to news about U.S. price movements per se, not to news about economic fundamentals.

effect on the correlation between the New York and Tokyo markets, do not favor this hypothesis.

The competing hypothesis is that Japanese traders correctly infer from New York price movements information that is relevant to the pricing of their own stocks. Lin and Ito find that the correlation across the markets goes up when the volatility in New York goes up, which they think may be evidence in favor of this second hypothesis. It is surprising, however, that the authors find no evidence that volatility in Tokyo is associated with volatility in New York, as they have found in earlier work on the foreign exchange market.[21] There is room for more research on the interaction of these variables. The use of direct data on the dispersion of beliefs among traders, as measured by the standard deviation of survey responses, might help.

Country Funds and Investor Sentiment

Most economists and finance specialists have long found unattractive the hypothesis that an important fraction of investors do not make full use of available information. After a decade of research into observed "anomalies" and some hard-to-explain upswings and crashes, however, there has recently been more serious consideration of the possible role of such factors as fads, bubbles, "noise traders," "feedback traders," and so on.

Gikas Hardouvelis, Rafael La Porta, and Thierry Wizman make a fascinating contribution to this volume in their study of country funds in chapter 8. These funds are well worth studying in their own right, as the leading wedge into some countries' emerging markets. By December 1992, U.S. investors could buy into twenty-six countries through one or more country funds traded on the New York Stock Exchange (NYSE) and American Stock Exchange (AMEX). The funds also offer a remarkable opportunity for one of the clearest tests to date of the Efficient Markets Hypothesis versus the hypothesis that noise traders are important.

It is always difficult to test whether the market price of a stock is equal to its fundamental value, because of the uncertainty regarding what is the correct model of the fundamental value. There is little doubt, however, that the market price of a fixed portfolio of equities ought to be equal to the net asset value of the portfolio, that is, the aggregate of the market prices of the individual stocks. Closed-end country funds are just such fixed portfolios, and yet their prices when traded in New York are observed to differ substantially from their net asset values expressed in dollars.

Previous authors have observed the discrepancy between country funds and their respective net asset values.[22] Hardouvelis, La Porta, and Wizman study

21. Engle, Ito, and Lin (1990) use the term "meteor showers" to describe volatility clusters that persist, not only from one trading day to the next, but from one time zone to the next.
22. For example, Bonser-Neal, Brauer, Neal, and Wheatley (1990) and Diwan, Senbet, and Errunza (1993).

how it moves through time. To summarize briefly the outcome of a systematic and thorough analysis, the New York prices of country funds are observed in the short run to behave far more like the New York prices of other U.S. securities than to behave like the aggregated net asset value of the individual foreign securities that constitute the portfolio. Specifically, when there is a fluctuation in the exchange rate between the dollar and the currency of the local country in question, the country-fund price tends in the short run to follow the dollar, not the local currency. When there is a fluctuation in the price of the world stock market, or small U.S. stocks, again the country-fund price tends in the short run to follow the world portfolio or the U.S. stocks, not its respective local national stock market. Only slowly over time does the price converge to the net asset value as in theory it should right away. The weekly autoregressive coefficient is estimated at .89, for a half-life of five weeks. It is difficult to reconcile this behavior with the hypothesis of an efficient and frictionless world capital market.

Hardouvelis, La Porta, and Wizman interpret the data in terms of a model that allows for the presence of irrational investors, or noise traders. Collectively, these investors swing between being under- and over-optimistic about investment opportunities in particular foreign countries. In this context, the discount or premium on a country fund becomes a measure of the spontaneous pessimism or optimism with which U.S. investors view the country in question, relative to the investors within that same country.

Moreover, the common component of country-fund discounts or premia across all New York-traded funds becomes an aggregate measure of general U.S. sentiment for all foreign countries, relative to local sentiment. A widespread interpretation of the specific timing of the 1982 international debt crisis is that domestic investors in such heavily indebted regions as Latin America became concerned about future prospects of their countries, and moved large amounts of money out, at a time when northern investors were still enthusiastically lending. As one observes the renewed surge of capital into less-developed countries during the period 1990–93, therefore, one should consider whether it is based on a degree of enthusiasm among northern investors that is not shared by the locals, who may be better informed. Hardouvelis, La Porta, and Wizman observe a shift from discount to premium in 1990 in the prices of many country funds, which they attribute to contagious enthusiasm beginning with the fall of the Berlin Wall. It is interesting to note that discounts have particularly diminished or disappeared in Latin America and Central Europe since 1990. (In East Asia, on the other hand, premiums have fallen since 1990, suggesting that their stock market booms may have been led by domestic investors, rather than by foreigners.) One possible interpretation is that discounts and premiums are diminishing everywhere as restrictions are removed and the markets become more efficient. Another, more troublesome, interpretation is that U.S. investors may in 1990 have entered a temporary wave of enthusiasm for countries in Latin America and Central Europe.

In any case, the broadest lesson to be drawn from the country-fund study by Hardouvelis, La Porta, and Wizman is the same as that to be drawn from the other contributions to this volume. International equity markets offer a wealth of new data, unique questions, and useful answers. Empirical studies should not merely treat foreign equities as one more asset to be added to the menu of investments considered by insular U.S. residents. They should, rather, take due account of the diversity of assets offered by countries around the world, the diversity of locales in which the universe of investors live, and the diversity of institutional peculiarities that characterize the markets in which assets and investors are brought together.

References

Adler, Michael, and Bernard Dumas. 1983. International portfolio choice and corporation finance: A survey. *Journal of Finance* 38:925–84.
Bollerslev, T., R. Engle, and J. Wooldridge. 1988. A capital asset pricing model with time-varying covariances. *Journal of Political Economy* 96:116–31.
Bonser-Neal, Catherine, Greggory Brauer, Robert Neal, and Simon Wheatley. 1990. International investment restrictions and closed-end country fund prices. *Journal of Finance* 45:523–47.
Brainard, William, and James Tobin. 1992. On the internationalization of portfolios. *Oxford Economic Papers* 44:533–65.
Branson, William, and Dale Henderson. 1985. The specification and influence of asset markets. In *Handbook of international economics,* eds. Ronald Jones and Peter Kenen, vol. 2. Amsterdam: North-Holland.
Campbell, J., S. Grossman, and J. Wang. 1993. Trading volume and serial correlation of stock returns. *Quarterly Journal of Economics* 108, no. A (November): 905–39.
Claessens, Stijn, and Sudarshan Gooptu, eds. 1993. *Portfolio investment in developing countries.* World Bank Discussion Papers, no. 228. Washington, D.C.: The World Bank.
Diwan, Ishac, Lemma Senbet, and Vihang Errunza. 1993. The pricing of country funds and their role in capital mobilization for emerging economies. PRE Working Paper no. 1058. The World Bank.
Dornbusch, Rudiger. 1983. Exchange risk and the macroeconomics of exchange rate determination. In *The internationalization of financial markets and national economic policy,* eds. R. Hawkins, R. Levich, and C. Wihlborg. Greenwich, Conn.: JAI Press.
Dumas, Bernard. 1993. Partial-equilibrium vs. general-equilibrium models of international capital market equilibrium. Working Paper no. 93-1. Wharton School, University of Pennsylvania.
Dumas, Bernard, and Bruno Solnik. 1993. The world price of exchange rate risk, NBER Working paper no. 4459. Cambridge, Mass.: National Bureau of Economic Research, September.
Engel, Charles, and Anthony Rodrigues. 1989. Tests of international CAPM with time-varying covariances. *Journal of Applied Econometrics* 4:119–38.
———. 1993. Test of mean-variance efficiency of international equity markets. *Oxford Economic Papers* 45:403–21.

Engel, Charles, Jeffrey Frankel, Kenneth Froot, and Anthony Rodrigues. 1994. The constrained asset share estimation (CASE) method: Testing mean-variance efficiency of the U.S. stock market. *Journal of Empirical Finance* 2, no. 1.

Engle, Robert, Takatoshi Ito, and Wen-Ling Lin. 1990. Meteor showers or heat waves? Heteroscedasticity of intra-daily volatility in the foreign exchange market. *Econometrica* 58:525–42.

Errunza, Vihang, and Etienne Losq. 1985. International asset pricing under mild segmentation: Theory and test. *Journal of Finance* 40:105–24.

Eun, C., and S. Shim. 1989. International transmission of stock market movements. *Journal of Financial and Quantitative Analysis* 24:241–56.

Ferson, Wayne, and Campbell Harvey. 1993. The risk and predictability of international equity returns. *Review of Financial Studies* 6:527–66.

———. 1994. Sources of risk and expected returns in international equity markets. *Journal of Banking and Finance*. Forthcoming.

Frankel, Jeffrey. 1982. In search of the exchange risk premium: A six-currency test assuming mean-variance optimization. *Journal of International Money and Finance* 1 (December): 255–74.

———. 1983. Estimation of portfolio-balance functions that are mean-variance optimizing: The mark and the dollar. *European Economic Review* 23, no. 3 (December): 315–27.

———. 1985. Portfolio shares as "Beta-Breakers": A test of CAPM. *Journal of Portfolio Management* 11, no. 4 (summer): 18–23.

Frankel, Jeffrey, and Charles Engel. 1984. Do investors optimize over the mean and variance of real returns? A six currency test. *Journal of International Economics* 17:309–23.

French, Kenneth, and James Poterba. 1991. Investor diversification and international equity markets. *American Economic Review* 81 (May): 222–26.

Froot, Kenneth. 1993. Currency hedging over long horizons: Empirical evidence. Paper presented at NBER Summer Institute, International Finance and Money, July 23, Cambridge, Massachusetts.

Giovannini, Alberto, and Philippe Jorion. 1989. The time variation of risk and return in the foreign exchange and stock markets. *Journal of Finance* 44, no. 2 (June): 307–25.

Golub, Stephen. 1991. International diversification of social and private risk: The U.S. and Japan. Swarthmore College, November. *Japan and the World Economy,* forthcoming.

Grauer, F. L. A., R. H. Litzenberger, and R. E. Stehle. 1976. Sharing rules and equilibrium in an international capital market under uncertainty. *Journal of Financial Economics* 3 (3): 233–56.

Harvey, Campbell. 1989. Time-varying conditional covariances in tests of asset pricing models. *Journal of Financial Economics* 24:289–317.

———. 1991. The world price of covariance risk. *The Journal of Finance* 41:111–57.

———. 1993. Portfolio enhancement using emerging markets and conditioning information. In *Portfolio investment in developing countries,* eds. Stijn Claessens and Sudarshan Gooptu. World Bank Discussion Papers, no. 228. Washington, D.C.: The World Bank.

King, Mervyn, and Sushil Wadhwani. 1990. Transmission of volatility between stock markets. *Review of Financial Studies* 3:5–33.

Kouri, Pentti, and Jorge de Macedo. 1978. Exchange rates and the international adjustment process. *Brookings Papers on Economic Activity* 1:111–50.

Obstfeld, Maurice. 1994. International capital mobility in the 1990s. In *Understanding interdependence: The macroeconomics of the open economy,* ed. Peter Kenen. Princeton, N.J.: Princeton University Press, forthcoming.

Perold, Andre, and Evan Schulman. 1988. The free lunch in currency hedging: Implications for investment policy and performance standards. *Financial Analysts Journal,* May/June, 45–50.

Roll, Richard. 1977. A critique of the asset pricing theory's tests; Part I on past and potential testability of the theory. *Journal of Financial Economics* 4:129–76.

Shiller, Robert, Fomiko Kon-ya, and Yoshiro Tsutsui. 1991. Investor behavior in the October 1987 stock market crash: The case of Japan. *Journal of the Japanese and International Economies* 5, no. 1 (March): 1–13.

Solnik, Bruno. 1974. An equilibrium model of the international capital market. *Journal of Economic Theory* 8 (4): 500–24.

Stock, James, and Mark Watson. 1992. A procedure for predicting recessions with leading indicators: Econometric issues and recent experience. NBER Working Paper no. 4014. Cambridge, Mass.: National Bureau of Economic Research.

Stulz, René. 1981a. A model of international asset pricing. *Journal of Financial Economics* 9:383–406.

———. 1981b. On the effects of barriers to international investment. *Journal of Finance* 36:923–34.

———. 1984. Pricing capital assets in an international setting: An introduction. *Journal of International Business Studies* 15:55–74.

Summers, Lawrence. 1985. On economics and finance. *Journal of Finance* 40, no. 3 (July): 633–35.

Tesar, Linda, and Ingrid Werner. 1992. Home bias and the globalization of securities markets. NBER Working Paper no. 4218. Cambridge, Mass.: National Bureau of Economic Research.

Thomas, S. H., and M. R. Wickens. 1993. An international CAPM for bones and equities. *Journal of International Money and Finance* 12, no. 2 (August): 390–412.

von Furstenberg, George, and B. N. Jeon. 1989. International stock price movements: Links and messages, *Brookings Papers on Economic Activity* 1:125–67.

I Asset Pricing and Home-Country Bias in Internationally Integrated Markets

1   A Test of the International CAPM Using Business Cycles Indicators as Instrumental Variables

Bernard Dumas

1.1   Introduction

Previous work by Dumas and Solnik (1993) has shown that a CAPM which incorporates foreign-exchange risk premia (a so-called international CAPM) is better capable empirically of explaining the structure of worldwide rates of return than is the classic CAPM. The test was performed on the conditional version of the two competing CAPMs. By that is meant that moments of rates of return were allowed to vary over time in relation to a number of lagged "instrumental variables." Dumas and Solnik used instrumental variables which were endogenous or "internal" to the financial market (lagged world market portfolio rate of return, dividend yield, bond yield, short-term rate of interest).

In the present paper, I aim to use as instruments economic variables which are "external" to the financial market, such as leading indicators of business cycles. This is an attempt to explain the behavior of the international stock market on the basis of economically meaningful variables which capture "the state of the economy."

The stock market is widely regarded as the best predictor of itself. A large body of empirical work shows that asset prices are predictors of the future level

Bernard Dumas is on the faculty of the H.E.C. School of Management (France). He also is research professor at the Fuqua School of Business, Duke University, a research associate of the National Bureau of Economic Research, and a research fellow of the Centre for Economic Policy Research and Delta.

Some of the data used in this paper were generously supplied by Lombard Odier, Jim Stock, and the Center for International Business Cycle Research at Columbia University. Sample GMM programs were provided by Wayne Ferson and Campbell Harvey. The author acknowledges their help with thanks. Useful comments were received from Bruno Solnik, Michael Rockinger, and the preconference and conference participants and discussants, especially Jeffrey Frankel, Gikas Hardouvelis, Bruce Lehmann, Richard Lyons, Campbell Harvey, Thierry Wizman, Charles Engel, Wayne Ferson, and Vihang Errunza. Here again, the author is grateful.

of activity or, generally, the future level of economic variables.[1] Several leading indexes of economic activity make use of this property of asset prices.[2]

It may, however, also be true that "external" variables can serve to explain asset returns. Fama and French (1989) show that much of the movement in "internal" variables is related to business conditions; for instance, the term structure spread peaks during recessions. Kandel and Stambaugh (1989) show that expected returns peak at the end of a recession, and Harvey (1991b) shows that the ratio of conditional mean return to variance is countercyclical. We show below that a particular set of leading indicators (which does not include asset prices) predicts the stock markets of four economically developed countries with an in-sample R^2 which is comparable (and in some cases superior) to that of "internal" variables.

From a theoretical standpoint, it should be clear that any intertemporal general-equilibrium model, such as the models of domestic or international business cycles that have appeared recently,[3] would generate asset prices that would be functions of the state variables of the economy. In these models, the conditional expected values of rates of return would be functions of state variables as well. Assuming that the mapping from state variables to asset prices is invertible, conditional expected returns must be functions of asset prices. This explains why the stock market predicts itself; a large enough number of asset prices can serve as proxy variables for the state variables.

In the course of this substitution, however, the model has lost some of its empirical content since the link to the underlying physical economy has been severed. Even if one found that stock returns are related to stock prices in the theoretical way, that would still leave open the question of the contemporaneous relationship of this perfectly working stock market to the economy. Does the stock market move of its own accord or does it remain in line with the conditions of physical production? More is achieved when underlying state variables are identified and expected returns are related to them, than when expected returns are related to asset prices. This paper is a preliminary investigation into the nature of "the state of the economy," as revealed by the behavior of asset returns.

1. Fama and Schwert (1977) show that asset returns predict inflation in the United States. Stambaugh (1988) has extracted the information concerning future economic variables that is contained in bond prices. Several authors have observed that stock prices lead gross national product (GNP): Fama (1981, 1990), Fama and Gibbons (1982), Geske and Roll (1983), and Barro (1990).

2. The list of NBER leading indicators includes, besides exchange rates, (a) the yield on a constant-maturity portfolio of ten-year U.S. Treasury bonds, (b) the spread between the interest rate on six-month corporate paper and the rate on six-month U.S. Treasury bills, and (c) the spread between the yield on a constant-maturity portfolio of ten-year U.S. T-bonds and the yield on one-year U.S. T-bonds. See Stock and Watson (1989). The Department of Commerce list includes, besides money supply, the Standard and Poor's 500 industrials index (see *Survey of Current Business,* current issues).

3. On the international side, see, for example, Backus, Kehoe, and Kydland (1993), Baxter and Crucini (1993), Canova (1993), and Dumas (1992).

Capital asset pricing models can serve as a tool, or sift, in the identification of state variables. First, one finds variables that can serve to condition returns (i.e., that have some power to predict rates of return). Second, one verifies whether the conditional distribution satisfies some asset-pricing restrictions. For instance, can the first moments of returns be made to match time-varying risk premia built on second moments, as the conditional form of the classic CAPM would suggest they should? If not, either the model is incorrect or the variables have been improperly chosen. The search for the relevant state variables, which will account for the time variability of asset returns, is also a search for the relevant model specification.

This paper is organized as follows. Section 1.2 is a short reminder of the "pricing kernel" or marginal-rate-of-substitution approach to CAPM tests. Section 1.3 explores the behavior of worldwide asset returns on the basis of U.S. instrumental variables. Section 1.4 does the same thing on the basis of country-specific instrumental variables. Section 1.5 concludes.

1.2   The "Pricing Kernel" Methodology

The "pricing-kernel" method, or marginal-rate-of-substitution method, initiated by Gallant and Tauchen (1989) and Hansen and Jagannathan (1991), was used in Bansal, Hsieh, and Viswanathan (1993) and generalized by Dumas and Solnik (1993) to test CAPMs.

1.2.1   The International CAPM

Let there be $L + 1$ countries, a set of $m = n + L + 1$ assets—other than the measurement-currency deposit—comprised of n equities or portfolios of equities, L nonmeasurement-currency currency deposits, and the world portfolio of equities which is the mth and last asset. The nonmeasurement-currency deposits are singled out by observing the above order in the list; that is, they are the $(n + 1)$st to $(n + L)$th assets.

The international capital asset pricing model is equation (14) in Adler and Dumas 1983:

$$(1) \quad E[r_{jt}|\Omega_{t-1}] = \sum_{i=1}^{L} \lambda_{i,\,t-1} \text{Cov}[r_{jt},\, r_{n+i,\,t}|\Omega_{t-1}] + \lambda_{m,t-1}\text{Cov}[r_{jt},r_{mt}|\Omega_{t-1}],$$

where r_{jt} is the nominal return on asset or portfolio j, $j = 1 \ldots m$, from time $t - 1$ to t, in excess of the rate of interest of the currency in which returns are measured, r_{mt} is the excess return on the world market portfolio, and Ω_{t-1} is the information set which investors use in choosing their portfolios. The time-varying coefficients $\lambda_{i,t-1}$, $i = 1 \ldots L$, are the *world prices of foreign exchange risk*. The time-varying coefficient $\lambda_{m,t-1}$ is the world price of market risk. The model takes into account the fact that investors of different countries view returns differently.

Equation (1) is the result of an aggregation over the several categories of investors. Equation (14) in Adler and Dumas (1983) provides an interpretation of the prices of risk. λ_m is a wealth-weighted harmonic mean of the nominal risk aversions of the investors of the various countries—the world nominal risk aversion, as it were. λ_i is equal to $1 - \lambda_m$ times the weight of country i in the world, where a country's weight is determined by its wealth times one minus its nominal risk tolerance.

By contrast, the classic CAPM ignores investor diversity and assumes, in effect, that everyone in the world translates returns into consumption as do the residents of the reference currency country. Hence, no exchange-risk hedging premium appears. In the above notations, the restriction of the international CAPM to the classic CAPM is stated as

(2) $$\lambda_{i,t-1} = 0 \; i = 1 \ldots L, \; \forall t.$$

In Dumas and Solnik (1993), a way has been found of writing the international CAPM in a parsimonious way that minimizes the number of parameters to be estimated. Introduce u_t, the unanticipated component of the market's marginal rate of substitution between nominal returns at date t and at date $t - 1$. u_t has the property that

(3) $$E[u_t|\Omega_{t-1}] = 0.$$

Define u_t as

(4) $$u_t = \lambda_{0,t-1} + \sum_{i=1}^{L} \lambda_{i,t-1} r_{n+i,t} + \lambda_{m,t-1} r_{mt}.$$

And define h_{jt} as

(5) $$h_{jt} = r_{jt} - r_{jt} u_t. \; j = 1, \ldots . m.$$

Then, Dumas and Solnik (1993) show that the international CAPM (1) may be rewritten as

(6) $$E[h_{jt}|\Omega_{t-1}] = 0, j = 1, \ldots m.$$

Equations (3) and (6) are the moment conditions used in the generalized method of moments (GMM) estimation.

1.2.2   Auxiliary Assumptions of the Econometric Analysis

In this subsection, we state two auxiliary assumptions that are needed for econometric purposes. They are identical to the auxiliary assumptions used in Dumas and Solnik (1993).

Assumption 1 of the empirical analysis: the information Ω_{t-1} is generated by a vector of instrumental variables Z_{t-1}.

Z_{t-1} is a row vector of l predetermined instrumental variables which reflect everything that is known to the investor. One goal of this paper is to identify the list of Z variables. Assumption 1 is a strong assumption which does not simply limit the information set of the econometrician: it limits the information set of the investors and, therefore, their strategy space.

Next, we specify the way in which the market prices, λ, move over time. We assume that the variables, Z, can serve as proxies for the state variables and that there exists an exact linear relationship between the λs and the Zs:

Assumption 2:

(7)
$$\lambda_{0,t-1} = -Z_{t-1}\delta,$$
$$\lambda_{i,t-1} = Z_{t-1}\phi_i, \, i = 1, \ldots L$$
$$\lambda_{m,t-1} = Z_{t-1}\phi_m.$$

Here the δs and ϕs are time-invariant vectors of weights which are estimated by the GMM, under the moment conditions (3) and (6).

Given Assumption 2 and the definition (4) of u_t, we have

(8)
$$u_t = -Z_{t-1}\delta + \sum_{i=1}^{L} z_{t-1}\phi_i \, r_{n+i,t} + z_{t-1} \, \phi_m \, r_{mt},$$

with u_t satisfying (3). Equation (8) serves to define u_t from now on.

1.2.3 Data

We consider the monthly excess return on equity and currency holdings measured in a common currency, the U.S. dollar. The excess return on an equity market is the return on that market (cum dividend) translated into dollars, minus the dollar one-month nominally risk-free rate. The return on a currency holding is the one-month interest rate[4] of that currency compounded by the exchange rate variation relative to the U.S. dollar, minus the dollar one-month risk-free rate.

In this study, we take four countries into account: Germany, the United Kingdom, Japan, and the United States. More precisely, we consider eight assets in addition to the U.S. dollar deposit: the equity index of each country,[5] a deutsche mark deposit, a pound sterling deposit, a yen deposit, and the world index of equities. In the CAPM, we include only three exchange risk premia—as many as we have exchange rates in the data set.

Available index level data cover the period January 1970 to December 1991, which is a 264-data-point series. However, we work with rates of return and in earlier work we needed to lag the rate of return on the world index by one month in the instrumental-variable set; that left 262 observations spanning March 1970 to December 1991. For the sake of comparability, we use here the same time series of returns.

---

4. These are Eurocurrency interest rates provided by Lombard Odier.
5. These are Morgan Stanley country indexes and the Morgan Stanley world index. See Harvey (1991a) for an appraisal of these indexes.

As we consider below various instrument sets, preliminary statistics will be provided concerning rates of return and their predictability.

1.3 U.S. Instrumental Variables

We first investigate a set of instruments common to all securities. We choose United States business-cycle variables as a common set. In the next section, we explore country-specific variables. The choice of U.S. variables as a common set is justified by figure 1.1, which plots coincident indicators of the business cycle in the four countries of our sample from 1948:01 to 1993:06.[6] It makes it plain that in most upturns and downturns the U.S. economy has led the two European economies of our sample. Japan has had at the most two downturns since the war; the United States has undergone downturns at about the same time. That the United States led other economies is confirmed by figure 1.2, which shows the cross-correlogram of coincident indicators between the United States and other countries.[7] Figure 1.2 reveals that the United States led Japan and Germany by at least twelve months and more strongly led the United Kingdom with a lead time of approximately four months. That fact also explains Harvey's (1991a) finding that U.S. stock market "internal" variables are at least as good predictors of worldwide rates of return as are country-specific "internal" variables.

Below we consider two sets of U.S. economic indicators: the Main Economic Indicators of the Organization for Economic Cooperation and Development (OECD) and the component indicators specifically selected by Stock and Watson (1993) to lead the U.S. cycles and predict recessions. Each time we consider a set of instrumental variables, predictability of returns is assessed by ordinary least squares (OLS), and conformity with the international and classic CAPMs is assessed by means of the GMM.

1.3.1 U.S. Main Economic Indicators (OECD)

I extracted from the OECD Main Economic Indicators (monthly data) the following variables in their seasonally adjusted version for the twenty years of our rate-of-return sample: (i) the U.S. level of total inventories in manufacturing industries (noted INV); (ii) U.S. residential construction put in place (RES); (iii) U.S. total value of retail sales (RSAL); (iv) U.S. percentage of unemployment out of the civilian labor force (UNMP);[8] (v) U.S. commercial bank loans (LOAN); and (vi) the U.S. money supply M3 (noted M3). All of

---

6. These are the coincident indicators calculated by the Center for International Business Cycle Research (CIBCR) as an overall measure of the overall performance of a country's economy.

7. These represent the correlation between the United States and other countries at various leads and lags, calculated after linear time detrending.

8. Business cycle experts know that unemployment lags the cycle. The use of this variable was not a good idea, but I refrained from making any changes to my original list for fear of accusations of data mining.

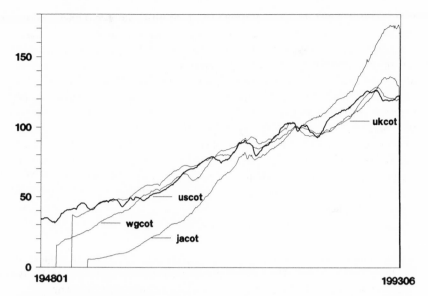

Fig. 1.1 Worldwide business cycles

Source: Center for International Business Cycle Research (CIBCR).
Note: the figure plots the indexes of coincident indicators (JACOT, UKCOT, WGCOT, USCOT) published by the CIBCR for the four countries investigated here.

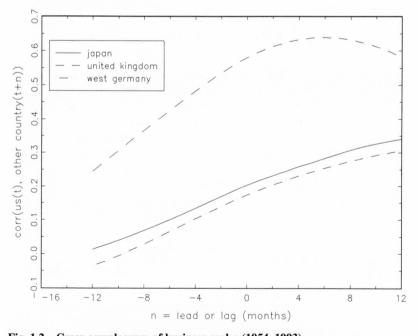

Fig. 1.2 Cross-correlogram of business cycles (1954–1993)

Note: The figure represents the cross-correlations of the U.S. coincident CIBCR indicator (USCOT) with the coincident indicators of other countries, after time detrending.

these were selected as being presumably "forward-looking variables." Series (iv) is naturally stationary. Other series were included in their first difference form. Even though it is properly classified as an "internal" variable, the lagged rate of return on the world market portfolio was added as an instrument in an attempt to capture potential lagged impacts of instruments on returns.[9]

Table 1.1 contains some descriptive statistics on rates of return, instrumental variables, and their ability to predict rates of return. I summarize in table 1.2 the R^2s that have been achieved by main economic indicators (column 2) and, for purposes of comparison, the R^2s that had been achieved by Dumas and Solnik (1993) by means of "internal" variables (column 1). It is observed that the predictive power of the Main Economic Indicators is generally lower than that of the "internal" financial variables. One variable has a consistent ability in predicting rates of return worldwide: the increase in U.S. inventories in manufacturing industries, with a positive increase of that variable being followed by lower returns.

Using these variables as instruments, I proceed to estimate the international and the classic CAPMs. The results appear in tables 1.3 and 1.4, respectively. The international CAPM yields a p-value of 0.0144 and is rejected. The classic CAPM produces a p-value of 0.0064 and is also rejected. It is not clear whether it is legitimate to test a hypothesis when the unrestricted model (in this case the international CAPM) is itself rejected. A Newey-West test does not reject the hypothesis that exchange-rate risk receives a zero price ($\phi_i = 0$, $i = 1 \ldots L$). (See table 1.5, p-value = 0.088.)

1.3.2   U.S. Leading Economic Indicators (National Bureau of Economic Research [NBER])

In a recent article, Stock and Watson (1993) proposed a leading index (called XLI2) which does not refer to financial variables and is instead constructed from the following leading indicators of the U.S. business cycle:[10] (i) housing authorizations (new private housing) in levels (HSBP);[11] (ii) average weekly hours of production workers in manufacturing, in level form (LPHRM); (iii) vendor performance: percentage of companies reporting slower deliveries, in levels (IVPAC); (iv) manufacturers' unfilled orders in the durable goods industries, 1982 dollars, smoothed[12] in growth rate form (MDU82); (v) the capacity utilization rate in manufacturing (Federal Reserve

---

9. The coefficient of this predictor will be found to be insignificant.

10. All variables are seasonally adjusted. In addition, Stock and Watson (1993) include the trade weighted nominal exchange rate between the United States and other countries as a leading indicator. We do not use it because it is a financial variable (although it obviously has real effects).

11. Observe that we use some of Stock and Watson's variables in level form, others in first-difference form. The issue of stationarity arises. There is no evidence that the level variables are nonstationary. However, there is a question of consistency in the comparisons; here we have housing authorizations in levels, whereas construction put in place—an MEI variable—was used in first-difference form in section 1.3. Further investigation is needed.

12. The series described as "smoothed" were passed through the filter $(1 + 2L + 2L^2 + L^3)$.

Table 1.1   **Summary Statistics Using U.S. Main Economic Indicators (MEIs) As Instrumental Variables (number of observations = 262)**

Securities	Mean of Excess Return	Standard Deviation of Excess Return
German stock market	0.0050726679	0.062362157
British stock market	0.0065975649	0.077541166
Japanese stock market	0.0090457824	0.065944529
U.S. stock market	0.0024764962	0.046825699
Deutsche mark	0.0017136374	0.034912228
British pound	0.0017428969	0.031856602
Japanese yen	0.0027198626	0.033234643
World stock market	0.0031789237	0.043619171

Instruments	Mean	Standard Deviation	Correlations						
Constant	1.00000	0.00000							
$rm, t-1$	0.0361454	0.521389	1.0	−0.15	0.11	0.026	0.13	−0.054	0.054
inv	0.00521380	0.0105418	−0.15	1.0	−0.21	−0.086	−0.18	0.14	0.11
res	0.00644040	0.0253341	0.11	−0.21	1.0	0.20	0.25	0.14	0.27
rsal	0.00633719	0.0132688	0.026	−0.086	0.20	1.0	0.038	0.097	0.15
unmp	6.69847	1.38235	0.13	−0.18	0.25	0.038	1.0	−0.25	0.14
loan	0.00774770	.00643937	−0.054	0.14	0.14	0.097	−0.25	1.0	0.41
M3	0.00733305	.00353889	0.054	0.11	0.27	0.15	0.14	0.41	1.0

Ordinary Least Squares with Heteroscedasticity Consistent Standard Errors (securities returns regressed on instruments; consistency is achieved by the Newey-West [NW] procedure)

German Stock Market				
Coefficients	Value	NW Standard Error	t-statistic	OLS Standard Error
Constant	0.00569285	0.0216447	0.263013	0.0222965
$rm, t-1$	0.00669026	0.00859968	0.777966	0.00746890
inv	−0.368126	0.243561	−1.51143	0.384939
res	0.0937675	0.152453	0.615060	0.167409
rsal	−0.326319	0.289070	−1.12886	0.295759
unmp	0.00189927	0.00285244	0.665842	0.00308242
loan	−0.0120132	0.618495	−0.0194233	0.698068
M3	−1.37839	1.10329	−1.24934	1.26840

R-squared is   0.236371

residual auto correlations (rho1~rho2~rho3~rho4~rho8~rho12~rho24~rho36)::
−0.018   −0.031   0.067   0.059   0.0027   −0.041   0.066   0.030

U.K. Stock Market				
Coefficients	Value	NW Standard Error	t-statistic	OLS Standard Error
Constant	0.00456223	0.0230321	0.198082	0.0275204
$rm, t-1$	0.00693558	0.00955990	0.725486	0.00921879

(*continued*)

Table 1.1   (continued)

		World Stock Market		
Coefficients	Value	NW Standard Error	t-statistic	OLS Standard Error
inv	−0.553277	0.451608	−1.22513	0.475126
res	0.126568	0.242514	0.521900	0.206631
rsal	−0.553975	0.360443	−1.53693	0.365052
unmp	0.00330507	0.00330871	0.998899	0.00380460
loan	−0.684188	0.682991	−1.00175	0.861619
M3	−1.29185	1.27644	−1.01207	1.56557

R-squared is   0.0378930

residual auto correlations (rho1~rho2~rho3~rho4~rho8~rho12~rho24~rho36)::
0.065   −0.11   0.043   0.0099   −0.041   −0.017   0.856   −0.067

		Japanese Stock Market		
Coefficients	Value	NW Standard Error	t-statistic	OLS Standard Error
Constant	−0.00782489	0.0253743	−0.308378	0.0233101
$rm, t-1$	0.0136144	0.00992300	1.37201	0.00780844
inv	−0.862245	0.230546	−3.74001	0.402438
res	0.0640068	0.174230	0.367371	0.175019
rsal	−0.268500	0.357431	−0.751195	.309204
unmp	0.00178737	0.00316203	0.565262	0.00322255
loan	−0.352924	0.598969	0.589220	0.729803
M3	1.01683	1.20467	0.844073	1.32606

R-squared is   0.0456416

residual auto correlations (rho1~rho2~rho3~rho4~rho8~rho12~rho24~rho36)::
−0.057   −0.019   0.036   0.030   0.062   0.075   −0.015   0.051

		U.S. Stock Market		
Coefficients	Value	NW Standard Error	t-statistic	OLS Standard Error
Constant	0.006669039	0.0168837	−0.396264	0.0165100
$rm, t-1$	0.00231443	0.00607610	0.380906	0.00553053
inv	−0.579509	0.195591	−2.96286	0.285037
res	0.00226372	0.119716	0.0189091	0.123962
rsal	−0.112179	0.234005	−0.479386	0.219002
unmp	0.00337828	0.00223428	1.51203	0.00228245
loan	−0.383116	0.444596	−0.861718	0.516902
M3	−0.935501	0.823839	−1.13554	0.939217

R-squared is   0.0504767

residual auto correlations (rho1~rho2~rho3~rho4~rho8~rho12~rho24~rho36):
−0.024   −0.064   −0.026   −0.049   −0.016   0.054   −0.020   −0.11

Deutsche Mark				
Coefficients	Value	NW Standard Error	t-statistic	OLS Standard Error
Constant	0.0258594	0.0111676	2.31557	0.0123199
$rm, t-1$	0.00801109	0.00404676	-1.97963	0.00412691
inv	-0.385613	0.148917	-2.58945	0.212696
res	0.0204019	0.0911840	0.223744	0.0925011
rsal	-0.201447	0.159687	-1.26152	0.163420
unmp	-0.00275891	0.00157580	-1.75080	0.00170318
loan	0.268681	0.402691	0.667214	0.385715
M3	-0.586607	0.605239	-0.969215	0.700848

R-squared is   0.0488795

residual auto correlations (rho1~rho2~rho3~rho4~rho8~rho12~rho24~rho36)::
0.028   0.10 -0.0038 0.021 -0.0049 0.034   0.049   0.056

British Pound				
Coefficients	Value	NW Standard Error	t-statistic	OLS Standard Error
Constant	0.0338504	0.0104436	3.24125	0.0111803
$rm, t-1$	-0.00303430	0.00378204	-0.802292	0.00374519
inv	-0.233203	0.109419	-2.13128	0.193023
res	0.0888226	0.0846396	1.04942	0.0839452
rsal	-0.220981	0.136461	-1.61937	0.148305
unmp	-0.00339392	0.00139092	-2.44005	0.00154564
loan	0.222244	0.318936	0.696829	0.350038
M3	-1.21933	0.543510	-2.24344	0.636023

R-squared is   0.0592174

residual auto correlations (rho1~rho2~rho3~rho4~rho8~rho12~rho24~rho36)::
0.066   0.067 -0.017 0.028 -0.084 -0.047 0.037   0.00080

Japanese Yen				
Coefficients	Value	NW Standard Error	t-statistic	OLS Standard Error
Constant	0.0110907	0.0120695	0.918900	0.0118473
$rm, t-1$	-0.000429227	0.00397897	-0.107874	0.00396862
inv	-0.365841	0.111626	-3.27740	0.204538
res	0.113531	0.0832779	1.36328	0.0889533
rsal	-0.213294	0.169312	-1.25977	0.157152
unmp	-0.000364428	0.00168879	-0.215793	0.00163785
loan	0.00795930	0.290915	0.0273595	0.370921
M3	-0.470191	0.575398	-0.817156	0.673967

R-squared is   0.0294043

residual auto correlations (rho1~rho2~rho3~rho4~rho8~rho12~rho24~rho36)::
0.048   0.041   0.080   0.068 -0.0037 0.096 -0.051 -0.052

(*continued*)

Table 1.1   (continued)

Coefficients	Value	NW Standard Error	t-statistic	OLS Standard Error
		World Stock Market		
Constant	−0.00802493	0.0160887	−0.498793	0.0153149
rm, $t-1$	0.00598386	0.00545754	1.09644	0.00513018
inv	−0.622000	0.183153	−3.39607	0.264404
res	0.0297202	0.117849	0.252190	0.114989
rsal	−0.293711	0.211799	−1.38674	0.203149
unmp	0.00311797	0.00202408	1.54044	0.00211723
loan	−0.00729195	0.440082	−0.0165695	0.479484
M3	−0.672124	0.776432	−0.865657	0.871228

R-squared is   0.584330

residual auto correlations (rho1~rho2~rho3~rho4~rho8~rho12~rho24~rho36):
−0.011   −0.049   0.021   −0.041   −0.013   −0.067   0.098   −0.095

Table 1.2   **Summary of Predictive Ability of Instruments**

	Dumas-Solnik	OECD Main Economic Indicators (table 1.1)	NBER XL12 Components (table 1.6)	NBER XL12 Delayed 1 Month	NBER XL12 Delayed 2 Months
			$R^2\%$		
Number of instruments (including constant)	6	8	7	7	7
German stock market	5.97	2.36	4.28	3.69	2.65
British stock market	10.28	3.79	12.18	10.20	5.03
Japanese stock market	7.93	4.56	9.27	7.86	7.40
U.S. stock market	9.60	5.05	7.96	4.55	4.42
Deutsche mark	10.63	4.89	4.07	4.52	3.12
British pound	11.24	5.92	3.14	3.62	2.61
Japanese yen	7.74	2.94	3.63	3.29	2.68
World stock market	11.33	5.84	10.17	5.86	4.99

	CIBCR Country Leading Indexes (LDTs) (table 1.9)	CIBCR Leading Index (LDT) Components
Number of instruments (including constant)	5	(number of instruments varies)
German stock market	2.76	2.19 (7)
British stock market	0.50	2.84 (9)
Japanese stock market	0.82	6.43 (7)
U.S. stock market	0.93	8.93 (10)
Deutsche mark	2.23	6.75 (16)
British pound	0.72	9.56 (18)
Japanese yen	0.06	10.39 (16)
World stock market	0.90	18.26 (30)

Table 1.3   **Estimation of the International CAPM with U.S. Main Economic Indicators as Instrumental Variables (number of observations = 262; number of factors = 4; degrees of freedom = 32)**

Generalized Method of Moments (GMM) Results, Stage 20			
Coefficients	Value	Standard Error	t-statistic
Linear form for $\lambda_{0,\,t-1}$ (see equation [7])			
Constant	−0.7624	0.3710	−2.0553
$rm, t-1$	0.0567	1.3231	0.0428
inv	27.9459	15.0797	1.8532
res	2.1540	2.1545	0.9998
rsal	−6.2960	4.9054	−1.2835
unmp	0.0185	0.0055	3.3873
loan	−2.7934	9.7046	−0.2878
M3	−34.0587	14.2208	−2.3950
Linear Forms for Market Prices of Risk, $\lambda_{m,t-1}$ and $\lambda_{i,t-1}$			
Constant			
$\lambda m, t-1$	53.8784	24.1627	2.2298
$\lambda 1, t-1$	45.0855	20.5153	2.1977
$\lambda 2, t-1$	−30.7942	20.7468	−1.4843
$\lambda 3, t-1$	−23.0563	9.9523	−2.3167
$rm\,(-1)$			
$\lambda m, t-1$	−160.2995	86.3428	−1.8565
$\lambda 1, t-1$	87.9048	83.4154	1.0538
$\lambda 2, t-1$	39.4347	75.9711	0.5191
$\lambda 3, t-1$	17.2105	34.7671	0.4950
inv			
$\lambda m, t-1$	−1390.1074	733.0540	−1.8963
$\lambda 1, t-1$	718.7262	727.4729	0.9880
$\lambda 1, t-1$	−229.0456	561.8708	−0.4076
$\lambda 1, t-1$	−148.8943	256.9847	−0.5794
res			
$\lambda m, t-1$	−206.5363	138.6434	−1.4897
$\lambda 1, t-1$	78.9526	159.1203	0.4962
$\lambda 2, t-1$	140.8913	169.2117	0.8326
$\lambda 3, t-1$	7.2748	82.5645	0.0881
rsal			
$\lambda m, t-1$	−157.2546	223.5246	−0.7035
$\lambda 1, t-1$	−99.0278	253.8506	−0.3901
$\lambda 1, t-1$	−59.7750	222.6823	−0.2684
$\lambda 1, t-1$	−206.2905	140.8505	−1.4646
unmp			
$\lambda m, t-1$	−0.8447	0.3391	−2.4906
$\lambda 1, t-1$	−0.4295	0.2883	−1.4897
$\lambda 2, t-1$	0.5240	0.2841	1.8446
$\lambda 3, t-1$	0.4676	0.1505	3.1062

(*continued*)

Table 1.3 (continued)

Generalized Method of Moments (GMM) Results, Stage 20

Coefficients	Value	Standard Error	t-statistic
	Linear Forms for Market Prices of Risk, $\lambda_{m,t-1}$ and $\lambda_{i,t-1}$		
loan			
$\lambda m, t-1$	705.1855	645.9489	1.0917
$\lambda 1, t-1$	117.8120	796.5030	0.1479
$\lambda 2, t-1$	−311.7085	734.6841	−0.4243
$\lambda 3, t-1$	−594.0021	371.0511	−1.6009
M3			
$\lambda m, t-1$	283.5984	1168.9769	0.2426
$\lambda 1, t-1$	−2710.4280	1559.4271	−1.7381
$\lambda 2, t-1$	350.1110	1346.4438	0.2600
$\lambda 3, t-1$	99.3373	664.8671	0.1494

Note: Number of iterations: 2; weighing matrix updated 20 times; chi-square : 51.923974; RIGHT TAIL p-value : 0.014421; degrees of freedom : 32.

Table 1.4 **Estimation of the Classic CAPM with U.S. Main Economic Indicators as Instrumental Variables (number of observations = 262; number of factors = 1; degrees of freedom = 56)**

Generalized Method of Moments Results, Stage 31

Coefficients	Value	Standard Error	t-statistic
	Linear form for $\lambda_{0,t-1}$ (see equation [7])		
Constant	−0.0590	0.1727	−0.3416
$rm, t-1$	−0.2638	0.5272	−0.5003
inv	8.0625	11.0876	0.7272
res	1.4246	1.2198	1.1679
rsal	−6.7746	3.1070	−2.1804
unmp	0.0023	0.0026	0.8853
loan	−0.3844	3.0409	−0.1264
M3	−2.0035	7.9628	−0.2516
	Linear Form of Market Price of Covariance Risk, $\lambda_{m,t-1}$		
Constant	−2.0280	7.9695	−0.2545
$rm, t-1$	14.2907	30.0824	0.4751
inv	−344.1557	126.6979	−2.7163
res	113.9686	72.0067	1.5828
rsal	−343.5483	121.5828	−2.8256
unmp	0.1899	0.1152	1.6485
loan	−81.3205	306.1997	−0.2656
M3	−379.7604	541.0834	−0.7019

Note: Number of iterations: 4; weighing matrix updated 31 times; chi-square : 85.755252; RIGHT TAIL p-value : 0.006427; degrees of freedom : 56.

Table 1.5   **Tests of Hypotheses**

Instruments	Specification	χ^2 Difference	Degrees of Freedom	p-value
U.S. MEI 8 instruments	linear	85.750564 −51.923974 33.826590	24	0.088
U.S. NBER 7 instruments	linear	86.702953 −39.961045 46.741908	21	0.001

Note: Statistics in this table test the hypothesis: $\phi_i = 0$, $i = 1, 2, 3$ against the alternative that the international CAPM holds. The various tests differ only in the set of the instrumental variables used.

Board), in first difference form (IPXMCA); and (vi) an index of help-wanted advertising in newspapers (the Conference Board), in growth rates (LHELL).

Table 1.6 reports the results of multiple OLS (and heteroscedasticity corrected) regressions of rates of return on these variables.[13] For purposes of comparison, the overall performance (R^2s) is transcribed in table 1.2. This set of instruments predicts stock returns worldwide about as well as the financial or internal variables used by Dumas and Solnik do. They predict currencies less well. The outstanding contribution to predictability is that of the indicator IVPAC (vendor performance) whose t-statistics in regressions of the various securities rates of return are, respectively, −2.72, −4.23, −2.96, −4.05, −0.138, −1.42, −1.62, −4.30. The signs are as expected: an increase in the number of firms reporting slower deliveries is followed by lower returns on securities. The larger values of t occur for stock returns. The forecasting of currencies presumably requires bilateral instrumental variables; U.S. business-cycle variables by themselves are insufficient. Another valuable contribution is that of HSBP (housing starts), also with the anticipated sign.

Many time series (280 series, precisely) were mined by Stock and Watson to select variables and their lags in order to make up an index that predicts the three-month increments in their U.S. index of coincident indicators (XCI, defined in Stock and Watson 1989). It turns out, however, that these variables (without lags) also predict U.S. and other stock returns about as well as internal variables do. That is not the result of data mining.[14]

---

13. The indicated variables were used in a vector autoregression (VAR) form by Stock and Watson to predict increments in their index of coincident indicators (XCI). I use here the raw variables, in the form described, without the VAR form and without lags. I did reconstruct the implied VAR coefficients that Stock and Watson used but found that the VAR form predicts securities returns with approximately the same degree of success as do the raw variables.

14. The correlations between monthly securities returns and one-month increments in the XCI are as follows:

German stock market	−0.074
British stock market	−0.073
Japanese stock market	0.046

Table 1.6   **Summary Statistics with U.S. NBER Variables as Instruments**

Instruments	Mean	Standard Deviation	Correlations					
Constant	1.00000	0.00000						
hsbp	121.004	32.6542	1.0	0.34	0.49	0.44	0.41	0.48
lphrm	40.2859	0.607544	0.34	1.0	0.45	0.38	0.30	0.23
ivpac	53.3844	13.0493	0.49	0.45	1.0	0.58	0.23	0.29
mdu82	0.00139399	0.0102974	0.44	0.38	0.58	1.0	0.27	0.31
ipxmca	−0.0164122	0.772366	0.41	0.30	0.23	0.27	1.0	0.49
lhell	−0.000517679	0.0316811	0.48	0.23	0.29	0.31	0.49	1.0

Ordinary Least Squares (OLS) with Heteroscedasticity Consistent Standard Errors (securities returns regressed on instruments; consistency is achieved by the Newey-West [NW] procedure)

German Stock Market

Coefficients	Value	NW Standard Error	t-statistic	OLS Standard Error
Constant	−0.390731	0.276101	−1.41518	0.285232
hsbp	0.000343379	0.000136858	2.50901	0.000149806
lphrm	0.0102116	0.00712679	1.43284	0.00722220
ivpac	−0.00107297	0.000393827	−2.72446	0.0000389195
mdu82	0.0304419	0.444454	0.0684928	0.469395
ipxmca	−0.00305786	0.00572859	−0.533789	0.00584667
lhell	−0.113002	0.159433	−0.708775	0.146780

R-squared is   0.0428200

residual auto correlations (rho1~rho2~rho3~rho4~rho8~rho12~rho24~rho36):
−0.031   −0.039   0.049   0.053   −0.0062   −0.036   0.056   0.036

U.K. Stock Market

Coefficients	Value	NW Standard Error	t-statistic	OLS Standard Error
Constant	−0.534844	0.308444	−1.73401	0.339701
hsbp	0.000559973	0.000184360	3.03739	0.000178414
lphrm	0.0147479	0.00770939	1.91298	0.00860139
ivpac	−0.00227316	0.000537946	−4.22562	0.000463518
mdu82	0.379958	0.548411	0.692834	0.559033
ipxmca	−0.0170324	0.0136970	−1.24351	0.00696319
lhell	−0.181394	0.159830	−1.13492	0.174810

R-squared is   0.121848

residual auto correlations (rho1~rho2~rho3~rho4~rho8~rho12~rho24~rho36):
−0.016   −0.15   0.038   −0.027   −0.050   −0.013   0.043   −0.0079

Japanese Stock Market				
Coefficients	Value	NW Standard Error	t-statistic	OLS Standard Error
Constant	−0.253508	0.320174	−0.791781	0.293657
hsbp	0.000750459	0.000148571	5.05119	0.000154231
lphrm	0.00563301	0.00822220	0.685097	0.00743553
ivpac	−0.00102859	0.000346998	−2.96424	0.000400692
mdu82	−0.288754	0.449197	−0.642822	0.483261
ipxmca	−0.00251334	0.00529847	−0.474353	0.00601938
lhell	−0.166150	0.141414	−1.17492	0.151116

R-squared is   0.0926722

residual auto correlations (rho1~rho2~rho3~rho4~rho8~rho12~rho24~rho36):
−0.020   −0.071   −0.0020   −0.011   0.043   0.073   0.0095   0.077

U.S. Stock Market				
Coefficients	Value	NW Standard Error	t-statistic	OLS Standard Error
Constant	−0.235663	0.215653	−1.09279	0.210016
hsbp	0.000251501	0.000108271	2.32289	0.000110302
lphrm	0.00660721	0.00542312	1.21834	0.00531770
ivpac	−0.00109923	0.000271581	−4.04752	0.000286564
mdu82	0.0564726	0.361858	0.156063	0.345615
ipxmca	−0.00219562	0.00430679	−0.509805	0.00430490
lhell	−0.187171	0.117017	−1.59952	0.108074

R-squared is   0.0795992

residual auto correlations (rho1~rho2~rho3~rho4~rho8~rho12~rho24~rho36):
−0.034   −0.090   −0.028   −0.052   −0.022   0.032   −0.0042   −0.088

Deutsche Mark				
Coefficients	Value	NW Standard Error	t-statistic	OLS Standard Error
Constant	−0.328134	0.137363	−2.38880	0.159854
hsbp	0.000193983	6.49824e-05	2.98516	8.39562e-05
lphrm	0.00766495	0.00353697	2.16710	0.00404757
ivpac	−3.82105e-05	0.000276595	−0.138146	0.000218118
mdu82	−0.328321	0.241348	−1.36036	0.263065
ipxmca	−0.00438420	0.00321052	−1.36557	0.00327667
lhell	−0.0215355	0.0852959	−0.252481	0.0822604

R-squared is   0.0407542

residual auto correlations (rho1~rho2~rho3~rho4~rho8~rho12~rho24~rho36):
−0.022   0.071   −0.010   0.018   −0.039   −0.00073   0.028   0.096

(*continued*)

Table 1.6   (continued)

	British Pound			
Coefficients	Value	NW Standard Error	t-statistic	OLS Standard Error
Constant	−0.332575	0.133099	−2.49870	0.146574
hsbp	0.000103983	5.95071e-05	1.74741	7.69820e-05
lphrm	0.00828977	0.00341368	2.42840	0.00371133
ivpac	−0.000231653	0.000163528	−1.41660	0.000199999
mdu82	0.0712808	0.212960	0.334714	0.241212
ipxmca	−0.000255775	0.00267844	−0.0954940	0.00300448
lhell	−0.0733277	0.0714012	−1.02698	0.0754270

R-squared is   0.0313697

residual auto correlations (rho1~rho2~rho3~rho4~rho8~rho12~rho24~rho36):
0.056   0.073   −0.016   0.036   −0.093   −0.046   −0.011   0.038

	Japanese Yen			
Coefficients	Value	NW Standard Error	t-statistic	OLS Standard Error
Constant	−0.159703	0.166350	−0.960047	0.152527
hsbp	0.000187078	6.24738e-05	2.99450	8.01082e-05
lphrm	0.00389288	0.00423289	0.919674	0.00386205
ivpac	−0.000316085	0.000194594	−1.62433	0.000208121
mdu82	−0.134085	0.244464	−0.548487	0.251008
ipxmca	−0.00347325	0.00299366	−1.16020	0.00312649
lhell	0.0734632	0.0826545	0.888798	0.0784901

R-squared is   0.0362787

residual auto correlations (rho1~rho2~rho3~rho4~rho8~rho12~rho24~rho36):
0.039   0.018   0.065   0.067   −0.015   0.094   −0.061   −0.030

	World Stock Market			
Coefficients	Value	NW Standard Error	t-statistic	OLS Standard Error
Constant	−0.304620	0.201082	−1.51490	0.193269
hsbp	0.000392649	9.90945e-05	3.96237	0.000101506
lphrm	0.00789062	0.00511004	1.54414	0.00489366
ivpac	−0.00108092	0.000251444	−4.29886	0.000263713
mdu82	−0.0322675	0.322532	−0.100044	0.318056
ipxmca	−0.00401874	0.00432539	−0.929105	0.00396162
lhell	−0.172625	0.102169	−1.68960	0.0994560

R-squared is   0.101723

residual auto correlations (rho1~rho2~rho3~rho4~rho8~rho12~rho24~rho36):
0.0092   −0.096   0.0014   −0.048   −0.031   0.051   0.015   −0.036

There is, of course, an issue concerning the precise timing of releases of economic data. Internal variables are observed in real time in the financial markets, whereas some economic variables are released several weeks after the end of the month. In the statistical analysis, we have simply used the data pertaining to month $t - 1$ to predict rates of return over the month $(t - 1, t)$. That procedure is not congruent with actual release dates. However, the variable that is most effective in bringing about predictive performance is vendor performance IVPAC. IVPAC is released by the National Association of Purchasing Managers a mere two days after the end of the month.

Even if economic data are released with some delay by statistical agencies and would, therefore, be available to external observers at that time only, it is also true that the investors, whose information set we are trying to represent, are not external observers and do not await actual releases. They enjoy the benefits of early estimates.

Furthermore, financial market prices and flows of goods and services act as aggregators of information faster than statistical agencies do. My goal in this paper is not to show that external economic variables are superior in their predictive ability to internal financial variables. I use them because I believe that their message is more meaningful. I am comfortable with the idea that news about economic variables may be "released" through the channel, inter alia, of financial market prices. Even then, I am interested in identifying the relevant economic variables.

The reader may nonetheless wish to know how the results would have been affected by a different assumption on the timing of releases. In order to provide that information to him or her, I have shown in table 1.2 the levels of R^2s attained when the Stock and Watson variables are delayed further by one and also two months. Not surprisingly, the predictive performance for stock returns deteriorates gradually.[15] The predictive performance for currencies, which was poor in the first place, is not markedly affected.

Tables 1.7 and 1.8 report on the tests of the two CAPMs based on the Stock and Watson leading variables. The overidentifying restrictions of the international CAPM are marginally accepted with a p-value of 0.067, and the classic CAPM is rejected with a p-value of 0.03.[16] A Newey-West test of the hypothesis of zero price on foreign-exchange risk is reported in table 1.5 and shows rejection (p-value = 0.0005). Foreign-exchange-risk premia are significant.

U.S. stock market	−0.027
Deutsche mark	−0.075
British pound	−0.073
Japanese yen	0.026
World stock market	−0.032

15. In my opinion, the gradual deterioration in predictive power that occurs confirms that earlier results were not pure chance and that they was some bona fide predictive power in the first place.

16. When the Stock-Watson instruments are lagged one month further, the international CAPM is marginally rejected (p-val = 3.9 percent) and the domestic CAPM is marginally accepted (p-val = 9.17 percent).

Table 1.7 **Estimation of the International CAPM with U.S. NBER Instrumental Variables (number of observations = 262; number of factors = 4; degrees of freedom = 28)**

Generalized Method of Moments (GMM) Results, Stage 19			
Coefficients	Value	Standard Error	t-statistic
Linear form for $\lambda_{0,\,t-1}$ (see equation [7])			
Constant	7.2346	3.9152	1.8478
hsbp	0.0176	0.0234	0.7530
lphrm	−0.1811	0.0957	−1.8915
ivpac	0.0030	0.0053	0.5681
mdu82	11.3602	5.6840	1.9986
ipxmca	−0.0063	0.0077	−0.8162
lhell	−1.5675	1.8945	−0.8274
Linear Forms for Market Prices of Risk, $\lambda_{m,t-1}$ and $\lambda_{m,t-1}$ and $\lambda_{i,\,t-1}$			
Constant			
$\lambda m, t-1$	−244.6722	300.3837	−0.8145
$\lambda 1, t-1$	−421.7032	230.8744	−1.8265
$\lambda 2, t-1$	361.2365	233.2194	1.5489
$\lambda 3, t-1$	−32.8439	151.6363	−0.2166
hsbp			
$\lambda m, t-1$	6.3348	2.0582	3.0779
$\lambda 1, t-1$	−1.7197	1.8737	−0.9178
$\lambda 2, t-1$	−1.0261	1.6096	−0.6374
$\lambda 3, t-1$	2.2875	0.9770	2.3414
lphrm			
$\lambda m, t-1$	4.0333	7.6146	0.5297
$\lambda 1, t-1$	11.0753	5.9827	1.8512
$\lambda 2, t-1$	−7.8050	5.9297	−1.3162
$\lambda 3, t-1$	0.9961	3.8104	0.2614
ivpac			
$\lambda m, t-1$	0.4265	0.3275	1.3021
$\lambda 1, t-1$	−0.1739	0.4019	−0.4327
$\lambda 2, t-1$	−0.7289	0.3564	−2.0453
$\lambda 3, t-1$	−0.4764	0.1738	−2.7418
mdu82			
$\lambda m, t-1$	−1518.8104	512.2532	−2.9650
$\lambda 1, t-1$	762.5102	432.8288	1.7617
$\lambda 2, t-1$	583.1863	426.5617	1.3672
$\lambda 3, t-1$	−105.5570	259.2887	−0.4071
ipxmca			
$\lambda m, t-1$	−0.6235	0.4303	−1.4488
$\lambda 1, t-1$	−1.1746	0.5937	1.9785
$\lambda 2, t-1$	−0.2372	0.4885	−0.4856
$\lambda 3, t-1$	0.3153	0.1770	1.7812

Table 1.7 (continued)

	Generalized Method of Moments (GMM) Results, Stage 19		
Coefficients	Value	Standard Error	t-statistic
lhell			
$\lambda m, t-1$	-200.9777	114.8282	-1.7502
$\lambda 1, t-1$	-227.7343	111.1008	-2.0498
$\lambda 2, t-1$	354.0376	126.1874	2.8056
$\lambda 3, t-1$	-171.5884	56.9768	-3.0116

Note: Number of iterations: 2; weighing matrix updated 19 times; chi-square: 39.961045; RIGHT TAIL p-value : 0.066658; degrees of freedom: 28.

Table 1.8 **Estimation of the Classic CAPM with U.S. NBER Instrumental Variables (number of observations = 262; number of factors = 1; degrees of freedom = 49)**

	Generalized Method of Moments Results, Stage 8		
Coefficients	Value	Standard Error	t-statistic
	Linear form for $\lambda_{0,\,t-1}$ (see equation [7])		
Constant	2.5886	1.8490	1.4000
hsbp	0.0087	0.0162	0.5388
lphrm	-0.0709	0.0469	-1.5126
ivpac	0.0056	0.0037	1.5079
mdu82	1.5476	3.2085	0.4823
ipxmca	-0.0082	0.0051	-1.6022
lhell	-1.4689	1.0460	-1.4044
	Linear Form of Market Price of Covariance Risk, $\lambda_{m,t-1}$		
Constant	-124.5130	117.8852	-1.0562
hsbp	2.4277	0.7155	3.3930
lphrm	3.3990	2.9848	1.1388
ivpac	-0.6296	0.1319	-4.7728
mdu82	61.8821	202.6053	0.3054
ipxmca	0.1011	0.1378	0.7339
lhell	-99.3850	44.9423	-2.2114

Note: Number of iterations: 4; weighing matrix updated 8 times; chi-square: 69.235898; RIGHT TAIL p-value: 0.029985; degrees of freedom: 49.

1.4   Worldwide Instrumental Variables

In tests of conditional CAPMs, it is crucial to predict well the market rate of return and, in tests of the international conditional CAPM, it is important to predict well the rates of return on currencies. Exchange rates are bilateral variables. Their prediction should not logically be based on unilateral instrumental variables, such as U.S. leading indicators. In this section, I consider instrumental variables reflecting the business cycles of the four countries of our sample. I use leading indexes of the four countries' cycles simultaneously.

Every month the Center for International Business Cycle Research (CIBCR) publishes a leading index of the business cycle for eleven countries. The growth rate of the index provides advance warning of a growth cycle upturn or downturn.[17] I used the leading indicators of Japan (JALDT), the United Kingdom (UKLDT), the former West Germany (WGLDT), and the United States (USLDT), in their growth rate form, as instrumental variables. The forecasting performance of the five variables (including a constant) is reported in table 1.9. R^2s are very low, of the order of 1 percent or 2 percent. It did not seem worthwhile to pursue a test of any CAPM.

The fact that a leading index shows poor forecasting performance for stock returns does not preclude the component series of the index from faring many times better. For instance, the Stock and Watson XLI2 (experimental leading index) predicts returns very poorly, but we reported in section 1.3.2 that its components provide the best forecasting basis that we have found so far. This remark applies even more in the case of the CIBCR indexes since they are meant to be qualitative predictors of upturns and downturns, not quantitative predictors of the subsequent movement in the business cycle.

Accordingly, I have also investigated the predictive ability of the series which compose the country leading indexes of the CIBCR. For each country, I used as instruments every component series that was available on a monthly basis. Then, for example, German stock returns were predicted on the basis of German instruments alone, but the deutsche mark/dollar return was predicted on the basis of German and U.S. instruments; the worldwide stock returns were predicted on the basis of all country instruments put together. In table 1.2 the column headed CIBCR leading index (LDT) components contains the R^2s obtained by this method. The number of instruments is large; yet the forecasting performance reached for stocks is no better than that of the NBER component series. For currencies, the performance is better (R^2s of the order of 10 percent). However, due to their large number, these instruments cannot be used to test CAPMs by the GMM.

Instruments ought to be selected in each country for the purpose of predicting increments in business-cycle coincident indicators. This would be a replication of the Stock and Watson procedure with worldwide data. Then the

---

17. Descriptions of various leading indicators are available in Lahiri and Moore (1991) and Moore (1992).

Table 1.9 **Summary Statistics with the CIBCR's Country Leading Indexes as Instruments**

Instruments	Mean	Standard Deviation	Correlations			
Constant	1.000000	0.000000				
JALDT	0.003146	0.013503	1.00	0.29	0.37	0.25
UKLDT	0.001078	0.006056	0.29	1.00	0.23	0.22
WGLDT	0.001533	0.005653	0.37	0.23	1.00	0.28
USLDT	0.002531	0.009265	0.25	0.22	0.28	1.00

Ordinary Least Squares with Heteroscedasticity Consistent Standard Errors (securities returns regressed on instruments; consistency is achieved by the Newey-West [NW] procedure)

German Stock Market

Coefficients	Value	NW Standard Error	t-statistic	OLS Standard Error
Constant	0.006115	0.004093	1.493955	0.004043
JALDT	−0.528313	0.307287	−1.719281	0.313727
UKLDT	0.856442	0.673679	1.271291	0.669450
WGLDT	1.028668	0.699139	1.471335	0.745461
USLDT	−0.742447	0.391963	−1.894175	0.438001

R-squared is   0.027619

residual auto correlations (rho1~rho2~rho3~rho4~rho8~rho12~rho24~rho36)::
0.01   −0.02   0.08   0.08   −0.04   −0.03   0.05   0.05

U.K. Stock Market

Coefficients	Value	NW Standard Error	t-statistic	OLS Standard Error
Constant	0.007672	0.006315	1.214889	0.005085
JALDT	−0.045286	0.480511	−0.094246	0.394588
UKLDT	−0.828986	1.006346	−0.823758	0.841997
WGLDT	−0.234803	0.911190	−0.257689	0.937598
USLDT	0.127008	0.705268	0.180084	0.550892

R-squared is   0.005056

residual auto correlations (rho1~rho2~rho3~rho4~rho8~rho12~rho24~rho36):
0.01   −0.08   0.06   0.00   −0.05   −0.00   0.07   −0.03

Japanese Stock Market

Coefficients	Value	NW Standard Error	t-statistic	OLS Standard Error
Constant	0.007704	0.004565	1.687841	0.004318
JALDT	0.128434	0.308548	0.416253	0.335046
UKLDT	0.502277	0.691403	0.726461	0.714943
WGLDT	−0.487162	0.745188	−0.653744	0.796118
USLDT	0.451507	0.458765	0.984179	0.467765

(*continued*)

Table 1.9 (continued)

R-squared is   0.008194

---

residual auto correlations (rho1~rho2~rho3~rho4~rho8~rho12~rho24~rho36):
0.05   0.0   0.06   0.05   0.08   0.08   −0.02   0.07

		U.S. Stock Market		
Coefficients	Value	NW Standard Error	*t*-statistic	OLS Standard Error
Constant	0.002766	0.003427	0.807155	0.003064
JALDT	0.094160	0.240852	0.390946	0.237778
UKLDT	0.072221	0.450946	0.160154	0.507384
WGLDT	−0.842245	0.582581	−1.445712	0.564994
USLDT	0.247814	0.331390	0.747801	0.331966

R-squared is   0.009287

---

residual auto correlations (rho1~rho2~rho3~rho4~rho8~rho12~rho24~rho36):
0.05   −0.03   0.01   0.00   −0.00   0.03   −0.03   −0.05

		Deutsche Mark		
Coefficients	Value	NW Standard Error	*t*-statistic	OLS Standard Error
Constant	0.002498	0.002209	1.130873	0.002270
JALDT	−0.093262	0.180581	−0.516453	0.176112
UKLDT	0.345475	0.321228	1.075484	0.375799
WGLDT	0.344474	0.477226	0.721825	0.418468
USLDT	−0.549694	0.232381	−2.365488	0.245874

R-squared is   0.022317

---

residual auto correlations (rho1~rho2~rho3~rho4~rho8~rho12~rho24~rho36):
0.04   0.09   0.02   0.05   −0.00   0.03   0.03   0.08

		British Pound		
Coefficients	Value	NW Standard Error	*t*-statistic	OLS Standard Error
Constant	0.002029	0.001968	1.030766	0.002087
JALDT	0.057912	0.152396	0.380009	0.161934
UKLDT	−0.191978	0.292474	−0.656395	0.345546
WGLDT	0.246833	0.383650	0.643380	0.384779
USLDT	−0.252616	0.219688	−1.149884	0.226080

R-squared is   0.007217

---

residual auto correlations (rho1~rho2~rho3~rho4~rho8~rho12~rho24~rho36):
0.10   0.08   0.02   0.06   −0.05   −0.00   0.02   0.03

		Japanese Yen		
Coefficients	Value	NW Standard Error	t-statistic	OLS Standard Error
Constant	0.002853	0.002193	1.300887	0.002184
JALDT	−0.036799	0.171975	−0.213981	0.169500
UKLDT	−0.013601	0.340779	−0.039911	0.361690
WGLDT	−0.087413	0.378062	−0.231214	0.402756
USLDT	0.051806	0.231718	0.223571	0.236642

R-squared is   0.000616

residual auto correlations (rho1~rho2~rho3~rho4~rho8~rho12~rho24~rho36):
0.07   0.05   0.08   0.10   0.02   0.10   −0.06   −0.04

		World Stock Market		
Coefficients	Value	NW Standard Error	t-statistic	OLS Standard Error
Constant	0.003171	0.003181	0.996848	0.002855
JALDT	0.109950	0.219190	0.501620	0.221523
UKLDT	0.113356	0.435592	0.260235	0.472700
WGLDT	−0.730282	0.514128	−1.420427	0.526371
USLDT	0.260565	0.325975	0.799338	0.309273

R-squared is   0.009033

residual auto correlations (rho1~rho2~rho3~rho4~rho8~rho12~rho24~rho36):
0.10   −0.03   0.04   −0.00   −0.01   0.05   −0.01   −0.03

selected instruments could be investigated for the ability to forecast securities returns. This will be left for future research.

1.5   Conclusion

This preliminary investigation was meant to highlight the links that exist between predicted activity levels and conditionally expected stock returns. The following conclusions emerge from it:

1. The nonfinancial leading indicators selected by Stock and Watson (1993) for the purpose of predicting United States business cycles also seem to offer some potential for the prediction of worldwide stock returns. Outstanding contributions to predictive power were made by the variables IVPAC (vendor performance) and HSBP (housing authorizations). Furthermore, the signs of these variables' coefficients made intuitive sense. IVPAC is an especially valuable predictor since its value is released a mere forty-eight hours after the end of the month.

2. Using the Stock and Watson instrument set, the international conditional CAPM was marginally not rejected while the classic conditional CAPM was rejected.

3. Other sets of instrumental variables that I have tried so far (U.S. Main Economic Indicators, CIBCR country leading indexes) have not proven as successful both in regard to their power of prediction and in regard to their ability to discriminate between asset-pricing models.

Other more subtle clues could be gathered from the data and could point the way toward future research. The first issue that I would like to raise concerns the link between predictability of returns and the power of asset-pricing tests. The OECD Main Economic Indicators (MEIs), as used here, have lower predictive power than did the Stock and Watson leading series, while these series in turn had a lower predictive ability than did the "internal" variables used by Dumas and Solnik and others (see table 1.2). In tests of asset prices, the MEIs rejected both the classic and the international models, while the Stock-Watson variables rejected one model and marginally did not reject the other. In Dumas and Solnik (1993), the discrimination between the two asset-pricing models was much sharper (the classic CAPM was rejected while the international one had a p-value of 22 percent). As we improve the degree of predictability, should we expect better discrimination between models? Since our goal is not to predict but to identify state variables of the economy and to determine which asset-pricing model is correct, how much importance should we give to the predictive power (the R^2) of the instruments?

The second issue concerns the choice of instrumental variables. In this respect it is important to avoid the pitfalls of data mining. That is the reason why I never modified my list of MEI indicators and why I chose to work with the Stock and Watson variables which have been preselected to predict activity and not to predict stock returns. This defense against accusations of data mining is all the stronger as the correlations between stock returns and activities levels are small (see note 14). As we attempt to predict worldwide stock returns, should we be content to use U.S. variables, such as those of Stock and Watson, on the grounds that the U.S. business cycle seems to lead other cycles? Or can we hope to attain greater predictability by using country-specific indicator variables? If so, should these variables be selected on the basis of their ability to predict local levels of activity?

A third issue that will deserve more scrutiny is the influence of time lags. Time lags are both of economic and statistical significance. Economically speaking, only innovation in a data series is capable of constituting news. News is the primary moving force behind realized returns. It is not clear, however, to what extent the past information and the lag structure that were identified as giving the best prediction of activity levels should also be relevant as determinants of conditionally expected returns. We did observe here (note 13) that the use of the Stock and Watson lags did not improve the predictability of returns.

Finally, from the point of view of the statistical specification, Thierry Wizman will point out in his comment that the levels, the first differences of indicator variables, and their first differences at different lags do not convey the same information concerning the stage of the business cycle the economy is in and do not have the same power to predict returns. How does one determine which specification is preferable for our purposes?

References

Adler, M., and B. Dumas. 1983. International portfolio choice and corporation finance: A synthesis. *Journal of Finance* 38:925–84.

Backus, D. K., P. J. Kehoe, and F. E. Kydland. 1993. International business cycles: Theory and evidence. Working paper, Stern School of Business, New York University.

Bansal, R., D. A. Hsieh, and S. Viswanathan. 1993. A new approach to international arbitrage pricing. *The Journal of Finance* 48:1719–47.

Barro, R. 1990. The stock market and investment. *Review of Financial Studies* 3:115–31.

Baxter, M., and M. J. Crucini. 1993. Explaining saving-investment correlations. *American Economic Review* 83 (3): 416–36.

Canova, F. 1993. Sources and propagation of international business cycles: Common shocks or transmission? CEPR Working Paper no. 781. London: Centre for Economic Policy Research.

Dumas, B. 1992. Dynamic equilibrium and the real exchange rate in a spatially separated world. *Review of Financial Studies* 5:153–80.

Dumas, B., and B. Solnik. 1993. The world price of foreign exchange risk. NBER Working Paper no. 4459. Cambridge, Mass.: National Bureau of Economic Research, September.

Fama, E. 1981. Stock returns, real activity, inflation and money. *American Economic Review* 71:545–65.

Fama, E. F., and K. R. French. 1989. Business conditions and expected returns on stocks and bonds. *Journal of Financial Economics* 25:23–50.

Fama, E., and M. Gibbons. 1982. Inflation, real returns and capital investment. *Journal of Monetary Economics* 9:297–323.

Fama, E., and W. Schwert. 1977. Asset returns and inflation. *Journal of Financial Economics* 5:115–46.

Gallant, R., and G. Tauchen. 1989. Semi-non parametric estimation of conditionally constrained heterogeneous processes: Asset pricing implications. *Econometrica* 57:1091–1120.

Geske, R., and R. Roll. 1983. The monetary and fiscal linkage between stock returns and inflation. *Journal of Finance* 38:1–33.

Hansen, L. P., and R. Jagannathan. 1991. Implications of security market data for models of dynamic economies. *Journal of Political Economy* 99:225–62.

Harvey, C. R. 1991a. The world price of covariance risk. *Journal of Finance* 46:111–59.

———. 1991b. The specification of conditional expectations. Working paper, Fuqua School of Business, Duke University.

Kandel, S., and R. F. Stambaugh. 1989. Expectations and volatility of long-horizon stock returns. Working Paper no. 12–89. Wharton School, University of Pennsylvania.

Lahiri, K., and G. H. Moore. 1991. *Leading economic indicators: New approaches and forecasting records.* Cambridge: Cambridge University Press.

Moore, G. H. 1992. *Leading indicators for the 1990s.* Homewood, Ill.: Dow Jones-Irwin.

Stambaugh, R. 1988. The information in forward rates: Implications for models of the term structure. *Journal of Financial Economics* 21:41–69.

Stock, J. H., and M. W. Watson. 1989. New indexes of leading and coincident economics indicators. *NBER Macroeconomics Annual,* 351–94.

———. 1993. A procedure for predicting recessions with leading indicators: Econometric issues and recent experience. In *Business cycles, indicators, and forecasting,* eds. J. H. Stock and M. W. Watson. Studies in Business Cycles, vol. 28, 95–156. Chicago: University of Chicago Press (for the NBER).

Comment   Campbell R. Harvey

The Contribution

Bernard Dumas's paper is important because it bridges finance and macroeconomics. I am sure that it will cause researchers to reevaluate the way that they specify the representative investor's conditioning information. Indeed, the idea of this paper is to explore the behavior of international stock market returns with "economically meaningful" variables. These variables will be called "external" or "macro" variables. This is in contrast to previous research which focuses on "internal" variables which are usually lagged financial returns. The paper poses and answers two questions: Do the external variables predict returns? and How does the use of external variables change the tests of the international CAPM?

Why Have Researchers Avoided Using Macro Variables?

Let me begin my discussion with an explanation of why previous research has focused on the use of financial variables as instruments. First, financial variables are available at time $t - 1$ (last day of month) and can be legitimately used to predict returns over the next month. This is in contrast to the variables used by Dumas. None of the macro variables is available on the last day of the month—not even the number of manufacturers reporting slower deliveries.

In conditional asset-pricing tests, it is crucial to have instruments that are strictly predetermined. None of the variables used in his asset-pricing tests are predetermined. In addition, it is hard to make the argument that all investors know the data before they are released. While they might in some countries, it is not the case in the United States. These macro data are very carefully protected before their release (usually at 8:30 A.M. EST). In addition, the innovations in the announcements affect both returns and volatility (see Harvey and Huang 1993). Hence, the values of the macro variables are not know in advance.

Campbell R. Harvey is associate professor of finance at the Fuqua School of Business, Duke University, and a research associate of the National Bureau of Economic Research.

The Advantages of Financial Variables as Instruments

Financial variables, on the other hand, are known on the last day of the month. In addition, asset-pricing theory suggests that financial variables should capture expectations of economic growth. A good example is interest rates. The price of the j-period discount bond, Q_j, is

$$Q_t^j = E[m_{t+j} | \Omega_{t-1}],$$

where m_{t+j} is the marginal rate of substitution between t and j, and Ω_{t-1} is the set of conditioning information that investors use to set prices at time $t - 1$. Hence, the term structure of interest rates is an ex ante measure of the marginal rate of substitution, and there has been considerable previous research confirming the relation between the term structure and the business cycle.

Most finance researchers avoid the use of macro variables. Even in consumption-based asset-pricing studies it is not unusual to project personal consumption growth rates (a macro variable) on a set of stock returns and use the resultant portfolio (a maximum correlation portfolio) for asset pricing.

The first reason research has avoided these variables has already been mentioned—the data are generally not available at the end of the month. Aside from violating the econometric assumptions, we lose the important link between asset pricing and real-world asset allocation.

Second, the data are filtered with Census X-11 seasonal adjustment program. This algorithm applies a series of centered moving averages, that is, it uses data in the future to determine the seasonal weights. In addition, the moving average changes in an ad hoc way through time. The use of future data for the seasonal weights makes even a one-year lag of the data technically nonpredetermined in the econometric sense.

Third, the macro data are subject to revisions. These revisions are often very substantial—especially when the data are first differenced. Technically, one should be using the first release of the data (unless one is willing to accept the assumption that economic agents know the data in advance).

Fourth, and most importantly, economic news is filtered by investors in forming expectations. The filter is applied to the innovation in the macro release (i.e., not the first difference as Dumas uses, but the deviation of the actual release from the market consensus expectation). In addition, the filter simultaneously considers many news events. The weights in the filter are potentially time-varying. That is, sometimes a decrease in unemployment is "bad" news if participants believe that there will be an increase in inflationary pressures, and sometimes a decrease in unemployment is good news! The filter is possibly nonlinear and fundamentally unobservable. It is unlikely that it can be proxied by a linear regression of returns on macro variables. The advantage of the financial variables is that this complicated process is collapsed into the predetermined asset price.

Predictability of Asset Returns

Expected equity returns are influenced by expected real activity. This is the main idea of Fama (1981, 1990) and Schwert (1990). Variables that forecast expected real activity should also forecast equity returns. Well-known examples are term structure variables and default risk measures.

Stock and Watson (1992) swept 280 economic series to isolate 7 which predict real activity. Data snooping is definitely an issue here. Although economic series were not swept for their ability to predict stock returns, there is a correlation between expected stock returns and expected real activity which has been documented in previous research.

Dumas identifies a number of series which "predict" stock returns: housing authorizations, growth in inventories, and the percentage of manufacturers reporting slower deliveries. If the data have been snooped, then we are stacking the deck against the asset-pricing model. Remember, the conditional asset-pricing model generates fitted expected returns. These model-fitted returns should mimic the statistical predictability in unrestricted regressions of asset returns on instruments. If the unrestricted regressions use snooped series, then it is no surprise that the asset-pricing model is rejected—it cannot be expected to explain snooped variation by changes in risk premiums and conditional betas!

The Econometric Model

The model is identical to Dumas and Solnik 1993. Let

$$E[r_{j,t}|\Omega_{t-1}] = \Lambda'_{t-1}E[r_{j,t}(f_t - E[f_t|\Omega_{t-1}]|\Omega_{t-1}],$$

where Λ = vector of prices of risk and f = factors (world excess return, FX excess returns).

A general way to test this model is to note

$$E[r_{j,t}|\Omega_{t-1}] = E[r_{j,t}u_t|\Omega_{t-1}],$$

where u_t is the relative innovation in the marginal rate of substitution (MRS). In terms of the Dumas and Solnik 1993 model,

$$u_t = \lambda_{0,t-1} + \Lambda'_{t-1}f_t,$$

where $\lambda_{0,t-1}$ is an intercept term.

However, some assumptions are required. Specifically, $\lambda_{0,t-1}$ is "whatever term is needed to bring about" equality. More precisely,

$$\lambda_{0,t-1} = -\Lambda'_{t-1}E[f_t|\Omega_{t-1}].$$

Some interpretation of this term would add to the paper.

The econometric assumptions include

$$\lambda_{0,t-1} = -Z_{t-1}D$$

and

$$\Lambda_{t-1} = Z_{t-1}\Phi,$$

where D and Φ are coefficient matrices and Z is the matrix of information variables. This amounts to assuming that the prices of risks are linear in the information set. For the tests, the innovation in the MRS is defined

$$u_t = -Z_{t-1}D + Z_{t-1}\Phi'f_t,$$

where the assumptions on the prices of risk are substituted into the definition of the innovation in the MRS.

However, the economic model imposes restrictions on the meaning of λ_0 and Λ. These restrictions are not imposed in the estimation. For example, in the case of the classic CAPM, $\Lambda = \lambda$, which is the conditionally expected excess return on the market divided by the conditional variance. That is, the coefficient has an economic definition which is not imposed in the estimation.

Dumas provides a "general test"—but we lose the ability to give intuitive interpretations to results. It is hard to answer questions like What are the model pricing errors? How well does the model do in accounting for the predictability in the asset returns? How well does the model explain the cross-section of expected returns? What do the fitted risk premiums look like? What do the fitted conditional covariances look like? What are the conditional betas? and What is the forecasted premium and covariance for the next period?

The cost of a general test is the inability to answer many of these questions. The approach is limited to verdicts such as "model rejected." In my opinion, the generality is not worth the cost. The model could be rejected but provide a useful approximation to the behavior of returns. It is impossible to measure the quality of the approximation using the approach in this paper. Nevertheless, this is only a comment on the econometric implementation. The main idea of the paper, to explicitly introduce macroeconomic variables into the conditioning information set, is a provocative one and is worthy of future research.

References

Dumas, Bernard, and Bruno Solnik. 1993. The world price of foreign exchange rate risk. NBER Working Paper no. 4459. Cambridge, Mass.: National Bureau of Economic Research, September.

Fama, Eugene F. 1981. Stock returns, real activity, inflation and money. *American Economic Review* 71:545–65.

———. 1990. Stock returns, expected returns, and real activity. *Journal of Finance* 45:1089–1108.

Harvey, Campbell R., and Roger D. Huang. 1993. Public information and fixed income volatility. Working paper, Duke University.

Schwert, G. William. 1990. Stock returns and real activity: A century of evidence. *Journal of Finance* 45:1237–57.

Stock, James H., and Mark W. Watson. 1992. A procedure for predicting recessions with leading indicators: Econometric issues and recent experience. NBER Working Paper no. 4014. Cambridge, Mass.: National Bureau of Economic Research.

Comment   Thierry A. Wizman

Most theories of asset pricing link the common movement in expected returns across different assets to a very small set of possible forces. These forces include (a) changes in volatility of dividends, volatility in dividend growth, or some broader measure of business-cycle risk (Fama and French 1989); (b) changes in risk aversion of a representative agent as aggregate wealth rises or falls (Marcus 1989); and (c) the risk of exogenous shifts in the demand of "noise traders" which must be accommodated by rational utility-maximizing traders (DeLong, Shleifer, Summers, and Waldmann 1990). The first two forces, and sometimes the third, are commonly associated with the cycle of boom and bust. For example, the degree of risk aversion may be higher in a recession, as might fundamental risk and noise-trader risk. Thus, it seems natural that we would want to use variables that are directly linked to the performance of the *real* economy in describing the behavior of excess returns through time. However, much of the literature on asset pricing has sought to link expected returns not to the underlying physical economy, but rather to other asset *price* variables such as interest rates, term structure spreads, quality spreads, and dividend yields. Professor Dumas seeks to restore the link with *quantity* variables in the context of the classic and international CAPM models of asset pricing. It is with this premise that the paper is at its most innovative and where the most potential for a new research agenda lies. I will structure my remarks around two issues: first, how to improve the power of the tests; second, how to make the premise of this approach and the motivations for using this model more convincing.

Choosing a Set of Instruments

As we know, the power of certain "internal" variables such as interest rates, dividend yields, interest-rate spreads, and quality spreads in predicting "in-sample" stock market returns has been established largely by repeated trial and error over the course of many papers (Keim and Stambaugh 1986; Campbell 1987; Campbell and Shiller 1988; Fama and French 1989; Chen 1991). In terms of R^2, the best that empirical economists can usually do in a multivariate predictive equation of monthly U.S. stock returns regressed on financial variables is about 12 percent (Harvey 1989; Hardouvelis and Wizman 1992). With

Thierry A. Wizman is investment officer and senior economist at Strategic Investment Partners, Inc.

quarterly returns, similarly specified equations yield R^2s of about 36 percent (Pesaran and Timmerman 1990). However, because some justifiable data-mining went into finding the set of explanatory variables that yield high R^2s, part of the multiple correlation may be spurious. As a result, the predictive equations typically used as a basis for testing the conditional form of the CAPMs may imbed statistical error, and this will bias the tests toward rejection. It makes sense, therefore, to select an alternative criterion, apart from the predictive power for stock market returns, for choosing state variables. One obvious criterion, given the arguments made above, is to choose variables with a direct relation to the real business cycle. Of course, if the test of the CAPM or international CAPM is to have some power, it would be nice if the same instruments help predict excess returns as well. Choosing a set of instruments that fulfill both criteria is the difficult part of the exercise Professor Dumas undertakes, because it requires the researcher to impose some discipline in his search. Specifically, we want to avoid introducing bias anew in the asset-pricing tests by mining the data for the best (highest R^2) predictive equation using a new set of "external" or "quantity" variables.

To Professor Dumas's credit, he handled the choice of instruments well, in my view. Instead of taking the reader through various specifications of stock returns regressed on various "external" variables on a hunt for the best fit, the author chooses to start with two *established* sets of nonfinancial variables. Although the point is not emphasized in the paper, the use of an established set of variables helps to deflect the criticism that any correlation between the stock market and these external variables is spurious. The two sets of candidate variables chosen are the OECD's main economic indicators for the United States (OECD-MEI) and the component indicators selected by Stock and Watson (1992) to lead the U.S. business cycle.

One suggestion here is that future research does not need to restrict its list of "external" variables to *leading* indicators only. Presumably, it is knowledge about the *phase* of the business cycle that helps us to predict stock returns. If this is so, including a corresponding predetermined set of *coincident* or *lagging* business indicators may provide a more powerful test of the orthogonality conditions implied by the conditional CAPMs because it would improve the fit of the predictive equation without sacrificing statistical integrity by overly mining the data. For example, industrial production indices, which are *coincident* indicators, have previously been shown also to help predict monthly stock returns. Also, the direction of exogenous fiscal and monetary policy may provide information on the current and future course of the economy over and above the indicators. Darrat (1990), for example, shows that changes in the cyclically adjusted budget deficit help forecast stock returns.

Transforming the Data

The first conclusion that the author draws is that while the Stock-Watson variables have the potential to predict not only U.S. but also international stock returns, the OECD-MEI variables do not share this property. At first, one might believe that this difference in predictive power is due to the temporal relation that these sets of variables have with respect to the U.S. business cycle: the Stock-Watson variables lead the cycle, while the OECD variables may lead, coincide, or slightly lag (as in the case of unemployment rates) the cycle. On second thought, however, the difference in predictive power may be an artifact of the way Professor Dumas transforms the variables, particularly the OECD-MEI variables. Specifically, my concern is with how stationarity of the instruments is achieved. As we know, stationarity is important if regressions of returns on the state variables are to have the standard asymptotic distributions. However, it is possible that a variable which carries information about the phase of the business cycle when it is expressed in *levels* or *de-trended level* loses this information when it is transformed into a first-difference, and only the most recent value of this first-difference is substituted in place of the level or de-trended level. This may be especially true of quantity variables measured in current dollars, since high-frequency changes in inflation rates may introduce noise in a measure of real economic activity (as in the case of *retail sales*). If the transformed variables no longer serve as summary statistics for the *phase* of the business cycle, they are rendered useless as state variables for the purpose of the exercise in Professor Dumas's paper.

To illustrate my point, notice that in table 1.1 of Professor Dumas's paper, where he reports the contemporaneous correlations between the six macroeconomic variables in the OECD-MEI, the correlations are relatively low. The average absolute value of cross-correlation among the set of instruments excluding the market return is 0.18. In table 1.6, on the other hand, the author reports the correlations among the Stock-Watson variables. Here, the correlations are higher. The average absolute value of the macroeconomic variables is 0.40. In light of my discussion above, these results are not surprising: three of the Stock-Watson variables are expressed in levels (housing authorizations, manufacturing hours, vendor performance), while the three that are expressed in growth rates (unfilled orders, capacity utilization, help wanted) are not measured in current dollars. In contrast, of the OECD-MEI variables, all but the unemployment rate are measured in current dollars. A strong indication that the method of transformation matters is seen in table 1.6: the predictive power of the Stock-Watson variables comes exclusively from the three variables measured in levels.

How can we improve the power of the OECD-MEI and Stock-Watson variables for U.S. and international stock market returns, while preserving stationarity? One possibility is to use de-trended levels in place of first-differences (growth rates) for the variables that are currently in first-difference (growth rate) form. Given the philosophical objections to using de-trended data in a unit-root world, another possibility is to use a higher-order lag specification in the predictive equations. That is, generalize the specification to include many lag values of the one-month first-difference (growth rate) on the right-hand side of the predictive equations. (Stock and Watson, for example, used five lags of their leading indicator variables in predicting U.S. recessions.) Although this will recover the low-frequency information previously lost, it will also expand the list of instrumental variables beyond what may be computationally feasible in the asset-pricing tests. The last (and probably best) possibility is to use longer-horizon first-differences or growth rates instead of the one-month first-differences or growth rates. Personal experience and intuition suggest that using the twelve- or eighteen-month growth rates of the macroeconomic variables would provide the greatest explanatory power for stock returns, since this periodicity closely matches the duration of U.S. business cycle downturns. If this is the case, we should be able to improve the R^2s of the predictive equations without surrendering computational ease and with a minimal amount of data mining. This would make the asset-pricing tests in Professor Dumas's paper more powerful and their results more convincing.

Having experimented with methods of transforming an established set of "external" variables, another way to make both the results and premise of this line of research more convincing is to address the issue of structural stability of the predictive equations. Professor Dumas does not address this issue, but it is important nonetheless. It turns out that when financial or "internal" variables such as interest rates, term structure spreads, and quality spreads are used to predict stock returns, most of the explanatory power comes from the period 1975–85 when the financial variables were most volatile. Moreover, in general, financial variables which have strong explanatory power in one part of the sample period do not always have explanatory power in another part. This may have to do with changes in monetary policy or changes in financial institutions over the postwar period. Finding that the properly transformed "external" variables (OECD-MEI and Stock-Watson) have a stable relationship to future stock returns and exchange-rate returns would strengthen Professor Dumas's case for using them over "internal" financial variables.

Additional Diagnostics and Experiments

The second principal finding in Professor Dumas's paper is that using the Stock-Watson instrument set, the conditional international CAPM was marginally not rejected while the conditional classic CAPM was rejected. This suggests that allowing for foreign exchange risk in a world with preferred local habitats matters. Also, recall that the specification in the theoretical section of Professor Dumas's paper is well motivated if the conditional covariances of the asset excess returns with the market return and exchange-rate returns move through time. What also motivates the specification is that the prices of risk are conditioned on the "external" variables. Given this, an interesting agenda for future research is to examine whether exchange-rate risk does in fact move significantly over time and whether these risks move with or are independent of world business cycles. Moreover, does one sort of exchange-rate risk, say, yen risk, move differently than, say, DM risk? These are important questions that may help to motivate empirical work using the ICAPM model over the traditional CAPM.

What also motivates Professor Dumas's specification is the idea that the prices of the various sources of risk are conditioned on the business cycle. Although Professor Dumas reports the coefficients from the estimated linear projection of the prices of risk on the instruments, a plot of the fitted values of the risk prices as they relate to international recessions and recoveries would be particularly helpful in ascertaining whether the prices of the various exchange-rate risks move in relation to business cycles in the various countries. Do the prices attached to yen risk, say, vary more with the cycle than prices attached to DM risk? Conducting these exercises would strengthen the premise of Professor Dumas's model by examining the nature of preferred habitats and how they might weaken or strengthen over time.

References

Campbell, John. 1987. Stock returns and the term structure. *Journal of Financial Economics* 18:373–99.
Campbell, John Y., and Robert J. Shiller. 1988. The dividend-price ratio and expectations of future dividends and discount factors. *Review of Financial Studies* 1:195–228.
Chen, Nai-Fu. 1991. Financial investment opportunities and the macroeconomy. *Journal of Finance* 46:529–54.
Darrat, A. F. 1990. Stock returns, money and fiscal deficits. *Journal of Financial and Quantitative Analysis* 25:387–98.
DeLong, J. Bradford, Andrei Shleifer, Lawrence H. Summers, and Robert Waldmann. 1990. Noise-trader risk in financial markets. *Journal of Political Economy* 98:107–18.
Fama, Eugene F., and Kenneth R. French. 1989. Business conditions and expected returns on stocks and bonds. *Journal of Financial Economics* 25:23–49.
Hardouvelis, Gikas A., and Thierry A. Wizman. 1992. The relative cost of capital of marginal firms over the business cycle. *Federal Reserve Bank of New York Quarterly Review* 17 (3): 44–58.
Harvey, Campbell. 1989. Time-varying conditional covariances in tests of asset pricing models. *Journal of Financial Economics* 24:289–317.
Keim, Donald B., and Robert F. Stambaugh. 1986. Predicting returns in the stock and bond markets. *Journal of Financial Economics* 17:357–90.
Marcus, Alan J. 1989. An equilibrium theory of excess volatility and mean reversion in stock market prices. NBER Working Paper no. 3106. Cambridge, Mass.: National Bureau of Economic Research, September.
Pesaran, M. H., and A. G. Timmerman. 1990. The statistical and economic significance of the predictability of excess returns on common stocks. Discussion Paper no. 26. Program in Applied Econometrics, University of California, Los Angeles.
Stock, James, and Mark W. Watson. 1992. A procedure for predicting recessions with leading indicators: Econometric issues and recent experience. NBER Working Paper no. 4014. Cambridge, Mass.: National Bureau of Economic Research, March.

2   An Exploratory Investigation of the Fundamental Determinants of National Equity Market Returns

Wayne Ferson and Campbell R. Harvey

This paper studies average and conditional expected returns in national equity markets and their relation to a number of fundamental country attributes. The attributes are organized into three groups. The first are relative valuation ratios, such as price-to-book-value, cash-flow, earnings, and dividends. The second group measures relative economic performance, and the third measures industry structure. We find that average returns across countries are related to the volatility of their price-to-book ratios. Predictable variation in returns is also related to relative gross domestic product (GDP), interest rate levels, and dividend-price ratios. We explore the hypothesis that cross-sectional variation in the country attributes proxies for variation in the sensitivity of national markets to global measures of economic risks. We test single-factor and two-factor models in which countries' conditional betas are assumed to be functions of the more important fundamental attributes.

2.1 Introduction

Asset-pricing theories postulate that cross-sectional differences in expected returns are linearly related to the covariances or betas of securities with marginal utility, which is a function of a set of economic risk factors. Firm-specific

Wayne Ferson is the Pigott-Paccar Professor of Finance in the Department of Finance and Business Economics at the University of Washington. Campbell R. Harvey is associate professor of finance at the Fuqua School of Business, Duke University, and a research associate of the National Bureau of Economic Research.

The authors are grateful to Jeffrey Frankel, Richard Lyons, Bruce Lehmann, an anonymous referee, and to the conference participants for helpful comments. They also appreciate the advice of Fred Fogg and Jaideep Khanna of Morgan Stanley on data issues. Ferson acknowledges financial support from the Pigott-Paccar professorship at the University of Washington. Harvey acknowledges financial support from a Batterymarch Fellowship.

59

attributes other than betas have traditionally served as alternative hypotheses in tests of these asset-pricing models at the "micro" level. A well-known example is the firm "size-effect," which first drew attention as an alternative to the capital asset pricing model (CAPM) of Sharpe (1964), Lintner (1965), and Black (1972). Additional examples include ratios of stock market price to earnings and the book value of equity (e.g., Basu 1977; Fama and French 1992; Chan, Hamao, and Lakonishok 1991). In the early 1990s, a flurry of research is attempting to understand the role of such firm-specific attributes in domestic asset pricing.

In contrast to research on foreign exchange markets, which has long been interested in predictability, research on international equity pricing has traditionally focused on average returns. Recently, however, studies have widened the focus to include the predictability of returns in different countries and the sources of this predictable variation (Harvey 1991b; Dumas and Solnik 1993; Ferson and Harvey 1993). This paper studies the relation between predictable variation and fundamental valuation ratios, measures of economic performance, and industry structure at the country level.

It is interesting that there is a divergence between the cross-sectional fundamental analysis that is important to investment practitioners (e.g., Rosenberg, Reid, and Lanstein 1985, Guerard and Takano 1990; Wadhwani and Shah 1993) and the perspective taken in most of the academic research on asset pricing. The evidence of Fama and French (1992) and others suggests that firm-specific attributes are important for explaining the cross section of domestic equity returns. This, of course, would be no surprise to many practitioners. One of the objectives of this paper is to begin to bridge the gap between the cross-sectional analysis of attributes conducted by practitioners and the beta pricing models for expected returns that are familiar to academics.

We estimate cross-sectional models, using fundamental attributes to predict future equity market returns. For example, the regressions ask whether lagged price-to-book ratios predict the next period's cross section of returns. The simplest international asset-pricing theories, based on perfect and integrated markets, imply that fundamental attributes should be useful in discriminating expected returns across countries only to the extent that they are proxies for the relevant risk exposures. We explore the hypothesis that fundamental ratios serve as proxies for conditional betas in national equity markets. We test single-factor and two-factor models in which countries' conditional betas are assumed to be functions of the fundamental attributes.

The paper is organized as follows. Section 2.2 describes the data. Section 2.3 presents some initial empirical results. Section 2.4 presents our empirical asset-pricing models, and section 2.5 offers concluding remarks.

2.2 The Data

2.2.1 National Equity Market Returns

Total returns for twenty-one countries are based on indexes from Morgan Stanley Capital International (MSCI). The returns are calculated with gross dividend reinvestment. They represent value-weighted portfolios of the larger firms traded on the national equity markets, and are designed to cover a minimum of 60 percent of the market capitalization. Returns are available from January 1970 except for Finland, Ireland, and New Zealand (which begin in February 1988). A value-weighted world market portfolio is constructed as the aggregate of the twenty-one countries.

2.2.2 Country Attributes

We examine three different groups of country attributes. The first are the relative valuation ratios. The second group measures country economic performance, and the third reflects industry structure. The data series are available from different starting dates, the earliest of which is January 1970. We conduct most of our analysis using the January 1976 through May 1993 period, for which all of the series are available. Here we motivate and briefly describe the variables. A data appendix contains more detailed descriptions of the data and sources.

Valuation Ratios

Measures of relative value have long been used by equity analysts in their attempt to discriminate high from low expected return stocks (e.g., Graham 1965). A number of investment services characterize the "styles" of equity managers as "value" or "growth" largely on the basis of similar valuation ratios for the stocks they buy (e.g., Haughton and Christopherson 1989). Quantitative stock selection models place a great deal of weight on valuation ratios for individual stocks in the United States and in other national markets (e.g., Rosenberg, Reid, and Lanstein 1985; Guerard and Takano 1990; Wadhwani and Shah 1993). With the recent work of Fama and French (1992) academics have become increasingly interested in valuation ratios. No previous study, however, has used such ratios at the country level to model the cross section of conditional expected returns as we do in this paper.

The usefulness of valuation ratios to predict stock returns may be related to mean reversion in the stock markets (Poterba and Summers 1988), time-varying risk and expected returns (Fama and French 1989), or investor sentiment (e.g., Shleifer and Summers 1990). At the country level, Stulz and Wasserfallen (1992) suggest that differences in stock market price levels, other things held fixed, may proxy for their relative investability. If expected returns differ across countries with investability, we might expect differences in valuation ratios to be related to differences in expected returns.[1]

We use four valuation ratios, obtained from MSCI. These are (a) earnings-to-price, (b) price-to-cash-flow, (c) price-to-book-value, and (d) dividend yield. Earnings-to-price was one of the first valuation ratios to attract attention as an alternative to the CAPM for individual stocks (Basu 1977). Our ratio is value-weighted across the firms in the MSCI universe. Chan, Hamao, and Lakonishok (1991) found that a ratio of price to cash flow had a stronger relation to individual stock returns in Japan than a ratio of price to earnings. Our price-to-cash ratio defines cash as accounting earnings plus depreciation. Like the price-to-book-value ratio, this is a value-weighted average across the firms. Finally, we examine dividend yields, which are the twelve-month moving sum of dividends divided by the current MSCI index level for each country.

Economic Performance Measures

We study four measures of country economic performance, designed to capture relative output, inflation, and future expected economic growth. Unlike the relative valuation measures, these variables come from outside the stock markets. The first is the ratio of lagged, quarterly gross domestic product (GDP) per capita to lagged quarterly GDP per capita for the Organization for Economic Cooperation and Development (OECD) countries, both measured in U.S. dollars. GDP per capita is studied by Harris and Opler (1990), who find that stock market returns reflect forecasts of future output. Our second measure is relative inflation, measured monthly as the ratio of country inflation (annual percentage changes in the local consumer price index [CPI]), to OECD annual inflation. Country inflation and inflation volatility, in relation to stock returns, are studied by Mandelker and Tandon (1985). A long-term interest rate and a term spread are the final economic performance measures. Harvey (1988, 1991a) has shown that the slope of the term structure contains forecasts of future economic growth rates in a number of countries. Bond yields and spreads for individual countries are also used in predictive models by Ferson and Harvey (1993), Solnik (1993), and Wadhwani and Shah (1993).[2]

Industry Structure Measures

We measure the industry structure of a country using the coefficients from regressing the country returns on international industry indices. We use the MSCI world industry portfolios to construct the industry indices. MSCI tracks

---

1. To the extent that such effects are concentrated in smaller shares, we may understate their importance by using the MSCI indexes, which are heavily weighted toward the larger and more liquid issues.

2. We use the long rate and the spread because their correlation is much lower than the correlation of the short rate and the spread, or the short rate and the long rate. While the long rates are highly persistent, appendix table 2A.1 shows that the sample autocorrelations damp out at longer lags.

thirty-eight industry groups. Industry factors are examined for explaining differences in stock return behavior across countries by Roll (1992) and Heston and Rouwenhorst (1993). Investment services, such as BARRA, use related industry structure measures in their models for individual stocks. BARRA uses as many as fifty-five industry groups. However, since our analysis is at the country level instead of the individual firm level, parsimony is important. We therefore aggregate the thirty-eight MSCI industry returns into four groups, as shown in figure 2.1. The industry groups are (*a*) natural resources, (*b*) construction and manufacturing, (*c*) transportation, communication, and energy, and (*d*) services, including financial. Summary statistics of the four industry-grouped portfolio returns are shown in the data appendix.

2.2.3 Global Risk Factors

We consider five global risk factors in our initial exploratory analysis, and focus on the two most important in our empirical asset-pricing models. Our choice of the factors follows previous theoretical and empirical work on international asset pricing. Stulz (1981b, 1984) and Adler and Dumas (1983) provide conditions under which a single-beta capital asset pricing model (CAPM) based on a world market portfolio holds globally, which motivates the use of a world equity market risk factor. A number of empirical studies have used a similar risk factor in a conditional asset-pricing context (e.g., Giovannini and Jorion 1989; Harvey 1991b; Ferson and Harvey 1993). The MSCI world return is the U.S. dollar world market return less the thirty-day Eurodollar rate.

Solnik (1974) showed that exchange risks should be "priced" in a world otherwise similar to that of the static CAPM, when purchasing power parity fails. Adler and Dumas (1983) present a model in which the world market portfolio and exchange risks are the relevant risk factors. The exchange risks can be broken down into a separate factor for each currency, as in Dumas and Solnik (1993), or can be approximated by a single variable, as in Ferson and Harvey (1993, 1994). Our second global risk factor, the G10 FX return, is the return to holding a portfolio of the currencies of the G10 countries (plus Switzerland) in excess of the thirty-day Eurodollar deposit rate. The currency return is the percentage change in the spot exchange rate plus the local currency, thirty-day Eurodeposit rate. The currency returns are trade-weighted to form a portfolio return (see Harvey 1993b for details of the construction). This measure is similar to the one used by Ferson and Harvey (1993, 1994), but it is measured directly as an excess return. This avoids the need to construct a mimicking portfolio for the factor in an asset-pricing model.

International equilibrium and arbitrage pricing (APT) models with several risk factors are described by Stulz (1981a), Hodrick (1981), Ross and Walsh (1983), and Bansal, Hsieh, and Viswanathan (1993) among others. The central intuition of such models is that only the pervasive sources of common variation should be priced. Korajczyk and Viallet (1989) and Heston, Rouwenhorst, and Wessels (1991) find evidence for several common sources of variation in U.S.

Number	Portfolio[†]	MSCI Composition
1	Natural Resoures	Forest Products & Paper (18) Gold Mines (19) Metals (Non-Ferrous) (26) Metals (Steel) (27) Misc. Materials & Commodities (28) Beverages & Tobacco (5) Food & Household Products (17)
2	Contruction and Manufacturing	Building Materials & Components (7) Construction & Housing (10) Appliances & Household Durables (2) Automobiles (3) Electrical & Electronics (12) Electronic Components & Instruments (13) Industrial Components (21) Machinery & Engineering (24) Aerospace & Military Technology (1) Chemicals (9) Merchandising (25) Textiles & Apparel (33) Wholesale & International Trade (38) Recreation, Other Consumer Goods (31)
3	Transportation/Communication/ Utilities/Energy	Transportation–Airlines (34) Transportation–Road & Rail (35) Transportation–Shipping (36) Broadcasting (6) Telecommunications (32) Utilities–Electrical & Gas (37) Energy Equipment & Services (14) Energy Sources (15)
4	Services and Financial Services	Banking (4) Financial Services (16) Insurance (22) Real Estate (30) Business & Public Services (8) Data Processing & Reproduction (11) Health & Personal Care (20) Leisure & Tourism (23)

Fig. 2.1   International industry portfolios
†An aggregation of thirty-seven Morgan Stanley Capital International industry portfolios. Each of the MSCI portfolios (numbers in parentheses) is valued-weighted. MCSI portfolio Multi-Industries (29) is not included in the aggregation. The aggregated portfolios represent returns to a portfolio that starts with an equally weighted investment in the MSCI categories in December 1969. Data are available through September 1991.

and European stocks, which suggests that a number of worldwide risk factors may be important. Ferson and Harvey (1993, 1994) find evidence that a number of global risk factors are useful in capturing both the cross section of average returns and the predictable variation of returns in national equity markets. Our additional factors are similar to theirs. The OIL return is the percentage change in the dollar price of oil minus the thirty-day Eurodollar deposit rate. The growth in OECD production is the percentage change in the OECD index of industrial production in member countries. OECD inflation is the percentage change in the OECD index of consumer prices in member countries. The data appendix provides more detailed descriptions of these variables.

2.2.4   World Information Variables

We are interested in the relation between predictability in country returns over time and the cross-sectional predictability using the fundamental attributes. We therefore include a number of worldwide information variables, similar to those which previous studies found can predict country returns over time. The variables are lagged values of the MSCI world market return, the G10 FX return, a world dividend yield, a short-term Eurodollar deposit rate, and a short-term structure measure taken from the Eurodollar market. The term spread is the difference between a ninety-day Eurodollar deposit rate and the thirty-day Eurodollar deposit rate. The short-term interest rate is the thirty-day Eurodollar deposit yield which is observed on the last day of the month.

As the predetermined variables follow previous studies using similar variables, there is a natural concern that their predictive ability arises spuriously from data mining. However, Solnik (1993) finds, using step ahead forecasts, that the predictability is economically significant. Ferson and Harvey (1993) find that a large fraction of the predictability is related to premiums for economic factor risks. Even so, the possibility of data mining remains an important caveat. Our methodology addresses this issue to some extent because it is robust to the specification of the expected factor premiums, as is explained below.

2.3   Preliminary Empirical Evidence

The appendix tables present summary statistics for the country returns and the fundamental attributes. We report the sample means, standard deviations, and autocorrelations. The monthly returns are measured in U.S. dollars. The sample period is 1975:01–1993:05, but for some of the countries and series the starting dates are later. Summary statistics are also reported for the MSCI world market index. As time series, the valuation ratios and most of the other fundamental attributes share the high degree of persistence that is familiar from the dividend yield series. However, the autocorrelations of the other series tend to damp out at longer lags more quickly than those of the dividend yields.

The appendix tables report the average correlations across countries of the valuation ratios and economic performance measures. For each country we calculate the time-series correlation matrix of the attributes. We then average these matrices across the countries. The highest absolute correlations are among the valuation ratios, which range from 0.69 to 0.79. The remaining correlations are all smaller than 0.51. The correlations between the valuation ratios and the measures of economic performance are generally much smaller than the correlations among the valuation ratios, which makes sense given the common price level in all of the valuation ratios. This suggests that some of the valuation ratios will be redundant in a time-series model, but there is not likely to be serious collinearity problems between the group of valuation ratios and the measures of economic performance.

The appendix tables record the measures of industry structure for each of the countries. These are obtained by regressing the country returns, over time, on the industry groups. The coefficients provide a simple measure of the extent to which the returns of a given country move in association with the global industry groups. Some of the industry loadings make intuitive sense. For example, Australia and Canada load heavily on natural resources, Germany on construction and manufacturing, while Hong Kong loads heavily on services, including financial. There are also examples of loadings that do not seem so intuitive. Furthermore, some of the loadings are negative. Negative loadings can be symptomatic of collinearity, or of missing factors. There is high, but not extremely high correlation between the industry groups (see the data appendix). If the four industry groups do not span the relevant factors, then the sum of the loadings should differ from 1.0 (Huberman and Kandel 1987). The coefficients are often less than 1.0, which suggests missing factors. This implies that the industry loadings should be used in conjunction with other attributes in an asset-pricing model.

Time-series plots of the valuation ratios for each country are shown in the data appendix figures. Each ratio is plotted on a graph with the corresponding ratio for the MSCI world market index as a reference series. The valuation ratios typically show no strong trends over the sample period. A number of the series show episodes of relatively high and low volatility, suggestive of conditional heteroscedasticity. The price-to-earnings ratios are the most volatile of the valuation ratios and are sometimes negative, due in large part to low and negative earnings during the world recession in 1992 (these graphs are truncated at zero and fifty).

We examine scatter plots of the average returns across countries, against the means and standard deviations of the fundamental attributes. Some of these are displayed in figure 2.2. Most of the plots show little relation among the variables. The plots do suggest a weak positive relation of average returns to the ratio of price to book value. Previous studies (e.g., Jaffe, Keim, and Westerfield 1989; Fama and French 1992) find a U-shaped relation between U.S. stock returns and their earnings-to-price ratios. We find no such pattern at the country level.

The strongest relations revealed by the scatter plots are between average returns and the standard deviation of the price-to-book ratio, and between average returns and the average term spread. The regression equations (standard errors in parentheses) are[3]

3. These are based on the 1976:01–1993:01 period shown in table 2.1. When we begin the samples in 1970:01 when available, the R^2 of the relation between average returns and the standard deviation of the price-to-book ratio increases to 25.7 percent.

(a) Mean equity return vs. standard deviation of equity return

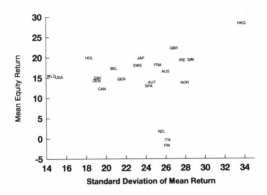

(b) Mean equity return vs. mean earnings to price

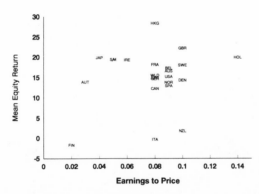

Fig. 2.2   Mean equity returns and the mean and volatility of attributes, January 1975 to May 1993 (221 observations).

Note: The Morgan Stanley Capital International (MSCI) returns are calculated with gross dividend reinvestment. Data exist for twenty-one countries. Value-weighted portfolios designed to cover a minimum of sixty returns are available from January 1970 except for Finland, Ireland, and New Zealand (which begin in February 1988). Earnings to price, price to cash, price to book, dividend to price, are value-weighted. Per capita GDP to OECD is the ratio of per capita annual GDP calculated in U.S. dollars for country to per capita annual OECD calculated in U.S. dollars. Inflation to OECD is the annual change in inflation for country *i* divided by the annual change in inflation for the OECD. The term spread is the long-term rate minus the short-term rate. Detailed descriptions and sources for all the variables are found in the data appendix.

(c) Mean equity return vs. standard deviation of earnings to price

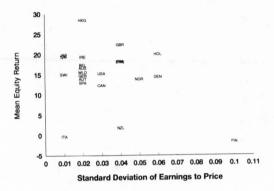

(d) Mean equity return vs. mean price to cash

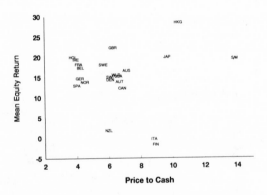

(e) Mean equity return vs. standard deviation of price to cash

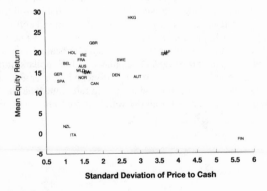

Fig. 2.2 (continued)

(f) Mean equity return vs. mean price to book

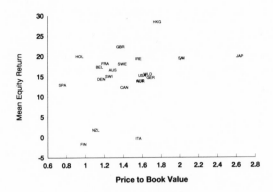

(g) Mean equity return vs. standard deviation of price to book

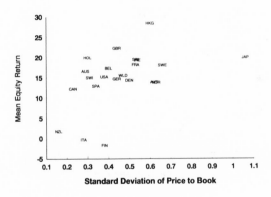

(h) Mean equity return vs. mean dividend yield

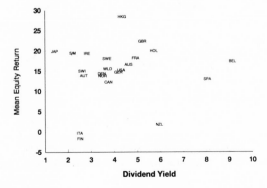

Fig. 2.2 (continued)

(i) Mean equity return vs. standard deviation of dividend yield

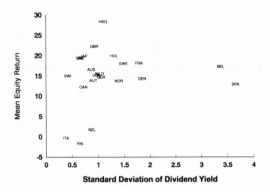

(j) Mean equity return vs. mean GDP to OECD GDP

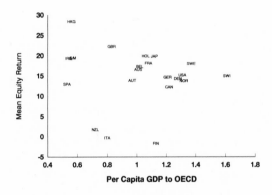

(k) Mean equity return vs. standard deviation of GDP to OECD GDP

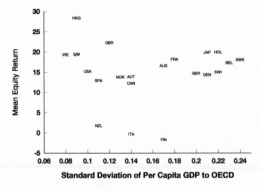

Fig. 2.2 (continued)

(l) Mean equity return vs. mean CPI to OECD CPI

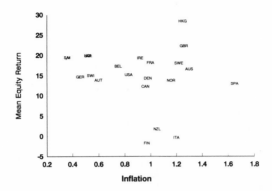

(m) Mean equity return vs. standard deviation of CPI to OECD CPI

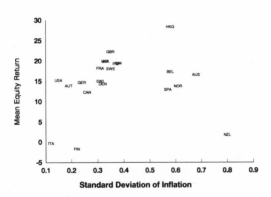

(n) Mean equity return vs. mean term spread

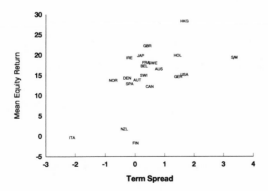

Fig. 2.2   (continued)

(o) Mean equity return vs. standard deviation of term spread

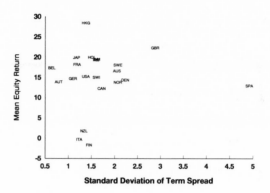

(p) Mean equity return vs. mean long-term rate

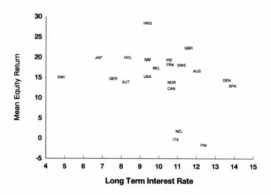

(q) Mean equity return vs. standard deviation of long-term rate

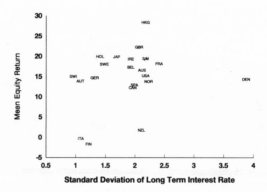

Fig. 2.2   (continued)

$$\text{avg}(R_i) = 6.7 + 17.7 \text{ sd}(P/B)_i + \varepsilon_i, R^2 = .23$$
$$(7.4), \text{ and}$$

$$\text{avg}(R_i) = 13.1 + 3.9 \text{ } TERM_i + \varepsilon_i, R^2 = .34.$$
$$(1.2).$$

These relations are stronger than the relation between the average returns and the standard deviation of the returns. The slope coefficient in that relation is 0.22 (standard error = 0.39) and the R^2 is 1.6 percent.[4] The positive relation of average returns to the term spreads should not be surprising, given previous evidence that both the slope of the term structure (Harvey 1991a) and stock returns (Harris and Opler 1990) forecast future economic growth in many countries.

It is interesting that the volatility of the price-to-book-value ratio is so strongly related to average returns, while stock return volatility shows little relation over this period. If variation over time in price-to-book ratios captures fluctuations of stock prices around "fundamental" values, then countries with higher price-to-book volatility may be countries where the risk of stock price departures from fundamentals is greater. If such deviations from fundamental values represent a risk that is priced in the market (e.g., Shleifer and Summers 1990), we would expect countries with higher volatility of price-to-fundamentals to have higher average returns.

The average relations shown in the scatter plots can be misleading if expected returns vary over time, as recent evidence suggests. The slopes in the cross-sectional relations represent a return premium associated with the attribute. Ferson and Harvey (1991) note that if the expected risk premium is time-varying, it is possible to find an average slope close to zero even though the conditional expected premium is important at some times. Table 2.1 summarizes cross-sectional predictive regressions of the country returns each month on the predetermined, fundamental attributes. The regression equation for month t is

$$(1) \qquad R_{it+1} = \gamma_{o,t+1} + + \sum_{j=1}^{K} \gamma_{j,t+1} A_{ij,t} + \varepsilon_{it+1} ; i = 1, \ldots, N,$$

where $\gamma_{o,t+1}$ is the intercept, the $\gamma_{j,t+1}$ are the slope coefficients, and $A_{ij,t}$ is the fundamental ratio j, $j = 1, \ldots, K$, for the country i in month t. The dating convention indicates that the fundamental attribute is public information at time t.[5] The slope coefficient $\gamma_{j,t+1}, j = 1, \ldots, K$ is the return on a maximum

---

4. Starting the sample in 1970:01 when available, the slope is 0.35 (standard error = 0.23) and the R^2 is .107.

5. The GDP and inflation variables are lagged fifteen months in these regressions to account for publication lag, and the interest rates are lagged one month. The industry structure variables are not predetermined, since they are estimated using regressions over the full sample period. However, they are constrained to be constant over time, which limits their predictive ability. We should not expect significant bias from including these measures, but we believe that future research should use alternative measures of industry structure which are predetermined.

Table 2.1   Cross-Sectional Regression Coefficients of Country Returns on Attributes: 1976:01–1993:01 (205 regressions)

Fundamental	Mean	Standard Deviation	t-ratio	Minimum	Maximum	1st-order Autocorrelation	Average Cross-Sectional R^2
Univariate models[a]							
Earnings to price	0.0360	0.4616	1.15	−1.578	1.723	0.105	0.078
Price to cash	0.0002	0.0058	0.55	−0.014	0.020	0.062	0.099
Price to book	−0.0010	0.0320	−0.47	−0.194	0.103	−0.111	0.083
Dividend to price	0.0009	0.0074	1.78	−0.021	0.032	0.148	0.066
Per capita GDP to OECD	−0.0084	0.0525	−2.29	−0.179	0.154	0.051	0.089
Inflation to OECD	0.0046	0.0391	1.73	−0.102	0.144	0.096	0.088
Term spread	0.0005	0.0081	1.45	−0.023	0.030	0.097	0.064
Long-term interest rate	−0.0002	0.0061	−0.48	−0.017	0.018	0.107	0.077
Industry 1 loading	−0.0072	0.0900	−1.18	−0.247	0.260	−0.006	0.087
Industry 2 loading	0.0006	0.0624	0.14	−0.147	0.211	0.003	0.088
Industry 3 loading	−0.0053	0.0495	−1.58	−0.164	0.157	0.043	0.079
Industry 4 loading	0.0089	0.0527	2.49	−0.141	0.256	0.088	0.092
Multivariate models[b]							
Earnings to price	−0.0111	0.7040	−0.23	−3.49	2.03	0.102	0.294
Price to cash	0.0012	0.0109	2.83	−0.029	0.079	0.114	0.294
Price to book	−0.0017	0.0440	−0.57	−0.111	0.154	0.062	0.294
Dividend to price	0.0010	0.0094	1.57	−0.028	0.034	0.083	0.294
Per capita GDP to OECD	−0.0064	0.0582	−1.57	−0.203	0.186	0.029	0.303
Inflation to OECD	0.0044	0.0555	1.14	−0.175	0.182	0.154	0.303
Term spread	−0.00002	0.0100	−0.03	−0.050	0.025	0.088	0.303
Long-term interest rate	−0.0010	0.0084	−1.75	−0.025	0.033	0.058	0.303

Industry 1 loading	0.0010	0.11	−0.405	0.572	0.077	0.317
Industry 2 loading	0.0074	0.87	−0.446	0.474	0.102	0.317
Industry 3 loading	0.0063	0.74	−0.346	0.461	0.101	0.317
Industry 4 loading	0.0125	1.66	−0.301	0.634	0.174	0.317
Price to cash	−0.0003	−0.45	−0.026	0.024	0.049	0.305
Dividend to price	0.0005	0.67	−0.044	0.028	0.213	0.305
Per capita GDP to OECD	−0.0063	−1.36	−0.247	0.239	0.168	0.305
Long-term interest rate	−0.0007	−1.67	−0.018	0.018	0.135	0.305
Price to cash	−0.0004	−0.79	−0.032	0.017	0.067	0.241
Per capita GDP to OECD	−0.0079	−1.99	−0.218	0.154	0.184	0.241
Long-term interest rate	−0.0008	−1.73	−0.019	0.017	0.110	0.241
Dividend to price	0.0007	1.25	−0.033	0.021	0.065	0.221
Per capita GDP to OECD	−0.0063	−1.61	−0.211	0.165	−0.002	0.221
Long-term interest rate	−0.0008	−1.88	−0.017	0.014	0.181	0.221
Dividend to price	0.0007	1.18	−0.033	0.026	0.067	0.286
Per capita GDP to OECD	−0.0040	−0.92	−0.207	0.178	−0.004	0.286
Long-term interest rate	−0.0007	−1.77	−0.017	0.017	0.176	0.286
Industry 4 loading	0.0034	0.91	−0.180	0.140	−0.056	0.286

Note: In the regressions from January 1975 to January 1977, there are fourteen countries (Austria, Finland, Italy, Ireland, New Zealand, Spain, and Switzerland are excluded). From February 1977 to February 1978, there are sixteen countries in the regressions (Finland, Italy, Ireland, New Zealand, and Spain are excluded). From March 1978 to April 1984, there are seventeen countries in the regressions (Finland, Italy, Ireland, and New Zealand are exluded). From May 1984 to January 1988, there are eighteen countries (Finland, Ireland, and New Zealand are exluded). From February 1988 to May 1990, there are twenty countries (Ireland is excluded). All twenty-one countries are used from June 1990. Per capita GDP to OECD is the ratio of per capita annual GDP calculated in U.S. dollars for the country to per capita annual OECD calculated in U.S. dollars. Inflation to OECD is the annual change in inflation for country *i* divided by the annual change in inflation for the OECD. The term spread is the long-term rate minus the short-term rate. The industry loadings are slope coefficients in the regressions of country returns on four industry returns: natural resources (loading 1), construction and manufacturing (loading 2), transportation/communication/energy and utilities (loading 3), and services and financial services (loading 4). Detailed descriptions and sources for all the variables are found in the data appendix.

[a] The univariate model is the cross-sectional regression of the returns in month *t* on the lagged attribute. Earnings to price, price to cash, price to book, dividend to price, term spread, long-term interest rate, and the industry loadings are lagged by one month. The per capita GDP to OECD GDP and the inflation to OECD inflation are lagged by fifteen months to allow for publication delays. Mean represents the average time-series cross-sectional coefficient on the attribute.

[b] The multivariate model is the cross-sectional regression of returns in month *t* on a group of lagged attributes.

correlation, zero net investment portfolio for the *j*th attribute, subject to zero cross-sectional correlation with the other attributes.[6] The portfolio weights depend only on the cross section of the attributes observed at time *t*. The expected values of the coefficients therefore represent expected return premia associated with the attributes.

Table 2.1 reports the mean, standard deviation, and other summary statistics for time series of the cross-sectional regression slopes and for the coefficients of determination of the regressions. There are 205 regressions, one for each month over the 1976:01–1993:01 sample period. To avoid the extreme outliers caused by near zero earnings, we use the ratio of earnings to price, rather than the inverse, in these regressions. Panel A of Table 2.1 reports univariate regressions. In panel B, multivariate regressions are shown, with each regression reported in a subpanel. The first three subpanels show regressions using the three main groups of fundamental attributes. The remaining subpanels show regressions which combine attributes across the three main groups. For the univariate regressions, the average of the cross-sectional *R*-squares varies from 6.4 to 9.9 percent. For the multivariate regressions, the average *R*-squares vary from 22.1 to 31.7 percent. While the average *R*-squares suggest that the cross-sectional predictive regressions have explanatory power, they should be interpreted with caution because they do not control for cross-sectional dependence of the error terms.

Table 2.1 reports *t*-ratios for the time-series average of each slope coefficient. The time-series average of the slopes is the same as the slope in the average relation, similar to those shown in figure 2.2. (However, the numbers in table 2.1 and figure 2.2 are multiplied by 1200, while those in the regressions are not, and the samples of firms differ between table 2.1 and figure 2.2.) The *t*-ratios are calculated as in Fama and MacBeth (1973), an approach which controls for cross-sectional dependence of the error terms. The *t*-ratios should be a better guide as to the significance of the average premia than the scatter plots of figure 2.2 (see Shanken 1992). For example, based on the scatter plots, the term spread showed a strong relation to average returns. However, term structure slopes are strongly positively dependent across countries, so the Fama-MacBeth *t*-ratios are reduced.[7] Table 2.1 also reports the standard deviations and the minimum and maximum values of the coefficients. The return premiums for the fundamental ratios vary substantially over the sample. This is not surprising, since the premiums are the realized excess returns of portfolios. Some of the premiums show significant autocorrelation, which implies time-variation in the conditional expected premiums. Recall that if the ex-

6. The maximum correlation and zero correlation condition with the other attributes is imposed only in a cross-sectional sense, and need not hold over time (see Shanken and Weinstein 1990 or Ferson and Harvey 1991).

7. The slope of the average relation, equal to 3.9, is not identical to .005*1200 = 6.0 in table 2.1 because the cross-sectional regressions for different months use different numbers of countries in table 2.1.

pected risk premium is time-varying, it is possible to find a small Fama-MacBeth t-ratio, even though the conditional expected premium is important.

Overall, a few of the fundamental attributes emerge as the more important cross-sectional predictors. We retain three of them for our subsequent investigations, based on the overall evidence. These are the ratio of per capita GDP to OECD per capita GDP, the dividend-to-price ratio, and the long-term interest rate. The price-to-cash-flow variable performs similarly to the dividend-to-price ratio, so we check the sensitivity of our main results to this substitution.

In table 2.2 we examine sample correlations between the slope coefficients from cross-sectional regressions on the three surviving attributes, and the contemporaneous values of the five global risk factors. If the levels of the fundamental ratios are proxies for the risk sensitivity of a national market to underlying risk factors, the cross-sectional regression slopes should jointly be proxies for the risk factors. Most of the correlations in table 2.2 are low, although some are statistically significant. Using the approximate standard error equal to $T^{-1/2}$ = 0.067, two of the fifteen simple correlations exceed three standard errors and four more exceed two standard errors. The multiple correlations, reported in the right-hand column and the bottom two rows of the table, are all less than 0.35, which corresponds to regression R-squares of about 10 percent or less.

Table 2.2	Correlations of Mimicking Portfolios Returns and Prespecified Factors: 1976:01–1993:01 (205 observations)			
Factor	γ YD	γ RGDP	γ LONG	Multiple
MSCI world excess return	−0.14	−0.07	−0.01	0.14
G10 excess FX return	0.07	−0.02	−0.32	0.32
Oil excess return	0.15	0.20	0.02	0.21
Growth OECD production	0.02	0.00	0.03	0.04
OECD inflation	−0.10	−0.03	0.09	0.13
2 factors	0.18	0.07	0.34	
5 factors	0.26	0.21	0.35	

Note: The mimicking portfolio returns, γ, are based on cross-sectional regressions of country returns on three lagged attributes: dividend yield, country per capita GDP to OECD GDP, and the long-term interest rate. GDP to OECD is the ratio of per capita GDP calculated in U.S. dollars for the country to per capita annual OECD calculated in U.S. dollars. In the cross-sectional regressions from January 1975 to January 1977, there are fourteen countries (Austria, Finland, Italy, Ireland, New Zealand, Spain, and Switzerland are excluded). From February 1977 to February 1978, there are sixteen countries in the regressions (Finland, Italy, Ireland, New Zealand, and Spain are excluded). From March 1978 to April 1984, there are seventeen countries in the regressions (Finland, Italy, Ireland, and New Zealand are excluded). From May 1984 to January 1988, there are eighteen countries (Finland, Ireland, and New Zealand are excluded). From February 1988 to May 1990, there are twenty countries (Ireland is excluded). All twenty-one countries are used from June 1990. The cross-setional slope coefficients are the mimicking portfolio returns. Time-series correlations are reported with five world risk factors: the excess return on the MSCI world market return, the excess return on a portfolio of currency investments in ten countries (see Harvey 1993b for details of the construction of this variable), the excess return to holding crude oil, growth in OECD industrial production, and the rate of change in OECD inflation.

(The two-factor case refers to the MSCI world excess return as the first factor and the G10 FX excess return is a second factor.)

There are a number of possible interpretations for the low correlations in table 2.2. One possibility is that the factors exclude some important priced risks. Another possibility is that the cross-sectional predictability using the attributes is not explained by a rational pricing model using the global risk factors in an integrated capital market. Yet a third possibility is that there is so much noise in the cross-sectional regression estimates of the return premiums that the true relation is obscured. It is likely that the cross-sectional regression slopes are noisy estimates, given the range of the values recorded in table 2.1. (See also Shanken and Weinstein 1990 in a domestic asset-pricing context.)

Our hypothesis is that expected returns, which are modeled in the cross-sectional regressions as a combination of the attributes multiplied by the conditional expected values of the γs, are equal to a combination of betas multiplied by conditional expected risk premia for the global risk factors. If this view is correct, there are a number of things that can cloud the relation between the cross-sectional slopes and the risk factors. Both time-series and cross-sectional variation in the ratios of betas to attributes can reduce the time-series correlation between the regression slopes and the risk factors. In order to obtain a clearer picture of the relation between the fundamental attributes and betas, we need to model the relation of the attributes to the betas explicitly.

Table 2.3 explores the time-series predictability of the national market returns in relation to the predetermined attributes. We report the results of time-series regressions for each country, on a constant, the vector of predetermined, world information variables (denoted by Z), and on the three own-country fundamental attributes (denoted by A). F-statistics examine the hypotheses that Z may be excluded or that the fundamental attributes may be excluded. The results are interesting and differ from previous studies. Harvey (1991b) found that world information variables were more important than country-specific variables for predicting the MSCI index returns over the 1970–89 period, while Ferson and Harvey (1993) found that both global and local information variables had marginal explanatory power. Solnik (1993) chose to use only local information variables. In table 2.3 we reject the hypothesis that the country attributes can be excluded when the world information variables are in the regressions, for eleven of the twenty-one countries at the 5 percent level, and five more at the 10 percent level. In contrast, we reject the hypothesis that the world information variables can be excluded, for one country only (Australia), at the 5 percent level. When we replace the dividend-to-price ratio with the ratio of price-to-cash-flow, the results are similar.[8]

There are several differences between the regressions in table 2.3 and previ-

---

8. Joint tests across the countries are complicated by the fact that the regressions for different countries use different sample periods. This also reduces the dependence across the separate regressions.

Table 2.3   World Information and Country Attributes for Predicting National Excess Equity Returns: 1976:01–1993:01 (205 observations)

Country i	Intercept	wr_{t-1}	$rg10fx_{t-1}$	$wdiv_{t-1}$	$e\$90\text{-}30_{t-1}$	$e\$30_t$	$div_{i,t-1}$	$rgdp_{i,t-1}$	$long_{i,t-1}$	$\bar{R}^2$	F-test Exclude World Z	F-test Exclude Local A
Australia	0.033	0.463	-0.072	0.013	0.030	-2.018	0.017	-0.144	-0.000	0.066	3.230	2.565
	(0.064)	(0.144)	(0.180)	(0.009)	(0.015)	(2.601)	(0.009)	(0.052)	(0.003)		[0.008]	[0.056]
Austria	0.150	0.245	-0.139	-0.004	0.033	1.327	-0.009	-0.076	-0.007	0.054	1.079	2.157
	(0.046)	(0.156)	(0.221)	(0.009)	(0.015)	(1.910)	(0.012)	(0.037)	(0.006)		[0.374]	[0.095]
Belgium	0.152	-0.107	-0.034	0.005	0.006	-2.277	0.005	-0.100	-0.009	0.095	0.670	6.230
	(0.038)	(0.110)	(0.167)	(0.012)	(0.013)	(2.610)	(0.004)	(0.028)	(0.004)		[0.647]	[0.000]
Canada	0.185	0.201	-0.072	0.003	0.026	2.224	0.028	-0.177	-0.010	0.058	1.592	3.988
	(0.058)	(0.070)	(0.106)	(0.007)	(0.014)	(2.619)	(0.015)	(0.055)	(0.004)		[0.164]	[0.009]
Denmark	0.072	-0.216	-0.064	-0.025	0.014	-2.036	0.006	-0.037	0.005	0.014	2.052	1.562
	(0.045)	(0.107)	(0.141)	(0.010)	(0.014)	(1.940)	(0.005)	(0.033)	(0.003)		[0.073]	[0.200]
Finland	0.526	0.393	-0.551	-0.069	0.017	-5.380	0.079	-0.308	-0.010	0.137	1.630	2.880
	(0.174)	(0.194)	(0.241)	(0.049)	(0.049)	(6.704)	(0.023)	(0.111)	(0.008)		[0.167]	[0.044]
France	0.205	-0.030	-0.149	-0.000	-0.005	2.678	0.014	-0.161	-0.010	0.057	0.437	5.051
	(0.051)	(0.119)	(0.183)	(0.013)	(0.019)	(3.133)	(0.008)	(0.039)	(0.004)		[0.822]	[0.002]
Germany	0.098	0.006	-0.269	0.000	0.011	-3.266	0.008	-0.078	-0.002	0.032	0.999	2.730
	(0.036)	(0.147)	(0.181)	(0.006)	(0.015)	(2.445)	(0.010)	(0.028)	(0.004)		[0.419]	[0.045]
Hong Kong	0.052	0.226	0.034	0.001	-0.009	2.992	0.016	-0.078	-0.009	0.015	0.554	2.055
	(0.073)	(0.154)	(0.268)	(0.009)	(0.028)	(5.028)	(0.008)	(0.081)	(0.007)		[0.735]	[0.107]
Ireland	0.611	-0.174	-0.024	-0.033	-0.033	-3.066	0.052	-0.902	-0.013	0.104	0.449	4.560
	(0.220)	(0.150)	(0.254)	(0.032)	(0.026)	(5.063)	(0.027)	(0.272)	(0.007)		[0.813]	[0.005]
Italy	-0.360	-0.454	0.308	-0.119	0.014	36.013	0.184	0.308	-0.022	0.068	1.240	2.070
	(0.671)	(0.271)	(0.326)	(0.099)	(0.057)	(14.506)	(0.069)	(0.430)	(0.016)		[0.317]	[0.129]
Japan	0.172	-0.043	0.112	-0.004	-0.001	0.225	0.004	-0.095	-0.007	0.033	0.127	3.746
	(0.053)	(0.154)	(0.180)	(0.012)	(0.014)	(2.906)	(0.017)	(0.029)	(0.006)		[0.986]	[0.012]

(*continued*)

Table 2.3 (continued)

Country i	Intercept	wr_{t-1}	$rg10fx_{t-1}$	$wdiv_{t-1}$	$e\$90\text{-}30_{t-1}$	$e\$30_t$	$div_{i,t-1}$	$rgdp_{i,t-1}$	$long_{i,t-1}$	$\bar{R}^2$	F-test Exclude World Z	F-test Exclude Local A
Netherlands	0.058 (0.024)	-0.043 (0.103)	-0.095 (0.127)	-0.003 (0.008)	0.010 (0.013)	-3.290 (1.648)	0.020 (0.007)	-0.078 (0.024)	-0.006 (0.003)	0.082	1.178 [0.321]	5.495 [0.001]
New Zealand	0.406 (0.499)	0.227 (0.280)	-0.192 (0.314)	-0.131 (0.085)	-0.100 (0.051)	3.874 (22.803)	0.031 (0.018)	-0.251 (0.753)	-0.008 (0.018)	0.072	1.743 [0.140]	1.291 [0.287]
Norway	0.141 (0.091)	0.108 (0.176)	-0.073 (0.201)	-0.011 (0.013)	0.012 (0.020)	2.713 (3.722)	0.007 (0.007)	-0.089 (0.060)	-0.002 (0.004)	-0.022	0.257 [0.936]	0.908 [0.438]
Singapore/Malaysia	0.031 (0.088)	0.112 (0.132)	-0.002 (0.192)	0.002 (0.010)	-0.004 (0.026)	4.722 (4.661)	0.013 (0.019)	0.015 (0.115)	-0.011 (0.006)	0.012	0.506 [0.771]	2.186 [0.091]
Spain	0.177 (0.065)	0.059 (0.148)	-0.089 (0.171)	-0.020 (0.014)	-0.013 (0.015)	0.313 (2.553)	0.007 (0.004)	-0.115 (0.050)	-0.007 (0.004)	0.039	0.743 [0.592]	3.289 [0.022]
Sweden	-0.024 (0.073)	0.250 (0.140)	-0.223 (0.176)	-0.011 (0.009)	0.002 (0.020)	-1.436 (2.890)	0.015 (0.007)	-0.052 (0.032)	0.009 (0.005)	0.027	1.400 [0.226]	2.396 [0.069]
Switzerland	0.070 (0.041)	-0.005 (0.115)	-0.097 (0.154)	-0.001 (0.006)	0.030 (0.016)	-3.682 (1.936)	0.009 (0.019)	-0.047 (0.018)	0.003 (0.004)	0.055	1.944 [0.089]	2.180 [0.092]
United Kingdom	0.036 (0.043)	0.144 (0.113)	-0.121 (0.149)	-0.021 (0.010)	0.017 (0.014)	1.443 (2.267)	0.043 (0.015)	-0.202 (0.064)	-0.002 (0.005)	0.059	1.240 [0.292]	4.923 [0.003]
United States	0.044 (0.056)	-0.008 (0.091)	-0.017 (0.106)	-0.016 (0.008)	-0.003 (0.012)	-5.090 (2.219)	0.033 (0.011)	-0.060 (0.053)	-0.001 (0.003)	0.018	1.331 [0.252]	2.682 [0.048]

Note: Time-series regressions begin in January 1976 or later depending on data availability. Returns are available from January 1970 except for Finland, Ireland, and New Zealand (which begin in February 1988). The instruments consist of two sets: the world Z and the attributes A. The world instruments are the lagged MSCI world return, the lagged change in a portfolio of ten currency returns, the lagged MSCI world dividend yield, the lagged spread between the ninety-day and thirty-day Eurodollar rates (based on average daily rates), and the thirty-day Eurodollar rate (quote last day of previous month). The attributes are the first lag of the local dividend yield, the fifteenth lag of the ratio of per capita GDP to OECD GDP, and the first lag of the long-term interest rate. Per capita GDP to OECD is the ratio of per capita annual GDP calculated in U.S. dollars for country to per capita annual OECD calculated in U.S. dollars. The long-term interest rate in Spain is only available from March 1978.

ous studies. The sample period is different, as table 2.3 refers to the 1976:01–1993:01 period (205 observations or fewer, depending on the country). The importance of the world information variables as predictors seems to diminish in such regressions when the 1970–75 period is excluded (see Ferson and Harvey 1993). Our fundamental attributes differ from the local information variables used in previous studies. In particular, the measure of relative GDP is a strong predictor of future stock returns in our regressions. The coefficient on this variable has a t-statistic larger than two for fourteen of the twenty-one countries.

We conclude from table 2.3 that the fundamental attributes are important in time-series as well as in cross-sectional predictive models. In time-series, they largely subsume the global information variables over this sample period. Ferson and Harvey (1993) found that beta variation contributed less to the time-series predictability of returns than risk premium variation for most countries, but they modeled the effect of local information variables through betas, and the effect of world information variables through the expected risk premia.[9] The results of table 2.2 and 2.3 lead us to an asset-pricing model in which global expected risk premiums are not restricted to depend only on our world information variables.

2.4   Conditional Asset Pricing

2.4.1   The Models

While international beta pricing models make strong assumptions about market integration, lack of frictions, and information efficiency, it is interesting to see how far one can go in modeling the relation of conditional returns to fundamental attributes and world information variables by using this standard framework. We hypothesize that conditional expected returns can be written as

$$(2) \qquad E(R_{it+1}|\Omega_t) = \lambda_o(\Omega_t) + \sum_{j=1}^{K} b_{ij}(\Omega_t)\lambda_j(\Omega_t),$$

where the $b_{ij}(\Omega_t)$ are the conditional regression betas of the country returns, R_{it+1}, measured in a common currency, on K global risk factors, $j = 1, \ldots, K$. The expected risk premia, $\lambda_j(\Omega_t)$, $j = 1, \ldots, K$, are the expected excess returns on *mimicking portfolios* for the risk factors.[10] The expectations are conditioned on a public information set, denoted by Ω_t. The intercept, $\lambda_o(\Omega_t)$, is

9. Ferson and Harvey motivated their assumption that the global risk premia depend only on world information variables by appealing to market integration. But they pointed out that their distinction between world and local market information variables was somewhat arbitrary. Expected risk premia may depend on the collection of the country attributes, as well as other public information variables, even in integrated equity markets.

10. Mimicking portfolios are defined as portfolios that may be substituted for the factors in a factor model regression, to measure the betas, and whose expected excess returns are the risk premiums. See Huberman, Kandel, and Stambaugh (1987), or Lehmann and Modest (1988).

the expected return of portfolios with all of their betas equal to zero. Equation (2) implies an expression for the expected *excess* returns:

$$(3) \qquad E(r_{it+1}|\Omega_t) = \sum_{j=1}^{K} \beta_{ij}(\Omega_t)\lambda_j(\Omega_t),$$

where the $\beta_{ij}(\Omega_t) = b_{ij}(\Omega_t) - b_{fj}(\Omega_t)$ are the conditional betas of the excess returns and the $b_{fj}(\Omega_t)$, $j = 1, \ldots, K$, are the conditional betas of a thirty-day Eurodollar deposit. Note that, according to equations (2) and (3), the only variables which differ across countries in the expressions for expected returns are the conditional betas of the country on the underlying risk factors. If rational expectations are assumed, then the difference between the actual returns at time $t + 1$ and the conditional expected returns, using information at time t, should not be predictable using information at time t. Therefore, if a cross-sectional regression of time $t + 1$ returns on variables known at time t, such as the fundamental attributes, has explanatory power, the model implies that the attributes measure the underlying betas.

In addition to evidence that expected country returns vary over time, there is evidence that the conditional covariances move over time in association with lagged variables (e.g., King, Sentana, and Wadhwani 1990; Harvey 1991b), and evidence of time-varying betas for international asset returns (e.g., Giovannini and Jorion 1987, 1989; Mark 1985; Ferson and Harvey 1993). Given the evidence in these studies and our tables, we allow for time-variation in both the expected risk premia and the conditional betas. Let $\Omega_t = \{Z_t, A_t^i, i = 1, \ldots, n, \phi_t\}$, where Z_t represents our global information variables, A_t^i the fundamental attributes of country i at time t, and ϕ_t any remaining public information that is relevant for conditional expected returns. We isolate the fundamental attributes from the other information to incorporate the idea that the variables with cross-sectional explanatory power for future returns are the variables which drive the conditional betas, $\beta_{ij}(\Omega_t)$. A parsimonious model, similar to one suggested by Ferson and Harvey (1993), assumes that the betas are functions only of the fundamental attributes. That is, we assume $\beta_{ij}(\Omega_t) = \beta_{ij}(A_t^i)$.[11] Taking the first term of a Taylor series, we use a linear function and model the conditional betas as

---

11. Some informal intuition for the impact of this restriction is suggested by Ferson and Harvey (1993). Assume that $E(r_{it+1}|\Omega_t)$ is a function $f(A_t^i, Y_t)$, where Y_t is the remaining public information, given A_t. Dropping the subscripts, consider an example where there is a single factor ($K = 1$), where β, λ, A^i, and Y are scalars, and where A^i is uncorrelated with Y. Writing $f(A^i, Y) = \beta(A^i, Y)\lambda(A^i, Y)$ and taking a first order Taylor series about the means, we have

$$\text{Var}(f) \approx [\lambda(\cdot)\partial\beta/\partial A^i + \beta(\cdot)\partial\lambda/\partial A^i]^2 \text{Var}(A^i) + [\lambda(\cdot)\partial\beta/\partial Y + \beta(\cdot)\partial\lambda/\partial Y]^2 \text{Var}(Y),$$

where $\lambda(\cdot)$ and $\beta(\cdot)$ are evaluated at the means. The first term captures the contribution of the fundamental attributes to the variance of country i's expected return, and the second term captures the contribution of the remaining public information. The assumption that the betas depend only on the local market information implies that $\partial\beta/\partial Y = 0$ in the second term. By setting $\partial\beta/\partial Y = 0$, we are ignoring what should be the smaller of the coefficients on the variance in the second term. This is because the square of an average risk premium is a small number, compared with the square of an average beta.

(4) $$\beta_{ij}(A_t^i) = b_{0ij} + B_{ij}{}' A_t^i.$$

The elements of the vector B_{ij} describe the response of the conditional beta of country i on factor j to the attributes which are the components of A_t^i.

Equation (4) allows the functional relation between the fundamental attributes and the betas to differ across countries, as was suggested by the evidence of table 2.2 and 2.3. The relation between attributes and betas for a given country is assumed to be stable over time, however, as B_{ij} is a vector of fixed coefficients. The relation may differ across countries because of differences in the accounting conventions used to compute earnings, depreciation, and book values, as well as other factors. For example, Kester and Luehrman (1989) and Ando and Auerbach (1990) argue that high cross-holdings of corporate shares in Japan inflate measured price-to-earnings ratios in that country.

The global beta pricing model (3), our model of the conditional betas (4), and rational expectations imply the following econometric model:

(5) $$r_{it+1} = \alpha_i + \sum_j \{b_{0ij} F_{jt+1} + B_{ij}{}' [A_t^i F_{jt+1}]\} + u_{i,t+1},$$

where F_{jt+1} is the excess return on the jth risk-factor–mimicking portfolio. The intercept, α_i, is an average pricing error similar to a Jensen's (1968) alpha, and should be zero if the model is well specified.

Using an ordinary least squares (OLS) regression to estimate (5) imposes moment conditions that identify $b_{0ij} + B_{ij}{}'A_t^i$ as a conditional beta. Indeed, these are the same conditions that would be imposed if the generalized method of moments (GMM) is used. To see this informally, consider the normal equations for a conditional regression coefficient given A, with the time and other subscripts suppressed:

(6) $$(F^* F^{*}{}')\beta^*(A) - F^* r' = w$$

$$E(w|A) = 0,$$

where $F^* = (1, F)'$ is a $(1 + K) \times T$ data matrix and $\beta^*(A) = (\alpha', \beta(A)')'$ is a $(1 + K)$ column vector of conditional regression coefficients. Using the GMM, the standard approach is to work with the weaker condition $E(w'A) = 0$, finding parameters which make the corresponding sample means close to zero. If the model is exactly identified, the sample means can be set equal to zero. Using the regression (5) to substitute for the term r in (6), it follows that $E(w'A) = 0$ if and only if $E(uF'A) = 0$. Since the OLS regression imposes the conditions that $E(u'F) = E(u) = E(uF'A) = 0$, it implies that $E(w'A) = 0$. Hence, $b_{0ij} + B_{ij}{}'A_t^i$, as estimated by regression (5), is a conditional beta.

To improve the power of tests using regression (5), we generalize the regression to provide specific alternative hypotheses. One interesting alternative hypothesis is that the fundamental attributes can predict returns, over and above their role as instruments for the betas. This alternative may provide powerful tests, in view of the traditional role of the attributes as alternatives to beta. In other words, we can address the question of whether the attributes represent country-specific determinants of expected returns, as in segmented capital markets, or proxies for country exposures to the global risk factors. For this alternative we replace the intercept in (5) with $\alpha_{it} = \alpha_{i0} + D_i' A_t^i$, and test the hypothesis that $D_i = 0$. A second alternative posits that the deviations between the "true" expected country returns and the model are linear functions of the world information variables. That is, we consider an alternative hypothesis with a time-varying conditional alpha: $\alpha_{it} = \alpha_{i0} + C_i' Z_t$.[12]

Under the null hypothesis, the regression model (5) should be robust to the form of the expected risk premiums, $E(F_{jt+1}|\Omega_t)$. To see this, write $F_{jt+1} = E(F_{jt+1}|\Omega_t) + \varepsilon_{jt+1}$ and note that the error term in (5) may be written, under the null hypothesis, as

$$(7) \qquad u_{it+1} = \{r_{it+1} - E(r_{it+1}|\Omega_t)\} - \beta(A_t^i)' \varepsilon_{t+1},$$

where $\beta(A_t^i)$ is the vector of conditional betas for country i and ε_{t+1} is the vector of unexpected factor excess returns. Since the $\beta(A_t^i)$ are, under the null hypothesis, the conditional betas given Ω_t, equation (7) implies that u_{it+1} is the error from projecting the unanticipated country return $\{r_{it+1} - E(r_{it+1}|\Omega_t)\}$ on the unanticipated factor excess returns, where $\beta(A_t^i)' \varepsilon_{t+1}$ is the projection. The error term u_{it+1} in (7) should be orthogonal to both the public information set Ω_t and the ex post factors, F_{jt+1}, and therefore to the right-hand-side variables in the regression (5). The expected risk premiums, $E(F_{jt+1}|\Omega_t)$, may depend on the world information variables, as in Ferson and Harvey (1993), or they may depend on the world variables and the country attributes, or possibly on all of Ω_t. The risk conditional premia could even be constant over time, and the regression (5) should still be well specified.

The robustness of the regression (5) is attractive, since the evidence suggests that it is restrictive to model the risk premia as functions only of our world information variables. Robustness to the functional form of the expected risk premia is also attractive given that linearity may be restrictive, and in view of the possibility that the relation between the expected factor risk premia and the predetermined variables could be subject to a data mining bias.

2.4.2 Asset-Pricing Results

Table 2.4 records the results of estimating the conditional asset-pricing models. The first panel shows results for a one-factor model, in which the MSCI world excess return is the factor. The second panel presents a two-factor model, using the world market portfolio and the G10 FX excess return as the second factor. F-statistics test for the significance of the products of the factors with the lagged fundamental attributes.

The results for the one-factor model confirm that the fundamental attributes

---

12. We also combined the alternative hypotheses, modeling $\alpha_{it} = \alpha_{i0} + C_i' Z_t + D_i' A_t^i$. The impressions from these tests are similar to the results reported below.

Table 2.4   National Attributes and Asset Pricing Using Dividend Yields, Economic Performance, and Long-Term Interest Rates, 1976:01–1993:01 (205 observations)

Country i	wr_t	$wr_t \times \text{div}_{i,t-1}$	$wr_t \times \text{rgdp}_{i,t-1}$	$wr_t \times \text{long}_{i,t-1}$	$\bar{R}^2$	F-test Exclude $wr_t \otimes A_{t-1}$
Australia	1.068	−0.434	1.670	0.012	0.282	4.568
	(1.452)	(0.182)	(0.818)	(0.052)		[0.004]
Austria	0.129	−0.142	−0.001	0.089	0.077	0.407
	(1.101)	(0.185)	(0.947)	(0.110)		[0.748]
Belgium	1.991	0.041	−0.604	−0.084	0.374	0.947
	(0.876)	(0.046)	(0.651)	(0.073)		[0.419]
Canada	−2.531	−0.116	2.045	0.127	0.499	5.717
	(1.326)	(0.253)	(1.468)	(0.044)		[0.001]
Denmark	0.850	−0.001	0.031	−0.015	0.251	0.163
	(0.931)	(0.089)	(0.685)	(0.034)		[0.921]
Finland	−5.180	−0.434	6.381	−0.138	0.126	1.405
	(3.749)	(0.353)	(3.526)	(0.262)		[0.250]
France	2.652	0.176	−0.626	−0.154	0.400	1.919
	(0.919)	(0.110)	(0.675)	(0.079)		[0.128]
Germany	0.984	0.035	−0.232	−0.003	0.289	0.058
	(0.822)	(0.123)	(0.582)	(0.095)		[0.981]
Hong Kong	1.027	−0.296	−0.145	0.135	0.196	3.791
	(1.413)	(0.187)	(1.795)	(0.068)		[0.011]
Ireland	9.731	0.449	−11.697	−0.332	0.367	4.165
	(2.832)	(0.214)	(3.589)	(0.113)		[0.008]
Italy	−2.569	0.208	1.322	0.192	0.619	0.413
	(9.243)	(0.892)	(6.376)	(0.415)		[0.745]
Japan	2.066	−0.376	−0.402	0.003	0.529	2.202
	(0.798)	(0.242)	(0.535)	(0.084)		[0.089]

(continued)

Table 2.4   (continued)

Country i	wr_t	$wr_t \times div_{i,t-1}$	$wr_t \times rgdp_{i,t-1}$	$wr_t \times long_{i,t-1}$	$\bar{R}^2$	F-test Exclude $wr_t \otimes A_{t-1}$
Netherlands	0.365 (0.346)	0.080 (0.088)	0.166 (0.420)	-0.009 (0.061)	0.524	1.461 [0.226]
New Zealand	2.082 (4.591)	0.033 (0.218)	-1.450 (0.796)	-0.061 (0.352)	0.029	0.186 [0.905]
Norway	-2.185 (1.662)	-0.062 (0.090)	2.072 (1.094)	0.061 (0.072)	0.282	1.483 [0.220]
Singapore/Malaysia	4.909 (1.403)	-0.631 (0.299)	-5.458 (1.720)	0.043 (0.059)	0.320	5.721 [0.001]
Spain	2.913 (1.140)	-0.056 (0.027)	-0.641 (1.056)	-0.092 (0.064)	0.337	4.161 [0.007]
Sweden	-1.383 (1.178)	-0.066 (0.072)	0.302 (0.594)	0.178 (0.072)	0.299	2.106 [0.101]
Switzerland	0.492 (0.746)	0.043 (0.154)	0.038 (0.351)	0.047 (0.076)	0.442	0.222 [0.881]
United Kingdom	0.285 (0.634)	-0.039 (0.129)	0.346 (0.982)	0.065 (0.059)	0.490	0.958 [0.413]
United States	-2.511 (1.370)	-0.104 (0.122)	2.693 (1.202)	0.026 (0.036)	0.642	3.767 [0.012]

Country i	wr_t	$wr_t \times div_{it-1}$	$wr_t \times rgdp_{it-1}$	$wr_t \times long_{it-1}$	$rg10_t$	$rg10_t \times div_{it-1}$	$rg10_t \times rgdp_{it-1}$	$rg10_t \times long_{it-1}$	$\bar{R}^2$	F-test Exclude $F_t \otimes A_{t-1}$
Australia	1.910 (1.111)	-0.414 (0.143)	1.044 (0.809)	-0.014 (0.051)	-4.666 (1.662)	0.378 (0.227)	2.274 (1.373)	0.053 (0.070)	0.306	3.894 [0.001]
Austria	-0.095 (0.987)	-0.252 (0.203)	0.562 (0.824)	0.053 (0.125)	1.252 (1.367)	0.314 (0.226)	-1.745 (1.234)	0.070 (0.161)	0.213	1.112 [0.357]
Belgium	2.251 (0.858)	0.012 (0.047)	-0.803 (0.559)	-0.083 (0.081)	-0.258 (0.881)	0.085 (0.226)	0.239 (0.574)	-0.007 (0.079)	0.470	1.971 [0.071]
Canada	-1.971 (1.379)	-0.065 (0.264)	1.650 (1.586)	0.109 (0.042)	-1.340 (1.576)	-0.001 (0.391)	0.519 (2.157)	0.042 (0.062)	0.509	3.044 [0.007]
Denmark	-0.161 (0.800)	-0.122 (0.091)	0.735 (0.612)	0.012 (0.032)	2.457 (0.984)	0.208 (0.148)	-1.367 (0.731)	-0.062 (0.057)	0.329	0.867 [0.520]
Finland	-5.212 (3.560)	-0.404 (0.255)	3.859 (2.866)	0.140 (0.172)	6.897 (7.008)	-0.579 (0.719)	1.319 (4.568)	-0.617 (0.246)	0.329	2.699 [0.022]
France	2.915 (0.731)	0.140 (0.115)	-0.868 (0.560)	-0.156 (0.072)	-0.396 (1.136)	0.104 (0.136)	0.330 (0.868)	0.025 (0.076)	0.466	1.467 [0.191]
Germany	0.768 (0.841)	-0.136 (0.131)	0.062 (0.578)	0.039 (0.100)	1.069 (0.902)	0.321 (0.170)	-0.723 (0.737)	-0.095 (0.096)	0.414	0.807 [0.566]
Hong Kong	0.542 (1.521)	-0.356 (0.169)	0.605 (1.852)	0.167 (0.078)	1.289 (2.971)	0.394 (0.307)	-3.629 (2.954)	-0.096 (0.124)	0.199	2.569 [0.020]
Ireland	8.494 (2.546)	0.465 (0.229)	-9.921 (3.333)	-0.316 (0.112)	2.012 (4.183)	-0.202 (0.619)	-2.676 (5.726)	0.017 (0.205)	0.364	2.362 [0.035]
Italy	-2.814 (8.375)	0.057 (0.854)	1.600 (5.887)	0.219 (0.367)	4.152 (8.552)	0.726 (0.712)	-3.668 (7.088)	-0.195 (0.292)	0.566	0.292 [0.936]
Japan	1.934 (1.138)	-0.541 (0.247)	-0.569 (0.739)	0.063 (0.081)	0.940 (1.272)	0.472 (0.243)	0.229 (0.772)	-0.200 (0.094)	0.571	2.321 [0.034]
Netherlands	0.517 (0.422)	0.028 (0.091)	0.214 (0.442)	-0.010 (0.066)	-0.257 (0.486)	0.127 (0.110)	-0.485 (0.620)	0.049 (0.070)	0.553	1.196 [0.310]

(continued)

Table 2.4 (continued)

New Zealand	-2.355	-0.081	12.347	-0.460	8.117	0.553	-36.321	1.265	0.138	1.596
	(5.068)	(0.245)	(10.864)	(0.367)	(6.480)	(0.308)	(19.142)	(0.665)		[0.165]
Norway	-2.118	-0.087	2.096	0.057	-0.272	0.079	-0.037	0.015	0.271	0.824
	(1.718)	(0.099)	(1.206)	(0.075)	(2.361)	(0.124)	(1.457)	(0.102)		[0.552]
Malaysia	4.999	-0.675	-5.053	0.023	-3.190	0.827	1.116	0.057	0.346	4.021
	(1.070)	(0.259)	(1.480)	(0.065)	(2.187)	(0.311)	(2.652)	(0.094)		[0.001]
Spain	2.261	-0.084	-0.035	-0.061	1.546	0.078	-2.380	-0.037	0.374	3.421
	(1.272)	(0.028)	(1.179)	(0.066)	(1.421)	(0.040)	(1.232)	(0.097)		[0.003]
Sweden	-1.817	-0.150	0.944	0.162	1.427	0.259	-2.038	0.042	0.308	2.137
	(1.218)	(0.088)	(0.673)	(0.071)	(1.654)	(0.127)	(0.711)	(0.110)		[0.051]
Switzerland	0.571	-0.177	0.088	0.093	-0.435	0.801	-0.561	-0.017	0.571	2.429
	(0.673)	(0.137)	(0.321)	(0.080)	(0.804)	(0.220)	(0.419)	(0.099)		[0.028]
United Kingdom	-0.232	-0.108	1.088	0.080	1.623	0.342	-2.613	-0.083	0.506	1.249
	(0.652)	(0.120)	(1.012)	(0.062)	(0.922)	(0.239)	(1.156)	(0.095)		[0.283]
United States	-2.630	-0.009	2.886	-0.017	2.613	0.072	-3.150	0.075	0.742	4.333
	(1.219)	(0.079)	(1.041)	(0.028)	(1.366)	(0.097)	(1.261)	(0.029)		[0.000]

Note: Time-series regressions begin in January 1976 or later depending on data availability. Returns are available from January 1976 except for Finland, Ireland, and New Zealand (which begin in February 1988). The returns are regressed on one factor (first panel) or two factors (second panel). The first factor is the excess MSCI world return. The second factor is the excess return on a portfolio of ten currency investments. The models regress the country return on the factor and the factor times each return. The three attributes are the first lag of the local dividend yield, the fifteenth lag of the ratio of per capita GDP to OECD GDP, and the first lag of the long-term attribute. Per capita GDP to OECD is the ratio of per capita annual GDP calculated in U.S. dollars for country to per capita annual OECD calculated in U.S. dollars. interest rate. The long-term interest rate in Spain is only available from March 1978. No intercept is included in the regression. Tests are presented that exclude the factor times each attribute.

are important when they enter the regression through the conditional betas. The tests reject the hypothesis of constant conditional betas, for seven countries at the 5 percent level and one more at the 10 percent level. In the two-factor model, the F-tests reject the exclusion of the product terms for ten of the countries, using a 5 percent level, and two more using a 10 percent level. The tests therefore show that using the attributes to model conditional betas improves the explanatory power of the regressions.[13]

Table 2.5 reports tests of the asset-pricing models against three alternative hypotheses. Testing for exclusion of the intercept α_i in equation (5), the tests produce only weak evidence against the models. In the one-factor model, the average pricing errors are significant at the 5 percent level for two countries, and at the 10 percent level for two more. These results are similar to those of Harvey (1991b) in testing a conditional version of a world CAPM.[14] In the two-factor model, none of the intercepts are significant at the 5 percent level, while three are significant at the 10 percent level.

Table 2.5 also reports the results of the tests against the alternative of a time-varying conditional alpha, using the fundamental attributes to model the time variation. These tests ask if the attributes represent country-specific determinants of expected returns, as in segmented capital markets, or proxies for country exposures to global risk factors. If the model captures the role of the fundamental attributes adequately through the conditional betas, we should find that the attribute variables do not provide additional explanatory power when added to the regression in an unrestricted way. In the one-factor model, the hypothesis that the model captures the information in the attributes through the betas is rejected at the 5 percent level for five countries, and at the 10 percent level for three more. In the two-factor model, the hypothesis can be rejected at the 5 percent level for only two countries, although it can be rejected at the 10 percent level for seven more. Thus, it appears that the conditional beta pricing model is only partially successful at capturing the explanatory power of the fundamental attributes.

The final tests in table 2.5 consider the alternative in which the model pricing errors are assumed to be a function of the world information variables. In the one-factor model, the exclusion hypothesis for these variables is rejected at the 5 percent level for five countries, and in the two-factor model the hypothesis is rejected for four countries.

2.5 Concluding Remarks

This paper analyses both the cross section of average returns and the time series of expected returns in twenty-one national equity markets, focusing on

---

13. We repeated the tests in table 2.4, where the dividend-to-price ratio is replaced by the price-to-cash-flow ratio. The results are generally similar, which shows some robustness of the results to the precise specification of the fundamental attributes.

14. Harvey (1991b) also conducted joint tests across the countries and did not reject that the average pricing errors are zero. Such joint tests would be complicated here because the sample periods for the countries are different.

Table 2.5   **Tests of Asset Pricing Models Using National Attributes: 1976:01–1993:01 (205 observations)**

Country	F-test Exclude Intercept	F-test Exclude Z	F-test Exclude A
One-factor model			
Australia	0.294	2.569	0.895
	[0.588]	[0.028]	[0.445]
Austria	0.228	2.273	3.171
	[0.633]	[0.049]	[0.026]
Belgium	0.363	1.311	4.066
	[0.548]	[0.261]	[0.008]
Canada	0.005	1.126	1.185
	[0.941]	[0.348]	[0.316]
Denmark	0.116	1.965	1.123
	[0.734]	[0.085]	[0.341]
Finland	2.880	2.410	1.917
	[0.095]	[0.048]	[0.138]
France	0.000	0.427	3.220
	[0.985]	[0.829]	[0.024]
Germany	0.005	1.131	1.496
	[0.945]	[0.345]	[0.217]
Hong Kong	4.067	0.629	0.698
	[0.045]	[0.678]	[0.555]
Ireland	0.089	0.238	2.218
	(0.766]	[0.945]	[0.091]
Italy	1.261	0.904	0.822
	[0.271]	[0.493]	[0.493]
Japan	0.563	0.096	2.176
	[0.454]	[0.993]	[0.092]
Netherlands	2.758	0.582	2.048
	[0.098]	[0.714]	[0.108]
New Zealand	0.621	2.459	0.760
	[0.434]	[0.044]	[0.521]
Norway	0.221	0.581	0.080
	[0.639]	[0.715]	[0.971]
Singapore/Malaysia	1.539	0.400	1.164
	[0.216]	[0.849]	[0.325]
Spain	0.008	0.836	1.222
	[0.929]	[0.526]	[0.303]
Sweden	0.820	2.703	2.039
	[0.366]	[0.022]	[0.110]
Switzerland	0.081	1.873	2.678
	[0.777]	[0.101]	[0.048]
United Kingdom	1.269	0.089	2.140
	[0.261]	[0.994]	[0.096]
United States	0.202	0.384	2.819
	[0.653]	[0.859]	[0.040]
Two-factor model			
Australia	0.670	2.952	0.707
	[0.414]	[0.014]	[0.549]

Table 2.5   (continued)

Country	F-test Exclude Intercept	F-test Exclude Z	F-test Exclude A
Austria	0.558	2.683	2.165
	[0.456]	[0.023]	[0.094]
Belgium	0.945	0.292	2.834
	[0.332]	[0.917]	[0.039]
Canada	0.037	0.714	1.413
	[0.847]	[0.613]	[0.240]
Denmark	0.030	1.443	2.706
	[0.862]	[0.210]	[0.047]
Finland	3.045	1.643	2.616
	[0.087]	[0.166]	[0.061]
France	0.053	0.625	2.046
	[0.818]	[0.681]	[0.109]
Germany	0.296	1.104	1.413
	[0.587]	[0.359]	[0.240]
Hong Kong	3.580	0.545	0.949
	[0.060]	[0.742]	[0.418]
Ireland	0.285	0.369	2.320
	[0.595]	[0.868]	[0.080]
Italy	1.266	0.902	0.856
	[0.272]	[0.496]	[0.478]
Japan	0.636	0.361	1.877
	[0.426]	[0.875]	[0.135]
Netherlands	3.835	0.183	2.429
	[0.052]	[0.969]	[0.067]
New Zealand	0.001	3.786	1.183
	[0.970]	[0.005]	[0.325]
Norway	0.314	0.685	0.028
	[0.576]	[0.636]	[0.994]
Singapore/Malaysia	1.248	0.376	1.522
	[0.265]	[0.865]	[0.210]
Spain	0.189	0.671	1.224
	[0.664]	[0.646]	[0.303]
Sweden	1.168	2.802	2.308
	[0.281]	[0.018]	[0.078]
Switzerland	0.998	1.062	2.486
	[0.319]	[0.383]	[0.062]
United Kingdom	0.726	0.191	1.800
	[0.395]	[0.966]	[0.148]
United States	1.025	1.879	2.188
	[0.313]	[0.100]	[0.091]

Note: A model is estimated with the world risk factor(s) and the product of the world risk factor(s) and the lagged country attributes. The first risk factor is the excess return on the MSCI world market portfolio. The second risk factor is the excess return on holding a trade-weighted portfolio of ten countries' currencies invested in local Eurodeposits. Three exclusion tests are presented: (*a*) exclude an intercept; (*b*) exclude the lagged world information (the lagged MSCI world return, the lagged change in a portfolio of ten currency returns, the lagged MSCI world dividend yield, the lagged spread between the ninety-day and thirty-day Eurodollar rates [based on average daily rates], and the thirty-day Eurodollar rate [quote last day of previous month]); (*c*) exclude the lagged country attributes (dividend yield, ratio of GDP to OECD GDP, and long-term interest rates).

the fundamental attributes of these economies. Our paper is the first to examine the relation of these attributes to asset pricing on a world economywide basis. We provide a framework that links the attribute analysis of investment practitioners to asset pricing theory.

We study three types of attributes. The first group includes traditional valuation ratios such as price-to-book-value, cash-flow, earnings, and dividends. The second group quantifies relative economic performance with measures such as relative GDP per capita, relative inflation, the term structure of interest rates, and long-term interest rates. Finally, we examine the industrial composition of each of the countries.

Our cross-sectional analysis suggests that the average country returns are related to the term structure of interest rates, which is a measure of expected economic performance. We also find a significant relation between the average returns and the volatility of the price-to-book-value ratios. If the variation in the price-to-book value represents movements of the stock price around fundamental values, then the countries with higher price-to-book-value volatility are the countries with the greatest departures from fundamental values. If this type of risk is priced, then this could account for our discovery of a positive relation between average country returns and the price-to-book-value volatility.

Our paper also provides evidence that the time series of expected returns is related to some of the fundamental attributes. We find that measures such as relative gross domestic product, interest-rate levels, and dividend-price ratios have the ability to predict returns in a number of countries.

The most important contribution of our work is to link the cross-sectional analysis of fundamental attributes and the time-series predictability in the framework of asset pricing theory. Asset managers often employ fundamental ratios to predict the cross section of expected returns. That is, the returns in one quarter for a large number of firms are regressed on attributes which are measured in the previous quarter. However, according to asset pricing theory, the only way to predict the cross section of expected returns is with the risk exposures. Therefore, the cross-sectional prediction based on attributes is linked to the cross-sectional prediction based on risk measures, from asset pricing theory. We explore the hypothesis that cross-sectional variation in the country attributes proxies for variation in the sensitivity of national markets to global measures of economic risk. We test single-factor and two-factor models in which countries' conditional betas are modeled as country-specific functions of the fundamental attributes.

When the betas are allowed to be functions of the attributes, the models are reasonably successful in capturing time-varying expected returns in the national equity markets. The average pricing errors for a single-factor specification are significant at the 5 percent level in only two of twenty-one countries. When a second factor is added, none of the twenty-one specifications is rejected using this test. However, there is some evidence that our model could be improved. In five of the twenty-one countries, the pricing errors from the one-factor model are partially predictable. Even when a second factor is added, there is some residual predictability in four of the twenty-one countries.

There are three natural directions for future research. First, while our model allows for changing betas and for the attributes to influence the changing betas, the structural relation between the attributes and the betas is fixed through time. A natural extension is to generalize this structural relation. Second, while we relate the betas to the level of the attributes, there is motivation for examining the volatility of the attributes. Our cross-sectional analysis indicated that the volatility of the price-to-book ratio is an important measure. A logical next step is to link the second moments of the attributes to the conditional betas. Finally, in our cross-sectional analysis we are limited by a relatively small sample of twenty-one countries. The framework that we have proposed can be immediately applied to individual firms. In addition to increased sample size, using individual firms will allow us to more precisely analyze the role of industrial composition as an economic attribute.

Data Appendix

Appendix tables 2A.1–2A.3 and appendix figures 2A.1–2A.4 describe our data and sources in more detail. IFS refers to International Financial Statistics. DataSt refers to Datastream, Ltd. OECD refers to the Organization for Economic Cooperation and Development.

Valuation Ratios

Value-weighted price-to-earnings ratios are available from MSCI starting in January 1970 except for Austria (January 1977), Finland (January 1988), Italy (April 1984), Ireland (May 1990), New Zealand (January 1988), Singapore/ Malaysia (December 1972), and Spain (January 1977). These are value-weighted averages of the ratios for the firms in the MSCI universe, based on the most recently available accounting data each month. Value-weighted price-to-cash earnings are defined as accounting earnings plus depreciation. These ratios are available beginning in January of 1970 except for Canada (December 1974), Finland (January 1988), France (September 1971), Hong Kong (December 1972), Ireland (May 1990), New Zealand (January 1988), Singapore/ Malaysia (December 1972), Spain (September 1971), and Switzerland (January 1977).

Value-weighted price-to-book-value ratios are available from January 1974 for all countries except Finland and New Zealand (both begin January 1988) and Ireland, which begins in May 1990. Dividend yields are the twelve-month moving sum of dividends divided by the current index level. The lagged value of the dividend yields are used. Dividend yields are available from January

1970 except for Finland and New Zealand (both begin January 1988), Hong Kong (January 1973), Ireland (May 1990), and Singapore/Malaysia (December 1972).

Economic Performance Measures

The ratio of lagged gross domestic product (GDP) per capita to lagged GDP per capita for the OECD countries is provided by the OECD, which provides quarterly OECD GDP figures for most of the countries. For some countries, the GDP data are only available on an annual basis. The ratio is lagged five quarters to account for publication lag. Since the data are observed quarterly (or annually), the monthly observations for each month in a quarter (or year) are the same. The population data are observed annually. The data sources and retrieval codes for the GDP data are listed below.

Country	Period	Frequency	Source	Code
AUS	1960Q1–1992Q4	Quarter	IFS	19399B.CZF...
AUT	1960Q1–1963Q4	Annual	IFS	12299B..ZF...
	1964Q1–1992Q4	Quarter	OECD	OE020000A
BEL	1960Q1–1969Q4	Annual	IFS	12499B..ZF...
	1970Q1–1992Q4	Annual	OECD	BGGDPCR.
CAN	1960Q1–1992Q4	Quarter	IFS	15699B.CZF...
DEN	1960Q1–1986Q4	Annual	IFS	12899B..ZF...
	1987Q1–1992Q4	Quarter	IFS	12899B..ZF...
FIN	1960Q1–1964Q4	Annual	IFS	17299B..ZF...
	1965Q1–1969Q4	Quarter	IMF	FNI99B..A
	1970Q1–1992Q4	Quarter	IFS	17299B..ZF...
FRA	1960Q1–1964Q4	Annual	IFS	13299B.CZF...
	1965Q1–1969Q4	Quarter	IFS	13299B.CZF...
	1970Q1–1992Q4	Quarter	OECD	FR104000B
GER	1960Q1–1992Q4	Quarter	IFS	13499A.CZF...
HKG	1960Q1–1992Q5	Annual	DataSt	HKEXTOTL
IRE	1960Q1–1969Q4	Annual	IFS	17899B..ZF...
	1970Q1–1970Q4	Annual	OECD	IRGDPCR.
ITA	1960Q1–1987Q4	Quarter	IFS	13699B.CZF...
	1988Q1–1992Q4	Quarter	OECD	IT301000B
JAP	1960Q1–1992Q4	Quarter	IFS	15899B.CZF...
HOL	1960Q1–1976Q4	Annual	IFS	13899B.CZF...
	1977Q1–1992Q4	Quarter	OECD	NL201000B
NZL	1960Q1–1969Q4	Annual	IFS	19699B..ZF...
	1970Q1–1992Q4	Annual	OECD	NZGDPCR.
NOR	1960Q1–1960Q4	Annual	IFS	14299B..ZF...
	1961Q1–1970Q4	Quarter	IFS	14299B..ZF...
	1971Q1–1977Q4	Annual	IFS	14299B..ZF...
	1978Q1–1986Q3	Quarter	IFS	14299B..ZF...
	1986Q4	Annual	IFS	14299B..ZF...
	1987Q1–1993Q1	Quarter	IFS	14299B..ZF...
SNG	1960Q1–1992Q4	Annual	IFS	57699B..ZF...
SPA	1960Q1–1969Q4	Annual	IFS	18499B..ZF...

Country	Period	Frequency	Source	Code
	1970Q1–1992Q4	Annual	OECD	ESGDPCR.
SWE	1960Q1–1979Q4	Annual	IFS	14499B..ZF...
	1980Q1–1992Q4	Quarter	IFS	14499B.ZF...
SWI	1960Q1–1966Q4	Annual	IFS	14699B.CZF...
	1967Q1–1969Q4	Quarter	IMF	SWI99B..A
	1970Q1–1993Q1	Quarter	IFS	14699B.CZF...
GBR	1960Q1–1992Q4	Quarter	IFS	11299B.CZF...
USA	1960Q1–1993Q1	Quarter	IFS	11199B.CZF...
WRD	1960Q1–1992Q4	Quarter	OECD	OC001000B

To obtain the measures of GDP per capita, the country GDP measures are divided by the following population series:

Country	Period	Frequency	Source	Code
AUS	1960Q1–1992Q4	Annual	IFS	19399Z..ZF...
AUT	1960Q1–1992Q4	Annual	IFS	12299Z..ZF...
BEL	1960Q1–1992Q4	Annual	IFS	12499Z..ZF...
CAN	1960Q1–1992Q4	Annual	IFS	15699Z..ZF...
DEN	1960Q1–1992Q4	Annual	IFS	12899Z..ZF...
FIN	1960Q1–1992Q4	Annual	IFS	17299Z..ZF...
FRA	1960Q1–1992Q4	Annual	IFS	13299Z..ZF...
GER	1960Q1–1992Q4	Annual	IFS	13499Z..ZF...
HKG	1973Q4–1992Q4	Annual	DataSt	HKTOTPOP
IRE	1960Q1–1992Q4	Annual	IFS	17899Z..ZF...
ITA	1960Q1–1992Q4	Annual	IFS	13699Z..ZF...
JAP	1960Q1–1992Q4	Annual	IFS	15899Z..ZF...
HOL	1960Q1–1992Q4	Annual	IFS	13899Z..ZF...
NZL	1960Q1–1992Q4	Annual	IFS	19699Z..ZF...
NOR	1960Q1–1992Q4	Annual	IFS	14299Z..ZF...
SNG	1960Q1–1992Q4	Annual	IFS	57699Z..ZF...
SPA	1960Q1–1992Q4	Annual	IFS	18499Z..ZF...
SWE	1960Q1–1992Q4	Annual	IFS	14499Z..ZF...
SWI	1960Q1–1992Q4	Annual	IFS	14699Z..ZF...
GBR	1960Q1–1992Q4	Annual	IFS	11299Z..ZF...
USA	1960Q1–1992Q4	Annual	IFS	11199Z..ZF...
WRD	1969Q4–1992Q4	Annual	OECD	OCDTOTPP
	1973Q4–1992Q4	Annual	DataSt	WDTOTPOP

The following currency exchange rate data are used to convert GDP in local currency to U.S. dollar terms. These series are national currency units per U.S. dollar, quarterly and annual averages, depending on the frequency of the GDP data. Period averages are used to better match the fact that GDP figures also represent an average over the period as opposed to a spot figure.

Country	Rate	Code	Country	Rate	Code
AUS	Market	193..RF.ZF...	ITA	Market	136..RF.ZF...
AUT	Official	122..RF.ZF...	JAP	Market	158..RF.ZF...
BEL	Market	124..RF.ZF...	HOL	Market	138..RF.ZF...
CAN	Market	156..RF.ZF...	NZL	Market	196..RF.ZF...
DEN	Market	128..RF.ZF...	NOR	Official	142..RF.ZF...
FIN	Official	172..RF.ZF...	SNG	Market	576..RF.ZF...
FRA	Official	132..RF.ZF...	SPA	Market	184..RF.ZF...
GER	Market	134..RF.ZF...	SWE	Official	144..RF.ZF...
HKG	Market	532..RF.ZF...	SWI	Official	146..RF.ZF...
IRE	Market	178..RF.ZF...	GBR	Market	112..RF.ZF...

The relative inflation measure is the ratio of annual percentage changes in the local consumer price index to annual percentage changes in the OECD CPI inflation series, available monthly for most of the countries. In predictive regressions, the variable is lagged five quarters to account for publication lag. The inflation series and their access codes are as follows:

Country	Period	Frequency	Source	Code
AUS	1957Q1–1993Q1	Quarter	IFS	19364...ZF...
AUT	1957Jan–1993Apr	Month	IFS	12264...ZF...
BEL	1957Jan–1993May	Month	IFS	12464...ZF...
CAN	1957Jan–1993Apr	Month	IFS	15664...ZF...
DEN	1957Q1–1966Q4	Quarter	IFS	12864...ZF...
	1967Jan–1993Mar	Month	IFS	12864...ZF...
FIN	1957Jan–1993Apr	Month	IFS	17264...ZF...
FRA	1957Jan–1993May	Month	IFS	13264...ZF...
GER	1957Jan–1993Apr	Month	IFS	13464...ZF...
HKG	1969Mar–1993Feb	Month	IFS	53264...ZF...
IRE	1957Q1–1993Q1	Quarter	IFS	17864...ZF...
	1969Q4–1993Q2	Quarter	OECD	IROCPCONF
ITA	1957Jan–1992Oct	Month	IFS	13664...ZF...
JAP	1957Jan–1993Apr	Month	IFS	15864...ZF...
HOL	1957Jan–1993Mar	Month	IFS	13864...ZF...
NZL	1957Q1–1993Q1	Quarter	IFS	19664...ZF...
NOR	1957Jan–1993Apr	Month	IFS	14264...ZF...
SNG	1968Jan–1993Apr	Month	IFS	57664...ZF...
SPA	1957Jan–1993Apr	Month	IFS	18464...ZF...
SWE	1957Jan–1993Mar	Month	IFS	14464...ZF...
SWI	1957Jan–1993May	Month	IFS	14664...ZF...
GBR	1957Jan–1993Feb	Month	IFS	11264...ZF...
USA	1957Jan–1993May	Month	IFS	11164...ZF...
WRD	1957Jan–1992Dec	Month	IFS	00164...ZF...

A long-term interest rate is measured for each country as an annualized percentage rate. In the predictive regressions, the long-term rate is lagged one month. For Hong Kong and Singapore, data are not available, so a U.S. rate was used. The sources and series codes are as follows:

Country	Period	Frequency	Source	Code	Description
AUS	1960Jan–1993May	Month	IFS	19361...ZF...	Treasury Bonds: 15 years
AUT	1971Jan–1993Apr	Month	IFS	12261...ZF...	Government bond yield
BEL	1960Jan–1993May	Month	IFS	12461...ZF...	Government bond yield
CAN	1960Jan–1993May	Month	IFS	15661...ZF...	Government bond yield > 10 yrs.
DEN	1960Jan–1993Apr	Month	IFS	12861...ZF...	Government bond yield
FIN	1972Jan–1993Apr	Month	OECD	FNOCLNG%	FN long-term rate-yield on taxable public bonds (3–6 YEARS) M. AVG. (P)
FRA	1960Jan–1993May	Month	IFS	13261...ZF...	Government bond yield (Moymens)
GER	1960Jan–1993Feb	Month	IFS	13461...ZF...	Public authorities bond yield
HKG	1960Jan–1993May	Month	IFS	11161...ZF...	Government bond yield: 10 yr.
IRE	1964Jan–1993May	Month	IFS	17861...ZF...	Government bond yield
ITA	1960Jan–1992Jun	Month	IFS	13661...ZF...	Government bond yield
JAP	1966Oct–1993Apr	Month	IFS	15861...ZF...	Government bond yield
HOL	1964Nov–1993May	Month	IFS	13861...ZF...	Government bond yield
NZL	1964Jan–1993May	Month	IFS	19661...ZF...	Government bond yield
NOR	1961Sep–1993May	Month	IFS	14261...ZF...	Government bond yield
SNG	1960Jan–1993May	Month	IFS	11161...ZF...	Government bond yield: 10 yr.
SPA	1978Mar–1993May	Month	IFS	18461...ZF...	Government bond yield
SWE	1960Jan–1993Apr	Month	IFS	14461...ZF...	Secondary Market: CENT. Government bonds: 5 yr.
SWI	1964Jan–1993May	Month	IFS	14661...ZF...	Government bond yield
GBR	1960Jan–1993Apr	Month	IFS	11261...ZF...	Government bond yield: long-term
USA	1960Jan–1993May	Month	IFS	11161...ZF...	Government bond yield: 10 yr.

Short-term interest rates for the various countries are used to construct a measure of the slope of the term structure. The term spread is the difference between the long-term interest rate and a short-term interest rate in each country. The term spread is lagged one month in the predictive regressions. The short-term interest rates are listed here together with their series codes:

Country	Period	Frequency	Source	Code	Description
AUS	1969Jul–1993May	Month	IFS	19360C..ZF...	13-weeks treasury bills
AUT	1960Jan–1993May	Month	OECD	OEOCSTIR	OE short-term interest rate—3-month vibor (monthly average) (P)
BEL	1960Jan–1993Jun	Month	IFS	12460C..ZF...	Treasury paper

CAN	1960Jan–1993Jun	Month	IFS	15660C..ZF...	Treasury bill rate
DEN	1960Jan–1993May	Month	OECD	DKOCSTIR	DK short-term interest rate—3-month interbank rate (P)
FIN	1977Dec–1993May	Month	IFS	17260B..ZF...	Average cost of CB debt
FRA	1970Jan–1986Jun	Month	IFS	13260BS.ZF...	Interbank money rate
	1986Jul–1993May	Month	IFS	13260C..ZF...	13-week Treasury bills
GER	1975Jul–1993Mar	Month	IFS	13460C..ZF...	Treasury bill rate
HKG	1974Sep–1993May	Month	IFS	11160CS.ZF...	Treasury bill rate (bond equivalent basis)
IRE	1972Mar–1993Apr	Month	IFS	17860C..ZF...	Exchequer bills
ITA	1977Mar–1993Mar	Month	IFS	13660C..ZF...	Treasury bills (weighted average before tax)
JAP	1960Jan–1977Jan	Month	IFS	15860B..ZF...	Call money rate
	1977Feb–1993May	Month	OECD	JPOCGEN%	JP short-term interest rate—3-month Gensaki rate—monthly average (P)
HOL	1968Dec–1990Aug	Month	IFS	13860C..ZF...	Treasury bill rate
NZL	1978Feb–1993May	Month	IFS	19660C..ZF...	New issue rate: 3-month Treasury bills
NOR	1971Aug–1993May	Month	IFS	14260B..ZF...	Call money rate
SNG	1972Apr–1993Apr	Month	IFS	57660B..ZF...	3-month interbank rate
SPA	1974Jan–1978Dec	Month	IFS	18460B..ZF...	Call money rate
	1979Jan–1993May	Month	IFS	18460C..ZF...	Treasury bill rate
SWE	1960Mar–1993Apr	Month	IFS	14460C..ZF...	3-month Treasury disc. notes
SWI	1975Sep–1979Dec	Month	IFS	14660B..ZF...	Call money rate
	1980Jan–1993May	Month	IFS	14660C..ZF...	Treasury bill rate
GBR	1974Jun–1993May	Month	IFS	11260CS.ZF...	Treasury bill rate bond equivalent
USA	1974Sep–1993May	Month	IFS	11160CS.ZF...	Treasury bill rate (bond equivalent basis)

Industry Structure Measures

These are the regression coefficients from regressing the country returns on the four groupings of the MSCI industry indexes, presented in figure 2.1. We use the MSCI world industry portfolios to construct the industry indexes. Each aggregate index is an equally weighted average of the returns of the MSCI industries in the group. MSCI tracks thirty-eight industry groups. These are: aerospace and military technology, appliances and household durables, automobiles, banking, beverages and tobacco, broadcasting and publishing, building materials and components, business and public services, chemicals, construction and housing, data processing and reproduction, electrical and electronics, electronic components and instruments, energy equipment and services, energy sources, financial services, food and household products, forest products and paper, gold mines, health and personal care, industrial components, insurance, leisure and tourism, machinery and engineering, merchandising, metals (nonferrous), metals (steel), miscellaneous materials and commodities, multi-industry, recreation, other consumer goods, real estate, telecommunication, textiles and apparel, transportation–airlines, transportation–road and rail, transportation–shipping, utilities–electrical and gas, and wholesale and international trade. All of the world industry indexes have a base value of 100 in December 1969. The indexes are calculated in U.S. dollars but do not include dividends. We group thirty-seven of the industry returns into the four groups shown in figure 2.1. The correlations of the four industry grouped portfolio returns are:

	IND1	IND2	IND3	IND4
IND1	1	0.69	0.71	0.64
IND2		1	0.81	0.90
IND3			1	0.78

World Information Variables

A short-term slope of the term structure is the difference between the ninety-day Eurodollar rate (Citibase FYUR3M) and the thirty-day Eurodollar deposit rate. The short-term interest rate is the thirty-day Eurodollar deposit yield. Both are monthly averages of daily quotes. The lagged values of the MSCI world stock market return, the dividend yield of the world stock market index, and the G10 FX return are also used.

Global Risk Factors

Data are available as early as January 1970 for some of the series; all are available by February 1971. The MSCI world return is the U.S. dollar world market return less the thirty-day Eurodollar rate. This series is from Datastream. The oil return is the percentage change in the U.S. dollar price of Saudi light crude, less the thirty-day Eurodollar deposit rate, which is available from the OECD from 1973. Prior to that date, the OECD series is constant, so we use the same oil price series as in Ferson and Harvey (1993, 1994) prior to 1973. This is the posted West Texas intermediate price from 1969 to 1973. Since the West Texas price reflects a different grade of oil than the Saudi light crude, the 1969–73 data is grossed down by a scale factor, based on the average price levels over the 1974–76 period. The G10 FX return is the return on holding a portfolio of currencies of the G10 countries (plus Switzerland) in excess of the thirty-day Eurodollar rate. The currency return is the percentage change in the spot exchange rate plus the local currency, thirty-day Eurodeposit rate. The portfolio weights are based on a one-year lag of a five-year moving average of trade sector weights. The numerator of the weight is the sum of the imports plus exports, and the denominator is the sum, over the countries, of the imports plus exports of each country, measured in a common currency (U.S. dollars). We use a five-year moving average of these weights, lagged by one year to insure that they are predetermined, public information. Further details of the index construction are presented by Harvey (1993b), who compares this measure with the Federal Reserve series of G10 exchange-rate changes that was used by Ferson and Harvey (1993, 1994). He finds that the correlation of the two series is in excess of 0.9.

The sample correlations of the global risk factors are:

	EXG10FX	EXOIL	dOECDIP	dOECDCPI
EXWRD	.36	−.09	−.14	−.11
EXG10FX		.03	.01	−.13
EXOIL			−.04	.09
dOECDIP				−.02

Table 2A.1   **Means, Standard Deviations, and Autocorrelations of International Equity Returns and Attributes: January 1975 to May 1993 (221 observations)**

Variable	Mean	Standard Deviation	Autocorrelation					
			ρ_1	ρ_2	ρ_3	ρ_4	ρ_{12}	ρ_{24}
Australia								
Equity return	16.60	26.02	0.03	−0.12	−0.04	0.04	−0.11	0.03
Earnings to price	0.09	0.02	0.93	0.85	0.79	0.74	0.22	0.13
Price to cash earnings	7.14	1.48	0.92	0.84	0.78	0.72	0.39	0.26
Price to book value	1.29	0.29	0.93	0.86	0.80	0.76	0.46	0.15
Dividend yield	4.63	0.87	0.93	0.86	0.81	0.76	0.20	−0.09
Per capita GDP to OECD	1.01	0.17	0.71	0.44	0.29	0.21	—	—
Inflation to OECD	1.30	0.68	0.98	0.95	0.91	0.87	0.41	−0.09
Term spread	0.81	2.05	0.93	0.85	0.78	0.74	0.32	−0.27
Long-term interest rate	12.03	2.12	0.98	0.96	0.94	0.91	0.75	0.39
Austria								
Equity return	13.90	24.63	0.14	0.01	0.05	0.11	0.02	0.03
Earnings to price	0.03	0.02	0.95	0.90	0.87	0.85	0.64	0.38
Price to cash earnings	6.70	2.94	0.96	0.91	0.87	0.83	0.49	0.14
Price to book value	1.58	0.62	0.97	0.92	0.88	0.86	0.58	0.23
Dividend yield	2.70	0.91	0.98	0.97	0.95	0.94	0.80	0.61
Per capita GDP to OECD	0.97	0.14	0.67	0.22	−0.12	−0.34	—	—
Inflation to OECD	0.60	0.19	0.93	0.86	0.79	0.71	0.27	0.00
Term spread	0.08	0.79	0.96	0.91	0.86	0.82	0.45	0.05
Long-term interest rate	8.24	1.08	0.99	0.96	0.93	0.90	0.61	0.14
Belgium								
Equity return	17.35	20.83	0.07	0.07	−0.02	0.02	0.00	0.02
Earnings to price	0.09	0.02	0.91	0.84	0.80	0.76	0.28	0.15
Price to cash earnings	4.25	1.06	0.97	0.93	0.90	0.88	0.67	0.48
Price to book value	1.15	0.40	0.98	0.96	0.95	0.93	0.85	0.69
Dividend yield	9.15	3.37	0.99	0.98	0.96	0.95	0.87	0.72
Per capita GDP to OECD	1.02	0.23	0.81	0.53	0.23	−0.06	—	—
Inflation to OECD	0.75	0.58	0.28	0.27	0.27	0.27	−0.18	0.03
Term spread	0.31	0.64	0.85	0.73	0.62	0.52	0.20	0.16
Long-term interest rate	9.86	1.93	0.99	0.98	0.96	0.95	0.76	0.37

Table 2A.1   (continued)

Variable	Mean	Standard Deviation	ρ_1	ρ_2	ρ_3	ρ_4	ρ_{12}	ρ_{24}
					Autocorrelation			
					Canada			
Equity return	12.29	19.61	−0.02	−0.06	0.06	−0.03	−0.09	0.09
Earnings to price	0.08	0.03	0.98	0.96	0.94	0.92	0.66	0.42
Price to cash earnings	6.86	1.80	0.97	0.93	0.89	0.84	0.45	0.28
Price to book value	1.41	0.23	0.94	0.88	0.84	0.79	0.37	0.02
Dividend yield	3.76	0.72	0.96	0.92	0.88	0.84	0.49	0.43
Per capita GDP to OECD	1.22	0.14	0.64	0.28	0.11	0.12	—	—
Inflation to OECD	0.96	0.26	0.95	0.90	0.84	0.76	−0.03	−0.30
Term spread	0.50	1.72	0.93	0.84	0.75	0.67	0.27	−0.21
Long-term interest rate	10.67	1.96	0.97	0.94	0.91	0.88	0.65	0.31
					Denmark			
Equity return	14.35	19.09	−0.06	0.07	0.05	0.05	−0.16	0.07
Earnings to price	0.10	0.06	0.97	0.93	0.90	0.86	0.55	0.55
Price to cash earnings	6.12	2.37	0.98	0.96	0.94	0.91	0.69	0.50
Price to book value	1.17	0.50	0.99	0.97	0.96	0.94	0.78	0.60
Dividend yield	3.48	1.85	0.99	0.99	0.98	0.97	0.88	0.71
Per capita GDP to OECD	1.28	0.21	0.74	0.36	0.08	−0.18	—	—
Inflation to OECD	0.98	0.32	0.92	0.84	0.75	0.67	0.23	0.11
Term spread	−0.26	2.23	0.91	0.86	0.80	0.74	0.22	−0.14
Long-term interest rate	13.60	3.88	0.98	0.97	0.96	0.94	0.82	0.69
					Finland			
Equity return	−1.68	26.10	0.22	−0.27	−0.14	−0.01	−0.00	0.35
Earnings to price	0.02	0.10	0.98	0.94	0.92	0.88	0.77	−0.44
Price to cash earnings	8.92	5.65	0.95	0.89	0.83	0.80	−0.05	−0.72
Price to book value	0.98	0.38	0.99	0.96	0.95	0.93	0.80	0.55
Dividend yield	2.53	0.65	0.90	0.75	0.62	0.50	0.26	−0.54
Per capita GDP to OECD	1.13	0.17	0.67	0.21	−0.11	−0.38	—	—
Inflation to OECD	0.97	0.22	0.95	0.92	0.90	0.86	0.45	−0.49
Term spread	0.02	1.45	0.80	0.51	0.28	0.18	0.11	−0.28
Long-term interest rate	12.39	1.22	0.94	0.84	0.72	0.59	0.21	0.07
					France			
Equity return	18.19	25.23	0.03	−0.02	0.12	0.05	−0.09	−0.02
Earnings to price	0.08	0.04	0.96	0.91	0.86	0.81	0.28	−0.24
Price to cash earnings	4.13	1.45	0.98	0.95	0.92	0.89	0.71	0.67
Price to book value	1.21	0.53	0.99	0.97	0.95	0.94	0.80	0.66
Dividend yield	4.93	1.79	0.98	0.96	0.94	0.92	0.79	0.58
Per capita GDP to OECD	1.08	0.18	0.72	0.35	0.5	−0.17	—	—
Inflation to OECD	1.00	0.31	0.99	0.96	0.94	0.91	0.75	0.57
Term spread	0.37	1.19	0.92	0.83	0.74	0.64	0.20	0.31
Long-term interest rate	10.60	2.41	0.99	0.98	0.96	0.94	0.76	0.41

(continued)

Table 2A.1 (continued)

Variable	Mean	Standard Deviation	Autocorrelation					
			ρ_1	ρ_2	ρ_3	ρ_4	ρ_{12}	ρ_{24}
Germany								
Equity return	14.71	21.59	−0.02	−0.01	0.11	0.08	−0.09	−0.00
Earnings to price	0.08	0.02	0.97	0.93	0.90	0.86	0.67	0.44
Price to cash earnings	4.20	0.83	0.95	0.90	0.84	0.78	0.51	0.35
Price to book value	1.69	0.44	0.97	0.94	0.91	0.88	0.63	0.32
Dividend yield	4.19	1.06	0.98	0.95	0.93	0.90	0.73	0.44
Per capita GDP to OECD	1.21	0.20	0.74	0.34	0.03	−0.21	—	—
Inflation to OECD	0.46	0.24	0.98	0.95	0.92	0.88	0.47	0.10
Term spread	1.47	1.10	0.95	0.90	0.87	0.83	0.55	0.14
Long-term interest rate	7.57	1.32	0.98	0.95	0.91	0.88	0.57	0.01
Hong Kong								
Equity return	28.43	33.74	0.05	−0.04	−0.04	−0.12	−0.01	0.00
Earnings to price	0.08	0.02	0.93	0.84	0.75	0.67	0.27	−0.23
Price to cash earnings	10.42	2.81	0.91	0.80	0.72	0.65	0.18	−0.32
Price to book value	1.76	0.60	0.94	0.88	0.81	0.76	0.36	−0.20
Dividend yield	4.35	1.10	0.91	0.80	0.69	0.61	0.24	−0.31
Per capita GDP to OECD	0.56	0.09	0.71	0.42	0.15	−0.09	—	—
Inflation to OECD	1.25	0.58	0.96	0.93	0.92	0.90	0.70	0.52
Term spread	1.68	1.38	0.93	0.82	0.73	0.65	0.37	0.08
Long-term interest rate	9.39	2.18	0.98	0.96	0.93	0.91	0.69	0.38
Ireland								
Equity return	19.36	27.73	0.09	0.09	0.16	0.11	−0.04	0.09
Earnings to price	0.06	0.02	0.93	0.87	0.80	0.73	0.44	−0.03
Price to cash earnings	3.96	1.51	0.96	0.92	0.87	0.83	0.41	−0.05
Price to book value	1.56	0.54	0.97	0.93	0.89	0.84	0.31	−0.31
Dividend yield	2.84	0.68	0.95	0.90	0.84	0.78	0.31	−0.28
Per capita GDP to OECD	0.54	0.08	0.66	0.22	−0.21	−0.39	—	—
Inflation to OECD	0.92	0.37	0.97	0.92	0.88	0.83	0.47	0.52
Term spread	−0.19	1.60	0.87	0.69	0.55	0.42	0.39	0.07
Long-term interest rate	10.55	1.93	0.97	0.91	0.85	0.79	0.57	0.49
Italy								
Equity return	−0.32	26.18	−0.16	−0.09	−0.05	0.18	−0.15	−0.37
Earnings to price	0.08	0.01	0.78	0.48	0.33	0.10	−0.36	0.08
Price to cash earnings	8.84	1.21	0.85	0.57	0.26	0.04	−0.31	0.64
Price to book value	1.56	0.28	0.85	0.56	0.22	0.01	0.11	0.44
Dividend yield	2.51	0.38	0.88	0.75	0.60	0.49	0.26	0.74
Per capita GDP to OECD	0.80	0.14	0.73	0.34	0.04	−0.12	—	—
Inflation to OECD	1.20	0.12	0.87	0.74	0.65	0.58	−0.34	0.68
Term spread	−2.10	1.24	0.67	0.62	0.51	0.36	−0.12	−0.74
Long-term interest rate	10.91	1.09	0.80	0.72	0.53	0.34	−0.70	0.04

Table 2A.1 (continued)

Variable	Mean	Standard Deviation	Autocorrelation					
			ρ_1	ρ_2	ρ_3	ρ_4	ρ_{12}	ρ_{24}
			Japan					
Equity return	19.89	23.54	0.04	−0.05	0.05	0.05	0.05	0.03
Earnings to price	0.04	0.01	0.99	0.98	0.97	0.96	0.86	0.74
Price to cash earnings	9.70	3.73	0.99	0.98	0.96	0.95	0.83	0.59
Price to book value	2.64	1.06	0.99	0.97	0.96	0.95	0.81	0.54
Dividend yield	1.43	0.73	0.99	0.99	0.99	0.98	0.97	0.93
Per capita GDP to OECD	1.12	0.21	0.76	0.42	0.15	−0.01	—	—
Inflation to OECD	0.52	0.33	0.96	0.94	0.91	0.89	0.66	0.50
Term spread	0.19	1.18	0.92	0.84	0.75	0.64	−0.13	−0.02
Long-term interest rate	6.79	1.69	0.98	0.96	0.94	0.91	0.71	0.30
			Netherlands					
Equity return	19.95	18.35	−0.02	−0.06	0.03	−0.07	0.04	−0.04
Earnings to price	0.14	0.06	0.97	0.95	0.92	0.89	0.59	0.48
Price to cash earnings	3.77	1.21	0.98	0.96	0.93	0.91	0.80	0.78
Price to book value	0.94	0.30	0.99	0.97	0.95	0.93	0.89	0.82
Dividend yield	5.73	1.31	0.97	0.94	0.92	0.89	0.74	0.58
Per capita GDP to OECD	1.06	0.22	0.81	0.53	0.27	0.01	—	—
Inflation to OECD	0.52	0.33	0.98	0.95	0.93	0.91	0.63	0.24
Term spread	1.45	1.51	0.85	0.75	0.65	0.56	0.36	0.05
Long-term interest rate	8.34	1.41	0.98	0.95	0.92	0.89	0.69	0.28
			New Zealand					
Equity return	1.80	25.56	−0.05	−0.06	−0.06	−0.13	−0.08	0.11
Earnings to price	0.10	0.04	0.85	0.70	0.61	0.54	−0.37	−0.31
Price to cash earnings	5.99	1.04	0.64	0.33	0.26	0.20	0.02	−0.12
Price to book value	1.11	0.16	0.85	0.70	0.57	0.46	−0.22	−0.32
Dividend yield	5.95	0.88	0.87	0.78	0.69	0.59	−0.25	−0.53
Per capita GDP to OECD	0.72	0.11	0.62	0.22	−0.07	−0.25	—	—
Inflation to OECD	1.05	0.80	0.95	0.90	0.89	0.87	0.41	0.63
Term spread	−0.36	1.34	0.95	0.91	0.86	0.81	0.26	0.10
Long-term interest rate	11.09	2.11	0.99	0.97	0.96	0.95	0.83	0.66
			Norway					
Equity return	13.81	27.96	0.12	−0.01	0.10	−0.06	−0.01	−0.02
Earnings to price	0.09	0.05	0.96	0.91	0.85	0.79	0.45	−0.07
Price to cash earnings	4.52	1.48	0.93	0.87	0.80	0.73	0.48	0.27
Price to book value	1.58	0.63	0.98	0.94	0.91	0.88	0.72	0.42
Dividend yield	3.51	1.40	0.98	0.95	0.92	0.89	0.61	0.29
Per capita GDP to OECD	1.32	0.13	0.64	0.23	−0.06	−0.32	—	—
Inflation to OECD	1.16	0.61	0.98	0.96	0.92	0.87	0.43	0.04
Term spread	−0.73	2.07	0.55	0.41	0.32	0.22	−0.11	−0.03
Long-term interest rate	10.68	2.23	0.99	0.98	0.97	0.96	0.88	0.67

(*continued*)

Table 2A.1   (continued)

Variable	Mean	Standard Deviation	Autocorrelation					
			ρ_1	ρ_2	ρ_3	ρ_4	ρ_{12}	ρ_{24}
			Singapore/Malaysia					
Equity return	19.48	28.58	0.13	0.04	−0.10	−0.01	0.04	0.02
Earnings to price	0.05	0.01	0.91	0.81	0.75	0.70	0.45	0.36
Price to cash earnings	13.90	3.66	0.93	0.87	0.81	0.72	0.19	0.14
Price to book value	2.02	0.53	0.95	0.88	0.80	0.74	0.45	0.16
Dividend yield	2.22	0.64	0.94	0.88	0.84	0.80	0.58	0.42
Per capita GDP to OECD	0.57	0.09	0.74	0.38	0.11	−0.12	—	—
Inflation to OECD	0.36	0.38	0.96	0.91	0.85	0.79	0.19	−0.07
Term spread	3.37	1.62	0.82	0.69	0.64	0.60	0.26	0.09
Long-term interest rate	9.39	2.18	0.98	0.96	0.93	0.91	0.69	0.38
			Spain					
Equity return	12.97	24.31	0.11	0.01	−0.06	0.07	−0.06	0.12
Earnings to price	0.09	0.02	0.94	0.87	0.80	0.74	0.45	0.03
Price to cash earnings	4.00	0.90	0.94	0.87	0.80	0.74	0.48	0.20
Price to book value	0.76	0.34	0.99	0.97	0.95	0.94	0.86	0.71
Dividend yield	8.06	3.65	0.99	0.97	0.96	0.95	0.85	0.69
Per capita GDP to OECD	0.53	0.11	0.77	0.39	0.00	−0.27	—	—
Inflation to OECD	1.65	0.57	0.97	0.93	0.88	0.82	0.22	−0.03
Term spread	−0.18	4.92	0.76	0.54	0.38	0.17	0.01	−0.04
Long-term interest rate	13.90	1.99	0.97	0.93	0.89	0.84	0.52	0.13
			Sweden					
Equity return	18.08	23.22	0.09	−0.00	0.05	−0.01	0.02	0.01
Earnings to price	0.10	0.04	0.97	0.94	0.91	0.87	0.50	0.12
Price to cash earnings	5.68	2.51	0.98	0.95	0.93	0.90	0.75	0.62
Price to book value	1.39	0.66	0.99	0.97	0.95	0.93	0.79	0.65
Dividend yield	3.70	1.49	0.98	0.96	0.94	0.92	0.79	0.62
Per capita GDP to OECD	1.37	0.24	0.78	0.46	0.18	−0.04	—	—
Inflation to OECD	1.22	0.35	0.93	0.87	0.78	0.70	0.07	−0.03
Term spread	0.61	2.07	0.87	0.75	0.65	0.57	0.16	0.07
Long-term interest rate	11.21	1.48	0.97	0.94	0.90	0.86	0.52	0.29
			Switzerland					
Equity return	15.03	19.18	0.04	−0.00	−0.00	0.01	−0.02	0.02
Earnings to price	0.08	0.01	0.95	0.89	0.84	0.79	0.49	0.38
Price to cash earnings	6.09	1.62	0.97	0.94	0.91	0.89	0.75	0.75
Price to book value	1.25	0.31	0.98	0.95	0.92	0.90	0.72	0.59
Dividend yield	2.62	0.42	0.95	0.90	0.84	0.80	0.55	0.37
Per capita GDP to OECD	1.61	0.22	0.57	0.08	−0.17	−0.30	—	—
Inflation to OECD	0.54	0.31	0.98	0.95	0.92	0.90	0.62	0.41
Term spread	0.30	1.61	0.93	0.89	0.84	0.79	0.45	−0.02
Long-term interest rate	4.81	0.96	0.98	0.96	0.93	0.90	0.66	0.23

Table 2A.1   (continued)

Variable	Mean	Standard Deviation	Autocorrelation					
			ρ_1	ρ_2	ρ_3	ρ_4	ρ_{12}	ρ_{24}
			United Kingdom					
Equity return	22.31	26.88	0.09	−0.12	0.03	−0.01	−0.07	0.08
Earnings to price	0.10	0.04	0.95	0.90	0.88	0.83	0.55	0.41
Price to cash earnings	6.29	1.78	0.97	0.94	0.91	0.88	0.73	0.61
Price to book value	1.37	0.44	0.98	0.96	0.94	0.92	0.85	0.77
Dividend yield	5.23	0.93	0.88	0.78	0.76	0.69	0.47	0.44
Per capita GDP to OECD	0.83	0.12	0.66	0.09	−0.44	−0.71	—	—
Inflation to OECD	1.26	0.35	0.97	0.91	0.84	0.77	0.27	0.11
Term spread	0.42	2.88	0.79	0.75	0.71	0.69	0.41	0.20
Long-term interest rate	11.58	2.07	0.98	0.94	0.91	0.88	0.73	0.59
			United States					
Equity return	15.23	15.32	0.00	−0.05	−0.07	−0.05	0.00	0.05
Earnings to price	0.09	0.03	0.98	0.97	0.95	0.93	0.73	0.60
Price to cash earnings	6.63	1.57	0.98	0.96	0.94	0.92	0.73	0.55
Price to book value	1.60	0.38	0.98	0.96	0.95	0.93	0.84	0.78
Dividend yield	4.31	0.97	0.98	0.96	0.94	0.92	0.77	0.62
Per capita GDP to OECD	1.31	0.10	0.70	0.49	0.35	0.22	—	—
Inflation to OECD	0.83	0.15	0.97	0.91	0.85	0.80	0.31	−0.06
Term spread	1.68	1.38	0.93	0.82	0.73	0.65	0.37	0.08
Long-term interest rate	9.39	2.18	0.98	0.96	0.93	0.91	0.69	0.38
			World					
Equity return	15.55	14.54	0.06	−0.06	−0.02	−0.04	0.02	0.07
Earnings to price	0.08	0.02	0.99	0.98	0.96	0.95	0.81	0.72
Price to cash earnings	6.48	1.43	0.98	0.96	0.93	0.91	0.76	0.71
Price to book value	1.66	0.47	0.99	0.97	0.96	0.95	0.85	0.74
Dividend yield	3.73	1.03	0.99	0.98	0.97	0.96	0.87	0.78

Note: Summary statistics use data that begin in January 1975 or later depending on data availability. Returns are available from January 1970 except for Finland, Ireland, and New Zealand (which begin in February 1988). Price to earnings ratios start in January 1970 except for Austria (January 1977), Finland (January 1988), Italy (April 1984), Ireland (May 1990), New Zealand (January 1988), Singapore/Malaysia (December 1972), and Spain (January 1977). The price to book ratios are available from January 1974 for all countries except Finland and New Zealand (both begin January 1988) and Ireland (May 1990). The price to cash ratios are available over the entire sample except for Canada (December 1974), Finland (January 1988), France (September 1971), Hong Kong (December 1972), Ireland (May 1990), New Zealand (January 1988), Singapore/Malaysia (December 1972), Spain (September 1971), and Switzerland (January 1977). Dividend yields are available from January 1970 except for Finland and New Zealand (both begin January 1988), Hong Kong (January 1973), Ireland (May 1990), and Singapore/Malaysia (December 1972). Per capita GDP to OECD is the ratio of per capita annual GDP calculated in U.S. dollars for country to per capita annual OECD calculated in U.S. dollars. The annual observations are observed quarterly except for Belgium, Denmark (annual through 1987Q4), Hong Kong, Netherlands and Norway (annual through 1976Q4), Singapore, and Spain. The population data are annual. The summary statistics for this variable are based on annual observations. Inflation to OECD is the annual change in inflation for country i divided by the annual change in inflation for the OECD. These monthly data are available from December 1969 for all countries. Monthly long-term interest rates begin in December 1969 except for Austria (January 1971), Finland (January 1972), and Spain (March 1978). Data were not avail-
(*continued*)

Table 2A.1   (continued)

able for Hong Kong and Singapore so the U.S. rate was used. The term spread is the long-term rate minus the short-term rate. Short-term interest rates begin in December 1969 except for Denmark (December 1974), Finland (December 1977), France (January 1970), Germany (December 1974), Hong Kong (September 1974 U.S. used), Ireland (November 1972), Italy (November 1977), Netherlands (December 1974), New Zealand (February 1978), Norway (August 1971), Singapore (August 1973), Spain (January 1974), Switzerland (December 1974), United Kingdom (January 1974), and United States (October 1974).

Table 2A.2   **Average Cross-Country Time-Series Correlations of Attributes 1975:01–1993:05 (221 observations)**

Attributes	EP	PC	PB	YD	RGDP	RCPI	TERM	LONG
Earnings to price	1.00							
Price to cash earnings	−0.79	1.00						
Price to book value	−0.51	0.69	1.00					
Dividend yield	0.69	−0.76	−0.79	1.00				
Per capita GDP to OECD	0.29	−0.27	−0.17	0.27	1.00			
Inflation to OECD	0.07	−0.11	−0.05	0.09	−0.14	1.00		
Term spread	−0.01	−0.04	−0.16	0.03	−0.03	−0.09	1.00	
Long-term interest rate	0.29	−0.28	−0.29	0.36	−0.07	0.4	0.00	1.00

Note: Time-series correlations of the attributes were calculated for each country. The statistics reported are the averages of these correlations across all the countries. The sample size is not the same for each country. Correlations use data that begin in January 1975 or later depending on data availability. Returns are available from January 1970 except for Finland, Ireland, and New Zealand (which begin in February 1988). Price to earnings ratios start in January 1970 except for Austria (January 1977), Finland (January 1988), Italy (April 1984), Ireland (May 1990), New Zealand (January 1988), Singapore/Malaysia (December 1972), and Spain (January 1977). The price to book ratios are available from January 1974 for all countries except Finland and New Zealand (both begin January 1988) and Ireland (May 1990). The price to cash ratios are available over the entire sample except for Canada (December 1974), Finland (January 1988), France (September 1971), Hong Kong (December 1972), Ireland (May 1990), New Zealand (January 1988), Singapore/Malaysia (December 1972), Spain (September 1971), and Switzerland (January 1977). Dividend yields are available from January 1970 except for Finland and New Zealand (both begin January 1988), Hong Kong (January 1973), Ireland (May 1990), Sinapore/Malaysia (December 1972). Per capita GDP to OECD is the ratio of per capita annual GDP calculated in U.S. dollars for country to per capita annual OECD calculated in U.S. dollars. The annual observations are observed quarterly except for Belgium, Denmark (annual through 1987Z4), Hong Kong, Netherlands and Norway (annual through 1976Q4), Singapore, and Spain. The population data are annual. The summary statistics for this variable are based on annual observations. Inflation to OECD is the annual change in inflation for country *i* divided by the annual change in inflation for the OECD. These monthly data are available from December 1969 for all countries. Monthly long-term interest rates begin in December 1969 except for Austria (January 1971), Finland (January 1972), and Spain (March 1978). Data were not available for Hong Kong and Singapore so the U.S. rate was used. The term spread is the long-term rate minus the short-term rate. Short-term interest rates begin in December 1969 except for Denmark (December 1974), Finland (December 1977), France (January 1970), Germany (December 1974), Hong Kong (September 1974 U.S. used), Ireland (November 1972), Italy (November 1977), Netherlands (December 1974), New Zealand (February 1978), Norway (August 1971), Singapore (August 1973), Spain (January 1974), Switzerland (December 1974), United Kingdom (January 1974), and United States (October 1974).

Table 2A.3   **International Industry Loadings for Twenty-One Equity Markets: 1975:01–1991:09 (202 observations)**

Country	Natural Resources	Construction and Manufacturing	Transportation, Communication, Energy	Services and Financial Services
Australia	0.52	0.13	0.05	0.10
Austria	0.19	0.42	0.04	−0.20
Belgium	0.22	0.35	−0.19	0.39
Canada	0.40	−0.18	0.50	0.16
Denmark	−0.05	0.24	0.18	0.21
Finland	1.01	−0.36	−0.02	0.20
France	0.27	0.47	0.01	0.23
Germany	0.04	0.68	−0.07	0.06
Hong Kong	0.01	−0.10	0.05	1.04
Ireland	0.32	−0.09	−0.39	0.93
Italy	−0.29	0.93	0.65	−0.42
Japan	0.03	0.59	−0.40	0.76
Netherlands	0.10	0.17	0.39	0.20
New Zealand	0.50	−0.71	1.38	−0.43
Norway	0.35	0.03	0.70	−0.11
Singapore/Mal	0.07	0.49	−0.08	0.51
Spain	0.03	0.30	−0.13	0.48
Sweden	0.04	0.50	0.10	0.13
Switzerland	0.15	0.42	−0.01	0.25
United Kingdom	0.23	0.14	−0.16	0.85
United States	−0.03	0.07	0.69	0.08

Note: The loadings are slope coefficients in the regressions of country returns on four industry returns: natural resources, construction and manufacturing, transportation/communication/energy and utilities, and services and financial services. The details of the industry portfolio construction are provided in figure 2.5. The regressions are run (when possible) from January 1975 through September 1991 (the last date of the industry returns). The returns for Finland, Ireland, and New Zealand begin in February 1988.

AUSTRALIA vs WORLD

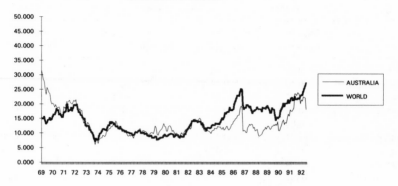

AUSTRIA vs WORLD

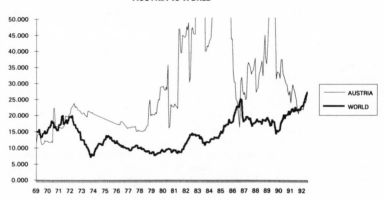

BELGIUM vs WORLD

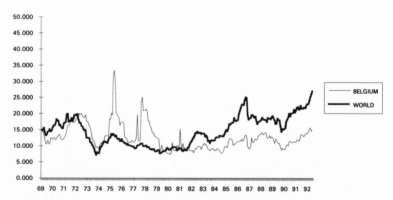

Fig. 2A.1   Price to earnings ratios, country versus world
Note: Value-weighted price to earnings ratios start in January 1970 except for Austria (January 1977), Finland (January 1988), Italy (April 1984), Ireland (May 1990), New Zealand (January 1988), Singapore/Malaysia (December 1972), and Spain (January 1977).

CANADA vs WORLD

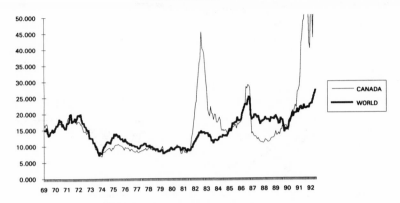

DENMARK vs WORLD

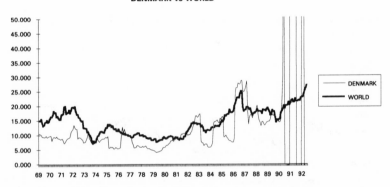

FINLAND vs WORLD

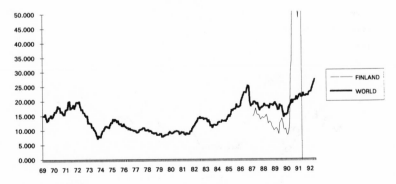

Fig. 2A.1   (continued)

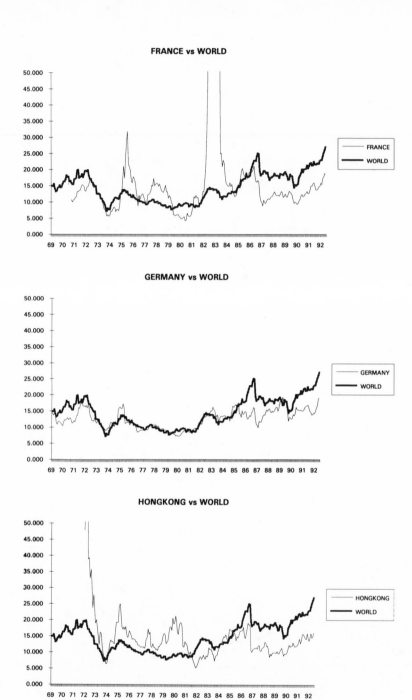

Fig. 2A.1 Price to earnings ratio (continued)

IRELAND vs WORLD

ITALY vs WORLD

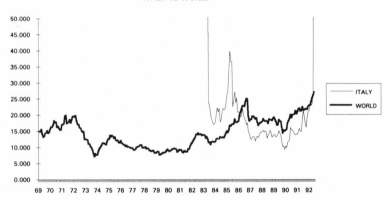

JAPAN vs WORLD

Fig. 2A.1   (continued)

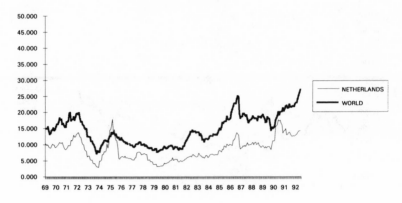

NETHERLANDS vs WORLD

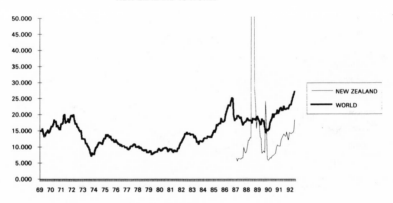

NEW ZEALAND vs WORLD

NORWAY vs WORLD

Fig. 2A.1   Price to earnings ratio (continued)

SINGAPORE/MALAYSIA vs WORLD

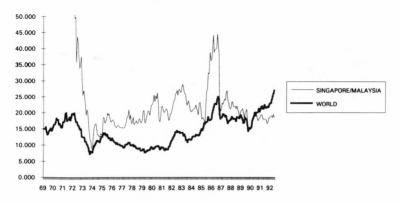

SPAIN vs WORLD

SWEDEN vs WORLD

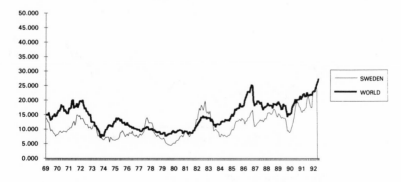

Fig. 2A.1   (continued)

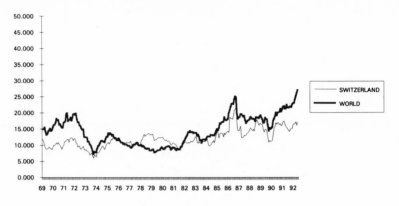

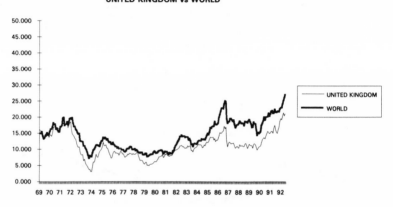

Fig. 2A.1   Price to earnings ratio (continued)

AUSTRALIA vs WORLD

AUSTRIA vs WORLD

BELGIUM vs WORLD

Fig. 2A.2   Price to cash earnings ratios, country versus world
Note: The value-weighted price to cash earnings (earnings plus depreciation) ratios are
available over the entire sample except for Canada (December 1974), Finland (January
1988), France (September 1971), Hong Kong (December 1972), Ireland (May 1990), New
Zealand (January 1988), Singapore/Malaysia (December 1972), Spain (September 1971),
and Switzerland (January 1977).

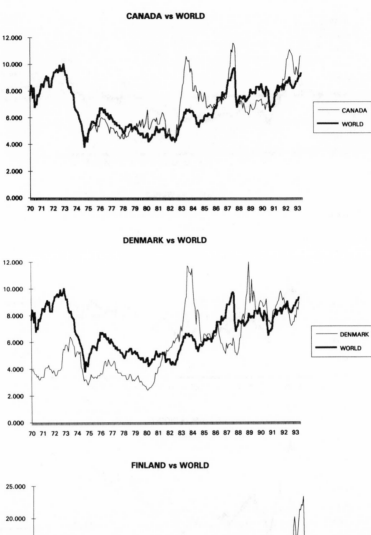

Fig. 2A.2   Price to cash earnings ratios (continued)

FRANCE vs WORLD

GERMANY vs WORLD

HONGKONG vs WORLD

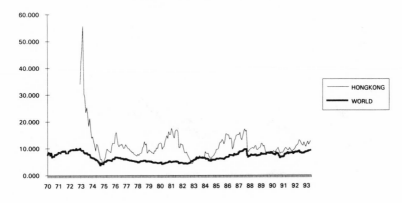

Fig. 2A.2   (continued)

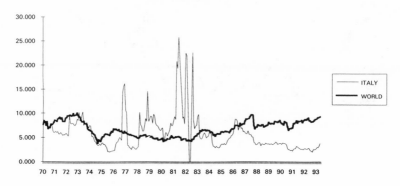

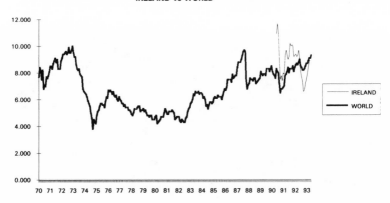

Fig. 2A.2   Price to cash earnings ratios (continued)

NETHERLANDS vs WORLD

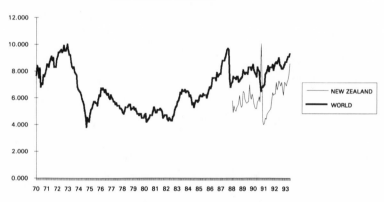

NEW ZEALAND vs WORLD

NORWAY vs WORLD

Fig. 2A.2   (continued)

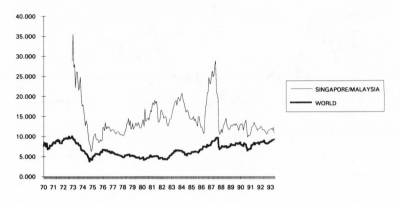

Fig. 2A.2   Price to cash earnings ratios (continued)

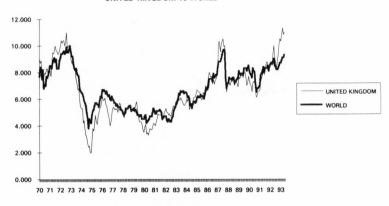

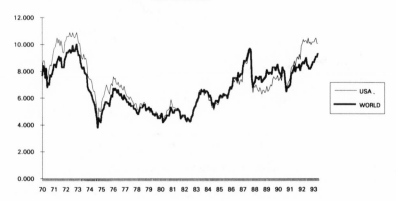

Fig. 2A.2   (continued)

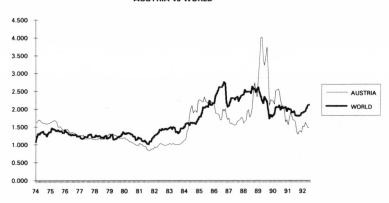

Fig. 2A.3 Price to book value ratios, country versus world
Note: The value-weighted price to book value ratios are available from January 1974 for all countries except Finland and New Zealand (both begin January 1988) and Ireland (May 1990).

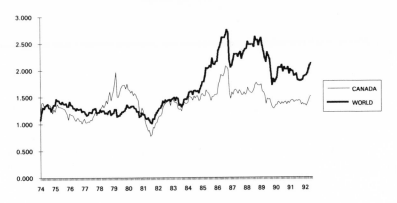

CANADA vs WORLD

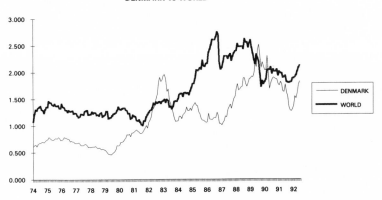

DENMARK vs WORLD

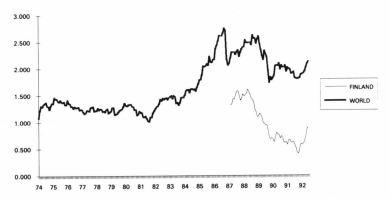

FINLAND vs WORLD

Fig. 2A.3   (continued)

FRANCE vs WORLD

GERMANY vs WORLD

HONGKONG vs WORLD

Fig. 2A.3 **Price to book value ratios** (continued)

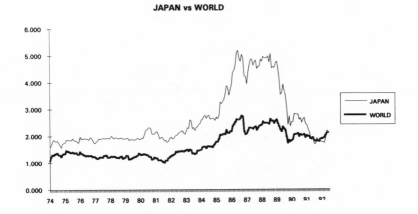

Fig. 2A.3 (continued)

NETHERLANDS vs WORLD

NEW ZEALAND vs WORLD

NORWAY vs WORLD

Fig. 2A.3   Price to book value ratios (continued)

Fig. 2A.3   (continued)

Fig. 2A.3   Price to book value ratios (continued)

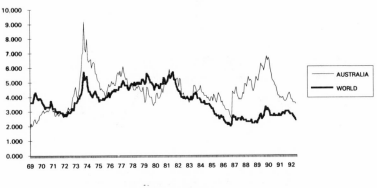

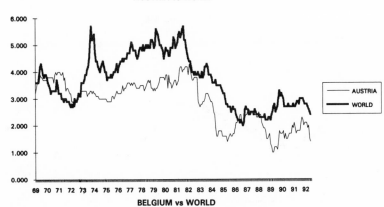

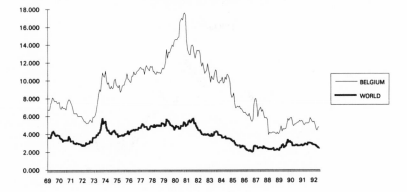

Fig. 2A.4   Dividend to price ratios, country versus world

Note: Dividend yields twelve-month moving sum of dividends divided by the current index level. They are available from January 1970 except for Finland and New Zealand (which both begin January 1988), Hong Kong (January 1973), Ireland (May 1990), and Singapore/ Malaysia (December 1972).

Fig. 2A.4   Dividend to price ratios (continued)

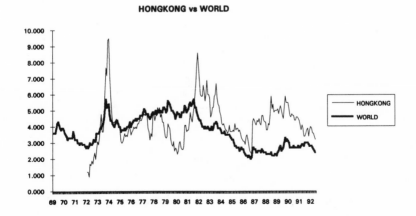

Fig. 2A.4   (continued)

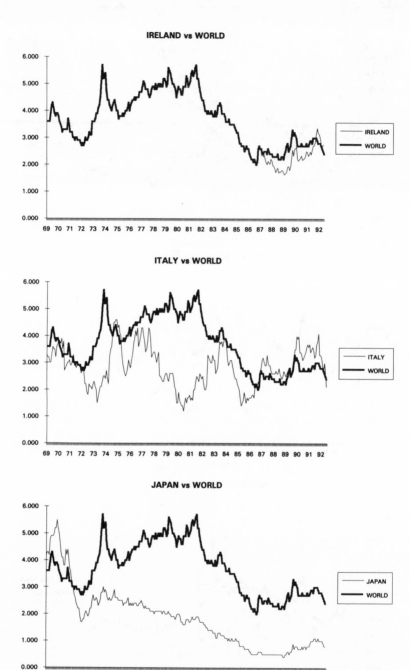

Fig. 2A.4   Dividend to price ratios (continued)

NETHERLANDS vs WORLD

NEW ZEALAND vs WORLD

NORWAY vs WORLD

Fig. 2A.4 (continued)

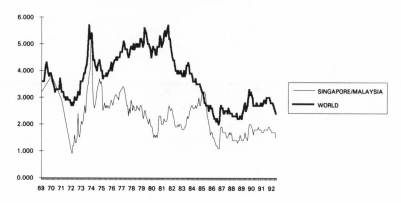

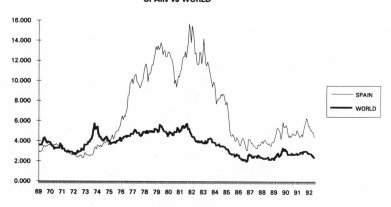

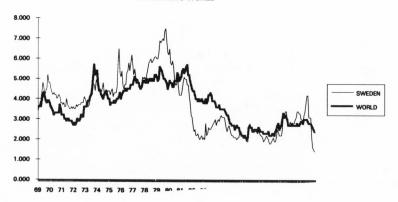

Fig. 2A.4 Dividend to price ratios (continued)

SWITZERLAND vs WORLD

UNITED KINGDOM vs WORLD

USA vs WORLD

Fig. 2A.4   (continued)

References

Adler, Michael, and Bernard Dumas. 1983. International portfolio selection and corpo-ration finance: A synthesis. *Journal of Finance* 38:925–84.

Ando, Albert, and Alan J. Auerbach. 1990. Cost of capital in Japan. *Journal of the Japanese and International Economies* 4:323–50.

Bansal, Ravi, David Hsieh, and S. Viswanathan. 1993. A new approach to international arbitrage pricing. *Journal of Finance* 48:1719–48.

Basu, Sanjoy. 1977. The investment performance of common stocks in relation to their price-earnings ratios: A test of the efficient markets hypothesis. *Journal of Finance* 32:663–82.

Black, Fischer. 1972. Capital market equilibrium with restricted borrowing. *Journal of Business* 45 (July): 444–54.

Bodurtha, James N., D. Chinhyung Cho, and Lemma W. Senbet. 1989. Economic forces and the stock market: An international perspective. *Global Finance Journal* 1:21–46.

Braun, Phillip, Dan Nelson, and Alan Sunier. 1991. Good news, bad news, volatility and betas. Working paper, University of Chicago.

Brown, Stephen J., and Toshiyuki Otsuki. 1990a. Macroeconomic factors and the Japa-nese equity markets: the CAPMD project. Chap. 8 in *Japanese Capital Markets,* eds. Edwin J. Elton and Martin J. Gruber, New York: Harper and Row. 175–92.

———. 1990b. A global asset pricing model. Working paper, New York University.

Campbell, John Y. 1987. Stock returns and the term structure. *Journal of Financial Economics* 18:373–400.

Chan, Louis K. C., Yasushi Hamao, and Josef Lakonishok. 1991. Fundamentals and stock returns in Japan. *Journal of Finance,* vol. 46, December.

Chen, Nai-fu, Richard R. Roll, and Stephen A. Ross. 1986. Economic forces and the stock market. *Journal of Business* 59:383–403.

Cho, David, C. Eun, and Lemma Senbet. 1986. International arbitrage pricing theory: An empirical investigation. *Journal of Finance* 41:313–29.

Cutler, David M., J. Poterba, and L. Summers. 1990. International evidence on the predictability of stock returns. Working paper, Massachusetts Institute of Tech-nology.

Dumas, Bernard, and Bruno Solnik. 1993. The world price of exchange rate risk. NBER Working Paper no. 4459. Cambridge, Mass.: National Bureau of Economic Re-search, September.

Fama, Eugene F. 1992. The cross-section of expected stock returns. *Journal of Fi-nance* 47:427–65.

———. 1993. 1993. Common risk factors in the returns on stocks and bonds. *Journal of Financial Economics* 33 (Feb.): 3–56.

Fama, Eugene F., and Kenneth R. French. 1989. Business conditions and expected stock returns. *Journal of Financial Economics* 25:23–50.

Fama, Eugene F., and James D. MacBeth. 1973. Risk, return and equilibrium: Empirical tests. *Journal of Political Economy* 81:607–36.

Ferson, Wayne E., and Campbell R. Harvey. 1991. The variation of economic risk pre-miums. *Journal of Political Economy* 99:385–415.

———. 1993. The risk and predictability of international equity returns. *Review of Financial Studies* 6:527–66.

———. 1994. Sources of risk and expected returns in international equity markets. *Journal of Banking and Finance.* Forthcoming.

French, Kenneth R., and James Poterba. 1991. Were Japanese stock prices too high? *Journal of Financial Economics* 29:337–64.

Giovannini, Alberto, and Philippe Jorion. 1987. Interest rates and risk premia in the stock market and in the foreign exchange market. *Journal of International Money and Finance* 6:107–23.

———. 1989. Time variation of risk and return in the foreign exchange and stock markets. *Journal of Finance* 44:307–25.

Graham, Benjamin. 1965. *The intelligent investor: A book of practical counsel.* 3rd ed. New York: McGraw Hill.

Guerard, John B., and Makoto Takano. 1990. Composite modelling in the Japanese equity markets. Working paper presented at the Berkeley program in finance, September.

Hamao, Yasushi. 1988. An empirical examination of arbitrage pricing theory: Using Japanese data. *Japan and the World Economy* 1:45–61.

Hansen, Lars P. 1982. Large sample properties of the generalized method of moments estimators. *Econometrica* 50:1029–54.

Harris, Thomas C., and Tim C. Opler. 1990. Stock market returns and real activity. Working paper, University of California, Los Angeles.

Harvey, Campbell R. 1988. The real term structure and consumption growth. *Journal of Financial Economics* 22:305–34.

———. 1991a. The term structure and world economic growth. *Journal of Fixed Income* 1:4–17.

———. 1991b. The world price of covariance risk. *Journal of Finance* 46: 111–57.

———. 1993a. Predictable risk and returns in emerging markets. Working paper, Duke University.

———. 1993b. Global risk exposure to a trade-weighted foreign currency index. Working paper, Duke University.

Harvey, Campbell R., Bruno Solnik, and Guofu Zhou. 1993. What determines expected international asset returns? Working paper, Duke University.

Haughton, Kelly, and Jon A. Christopherson. 1989. Equity style indexes: Tools for better performance evaluation and plan management. Working paper, Frank Russell Corporation.

Heston, Steven, and Geert Rouwenhorst. 1993. Does industrial structure explain the benefits of international diversification? Working paper, Yale School of Organization and Management.

Heston, Steven, Geert Rouwenhorst, and Roberto E. Wessels. 1991. The structure of international stock returns. Working paper, Yale School of Organization and Management, October.

Hodrick, Robert J. 1981. Intertemporal asset pricing with time-varying risk premia. *Journal of International Economics* 11:573–87.

Huberman, Gur, and Shmuel A. Kandel. 1987. Mean variance spanning. *Journal of Finance* 42:383–88.

Huberman, Gur, Shmuel A. Kandel, and Robert F. Stambaugh. 1987. Mimicking portfolios and exact arbitrage pricing. *Journal of Finance* 42:1–10.

Jaffe, Jeffrey, Donald B. Keim, and Randolph Westerfield. 1989. Earnings yields, market values and stock returns. *Journal of Finance* 44:135–48.

Jensen, Michael C. 1968. The performance of mutual funds in the period 1945–1964. *Journal of Finance* 23:389–446.

Jorion, Philippe. 1991. The pricing of exchange risk in the stock market. *Journal of Financial and Quantitative Analysis* 26:363–76.

Kester, Carl W., and Timothy A. Luehrman. 1989. Real interest rates and the cost of capital. *Japan and the World Economy* 1:279–301.

King, Mervyn, Enrique Sentana, and Sushil Wadhwani. 1990. A Heteroscedastic factor model of asset returns and risk premia with time-varying volatility: An application to sixteen world stock markets. Working paper, London School of Economics, May.

Korajczyk, Robert A., and Claude J. Viallet. 1989. An empirical investigation of international asset pricing. *Review of Financial Studies* 2:553–86.

———. 1992. Equity risk premia and the pricing of foreign exchange risk. *Journal of International Economics* 33 (November): 199–219.

Lehmann, Bruce N., and Modest, David M. 1988. The empirical foundations of the arbitrage pricing theory. *Journal of Financial Economics* 21:213–54.

Lintner, John. 1965. The valuation of assets and the selection of risky investments in stock portfolios and capital budgets. *Review of Economics and Statistics* 47:13–37.

Mandelker, Gershon, and Kishore Tandon. 1985. Common stock returns, real activity and inflation: Some international evidence. *Journal of International Money and Finance* 4:267–86.

Mark, Nelson C. 1985. On time-varying risk premia in the foreign exchange market: An econometric analysis. *Journal of Monetary Economics* 16:3–18.

Merton, Robert C. 1973. An intertemporal capital asset pricing model. *Econometrica* 41:867–87.

Poterba, James M., and Lawrence H. Summers. 1988. Mean reversion in stock prices: Evidence and implications. *Journal of Financial Economics* 22:27–60.

Roll, Richard. 1977. A critique of the asset pricing theory's tests—Part I: On past and potential testability of the theory. *Journal of Financial Economics* 4:349–57.

———. 1992. Industrial structure and the comparative behavior of international stock market indexes. *Journal of Finance* 47:3–42.

Rosenberg, B., K. Reid, and R. Lanstein. 1985. Persuasive evidence of market inefficiency. *Journal of Portfolio Management* 3:9–17.

Ross, Stephen A. and Michael Walsh. 1983. A simple approach to the pricing of risky assets with uncertain exchange rates. In *The internationalization of financial markets and national economic policy,* eds. R. Hawkins, R. Levich, and C. Wihlborg. Greenwich, Conn.: JAI Press.

Shanken, Jay. 1990. Intertemporal asset pricing: An empirical investigation. *Journal of Econometrics* 45:99–120.

Shanken, Jay. 1992. On the estimation of beta pricing models. *Review of Financial Studies* 5:1–34.

Shanken, Jay, and Mark I. Weinstein. 1990. Macroeconomic variables and asset pricing: Estimation and tests. Working paper, University of Rochester.

Sharpe, William F. 1964. Capital asset prices: A theory of market equilibrium under conditions of risk. *Journal of Finance* 19:425–42.

Shleifer, Andrei, and Lawrence H. Summers. 1990. The noise trader approach to finance. *Journal of Economic Perspectives* 4:19–33.

Solnik, Bruno. 1974. An equilibrium model of the international capital market. *Journal of Economic Theory* 8:500–24.

———. 1993. The unconditional performance of international asset allocation strategies using conditioning information. *Journal of Empirical Finance* 1:33–55.

Stulz, René M. 1981a. A model of international asset pricing. *Journal of Financial Economics* 9:383–406.

———. 1981b. On the effects of barriers to international investment. *Journal of Finance* 36:923–34.

———. 1984. Pricing capital assets in an international setting: An introduction. *Journal of International Business Studies* 15:55–74.

Stulz, René M., and Walter Wasserfallen. 1992. Foreign equity investment restrictions: Theory and evidence. Working paper, Ohio State University.

Wadhwani, Sushil, and Mushtaq Shah. 1993. Valuation indicators and stock market prediction: I. Working paper, Goldman Sachs International, Ltd., London.

Comment   Bruce N. Lehmann

To many mainstream financial economists, it is natural to view international finance as providing a different asset menu for an otherwise conventional asset allocation analysis. The Ferson and Harvey paper has this flavor, seeking to interpret comovements in equity returns across countries in terms of the kinds of risk/return models that have proved useful in domestic U.S. equity market studies. This approach is congenial for one (such as I) schooled in conventional asset allocation analysis.

The principal tool used in this paper is the ubiquitous factor model for asset returns. Factor models for any asset menu have three components: sources of risk that impinge on most of the asset menu, variables that reflect the asset risk exposures to these common sources of risk, and return components that are largely specific to a small subset of the asset menu. This decomposition has provided a useful framework for organizing facts about asset return comovements and the structure of expected returns.

Factor model builders follow one of three strategies to get at the heart of these models—the sources of risk and risk exposures. One strategy is to postulate asset attributes that measure risk exposures and implicitly measure the common risk factors. Another approach is to postulate common risk factors and implicitly measure the corresponding asset risk exposures. The third procedure is to implicitly measure both risk factors and asset risk exposures from the covariance structure of asset returns.

The main contributions of this paper are factor models of the first two kinds for national equity index returns. The principal focus is on several country attributes as candidate measures of country risk exposures to global risk factors. Ferson and Harvey also postulate two kinds of global risk factors: a pair of proxies for the variables in the international CAPM and a set of international industry index returns. No new methods are required for this investigation—the principal decisions made by the authors involve the choices of these sets of variables.

There is no natural measure of success in an exploratory model-fitting exercise of this sort. I find it useful to think in terms of two criteria: how well the model fits international equity returns and how much insight the model provides about them. Model fit is determined by the choices of the variables included in the analysis. Accordingly, my main questions involve these choices, particularly with regard to their suitability in an international application. My discussion consists of a brief description of these choices followed by a discussion of their consequences.

Probably the main challenge confronting any risk-based international asset-pricing model is the possibility that actual markets are partially or totally seg-

Bruce N. Lehmann is professor of economics and finance at the Graduate School of International Relations and Pacific Studies at the University of California, San Diego.

mented. This prospect is very real in light of the apparent benefits of global diversification and investors' apparent abstention from exploiting them, the so-called home-country bias problem. Hence, the other focus of my comment is how well the Ferson and Harvey analysis informs us about this question. One might hope for insight into this issue from this exploration.

The Selection of Country Attributes

The principal contribution of this paper is the investigation of several heretofore unused country attributes in international applications. These attributes fall into three categories: valuation ratios, economic performance indicators, and industry exposure measures, all at the country level. I will discuss each of these choices in turn.

Valuation Ratios

As is now commonplace in asset-pricing applications, Ferson and Harvey use financial ratios that have proved useful in studies of cross-sectional variation in expected U.S. equity returns. They use ratios like earnings and dividend yields, the ratio of the market value to the book value of equity, and the ratio of price to cash flow (in place of earnings). The novelty in the present application is that these variables are not *firm* attributes as in most research but rather represent *country* attributes in this application.

Ferson and Harvey use these attributes because they are plausible risk exposure indicators.[1] For example, dividend and earnings yields are plausible indicators of expected returns, particularly for the cash cows (i.e., mature firms with no uncertain growth opportunities) that populate corporate finance textbooks. Replacing earnings with cash flow is reasonable given cross-country differences in the treatment of depreciation.[2] Similarly, the ratio of equity market values to their book values is also a plausible value indicator—if book value equals the market value of firm capital (i.e., historical cost of capital investment equals the market value of capital), this ratio is the expected present value of growth opportunities, another textbook valuation measure. After preliminary data analysis, they settle on dividend yield as the representative of this group.[3]

---

1. Of course, these variables were "asset pricing anomalies" before they were transformed into "valuation ratios." These security characteristics helped explain expected returns after risk adjustments using the capital asset pricing model (CAPM) or the arbitrage pricing theory (APT) in violation of these theories. The major missing anomaly from the Ferson and Harvey list is size or market capitalization, which appears in the numerator or denominator of each of the valuation ratios.

2. It might be better to use cash-flow yield instead of price/cash flow. It also would be better to measure cash flow (i.e., net income calculated on a realized basis) rather than earnings plus depreciation, since the latter takes no account of cross-country differences in accruals and other accounting practices. Unfortunately, cross-country data on realized net income are hard to come by, although such data are available from several commercial vendors.

3. Ferson and Harvey also informally study the role of the volatility of attributes such as market to book. While they highlight some suggestive regressions, these results are not subjected to the kind of scrutiny afforded those obtained from the other attributes.

It might be useful at this point to reflect on what these variables measure in an international setting. I neither question the risk exposure interpretation of these valuation ratios nor do I dwell on potentially important international differences in accounting measurement. Rather, I wonder about cross-country differences in dividend setting and earnings retention practices.

For example, consider the role of dividend policy in the agency cost models of Rozeff (1982) and Easterbrook (1984). In these models, dividend payments are a device forcing the production of information about the firm. The basic idea is that the payment of regular cash dividends requires firms to obtain more frequent debt and equity funding in the capital markets. The concomitant scrutiny by lending institutions, investment banks, and potential outside investors constitutes information production that might help reduce agency costs.

There are substantial cross-country differences in the capital market mechanisms designed to cope with these agency problems. For example, dividend payouts in Japan are quite low by world standards. Japanese institutional arrangements provide for other means of reducing agency costs within corporate cross-ownership structures like *keiretsu,* particularly in the form of monitoring by trust and long-term banks. By contrast, agency problems in Spain may be more severe than in Japan because of the absence of such institutional arrangements, perhaps accounting for Spain's relatively high dividend yield.

Problems of this sort potentially infect all of these valuation ratios. In the absence of new equity issues or asset write-downs, dividends, earnings, and book values are all related by the arithmetic accounting relation:

$$\text{Change in Book Value} = \text{Earnings} - \text{Dividend Payments}$$

Similarly, there are international differences in the time scale of these numbers—countries may have quarterly, semiannual, or annual payment and information release patterns. There might be some payoff to thinking about minutiae of this sort in order to more precisely measure putative country risk exposures.

It might also be advisable to distinguish the international and domestic components of earnings and cash flows to shed more light on the segmentation/integration question. While it might be hard to differentiate the domestic content of revenues and costs (i.e., the sale of traded and nontraded goods produced with traded and nontraded factors of production), it would certainly be desirable to move as far in this direction as possible. Dividing expected returns indicators like earnings yield into traded and nontraded components would certainly facilitate more powerful and economically interesting tests of the extent to which country cash flows are priced internationally or in segmented domestic markets.

National Economic Performance Measures

It is also now commonplace to use both macroeconomic variables and asset prices from other markets like bond and foreign exchange markets as risk factors in domestic asset pricing applications. Ferson and Harvey use a conventional variable set: the GDP growth rates, inflation rates, and long-term bond yields and yield spreads.[4]

However, Ferson and Harvey use these variables in an unusual and novel way. In most asset-pricing applications, such variables measure time-series risk factors. In contrast, Ferson and Harvey assume that the magnitudes of the macroeconomic variables relative to world values measure country risk exposures to world macroeconomic risk factors. Similarly, they take domestic bond yields and yield spreads to measure country exposure to long-run world growth risks. After preliminary data analysis, they settle on relative GDP growth and the long-term bond yield as representatives of this group.

It is hard to think about these economic performance indicators as measures of country risk exposure. There is a natural analogy between the relative GDP measure and the kind of industry analysis found, for example, in the commercial BARRA multifactor model (see Rosenberg 1974 and Rosenberg and Marathe 1979) and in unpublished work by Kale, Hakansson, and Platt (1991). Industry models of this sort measure the exposure to industry risk by the fraction of firm revenues from a given industry segment and implicitly measure industry risk factors from cross-sectional return regressions. This useful analogy suggests that we might think of relative GDP as measuring the fraction of world income from a given country "segment," measuring exposure to world income risk.[5]

The question of whether these variables measure risk factors or exposure to risk factors is really a restatement of the segmentation/integration question. Perhaps relative GDP and domestic bond yields do measure country risk exposure to global risk factors but surely a reasonable alternative hypothesis is that these variables measure domestic risk factors that are "priced" in (perhaps segmented) domestic equity markets. One might hope for sharper insights into this question from this investigation.[6]

Country Industry Exposure Measures

The final country attributes considered by Ferson and Harvey are country industry exposures. They measure these attributes by linear regression using data on the thirty-eight Morgan Stanley Capital International (MSCI) world industry portfolios as risk factors. For reasons of parsimony, they aggregate these portfolios into four groups: natural resources; construction and manufacturing; transportation, communication, utilities, and energy; and services in-

4. One can imagine other choices, such as relative real or nominal exchange rates or real wage differentials.

5. The interpretation of the long-term bond yield in this fashion is a bit more strained. Ferson and Harvey think of long-term yields as capturing real return differentials arising from different growth risks. However, a reasonable implication of the notion is that bond yield differentials should satisfy some asset-pricing model if capital markets are integrated. It would then be natural to ask whether yields would be plausible national equity risk exposures in such a model.

6. For example, Ferson and Harvey could apply the formal tests of integration and segmentation discussed in Jorion and Schwartz (1986) and Wheatley (1988).

cluding financial services. They then regress the national equity index returns on these four aggregated world industry portfolio returns, and the estimated time-series regression coefficients constitute the country industry exposures.

It has certainly become interesting to examine industry returns in an international setting in light of the results of Roll (1992) and Heston and Rouwenhorst (1993). Accordingly, it is not surprising that Ferson and Harvey sought to examine industry components in this paper. Nevertheless, their industry analysis is really out of character with the remainder of the paper. The other country attributes vary over time and, in some specifications, risk factor exposures are modeled as varying over time with these attributes. Country industry exposures that are time invariant regression coefficients are just in a different league from the other dynamic characteristics and it is probably better to wait for better and more appropriate data in order to investigate these issues.[7]

The Global Risk Factors

Ferson and Harvey make conventional choices in this domain. The two main global risk factors are commonly used in empirical work: the MSCI world index and the trade-weighted G10 currency return. These factors naturally arise from a loose reading of the international CAPM literature, particularly the well-known equation (14) of Adler and Dumas (1983).[8] There is a secondary set of world factors employed in some of the specifications: the world oil return along with OECD inflation and production growth.

There is little to note about these choices save for the recapitulation of the puzzles that arise when one thinks about an international CAPM along these lines. There are easy and hard empirical challenges confronting such a model. The easy ones involve cross-country variation in mean returns—sample mean country index returns are imprecisely measured and generally cluster around four values (0, 12, 16, and 20 percent). Accordingly, it is typically not hard for a one- or two-dimensional model to fit these features of the data.

By contrast, the other challenge is the poor fit of the one-, two-, and five-factor models. The time-series R^2s are small and the incremental time-series R^2 after the MSCI index is negligible for most countries. These numbers are much smaller than those for U.S. sector portfolios and on the order of the time-series R^2s for individual securities in U.S. asset-pricing applications. This is just another way of stating the "home-country bias" question: why don't investors systematically eliminate this measured residual country risk through diversification? It remains difficult to imagine how rational world risk premiums can account for this puzzle in the context of the international CAPM.

---

7. Once again, see Rosenberg (1974), Rosenberg and Marathe (1979), and Kale, Hakansson, and Platt (1991) for a possible formulation.

8. The phrase "loose reading" merely constitutes an application of the well-known Roll (1977) critique to the MSCI index and the observation that the international CAPM requires a separate exchange rate hedging term for each country of origin. Ferson and Harvey note both points.

Dynamic Asset Allocation Implications of the Factor Models

Ferson and Harvey presume that country index returns follow a factor model. Standard factor models for security returns take the form

$$R_{it+1} = a_{it+1} + \sum_{k=1}^{K} b_{ikt+1} R_{kt+1} + \varepsilon_{it+1}; \ E\{\varepsilon_{it+1}|R_{kt+1}\} = 0,$$

where R_{it+1} is the percentage return of security i in period $t + 1$, a_{it+1} is the unsystematic portion of the expected return of security i as of time t, b_{ikt+1} security i's exposure to the kth common factor as of time t, R_{kt+1} is the percentage return of the mimicking portfolio for the kth common factor (i.e., the portfolio that perfectly tracks the kth common factor during time period $t + 1$), and ε_{it+1} is security i's residual return. In international CAPM applications where i represents country indices, these residuals are only weakly correlated, yet another restatement of the home-country-bias puzzle.

If one thinks of these models as tools for international asset allocation, it is worth discussing how one would produce portfolios based on the country attributes in actual practice. These portfolios have returns that implicitly measure the common risk factors associated with the country attributes. The weights of these mimicking portfolios are chosen to give the portfolios unit exposure to the factor being tracked, to give zero exposure to the others, and to satisfy some (usually minimum variance) optimality criterion. In principle, portfolios with these qualities track the appropriate risk factors with negligible error.

Several of the factor loadings exhibit substantial short-run volatility due to their dependence on national equity values and bond yields. Accordingly, mimicking portfolios for these risk exposure measures have weights that vary substantially over time, requiring frequent rebalancing. Asset allocation models with these kinds of factor loading dynamics implicitly require very active portfolio strategies. That is, these factor models are, in part, "tactical" models for country timing.[9]

Some Concluding Observations

This paper answers some questions and suggests others. On the positive side, Ferson and Harvey document several potential uses of different country attributes in global asset allocation models. Two kinds of country attributes—national valuation ratios and economic performance measures—yield some marginally significant risk premiums when treated as factor loadings and are sometimes significant at conventional levels when used as explanatory variables for conditional betas on the MSCI world index and the trade-weighted G10 currency return. On the negative side, the measured correlations and risk premiums are often small, suggesting that even "statistically significant" results may not represent economically important ones.

---

9. This issue is also discussed in Hardy (1990).

This international evidence stands in sharp contrast to the domestic U.S. asset-pricing evidence that motivated the selection of variables to a considerable extent. Cross-firm differences in earnings and dividend yield, market capitalization, and market/book ratios play both economically and statistically important roles in accounting for both unconditional expected returns and return predictability in U.S. data. Similarly, time-series variation in long-term yields, yield spreads, and industrial production growth play an important part in domestic macrofactor models. Just as international asset-pricing models fit poorly compared with their domestic counterparts, so these models based on country attributes fare worse than the domestic models on which they were based.

How should one measure success in this kind of exercise, particularly since the observations made above seem somewhat subjective? One way is to nest this integrated international asset-pricing model into one with segmented domestic components. Appropriate tests can be based on the hypothesized homogeneity of risk premiums across countries. Such tests seem to be a sensible way to organize international equity return data to provide insight into some of the key questions in international asset pricing.[10] I venture to guess that the home-country-bias problem will deepen as a result of such an effort.

References

Adler, Michael, and Bernard Dumas. 1983. International portfolio selection and corporate finance: A synthesis. *Journal of Finance* 38:925–84.

Easterbrook, Frank H. 1984. Two agency cost explanations of dividends. *American Economic Review* 74:650–59.

Hardy, Daniel C. 1990. Market timing and international diversification. *Journal of Portfolio Management* 16:23–27.

Heston, Steven L., and K. Geert Rouwenhorst. 1993. Does industrial structure explain the benefits of international diversification? Working paper, School of Organization and Management, Yale University.

Jorion, Philippe, and Eduardo S. Schwartz. 1986. Integration vs. segmentation in the Canadian stock market. *Journal of Finance* 41:603–16.

Kale, Jivendra K., Nils H. Hakansson, and Gerald W. Platt. 1991. Industry vs. other factors in risk prediction. Finance Working Paper no. 201. University of California, Berkeley, Institute of Business and Economic Research.

Roll, Richard W. 1977. A critique of the asset pricing theory's tests—Part I: On past and potential testability of the theory. *Journal of Financial Economics* 4:129–76.

———. 1992. Industrial structure and the comparative behavior of international stock market indices. *Journal of Finance* 47:3–42.

Rosenberg, Barr. 1974. Extra-market components of covariance in security returns. *Journal of Financial and Quantitative Analysis* 9:263–74.

10. More powerful and more ambitious tests can be constructed by collecting more data. In particular, data on individual securities or sector portfolios within asset markets could be used in more powerful tests for segmentation and integration within and across asset markets. Models in which factors are based on market prices such as yields and yield spreads are particularly easy to implement. Such factors require neither mimicking portfolio construction (because their returns are already perfectly correlated with particular asset returns, themselves) nor risk premium estimation since they are already priced in the market.

Rosenberg, Barr, and Vinay Marathe. 1979. Tests of capital asset pricing hypotheses. In *Research in finance: A research annual.* Vol. 1:115–223. Greenwich, Conn.: JAI Press.

Rozeff, Michael. 1982. Growth, beta, and agency costs as determinants of dividend payout ratios. *Journal of Financial Research* 5:249–59.

Wheatley, Simon. 1988. Some tests of international equity integration. *Journal of Financial Economics* 21:177–212.

Comment   Richard K. Lyons

My intent with these comments is to complement those of the other discussant, Bruce Lehmann. His are directed at what I would refer to as the production side of the paper, issues such as pushing the research further and polishing what is already there. I will address the perspective of a consumer of this area of research: What does the measured predictability tell us? And how does this study relate to the research on exchange rates mentioned in the authors' introduction?

The paper's evidence of predictable excess returns in international equities—an important contribution—leads naturally to the question: Is it risk? The paper goes on to present evidence consistent with a factor-model representation of risk premia. One is left, however, with the usual concern about whether the seeming black box of the factor model is in fact capturing risk.

Three Asset Classes

Here, in my view, the black box is a little larger than usual. This view is tied largely to the fact that the paper measures returns in dollars. Digressing slightly, most of the literature on global asset allocation makes the point that there are (at least) three distinct asset classes to choose from: currency-hedged equities, currency-hedged bonds, and currencies. That is, nonzero currency positions are viewed as an active management decision, rather than viewing the unhedged position as a benchmark. Accordingly, the inputs to models such as the Black-Litterman global asset allocation model (Goldman-Sachs) are beliefs regarding each of these classes—separately. The paper as currently written confounds the first class with the third class by including the currency component in realized returns.

A Two-by-Two View

What is needed is a clearer decomposition, not just for the practitioner, but also to help researchers determine whether predictability is coming from risk premia. Consider figure 2C.1, a two-by-two diagram. In my judgment, there is

Richard K. Lyons is professor at the Haas School of Business at the University of California, Berkeley.

	Structural Models **—Risk**	**Statistical Models** **—Inefficiency?**
Equities – Curr. Hedged		
Currencies		

Fig. 2C.1   Two-by-two diagram

insufficient evidence in the paper to place the results in the upper-left-hand cell of figure 2C.1, which is the natural tendency. We know from statistical models of foreign exchange that predictable excess returns exist in that asset class; and researchers have been struggling for years to find models of a risk premium that can account for the predictability, with little success. It is possible that the predictability the authors find comes from the currency component of dollar equity returns.

Final Thoughts

Even if the authors were to effect a decomposition, one might still debate whether to place the equity evidence in the left-hand versus the right-hand cell of row 1 of figure 2C.1. As the authors point out, international factor models make strong assumptions about integration, information, and lack of frictions that are even more strained here than in the context of a domestic pricing model and U.S. data.

In the end, there is no doubt that the authors advance the literature. They extend past work on predictable variation, and demonstrate a clear link between country attributes and beta pricing models. My comments are not intended to detract from their results, but rather to provide a perspective for consumers of their work.

3   Tests of CAPM on an International Portfolio of Bonds and Stocks

Charles M. Engel

3.1   Introduction

Portfolio-balance models of international asset markets have enjoyed little success empirically.[1] These studies frequently investigate a very limited menu of assets, and often impose the assumption of a representative investor.[2] This study takes a step toward dealing with those problems by allowing some investor heterogeneity, and by allowing investors to choose from a menu of assets that includes bonds and stocks in a mean-variance optimizing framework.

The model consists of U.S., German, and Japanese residents who can invest in equities and bonds from each of these countries. Investors can be different because they have different degrees of aversion to risk. More important, within each country nominal prices paid by consumers (denominated in the home currency) are assumed to be known with certainty. This is the key assumption in Solnik's (1974) capital asset pricing model (CAPM). Investors in each country are concerned with maximizing a function of the mean and variance of the returns on their portfolios, where the returns are expressed in the currency of the investors' residence. Thus, U.S. investors hold the portfolio that is efficient in terms of the mean and variance of dollar returns, Germans in terms of mark returns, and Japanese in terms of yen returns.

The estimation technique is closely related to the CASE (constrained asset

Charles M. Engel is professor of economics at the University of Washington and a research associate of the National Bureau of Economic Research.

Helpful comments were supplied by Geert Bekaert, Bernard Dumas, Jeff Frankel, and Bill Schwert. The author thanks Anthony Rodrigues for preparing the bond data for this paper, and for many useful discussions. He also thanks John McConnell for excellent research assistance.

1. See Frankel (1988) or Glassman and Riddick (1993) for recent surveys.

2. Although, notably, Frankel (1982) does allow heterogeneity of investors. Recent papers by Thomas and Wickens (1993) and Clare, O'Brien, Smith, and Thomas (1993) test international CAPM with stocks and bonds, but with representative investors.

share efficiency) method introduced by Frankel (1982) and elaborated by Engel, Frankel, Froot, and Rodrigues (1993). The mean-variance optimizing model expresses equilibrium asset returns as a function of asset supplies and the covariance of returns. Hence, there is a constraint relating the mean of returns and the variance of returns. The CASE method estimates the mean-variance model imposing this constraint. The covariance of returns is modeled to follow a multivariate GARCH process.

One of the difficulties in taking such a model to the data is that there is scanty time-series evidence on the portfolio holdings of investors in each country. We do not know, for example, what proportion of Germans' portfolios is held in Japanese equities, or U.S. bonds.[3] We do have data on the total value of equities and bonds from each country held in the market, but not a breakdown of who holds these assets. Section 3.2 shows how we can estimate all the parameters of the equilibrium model using only the data on asset supplies and data that measure the wealth of residents in the United States relative to that of Germans and Japanese. The data used in this paper have been available and have been used in previous studies. The supplies of bonds from each country are constructed as in Frankel (1982). The supply of nominal dollar assets from the United States, for example, increases as the government runs budget deficits. These numbers are adjusted for foreign exchange intervention by central banks, and for issues of Treasury bonds denominated in foreign currencies. The international equity data have been used in Engel and Rodrigues (1993). The value of U.S. equities is represented by the total capitalization on the major stock exchanges as calculated by Morgan Stanley's *Capital International Perspectives*. The shares of wealth are calculated as in Frankel (1982)—the value of financial assets issued in a country, adjusted by the accumulated current account balance of the country.

The Solnik model implies that investors' portfolios differ only in terms of their holdings of bonds. If we had data on portfolios from different countries, we would undoubtedly reject this implication of the Solnik model. However, we might still hope that the equilibrium model was useful in explaining risk premia. In fact, our test of the equilibrium model rejects CAPM relative to an alternative that allows diversity in equity as well as bond holdings. Probably the greatest advantage of the CASE method is that it allows CAPM to be tested against a variety of plausible alternative models based on asset demand functions. Models need only require that asset demands be functions of expected returns and nest CAPM to serve as alternatives. In section 3.6, CAPM is tested against several alternatives. CAPM holds up well against alternative models in which investors' portfolios differ only in their holdings of bonds. But when we build an alternative model based on asset demands which differ across countries in bond and equity shares, CAPM is strongly rejected. While our CAPM model allows investor heterogeneity, apparently it does not allow enough.

---

3. Tesar and Werner (chap. 4 in this volume) have a limited collection of such data.

There are many severe limitations to the study undertaken here, both theoretical and empirical. While the estimation undertaken here involves some significant advances over previous literature, it still imposes strong restrictions. On the theory side, the model assumes that investors look only one period into the future to maximize a function of the mean and variance of their wealth. It is a partial equilibrium model, in the classification of Dumas (1993). Investors in different countries are assumed to face perfect international capital markets with no informational asymmetries. The data used in the study are crude. The measurement of bonds and equities entails some leaps of faith, and the supplies of other assets—real property, consumer durables, etc.—are not even considered. Furthermore, there is a high degree of aggregation involved in measuring both the supplies of assets and their returns.

Section 3.2 describes the theoretical model, and derives a form of the model that can be estimated. It also contains a brief discussion relating the mean-variance framework to a more general intertemporal approach. Section 3.3 discusses the actual empirical implementation of the model. Section 3.4 presents the results of the estimation, and displays time series of the risk premia implied for the various assets.

The portfolio balance model is an alternative to the popular model of interest parity, in which domestic and foreign assets are considered perfect substitutes. This presents some inherent difficulties of interpretation in the context of our model with heterogeneous investors, which are discussed in section 3.5. These problems are discussed, and some representations of the risk-neutral model are derived to serve as null hypotheses against the CAPM of risk-averse agents.

Section 3.6 presents the test of CAPM against alternative models of asset demand. The concluding section attempts to summarize what this study accomplishes and what would be the most fruitful directions in which to proceed in future research.

3.2   The Theoretical Model

The model estimated in this paper assumes that investors in each country face nominal consumer prices that are fixed in terms of their home currency. While that may not be a description that accords exactly with reality, Engel (1993) shows that this assumption is much more justifiable than the alternative assumption that is usually incorporated in international financial models—that the domestic currency price of any good is equal to the exchange rate times the foreign currency price of that good.

Dumas, in his 1993 survey, refers to this approach as the "Solnik special case," because Solnik (1974) derives his model of international asset pricing under this assumption. Indeed, the presentation in this section is very similar to Dumas's presentation of the Solnik model. The models are not identical because of slightly differing assumptions about the distribution of asset returns.

There are six assets—dollar bonds, U.S. equities, deutsche mark bonds, German equities, Japanese bonds, and Japanese equities. Time is discrete.

Table 3.1 lists the variables used in the derivations below.

The own currency returns on bonds between time t and time $t + 1$ are assumed to be known with certainty at time t, but the returns on equities are not in the time t information set.

U.S. investors are assumed to have a one-period horizon and to maximize a function of the mean and variance of the real value of their wealth. However, since prices are assumed to be fixed in dollar terms for U.S. residents, this is equivalent to maximizing a function of the dollar value of their wealth.

Let W_{t+1}^u equal dollar wealth of U.S. investors in period $t + 1$. At time t, investors in the United States maximize $F^{US}(E_t(W_{t+1}^u), V_t(W_{t+1}^u))$. In this expression, E_t refers to expectations formed conditional on time t information. V_t is the variance conditional on time t information. We assume the derivative of F^{US} with respect to its first argument, F_1^{US}, is greater than zero, and that the derivative of F^{US} with respect to its second argument, F_2^{US}, is negative.

Following Frankel and Engel (1984), we can write the result of the maximization problem as

(1) $$\lambda_t^u = \rho_{US}^{-1}\Omega_t^{-1}E_tZ_{t+1}^{US}$$

In equation (1) we have

$$Z_{t+1} = \begin{bmatrix} R_{t+1}^u - (1 + i_{t+1}^u) \\ R_{t+1}^g\dfrac{S_{t+1}^g}{S_t^g} - (1 + i_{t+1}^u) \\ (1 + i_{t+1}^g)\dfrac{S_{t+1}^g}{S_t^g} - (1 + i_{t+1}^u) \\ R_{t+1}^j\dfrac{S_{t+1}^j}{S_t^j} - (1 + i_{t+1}^u) \\ (1 + i_{t+1}^j)\dfrac{S_{t+1}^j}{S_t^j} - (1 + i_{t+1}^u) \end{bmatrix}$$

$$\Omega_t \equiv V_t(Z_{t+1}) = E_t[(Z_{t+1} - E_tZ_{t+1})(Z_{t+1} - E_tZ_{t+1})'],$$
$$\rho_{US} = -2F_2^{US}W/F_1^{US},$$

and λ_t^u is the column vector that has in the first position the share of wealth invested by U.S. investors in U.S. equities, the share invested in German equities in the second position, the share in mark bonds in the third position, the share in Japanese equities in the fourth position, and the share in Japanese bonds in the fifth position.

We will assume, as in Frankel (1982), that ρ_{US} (and ρ_G and ρ_J, defined later) are constant. These correspond to what Dumas (1993) calls "the market average degree of risk aversion," and can be considered a taste parameter. The degree of risk aversion can be different across countries.

Table 3.1

i_{t+1}^u	$\equiv$	the dollar return on dollar bonds between time t and $t+1$
i_{t+1}^g	$\equiv$	the mark return on mark bonds
i_{t+1}^j	$\equiv$	the yen return on yen bonds
R_{t+1}^u	$\equiv$	the gross dollar return on U.S. equities
R_{t+1}^g	$\equiv$	the gross mark return on German equities
R_{t+1}^j	$\equiv$	the gross yen return on Japanese equities
S_t^g	$\equiv$	the dollar/mark exchange rate at time t
S_t^j	$\equiv$	the dollar/yen exchange rate
μ_t^u	$\equiv$	$W_t^u/(S_t^j W_t^j + S_t^g W_t^g + W_t^u)$, share of U.S. wealth in total world wealth
μ_t^g	$\equiv$	$S_t^g W_t^g/(S_t^j W_t^j + S_t^g W_t^g + W_t^u)$, share of German wealth in total world wealth
μ_t^j	$\equiv$	$S_t^j W_t^j/(S_t^j W_t^j + S_t^g W_t^g + W_t^u)$, share of Japanese wealth in total world wealth

Let $r_{t+1} \equiv \ln(R_{t+1})$, so that $R_{t+1} = \exp(r_{t+1})$. Now, we assume that r_{t+1} is distributed normally, conditional on the time t information. So, we have that

$$E_t R_{t+1} = E_t \exp(r_{t+1}) = \exp(E_t r_{t+1} + \sigma_t^u/2),$$

where $\sigma_t^u = V_t(r_{t+1})$.

Then, note that for small values of $E_t r_{t+1}$ and $\sigma_t^u/2$, we can approximate

$$E_t R_{t+1} = \exp(E_t r_{t+1} + \sigma_t/2) \cong 1 + E_t r_{t+1} + \sigma_t^u/2.$$

Using similar approximations, and using lower-case letters to denote the natural logs of the variables in upper cases, we have

$$E_t Z_{t+1} \cong E_t z_{t+1} + D_t, \text{ where}$$

$$z_{t+1} \equiv \begin{bmatrix} r_{t+1}^u - i_{t+1}^u \\ r_{t+1}^g + s_{t+1}^g - s_t^g - i_{t+1}^u \\ i_{t+1}^g + s_{t+1}^g - s_t^g - i_{t+1}^u \\ r_{t+1}^j + s_{t+1}^j - s_t^j - i_{t+1}^u \\ i_{t+1}^j + s_{t+1}^j - s_t^j - i_{t+1}^u \end{bmatrix}$$

$$\Omega_t = V_t(Z_{t+1}) \cong V_t(z_{t+1})$$

and

$D_t = \text{diag}(\Omega_t)/2$, where diag( ) refers to the diagonal elements of a matrix.

So, we can rewrite equation (1) as

(2) $$\lambda_t^u = \rho_{US}^{-1}\Omega_t^{-1}(E_t z_{t+1} + D_t).$$

Now, assume Germans maximize $F^G(E_t(W_{t+1}^g), V_t(W_{t+1}^g))$, where W^g represents the mark value of wealth held by Germans. After a bit of algebraic manipulation, the vector of asset demands by Germans can be expressed as

(3) $$\lambda_t^g = \rho_G^{-1}\Omega_t^{-1}(E_t z_{t+1} + D_t) + (1 - \rho_G^{-1})e_3,$$

where e_j is a vector of length five that has a one in the jth position and zeros elsewhere.

Japanese investors, who maximize a function of wealth expressed in yen terms, have asset demands given by

(4) $$\lambda_t^j = \rho_J^{-1}\Omega_t^{-1}(E_t z_{t+1} + D_t) + (1 - \rho_J^{-1})e_5.$$

Note that in the Solnik model, if the degree of risk aversion is the same across investors, they all hold identical shares of equities. Their portfolios differ only in their holdings of bonds. Even if they have different degrees of risk aversion, there is no bias toward domestic equities in the investors' portfolios. This contradicts the evidence we have on international equity holdings (see, for example, Tesar and Werner, chap. 4 in this volume), so this model is not the most useful one for explaining the portfolio holdings of individuals in each country. Still, it may be useful in explaining the aggregate behavior of asset returns.

Then, taking a weighted average, using the wealth shares as weights, we have

(5) $$\lambda_t = (\mu_t^j\rho_J^{-1}+\mu_t^g\rho_{US}^{-1}+\mu_t^u\rho_{US}^{-1})\Omega_t^{-1}(E_t z_{t+1} + D_t) + \mu_t^g(1 - \rho_G^{-1})e_3$$
$$+ \mu_t^j(1 - \rho_J^{-1})e_5.$$

The vector λ_t contains the aggregate shares of the assets. While we do not have time-series data on the shares for each country, we have data on λ_t, and so it is possible to estimate equation (5). This equation can be interpreted as a relation between the aggregate supplies of the assets and their expected returns and variances.

3.2   A Note on the Generality of the Mean-Variance Model

The model that we estimate in this paper is a version of the popular mean-variance optimizing model. This model rests on some assumptions that are not very general. The strongest of the assumptions is that investors' horizons are only one period into the future.

It is interesting to compare our model with that of Campbell (1993), who derives a log-linear approximation for a very general intertemporal asset-pricing model. Campbell assumes that all investors evaluate real returns in the same way—as opposed to our model, in which real returns are different for U.S. investors, Japanese investors, and German investors.

In order to focus on the effects of assuming a one-period horizon, we shall follow Campbell and examine a version of the model in which all consumers evaluate returns in the same real terms. This would be equivalent to assuming that all investors evaluate returns in terms of the same currency, and that nominal goods prices are constant in terms of that currency.

So, we will assume investors evaluate returns in dollars. In that case, we can derive from equation (2) that

(6) $$E_t z_{t+1} = \rho\Omega_t\lambda_t - D_t.$$

Let z_i represent the excess return on the ith asset. The expected return can be written

$$E_t z_{i, t+1} = \rho \Omega_{it}' \lambda_t - var_t(z_{i, t+1})/2.$$

In this equation, var_t refers to the conditional variance, and Ω_{it}' is the ith row of Ω_t.

We can write

$$\Omega_{it}' \lambda_t = \sum_{j=1}^{n} Cov_t(z_{i, t+1}, z_{j, t+1}) \lambda_j = Cov_t(z_{i, t+1}, \sum_{j=1}^{n} z_{j, t+1} \lambda_j)$$

$$= Cov_t(z_{i, t+1}, z_{m, t+1}).$$

Cov_t refers to the conditional covariance, and $z_{m, t+1}$, which is defined to equal $\sum_{j=1}^{n} z_{j, t+1} \lambda_j$, is the excess return on the market portfolio. So, we can write

(7) $$E_t z_{i, t+1} = \rho Cov_t(z_{i, t+1}, z_{m, t+1}) - var_t(z_{i, t+1})/2.$$

Compare this to Campbell's equation (25) for the general intertemporal model:

(8) $$E_t z_{i, t+1} = \rho Cov_t(z_{i, t+1}, z_{m, t+1}) - var_t(z_{i, t+1})/2 + (\rho - 1)V_{ih, t},$$

where

$$V_{ih, t} \equiv Cov_t(z_{i, t+1}, (E_{t+1} - E_t) \sum_{j=1}^{\infty} \beta^j z_{m, t+j+1}).$$

β is the discount factor for consumers' utility. Campbell's equation is derived assuming that Ω_t is constant over time, but Restoy (1992) has shown that equation (8) holds even when variances follow a GARCH process.

Clearly the only difference between the mean-variance model of equation (7) and the intertemporal model is the term $(\rho - 1)V_{ih, t}$. This term does not appear in the simple mean-variance model because it involves an evaluation of the distribution of returns more than one period into the future. Extending the empirical model to include the intertemporal term is potentially important, but difficult and left to future research. However, note that Restoy (1992) finds that the mean-variance model is able to "explain the overwhelming majority of the mean and the variability of the equilibrium portfolio weights" in a simulation exercise.[4]

3.3 The Empirical Model

The easiest way to understand the CASE method of estimating CAPM is to rewrite equation (5) so that it is expressed as a model that determines expected returns:

---

4. I would like to thank Geert Bekaert for pointing out an error in this section in the version of the paper presented at the conference.

(9) $E_t z_{t+1} = -D_t + (\mu_t^j \rho_J^{-1} + \mu_t^g \rho_G^{-1} + \mu_t^u \rho_{US}^{-1})^{-1} [\Omega_t \lambda_t - \mu_t^g (1 - \rho_G^{-1}) \Omega_t e_3$
$- \mu_t^j (1 - \rho_J^{-1}) \Omega_t e_5].$

Under rational expectations, the actual value of z_{t+1} is equal to its expected value plus a random error term:

$$z_{t+1} = E_t z_{t+1} + \varepsilon_{t+1}.$$

The CASE method maximizes the likelihood of the observed z_{t+1}. Note that when equation (9) is estimated, the system of five equations incorporates cross-equation constraints between the mean and the variance.

There are four versions of the model estimated here:

Model 1

This version estimates all of the parameters of equation (9)—the three values of ρ, and the parameters of the variance matrix, Ω_t. It is the most general version of the model estimated. It allows investors across countries to differ not only in the currency of denomination in which they evaluate returns, but also their degree of risk aversion.

Model 2

Here we constrain ρ to be equal across countries. Then, using equation (9), we can write

(10) $E_t z_{t+1} = -D_t + \rho \Omega_t \lambda_t + \mu_t^g (1 - \rho) \Omega_t e_3 + \mu_t^j (1 - \rho) \Omega_t e_5.$

Model 3

Here we assume μ^i is constant over time for each of the three countries. We do not use data on μ^i, and instead treat the wealth shares as parameters. Since our measures of wealth shares may be unreliable, this is a simple alternative way of "measuring" the shares of wealth. However, in this case, neither the μ^i nor the ρ_i is identified. We can write equation (24) as

(11) $E_t z_{t+1} = -D_t + \alpha \Omega_t \lambda_t - \gamma_1 \Omega_t e_3 - \gamma_2 \Omega_t e_5.$

The parameters to be estimated are α, γ_1, γ_2, and the parameters of Ω_t. In the case in which the degree of risk aversion is the same across countries, α is a measure of the degree of risk aversion.

Model 4

The last model we consider abandons the assumption of investor heterogeneity and assumes that all investors are concerned only with dollar returns. So we can use equation (2) to derive the equation determining equilibrium expected returns under these assumptions. We presented this model in section 3.2 as equation (6) and repeat it here for convenience:

(12) $E_t z_{t+1} = \rho \Omega_t \lambda_t - D_t.$

The mean-variance optimizing framework yields an equilibrium relation between the expected returns and the variance of returns, such as in equation (9). However, the model is not completely closed. While the relation between means and variances is determined, the level of the returns or the variances is not determined within the model. For example, Harvey (1989) posits that the expected returns are linear functions of data in investors' information set. The equilibrium condition for expected returns would then determine the behavior of the covariance matrix of returns. Our approach takes the opposite tack. We specify a model for the covariance matrix, and then the equilibrium condition determines the expected returns.

Since the mean-variance framework does not specify what model of variances is appropriate, we are free to choose among competing models of variances. Bollerslev's (1986) GARCH model appears to describe the behavior of the variances of returns on financial assets remarkably well in a number of settings, so we estimate a version of that model.

Our GARCH model for Ω_t follows the positive-definite specification in Engel and Rodrigues (1989):

(13) $$\Omega_t = P'P + G\varepsilon_t\varepsilon_t'G + H\Omega_{t-1}H.$$

In this equation, P is an upper triangular matrix, and G and H are diagonal matrices.

This is an example of a multivariate GARCH(1,1) model: the covariance matrix at time t depends on one lag of the cross-product matrix of error terms and one lag of the covariance matrix. In general, Ω_t could be made to depend on m lags of $\varepsilon\varepsilon'$ and n lags of Ω_t. Furthermore, the dependence on $\varepsilon_t\varepsilon_t'$ and Ω_{t-1} is restrictive. Each element of Ω_t could more generally depend independently on each element of $\varepsilon_t\varepsilon_t'$ and each element of Ω_{t-1}. However, such a model would involve an extremely large number of parameters. The model described in equation (27) involves the estimation of twenty-five parameters—fifteen in the P matrix and five each in the G and H matrices.

3.4   Results of Estimation

The estimates of the models are presented in tables 3.2–3.5.

The first set of parameters reported in each table are the estimates of the risk aversion parameter. Model 1 allows the degree of risk aversion to be different across countries. The estimates for ρ_{US}, ρ_G, and ρ_J reported in table 3.2 are not very economically sensible. Two of the estimates are negative. The mean-variance model assumes that higher variance is less desirable, which implies that ρ should be positive.

Furthermore, we can test the hypothesis that the ρ coefficients are equal for all investors against the alternative of table 3.2 that they are different. This can

Table 3.2   **GARCH-CAPM Model with Rho Different across Countries (model 1)**

Rho (United States, Germany, Japan)

−1.3565e-07	−3.2690e-07	3.7562e-08		

P'P matrix

0.00059049	0.00016524	−1.7010e-05	0.00020655	−2.9160e-05
0.00016524	0.00031849	0.00016684	0.00026570	0.00016344
−1.7010e-05	0.00016684	0.00021890	0.00013559	0.00017095
0.00020655	0.00026570	0.00013559	0.00068145	0.00029210
−2.9160e-05	0.00016344	0.00017095	0.00029210	0.00028625

Diagonal elements of G matrix

−0.024400	0.14830	0.19370	0.42910	0.35240

Diagonal elements of H matrix

0.84760	0.95300	0.90130	0.82470	0.82200

Log-likelihood value

2469.47942

Table 3.3   **GARCH-CAPM Model with Rho Equal across Countries (model 2)**

Rho

4.6540

P'P matrix

0.00054260	0.00014092	−2.0086e-05	0.00018704	−3.4940e-05
0.00014092	0.00028210	0.00016825	0.00026609	0.00018164
−2.0086e-05	0.00016825	0.00022854	0.00013989	0.00018902
0.00018704	0.00026609	0.00013989	0.00068100	0.00031419
−3.4940e-05	0.00018164	0.00018902	0.00031419	0.00031561

Diagonal elements of G matrix

−0.039763	0.087661	0.17620	0.40677	0.37041

Diagonal elements of H matrix

0.86051	0.96511	0.90048	0.83463	0.80805

Log-likelihood value

2467.45718

be easily done with a likelihood ratio test, since table 3.3 estimates the constrained model. The value of the χ^2 test with two degrees of freedom is 4.056. The 5 percent critical value is 5.91, so we cannot reject the null hypothesis of equal values of ρ at this level.

In fact, the likelihood value for Model 1 is not as dependent on the actual values of the ρs as it is on their relative values. If we let ρ be different across countries, we are unable to reject some extremely implausible values. For example, we cannot reject $\rho_{US} = 1414$, $\rho_G = 126$, and $\rho_J = 1.6$.

Based both on the statistical test and the economic plausibility of the estimates, the restricted model—Model 2—is preferred to Model 1. Table 3.3 shows that the estimate of ρ in Model 2 is 4.65. This is not an unreasonable estimate for the degree of relative risk aversion of investors. It falls within the range usually considered plausible. It is also consistent with the estimates from

Table 3.4   **GARCH-CAPM Model with Wealth Shares Constant (model 3)**

Alpha
  4.03400
Gamma
  −1.11955

−1.11955	0.739053			

$P'P$ matrix

0.000561370	0.000149152	−2.04214e-05	0.000190815	−3.82150e-05
0.000149152	0.000295907	0.000170993	0.000273723	0.000181881
−2.04214e-05	0.000170993	0.000232242	0.000145623	0.000192640
0.000190815	0.000273723	0.000145623	0.000701762	0.000321168
−3.82150e-05	0.000181881	0.000192640	0.000321168	0.000322825

Diagonal elements of G matrix

−0.0363077	0.105138	0.179205	0.417467	0.366548

Diagonal elements of H matrix

0.855632	0.961629	0.898721	0.826812	0.806122

Log-likelihood value
  2467.61284

Table 3.5   **GARCH-CAPM Model in Dollar Terms (model 4)**

Rho
  4.09263

$P'P$ matrix

0.000559210	0.000147301	−2.12924e-05	0.000190461	−3.82462e-05
0.000147301	0.000292889	0.000170081	0.000272490	0.000181657
−2.12924e-05	0.000170081	0.000231566	0.000144383	0.000192179
0.000190461	0.000272490	0.000144383	0.000698603	0.000320088
−3.82462e-05	0.000181657	0.000192179	0.000320088	0.000322144

Diagonal elements of G matrix

−0.0374155	0.101296	0.177600	0.416692	0.367108

Diagonal elements of H matrix

0.856192	0.962377	0.899183	0.827584	0.806167

Log-likelihood value
  2467.51288

models 3 and 4. Model 3—which treats the wealth shares as unobserved constants—estimates the degree of risk aversion to equal 4.03. (Recall when reading table 3.4 that the coefficient of risk aversion in Model 3 is the parameter α.) When we assume all investors consider returns in dollar terms—as in Model 4—the estimate of ρ is 4.09, as reported in table 3.5.

Inspection of tables 3.1–3.4 shows that the parameters of the variance matrix, Ω_t, are not very different across the models. The matrix P from equation (13) is what was actually estimated by the maximum likelihood procedure, but we report $P'P$ in the tables because it is more easily interpreted. $P'P$ is the constant part of Ω_t.

The GARCH specification seems to be plausible in this model. Most of the elements of the H matrix were close to one, which indicates a high degree of persistence in the variance. One way to test GARCH is to perform a likelihood ratio test relative to a more restrictive model of the variance. Table 3.6 reports the results of testing the GARCH specification against a simple ARCH specification in which the matrix H in equation (13) is constrained to be zero. This imposes five restrictions on the GARCH model. As table 3.6 indicates, the restricted null hypothesis is rejected at the 1 percent level for each of models 1–4.

Figures 3.1 and 3.2 plot the diagonal elements of the Ω_t matrix for Model 2. The time series of the variances for the other models are very similar to the ones for Model 2. In figure 3.1 the variances of the returns on U.S., German, and Japanese equities relative to U.S. bonds are plotted. As can be seen, the variance of U.S. equities is much more stable that the variances for the other equities. In the GARCH model, the $1 - 1$ element in both the G and H matrices is small in absolute value. This leads to the fact that the variance does not respond much to past shocks, and changes in the variance are not persistent. On the other hand, figure 3.1 shows us that toward the end of the sample the variance of Japanese equities fluctuated a lot and at times got relatively large. Recall that in measuring returns on Japanese and German equities relative to U.S. bonds a correction for exchange rate changes is made, while that is not needed when measuring the return on U.S. equities relative to U.S. bonds.

The variances of returns on German and Japanese bonds relative to the returns on U.S. bonds are plotted in figure 3.2. Interestingly, the variance of Japanese bonds fluctuates much more than the variance of German bonds. The variance is much more unstable near the beginning of the sample period (while the variance of returns on Japanese equities gyrated the most at the end of the sample).

Figures 3.3 and 3.4 plot the point estimates of the risk premia. These risk premia are calculated from the point of view of U.S. investors. The risk premia are the difference between the expected returns from equation (9) and the risk neutral expected return for U.S. investors, which is obtained from equation (6) setting ρ equal to zero.

In some cases the risk premia are very large. (The numbers on the graph are the risk premia on a monthly basis. Multiplying them by 1200 gives the risk premia in percentage terms at annual rates.) The risk premia on equities are much larger than the risk premia on bonds. Furthermore, the risk premia vary a great deal over time. Comparing figure 3.3 to figure 3.1, it is clear that the risk premia track the variance of returns, particularly for the Japanese equity markets. The risk premia reached extremely high levels in 1990 on Japanese equities, which reflects the fact that the estimated variance was large in that year. The average risk premium on Japanese equities (in annualized rates of return) is 6.07 percent. For U.S. equities it is 5.01 percent, and 3.36 percent is the average risk premium for German equities.

The risk premia on equities are always positive, but in a few time periods the risk premia on the bonds are actually negative. The risk premia on bonds in this model are simply the foreign exchange risk premia. They also show

Table 3.6   **Test of Significance of GARCH Coefficients (likelihood ratio tests, 5 degrees of freedom)**

Model	Chi-Square Statistic
Model 1	26.740
Model 2	24.174
Model 3	24.039
Model 4	24.050

Note: All statistics significant at 1 percent level.

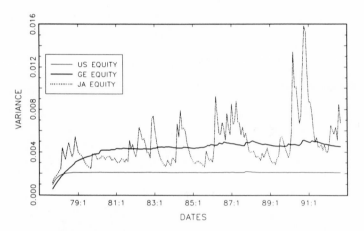

Fig. 3.1   Variance of equity returns relative to U.S. bonds

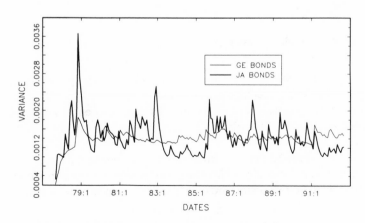

Fig. 3.2   Variance of bond returns relative to U.S. bonds

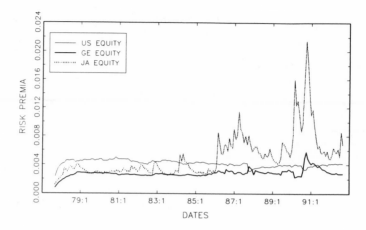

Fig. 3.3   Risk premia on equity returns relative to U.S. bonds

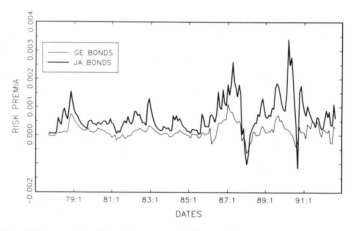

Fig. 3.4   Risk premia of bond returns relative to U.S. bonds

much time variation. At times they are fairly large, reaching a maximum of approximately four percentage points on the yen in 1990. Note, however, that the average risk premia—0.18 percent for German bonds and 0.79 percent for Japanese bonds—are an order of magnitude smaller than the equity risk premia.

However, figures 3.3 and 3.4 present only the point estimates of the risk premia, and do not include confidence intervals. The evidence in section 3.5 suggests that these risk premia are only marginally statistically significant.

3.5   Tests of the Null Hypothesis of Interest Parity

If investors perceive foreign and domestic assets to be perfect substitutes, then a change in the composition of asset supplies (as opposed to a change in the total supply of assets) will have no effect on the asset returns. Suppose investors choose their portfolio only on the basis of expected return. In equilibrium, the assets must have the same expected rate of return. Thus, in equilibrium, investors are indifferent to the assets (the assets are perfect substitutes), and the composition of their optimal portfolio is indeterminate. A change in the composition does not affect their welfare, and does not affect their asset demands. Thus, sterilized intervention in foreign exchange markets, which has the effect of changing the composition of the asset supplies, would have no effect on expected returns.

In our model, investors in general are concerned with both the mean and the variance of returns on their portfolios. The case in which they are concerned only with expected returns is the case in which ρ equals zero. We shall test the null hypothesis that consumers care only about expected return and not risk.

Consider first the version of the model in which all investors have the same degree of risk aversion—Model 2. That is, ρ is the same across all three countries. Then, the mean-variance equilibrium is given by equation (10). If we constrain ρ to equal zero in that equation, then we have the null hypothesis of

$$(14) \qquad E_t z_{t+1} = -D_t + \mu_t^g \Omega_t e_3 + \mu_t^j \Omega_t e_5.$$

Since the version of the model in which ρ is the same across all countries is a constrained version of the most general mean-variance model, then equation (14) also represents the null hypothesis for the general model (given in equation [9]).

We estimate two other versions of the mean-variance model. Model 3, as mentioned above, treats the shares of wealth as constant but unobserved. The model is given by equation (11). If ρ is the same for investors in all countries, then $\alpha = \rho$. So, the null hypothesis of risk neutrality can be written as

$$(15) \qquad E_t z_{t+1} = -D_t + \gamma_1 \Omega_t e_3 + \gamma_2 \Omega_t e_5.$$

The final version of the mean-variance model that we estimate is the one in which all investors evaluate returns in dollar terms—Model 4. Equation (12) shows the equation for equilibrium expected returns in this case. The null hypothesis then, is simply

$$(16) \qquad E_t z_{t+1} = -D_t.$$

So, equation (14) is the null hypothesis for Model 1 and Model 2, equation (15) is the null for Model 3, and equation (16) is the null for Model 4.

However, we have finessed a serious issue for the models in which investors assess asset returns in terms of different currencies. If investors are risk neutral, they require that expected returns expressed in terms of their domestic currency be equal. However, if expected returns are equal in dollar terms, then they will not be equal in yen terms or mark terms unless the exchange rates are constant. This is simply a consequence of Siegel's (1972) paradox (see Engel 1984, 1992 for a discussion).

The derivation of equation (9) does not go through when investors in one or more countries are risk neutral. The derivation proceeded by calculating the asset demands, adding these across countries, and equating asset demands to asset supplies. However, when investors are risk neutral, their asset demands are indeterminate. If expected returns on the assets (in terms of their home currency) are different from each other, they would want to take an infinite negative position in assets with lower expected returns and an infinite positive position in assets that have higher expected returns. If all assets have the same expected returns, then they are perfect substitutes, so the investor will not care about the composition of his portfolio. Hence, the derivation that uses the determinate asset demands when $\rho \neq 0$ does not work when $\rho = 0$.

If investors in different countries are risk neutral, then there is no equilibrium in the model presented here. Since it is not possible for expected returns to be equalized in more than one currency, then investors in at least one country would end up taking infinite positions.

So, we will consider three separate null hypotheses for our mean-variance model. One is that U.S. residents are risk neutral, so that expected returns are equalized in dollar terms. The other two null hypotheses are that expected returns are equalized in mark terms and in yen terms. The first of three hypotheses is given by equation (16), which was explicitly the null hypothesis when all investors considered returns in dollar terms. The second two null hypotheses can be expressed as

(17) $$E_t z_{t+1} = -D_t + \Omega_t e_3.$$

and

(18) $$E_t z_{t+1} = -D_t + \Omega_t e_5.$$

Equations (16), (17), and (18) can represent alternative versions of the null hypothesis for models 1 and 3 (expressed in equations [9] and [11]). Model 4—the one in which investors consider returns in dollar terms—admits only equation (16) as a restriction.

The foregoing discussion suggests that the model in which ρ is restricted to be equal across countries will not have an equilibrium in which $\rho = 0$. However, we still will treat equation (14) as the null hypothesis for this model. Note that equation (14) is a weighted average of equations (16), (17), and (18), where the weights are given by the wealth shares. Equation (14) should be considered the limit as ρ goes to zero across investors. It is approximately correct when ρ is approximately zero. The same argument can be used to justify equation (15) as a null hypothesis for the model expressed in equation (11).

To sum up:

Model 1. The general mean-variance model given by equation (9) will be tested against the null hypotheses of equations (14), (16), (17), and (18).

Model 2. The mean-variance model in which ρ is restricted to be equal across countries, equation (10), will be tested against the null hypothesis of equation (14).

Model 3. The version of the mean-variance model in which the wealth shares are treated as constant—equation (11)—will be tested against the null hypotheses of equations (15), (16), (17), and (18).

Model 4. The version of the mean-variance model in which investors evaluate assets in dollar terms, given by equation (12), will be tested against the null hypothesis of equation (16).

The results of these tests are reported in table 3.7. The null hypothesis of perfect substitutability of assets is not rejected at the 5 percent level for any model.

All but equation (18) can be rejected as null hypotheses at the 10 percent level when Model 1 is the alternative hypothesis. The *p*-value in all cases is close to 0.10, so there is some weak support for Model 1 against the null of risk neutrality.

For Model 2, the *p*-value is about 0.12. Since we were unable to reject the null that the coefficient of risk aversion was equal across countries, it is not surprising that models 1 and 2 have about equal strength against the null of risk neutrality.

It is something of a success that the estimated value of ρ is so close to being significant at the 10 percent level. There are many tests which reject the perfect substitutability, interest parity model. But, none of these tests that reject perfect substitutability are nested in a mean-variance portfolio balance framework. For example, Frankel (1982), who does estimate a mean-variance model, finds that if he restricts his estimate of ρ to be nonnegative, the maximum likelihood estimate of ρ is zero. Clearly, then, he would not reject a null hypothesis of $\rho = 0$ at any level of significance.

Our model performs better than Frankel's because we include both equities and bonds, and because we allow a more general model of Ω_t.[5]

Model 3 is unable to reject the null of perfect substitutability at standard levels of significance.

Model 4 rejects perfect substitutability at the 10 percent level. It might seem interesting to test the assumptions underlying Model 4. That is, does Model 4, which assumes that investors assess returns in dollar terms, outperform Model 2, which assumes that investors evaluate returns in their home currency? Unfortunately, Model 4 is not nested in Model 1 or Model 2, so such a test is not possible.

Model 4 is nested in Model 3, the model which treats the wealth shares as constant and unobserved. Comparing equation (11) with equation (12), the restrictions that Model 4 places on Model 3 are that $\gamma_1 = 0$ and $\gamma_2 = 0$. The likelihood-ratio (LR) test statistic for this restriction is distributed χ^2 with two degrees of freedom. The value of the test statistic is 0.200, which means that the null hypothesis is not rejected. So we cannot reject the hypothesis that all investors evaluate returns in dollar terms. However, equation (11) is not a very strong version of the model in which investors evaluate returns in terms of

---

5. Frankel assumes Ω_t is constant.

Table 3.7   **LR Tests of Null Hypothesis of Perfect Substitutability: Chi-Square Statistics (p-value in parentheses)**

Model	Null 14	Null 15	Null 16	Null 17	Null 18
Model 1	6.433 (0.092)		6.714 (0.082)	6.719 (0.081)	5.955 (0.114)
Model 2	2.388 (0.122)				
Model 3		1.640 (0.200)	2.981 (0.395)	2.986 (0.394)	2.222 (0.528)
Model 4			2.781 (0.095)		

different currencies. It does not use the data on shares of wealth, and treats those shares as constants. It performs the worst of all the models against the null of perfect substitutability. So we really cannot decisively evaluate the merits of allowing investor heterogeneity.

3.6   Tests of CAPM against Alternative Models of the Risk Premia

The CASE method of estimating the CAPM is formulated in such a way that it is natural to compare the asset demand functions from CAPM with more general asset demand functions. Unlike many other tests of CAPM, the alternative models have a natural interpretation and can provide some guidance on the nature of the failure of the mean-variance model if CAPM is rejected.

Any asset demand function that nests the asset demand functions derived above—equations (2), (3), and (4)—can serve as the alternative model to CAPM. That means, practically speaking, that the only requirement is that asset demands depend on expected returns with time-varying coefficients. Thus, in principle, we could use the CASE method to test CAPM against a wide variety of alternatives—models based more directly on intertemporal optimization, models based on noise traders, etc.

In practice, because of limitations on the number of observations of returns and asset supplies, it is useful to consider alternative models that do not have too many parameters. This can be accomplished by considering models which are similar in form to CAPM, but do not impose all of the CAPM restrictions.

Thus, initially, we consider models in which the asset demand equations in the three countries take exactly the form of equations (2), (3), and (4), except that the coefficients on expected returns need not be proportional to the variance of returns. We will test only the version of CAPM in which the degree of risk aversion is assumed to be equal across countries. For that version, we can write the alternative model as

(19) $$\lambda_t^u = A_t^{-1} (E_t z_{t+1} + D_t)$$

(20) $$\lambda_t^g = A_t^{-1} (E_t z_{t+1} + D_t) + a_G e_3$$

(21) $$\lambda_t^j = A_t^{-1} (E_t z_{t+1} + D_t) + a_J e_5.$$

In the alternative model, asset demands are functions of expected returns, but the coefficients, A_t^{-1}, are not constrained to be proportional to the inverse of the variance of returns. As with the Solnik model, we assume in the alternative that the portfolios of investors in different countries differ only in their holdings of nominal bonds.

Aggregating across countries gives us

$$\lambda_t = A_t^{-1} (E_t z_{t+1} + D_t) + \mu_t^g a_G e_3 + \mu_t^j a_J e_5.$$

This can be rewritten as

(22) $$E_t z_{t+1} = -D_t + A_t \lambda_t - \mu_t^g a_G A_t e_3 - \mu_t^j a_J A_t e_5.$$

The matrix of coefficients, A_t, is unconstrained. However, for formal hypothesis testing, it is useful if model (10) is nested in model (22). So, we hypothesize that A_t evolves according to

(23) $$A_t = Q'Q + J \varepsilon_t \varepsilon_t' J + K A_{t-1} K.$$

We will assume that the variance of the error terms in the alternative model follows a GARCH process as in equation (13).

Thus, the CAPM described in equations (10) and (13) imposes the following restrictions on the alternative model described by equations (22), (23), and (13):

$$\rho^{1/2} P = Q$$

$$\rho^{1/2} G = J$$

$$\rho^{1/2} H = K, \text{ and}$$

$$\rho^{-1} - 1 = a_G = a_J.$$

So, CAPM places twenty-six restrictions on the alternative model.

The alternative model was estimated by maximum likelihood methods. The value of the log of the likelihood is 2481.9026. Thus, comparing this likelihood value with the one given in table 3.3, the test statistic for the CAPM is 28.89. This statistic has a chi-square distribution with twenty-six degrees of freedom. The p-value for this statistic is 0.316, which means we would not reject CAPM at conventional levels of confidence.

We now consider two generalizations of equation (22). In the first, we posit that the asset demands do not depend simply on the expected excess returns, $E_t z_{t+1} + D_t$. Instead, there may be a vector of constant risk premia, c, so that we replace equation (22) with

(24) $$E_t z_{t+1} = c - D_t + A_t \lambda_t - \mu_t^g a_G A_t e_3 - \mu_t^j a_J A_t e_5.$$

CAPM places thirty-one restrictions on this alternative—those listed above, and the restriction that $c = 0$. This test of CAPM is directly analogous to the tests for significant "pricing errors" in, for example, Gibbons, Ross, and Shanken (1989) and Ferson and Harvey (chap. 2 in this volume).

This model was also estimated by maximum likelihood methods. The value of the log of the likelihood is 2482.6712. The chi-square statistic with thirty-one degrees of freedom is 30.428, which has a p-value of 0.495. So, again, we would not reject CAPM.

Another alternative is to retain equation (19) to describe asset demand by U.S. residents, but to replace equations (20) and (21) with

$$(25) \qquad \lambda_t^g = A_t^{-1}(E_t z_{t+1} + D_t) + a_G$$

$$(26) \qquad \lambda_t^j = A_t^{-1}(E_t z_{t+1} + D_t) + a_J.$$

In these equations, a_G and a_J are vectors. These equations differ from (20) and (21) by allowing more investor heterogeneity across countries. Each of the portfolio shares may differ between investors across countries—rather than just the bond holdings as in the Solnik model and in the alternative given by equation (22). Thus, aggregating equations (19), (25), and (26), and rewriting in terms of expected returns, we get

$$(27) \qquad E_t z_{t+1} = -D_t + A_t \lambda_t - \mu_t^g A_t a_G - \mu_t^j A_t a_J.$$

The CAPM model places thirty-four restrictions on equation (27). The model of equation (27) was estimated using maximum likelihood techniques. When the vectors a_G and a_J were left unconstrained, the point estimates of the portfolio shares were implausible. So, the model was estimated constraining the elements of a_G and a_J to lie between -1 and 1. This restriction is arbitrary, and is not incorporated in the optimization problems of agents, but it yields somewhat more plausible estimates of the optimal portfolio shares.

The value of the log of the likelihood in this case was 2499.8842. This gives us a chi-square statistic (thirty-four degrees of freedom) of 64.854. The p-value for this statistic is .0011. We reject CAPM at the 1 percent level.

So, we reject CAPM precisely because the Solnik model does not allow enough diversity across investors in their holdings of equities. However, it would not be correct to conclude that a model that has home-country bias in both equities and bonds outperforms the Solnik model. That is because our estimates of a_G and a_J are not consistent with home-country bias.

The vectors a_G and a_J represent the constant difference between the shares held by Americans on the one hand, and by Germans and Japanese, respectively, on the other. Our estimate of a_G shows that Germans would hold the fraction 0.23857 *more* of their portfolio in U.S. equities than Americans. Furthermore, they would hold -1.0 less of German equities, and -1.0 less of Japanese equities than Americans. On the other hand, there would be home bias in bond holdings—they would hold 1.0 more of German bonds. They would hold -0.31843 less of Japanese bonds, but they would hold 2.07988 more of U.S. bonds. (Recall that U.S. bonds are the residual asset. So, while the estimation constrained the elements of a_G to lie between -1 and 1, the difference between the share of U.S. bonds held by Germans and Americans is not so constrained.)

Likewise, the estimated difference between the Japanese and American portfolio is not indicative of home-country bias in equity holdings. While we do estimate that Japanese hold -1.0 less of U.S. equities than Americans, they also hold less of both German and Japanese equities. The difference between the American and Japanese share of German equities is very small: -0.00047, and of Japanese equities, -0.06301. But Japanese are also estimated to hold smaller shares of German bonds and Japanese bonds, the differences being -0.20343 and -0.12084, respectively. But Japanese are estimated to hold much more of American bonds. The difference in the portfolio shares is 2.38784.

So, in fact, a general asset demand model that allows for diversity in equity holdings can significantly outperform CAPM. But the failure of CAPM is not due to the well-known problem of home-country bias in equity holdings.

3.7 Conclusions

There are three main conclusions to be drawn from this paper.

First, the version of international CAPM presented here performs better than many versions estimated previously. Section 3.5 shows that the model has some weak power in predicting excess returns, whereas almost all previous studies have found that international versions of CAPM have little or no power. The models presented here differ from past models by allowing a broader menu of assets—equities and bonds—and by allowing some investor heterogeneity.

Second, the version of CAPM estimated here—the Solnik model—does not allow for enough investor heterogeneity. Section 3.6 presents a number of tests of CAPM against alternative models of asset demand. The alternative models do not impose the constraint between means of returns and variances of returns that is the hallmark of the CAPM.

Some of these alternative models do not significantly outperform CAPM. Specifically, CAPM cannot be rejected in favor of models which still impose the Solnik result—that portfolios of investors in different countries differ in their bond shares but not their equity shares. But the alternative models need not impose the Solnik result. So, when the alternative model is generalized so that it does not impose the CAPM constraint between means and variances, and does not impose the Solnik result, CAPM is rejected.

The third major conclusion regards the usefulness of the CASE approach to testing the CAPM. In the CASE method, the alternative models are all built up explicitly from asset demand functions. In section 3.6, we considered several different models of asset demands. In each case, we built an equilibrium model from those asset demand functions that served as an alternative to CAPM. In some of the cases, we were not able to reject CAPM. But when we altered our model of asset demand in a plausible way, we arrived at an equilibrium model which rejects CAPM. The advantage of the CASE approach is that we know very explicitly the economic behavior behind the alternative equilibrium models. When we fail to reject CAPM, we realize that it is not because CAPM is an acceptable model, but because the alternative model is as unacceptable as CAPM. When we reject CAPM, we know precisely the nature of the alternative model that is better able to explain expected asset returns. In this case, we have learned that CAPM must be generalized in a way to allow cross-country investor heterogeneity in equity demand. Perhaps incorporating capital controls or asymmetric information into the CAPM will prove helpful, but this is left for future work.

Appendix

Foreign Exchange Rate

The foreign exchange rates that were used in calculating rates of return and in converting local currency values into dollar values were taken from the data base at the Federal Reserve Bank of New York. They are the 9 A.M. bid rates from the last day of the month.

Equity Data

The value of outstanding shares in each of the three markets comes from monthly issues of Morgan Stanley's *Capital International Perspectives*. These figures are provided in domestic currency terms. I thank William Schwert for pointing out that these numbers must be interpreted cautiously because they do not correct adequately for cross-holding of shares, a particular problem in Japan.

The return on equities in local currency terms was taken from the same source. The returns are on the index for each country with dividends reinvested.

Bond Data

The construction of the data on bonds closely follows Frankel (1982). For each country, the cumulative foreign exchange rate intervention is computed, on a benchmark of foreign exchange holdings in March 1973. That cumulative foreign exchange intervention is added to outstanding government debt, while foreign government holdings of the currency are subtracted.

Germany

dmasst = dmdebt + bbint − ndmcb

dmdebt = German central government debt excluding social security contributions. Bundesbank Monthly Report, table VII.

dbbint = (DM/\$ exchange rate, IFS line ae) × (Δforeign exchange holdings, IFS line 1dd + SDR holdings, IFS line 1bd + Reserve position at IMF, IFS line cd − (SDR Holdings + Reserve position at IMF)$_{t-1}$ × (\$/SDR)/(\$/SDR)$_{t-1}$, IFS line sa − ΔSDR allocations, IFS line 1bd × (\$/SDR))

bbint − ∑ dbbint + 32.324 × (DM/\$)$_{1973:3}$

ndmcb is derived from the International Monetary Fund (IMF) Annual Report.

Japan

ynasst = yndebt + bjint − njncb

yndebt = ∑ Japanese central government deficit interpolated monthly, Bank of Japan, Economic Statistics Monthly, table 82.

dbjint = (Yen/\$ exchange rate, IFS line ae) × (Δforeign exchange holdings, IFS line 1dd + SDR holdings, IFS line 1bd + Reserve position at IMF, IFS line cd − (SDR Holdings + Reserve position at IMF)$_{t-1}$ × (\$/SDR)/(\$/SDR)$_{t-1}$, IFS line sa − ΔSDR allocations, IFS line 1bd × (\$/SDR))

bjint − ∑ dbjint + 18.125 × (Yen/\$)$_{1973:3}$

nyncb is derived from the IMF Annual Report.

United States

doasst = dodebt + fedint − ndolcb

dodebt = Federal debt, month end from Board of Governors Flow of Funds − carter

carter = 1.5952 in 78:12 and 1.3515 in 79:3, the Carter bonds

dfedint = Δforeign exchange holdings, IFS line 1dd + SDR holdings, IFS line 1bd + Reserve position at IMF, IFS line cd − (SDR Holdings + Reserve position at IMF)$_{t-1}$ − ΔSDR allocations, IFS line 1bd × (\$/SDR))

fedint = ∑ dfedint + 14.366

ndolcb is derived from the IMF Annual Report.

Wealth Data

Outside wealth is measured by adding government debt and the stock market value to the cumulated current account surplus on Frankel's benchmark wealth.

The monthly current account is interpolated from IFS line 77ad.

Interest Rates

Interest rates are one-month Eurocurrency rates obtained from the Bank for International Settlements tape.

References

Bollerslev, Tim. 1986. Generalized autoregressive conditional heteroscedasticity. *Journal of Econometrics* 31:307–27.
Campbell, John Y. 1993. Intertemporal asset pricing without consumption data. *American Economic Review* 83:487–512.
Clare, Andrew, Raymond O'Brien, Peter N. Smith, and Stephen Thomas. 1993. Global macroeconomic shocks, time-varying covariances and tests of the ICAPM. Working paper, Department of Economics, University of West London.
Dumas, Bernard. 1993. Partial equilibrium vs. general equilibrium models of international capital market equilibrium. Working Paper no. 93-1. Wharton School, University of Pennsylvania.
Engel, Charles M. 1984. Testing for the absence of expected real profits from forward market speculation. *Journal of International Economics* 17:299–308.
———. 1992. On the foreign exchange risk premium in a general equilibrium model. *Journal of International Economics* 32:305–19.
———. 1993. Real exchange rates and relative prices: An empirical investigation. *Journal of Monetary Economics* 32:35–50.
Engel, Charles M., Jeffrey A. Frankel, Kenneth A. Froot, and Anthony P. Rodrigues. 1993. The constrained asset share estimation (CASE) method: Testing mean-variance efficiency of the U.S. stock market. NBER Working Paper no. 4294. Cambridge, Mass.: National Bureau of Economic Research.
Engel, Charles M., and Anthony P. Rodrigues. 1989. Tests of international CAPM with time-varying covariances. *Journal of Applied Econometrics* 4:119–38.
———. 1993. Tests of mean-variance efficiency of international equity markets. *Oxford Economic Papers* 45:403–21.
Frankel, Jeffrey A. 1982. In search of the exchange risk premium: A six-currency test assuming mean-variance optimization. *Journal of International Money and Finance* 1:255–74.
———. 1988. Recent estimates of time-variation in the conditional variance and in the exchange risk premium. *Journal of International Money and Finance* 7:115–25.
Frankel, Jeffrey A., and Charles M. Engel. 1984. Do asset demand functions optimize over the mean and variance of real returns? A six-currency test. *Journal of International Economics* 17:309–23.
Gibbons, Michael R., Stephen A. Ross, and Jay Shanken. 1989. A test of the efficiency of a given portfolio. *Econometrica* 57:1121–52.
Glassman, Debra A., and Leigh A. Riddick. 1993. Why empirical international portfolio models fail. University of Washington. Manuscript.
Harvey, Campbell. 1989. Time varying conditional covariances in tests of asset pricing models. *Journal of Financial Economics* 24:289–317.
Restoy, Fernando. 1992. Optimal portfolio policies under time-dependent returns. Research Department, Bank of Spain. Manuscript.
Siegel, Jeremy. 1972. Risk, interest rates and the forward exchange. *Quarterly Journal of Economics* 86:303–9.
Solnik, Bruno. 1974. An equilibrium model of the international capital market. *Journal of Economic Theory* 8:500–524.
Thomas, S. H., and M. R. Wickens. 1993. An international CAPM for bonds and equities. *Journal of International Money and Finance* 12:390–412.

Comment   G. William Schwert

Introduction

I would like to begin by thanking Charles Engel for clearly listing the major limitations of this paper in his introduction. Moreover, throughout the paper he is clear to explain how his assumptions lead to the model formulations he tests. Overall, this is a paper that is easy to read and understand. Readers who are not familiar with the past work of Jeffrey Frankel on the use of portfolio share information to test the capital asset pricing model (CAPM) will find Engel's explanation and application of this model to be a useful introduction to this line of research.

Engel uses monthly data on rates of return to aggregate portfolios of stocks and bonds for three countries: the United States, Germany, and Japan (I believe the sample period is 1977–92, but it is never explicitly mentioned in the paper). He also uses data on the aggregate value of the stocks and bonds from these countries in some of his tests to impose constraints on his specification of the CAPM (this is the general strategy followed by Frankel 1982 and several subsequent authors).

As a small point, it is worth noting that care must be taken in using the Morgan Stanley *Capital International Perspectives* data on the aggregate value of country stock markets because they do not adjust for interfirm holdings of stock. Particularly in Japan, this problem leads to substantial overestimation of aggregate value (see, for example, French and Poterba 1991).

To model the conditional covariance matrix of the six assets, Engel uses a special form of the multivariate GARCH(1,1) model which assures that the covariance matrix is positive definite. Consistent with much prior work in this area, Engel finds that there is persistence in the conditional variance of returns to stocks and bonds.

Engel does not assume that purchasing power parity (PPP) holds, and he assumes that home country consumption prices are certain, so he uses the Solnik 1974 international CAPM. The unusual prediction from this model is that investors will hold differential amounts of bonds, but the same basket of equities. He relaxes this assumption in some of the empirical tests in section 3.6 by allowing domestic equity shares to differ from conventional CAPM predictions by a constant for Germany and Japan. Not surprisingly, Engel finds that these additional parameters are reliably different from zero (perhaps showing the type of home-country bias that has been found in many other papers).

Engel finds several other results that are not surprising. For example, he is unable to get a precise estimate of the risk aversion parameter ρ. Also, there is relatively weak power to discriminate among the competing models he consid-

G. William Schwert is the Gleason Professor of Finance and Statistics at the William E. Simon Graduate School of Business Administration, University of Rochester, and a research associate of the National Bureau of Economic Research.

ers in sections 3.5 and 3.6. In particular, there is not much evidence of a positive risk premium. This result is not surprising. As noted by Merton (1980), long time series are needed to derive precise estimates of unconditional expected stock returns because the volatility of stock returns is so large. Using only sixteen years of data (a limitation that is due largely to the desire to have data on all three countries' stock and bond markets) means that it is virtually impossible for Engel to get precise estimates of risk premiums.

How Does This Paper Relate to International Finance?

What Makes International Finance Different?

There are several things that distinguish *international* finance from the broad finance literature. First, there are potentially unusual consumption preferences or opportunities that differ systematically across groups of investors sorted by their home country. Often, regulation, taxes, or transaction costs may cause particular country investors to want to hold unusual portfolios of tradable securities compared with the predictions of typical portfolio models (e.g., the standard CAPM that is the benchmark in this paper).

Constraints on the investment opportunity set facing investors in different countries provide a second reason to focus on international finance. Nontraded assets, such as human capital, are obvious reasons why investors might choose different asset allocations in different countries (see Baxter and Jermann 1993). As discussed in the paper by Campbell and Froot (chap. 6 in this volume), market microstructure differences, such as securities transaction taxes, could also alter asset allocations (see also Schwert and Seguin 1993).

Lacking unusual consumption or investment opportunities that differ systematically across countries, the standard models of finance, such as the CAPM, should be equally as valid across countries as within countries. Therefore, Engel uses as his benchmark model the CAPM with integrated equity markets, but potentially segmented bond markets (because of the failure of PPP). As mentioned above, the data rejects even this form of the CAPM.

What Have We Learned about International Finance?

While Engel's results are suggestive that international constraints or differences might alter asset demands, I am skeptical that this inference is robust. For example, if we could obtain data on the stock holdings of investors in Rochester, New York, San Jose, California, and Seattle, Washington, I suspect that we would find concentrations of Kodak, Xerox, or Bausch & Lomb; silicon valley companies; and Microsoft, Boeing, or Weyerhauser, respectively. These examples have no legal barriers to capital flows or sources of exchange rate or political risk that are usually relied on to explain "home-country bias" in international asset-pricing models.

What this suggests is that tests for "international effects" based on simple models (e.g., the CAPM) should be calibrated using noninternational data. Given the many sources of evidence that the simple two-period CAPM is not adequate to describe risk-return relations within the set of NYSE-listed stocks (e.g., Fama and French 1993), it is not surprising that it also does not fit the data on portfolio shares.[1] The special implications about optimal portfolio shares from the CAPM used by Frankel (1982) and Engel are likely to be very sensitive to departures from the simple assumptions of the CAPM.

Moreover, if I were to identify a set of countries that are *least* likely to have significant artificial impediments to cross-country trading of financial assets, it would include the United States, Germany, and Japan (probably supplemented by the United Kingdom). Thus, if one were to think about the ideal experiment to identify some form of market segmentation due to international factors, it would not use data from the countries used by Engel.

Thus, while I believe that his empirical results reject the CAPM as an adequate joint description of the means and covariances of country portfolios of stocks, along with the implications for asset holdings, I doubt that this evidence tells us much about the factors that are peculiar to models of international asset pricing.

References

Baxter, Marianne, and Urban J. Jermann. 1993. The international diversification puzzle is worse than you think. Unpublished working paper, University of Virginia.

Fama, Eugene F. 1993. Multifactor portfolio efficiency and multifactor asset pricing. Unpublished working paper, University of Chicago.

Fama, Eugene F., and Kenneth R. French. 1993. Common risk factors in the returns on stocks and bonds. *Journal of Financial Economics* 33 (February): 3–56.

Frankel, Jeffrey A. 1982. In search of the exchange risk premium: A six-currency test assuming mean-variance optimization. *Journal of International Money and Finance* 7:115–25.

French, Kenneth R., and James M. Poterba. 1991. Were Japanese stock prices too high? *Journal of Financial Economics* 29 (October): 337–63.

Merton, Robert C. 1980. On estimating the expected return on the market: An exploratory investigation. *Journal of Financial Economics* 8:323–61.

Schwert, G. William, and Paul J. Seguin. 1993. Securities transaction taxes: An overview of costs, benefits and unresolved questions. *Financial Analysts Journal*, September/October.

Solnik, Bruno. 1974. An equilibrium model of the international capital market. *Journal of Economic Theory* 8:500–524.

---

1. Fama (1993) discusses the structure of efficient portfolios in the context of a multifactor asset-pricing model.

Comment   Geert Bekaert

In his excellent paper, Engel tests a version of the international CAPM using a technique that builds on the portfolio balance framework of Frankel (1982). The introduction of the paper contains a careful discussion of the limitations that this approach faces. Frankel, in his introduction to this volume, also provides an extensive discussion of the advantages and disadvantages of the approach followed by Engel relative to alternative approaches. To avoid merely reiterating the arguments given there, I will focus on just two issues.

I will start by reflecting on the nondynamic nature of the model and its likely implications for the ability of the model to explain time-variation in expected returns. In doing so, I will provide *empirical* estimates of the variability of risk premiums on equity and foreign exchange returns. The second issue concerns the presence of some form of investor heterogeneity in Engel's model. Since prices are fixed and exchange rate movements are random, the model effectively does not impose purchasing power parity (PPP). Although this "Solnik assumption" is a somewhat ad hoc way of introducing PPP deviations, it remains a fact that PPP is grossly violated in the data. Hence, the model is at least a priori more consistent with a world in which nominal and real exchange rates are very highly correlated than most theoretical models in which the PPP assumption assures that real expected returns are equalized across countries. Below I will attempt to put the importance of PPP deviations in a different perspective by examining empirically the relative importance of PPP deviations versus real interest differentials as determinants of risk premiums in foreign exchange returns.

Comparison with a Dynamic Model

Engel motivates the nondynamic nature of the model by comparing the expected return equation to a reduced form equation in a recent paper by Campbell (1993), which is reproduced here:

$$(1) \qquad E_t z_{i,\,t+1} = \rho \mathrm{cov}_t(z_{i,t+1}, z_{m,t+1}) - \frac{\mathrm{var}_t(z_{i,t+1})}{2} + (\rho - 1)V_{ih,t}.$$

The first term is the standard covariance with the market portfolio return with ρ being the coefficient of risk aversion or the price of risk; the second term is a Jensen's inequality term which would be present under risk neutrality as well. Both are present in Engel's framework. The last term is the "dynamic term," which is not present in the model of this paper:

$$(2) \qquad V_{ih,t} \equiv \mathrm{cov}_t(z_{i,t+1}, (E_{t+1} - E_t)\sum_{j=1}^{\infty}\beta^j z_{m,t+1+j}).$$

Geert Bekaert is assistant professor of finance at the Graduate School of Business, Stanford University.

The author thanks Jeffrey Frankel and Bob Hodrick for helpful suggestions.

A positive correlation between the asset return and news about future returns on the market increases expected returns when agents are more risk averse than log-utility but lowers expected returns for less risk averse ($\rho < 1$) agents.

Numerous studies have shown that equity returns are predictable using various financial variables. The ultimate goal of this paper is to provide an explanation for this observed statistical predictability. What I will try to show below is that the model here is very far from explaining the observed time-variation of expected returns. The analysis in Campbell (1993) suggests that ignoring the dynamic term in (2) might be part of the problem.

Campbell assumes that the return on the market is the first element of a K-element state vector, which follows a vector autoregressive law of motion (VAR). This implies that the dynamic term follows a factor model with the risks factors being the correlations between the VAR's residuals and the asset return and the risk prices being nonlinear functions of the VAR parameters. Since financial variables with strong predictive power for the market return can be included in the VAR, the dynamic term can potentially account for a major fraction of the predictable variation in returns.

The Empirical Variability of Risk Premiums

In what follows, I focus on the foreign exchange risk premium. It is well-known that, using the usual logarithmic approximations, this risk premium will be a component of the expected excess return on *any* foreign investment, that is,

$$(3) \qquad [E_t(r_{t+1}) - i_t] \approx [E_t(s_{t+1}) - f_t] + [E_t(r_{t+1}^*) - i_t^*],$$

where r_{t+1} represents the return on Japanese or German equity in dollars, i_t (i_t^*) is the U.S. (foreign) interest rate, s_t (f_t) is the dollar per foreign currency spot (forward) rate, and r_{t+1}^* is the local currency equity return. The expected excess dollar return has two components: the risk premium in the forward market and the risk premium of Japanese or German equity returns over the Japanese or German nominal interest rate. In Bekaert and Hodrick (1992), we show that both components are predictable using variables such as dividend yields and forward premiums. Hence, explaining risk premiums on foreign equity investments requires an investigation of risk premiums in the forward market.

As is well-known, the puzzle in the foreign exchange market is the *variability* of the risk premium, not its mean. How can we empirically estimate the variability of this risk premium? One way is to project foreign exchange returns linearly on a number of forecasting variables and compute the standard deviation of the fitted value. This approach implicitly assumes that expectations are linear functions of the information set and that the full information set is comprised of the variables used in the projection. These assumptions are less damaging than they seem. First, adding other variables to the information set will only lead to *larger* estimates of the variability of the risk premium. Second, when nonlinear functions are approximated by polynomials, adding the higher-order terms to the regression can likewise not decrease explanatory power. Hence, our estimate here can be considered a lower bound for the standard deviation of the risk premium.

Let $Y_t = [\Delta s_t^1, \Delta s_t^2, \Delta s_t^3, fp_{t,n}^1, fp_{t,n}^2, fp_{t,n}^3]'$, where Δs_t refers to exchange rate changes and fp_t is the forward premium (or interest differential) over n periods for $n = 4,13$. The superscripts 1,2,3 stand for yen, mark, and pound exchange rates, all measured in dollars per foreign currency. I sample Y_t weekly, run a vector autoregression and use its dynamics to compute the implied risk premium for monthly and quarterly forward contracts as[1]

$$(4) \qquad rp_{t,n}^i = E_t[\sum_{j=1}^{n} \Delta s_{t+j}^i - fp_{t,n}^i] \ i = 1,2,3.$$

In figure 3C.1, the implied monthly premiums are plotted for the 1975 to mid-1991 sample period. There is substantial time-variation in expected returns, although the unconditional mean is close to zero. Since the VAR is log-linear, it can be used to infer cross-rate expected returns. These returns are plotted in figure 3C.2. Finally, table 3C.1 reports the standard deviation and autocorrelations of the implied monthly and quarterly risk premiums.

Some striking facts emerge. First, the implied risk premiums are highly variable and very persistent despite the serial uncorrelatedness of actual returns. Second, the variability of the risk premium is of the order of 10 percent a year in all markets, including cross-rates. The well-known forward market puzzle is not a dollar phenomenon! The numbers I report are standard deviations and the unconditional mean is insignificantly different from zero; consequently, about 95 percent of the observations are between -20 percent and 20 percent. Is Engel's model explaining this huge variability? From the graphs in Engel's paper, the largest risk premium that occurs, annualized, is smaller than 5 percent. Hence, the variability of the risk premium generated by the model is at least an order of magnitude smaller than what is observed in the data. The graphs also show that the estimated variability of equity premiums is larger, in particular for Japanese equity, but never are the model's risk premiums higher than 25 percent. Using similar methods, empirical estimates of the equity premium variability are of the order of 40 to 60 percent. Hence, looking at this implied moment gives a much more dramatic sense of the failure of the model to account for the data.

I do want to caution that the empirical results reported above are based on statistical estimates using data sets that have been used by numerous researchers, so that there might be problems of data snooping. Also, this time-variation in ex ante returns need not be interpreted as a "risk premium"; it could also be caused by persistent fads or it might partially reflect peso problems (see below).

---

1. For more details, see Bekaert (1993).

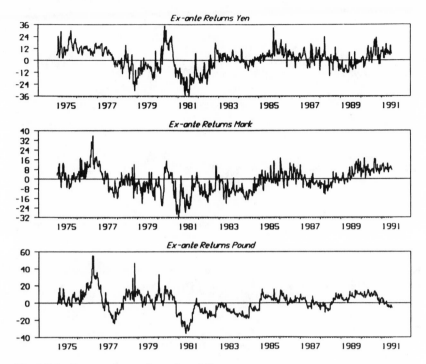

Fig. 3C.1   Ex ante forward market dollar returns

The Importance of PPP Deviations

Consider the following decomposition of foreign exchange returns:

$$[s_{t+1} - f_t] = [s_{t+1} - s_t + i_t^* - i_t] \equiv [\Delta q_{t+1} + r_{t+1}^* - r_{t+1}],$$

where Δq_{t+1} are (logarithmic) real exchange rate changes, r_{t+1}^* (r_{t+1}) the ex post real interest rate in the foreign country (the United States), defined as the nominal interest rate minus the inflation rate. The first equality follows from covered interest rate parity, the second from subtracting and adding relative inflation rates. Taking expectations, this equation decomposes the risk premium into expected real exchange rate changes and expected real interest differentials. In models based on PPP, real exchange rate changes are set to zero and the risk premium is totally driven by real interest rate differentials.

If the real exchange rate is martingale, that is, $E_t[\Delta q_{t+1}] = 0$, the PPP assumption would be a harmless simplifying assumption. Recent evidence in Cumby and Huizinga (1991), however, suggests that real exchange rate changes contain a substantial predictable component. Table 3C.2, reproduced from Bekaert (1994), offers an informal estimate of the relative contributions of expected real exchange rate changes and real interest differentials. To obtain

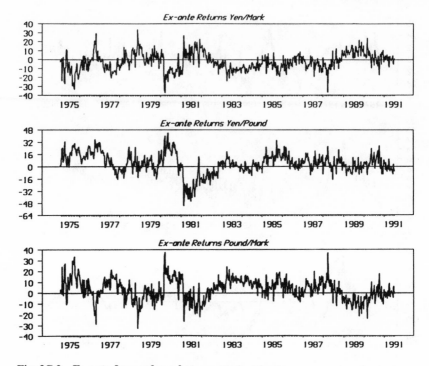

Fig. 3C.2 Ex ante forward market cross-rate returns

Table 3C.1   **Properties of the Implied Risk Premiums: Sample Period: January 1975–July 1991 (weekly data)**

A: Standard Deviations/Autocorrelations of Implied Risk Premiums

	$rp^1_{t,4}$	$rp^2_{t,4}$	$rp^3_{t,4}$	$rp^1_{t,13}$	$rp^2_{t,13}$	$rp^3_{t,13}$
σ	11.125	9.199	11.513	9.923	7.788	10.350
	(2.701)	(3.007)	(4.223)	(3.132)	(3.794)	(4.764)
ac_1	.887	.872	.935	.959	.959	.965
	(.062)	(.090)	(.035)	(.019)	(.030)	(.017)
ac_2	.786	.775	.891	.927	.926	.936
	(.110)	(.151)	(.052)	(.034)	(.052)	(.030)
ac_3	.743	.740	.851	.902	.904	.908
	(.125)	(.165)	(.065)	(.044)	(.063)	(.042)
ac_5	.681	.691	.782	.859	.865	.855
	(.139)	(.177)	(.084)	(.060)	(.081)	(.063)
ac_{13}	.528	.557	.567	.720	.738	.679
	(.153)	(.194)	(.133)	(.110)	(.134)	(.125)

Table 3C.1   (continued)

B: Standard Deviations of Cross-Rate Risk Premiums

	$rp_{t,4}^2\text{-}rp_{t,4}^1$	$rp_{t,4}^3\text{-}rp_{t,4}^1$	$rp_{t,4}^3\text{-}rp_{t,4}^2$	$rp_{t,13}^2\text{-}rp_{t,13}^1$	$rp_{t,13}^3\text{-}rp_{t,13}^1$	$rp_{t,13}^3\text{-}rp_{t,13}^2$
σ	9.773	12.133	7.575	8.138	10.663	5.423
	(2.392)	(2.738)	(2.143)	(2.555)	(2.999)	(2.432)

Notes: The standard deviation (σ) and autocorrelations (ac_n) of the risk premium (panel A) are computed from the dynamics of a second order VAR. The same methodology is used to compute the standard deviations of the cross-rate risk premiums in panel B. The exchange rate and interests rate data used are described in Bekaert (1993). The returns are annualized by multiplying by 1200 for monthly, by 400 for quarterly data.

Table 3C.2   **Relative Variability of Expected PPP Deviations and Real Interest Differentials for the Dollar/Yen Rate: Sample Period: 1972:02–1989:04 (quarterly data)**

	$\Delta s\text{-}fp$	Δq	$r^*\text{-}r$	$(\Delta q, r^*r)$
$\sigma^2[.]$	696.093	647.063	10.380	19.325
$\sigma^2[E_t[.]]$	122.703	81.059	4.853	18.396

Notes: The symbols *fb*, Δq, and $r^*\text{-}r$ indicate, respectively, the (logarithmic) difference between the future spot and current forward rate, real exchange rate changes, and the real interest differential between the United States and Japan. The data are further described in Bekaert (1993). σ^2 denotes the sample variance. The conditional expectation $E_t[.]$ is computed from the projection of the variable in the column onto a constant, lagged real exchange rate changes, the lagged forward premium, and the lagged inflation differential. The last column contains the sample covariance between (expected) real exchange rate changes and the (expected) real interest differential. All variables are multiplied by 400 to obtain annualized numbers.

estimates of expected values, I simply projected $fb_{t+1} = s_{t+1} - f_t$, Δq_{t+1}, and $r_{t+1}^* - r_{t+1}$ onto a number of information variables consisting of the lagged real exchange rate, the lagged forward premium, and the lagged inflation differential using quarterly data for the United States and Japan. The table reveals that the predictability of real interest differentials is indeed higher than the predictability of real exchange rates. However, the total variance of real interest differentials is dwarfed by the total variance of real exchange rate changes. According to the table, only 4 percent of the total variance of the risk premium can be fully accounted for by ex ante real interest differentials. Hence, models that rely on PPP should not hope to explain much of the variability of expected foreign exchange returns. Although the table reports results for the yen only, this result is robust to various periods, currencies, and information variables (see Gokey 1993). As a consequence, when Engel, unlike most of the literature, chose not to impose PPP, it was a very wise decision.

Concluding Comments

First, I want to point out that all the computations here *and* Engel's model crucially rely on the assumption of *rational expectations*. It is conceivable that the estimates of the variance of the risk premiums, reported above, are grossly overestimated because of "peso problems." We do not have large enough samples to experience all of the events on which agents place prior probability, and to have sample moments converge to their population moments. More generally, when the true model of the world is evolving over time, ex ante expectations can appear biased ex post, although they were formed rationally. Several researchers have pointed out that market participants in foreign exchange markets seem to make systematic forecast errors. This is not surprising in a complex environment where agents, say, anticipate shifts in monetary policy, which do not occur frequently or never materialize. The recent currency turmoil in Europe, for example, has dramatized the importance of monetary policy in shaping the expectations of the major players in financial markets in general and currency markets in particular. Although some research is emerging that tries to address this issue (Engel and Hamilton 1990; Kaminsky 1993; and Evans and Lewis 1993), much more is needed.

Of more direct relevance to this paper, the idea that there are policy regime switches implies that the conditional variance process is likely to be severely misspecified. For instance, Cai (1992) shows that if a shift in the unconditional variance of an interest rate process is allowed for, the estimated GARCH coefficients change dramatically. Since the sample of this paper includes the 1979–82 monetary policy shift in the United States, and money market instruments are part of the assets considered, a different conditional variance specification is likely to substantially affect the maximum likelihood estimates of the model. After all, it is the time-variation of the second moments that largely drives expected returns in this model.

Finally, I want to recall the main result of the paper: the model is rejected only versus an alternative that allows for more diversity across investors in their holdings of equities. In particular, it is the diversity that makes people hold disproportionate amounts of their own equity that has the power to reject the model. This brings us back to the enormously hot topic of "home bias" in asset choice. What might cause this diversity? One obvious candidate is simply location and the differential-transactions cost that comes with buying assets in different markets, including informational costs. It is perhaps no coincidence that with increasingly faster and cheaper access to foreign stocks, partially through the evolution in telecommunications and computers, and with information flowing more frequently and faster throughout the world, portfolios have become more and more "international." Currently, we do not have very good economic models to think about these issues and Engel's paper has once again confirmed that this is where international economists should direct their research efforts.

The internationalization of equity markets might also be related to the dismantling of numerous regulatory barriers to investment over the last decade. Engel's model assumes full market integration, which might be a tenuous assumption, especially in the early part of the sample, when Japanese capital markets were subject to severe regulatory restrictions. Ideally, the model should allow for partial segmentation in the early part of the sample and integrated capital markets for the later part of the sample. Such a model with time-varying degrees of segmentation is developed in Bekaert and Harvey (1993).

References

Bekaert, G. 1993. The time-variation of expected returns and volatility in foreign exchange markets. Stanford University, Graduate School of Business. Manuscript.
———. 1994. Exchange rate volatility and deviations from unbiasedness in a cash-in-advance model. *Journal of International Economics* 36 (April): 29–52.
Bekaert, G., and C. Harvey. 1993. Time-varying world market integration. Stanford University, Graduate School of Business. Manuscript.
Bekaert, G., and R. Hodrick. 1992. Characterizing predictable components in excess returns on equity and foreign exchange markets. *Journal of Finance* 47:467–509.
Cai, J. 1992. A Markov model of unconditional variance in ARCH. Northwestern University. Manuscript.
Cambell, John Y. 1993. Intertemporal asset pricing without consumption data. *The American Economic Review,* June, 487–512.
Cumby, R., and J. Huizinga. 1991. The predictability of real exchange rates in the short and the long run. *Japan and the World Economy* 3:17–38.
Engel, C., and J. Hamilton. 1990. Long swings in the exchange rate: Are they in the data and do markets know it? *American Economic Review* 80:689–713.
Evans, M., and K. Lewis. 1993. Do long swings in the dollar affect estimates of the risk premia? The Wharton School. Manuscript.
Frankel, Jeffrey A. 1982. In search of the exchange risk premium: A six-currency test assuming mean-variance optimization. *Journal of International Money and Finance* 1:255–74.
Gokey, T. 1993. What explains the risk premium in foreign exchange returns? *Journal of International Money and Finance.* Forthcoming.
Kaminsky, G. 1993. Is there a peso problem? Evidence from the dollar/pound exchange rate, 1976–1987. *American Economic Review* 83:450–72.

4 International Equity Transactions and U.S. Portfolio Choice

Linda L. Tesar and Ingrid M. Werner

4.1 Introduction

The gain from diversification of investment portfolios across national markets is by now a well-established fact. Studies published in the late 1960s and early 1970s demonstrated that investors would be rewarded for holding a global set of assets rather than skewing their portfolios toward domestic investments (see Grubel 1968; Levy and Sarnat 1970; and Solnik 1974). Since that time, fixed barriers to international investment—such as government controls on cross-border capital flows, difficulties in obtaining information about foreign markets, and differences in financial institutions—have gradually declined. However, as of 1991, the share of portfolio investment allocated to foreign assets by the United States and Canada has remained at less than 5 percent of their total portfolios (Tesar and Werner 1994a). Somewhat surprisingly, the turnover rate on the component of portfolios allocated to international equities is substantially larger than the turnover rate on national equity markets. This suggests that variable transactions costs are unlikely to be the main cause for home bias in portfolio allocations. Therefore models of international portfolio choice must provide explanations *both* for the heterogeneity in national port-

Linda L. Tesar is assistant professor of economics at the University of California at Santa Barbara and faculty research fellow of the National Bureau of Economic Research. Ingrid M. Werner is associate professor of finance at the Graduate School of Business, Stanford University, research fellow of the Institute for International Economic Studies, Stockholm University, faculty research fellow of the National Bureau of Economic Research, and Robert M. and Ann T. Bass faculty fellow for 1993–94.

The authors thank Bernard Dumas, Geert Bekaert, Jeff Frankel, Danny Quah, Peter Reiss, Doug Steigerwald, and our discussants, Philippe Jorion and Richard Levich, for invaluable comments and suggestions. We also thank Tiff Macklem of the Bank of Canada and Hartmut Draeger of the Deutsche Bundesbank for their assistance. Richard Crabb and Jon Riddle both provided excellent research assistance. Any remaining errors are our own responsibility.

folios, in particular the bias toward domestic securities, and the high volume of transactions in international securities markets.

To gain further insight into the behavior of international investors, we examine the time-series patterns of bilateral equity flows between five large Organization for Economic Cooperation and Development (OECD) countries: Canada, Germany, Japan, the United Kingdom, and the United States. Our study uses quarterly data drawn from Statistics Canada and the U.S. Department of the Treasury. This research makes a number of contributions to the existing literature on international portfolio investment. First, our data allow us to identify the nationality of the investors involved in cross-border transactions. Thus we are able to study potential differences in investment behavior across investors from different countries. Second, having data on bilateral securities transactions (rather than aggregate portfolio inflows and outflows) allows us to examine how each investor allocates these funds across markets. Finally, our study examines the actual portfolio choice of U.S. investors. Thus we can test models of portfolio choice directly using both the information about asset allocations and returns. Our results suggest that existing models of international portfolio choice are not supported by the data. It is our hope that these findings will help guide the development of new models of portfolio choice that are more consistent with the observed behavior of investors in international equity markets.

In section 4.2 we summarize the rules governing U.S. reporting of international securities transactions. In section 4.3 we examine net equity flows reported by Canadian and U.S. reporting agencies. We find that net equity flows to and from the United Kingdom account for the majority of flows across U.S. borders, while flows to and from the United States account for most of the net equity flows across Canadian borders. In a simple frictionless world, net equity flows result from changes in investors' perceptions about expected returns to, and the risk of, individual markets. If investors across countries shared the same views, one would expect net acquisitions of equity to be synchronized across investors and over markets. We find very little evidence in the data for such a consensus among investors. Perhaps even more puzzling is that net purchases are strongly positively autocorrelated, suggesting that portfolios adjust sluggishly over time. This could be explained by very slow moving state variables driving the perceived investment opportunity set, or by frictions that prevent a rapid adjustment of portfolios in response to altered expectations.

In section 4.4 we construct estimates of U.S. investment positions in foreign equities and foreign investment positions in U.S. equities. During the sample U.S. holdings of foreign equity increased at a modest pace. Foreign holdings of U.S. equity exhibited a more rapid increase and by the end of the sample reached a level of roughly 10 percent of U.S. market capitalization. In section 4.5 we combine these estimates of investment positions with gross transactions volumes to create a measure of turnover in foreign equity. Two basic conclusions emerge. First, gross trading volume in foreign equity is substantially larger than the corresponding net acquisitions of equity. Second, we find that the rate at which foreign investors turn over their U.S. equity portfolios is roughly at par with the average turnover rate in U.S. markets. In contrast, U.S. investors appear to be trading more frequently on their portfolio of foreign equities, particularly Japanese and British equities, than the average transactions rate on U.S. stock exchanges. U.S. turnover rates in foreign equity also tend to exceed the average turnover rates in the markets where transactions take place.

In sections 4.6 and 4.7 we combine our data on net purchases with excess returns to test some simple models of portfolio choice. We find that U.S. net purchases show very little significant comovement with equity returns, interest rates, dividend yields, exchange rates, and measures of investor wealth. We then use our estimates of international investment positions to test whether U.S. investors allocate portfolios according to the capital asset pricing model (CAPM). Our data strongly reject this hypothesis.

4.2   Reporting of International Securities Transactions

Our data on equity flows are collected from Statistics Canada and the U.S. Department of the Treasury.[1] Foreign direct investment activity is excluded from this data. Statistics Canada reports quarterly net transactions in foreign and domestic bonds and equities between Canadian residents and residents of the United States, the United Kingdom, Japan, and the European Community (EC) excluding the United Kingdom. The U.S. Treasury Bulletin reports quarterly data on purchases and sales of equities and bonds between U.S. residents and foreign residents from Canada, Germany, Japan, and the United Kingdom, and from a large number of other countries. The sample period is 1978:01–1991:03.[2] Data from the U.S. Treasury appear to be the most comprehensive of the data sets (see Tesar and Werner 1992). Appendix A briefly summarizes the reporting requirements specified by the U.S. government.[3] Reports are filed monthly with the Treasury Department covering transactions with foreigners in long-term marketable securities. A foreigner is any individual, partnership, association, corporation, or other organization located outside the United States.[4]

---

1. Data on corporate and government bonds are available from the same source.

2. The Deutsche Bundesbank reports quarterly purchases and sales of equities and bonds between German residents and residents of Canada, Japan, the United Kingdom, the United States, and a broad set of other countries. We excluded the German data from our analysis to conserve space. We have not been able to find similar bilateral data on international portfolio transactions for the United Kingdom and Japan.

3. This is extracted from *Instructions for preparation of monthly form S, international capital form S*. OMB no. 1505-0001, Treasury Department, Office of the Assistant Secretary for Economic Policy, 1991. We do not have access to the corresponding documentation for Canada. Discussions with representatives from the Bank of Canada lead us to believe that the reporting requirements in Canada are similar.

4. Note that the data reflect the residency of the party involved in the transaction and not the country of origin of the security itself.

Before going on to the analysis, we should mention some of the shortcomings of the data. First, there is no explicit penalty for failing to report securities transactions to the regulatory agencies. However, the securities brokers we have spoken with indicate that they are unlikely to "overlook" reporting requirements, as they wish to stay on friendly terms with reporting agencies. In fact, they are more likely to bend over backwards to remain in compliance. Second, the rapid expansion of markets and the development of new types of financial instruments make it difficult for the reporting agencies to keep pace with the volume of flows.[5] Third, the data may not reflect the transactions of foreign-based firms which are transacting on behalf of domestic residents. An important example are U.S. mutual funds domiciled offshore.[6] Finally, the initial deposit of American Depository Receipts (ADRs) and global Depository Receipts (GDRs) on domestic markets is reflected in the data; however, the subsequent reissue and ultimate trading of these essentially foreign securities by domestic residents is not picked up by our data sources.

Despite these problems, the data provide a wealth of information about international portfolio investment. It is unlikely that the data reflect *all* cross-border securities transactions. However, as long as there is no systematic bias between the reporting of purchases and sales, and there is little reason to suspect such bias during the time period we study, our data can be interpreted as reflecting the investment choices of those investors who report their transactions to official agencies. As will be seen below, to the extent that gross cross-border transactions are underreported, some of the evidence on the magnitude of transactions in foreign equity and turnover becomes even more puzzling.

We will apply two basic concepts to the data on equity transactions. The first, *net equity flows,* is the change in a country's net holdings of foreign equity. We define U.S. residents' net purchases of Canadian securities as gross purchases of foreign securities from Canadian residents *minus* gross sales of foreign securities to Canadian residents. Similarly, Canadian residents' net purchases of U.S. securities are defined as the gross sales of domestic (U.S.) securities by Canadians *minus* the gross purchases by U.S. residents of domestic (U.S.) securities from Canadians. The second concept, *gross equity flows* or *transactions,* is the volume of cross-border equity trading. We define transactions in foreign equity by U.S. residents to be the sum of U.S. residents' purchases of foreign equity from and U.S. residents' sales of foreign equity to foreign residents. Transactions in U.S. equity by foreign residents are similarly defined.

We did some basic cross-checking of the correspondence between comparable series reported by Statistics Canada and the U.S. Treasury. The reported

---

5. See Stekler and Truman (1992) for a complete description of the problems involved in collecting data on portfolio flows.

6. It is our understanding that in 1992 the United States began collecting data on offshore U.S. brokerages.

net equity flows are significantly positively correlated.[7] It does, however, appear that the average quarterly net purchases of U.S. shares reported by Statistics Canada are less than half of those reported by the U.S. Treasury. No discrepancy of similar magnitude is present for the reported U.S. net purchases of Canadian equity.[8] This may reflect a tendency for Canadian investors to misreport their purchases of U.S. equity. One might suspect that the reason is to avoid taxation or circumvent quantitative capital controls. It is of course also possible that the reporting requirements differ in the two countries. The asymmetric evidence of underreporting, however, is difficult to reconcile with such an explanation.

To facilitate comparisons between equity flows reported by the two official sources, we report all flows in millions of U.S. dollars. The Canadian data are translated into U.S. dollars using the average quarterly exchange rate drawn from the International Financial Statistics (IFS) data base. We produce descriptive statistics for real flows expressed in December 1977 prices. These are computed by deflating nominal flows using the average monthly seasonally adjusted consumer price index for each quarter from Citibase.

4.3 Net Equity Flows

4.3.1 Net Equity Flows Crossing the U.S. Border

Figures 4.1A and 4.1B show net equity flows crossing U.S. borders. These flows became more volatile after the mid-1980s, primarily due to fluctuations in U.S. purchases of Japanese and British equity. Figure 4.1B shows that the same two countries also exhibit the most volatile net purchases of U.S. equity. Note the large sale of U.S. equity by British residents during the fourth quarter of 1987—the quarter including the stock market crash. It is interesting that investors from the other countries did not simultaneously dump U.S. stocks. We will document that such heterogeneity in investor responses across countries appears to be a characteristic of international investment behavior.

Table 4.1A shows that the United Kingdom is the most important counterpart in cross-border equity transactions with the United States. U.S. investors bought on average 169 million constant dollars worth of equity from the United Kingdom per quarter during the 1978:01–1991:03 period. Quarterly net purchases from Canada were less than half that at $74 million, and U.S. investors bought $27 million of equity per quarter from Germany. While average quarterly net flows from the United States to Japan have been modest at $49 mil-

---

7. The correlation between U.S. net purchases of Canadian equity reported by the two data sources is 0.853. The correlation between reports of Canadian net purchases of U.S. equity is somewhat smaller at 0.518.

8. Tesar and Werner (1992) show that the Canadian investment position in the United States reported by Statistics Canada is considerably smaller than the Canadian investment position reported by the U.S. Treasury.

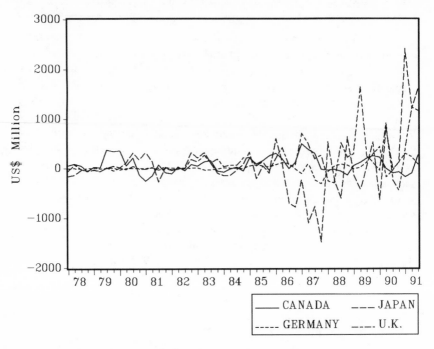

Fig. 4.1A   Net U.S. purchases of foreign equity
Source: U.S. Treasury Bulletin (1977 = 100).

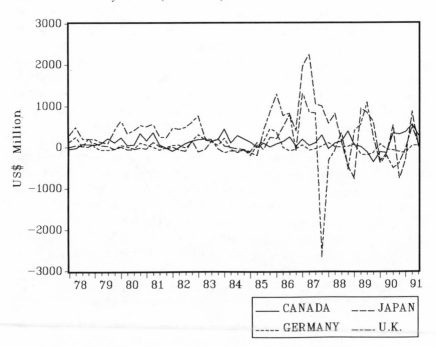

Fig. 4.1B   Net foreign purchases of U.S. equity
Source: U.S. Treasury Bulletin (1977 = 100).

Table 4.1A   Net Equity Flows Crossing the U.S. Border 1978:01–1991:03

Variable[b]	Mean	Standard Deviation	Maximum	Minimum	AR(1)[a]	AR(2)[a]	AR(3)[a]	AR(4)[a]	Ljung-Box(4) p-value
U.S. purchases of foreign equity									
Canada	74.0	163.8	503.3	−254.4	0.54*	0.20	−0.06	−0.15	0.000
Germany	26.8	113.0	439.2	−311.4	0.39*	−0.04	−0.05	0.14	0.038
Japan	48.6	592.3	2415.3	−1486.9	0.32*	0.32*	0.25	0.04	0.004
United Kingdom	169.4	370.8	1678.6	−461.3	0.27	−0.09	−0.00	0.13	0.238
Foreign purchases of U.S. equity									
Canada	120.3	161.9	553.1	−364.1	0.43*	0.28*	−0.05	−0.29	0.000
Germany	25.0	131.9	450.4	−208.7	0.45*	0.10	−0.12	−0.13	0.007
Japan	200.1	540.5	2256.0	−796.5	0.54*	0.28*	0.28*	0.20	0.000
United Kingdom	234.8	585.4	1347.3	−2692.1	0.25	0.10	−0.21	0.17	0.072

Source: U.S. Treasury Bulletin.

Note: Units are million U.S. dollars (1977 = 100). AR(1) = autoregression coefficient at lag 1 (lag 2, lag 3, lag 4).

[a]An asterisk indicates significance at the 5 percent level.

[b]Nominal purchases are deflated using the average quarterly consumer price index from Citibase (1977 = 100).

lion, their volatility has been exceptionally high. The table also reports statistics on net purchases of U.S. equity by Canadian, German, Japanese, and British investors. British and Japanese investors have been the dominant foreign investors in U.S. equity, acquiring on average $235 million (41 percent of total inflow) and $200 million (34 percent of total inflow), respectively, per quarter. Canadian investors bought on average 120 million constant U.S. dollars of equity per quarter while German investors spent $25 million per quarter. Note that the combined average quarterly net investment in U.S. equity by foreign investors of $580 million is almost twice as large as the combined average net investment in foreign equity by U.S. investors of $319 million. Thus, net purchases of U.S. equity by foreign residents contributed to financing the U.S. current account deficits of the 1980s and early 1990s.

4.3.2   Net Equity Flows Crossing the Canadian Border

Net equity flows crossing the Canadian border are illustrated in figures 4.1C and 4.1D. Related descriptive statistics are presented in table 4.1B. From Canada's perspective, the United States is its largest trading partner in terms of equity transactions. Canadian average net purchases of U.S. equity of $55 million are more than twice as large as net purchases of British equity at $21 million. U.S. investors provide 85 percent of the average equity flows to Canada. Net purchases by EC residents account for roughly 20 percent of U.S. net purchases. Note that bilateral equity flows between the United States and Canada are not only the largest in magnitude (relative to the other countries) but also exhibit the most volatility. Japanese net equity investment was modest while British investors on average withdrew funds from the Canadian equity market. Net average quarterly equity flows crossing the Canadian border were virtually balanced during this period.

4.3.3   Autocorrelation of Net Equity Flows

The data on U.S. and Canadian net purchases exhibit substantial positive autocorrelation. In only one case, Canadian net purchases of EC equity, do we observe a significantly negative autocorrelation coefficient. This persistence in net purchases may be evidence that investors adjust their portfolios gradually over time. If this is indeed the case, such dynamic adjustments should be incorporated into the development and testing of models of portfolio choice.

The serial correlation of net acquisitions of equity also affects our inference based on simple correlations of net equity flows across markets. We report correlation coefficients since they have the advantage of being unit-free. However, the calculation of appropriate standard errors of the estimated correlation coefficients between time series with serial correlation is not straightforward. Instead we base our inference on the covariance between the time series, and correct the corresponding standard errors for autocorrelation using a method proposed by Newey and West (1987). The method is outlined in appendix B.

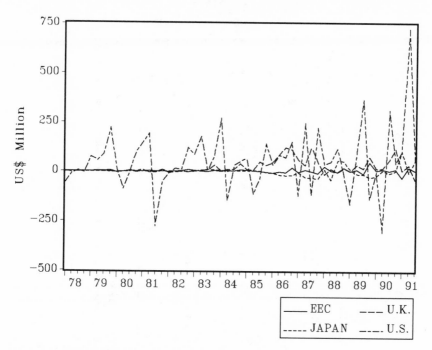

Fig. 4.1C   Net Canadian purchases of foreign equity
Source: Statistics Canada (1977 = 100).

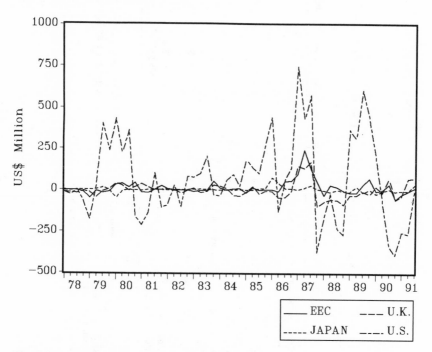

Fig. 4.1D   Net foreign purchases of Canadian equity
Source: Statistics Canada (1977 = 100).

Table 4.1B Net Equity Flows Crossing the Canadian Border 1978:01–1991:03

Variable[a]	Mean	Standard Deviation	Maximum	Minimum	AR(1)[b]	AR(2)[b]	AR(3)[b]	AR(4)[b]	Ljung-Box(4) p-value
Canadian purchases of foreign equity									
European Community excluding United Kingdom	3.5	10.3	46.6	−30.0	−0.30*	0.16	−0.02	0.13	0.098
Japan	0.9	23.2	105.1	−43.5	0.14	0.26	0.02	−0.18	0.128
United Kingdom	21.3	36.2	127.3	−40.3	0.49*	0.39*	0.32	0.38*	0.004
United States	54.5	160.9	726.7	−307.7	−0.14	−0.02	−0.03	−0.09	0.238
Foreign purchases of Canadian equity									
European Community excluding United Kingdom	12.3	45.3	240.8	−58.1	0.56*	0.23	0.09	−0.02	0.789
Japan	1.6	16.5	74.9	−52.8	0.30*	0.10	0.02	0.05	0.190
United Kingdom	−2.1	51.0	169.7	−100.0	0.39*	0.06	−0.22	−0.15	0.010
United States	67.6	257.2	752.8	−394.5	0.48*	0.22	−0.15	−0.24	0.000

Source: Statistics Canada.

Note: Units are million U.S. dollars (1977 = 100). AR(1) = autoregression coefficient at lag 1 (lag 2, lag 3, lag 4).

[a]Nominal purchases are translated into U.S. dollars using the average quarterly exchange rate from Citibase. Dollar purchases are deflated using the average quarterly consumer price index from Citibase (1977 = 100).

[b]An asterisk indicates significance at the 5 percent level.

Our null hypothesis is that the estimated covariances are zero, or that net equity flows are uncorrelated.

4.3.4 Correlations of Net Equity Flows across Markets

In tables 4.2A and 4.2B, we report the correlations among real net equity flows to investigate the extent to which net acquisitions of equity are synchronized across investors from different countries. Suppose that investors follow a simple mean-variance model for asset allocation, and that for exogenous reasons they start with a portfolio of primarily domestic securities. In such a world, the decision to invest in foreign equity can be prompted by an expectation that the return to foreign equity will exceed the return on domestic equity or that the inclusion of foreign equity in the portfolio will reduce risk.

To the extent that cross-border investment is driven solely by differences in expected returns, we expect to see a negative contemporaneous correlation between domestic investors' net purchases of foreign equity and foreign investors' net purchases of domestic equity. Moreover, investors would channel funds into the same "foreign" market simultaneously. If, on the other hand, cross-border investment is driven primarily by the desire to diversify across markets, the correlation between net equity purchases crossing a border from different directions might very well be positive. The diversification motive might, alternatively, make different investors target different foreign markets for their investment, which means that the cross-sectional correlations could be positive or negative.

Of course, portfolio flows between countries are part of the larger picture of trade and financial linkages that connect open economies. If equity flows are in some sense the "residual" component of the capital account, net equity flows may be determined by factors quite separate from the simple mean-variance trade-offs discussed above.

The first panel of table 4.2A shows the correlation between quarterly net purchases of foreign equity by U.S. residents. The marginal significance levels give the probability that the estimated covariance is zero. U.S. net purchases of equity from Canadian and Japanese residents are negatively correlated, while the rest of the pair-wise correlations of net purchases are positive. In no case are the covariances significantly different from zero. Correlation of foreign investors' net purchases of U.S. equity, reported in the second panel of the table, have mixed signs, but again none of the covariances are significant. Thus, there appears to be little synchronization in foreign investment in U.S. equity. The bottom panel reports the correlations between U.S. net acquisitions of foreign equity and foreign acquisitions of U.S. equity. If U.S. and Canadian investors concur, for example, that it is appropriate to reallocate the portfolio between U.S. and Canadian equity, we anticipate that the correlations will be negative. While the majority of correlations are in fact negative, none of the covariances are significantly different from zero.

A somewhat different picture emerges from the correlation between cross-

Table 4.2A   Correlations: Net Equity Flows Crossing the U.S. Border 1978:01–1991:03

	Correlation	Marginal Significance Level[a]	Correlation	Marginal Significance Level[a]	Correlation	Marginal Significance Level[a]
U.S. purchases of equity from:	Germany		Japan		United Kingdom	
Canada	0.00	1.00	−0.19	0.16	0.19	0.16
Germany			0.35	0.15	0.04	0.39
Japan					0.23	0.49
Purchases of U.S. equity by:	Germany		Japan		United Kingdom	
Canada	0.02	0.87	−0.05	0.64	−0.18	0.15
Germany			−0.14	0.20	0.20	0.27
Japan					0.20	0.15

Investor Agreement between the United States and:

Canada		Germany		Japan		United Kingdom	
Correlation	MSL[a]	Correlation	MSL[a]	Correlation	MSL[a]	Correlation	MSL[a]
−0.32	0.19	−0.13	0.23	−0.37	0.25	0.15	0.23

Source: U.S. Treasury bulletin.
Note: Units: Million U.S. dollars (1977 = 100).
[a]The marginal significance level (MSL) gives the probability under the null that the covariance is zero.

border flows for Canada in table 4.2B. The correlation between Canadian net purchases of foreign equity in the first panel are of mixed signs, suggesting more of a reallocation across markets rather than a general increase in Canadian holdings of all foreign equity. None of the covariances are, however, significantly different from zero. The consistently positive correlations in the second panel indicate that there appears to be a consensus among British, EC, and U.S. investors about the appropriate timing of investment in Canadian equities. However, the mixed signs and the high marginal significance levels in the bottom panel suggest that Canadian investors do not agree with the investors in the other countries.

The overwhelming impression from tables 4.2A and 4.2B is the lack of significant correlation among net equity flows.[9] Given the general nature of the alternative hypothesis and that the sample is rather limited, we do not expect to have much power against the null. The absence of comovement in net equity flows may indicate that the decisions about international portfolio choice are guided primarily by the diversification motive. This conclusion is somewhat contradicted by the high volume of cross-border investment between countries

9. In examining the correlations between U.S. net purchases of equity from nineteen countries, including fifteen emerging stock markets, Tesar and Werner (1994b) also find little or no correlation between net purchases from different markets.

Table 4.2B   **Correlations: Net Equity Flows Crossing the Canadian Border 1978:01–1991:03**

	Correlation	Marginal Significance Level[a]	Correlation	Marginal Significance Level[a]	Correlation	Marginal Significance Level[a]
Canadian purchases of equity from:	Japan		United Kingdom		United States	
EC excluding United Kingdom	−0.26	0.46	0.16	0.44	−0.02	0.93
Japan			−0.41	0.14	−0.06	0.27
United Kingdom					0.04	0.48
Purchases of Canadian equity by:	Japan		United Kingdom		United States	
EC excluding United Kingdom	0.11	0.40	0.59	0.24	0.44	0.18
Japan			0.09	0.57	0.12	0.51
United Kingdom					0.44	0.35

Investor Agreement between Canada and:

EC excluding United Kingdom		Japan		United Kingdom		United States	
Correlation	MSL[a]	Correlation	MSL[a]	Correlation	MSL[a]	Correlation	MSL[a]
0.06	0.54	−0.06	0.67	0.09	0.67	−0.24	0.23

Source: Statistics Canada.

Note: Units are million U.S. dollars (1977 = 100).

[a]The marginal significance level (MSL) gives the probability under the null that the covariance is zero.

whose stock markets are highly positively correlated, that is, Canada and the United States. Another potential explanation is that investors' strategies for portfolio allocation differ substantially across countries. Alternatively, net equity purchases may be mainly affected by more general macroeconomic conditions such as business cycle fluctuations, the differential between output growth at home and abroad, or fiscal policies.

4.4   Cumulated Foreign Investment Positions

In the remainder of this paper we concentrate on equity flows to and from the United States as reported by the U.S. Treasury. Using our bilateral data on net purchases of equity, we construct a quarterly time series of U.S. foreign investment positions. Such data are not available from published sources.[10] The

10. The Department of Commerce reports only the investment position on an annual basis for a limited number of countries. Their reported series are constructed in a way similar to the method we propose below.

time series are interesting for two reasons. First, they provide information about the allocation of the U.S. investment portfolio across global markets. Second, the investment positions are the relevant base for thinking about turnover rates on foreign equity investments.

To create an investment position series from U.S. net purchases of equity, we cumulate net purchases starting from an initial investment position, which we take as the investment position at the end of 1977 as estimated by the Department of Commerce. At the end of 1977, the reported U.S. investment position was $4,971 million in Canada, $350 million in Japan, and $4,485 million in Western Europe. We allocate the Western Europe position over Germany and the United Kingdom according to their relative market sizes at the end of 1977.[11] The resulting position is $1,794 million in Germany and $2,691 million in the United Kingdom. Starting from these initial values, denoted X_0^i, the quarterly investment position is created using the following algorithm:

$$(1) \qquad X_{t+1}^i = X_t^i(1+R_{t+1}^i) + NP_{t,\,t+1}^i,$$

where X_t^i is the U.S. investment position in market i at t, R_{t+1}^i is the gross return (including dividends) on equity in market i over the quarter, and $NP_{t,\,t+1}^i$ represents quarterly net purchases of U.S. investors from market i.[12] Using the data on net foreign purchases of U.S. equity, the same algorithm can be used to generate the investment position of foreign investors in the United States.[13]

The resulting series for U.S. investment positions across foreign markets as a fraction of the U.S. market capitalization are plotted in figure 4.2A.[14] According to our estimates, the U.S. international investment position increased from 1.3 percent of U.S. equity market capitalization in the first quarter of 1978 to 3.9 percent by the third quarter of 1991. This increase can largely be accounted for by the growing U.S. investment position in the United Kingdom, which went from 0.3 percent in 1978:01 to 1.7 percent at the end of the sample. U.S. holdings of Canadian equity increased sharply from 0.7 in 1978:01 to 1.6 percent in the first quarter of 1980, but have since fallen to a level of 1.2 percent. The U.S. investment positions in Germany and Japan remained stable and low at around 0.5 percent throughout the sample period.

11. According to Morgan Stanley Capital International, the market capitalization of Germany was $65.1 billion, and that of the United Kingdom was $96.4 billion in the fourth quarter of 1977. We apply the weights of 40 percent and 60 percent to Germany and the United Kingdom, respectively, for the initial values of our Western Europe aggregate.

12. Gross returns are calculated using stock market indices from Morgan Stanley Capital International.

13. As initial values, we use the reported foreign investment positions (assuming a 60-40 split between the United Kingdom and Germany): Canada, $5,671 million; Japan, $594 million; Germany, $17,083 million; and the United Kingdom, $11,389 million.

14. Our estimates of the U.S. investment position are slightly lower than those reported by the Department of Commerce. At the end of 1990, they estimate the foreign investment position in Canada and Western Europe combined to be $86,510 million. Our estimate is $85,907 million. The Department of Commerce stopped reporting the U.S. investment position in Japan in 1987 since they perceived the position to be grossly underestimated.

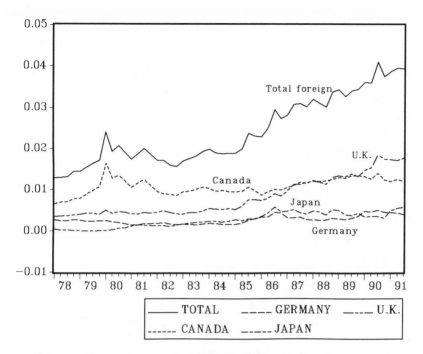

Fig. 4.2A   U.S. equity investment position in foreign equity
Note: U.S. equity investment position as a fraction of U.S. market capitalization.

The investment positions of foreign investors in the United States as fractions of U.S. market capitalization are reported in figure 4.2B.[15] Total foreign holdings of U.S. equity increased steadily over the sample from a level of 4.3 percent at the outset to a level of 11.5 percent by the end of the sample. All countries increased their investment positions in the United States, but the most dominant contributors to U.S. risk capital were British investors whose equity holdings went from 2.1 to 5.6 percent of U.S. market capitalization over the 1978–91 period. The Japanese investment position began to rise in the mid-1980s and reached a level of 1.1 percent of U.S. market capitalization by the third quarter of 1991. This late start can in part be explained by the relaxation of capital controls which took place in Japan in the mid-1980s.[16] Canadians

15. Our estimated investment positions of foreign investors in the United States are larger than those reported by the Department of Commerce. They estimate the total foreign investment position by these countries at the end of 1990 to be $188,967 million. Our estimate is substantially larger at $256,004 million. This is a bit surprising since our algorithm tends to bias the estimated position downwards by not crediting capital gains to equity acquired during the quarter of purchase. On the other hand, we assume that all dividends from foreign equity investment are reinvested, which may make the investment position too large.
16. See Riddle (1992) for a discussion of capital controls in the five countries in our sample.

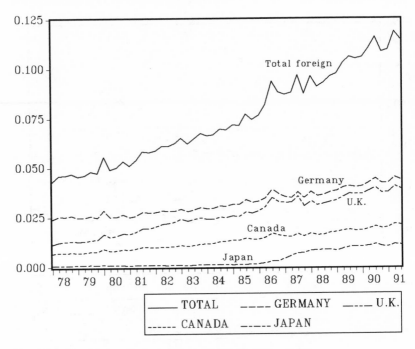

Fig. 4.2B   Foreign equity investment position in U.S. equity
Note: Foreign equity investment position as a fraction of U.S. market capitalization.

and Germans held 2.1 and 2.7 percent, respectively, of the U.S. equity market by the end of the sample.

Although the data display a steadily increasing level of investment in foreign equity markets by U.S. investors, the fraction of U.S. wealth allocated to foreign markets by U.S. investors is still very limited. According to our estimates, over 96 percent of U.S. wealth was invested in U.S. equity in 1991. Home bias is still very much a feature of international equity markets.

4.5   Gross Equity Flows and Turnover

Table 4.3 provides descriptive statistics on gross cross-border equity trading. We report the real value of transactions by U.S. residents in Canadian, German, Japanese, and British equity as well as the value of transactions in U.S. equity by residents from Canada, Germany, Japan, and the United Kingdom. As a benchmark, we also report the combined quarterly real trading volume in the United States, defined as the trading volume on the American Stock Exchange, NASDAQ (National Association of Securities Dealers Automated Quotations), and the New York Stock Exchange. The first three columns report the means, standard deviations, and coefficients of variation, respectively, for the

Table 4.3   Gross Cross-Border Equity Trading 1978:01–1991:03

Variable	1978:01–1991:03 (55 observations)			1978:01–1984:04 (28 observations)			1985:01–1991:03 (27 observations)		
	Mean	Standard Deviation	Standard Deviation/ Mean	Mean	Standard Deviation	Standard Deviation/ Mean	Mean	Standard Deviation	Standard Deviation/ Mean
Real transactions by U.S. residents in equity from[a]									
Canada	1097	528	0.48	774	314	0.40	1432	498	0.35
Germany	495	536	1.08	90	58	0.65	916	483	0.53
Japan	3239	3009	0.93	790	421	0.53	5778	2338	0.40
United Kingdom	4067	4251	1.05	633	335	0.53	7628	3398	0.45
Real transactions in U.S. equity by residents from[a]									
Canada	3399	1810	0.53	1895	651	0.34	4960	1183	0.24
Germany	1187	529	0.45	834	300	0.36	1553	463	0.30
Japan	3918	5227	1.33	325	152	0.47	7645	5328	0.70
United Kingdom	6555	4457	0.68	2740	1257	0.46	10512	2771	0.26
Total real transactions in U.S. equity[a]	170311	85071	0.50	98480	37123	0.38	244801	47757	0.20

Source: U.S. Treasury Bulletin.

Note: Units are million U.S. dollars (1977 = 100).

[a]Nominal gross flows are deflated using the average quarterly consumer price index from Citibase.

entire period, 1978:01–1991:03. Results for subsamples are reported in columns four through nine.

The numbers in the first column indicate that the largest average volume of transactions is between U.S. and British citizens. The second largest volume is transactions between U.S. and Japanese citizens, followed by U.S. transactions in equity with Canadians and Germans. This ranking holds regardless of whether transactions involve U.S. or foreign equity. By comparing the results in table 4.3 with our figures on net equity flows in table 4.1A, it is clear that the gross transactions volume vastly exceeds the corresponding net transactions volume. Gross quarterly transactions range from eighteen (U.S. transactions with German citizens) to sixty-seven (U.S. transactions with Japanese citizens) times the average quarterly net bilateral equity flows. Comparing the two subperiods, we also find a large increase in average quarterly transactions over time. Looking across U.S. residents' transactions in foreign equity, the increase is 1105 percent in British equity, 919 percent in German, 631 percent in Japanese, and 85 percent in Canadian. Correspondingly, the quarterly level of transactions in U.S. equity went up by 2253 percent for Japanese residents, 284 percent for British, 162 percent for Canadian, and 86 percent for German.

The volume of gross cross-border equity trading displays considerable variation over time. In terms of volatility relative to the mean, U.S. residents' transactions in foreign equity from Germany, Japan, and the United Kingdom are each about twice as high as the volatility (compared to the mean) of their transactions in Canadian equity. An even higher volatility compared with the mean is evident in Japanese transactions in U.S. equity. Although the volatility of transactions went up dramatically from the earlier to the later part of the sample, the coefficients of variation for the two subsamples fell in all cases except Japanese transactions in U.S. equity, where the volatility almost doubled. Interestingly, the same pattern of declining coefficients of variation appears in U.S. transactions in emerging stock markets (Tesar and Werner 1993b). The data seem to indicate that as U.S. investors increase their investment position in a particular market, their transactions volume (relative to the mean level of transactions) declines.

By cumulating the (nominal) quarterly gross cross-border transactions over each year and dividing by the estimated dollar investment position we obtain the turnover rates for cross-border equity trading. Table 4.4 reports the annual turnover rates (in percent) for each year from 1982 to 1990. The first striking observation is that turnover rates for foreign investments are higher than the turnover rate in the investor's home market and in the market where trading takes place. Interestingly, the most extreme cases are Japanese investors' turnover rates in the U.S. equity market, with an average of 334 percent, and U.S. investors' turnover in Japanese equities of 377 percent. One possible explanation for these extraordinarily high numbers is that the base, or the investment position, is underestimated. However, one would have to increase sixfold the estimated positions of U.S. investors in Japan and Japanese investors in the United States to get turnover rates at par with the benchmarks. Also, U.S. in-

Table 4.4   **Turnover in Cross-Border Equity Trading (percent)**

Turnover	1982	1983	1984	1985	1986	1987	1988	1989	1990	Mean
U.S. market[a]	44	48	48	55	65	93	56	53	49	57
Canadians in U.S.[b]	86	98	89	89	103	122	85	88	69	92
Germans in U.S.[b]	17	28	22	17	21	29	20	23	17	21
Japanese in U.S.[b]	181	229	151	348	502	658	513	228	198	334
British in U.S.[b]	49	54	49	53	65	87	65	67	60	61
Foreigners in U.S.[b]	49	57	51	55	73	117	98	75	65	71
Canadian market[a]	14	17	15	20	11	35	24	25	23	20
Americans in Canada[b]	29	33	29	38	47	60	33	29	26	36
German market[a]	24	44	42	54	72	279	151	106	97	97
Americans in Germany[b]	27	51	33	47	74	105	69	72	105	65
Japanese market[a]	35	127	35	36	28	75	60	63	49	56
Americans in Japan[b]	298	272	257	244	254	405	450	556	654	377
U.K. market[a]	31	36	37	38	57	107	66	44	42	51
Americans in U.K.[b]	72	96	97	109	182	235	174	209	193	152
Americans abroad[b]	61	75	76	87	129	181	150	170	165	122

[a]From "Anatomy of World Markets," 1991, Goldman Sachs Investment Research, table 1.18, p. 17.
[b]Authors' estimates based on gross transactions as reported by the U.S. Treasury and authors' own estimates of investment positions based on cumulated net purchases of equity. We take the annual averages of our estimated investment positions as the base and the annual transactions volume to be the quarterly transactions cumulated over the year.

vestors trading in British equity and Canadian investors trading in U.S. equity turn over their positions at a substantially higher rate than they do in their home markets. These turnover rates are also higher than the average turnover rates in the United Kingdom and the United States, respectively. The only exception is German investors, who transact at a very modest average rate of 21 percent in the United States. Based on the last column, which gives the mean turnover rate over the entire period, it appears that U.S. investors have a larger tendency to "churn" their portfolios of foreign securities than foreign investors trading in U.S. equity.[17]

Another message from the table is that turnover rates vary, both across different markets and across time. For instance, the average turnover rate for Germany at 97 percent is substantially higher than that of the other countries. The Canadian market is at the other extreme, with an average turnover rate of 20 percent. Turnover also varies over time for most markets. All markets experienced a temporary increase in turnover after the stock market crash in 1987.

The heterogeneity in turnover rates for foreign investments is seen most easily in figures 4.3A and 4.3B, which illustrate U.S. investors' turnover rates

17. Tesar and Werner (1994a) discuss the high turnover rate on foreign equity holdings in more detail.

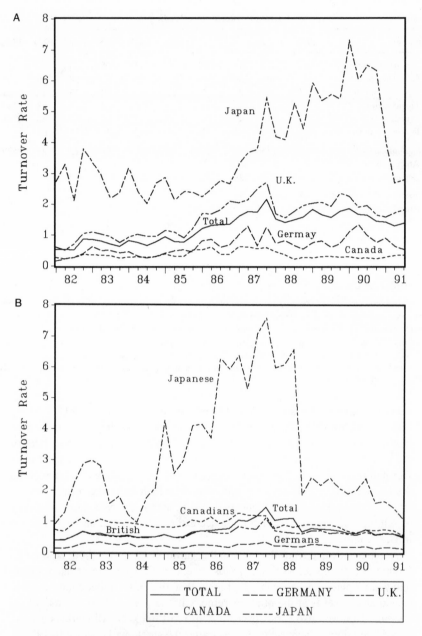

Fig. 4.3 **(A) U.S. investors' turnover rates in foreign equity; (B) Foreign investors' turnover rates in U.S. equity**

Note: Transactions divided by the investment position.

in foreign equity and foreign investors' turnover rates in U.S. equity in the 1982:01–1991:03 period. Turning first to figure 4.3A, we see that U.S. investors' turnover rate on the Japanese market is substantially larger than in other markets, and that there is a large increase in the turnover rate in the 1987–90 period, followed by a sudden drop in the second quarter of 1991. The time variation in turnover rates is even more dramatic in figure 4.3B. The turnover rate on U.S. equity holdings by Japanese investors increased roughly 800 percent between 1984 and 1987, falling off suddenly in the fourth quarter of 1988.

Several things should be kept in mind in comparing turnover rates across markets and over time. First, the numbers used in creating our measures of turnover rates may contain substantial measurement errors. Second, differences in regulations across countries and changes in regulations over time may affect where an investor chooses to conduct his or her financial transactions. This in turn may affect whether the transaction is considered a transaction with a domestic resident (in which case it will not be reported) or with a foreign resident. Finally, the transactions data include derivative securities. In periods of volatile returns in equity markets, investors may hedge their portfolios, effectively transacting several times on the same underlying investment position.

Whatever the source of the variation in turnover rates, the high volume of transactions and the high turnover rates in cross-border equity trading make it difficult to ascribe the home-bias puzzle to high variable transactions costs. The high turnover rates also give some indication that foreign equity investment may be dominated by institutional investors who face lower transactions costs than the average investor.

4.6 What Drives U.S. Net Equity Flows?

Even though we have seen no strong patterns of comovement between net equity flows, it is still possible that international equity purchases are sensitive to variables such as returns and risk. Table 4.5 reports the correlations of U.S. net purchases of equity from Canada, Germany, Japan, and the United Kingdom with four sets of financial variables.[18] The marginal significance levels refer to the probability that the estimated covariances are zero.

The first set of variables are contemporaneous changes (in absolute terms) in the market capitalization of the United States and each of the foreign markets. Changes in U.S. market capitalization proxy for changes in the wealth of U.S. investors. If U.S. investors follow a strategy of holding a constant fraction of their wealth in foreign equity, an increase in wealth would be associated with increased purchases of foreign equity. Judging from the consistently positive correlations in the first row of the table, this hypothesis has some support in

18. We use the following data sources. Data on market capitalization, equity returns, and dividend yields are calculated from the stock market indices published by Morgan Stanley Capital International. Treasury bill returns are from the Center for Research in Security Prices (CRSP) and exchange rates are from Citibase.

Table 4.5   Correlations of Net U.S. Equity Flows and Financial Variables 1978:01–1991:03

| | Net U.S. Purchases of Equity from: | | | | | | | |
| | Canada | | Germany | | Japan | | United Kingdom | |
Financial Variable	Correlation[b]	Marginal Significance Level[a]	Correlation[b]	Marginal Significance Level[a]	Correlation[b]	Marginal Significance Level[a]	Correlation[b]	Marginal Significance Level[a]
Changes in market capitalization:								
United States	0.30	0.21	0.21	0.16	0.46	0.11	0.23	0.10
Foreign	0.32	0.17	0.45	0.15	0.22	0.30	0.17	0.15
Average equity returns and betas with U.S. market:								
U.S. return	0.30	0.19	0.14	0.17	0.33	0.08	0.17	0.06
Foreign return	0.26	0.15	0.37	0.11	0.20	0.16	0.09	0.24
Foreign beta[c]	-0.12	0.17	0.29	0.23	0.12	0.41	0.04	0.89
Average dividend yields and interest rates:								
U.S. yield	-0.27	0.13	-0.20	0.41	-0.06	0.83	-0.45*	0.03
Foreign yield	-0.40	0.09	-0.08	0.33	0.01	0.97	0.10	0.51
30-day U.S. T-bill	-0.27	0.25	-0.10	0.63	-0.04	0.88	-0.26	0.15
90-day U.S. T-bill	-0.31	0.20	-0.11	0.49	-0.04	0.85	-0.24	0.19
Average exchange rate:[d]								
(i) Returns								
Trade-weighted	-0.36	0.12	0.09	0.47	0.15	0.26	0.14	0.42
Bilateral	-0.07	0.42	0.06	0.62	0.01	0.87	-0.15	0.41
(ii) Levels								
Trade-weighted	0.07*	0.01	-0.06	0.71	-0.11	0.52	-0.04	0.69
Bilateral	0.31	0.23	-0.11	0.61	-0.07	0.79	-0.22	0.17

Sources: Net purchases of equity come from the U.S. Treasury Bulletin. Stock market returns, dividend yields, and market capitalizations come from Morgan Stanley Capital International. T-bill returns are from the Center for Research in Security Prices (CRSP) and exchange rates are from Citibase.

[a]The marginal significance level gives the probability under the null that the covariance is zero.

[b]An asterisk (underlined coefficient) indicates that the covariance is significantly different from zero at 5 (10) percent.

[c]Authors' estimates of beta defined as the covariance of the return on the foreign market with the U.S. market, divided by the variance of the return to the U.S. market. Estimates are made on rolling sixty-month samples of excess returns using data from Morgan Stanley Capital International and CRSP.

[d]Note that the U.S. exchange rate is expressed as U.S. dollars per pound.

the data. For U.S. investment in the United Kingdom, the covariance is significantly different from zero at the 10 percent level. Media tend to follow high growth markets, and to the extent that U.S. investors follow the advice of investing in such markets they would increase their equity purchases as foreign market capitalization increases. The correlation coefficients in the second row of the table are all positive, but the association is not significant.

The second set of variables is related to the returns on equity in the respective markets. Models of portfolio allocation relate investment decisions to expected returns and risk. In this simple illustration, we view the average realized monthly excess return over the quarter as a rough proxy for expected future returns. If the decision to invest in equity hinges on the investor's expectation of returns, one would expect that increases in U.S. returns should tend to decrease foreign equity purchases, while increases in foreign returns should increase net equity purchases from abroad. The results show that net equity flows generally are positively correlated with *both* U.S. and foreign returns. U.S. purchases of equity from Japan and the United Kingdom covary positively with the return on the U.S. market. Part of the explanation for the positive correlation might be that U.S. equity returns are highly correlated with changes in U.S. wealth. Although U.S. net equity purchases are consistently positively correlated with the return on foreign markets, none of the marginal significance levels are lower than 10 percent.

To capture the impact of risk on foreign investment, we measure the correlation between net purchases and the beta of the foreign market. Beta is measured as the covariance between excess returns on the foreign market and the U.S. market divided by the variance of excess return in the U.S. market based on sixty-month (five-year) rolling samples. One would expect that U.S. investors would decrease their purchases of equity from a market when that market covaries more strongly with the U.S. market. There is no evidence for such a pattern in the data.

It is often suggested by policymakers and the financial press that recent increases in capital outflows from the United States can be explained by historically low domestic interest rates. To check whether this is borne out by the data, we correlate net purchases with U.S. and foreign dividend yields and U.S. interest rates. A majority of the estimated correlations are negative, as predicted, but only in the case of U.S. investment in the United Kingdom does the marginal significance level imply that we reject the null hypothesis of no association. The correlations between U.S. net purchases and foreign yields have mixed signs. For U.S. acquisitions of Canadian equity, the association is significantly negative. We finally investigate the correlation between returns to and levels of trade-weighted and bilateral exchange rates and net equity flows. Bilateral exchange rates seem generally to be of limited importance for cross-border investment decisions. The level of the trade-weighted U.S. dollar is significantly positively related to U.S. net purchases of Canadian equity, but the value of the dollar has no significant impact on purchases of equity from other countries.[19]

Of the financial variables we examine, very few are significantly associated with acquisitions of foreign equity by U.S. investors. Granted, our measures of expected returns and risk are crude and might not adequately capture the importance of such variables in general for international portfolio transactions. In addition, simple correlations do not capture the investor's problem of trading off risk and return across financial assets. It is still puzzling that the data display so little systematic comovement between equity flows and simple measures of return and risk. We turn to a more explicit test of portfolio allocation in the next section.

4.7 Do U.S. Investors Allocate Their Portfolios according to the CAPM?

Recent tests of international asset-pricing models yield mixed results about the extent of global market integration and the validity of the CAPM in an international context (Frankel 1982; Wheatley 1988; Engel and Rodrigues 1989, 1992; Korajczyk and Viallet 1989; Harvey 1991; Cooper and Kaplanis 1994; Ferson and Harvey 1991; Dumas and Solnik 1992; Heston, Rouwenhorst, and Wessels 1992; Harvey 1993). We combine our estimates of the *actual* international investment positions of U.S. investors in foreign equities with data on equity returns to test whether the observed U.S. portfolio allocation satisfies the first-order conditions of maximization in a simple CAPM world. This amounts to testing whether the portfolio chosen by U.S. investors is mean-variance efficient.

Consider the set of first-order conditions dictating the demand for risky assets in a standard capital asset pricing model (Merton 1973):

$$(2) \qquad\qquad v_{t+1} = \gamma \Omega x_t,$$

where x_t is a vector of portfolio allocations chosen by the investor at t, γ is the risk aversion of the investor, Ω is the covariance matrix of excess returns, and v_{t+1} is a vector of expected excess returns between t and $t + 1$. When preferences are isoelastic, γ is the coefficient of relative risk aversion and x_t corresponds to shares of wealth.

The traditional way of implementing empirical tests of the CAPM involves aggregating similar conditions across all investors, exploiting the fact that the market portfolio equals the market-capitalization weighted average of returns to individual equity markets. We will instead exploit our information on portfolio allocations to directly test the implications of the model on the first-order condition for maximization of one group of investors, namely, U.S. residents. If the model accurately describes investment behavior, the first-order condi-

---

19. Froot and Stein (1991) find no significant relationship between the value of the dollar and aggregate portfolio *inflows*.

tions in equation (2) should be satisfied for each investor in international equity markets.

Our empirical implementation follows Engel and Rodrigues (1992). We assume that U.S. investors have access to a constant risk-free rate, r. Let $R_{t+1} - r$ denote the realized excess return on equity. If expectations are rational, it follows that

$$(3) \qquad R_{t+1} - r = v_{t+1} + \varepsilon_{t+1},$$

where ε_{t+1} is a white noise error term. The first-order conditions can then be restated as

$$(4) \qquad R_{t+1} - r = \gamma \Omega x_t + \varepsilon_{t+1}.$$

The corresponding unrestricted model is

$$(5) \qquad R_{t+1} - r = Bx_t + \varepsilon_{t+1},$$

where B is a matrix of regression coefficients of the same dimension as the covariance matrix.

Under the null, the covariance matrix of the residuals, $\varepsilon\varepsilon'$, is equal to the covariance matrix of excess returns, Ω. Thus, the restrictions we test are that the regression coefficients in the matrix B are proportional to the covariance matrix of the residuals. The unidentified constant of proportionality is equal to the coefficient of risk aversion of U.S. investors. Under the assumption that the covariance matrix is constant over time, the test involves first estimating the unrestricted system in equation (5) using full information maximum likelihood (FIML). The system of equations is then reestimated, imposing the constraints implied by the model. We use a likelihood-ratio test to see whether the data reject the null hypothesis that the constraints implied by the model hold. The likelihood-ratio (LR) statistic has an asymptotic $\chi^2(q)$ distribution, where q is the number of restrictions imposed.

The results from the FIML estimation of the five-equation system of excess returns on U.S. portfolio shares are given in table 4.6. The model assumes that investors have preferences with constant relative risk aversion, and that x_t corresponds to shares of wealth invested in Canada, Germany, Japan, the United Kingdom, and the United States, respectively. As a proxy for U.S. wealth, we use the U.S. market capitalization plus the total foreign investment position of U.S. investors *minus* the total investment position by foreign investors in the United States. The top panel of the table reports the estimated regression coefficients and the corresponding standard errors. Few of them are significantly different from zero, which is to be expected given the well-known difficulty of explaining the ex post variation in excess equity returns. The covariance matrix of the residuals is given in the lower panel in table 4.6. Covariances are multiplied by 100. Note that there is considerable variation in the ratios of estimated coefficients, b_{ij}, to the corresponding elements of the covariance matrix, s_{ij}. Under the null hypothesis that the model is correct, all those ratios should be equal.

Table 4.6   Regressions of Excess Returns on U.S. Portfolio Shares

Investment Position Equation	Canada (standard error)	Germany (standard error)	Japan (standard error)	United Kingdom (standard error)	United States (standard error)
Estimated coefficients:[a]					
Canada	10.053	15.200	4.343	-8.184	-0.085
	(27.479)	(62.609)	(27.563)	(20.403)	(0.318)
Germany	-0.986	56.412	21.987	-16.519	-0.051
	(53.261)	(67.497)	(27.972)	(28.770)	(0.507)
Japan	-2.947	35.781	59.197 *	-27.294	0.035
	(25.935)	(34.962)	(24.152)	(15.009)	(0.248)
United Kingdom	1.482	23.405	6.471	-5.787	-0.025
	(18.945)	(70.488)	(36.440)	(26.984)	(0.249)
United States	-2.204	-5.556	10.472	-0.955	0.039
	(32.846)	(63.131)	(27.948)	(28.127)	(0.337)
Covariance matrix of residuals (×100):					
Canada	1.039				
Germany	0.198	1.104			
Japan	0.323	0.245	0.815		
United Kingdom	0.590	0.408	0.423	0.893	
United States	0.604	0.306	0.295	0.438	0.692
Log-likelihood:	307.67				

Sources: The initial investment position was taken from the Department of Commerce, Survey of Current Business. We used net equity flows reported in the U.S. Treasury Bulletin to create the quarterly investment positions of U.S. investors. The U.S. market capitalization as well as returns on equity indices came from Morgan Stanley Capital International. T-bill returns are from CRSP.

Note: Specification: $R(t+1) - r = B^*x(t) + e(t+1)$.

[a]An asterisk (underlined coefficient) indicates significance at the 5 (10) percent level.

It is possible to design the set of constraints of the model in several ways. In principle, the best way to test the model would be to let the constraints be $b_{ij} = \gamma s_{ij}$. Since we do not know the coefficient of risk aversion, this constraint cannot be tested without assigning an ad hoc value for γ. Alternatively, the constraint can be expressed as b_{ij}/s_{ij}, equal for all i, j. Engel and Rodrigues (1992) argue, based on results in Gregory and Veall (1985), that tests based on products rather than tests based on quotients result in more power. We follow their suggestion and specify the constraints to be of the form $b_{ij}s_{kl} = b_{kl}s_{ij}$, for all i, j. This leaves us with the problem of choosing the benchmark, k, l. We use $b_{jap, jap}$ and $s_{jap, jap}$, since both these estimated coefficients are significantly different from zero.

The log-likelihood value for the unrestricted system is 307.67. When the twenty-four constraints implied by the model are imposed, the resulting value of the log likelihood is 284.18. Our results give the LR statistic a value of 46.99, which for a $\chi^2(24)$ has a p-value of 0.003. The data thus strongly reject the null hypothesis that U.S. investors follow the CAPM in their portfolio allocation. Another way of interpreting the result is that the U.S. equity investment portfolio is not mean-variance efficient.

To check the robustness of our result, we grouped countries into regions. First, we aggregated Germany and the United Kingdom into "Europe." This should reduce the problem of erroneously classifying trading in German securities which takes place in London as transactions in U.K. shares. Combining our new European aggregate with Canada, Japan, and the United States implies a four-by-four system. Market-capitalization-weighted return series were generated for Europe, and the U.S. investment position in Germany was added to the fraction of wealth allocated to the U.K. market. To conserve space, we do not report the estimated coefficients. The only significant parameters are in the equation for excess returns on the Japanese market; the coefficient on the Europe weight is significantly negative, and the coefficient on the Japan weight is significantly positive at 5 percent. The resulting LR statistic was 33.43, which for a $\chi^2(15)$ has a p-value of 0.004. Finally, we also considered North America (Canada and the United States) as one region. If Canadian residents are in fact conducting many of their transactions in New York, it may be that little information is lost in the aggregation. Again, to conserve space, the estimated coefficients of the resulting three-by-three system are not reported. All three coefficients in the equation for excess returns in Japan are significant, but none of the other estimated parameters are significant. The LR statistic was in this case 26.52, which for a $\chi^2(8)$ has a p-value of 0.001.

The null hypothesis that U.S. investors follow the simple CAPM in allocating their investment portfolio is thus strongly rejected by the data. Even when we try to reduce potential reporting problems by aggregating markets into regions, we still strongly reject. Engel and Rodrigues (1992) were not able to reject that the market-capitalization-weighted portfolio was mean-variance efficient using monthly data on market capitalizations and excess returns from ten countries. Beyond the differences in data frequency and sample countries, a possible explanation for our stronger result is that we study the investment behavior of one particular group of investors, whereas Engel and Rodrigues capture the behavior of the marginal investor in each market, wherever that investor may reside.

4.8 Conclusion

In this paper we examine cross-border equity flows in Canada, Germany, Japan, the United Kingdom, and the United States. To our knowledge, this is among the first studies to combine information about the return to equity investment with the actual portfolio allocations of international investors. In many respects, our results are negative. Observed adjustments in international portfolios are not consistent with the first-order conditions of the CAPM. Neither do investors across countries seem to behave in unison; country- and investor-specific factors seem to play an important role in portfolio allocations. Net equity flows to and from the United Kingdom account for the majority of all flows across U.S. borders. Flows to and from the United Kingdom account for most of the flows across Canadian borders. Finally, U.S. residents appear to churn their holdings of foreign assets, while the turnover rate on foreign holdings of U.S. equities is more closely in line with the average turnover rate on the U.S. market. We conclude that there is a considerable amount of heterogeneity in international investment behavior.

The data strongly reject that U.S. investors' portfolios are mean-variance efficient. Previous studies have had only limited success in rejecting the CAPM based on international data. This highlights the difference between the norm in the finance literature, which involves basing tests solely on relationships among rates of return as opposed to testing the actual portfolio-allocation strategies of investors. When trying to understand international portfolio choice, research should focus on combining the price data with the actual portfolio investment made by international investors. To facilitate this task, it is imperative that researchers obtain more detailed data on international securities transactions.

One possible explanation for our failure to confirm even the most basic predictions of simple models of portfolio choice is that cross-border equity flows are underreported to official agencies, and therefore our data are not representative of investor behavior. This may indeed be the case; however, equity investment by the countries included in our sample now accounts for over 10 percent of all transactions on U.S. stock exchanges. If these data are to be considered suspect, one has to question the validity of any analysis using balance of payments data. It is possible that reporting problems make it difficult to find linkages between returns and portfolio allocations. Given that the results are robust to aggregating across regions, which should reduce such problems, the evidence seems more convincing.

Another possibility is that existing models of portfolio allocation can be thought of as descriptions of "mature" investors making marginal changes in an already well-diversified portfolio. As of the 1990s, national portfolios remained strongly biased toward domestic securities. The problem facing investors is how to move their existing holding of equity toward a better diversified portfolio, while still remaining sensitive to high-frequency changes in returns. Thus, our research points to the need for new models of portfolio choice which can explain the dynamics of portfolio adjustment.

Appendix A
U.S. Reporting of International Securities Transactions

Each month, all transactions between U.S. and foreign residents in long-term marketable securities must be recorded on a form ("International Capital Form S") which is then filed with the Treasury Department. Reporting is required by law for "all banks, other depository institutions . . . , International Banking Facilities (IBFs), bank holding companies, brokers, dealers, nonbanking enterprises or other persons in the United States . . . , who on their own behalf, or on behalf of customers, engage in transaction in long-term securities DIRECTLY with foreigners" (Treasury Department 1991, 1). Reports are also required by brokers and institutions who intermediate transactions between a domestic client (private investors or another broker or dealer) and a foreigner. A foreigner is any individual, partnership, association, corporation, or other organization located outside the United States. Under these guidelines, branches of American brokers and dealers located in foreign countries are considered foreigners. Exemption from reporting is granted when the grand total of purchases *or* sales of all long-term securities falls below $2 million during the reporting month.

The definition of long-term marketable securities includes public and private issues of debt and equity with maturity of more than one year from date of issue. It includes "common and preferred stocks or investment company shares, rights, scrip, bonds, debentures, Floating Rate Notes (FRNs), Continually-Offered Medium Term Notes, Collateralized Mortgage Obligations (CMOs), zero-coupon bonds and notes, equipment trust certificates and similar long-term marketable corporate debt instruments issued by entities located in the United States or in a foreign country; marketable long-term debt obligations of the U.S. Treasury, Federal Financing Bank, United States Government–owned corporations, and Federally-sponsored agencies; and marketable long-term obligations of state and local government or of governments of foreign countries, including any agencies, corporations, financial institutions, or other instrumentalities thereof." It also includes "American Depository Receipts (ADRs), when issued by, or surrendered to, Depositories of ADRs; options and warrants to purchase and/or sell long-term securities and certificates or receipts representing an interest in particular coupon or principal payments of marketable U.S. Treasury securities" (Treasury Department 1991, 4). Reports cover new security issues, direct placements, and securities issued under Shelf Registration provisions. The rule is that the geographic *location* of the issuing entity determines the classification of a security as domestic or foreign. Thus, equity issued by a U.S. subsidiary (branch or agency) of a foreign-based firm is considered domestic equity.

Transactions with foreigners in options and warrants should be reported regardless of the maturity of the option and warrant (Treasury Department 1991, 4). When options and warrants are issued by an entity other than the issuer of the underlying security, the option and warrant is classified according to the location of its own issuer. Form S gives the following example: "A dealer located in New York writes put/call warrants on a British stock, e.g., British Telecom, and sells the warrants to foreigners. The sale of the warrants should be reported as purchases by foreigners of a domestic corporate bond. At the time the warrants are exercised, the transactions would be recorded as a purchase/sale, as appropriate, of foreign stock to which the warrants applied" (Treasury Department 1991, 5). Options and warrants are bundled with the underlying class of securities, that is, corporate equity, corporate bonds, marketable Treasury and Federal Financing Bank bonds and notes, and bonds of U.S. government corporations and federally sponsored agencies in the aggregated data.

Appendix B
Calculating Robust Standard Errors of Covariances

Although our sample is rather short, we rely on asymptotic theory to derive the formula for robust standard errors of covariances. If x_t and y_t denote the demeaned time series, and we define z_t to be the product of these series, $x_t y_t$, then

(6)
$$\sqrt{T}\left[\frac{1}{T}\sum_{t=1}^{T}z_t\right] \rightarrow N(E_t(x_t y_t), V),$$

where $V = \lim_{T \to \infty} \text{Var}(\frac{1}{\sqrt{T}}\sum_{t=1}^{T}z_t)$. We estimate V as

(7)
$$\hat{V}_T = \frac{1}{T}\sum_{t=1}^{T}\left((z_t - \bar{z}_T)^2 + 2\sum_{l=1}^{k(l)}W_T(l)(z_t - \bar{z}_T)(z_{t-l} - \bar{z}_T)\right),$$

where $\bar{z}_T \equiv \frac{1}{T}\sum_{t=1}^{T}z_t$, $k(l)$ is of order $T^{1/4}$, and $W_T(l) = [1 - l/(T + 1)]$. Our time series have fifty-five observations, and we use six lags in estimating $\hat{V}$ ($2 \cdot (55)^{1/4}$). Under the null that the series are uncorrelated, $\bar{z}_T \equiv 0$. We thus set this to zero in the formula for calculating $\hat{V}$. The random variable $[\sqrt{T}\widehat{cov}/\sqrt{\hat{V}}]$ has a standard normal distribution, $N(0,1)$, under the null hypothesis. The reported marginal significance levels refer to this distribution.

References

Adler, M., and B. Dumas. 1983. International portfolio choice and corporation finance: A synthesis. *Journal of Finance* 38:925–84.

Cooper, I. A., and E. Kaplanis. 1994. Home bias in equity portfolios, inflation hedging and international capital market equilibrium. *Review of Financial Studies* 7, no. 1:45–60.

Dumas, B. 1993. Partial equilibrium vs. general-equilibrium models of international capital market equilibrium. Working Paper no. 93–1. Wharton School, University of Pennsylvania.

Dumas, B., and B. Solnik. 1992. The world price of exchange rate risk. Working paper, HEC School of Management, France.

Engel, C. M., and A. P. Rodrigues. 1989. Tests of international CAPM with time-varying covariances. *Journal of Applied Econometrics* 4:119–38.

———. 1992. Tests of mean-variance efficiency of international equity markets. Working paper, University of Chicago.

Ferson, W. E., and C. R. Harvey. 1991. The risk and predictability of international equity returns. Working paper, University of Chicago.

Frankel, J. 1982. In search of the exchange risk premium: A six-currency test assuming mean-variance optimization. *Journal of International Money and Finance* 1:255–74.

French, K., and J. Poterba. 1991. Investor diversification and international equity markets. *The American Economic Review* 81:222–26.

Froot, K. A., and J. C. Stein. 1991. Exchange rates and foreign direct investment: An imperfect capital markets approach. *The Quarterly Journal of Economics,* November, 1191–1217.

Gregory, A., and M. Veall. 1985. Formulating Wald tests of nonlinear restrictions. *Econometrica* 6:1465–68.

Grubel, H. G. 1968. Internationally diversified portfolios. *The American Economic Review* 58:1299–1314.

Harvey, C. R. 1991. The world price of covariance risk. *The Journal of Finance* 41:111–57.

———. 1993. Predictable risk and returns in emerging markets. Working paper, Duke University.

Heston, S. L., K. G. Rouwenhorst, and R. E. Wessels. 1992. The structure of international stock returns. Working paper, Yale University.

Korajczyk, R. A., and C. J. Viallet. 1989. An empirical investigation of international asset pricing. *The Review of Financial Studies* 2:553–85.

Levy, H., and M. Sarnat. 1970. International diversification of investment portfolios. *The American Economic Review* 50:668–75.

Merton, R. E. 1973. An intertemporal capital asset pricing model. *Econometrica* 41:867–87.

Newey, W., and K. West. 1987. A simple positive semi-definite heteroscedasticity and autocorrelation consistent covariance matrix. *Econometrica* 55:703–8.

Riddle, J. 1992. Controls on international securities transactions. Working paper, University of California, Santa Barbara.

Solnik, B. H. 1974. Why not diversify internationally rather than domestically? *Financial Analysts Journal* 30:91–135.

Stekler, L., and E. M. Truman. 1992. The adequacy of the data on U.S. international financial transactions: A Federal Reserve perspective. International Finance Discussion Paper no. 430. Board of Governors of the Federal Reserve System.

Tesar, L. L., and I. M. Werner. 1992. Home bias and the globalization of securities markets. NBER Working Paper no. 4218. Cambridge, Mass.: National Bureau of Economic Research.

———. 1994a. Home bias and high turnover. *Journal of International Money and Finance*, forthcoming.

———. 1994b. U.S. equity investment in emerging stock markets. *World Bank Economic Review*, forthcoming.

Treasury Department. Office of the Assistant Secretary for Economic Policy. 1991. *Instructions for preparation of monthly form S, international capital form S*. OMB no. 1505–0001. Washington, D.C.

Wheatley, S. 1988. Some tests of international equity integration. *The Journal of Finan-*

Comment   Philippe Jorion

The main contribution of the Tesar-Werner paper is the detailed analysis of a data base of foreign investment positions hitherto ignored by academics. The data analysis confirms that domestic investors hold a disproportionately small amount of foreign investment, and provides useful evidence of changing patterns of international investments.

The Home-Bias Puzzle

The foreign portfolio positions reported in the Tesar-Werner paper can be compared to the foreign investment position (FPI) of pension funds all over the world. These positions, presented in table 4C.1 and taken from Adler and Jorion (1992), cover more countries than the Tesar-Werner study, but are restricted to one class of institutional investors.

The striking feature of this table is the low proportion generally invested in foreign assets. In the United States, for instance, pension funds have invested only 4 percent of their assets abroad. A second feature of the table is that the foreign portfolio investment ratios are growing rapidly for all countries, except for Canada, where pension funds are subject to a 10 percent foreign asset limit that is currently binding.

To put these FPI ratios in perspective, market capitalization ratios are reported in table 4C.2. In terms of market capitalization, nondollar stocks and bonds account for 66.7 percent and 57.5 percent, respectively, of the world market in 1990. The portfolios of U.S. pension funds, therefore, are much closer to purely domestic portfolios than to capitalization-weighted world indices.

Philippe Jorion is with the Graduate School of Management at the University of California at Irvine.

Table 4C.1   **Foreign Investment by Pension Funds (percentage of assets invested abroad)**

Country	1980	1985	1990
Canada	7	7	8
France	1	2	5
Germany	2	3	5
Japan	1	4	8
Netherlands	4	6	11
United Kingdom	9	15	26
United States	1	2	4
Total	2	4	8
($ billion)	19	95	347

Source: InterSec Research, Stamford, Connecticut. Pension fund data include public and private funds.

Table 4C.2   **Size of Major Stock and Bond Markets (percentage of total world market capitalization)**

Country	Stocks			Bonds		
	1980	1985	1990	1980	1985	1990
Canada	4.7	3.6	2.6	3.2	2.1	2.3
France	2.2	1.9	3.5	4.0	2.9	4.2
Germany	2.9	4.4	4.0	10.3	6.4	7.0
Japan	14.7	22.5	33.2	20.1	17.5	18.1
Netherlands	1.0	1.3	1.4	1.4	1.0	1.3
United Kingdom	7.8	8.1	10.4	7.8	3.2	2.1
United States	56.8	48.4	33.3	29.5	46.8	42.5
Other	9.9	9.7	11.5	23.7	20.1	22.5
Total size ($ billion)	2430	4039	8444	2706	5933	10368

Source: Morgan Stanley Capital International for stock market data; Ibbotson and Associates for 1980 bond market data; Salomon Brothers for 1985, 1990 bond market data.

Therefore, the actual proportions invested in foreign assets appear to be much lower than the proportions implied by either market capitalization or import penetration. These results are confirmed by the analysis of Tesar and Werner, using a more comprehensive data set collected by U.S., Canadian, and German governments, and covering all capital flows into long-term securities.

Net Equity Flows

While the authors do a commendable job of describing the data, the paper provides little theoretical guidance as to how flows should change over time.

This, however, is more a reflection of the present state of finance models that focus almost exclusively on price, or rather rates, of returns, rather than on transaction volumes. As a result, there is little theory to draw from.

In the absence of theoretical models that explain capital flows, two competing explanations are given for correlations between capital flows:

1. If flows are driven by homogeneous expectations, we should expect *negative correlations* between capital flows. This corresponds, for instance to a situation where both U.S. and Japanese investors think the U.S. stock market will outperform the Japanese market and, as a result, Japanese investors buy U.S. stocks, and U.S. investors simultaneously sell Japanese stocks.

2. If flows are driven by diversification motives, we should expect *positive correlations* between capital flows. This corresponds, for instance, to situations where both U.S. and Japanese investors invest in each other's market.

Let me offer, however, two words of caution about empirical tests. First, these flows are highly autocorrelated. As a result, rejections of the hypothesis of zero correlations are misleading, because they assume independent observations, which is not the case. Second, it should be recognized that these flows are constrained by balance of payment considerations. When the United States runs a large balance of trade (BT), or current account, deficit with Japan, this *must* be balanced by a capital account surplus. Financing can occur through portfolio inflows into bank accounts, bonds, or stocks, through direct investment, or through government intervention. While there is no indication of which account will be affected, we know that the net of all capital inflows into the United States must be positive. This would be consistent, for instance, with a situation where Japanese investors buy U.S. stocks and U.S. investors sell foreign stocks, which translates into a *negative correlation*. Therefore, BT deficits may imply negative correlations between capital flows. While the balance of payment only constrains flows netted across assets and countries, certain patterns are clearly ruled out.

Indeed, this is what we observe in the data. Over 1988–91, the United States had an average BT deficit of $50 billion, $10 billion, and $10 billion with Japan, Germany, and Canada, respectively, and a small BT surplus of $3 billion with the United Kingdom. Correlations of flows with these respective countries appear to be perfectly in line with the sign of the BT. This is not to say that the sign of correlations are uniquely determined by balance of payment data, but rather serves as a reminder that aggregate flow data do impose constraints on the patterns of capital flows.

Gross Equity Flows

In this section, the authors remark that gross equity flows, which consist of the total of purchases and sales, seem to have increased over time. This, however, cannot be interpreted as a sign of increased turnover, since the paper subsequently shows that the total foreign investment position of U.S. investors has increased over time. Turnover is usually associated with transactions as a proportion of assets, and could actually be constant over time.

Another puzzling statement is the assertion that variable trading costs cannot explain home-country bias because the volume of trading has increased over time. It is not clear how variable transaction costs, in one shape or another, can have anything to do with home-country bias, since they affect domestic and foreign investors in a symmetric fashion. If home bias is to be explained at all, it must be related to asymmetries in international capital markets, such as exchange risk, capital restrictions, or asymmetric information.

Asset-Pricing Tests

The last part of the paper claims to test an asset-pricing model and to find stronger results than previous research. The methodology consists of estimating an unrestricted model

$$(1) \qquad r_t = Bx_t + \varepsilon_t,$$

where r_t represents a vector of excess returns, and x_t is a vector of asset shares. If the standard capital asset pricing model (CAPM) holds, we can write

$$(2) \qquad r_t = \rho \Omega x_t + \varepsilon_t,$$

where ρ represents the constant relative risk aversion, and Ω is precisely the variance-covariance matrix of the error terms $V(\varepsilon_t)$. Following Frankel 1982, the authors test the restriction that

$$(3) \qquad B = \rho \Omega.$$

The methodology is by now standard, and has been extended to time-varying second moments by Giovannini and Jorion (1989), among others.

Two major points should be made here. First is the interpretation of the tests. The authors take x_t as the vector of U.S. investment positions. As a result, the tests should properly be interpreted as tests of the mean-variance efficiency of the portfolio of a representative U.S. investor, *not* as a test of the CAPM. Testing the CAPM involves setting the weights to those of the world market portfolio, if all investors display logarithmic utility function, or to those of a market portfolio optimally hedged against currency risk, in the more general case. The tests presented here can be viewed as a measure of the mean-variance inefficiency of U.S. investments, or of the performance loss due to insufficient international diversification. The conclusion that stronger tests of the CAPM can be achieved using actual positions hardly seems justified.

A second point concerns the statistical tests. The restrictions imposed by the model can be tested by maximum likelihood, for instance, by comparing the values of the maximized likelihood functions with and without the restrictions. Alternatively, an LM test or a Wald test can be used. The authors test the constraint that $b_{ij}\omega_{kl} = b_{kl}\omega_{ij}$, where ω_{ij} are assumed known. This raises a number of issues. First, the elements of the variance-covariance matrix Ω are measured with error, which should be reflected in the test statistic. Second, the chi-square test is only valid asymptotically. In practice, it will reject too often in small samples, which is the case here since the experiment involves only fifty-five quarters and twenty-five parameters. To give an idea of the bias, consider the bias arising from approximating an F distribution by a chi-square distribution. The 5 percent critical value for a $\chi^2(24)$ is 36.41, which, when evaluated relative to an $F(24,20)$ distribution, has a marginal significance level of only 17 percent. Thus with a statistic sample value slightly above 36.41, one would conclude that the hypothesis of interest is rejected, whereas rejection would not occur with the more appropriate distribution.

Therefore, it is highly unlikely that this test of the mean-variance efficiency can lead to credible rejections. Tests involving stock prices and based on unconditional moments, as in Harvey (1991), have seldom rejected any hypothesis of interest in previous research. These results could be ascribed to the low power resulting from high stock return volatility, and are the reason why researchers have turned to more informative tests based on time-varying moments.

Conclusions

This paper makes an interesting contribution to the growing literature on international investments by attracting the attention of researchers to a potentially useful data base of U.S. and foreign investment positions. While I applaud the attempt to shed light on the home-bias puzzle, the empirical tests in the latter part of the paper can be criticized on several grounds. Empirical tests of the mean-variance efficiency of stock portfolios are likely to be uninformative unless complemented by conditioning information.

Finally, the paper takes an empirical approach to the data because of the lack of theoretical guidance as to what should drive transaction volume in financial markets. This clearly shows an important gap in finance theory, and points to the need for future theoretical work in this direction. In general, volume can be driven by investors' disagreement about expected returns. Alternatively, another view is that international capital flows are primarily responding to changes in capital restrictions, and are slowly building up after the effective removal of investment barriers in the late 1980s.

References

Adler, M., and P. Jorion. 1992. Foreign portfolio investment. In *The new Palgrave dictionary of money and finance,* eds. P. Newman, M. Milgate, and J. Eatwell. London: Macmillan.

Frankel, J. 1982. In search of the exchange risk premium: A six-currency test assuming mean-variance optimization. *Journal of International Money and Finance* 1:255–74.

Giovannini, A., and P. Jorion. 1989. The time-variation of risk and return in the foreign exchange and stock markets. *Journal of Finance* 44:307–25.

Harvey, C. 1991. The world price of covariance risk. *Journal of Finance* 46:111–57.

Comment   Richard Levich

Text

In his 1968 paper, Herbert Grubel verified an empirical regularity that most economists would have confidently predicted: that the correlation of equity market returns across countries is less than unity and sometimes substantially so. These results implied that investors had strong incentives to hold diversified international stock portfolios. Yet they do not diversify fully, in fact. Thus Grubel's analysis fit comfortably into a common problem in financial model building—a stylized model of economic behavior producing results at variance with the behavior of real-world economic agents. For the past several years, economists have attempted to reconcile the predictions of the stylized international portfolio choice models, and the observed tendency of investors to hold portfolios biased toward domestic securities.[1] The paper by Tesar and Werner hopes to add to our understanding of investor choices by analyzing a new set of data on international capital *flows* among several countries: the United States, Canada, Germany, Japan, and the United Kingdom.

Any prospective reader of a paper with this title might suspect that this task of linking information about capital *flows* to models of *stock* allocation of assets would be difficult. The authors are aware of these difficulties. They themselves raise several caveats suggesting that the researcher must proceed carefully with accurately measured data.

I admire the authors for uncovering a new data base assembled from U.S. Treasury, Bank of Canada, and Bundesbank sources, and subjecting it to a thorough and creative data analysis. However, in the end I retain doubts that this new data base is sufficient to permit valid inferences (let alone conclusions) on investor portfolio choices—their adjustment over time or their stock allocation at a point in time. I am still more pessimistic, feeling that any method—short of directly surveying individual investors (not institutions)—will be unsuccessful in gauging the nature of international portfolio allocations at the level of specificity our stylized models require.

My comments focus on the first three sections of the paper. My major theme is to underscore the apprehension that readers should harbor with respect to research on international capital flows and portfolio allocations. But I will also try to offer constructive advice on how this new data base and related data might be used to analyze various aspects of international portfolio choice models.

Richard Levich is professor of finance and international business at the Stern School of Business, New York University, and a research associate of the National Bureau of Economic Research.

1. See Uppal (1992) for a survey of this research. Uppal argues that several plausible explanations—a desire to hedge domestic inflation, prevailing institutional barriers to foreign investment, and discriminatory tax treatment on income from foreign versus domestic assets—are not sufficient to resolve the findings of a home-country bias.

Data Description

In section 4.2 of their paper, Tesar and Werner acknowledge that there are some shortcomings of their data, and they discuss several of them. But other potentially serious problems may remain. Consider the case of Fidelity Investments, headquartered in Boston, Massachusetts, which has just received a $1 million purchase in its open-end Europe Fund.

To begin, the documentation of the U.S. Treasury data base (on which the authors base much of their analysis) explains that it covers "DIRECT transactions" between residents of two countries.[2] Is it the implication that "INDIRECT" transactions are not covered? In particular, suppose Fidelity Investments transfers the $1 million via the foreign exchange market to a bank account in London, an action recorded in the balance of payments as a short-term capital flow. Days later, Fidelity's affiliate in London (a British entity) buys shares on the London exchange—a transaction between two British residents, entered neither in the balance of payments nor in the U.S. Treasury's data base. For various reasons (market liquidity, depth, legal restrictions on removing physical shares from the country) most institutional investors hold the true equity shares in the native country rather than in American Depository Receipts (ADRs) in the United States. If coverage for these transactions is lacking, the U.S. Treasury data could be quite misleading. In note 6, the authors refer to a procedural change in 1992 intended to address this problem. But data prior to 1992 could reflect substantial undercoverage of cross-border equity investments.[3]

Continuing to follow this $1 million cross-border flow, our natural inclination is to classify the shares purchased in London as those of a U.K. firm. But the shares could easily be those of a German, French, or Italian firm. The authors' data sources identify London as the location of the *market,* not of the identity of the headquarters from which the shares were purchased. This uncertainty in identifying the portfolio allocation by country is particularly a problem for cross-border flows to London where shares of many non-British firms are traded. And even if the shares are those of a U.K. firm, it could very likely be a multinational corporation, with few revenues and productive operations in the United Kingdom itself.[4]

Finally, the presentation of the data inclines us to believe that the *owner* of the shares in Fidelity's Europe Fund is American, but this need not be the case. He could be French (Bernard Dumas), Swedish (Ingrid Werner), Swiss (René

---

2. Uppercase letters as in original U.S. Treasury documents.

3. The authors discuss that if Fidelity Boston buys ADR shares from an American, this is *not covered* in the U.S. Treasury data base. This does not impact their estimates of global portfolio allocations, but it biases downward their estimate of trading volume in foreign securities.

4. There is also the further implicit assumption that London is the "dominant" market for the trading and pricing of these shares. But in some cases (e.g., Sony, Telephonos de Mexico, Royal Dutch Petroleum) it is claimed that the market in the domestic headquarters country is really a satellite market, with the bulk of trading and price determination taking place elsewhere.

Stulz), or a person of some other nationality and prospective cash flow pattern who happens to use Fidelity Boston as his or her investment intermediary. This is particularly a problem for data on capital flows emanating from London and Switzerland, where it is well-known that investment funds from around the world have been managed for centuries. For example, Baring Securities reports that over one-half of all foreign equity investments are held in Swiss and U.K. portfolios.[5] Does this reflect closer adherence by Swiss and British investors to models of international portfolio choice, or their niche activity (investment funds management) within the financial services industry? While the former could be true, the data undoubtedly reflect the latter effect as well.

Net Equity Flows: Cross Border

Assuming that the raw data are meaningful, the analysis of cross-border equity flows is interesting, offering us a varied pattern of behaviors rich in interpretation. But as the authors acknowledge—this is part of the problem. Because any pattern of time-series correlation and cross-country correlation is conceivable and rational, the data are fundamentally descriptive. The authors take their results to suggest that heterogeneous motives or allocation rules may be guiding investors in different countries. However, even this interpretation, I feel, can be challenged.

International portfolio transactions can reflect either stock adjustments or flow adjustments, each taken in response to a particular portfolio optimization decision framework. Stock adjustments represent transactions to rebalance long-term equilibrium portfolio allocations. These could stem from the sudden lifting of investment barriers or one-time, permanent changes in investor wealth, appetite for risk taking, assessment of country risk, and so forth. Despite assumptions in portfolio-balance models, these portfolios adjustments *cannot* be made instantaneously. Take, for example, the windfall earned by oil-exporting countries in the 1970s. Initially, OPEC investors behaved conservatively with investments in short-term deposits and government securities. Only gradually did the investment mix change to include longer-term portfolio and direct investments.[6]

Flow adjustments, on the other hand, may result from a permanent change in the domestic savings rate, the growth of domestic real income, or the growth rate of foreign market capitalization. Each of these factors could lead to a higher volume of cross-border investment flows to keep portfolio allocations at their target proportion.

Dividing cross-border portfolio transactions between stock and flow adjustments may be a convenient way to organize our thinking about the data, but we should not overlook the possibility that asset-demand functions (the portfolio

---

5. Baring Securities (1992), 69.
6. Lifting the investment sterling restriction in 1979 appears to be reflected in the U.K. series, but the gradual Japanese liberalization of foreign investments in the 1980s does not.

optimization objective) might be subject to change. Our stylized models rely on the presumption that investors are following a single portfolio optimization rule in an integrated world capital market. But global investors are more likely seeking some mixture of (a) expected value gains associated with market segmentation and the fact that some markets have a limited following or some barriers to investment, and (b) portfolio diversification gains associated with markets that have imperfect correlation.

I have two main concerns here. One is that the flow data of the U.S. Treasury mixes both stock and flow adjustments. The authors' tests of the determinants of cross-border flows focus primarily on the flow determinants. However, because foreign stocks are so underrepresented in U.S. portfolios, there is a presumption that a large stock adjustment is taking place. My second concern is that while our models of international asset allocation are based on *individual's* portfolios, foreign transactions are dominated by *institutions*. Institutional managers have their own performance evaluation criteria and objectives that may not coincide with uniform portfolio allocation rules deemed optimal for individuals. This is not necessarily bad since individuals can reach their own investment objectives by offsetting or supplementing positions taken by institutional managers.

Gross Cross-Border Training

This section and the remainder of the paper rely on U.S. Treasury data only. The rationale for examining gross cross-border trading is not made completely clear, although it seems directed at supporting the notion that foreign trading is inexpensive, and therefore not responsible for the home-country bias in portfolios. As suggested earlier, the data may not be fully up to this task. What if Fidelity Investments buys and sells securities actively in London on behalf of American investors? These ultimately represent foreign trading activity, but may not be reflected in the U.S. Treasury data.

In one sense the authors' result—that gross turnover in foreign equities is large relative to U.S. domestic trading—is not surprising. We suspect that foreign trading is dominated by institutions and that institutions trade roughly four times as much as individuals in the U.S. domestic market.[7] Other estimates from Baring Securities on gross turnover (measured as trading volume relative to the market value of shares held) place foreign turnover activity at 2.29 (in 1991, all countries) compared with 0.81 in domestic turnover.[8]

It is worth noting the tremendous cross-sectional variation in turnover when measured by trading volume as a percentage of a market capitalization.[9] At the low end of the turnover statistics, we find Chile (6.0 percent), Brazil (6.1 per-

7. New York Stock Exchange data report that institutions and individuals each own roughly 50 percent of U.S. securities. However, institutions account for 80 percent of trading volume versus 20 percent for individuals.
8. Baring Securities (1992), 67.
9. These statistics reflect trading in 1990. See Goldman Sachs (1991), 17.

cent), Philippines (8.1 percent), and Mexico (8.8 percent). At the high end are Taiwan (709.6 percent), Thailand (102.2 percent), Germany (92.1 percent), and Switzerland (73.7 percent). For the sake of comparison, U.S. turnover in 1990 was 49.2 percent of market capitalization. The wide variation in turnover gives foundation to the adage "Global investors 'trade' in mature markets and invest in developing markets."

While implying nothing about causality, a significant relationship can be measured between the volatility of stock returns and the percentage of foreign trading activity in the market.[10] With no foreign activity, price volatility is measured at 12 percent per annum. Each 1 percent additional foreign trading implies 0.35 percent additional price volatility. The Netherlands stock market is at one extreme with roughly 85 percent of trading volume attributable to foreign activity. The United States is at the other extreme, with only 10 percent of trading activity attributable to foreigners.

What Drives U.S. Net Equity Flows?

The exploratory analysis in this section of the paper is interesting. One problem referred to earlier is the reliance on flow variables rather than stock adjustment variables. Along these lines, a variable related to the onset of global offerings could be useful. This might include the volume of foreign initial public offerings, or a measure of foreign privatization issues. An additional flow variable that might be tried is a country sentiment index derived from the pricing of closed-end country funds.

Conclusions

The authors have developed a new data base with the potential to examine three distinct issues in international investment models: (a) identify the nationality of investors in cross-border investment, (b) identify the country-specific determinants of portfolio choices, and (c) examine the actual portfolio choices of investors rather than imposing market clearing conditions that may be ad hoc or wrong. Regarding the first two issues, the limitations of the data base are such that all we know for certain is that a transaction between country x and country y occurred. We are not certain that the investor resides in or consumes in country x or that the firm is headquartered or does business in country y. Moreover, we are not certain that the data coverage includes portfolio transactions that take place within the foreign country after a short-term international money market transaction. Thus the possibilities for learning about these two issues appear doubtful.

As for the third area of exploration, the authors' attempt to examine actual portfolio choices deserves high praise. Too often we have been offered a method of international portfolio allocations that logically cannot satisfy a market clearing condition. For example, looking only at the correlation of re-

10. These calculations are from Baring Securities (1992), 70.

turns in the 1960s and 1970s would have led us to weight heavily on small markets largely uncorrelated with the U.S. index, or segmented markets that offered unusually high returns. Logically, the world cannot invest a large share in countries that are small or countries that erect substantial barriers to foreign investment. However, a naive, passive weighting system, such as weighting according to gross domestic product (GDP) shares also has its flaws. All countries do not have equity market capitalizations in proportion to their GDP weights. Even an international allocation system based on market capitalization has its difficulties. Many countries restrict market ownership by foreigners, and market capitalization may be a noisy measure of size because of the cross-holding effect.[11]

Investor allocation of investments across countries very likely reflects a complicated trade-off involving numerous factors. Investors typically feel that a country must pass a critical threshold with respect to capital controls, clearing and settlement procedures, auditing standards, accounting transparency, and so forth before the *ability* to invest translates into a *willingness* to invest. Fixed set-up costs for an equity research unit and funds manager and due diligence costs imply that a market must reach a critical size before "coverage" of the market beings. As a practical matter, that means that many of the world's smaller markets are omitted.[12] The International Finance Corporation, which began its *Emerging Stock Markets Factbook* and data base in only 1987, is a good case example.

An alternative approach to measuring portfolio allocation would put greater emphasis on surveys of individual investors. The data show that in the United States, the top one hundred pension funds hold about 10 percent of their funds in foreign assets while individuals hold directly only 2 percent in foreign assets. These may be better estimates of actual positions than those derived from Treasury or balance of payments data, although they are still subject to their own estimation problems.

References

Baring Securities. 1992. *Cross-border capital flows: 1991/92 review.* London: Baring Securities.
Choi, Frederick D. S., and Richard M. Levich. 1990. *The capital market effects of international accounting diversity.* Homewood, Ill.: Dow Jones-Irwin.
French, Kenneth, and James Poterba. 1989. Are Japanese stock prices too high? NBER Summer Institute, August. Manuscript.
Goldman Sachs International Limited. 1991. *Anatomy of world markets.* London: Goldman Sachs International Limited.

11. If firm A owns x percent of the shares of firm B, the market values of A + B overstate the amount of capital needed to buy both firms by the fraction (x percent) of B's value. The overstatement is amplified when B also owns an interest in A. Cross-holding along these lines is significant in Germany and Japan. See French and Poterba (1989).

12. See Choi and Levich (1990) for further discussion of the international investment process.

Grubel, Herbert G. 1968. Internationally diversified portfolios: Welfare gains and capital flows. *American Economic Review* 58:1299–1314.

International Finance Corporation (IFC). 1987. *Emerging markets factbook.* Washington, D.C.: International Finance Corporation.

Uppal, Raman. 1992. The economic determinants of the home country bias in investors' portfolios: A survey. *Journal of International Financial Management and Accounting,* no. 3 (autumn): 171–89.

II

Trading Volume, Location,
Emerging Markets, Taxes,
Controls, and Other
Imperfections

5   The Effect of Barriers to Equity Investment in Developing Countries

Stijn Claessens and Moon-Whoan Rhee

5.1   Introduction

Equity portfolio flows to developing countries have increased sharply in magnitude in recent years, especially to the so-called emerging countries. Total equity flows to developing countries are estimated to have been $13.2 billion in 1993, quadruple that of three years earlier (table 5.1). Equity flows are quite concentrated among a small group of emerging countries (e.g., Latin America received about 60 percent of all equity flows to developing countries in 1993). Though relatively still small for developing countries on aggregate (about 7 percent of the aggregate net financing they received in 1993), these flows are an important source of finance for some developing countries.

Equity flows have taken place in a number of forms: direct equity purchases by investors in the host stock markets, investments through country funds, issue of rights on equities held by depository institutions (American and global depository receipts [ADRs and GDRs]),[1] and direct foreign equity offerings. In the last three years equity flows have taken place largely through depository receipts. The volume of ADRs/GDRs issued for equity claims of developing countries is estimated to have been about $18.2 billion over 1989–93.[2] Until

Stijn Claessens is an economist at the World Bank. Moon-Whoan Rhee is assistant professor at the Department of Business Administration, Kyung Hee University, and is on leave from Towson State University.

The authors would like to thank Michael Dooley, Donald Lessard, Jeffrey Frankel, and the participants at the preconference and the conference for their comments, and Joon Y. Park for computer support. The views expressed are those of the authors and do not necessarily express the opinions of the institutions they are affiliated with. This paper is funded in part through the World Bank research grant RPO 678–01.

1. ADRs and GDRs are receipts issued by financial intermediaries in industrial countries against shares held in custody by these intermediaries in the developing countries.

2. This includes direct offerings on foreign capital markets by corporations in developing countries outside the ADR/GDR structure (under Rule 144A in the United States). These have been minimal, however.

Table 5.1   Equity Flows to Developing Countries (millions of dollars, estimates)

Type of Flow	1989	1990	1991	1992	1993[a]	Total 1989–93[a]
Country funds	$2.2	$2.9	$1.2	$1.3	$2.7	$10.3
ADRs/GDRs	—	$0.1	$4.9	$5.9	$7.3	$18.2
Direct equity	$1.3	$0.8	$1.5	$5.8	$3.2	$12.6
Total	$3.5	$3.8	$7.6	$13.0	$13.2	$41.1

Source: World Debt Tables (1993).
[a]estimated for 1993.

recently, next in importance were (closed-end) country funds: during 1989–93, new country funds were created for developing countries with an aggregated size of $10.3 billion. The sharpest relative increase in the last few years has been direct purchases of equities: these were about $5.8 billion in 1992, up from $0.8 billion in 1990, and were second in importance from 1989 through 1993.

The increased importance of direct equity purchases by foreigners on emerging stock markets may be attributed in part to the progressive removal of barriers by developing countries on foreign participation in their stock markets. Many developing countries have removed restrictions on foreign ownership, liberalized capital account transactions, improved their accounting and information standards, and in general have made it easier for foreigners to gain access to their markets (see, further, for example, Mathieson and Rojas-Suárez 1993 and Reisen and Fischer 1993). Particularly in Europe and Latin America, many countries now have very few or no restrictions on access by foreigners to their markets and treat foreign investors in most ways identical to domestic investors.

At the same time, returns on stock markets in emerging countries have been high; for example, the International Finance Corporation (IFC) composite index for Latin America was up 294.2 percent over 1988–92, compared to 108.4 percent for the Standard and Poor's 500 (S&P 500). This also may have been a factor motivating the larger inflows of foreign equity. At the same time, however, the volatility of rates of return has been high, reaching, for example, more than 100 percent for Argentina.

The increase of these equity flows to a number of developing countries and the opening up of their stock markets raise a number of issues. An important one is the effect of the removal of barriers on the risk-return trade-off in these markets, that is, how much has the risk-return trade-off changed? The purpose of this paper is to investigate this question and to quantify the effects of barriers to access by foreign investors on stock prices and rates of return.

To answer this question, we use the newly created indexes by the IFC Emerging Markets Data Base (EMDB) on the degree of foreign access or "investability." The IFC investability indexes capture for each stock the barriers to free access by foreigners (general inflow or outflow restrictions, general or sector-specific ownership restrictions, remittance restrictions, other exchange restrictions, restrictions on capital structure, etc.). These indexes should thus be a good indicator of the relative importance of barriers across securities at a given point in time in one market or across a number of markets, or of changes in barriers over time.

Summarizing our results, we find a positive relationship between price-earnings (P/E) ratios and the degree of access for almost all the countries. For four out of the seven markets we study in detail, this result is robust to the inclusion of the world beta and the degree of international spanning of the domestic market. Only for Jordan and Mexico, however, is this result robust to the inclusion of the additional factor of the supply of stocks. For the relationship between rates of return and the investability index, we find evidence of a negative sign for Jordan only, which is also less robust. For other countries, we do not find that abnormal stock returns are related in a systematic fashion to a stock's investability index.

The outline of this paper is as follows. Section 5.2 presents an overview of possible analytical frameworks. Section 5.3 describes the data we use and provides some statistics on the rates of return. We then perform the Stehle (1977) test for market segmentation or integration for each market to investigate whether these markets indeed show signs of being segmented. Section 5.4 provides the empirical results of these tests of market integration and market segmentation. We then describe in section 5.5 the concept of the investability index as developed by the IFC and provide some statistics on the investability indexes. In section 5.6 we perform the tests on the (cross-sectional and time-series) relationship between the P/E ratio and the rate of return on an individual stock on the one hand and the level of its investability index on the other hand, and we perform some robustness tests. Section 5.7 concludes.

5.2   Overview of Possible Analytical Models

Tests assuming no barriers. Without barriers, international integration tests can be performed using the various international asset pricing models that have been developed. Past empirical tests along these lines specifically concerned with developing countries—and which assume no barriers—are, for example, Lessard (1973, 1974); Divecha, Drach, and Stefek (1992); Bekaert (1993); Buckberg (1993); Diwan, Errunza, and Senbet (1993b); de Santis (1993); Harvey (1993); and Tesar and Werner (1993). All the papers find that there are significant diversification benefits available from investing in developing countries. Most of these tests, however, use a specific asset pricing model which assumes full integration. As a result, one doesn't know whether these diversification benefits can be achieved.

Tests assuming barriers. Without explicitly incorporating the type and severity of barriers in an asset pricing model, several papers have investigated market integration (or segmentation) using the test developed by Stehle (1977). The advantage of the Stehle methodology is that it allows for tests of both full integration and full segmentation. Jorion and Schwartz (1986), focusing on interlisted stocks, reject full market integration between Canada and the United States using this test, something which they attribute to legal barriers. Mittoo (1992) investigates the same issue and finds segmentation pre-1981, but integration afterward, especially for interlisted stocks.

With barriers, assets in different markets may have different expected rates of return even when their risk characteristics are the same. One way of testing integration in the presence of barriers is to model the barriers explicitly, derive the resulting theoretical equilibrium asset prices, and verify the model using actual asset prices. Following Jorion and Schwartz (1986), barriers can be classified into indirect barriers, arising from differences in available information, transaction costs, accounting standards, etc.; and legal barriers, arising from the different judicial status of foreign and domestic investors—for example, ownership restrictions and taxes. Typically only legal barriers are incorporated in asset pricing models, as these can easily be modeled explicitly.[3]

Theoretical models here are Black (1974, 1978); Stulz (1981); and Errunza and Losq (1985, 1989). For imperfectly accessible stocks (i.e., foreigners can own stocks up to a fraction δ less than 1), Eun and Janakiramanan (1986) and Stulz and Wasserfallen (1992) develop models. These papers find theoretical "mispricing" resulting from the barriers given the specific asset pricing model used. As expected, the analytical predictions on asset pricing with barriers crucially depend on the type of market segmentation.

There are some empirical investigations building on these models for industrial countries. Hietala (1989) investigates the pricing of individual Finnish stocks which can be owned by foreign as well as domestic investors (unrestricted) versus stocks which can be owned only by domestic investors (restricted). Other papers have applied these tests to developing countries. Errunza and Losq (1985) find tentative empirical support for a hypothesis of mild[4] market segmentation. Errunza, Losq, and Padmanabhan (1992) find that many emerging markets are neither completely integrated with nor completely segmented from industrial countries.

For imperfectly accessible stocks, Stulz and Wasserfallen (1992) test their model for Swiss stocks and find that a relaxation of investment barriers substantially lowers the value of the shares available to foreigners relative only to the value of the shares available to all investors. Bailey and Jagtiani (1992) use

---

3. For these reasons, Bekaert (1993) employs a nonparametric approach for testing the relationships between barriers and measures of market integration.

4. Defined as a situation where the industrial countries' security markets are well integrated, and developing-country investors can invest in all these (foreign) security markets, but foreign investors cannot vice versa invest in developing countries.

this model to investigate differential pricing of restricted and unrestricted stocks for Thailand. They find that cross-sectional difference in the severity of foreign ownership explains some of the variation in the premiums of unrestricted shares over restricted shares, leading to a mildly segmented capital market.

5.3 The Rate of Return Data

The raw data we have cover twenty emerging markets. The price and rate of return data are generally available from 1975 on. Tables 5.2 and 5.3 provide some basic statistics for the rates of return on the IFC indexes and other market data in these emerging markets over the period 1989–92. Appendix A describes the criteria used for creating the indexes.

As can be observed from table 5.2, the IFC indexes have in general increased, for some countries by multiple factors (e.g., Argentina). There is also a great variation in the market capitalization across countries.[5] The rates of return in emerging markets in general are high, but so are the standard deviations (table 5.3). The highest rate of return is for Argentina, more than 100 percent on an annual basis. However, Argentina also has the highest standard deviation, almost 130 percent, and the highest range. In general, the rates of return and standard deviations for the emerging markets are much higher than those for the industrial countries. Table 5.3 also provides the skewness and kurtosis measures, which indicate that the rates of return are not likely drawn from normal distributions. Jarque-Bera tests for normality bear this out: for most markets it rejects normality (see, further, Claessens, Dasgupta, and Glen 1993).

Table 5.4 provides some cross-sectional information on the monthly rates of return of the individual stocks for each market (the methodology used for creating the individual stocks' rates of return is described in Claessens, Dasgupta, and Glen 1993). There is a great cross-sectional variation in the monthly rates of return behavior. Autocorrelation coefficients likewise vary over a wide range.

5.4 Test of Market Segmentation

We first use the model of Stehle (1977), as also applied by Jorion and Schwartz (1986); Errunza, Losq, and Padmanabhan (1992); and Mittoo (1992), to separately investigate the hypothesis of market integration or segmentation for each emerging market. The Stehle model assumes that the capital asset pricing model (CAPM) holds and that exchange risk is not priced. The test

---

5. It is important to note that the IFC indexes cover only a subset of all stocks listed on the various exchanges, varying between 39 percent (Turkey) and 90 percent (Colombia) in terms of market capitalization. Typically, because of its selection criteria, the IFC index will be weighted toward the larger market capitalization and more liquidly traded stocks.

Table 5.2   International Finance Corporation (IFC) Indexes and Other Data for Each Market: January 1989 and December 1992 (millions of U.S. dollars, unless otherwise noted)

Country	IFC Stocks		IFC Index		IFC Price/Earnings Ratio		IFC Price/Book Value Ratio		IFC Market Capitalization		IFC Value Traded		Total Market Capitalization		Exchange Rate	
India	...	63	...	59.03	...	12.19	...	1.60	...	8661.31	...	259.65	...	12037.54	...	2063.50
Indonesia	60	62	233.25	415.96	18.18	33.74	2.6	14.74	11624.16	25365.18	1068.88	...	2518.98	65118.90	15.16	28.68
Korea	61	91	730.26	518.61	38.46	21.43	2.75	1.06	54828.72	66461.02	5556.64	6006.51	94233.33	107447.97	680.00	788.40
Malaysia	62	62	134.12	226.89	36.52	21.84	2.30	2.53	20176.60	47940.53	188.03	773.27	25175.59	94003.82	2.73	2.62
Pakistan	50	58	176.52	455.14	7.32	21.86	1.21	2.55	825.72	3773.68	6.33	32.74	2427.11	8028.36	18.95	25.50
Philippines	18	30	1526.25	2056.78	12.34	14.13	2.81	2.45	2590.98	8167.09	65.20	83.70	4123.46	13794.50	20.61	25.60
Taiwan	62	70	866.08	503.74	42.60	16.57	8.35	2.15	90820.99	60454.10	15156.36	3171.63	139174.36	101124.43	27.65	25.17
Thailand	29	51	376.89	900.42	12.83	13.93	2.15	2.52	6476.44	28368.39	321.99	1876.84	9875.27	58258.87	25.39	25.49
Greece	26	32	226.14	537.42	10.12	6.89	1.63	1.67	2289.03	5376.53	8.22	112.20	3922.75	9488.60	155.00	215.30
Jordan	25	27	132.93	181.79	15.78	14.49	1.48	1.61	1697.46	1987.65	41.29	70.16	2320.86	3365.03	0.48	0.67
Portugal	23	30	637.84	503.06	15.05	9.05	2.77	1.02	4117.01	4867.61	14.57	52.25	6626.11	9213.36	152.47	146.92
Turkey	18	25	134.41	227.01	2.26	6.95	1.48	1.29	718.91	3872.42	2.32	158.33	1115.90	9930.80	1855.00	8540.00
Argentina	24	29	188.10	1253.14	0.55	37.99	0.08	1.20	1243.96	14292.60	16.23	1111.52	1876.49	18632.57	0.00	1.00
Brazil	56	69	95.00	158.92	4.57	-24.43	0.46	0.37	10516.38	23199.80	388.06	803.25	24280.00	45261.38	0.99	12243.00
Chile	26	35	754.93	3315.58	4.10	12.99	0.78	1.71	4923.25	21932.54	22.14	96.08	7601.91	29643.89	245.00	382.33
Colombia	21	20	359.32	2171.64	5.39	27.95	0.97	1.73	1036.14	5107.24	3.43	23.40	1144.98	5681.19	343.00	811.77
Mexico	52	62	462.19	2608.21	3.47	12.28	0.58	1.99	8828.23	66108.21	145.06	1806.25	13655.43	139060.77	2.30	3.12
Venezuela	13	17	147.85	523.61	8.80	15.63	1.89	1.61	1279.38	4997.28	12.26	95.73	1878.43	7599.70	38.30	78.16
Nigeria	15	24	33.82	64.43	5.61	8.98	1.16	1.74	397.69	796.97	0.10	0.72	752.72	1220.73	6.90	21.50
Zimbabwe	...	17	...	384.76	...	2.03	...	0.31	...	267.97	...	0.44	...	627.63	...	5.48

Source: EMDB.

Note: The first column under each heading refers to January 1989 and the second to December 1992. The (double) columns are: number of stocks, level of the IFC index (1984 = 100), IFC P/E ratio, IFC P/BV ratio, IFC market capitalization, IFC value traded, total market capitalization, and exchange rate (LC/$). The P/E ratios can be misleading in high inflation countries (such as Argentina and Brazil in the late 1980s, as the earnings are measured as the average flow over the past twelve months, and prices are taken at the end of the periods). Similarly, P/BV ratios can be misleading in a highly inflationary environment.

Table 5.3   **Statistic on the Index Rates of Return (1989–1992), by Country (annual percentage changes)**

Country	N	Meanchg	Stdchg	Minchg	Maxchg	Skewchg	Kurtchg	Autocorr
India	35	−16.6	32.1	−250.6	224.9	0.18	0.12	0.25
Indonesia	48	22.2	39.6	−292.6	423.2	0.60	0.92	0.17
Korea	48	−4.4	31.3	−230.9	319.0	0.94	1.23	−0.18
Malaysia	48	17.6	21.7	−186.8	155.9	−0.56	0.36	−0.10
Pakistan	48	28.7	31.0	−189.9	423.2	1.64	5.19	0.28
Philippines	48	14.2	34.7	−351.6	325.0	−0.17	1.59	0.34
Taiwan	48	3.7	49.2	−409.6	359.5	0.14	0.18	0.18
Thailand	48	29.1	29.6	−270.0	201.7	−0.59	0.28	0.25
Greece	48	31.4	53.4	−206.8	702.9	1.83	4.01	0.13
Jordan	48	11.8	20.2	−154.1	193.9	−0.18	0.93	−0.16
Portugal	48	−2.4	25.4	−170.1	348.3	1.34	4.31	0.06
Turkey	48	33.6	70.5	−377.4	829.5	1.12	1.46	0.22
Argentina	48	109.0	129.5	−779.4	2137.3	2.34	8.98	−0.12
Brazil	48	41.8	83.4	−682.7	573.8	0.06	−0.14	−0.09
Chile	48	43.5	26.0	−109.7	255.4	0.24	−0.68	0.41
Colombia	48	53.4	39.6	−209.5	448.1	1.61	2.83	0.52
Mexico	48	47.5	27.0	−170.1	235.9	−0.02	−0.37	0.16
Venezuela	48	48.1	54.1	−313.8	582.6	0.62	1.15	0.33
Nigeria	48	16.1	30.2	−507.1	226.0	−2.98	13.54	0.15
Zimbabwe	35	−29.0	31.4	−276.6	180.4	−0.34	−0.42	0.29

Note: The monthly rates are multiplied by 12 to obtain the yearly rates. The standard deviation is obtained by multiplying the monthly standard deviation with the square root of 12. N is the number of months, Meanchg refers to the mean change in the rate of return, Stdchg to the standard deviation of the rate of return, Minchg and Maxchg to the minimum and maximum change in the rate of return, Skewchg to the skewness coefficient, Kurtchg to the kurtosis coefficient, and Autocorr to the first order autocorrelation. First observation for Indonesia and Zimbabwe is January 1990.

requires running the following regressions. First, we project the rate of return of the domestic IFC market indexes, $j, = 1, \ldots, K$, on the rate of return on a world portfolio index, here approximated by the Morgan Stanley Capital International (MSCI) world index (the net dividends reinvested series), to get the orthogonal component in the domestic index (note that all time subscripts are omitted):

$$(1) \qquad R_j = \alpha_{0,j} + \alpha_{1,j} R_w + V_{j-w},$$

where R_j is the rate of return on the index in market j, R_w is the rate of return of the world index, and V_{j-w} is the component orthogonal to the projection of R_j on R_w.

We then regress the world rate of return on the various IFC indexes' rates of return to get the orthogonal components here:

$$(2) \qquad R_w = \delta_{0,j} + \delta_{1,j} R_j + V_{w-j},$$

where V_{w-j} is the component orthogonal to the projection of R_w on R_j.

Table 5.4 Minimum and Maximum Values of Cross-Sectional Values of Monthly Time Series of Rates of Return for All Stocks

Country	Years	Avail	Lmean–Hmean		Lstd–Hstd		Lmin–Hmin		Lmax–Hmax		Lautolag–Hautolag	
India	90–92	90	−0.085	0.388	0.013	2.182	−0.776	−0.010	0.007	12.484	−0.838	0.569
Indonesia	76–92	69	−0.005	0.078	0.074	0.386	−0.565	−0.131	0.265	2.910	−0.304	0.248
Korea	76–92	105	−0.027	0.057	0.054	0.223	−0.648	−0.071	0.084	1.342	−0.696	0.244
Malaysia	86–92	75	−0.028	0.072	0.045	0.332	−0.499	−0.069	0.109	2.037	−0.538	0.463
Pakistan	85–92	77	−0.046	0.096	0.040	0.263	−0.443	−0.062	0.069	1.093	−0.418	0.340
Philippines	85–92	34	−0.092	0.079	0.037	0.352	−0.593	−0.085	0.000	2.848	−0.350	0.478
Taiwan	85–92	77	−0.036	0.055	0.108	0.305	−0.725	−0.172	0.205	1.685	−0.260	0.271
Thailand	76–92	58	−0.030	0.104	0.063	0.389	−0.517	−0.137	0.138	1.774	−0.448	0.366
Greece	76–92	34	−0.054	0.043	0.050	0.235	−0.497	−0.049	0.042	1.408	−0.310	0.416
Jordan	78–92	30	−0.023	0.106	0.057	0.170	−0.468	−0.110	0.139	0.753	−0.374	0.250
Portugal	86–92	30	−0.051	0.066	0.074	0.324	−0.758	−0.124	0.118	1.885	−0.423	0.275
Turkey	87–92	25	−0.084	0.094	0.140	0.389	−0.466	−0.251	0.241	2.274	−0.228	0.415
Brazil	76–87	80	−0.091	0.208	0.117	0.753	−4.538	−0.180	0.000	3.628	−0.411	0.646
Chile	76–92	44	−0.017	0.075	0.097	0.348	−0.798	−0.109	0.213	3.011	−0.254	0.387
Colombia	85–92	22	−0.050	0.057	0.082	0.367	−0.475	−0.103	0.000	3.209	−0.220	0.402
Mexico	76–92	83	−0.046	0.099	0.019	0.501	−1.000	−0.012	0.064	3.695	−0.333	0.449
Venezuela	85–92	17	−0.016	0.075	0.144	0.316	−0.572	−0.301	0.273	1.955	−0.361	0.236
Nigeria	85–92	25	−0.051	0.057	0.093	0.174	−0.621	−0.392	0.145	0.784	−0.077	0.327
Zimbabwe	76–92	21	−0.097	0.048	0.107	0.250	−0.643	−0.040	0.130	1.239	−0.408	0.267

Note: Avail is the number of stocks for which data are available during the period. Lmean is the lowest mean rate of return for any stock in a market, and Hmean the highest rate of return. Lstd is the lowest standard deviation of the rates of return across all stocks in a given market, Hstd the highest. Lmin is the lowest minimum rate of return across all stocks in a given market; Hmin is the highest minimum rate of return in a given market. Similarly for Lmax and Hmax, the highest. Autolag is the first autocorrelation, with Lautolag the lowest and Hautolag the highest in a given market. No data on individual stock rate of return were available for Argentina.

The Stehle test then involves two cross-section tests, using the orthogonal components of the regressions (1) and (2). Under full integration, the parameter on the slope coefficients (denoted here by $\beta_{i,j-w}$) of the individual stocks' rates of return on the orthogonal component of the regression of the local index on the world portfolio should not be significantly different from zero. Under complete segmentation, the parameter on the slope coefficients (denoted here by $\beta_{i,w-j}$) of the individual stocks' rates of return on the orthogonal component of the regression of the world portfolio on the local index should be not be significantly different from zero. In other words, assuming complete integration or complete segmentation, equation (3) or (4) should hold for the rate of return on stock i in market j:

$$(3) \qquad E(R_{i,j}) = \gamma_{0,j} + \gamma_{1,j}\beta_{i,j,w} + \gamma_{2,j}\beta_{i,j-w}$$

$$(4) \qquad E(R_{i,j}) = \eta_{0,j} + \eta_{1,j}\beta_{i,j} + \eta_{2,j}\beta_{i,w-j},$$

where $R_{i,j}$ is the return on stock i in market $j, i = 1,..N_j$, where N_j is the number of stocks in market j. Under complete integration, $\gamma_2 = 0$ and $\eta_2 \neq 0$, and under complete segmentation $\eta_2 = 0$ and $\gamma_2 \neq 0$.

Since we have actual rates of return, we need to decompose the rates of return in an expected component and an unexpected component. Under complete integration

$$(5) \qquad R_{i,j} = E(R_{i,j}) + \beta_{i,j,w}[R_w - E(R_w)] + \beta_{i,j-w} V_{j-w} + \varepsilon_{i,j}.$$

Under complete segmentation

$$(6) \qquad R_{i,j} = E(R_{i,j}) + \beta_{i,j}[R_j - E(R_j)] + \beta_{i,w-j} V_{w-j} + \theta_{i,j}.$$

Substituting equation (3) into (5) and (4) into (6) we get two equations which give us the empirical model under market integration (7) and under segmentation (8), respectively:

$$(7) \qquad R_{i,j} = \gamma_{0,j}(1 - \beta_{i,j,w}) + \gamma_{2,j}\beta_{i,j-w} + \beta_{i,j,w}R_w + \beta_{i,j-w}V_{j-w} + \varepsilon_{i,j}$$

$$(8) \qquad R_{i,j} = \eta_{0,j}(1 - \beta_{i,j}) + \eta_{2,j}\beta_{i,w-j} + \beta_{i,j}R_j + \beta_{i,w-j}V_{w-j} + \theta_{i,j}.$$

Estimating these equations using the two-pass approach often used in empirical studies of traditional asset pricing models (see Fama 1991) is not straightforward here since the βs are measured with error—there is thus an errors-in-the-variables problem—and the cross-section equations (7) and (8) are biased. To overcome this problem, cross-section tests traditionally have been done using portfolios of stocks, in the expectation that the formation of portfolios will reduce the measurement error (the Fama-Macbeth [1973] method). Because of the limited data we have here, this is difficult (there are few stocks for each country with complete data on rates of return, on average less than twenty). We therefore use the rates of return on the individual stocks directly.

We use the nonlinear, seemingly unrelated regression (SUR) technique, which is asymptotically efficient and equivalent to the maximum likelihood estimation (MLE) method (see, further, Gibbons 1980 and 1982).[6] This method is consistent, but may not have good small sample properties. We therefore use all securities which are consistently available in a given market over the 1989–92 period. We estimate for each market N equations (N being the number of securities in the market) as a system of equations with cross-equation restrictions on the γ and η coefficients in each market and no restrictions on the βs (except that they are constant over time). The estimation technique allows for correction of heteroscedasticity across the stocks and exploits the contemporaneously correlated errors. The parameter estimates and other statistics are in table 5.5.

The R^2s for the segmentation and integration tests (last column) vary between 0.18 (Jordan) and 0.74 (Nigeria) and are of similar magnitude (by country) for the two tests (reflecting the fact that the two systems are basically run with the same set of fundamental variables). The integration hypothesis is rejected at the 5 percent level for ten out of the sixteen countries for which we have consistent data.[7] The segmentation hypothesis is not rejected at the 5 percent level for all countries and at the 10 percent level for only three countries (India, Korea, and the Philippines). For two countries, the segmentation test did not converge (Colombia and Malaysia). Combining the two tests, market integration can and market segmentation cannot be rejected (at the 5 percent level) for eight countries (Brazil, Greece, Korea, Mexico, Pakistan, the Philippines, Taiwan, and Thailand). For six countries neither market segmentation nor market integration can be rejected (Chile, India, Jordan, Nigeria, Venezuela, and Zimbabwe), possibly indicating a low power of our test.

The results of these estimation techniques can be compared with the results for Canada–United States: Jorion and Schwartz (1986) find strong evidence of market segmentation, and Mittoo (1992) finds evidence of market segmentation for the pre-1981 period, but integration for the post-1981 period. For developing countries, Errunza, Losq, and Padmanabhan (1992), using IFC EMDB data over the 1976–87 period, reject complete market integration for all eight developing countries they study and reject complete market segmentation of five of these eight countries (Brazil, Chile, Greece, Korea, and Mexico). They conclude that "mild" segmentation best describes the market structure for these five countries. Compared to their results, we find that relatively fewer countries are not integrated (ten out of sixteen compared to eight out of eight), but more are segmented (fourteen out of the fourteen markets which converged compared to their five out of eight).

---

6. We use the SAS routine SYSNLIN (version 5.0) for the nonlinear seemingly unrelated regression (NLSUR). Other approaches are the MLE method of Litzenberger and Ramaswamy (1979), the procedure outlined in Gibbons (1980), and the odd/even instrumental variable approach of Mankiw and Shapiro (1986). We did use the odd/even method but this method had a lower power as it could reject neither market segmentation nor integration for any of the countries.

7. Data for individual stock rates of return are missing for Argentina for all years; for Turkey and Indonesia, data were only available since 1987 and 1990, respectively; for Portugal no stock has data available consistently for the 1989–92 period.

Table 5.5   Slope Coefficients for the Integration and Segmentation Tests

	N	Integration				Segmentation			
		$\gamma_{0,j}$	$\gamma_{2,j}$	R^2	I	$\eta_{0,j}$	$\eta_{2,j}$	R^2	S
Indonesia	18	0.0333 (0.002)	−0.0265 (0.067)	0.46	not reject	0.0121 (0.786)	−0.1956 (0.076)	0.46	not reject
Korea	22	−0.0106 (0.144)	0.0279 (0.0001)	0.40	reject	0.1841 (0.163)	0.2604 (0.053)	0.40	not reject
Malaysia	29	0.0089 (0.221)	0.0154 (0.0001)	0.37	reject	NC			
Pakistan	31	0.0132 (0.012)	0.0108 (0.042)	0.29	reject	−2.623 (0.896)	5.954 (0.895)	0.28	not reject
Philippines	16	−0.0243 (0.015)	0.0478 (0.0001)	0.30	reject	0.0523 (0.335)	0.194 (0.079)	0.29	not reject
Taiwan	20	−0.0148 (0.107)	0.045 (0.0001)	0.68	reject	−0.0674 (0.079)	0.490 (0.389)	0.68	not reject
Thailand	9	0.0560 (0.036)	0.0215 (0.003)	0.46	reject	0.211 (0.525)	0.546 (0.301)	0.47	not reject
Greece	8	−0.035 (0.067)	0.0545 (0.0001)	0.55	reject	−0.152 (0.605)	0.522 (0.418)	0.56	not reject
Jordan	9	−0.0056 (0.460)	0.0092 (0.203)	0.18	not reject	0.059 (0.586)	−0.362 (0.575)	0.19	not reject

(*continued*)

Table 5.5   (continued)

		Integration				Segmentation			
	N	$\gamma_{0,j}$	$\gamma_{2,j}$	R^2	I	$\eta_{0,j}$	$\eta_{2,j}$	R^2	S
Brazil	18	-0.002 (0.799)	0.0375 (0.0001)	0.45	reject	-12.54 (0.977)	-8.798 (0.977)	0.45	not reject
Chile	22	0.0627 (0.005)	-.0024 (0.877)	0.37	not reject	0.188 (0.744)	-2.020 (0.489)	0.40	not reject
Colombia	20	0.0077 (0.234)	0.0435 (0.0001)	0.33	reject	NC			
Mexico	21	0.0227 (0.042)	0.0466 (0.0001)	0.32	reject	0.158 (0.941)	-6.748 (0.927)	0.32	not reject
Venezuela	12	0.0100 (0.479)	0.0199 (0.390)	0.36	not reject	0.0073 (0.941)	0.940 (0.199)	0.36	not reject
Nigeria	14	1.196 (0.808)	-0.914 (0.807)	0.74	not reject	6.622 (0.962)	-5.914 (0.961)	0.74	not reject
Zimbabwe	10	0.0006 (0.969)	0.0059 (0.805)	0.22	not reject	0.006 (0.673)	-0.030 (0.176)	0.22	not reject

Note: Approximate p-values (for the t-statistics) are in parentheses. In spite of using many different starting values for the parameters, and even after the maximum iterations were increased up to 2000 and the convergence criteria were raised to 0.0001, no convergence (NC) was obtained for Colombia and Malaysia for the segmentation test. R^2s are obtained as one minus the ratio of sum of squared residual (totaled for all equations) over sum of squared totals (totaled for all equations).

It is worth noting that the overall fit of both cross-section equation (5) as well as (6) improves over time.[8] The fact that both the complete segmentation model as well as the complete integration model describe the cross-sectional behavior of returns better as time progresses is somewhat puzzling. A priori, we expected that the integration model would have performed better over time—as countries opened up—and the segmentation model worse. One explanation is that both equations essentially use the same set of explanatory variables, world and local rates of return, and consequently that the behavior over time of the overall fit has to be similar.

5.5   Barriers and the Investability Indexes

This section provides some statistics on the investability indexes. Barriers to access by foreigners are more severe for developing countries than for industrial countries. While many developing countries have liberalized in recent years, in the past many had—and some still have—capital controls affecting the general ability to invest in and repatriate capital out of the host country, restrictions on foreign investment (e.g., restrictions on the general permissible share of foreign ownership), and other sector or company-specific ownership restrictions.

In addition to these legal barriers, other barriers likely limit foreigners' access to these markets.[9] The IFC investability indexes are, however, only concerned with legal barriers. In particular, the investability indexes are compiled on the basis of information on type (and/or changes) of identifiable barriers (in or out, ownership restrictions, remittance restrictions, other foreign exchange restrictions, restrictions on capital structure, etc.). Typically, however, the index reflects the share of stocks which can be held by foreigners, that is, the δ-constraint. Indirect barriers are not incorporated in the index (even though the IFC categorizes the severity of these indirect barriers by market; see the IFC *Emerging Markets Factbook*, 1993). Appendix B describes the method used for creating the investability indexes and the restrictions in place as of the end of 1992 for some selected emerging markets.

8. We estimate the cross-section equations (5) and (6) for every month during the period December 1988–December 1992, where we use estimates of the various betas obtained from using the previous three years of data (instead of running it as systems with constant betas). We then measure the degree of improvement over time in overall fit for each country through the correlations of the R^2s of the cross-section equations with an index which runs from one (first cross-section equation) to forty-nine (last cross-section equation). For both equations (5) and (6), fourteen out of the sixteen correlations are positive (six of which are significantly so at the 5 percent level).

9. For example, there can be restrictions imposed on investors by the home country (e.g., restrictions on the share of foreign assets held by pension funds) and other regulatory and accounting standards in the home country. Also, indirect barriers may exist, such as the efficiency of the domestic stock (and other financial) markets; the regulatory, accounting, enforcement, etc., standards in the host country; the different forms of sovereign (or transfer) risk; and taxes (see Demirguc-Kunt and Huizinga 1992) and other transaction costs. We do not analyze these restrictions.

The investability indexes are available from December 1989, initially for ten of the twenty markets in the EMDB and later for eighteen. The investability indexes take on values between 0.0 (complete lack of access by foreigners) and 1.0 (complete access). Table 5.6 provides information (the number of stocks, the mean level, the standard deviation, the range, and the skewness of the indexes) on the cross-sectional distributions of the investability index within a given country, at different points in time. Figure 5.1 provides the time-series plots for the mean and cross-sectional standard deviation for the seven countries which have consistent data for the investability index and the stock rates of return since 1989 (Chile had missing data for 1991 and thus could not be plotted). As can be observed from the figure and also by comparing the three panels of table 5.6, there are sharp movements over time in the degree to which foreigners can access these markets. For Mexico, for example, the index goes up from an average of 0.10 in January 1989 to 0.61 at the end of 1992 and further to 0.80 in March 1993. Similarly, the average for Brazil goes up from 0.18 to 0.53. Except for Malaysia, the cross-sectional mean is lower in Asia, an indication that few markets in this region have opened up.

The cross-sectional standard deviation of the index at the end of 1992 varies greatly, from 0.00 for Taiwan to 0.51 for Colombia, Greece, and Venezuela. In general, the cross-sectional standard deviation is lower in Asia (even though less so for Pakistan, the Philippines, and Malaysia), an indication that these countries have mostly marketwide, not sector- or stock-specific restrictions.

The time-series plots of the cross-section variation and table 5.7 show that European and Latin American countries have seen the greatest variation over time in the mean index (the standard deviation of the mean index [Stdmn] in table 5.7 is higher for European countries, except Jordan, and Latin American countries, except Venezuela). Asian countries have the least variation over time. Also taking into account the low cross-sectional variation in Asian countries, this reflects that those Asian countries which opened up during this period did so in a marketwide fashion. Altogether there are four markets which have little time-series variation in access (i.e., for which in table 5.7 the Stdmn ≤ 0.04), but a reasonable cross-sectional variation (i.e., for which, according to table 5.6, the Std ≥ 0.16 at any point in time and for which we have complete data on rates of return and investability indexes): Jordan, Malaysia, the Philippines, and Thailand. Of these four, Jordan has the lowest mean index, 0.09 at the end of 1992.

5.6   Tests of the Relationship between the Investability Indexes, P/E Ratios, and Rates of Return

So far, we have found evidence of market segmentation for about ten markets. We now proceed to more formally incorporate barriers in our empirical tests, using the models of Eun and Janakiramanan (1986) and Stulz and Wasserfallen (1992), and the application of these models by Bailey and Jagtiani

Table 5.6   **Cross-Sectional Analysis of the Investability Index for Each Country in January 1989, June 1990, and December 1992**

Country	Date	Number of Stocks	Mean Level	Standard Deviation	Range (= maximum)	Skewness
Malaysia	8901	62	0.84	0.34	1.00	−1.74136
Philippines	8901	18	0.28	0.46	1.00	1.08486
Thailand	8901	29	0.30	0.20	1.00	1.14879
Greece	8901	26	0.31	0.47	1.00	0.88525
Jordan	8901	25	0.10	0.20	0.49	1.59749
Portugal	8901	23	0.74	0.45	1.00	−1.16667
Argentina	8901	24	0.58	0.50	1.00	−0.36103
Brazil	8901	56	0.18	0.19	0.56	0.31331
Chile	8901	26	0.09	0.12	0.25	0.68705
Mexico	8901	52	0.10	0.30	1.00	2.82184
Malaysia	9006	62	0.86	0.32	1.00	−2.03384
Philippines	9006	29	0.22	0.41	1.00	1.43347
Thailand	9006	34	0.29	0.21	1.00	0.91982
Greece	9006	26	0.77	0.43	1.00	−1.35763
Jordan	9006	25	0.10	0.20	0.49	1.59749
Portugal	9006	27	0.67	0.48	1.00	−0.75423
Turkey	9006	18	0.89	0.32	1.00	−2.70579
Argentina	9006	24	0.42	0.50	1.00	0.36103
Brazil	9006	56	0.10	0.17	0.50	1.22881
Chile	9006	28	0.08	0.12	0.25	0.80870
Mexico	9006	54	0.56	0.50	1.00	−0.23005
Venezuela	9006	13	0.38	0.51	1.00	0.53859
India	9212	63	0.26	0.25	0.49	−0.09769
Indonesia	9212	62	0.15	0.12	0.24	−0.62193
Korea	9212	91	0.10	0.02	0.24	0.25280
Malaysia	9212	62	0.85	0.33	1.00	−1.87221
Pakistan	9212	58	0.09	0.28	1.00	3.02748
Philippines	9212	30	0.25	0.43	1.00	1.24847
Taiwan	9212	70	0.03	0.00	0.05	−5.67578
Thailand	9212	51	0.27	0.16	0.50	−0.31587
Greece	9212	32	0.47	0.51	1.00	0.13149
Jordan	9212	27	0.09	0.19	0.49	1.71783
Portugal	9212	30	0.38	0.48	1.00	0.56336
Turkey	9212	25	0.80	0.41	1.00	−1.59749
Argentina	9212	29	0.79	0.41	1.00	−1.52730
Brazil	9212	69	0.53	0.47	1.00	−0.12553
Chile	9212	35	0.14	0.13	0.25	−0.17986
Colombia	9212	20	0.50	0.51	1.00	0.00000
Mexico	9212	66	0.61	0.49	1.00	−0.44428
Venezuela	9212	17	0.41	0.51	1.00	0.39424

Note: Statistics provide the cross-sectional distribution of the investability index at a given point in time. The cross-sectional minimum is 0.0 in all markets. No data were available for Nigeria and Zimbabwe.

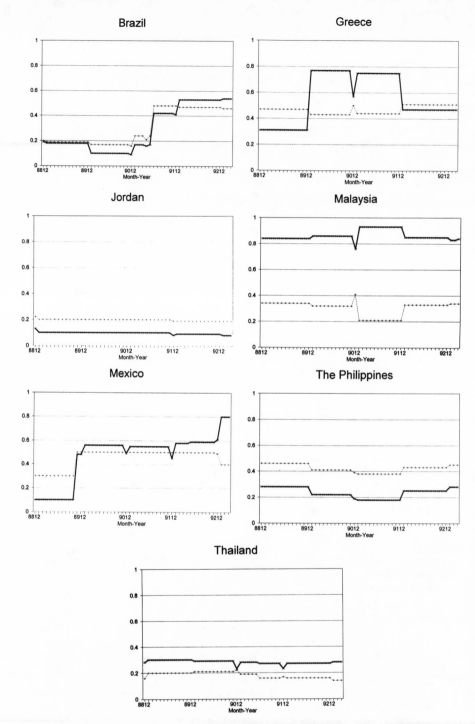

Fig. 5.1   Mean and standard deviation of the investability indexes (by country)
Note: ++ = mean; ———— = standard deviation.

Table 5.7   Time-Series Analysis of the Cross-Sectional Mean of the Investability
              Indexes

Country	N	Mean	Stdmn	Minmn	Maxmn
India	31	0.20	0.07	0.10	0.37
Indonesia	5	0.14	0.01	0.14	0.15
Korea	15	0.10	0.00	0.09	0.10
Malaysia	52	0.87	0.04	0.76	0.93
Pakistan	25	0.09	0.01	0.09	0.13
Philippines	52	0.23	0.04	0.18	0.28
Taiwan	27	0.03	0.00	0.03	0.03
Thailand	52	0.28	0.02	0.23	0.30
Greece	52	0.56	0.19	0.31	0.77
Jordan	52	0.10	0.01	0.08	0.13
Portugal	52	0.57	0.14	0.38	0.83
Turkey	44	0.79	0.10	0.56	0.89
Argentina	52	0.61	0.15	0.33	0.79
Brazil	52	0.30	0.18	0.09	0.54
Chile	40	0.10	0.03	0.06	0.14
Colombia	26	0.38	0.12	0.25	0.50
Mexico	52	0.47	0.21	0.10	0.80
Venezuela	39	0.41	0.03	0.31	0.44

Note: The statistics apply to the time series of the mean value of the investability index for a given market. Chile has missing data for 1991. Stdmn refers to the standard deviation of the mean index, Minmn to the minimum of the mean index, and Maxmn to the maximum of the mean index.

(1992). We start with the assumption that the world and the emerging country have the same numeraire (dollars) so that exchange risk is not priced. Consequently, we focus on the dollar rates of return. We further assume that the residents of the emerging countries have full access to foreign financial markets and foreign stocks. The high levels of flight capital observed for many developing countries indicate that this is a reasonable assumption. Foreigners are, however, restricted from full access to the emerging markets and can invest only up to a fraction δ measured by the investability index.

When the δ-constraint is binding, two prices for the same security will occur: a "domestic" price for that share of the stock which can only be held by domestic residents, and a "foreign" price for the share of the stock which can be held by both foreigners and domestic residents. Compared to a situation with no restrictions, a discount can arise for the domestic price and a premium for the foreign price. The ratio of foreign to domestic prices will, among others, depend on the supply of both classes of shares, relative to domestic and foreign investors' wealth.

Apart from the fact whether the constraint on ownership is binding on the foreigners—which we assume it is—the degree to which the domestic market offers unique risk-return characteristics from a world capital market point of view plays an important role in determining the existence and size of the discount and premium. If the domestic market can be mimicked perfectly using world assets, then foreigners will not be willing to pay a premium for emerging markets' stocks. And if domestic residents can lay off the risk of their emerging market stocks through positions in stocks available in the world capital markets, then they do not require a discount on emerging market stocks, even if they are forced to hold them because of the δ-constraint.[10]

We test these relationships using individual stocks' P/E ratios and rates of return for the seven countries for which we have consistent data on returns and investability indexes.[11] Since we are not studying unrestricted and restricted shares of the same firm, but rather shares of individual firms which vary in their degree of restrictiveness, we cannot calculate the ratio of foreign to domestic prices here.[12] However, we can study the price-earning ratio of a stock. Similarly, we can use domestic rates of return (instead of the difference between the returns to foreign and domestic shareholders).

We estimate mimicking portfolios on the basis of the IFC index for the emerging market and the MSCI indexes for thirteen industrial countries. Specifically, the mimicking portfolios are created through ordinary least squares (OLS) regressions of (the rates of return on) the indexes on (the rates of return on) the thirteen MSCI indexes. We then use the predicted values from this regression as the rates of return on the mimicking portfolio.[13] As in Stulz and Wasserfallen (1992) and Bailey and Jagtiani (1992), we also include in the estimations a size (or supply) variable, here taken as the log of the market capitalization of each stock, $MV_{i,t}$. Finally, we use actual instead of expected P/E ratios or returns.

We thus model the P/E ratio, or alternatively, the (excess) rate of return of domestic stock i in market j, as

$$(9) \qquad (P/E)_{i,t} = \alpha_{0,t} + \alpha_{1,t}\delta_{i,t} + \alpha_{2,t}\beta_{i,w,t}$$

$$+ \alpha_{3,t}[\beta_{i,j,t} - \beta_{i,a,t}] + \alpha_{4,t}MV_{i,t} + \varepsilon_{i,t},$$

where $\delta_{i,t}$ indicates the share foreigners can buy of a particular stock i at time t (the investability index), $\beta_{i,w}$ is the slope coefficient of stock i on the world

---

10. Notice that this approach resembles segmentation/integration tests where the residual of a projection of the local return on the world return (and vice versa) was used. Here the local index is mimicked more generally using (in principle) all worldwide traded assets. Since barriers and associated "mispricing" of individual securities can affect the overall domestic stock market, (announcements of) barriers on individual securities can lead to a marketwide effect through "spillover" effects (see, further, Eun, Claessens, and Jun 1993). We do not attempt to control for these effects.

11. The results for seven other countries are available upon request.

12. Even though we have some stocks of the same firm (e.g., Telmex shares A, B, C, and L) which differ in degree of investability, the sample of such stocks is small. Other foreign prices are available in the form of country-fund and ADR prices. For an analysis of country-fund prices, see Hardouvelis, La Porta, and Wizman (chap. 8 in this volume) and Diwan, Errunza, and Senbet (1993a, 1993b).

13. The mimicking is, as expected, generally poor as these markets have a low correlation with markets of industrial countries. The residual domestic risks are consequently quite large.

portfolio (here the MSCI world index), $\beta_{i,a}$ is the slope coefficient of stock i on the mimicking portfolio A, $\beta_{i,j}$ is the slope coefficient of stock i on the local market index j (note that the αs are not stock specific), and where the subscript t for the β-coefficients indicates that these are estimates updated every month using the previous three years of data. The difference between $\beta_{i,j}$ and $\beta_{i,a}$ represents the domestic risk that cannot be hedged through positions in foreign assets. When there is no residual risk to bear, $\beta_{i,j} - \beta_{i,a} = 0$ and the world CAPM prevails. To estimate the betas, we regress the rates of return during the three-year period preceding the date on the respective indexes.

The coefficients $\alpha_{1,t}$ depend on the relative risk aversion, the wealth of both foreign and domestic investors, and the total supply of restricted and unrestricted shares. The prior is, when the access constraint is binding, that the coefficients $\alpha_{1,t}$ are positive (an increase in δ relaxes the foreign constraint, decreases the required rate of return, and increases the P/E ratio). The coefficients $\alpha_{2,t}$ represent the world market price of risk and are expected to be negative. The coefficients $\alpha_{3,t}$ are expected to be negative as a decrease in the ability to mimic local risk increases the required rate of return and lowers the P/E ratio. Finally, $\alpha_{4,t}$ are expected to be positive as an increase in the supply of assets, keeping liquidity constant, raises the required rate of return and lowers the P/E ratio. When using the rate of return as the dependent variable, the signs of the α-coefficients are expected to take the opposite value.

We do not impose time-series restrictions on the coefficients $\alpha_{0,t} - \alpha_{4,t}$ for each market, that is, we do not use the SUR technique we used for the integration/segmentation tests. Rather we employ the Fama-MacBeth (1973) methodology where we estimate a separate cross-section equation for each month in the 1989–92 period for each market and then calculate averages, standard deviation, etc., of the time series of the slope coefficients.[14]

The results for the P/E ratio alone are in the first panel of table 5.8, which reports the means of the slope coefficients, the t-value for the time-series means, and the means of the individual t-values. The other panels cover the results when we include different combinations of the other right-hand-side variables. The results for the rates of return are in table 5.9.

The results for regressions of the P/E ratios on the index alone confirm the notion that the P/E ratio is positively related to the degree of access by foreigners, suggesting that barriers to access have a negative impact on prices. As measured by the t-value for the mean slope coefficient, for all seven countries, the mean slope is significantly positive (with Brazil marginally). When including other explanatory variables, we find that the positive sign for δ is robust to the inclusion of the world beta and the degree of international spanning of the

---

14. The main reason we use the Fama-MacBeth methodology is that equation (9) is not formally derived from any rate of return generating process. As a result, the restrictions which would need to be imposed on the coefficients in an SUR are unclear and the more traditional Fama-Macbeth method is preferred.

Table 5.8   Time-Series Summary of Cross-Sectional Regressions of Price/Earnings Ratio (P/E) against Investability Index (1989–1992)

	MN δ	T δ	MN T δ	β_w	$T\beta_w$	$MN\,T\beta_w$	$MN\,\beta_j - \beta_a$	$T\,\beta_j - \beta_a$	$MN\,T\,\beta_j - \beta_a$	MN MV	T MV	MN T MV
Malaysia	40.45	2.65	-0.04									
Philippines	57.62	3.45	1.08									
Thailand	5.1	3.83	0.64									
Greece	28.31	3.06	1									
Jordan	125.87	3.26	0.23									
Brazil	9.18	1.94	0.12									
Mexico	6.19	4.13	0.98									
Malaysia	53.17	1.71	-0.06	37.44	0.78	0.23						
Philippines	-52.22	-3.18	-0.28	54.88	2.87	-0.23						
Thailand	-25.73	-8.52	-1.01	10.99	9.02	1.44						
Greece	140.18	1.85	0.76	-109.3	-1.63	-0.71						
Jordan	4.2	1.02	-0.01	11.74	3.41	0.21						
Brazil	7.33	2.17	0.3	-0.33	-0.48	-0.39						
Mexico	11.69	3.6	0.38	-1.95	-0.76	0						
Malaysia	71.11	1.62	-0.1				-17.9	-0.3	0.37			
Philippines	10.66	1.89	-0.24				-82.77	-3.05	-1.39			
Thailand	-9.53	-5.89	-0.31				11.9	7.71	1.94			
Greece	288.19	1.64	0.21				236.21	1.56	-1.02			
Jordan	26.31	2.24	-0.08				3.28	0.4	-0.45			
Brazil	10.58	2.33	0.55				-3.25	-4.92	-1.02			
Mexico	9.75	4.77	0.48				-5.49	-2.08	-0.25			

Malaysia	-2.3	-0.15	-0.17				-16.31	-2.73	0.31
Philippines	-38.41	-2.4	0.04				0.77	0.31	-0.77
Thailand	-13.47	-7.35	-0.47				1.29	4.6	0.55
Greece	-65.12	-1.55	0.28				60.61	1.81	0.17
Jordan	43.6	4.53	0.45				-6.58	-5.34	-0.51
Brazil	-13.99	-2.27	-0.93				3.15	4.37	1.81
Mexico	10.46	2.67	0				0.07	0.05	0.69

Malaysia	66.62	1.52	-0.08	16.33	0.34	0.37	-10.28	-0.16	0.51
Philippines	4.2	1.13	0.04	13.16	2.1	-0.75	-77.76	-3.04	-1.22
Thailand	-18.4	-6.17	-0.58	4.51	4.36	0.41	9.38	6.2	1.11
Greece	370	1.71	0.35	-108.1	-1.68	-1.21	240.34	1.6	-1.06
Jordan	16.97	1.82	-0.02	31.29	3.03	0.21	14.94	1.29	-0.25
Brazil	10.43	2.22	0.67	-2.18	-3.36	-0.79	-3.92	-6.26	-1.39
Mexico	12.31	4.06	0.57	-4.34	-1.07	-0.11	-5.56	-1.7	-0.45

Malaysia	22.94	0.97	-0.13	35.19	0.75	0.18	-7.15	-1.38	0.4
Philippines	17.06	2.33	0.28	85.15	2.97	0.07	-25.4	-3.32	-0.87
Thailand	-27.16	-8.59	-1.17	11.95	10.11	1.61	1.68	7.89	0.96
Greece	-35.86	-0.6	0.35	-32.24	-0.78	-0.45	51.08	1.71	0.16
Jordan	51.39	4.54	0.54	20.06	4.63	0.34	-9.28	-5.09	-0.57
Brazil	-0.23	-0.07	-0.64	-0.01	-0.01	-0.29	2.29	7.1	2.01
Mexico	11.6	2.67	0.07	-1.96	-0.8	-0.18	0.14	0.11	0.64

(*continued*)

Table 5.8 (continued)

	MN δ	T δ	MN T δ	β_w	T β_w	MN T β_w	MN β_j−β_a	T β_j−β_a	MN T β_j−β_a	MN MV	T MV	MN T MV
Malaysia	25.87	0.71	−0.19				−19.77	−0.33	0.34	−16.92	−2.69	0.28
Philippines	21.82	3.12	0.32				−83.72	−3.08	−1.54	−4.14	−3.04	−0.95
Thailand	−10.64	−5.92	−0.4				11.85	7.19	1.58	−0.13	−0.72	0.06
Greece	174.61	1.59	0.02				218.29	1.57	−0.86	47.36	1.79	−0.08
Jordan	32.21	4.07	0.49				3.94	0.47	−0.53	−1.55	−0.98	−0.55
Brazil	5.47	0.84	−0.34				−2.9	−3.09	−0.61	1.5	3.36	1.68
Mexico	10.57	2.91	0.09				−5.46	−1.91	−0.44	−0.62	−0.39	0.65
Malaysia	35.48	0.97	−0.16	14.46	0.31	0.34	−10.87	−0.16	0.51	−7.93	−1.45	0.34
Philippines	39	3.06	0.47	32.96	2.62	−0.41	−74.07	−2.99	−1.22	−14.25	−3.19	−0.8
Thailand	−21.33	−6.18	−0.71	6.46	4.37	0.57	8.23	4.56	0.57	0.5	1.99	0.34
Greece	235.3	1.68	0.06	−53.95	−1.24	−0.75	227.95	1.63	−0.84	35.29	1.71	0.11
Jordan	32.15	3.51	0.53	37.82	3.68	0.34	16.36	1.43	−0.35	−3.63	−1.89	−0.55
Brazil	5.88	0.91	−0.19	−1.37	−2.13	−0.7	−3.02	−3.12	−0.89	1.51	3.29	1.45
Mexico	12.47	2.93	0.23	−4.31	−1.13	−0.22	−5.73	−1.68	−0.62	−0.17	−0.11	0.67

Note: MN stands for the time-series mean of the cross-sectional regression coefficients. Std represents the standard deviation of the cross-sectional regression coefficients. T stands for the *t*-value of the mean of the time-series of coefficients, i.e., mean*sqrt(n)/std. MN T stands for the mean of the *t*-values of the individual cross-sectional regressions. We use stocks with complete observations from 1/86 through 12/92. δ stands for the investability index. β_w are world betas. β_j are the betas against the local index and β_a are the betas from the mimicking portfolios. MV are one-month lagged log market values. For the number of stocks, see table 5.6 on the investability index. Results are similar when using local betas and betas from mimicking portfolios separately rather than taking the difference between them.

Table 5.9   Time-Series Summary of Cross-Sectional Regressions of Rates of Return against Investability Index (1989–1992)

	MN δ	T δ	MN T δ	β_w	T β_w	MN T β_w	MN $\beta_j-\beta_a$	T $\beta_j-\beta_a$	MN T $\beta_j-\beta_a$	MN MV	T MV	MN T MV
Malaysia	0.02	1.77	0.13									
Philippines	0.02	1.7	0.35									
Thailand	0.13	4.28	0.48									
Greece	0.03	2.3	0.55									
Jordan	−0.03	−2.05	−0.2									
Brazil	0.02	0.68	0.14									
Mexico	0.01	1.08	0.1									
Malaysia	0.02	1.48	0.09	−0.01	−0.7	−0.16						
Philippines	0.02	1.94	0.42	0	−0.1	−0.08						
Thailand	0.1	2.82	0.44	−0.02	−0.69	−0.12						
Greece	0.03	2.2	0.59	0	0.35	0.18						
Jordan	−0.04	−1.98	−0.22	0.03	1.86	0.25						
Brazil	0	−0.08	−0.01	−0.03	−2.08	−0.28						
Mexico	0.01	0.91	0.06	0.01	1.01	0.27						
Malaysia	0.02	1.65	0.12				0.01	0.91	0.02			
Philippines	0.02	2	0.41				−0.01	−0.98	−0.34			
Thailand	0.12	3.19	0.44				0	−0.14	0			
Greece	0.02	1.82	0.6				−0.01	−0.86	−0.11			
Jordan	−0.02	−1.09	−0.16				0.03	1.56	0.02			
Brazil	0.04	0.89	0.08				−0.01	−0.6	−0.05			
Mexico	0.02	1.41	0.16				−0.01	−1.65	−0.3			

(*continued*)

Table 5.9 (continued)

	MN δ	T δ	MN T δ	β_w	T β_w	MN T β_w	MN $\beta_j - \beta_a$	T $\beta_j - \beta_a$	MN T $\beta_j - \beta_a$	MN MV	T MV	MN T MV
Malaysia	0.01	1.49	0.12							0	−1	0.11
Philippines	0.03	2.69	0.29							0	−0.71	−0.01
Thailand	0.13	3.83	0.46							0	0.69	0.18
Greece	0.03	2.02	0.43							0	−0.54	−0.14
Jordan	0	0.06	0.01							−0.01	−0.93	−0.09
Brazil	0.02	0.57	0.06							0	0.12	0.1
Mexico	0	−0.36	−0.11							0.01	2.04	0.47
Malaysia	0.02	1.46	0.09	0	−0.11	−0.08	0.01	0.69	−0.02			
Philippines	0.03	2.32	0.47	−0.01	−0.69	−0.15	0	−0.15	−0.21			
Thailand	0.1	2.28	0.32	−0.03	−0.95	−0.08	0.01	0.32	−0.08			
Greece	0.03	1.75	0.55	0	−0.2	0.15	−0.01	−0.58	−0.01			
Jordan	−0.02	−1.38	−0.13	0.05	3.25	0.29	0.05	2.61	0.2			
Brazil	0.02	0.45	0	−0.03	−2.26	−0.18	−0.02	−1.51	−0.2			
Mexico	0.01	0.96	0.15	0.02	1.26	0.34	−0.01	−1.42	−0.38			
Malaysia	0.01	1.27	0.1	0	−0.01	−0.05				0	−1.07	0.09
Philippines	0.04	2.97	0.39	0.01	0.67	0				−0.01	−1.15	−0.05
Thailand	0.09	2.22	0.46	−0.01	−0.33	−0.13				0	0.67	0.05
Greece	0.05	2.74	0.59	0.02	1.14	0.33				−0.01	−1.75	−0.31

	MN	T	Std	MN	T	δ	MN	T		MN	T	
Jordan	0.02	0.67	0.09	0.04	2.05	0.34				−0.01	−1.59	−0.19
Brazil	−0.01	−0.23	−0.06	−0.03	−1.97	−0.28				0	0.27	0.07
Mexico	−0.01	−0.55	−0.15	0.02	1.08	0.31				0.01	2.22	0.49
Malaysia	0.01	1.34	0.12				0.02	1.14	0.05	0	−1.01	0.11
Philippines	0.03	3.03	0.37				−0.01	−1.11	−0.35	0	−0.76	−0.05
Thailand	0.11	2.79	0.4				−0.01	−0.26	−0.13	0	−0.07	0.03
Greece	0.03	2.02	0.64				−0.02	−1.15	−0.32	−0.01	−1.01	−0.33
Jordan	−0.01	−0.19	0.06				0.02	1.09	−0.06	0	−0.21	−0.11
Brazil	−0.03	−0.77	−0.07				0	0.36	0.05	0.01	0.48	0.08
Mexico	0	−0.14	−0.06				−0.02	−2.47	−0.39	0.01	2.39	0.52
Malaysia	0.01	1.24	0.1	0	0.37	0.01	0.01	0.87	0.02	0	−1.11	0.09
Philippines	0.04	3.36	0.45	0	0.14	−0.06	0	−0.11	−0.18	−0.01	−1.14	−0.05
Thailand	0.04	0.72	0.2	0.01	0.31	0	−0.01	−0.2	−0.3	0	0.46	0.04
Greece	0.04	2.35	0.67	0.01	0.35	0.19	−0.02	−0.72	−0.15	−0.01	−1.91	−0.46
Jordan	0.01	0.4	0.15	0.06	3.17	0.37	0.05	2.35	0.14	−0.01	−1.01	−0.21
Brazil	−0.01	−0.36	−0.06	−0.02	−1.85	−0.12	−0.01	−0.69	−0.09	0	0.08	0
Mexico	−0.01	−0.49	−0.11	0.02	1.31	0.39	−0.02	−1.88	−0.43	0.01	2.44	0.54

Note: MN stands for the time-series mean of the cross-sectional regression coefficients. Std represents the standard deviation of the cross-sectional regression coefficients. T stands for the t-value of the mean of the times-series of coefficients, i.e., mean*sqrt(n)/std. MN T stands for the mean of the individual cross-sectional regressions. We use stocks with complete observations from 1/86 through 12/92. δ stands for the investability index. β_w are world betas. β_j are the betas against the local index and β_a are the betas from the mimicking portfolios. MV are one-month lagged log market values. For the number of stocks, see table 5.6 on the investability index. Results are similar when using local betas and betas from mimicking portfolios separately rather than taking the difference between them.

domestic market for four markets. Only for Jordan and Mexico is the positive sign for δ maintained across all regression specifications. For the other countries the sign for δ at times turns negative, for example, when including the lagged (log) market value, the third panel. For Jordan, the signs for the other explanatory variables are not always as expected, for example, several of the βs have positive signs. In the case of Mexico, the signs for the βs are, as hypothesized, all negative (e.g., see the very last line of table 5.8).

The t-values for the time-series means show that there are quite a number of significant coefficients. For example, for the regression which includes all explanatory variables (the last panel of table 5.8), fourteen out of twenty-eight coefficients are significant on the basis of the t-values for the mean (the mean of the individual t-values shows, however, that many of the individual regression coefficients were insignificant). But the signs are often not as expected.

For the rates of return, Jordan is the only country which has the expected negative sign for δ (first panel, table 5.9). This negative sign is robust, but loses significance, when including β_w and $\beta_j - \beta_a$, which themselves also have the expected positive and often significant signs. The negative sign for δ disappears when the lagged (log) market value is included. For none of the other markets do we find that returns are negatively related to the investability indexes in a consistent fashion.

The degree to which the model explains the cross-section variation in the P/E-ratios and rates of return varies greatly across equations and countries. While in general we have low explanatory power, with the time-series mean of the adjusted R^2s mostly reaching less than 10 percent, at times the mean adjusted R^2 reaches 70 to 80 percent (figures are not reported).

Our findings may be better understood by referring back to figure 5.1. This figure showed that there is much erratic behavior in the investability indexes, with large swings from month to month for some countries; for example, for Greece in late 1990 the mean index falls in one month from 0.77 to 0.57 and then goes back up to 0.75, casting some doubt on the manner in which these data were constructed. More important, as was noted before, only for Jordan is the mean index stable and low, while at the same displaying a relatively large cross-sectional variation.

The behavior of the indexes may explain why we only find consistent results for both P/E ratios and rates of return for Jordan. For three of the four countries where the investability index was stable while still displaying relatively large cross-sectional variation, the access constraint likely did not bind (Malaysia, the Philippines, and Thailand). This implies one would not expect a cross-sectional relationship between returns and the indexes. For the other countries, the investability indexes were not stable (the mean increased for Brazil and Mexico and behaved erraticly for Greece). This could imply that time-series effects (of opening up or closing of the markets, or of data problems) confounded the cross-sectional relationship between returns and the investability indexes. Put differently, the ex post rates of return are likely a poor proxy of the ex ante rates of return. A positive relationship between the P/E ratio and the investability indexes could still be maintained if countries opened up (e.g., Brazil and Mexico), however, since then both the cross-sectional and time-series effects would go the same way.

To control for the time-series effects of marketwide opening up, we standardize the P/E ratio of each stock in a given market by dividing it by the market-average P/E ratio. In this way, we control for changes in the P/E ratio of each stock for marketwide developments which may be related to the opening up of the market. Admittedly, this is a crude way of proxying for events which affect a particular stock's P/E ratio over time, but it should provide some indication of how robust our results are to the time-series behavior of the P/E ratios.

The results are reported in table 5.10. Comparing the coefficients in table 5.10 with those of table 5.8, we find that the cross-sectional relationship between a stock's P/E ratio and its δ is robust to this standardization. While, as expected, the slope coefficients drop significantly, the t-values are not affected. If anything, the cross-sectional effect of δ on the P/E ratio is significant at higher levels than in table 5.8. By multiplying the slope coefficients with the mean level of δ (from table 5.7), the relative sensitivity of a stock's P/E ratio with respect to δ can be compared across countries. Excluding Thailand (which has a very low slope coefficient), the mean sensitivity is 0.91, with a standard deviation of only 0.44, indicating some evidence of a common pattern.

We also perform a second robustness test. This involves controlling for the stocks' industry (sector).[15] Our previous results may be capturing differences in P/E ratios by industry to the extent that foreign ownership restrictions differ systematically by industry. Since we often have a limited number of stocks for each country, we cannot control for each industry without running out a degrees of freedom. We therefore classify stocks in two groups: nonbank and bank. Ownership restrictions appear to differ most systematically between these two groups. We perform this second robustness test for two countries, Malaysia and Brazil. Malaysia has twenty-three stocks in nonbank and six in bank. The nonbank group has a much higher δ (100 percent) than the bank group (30 percent): the P/E ratio for nonbank is on average about twice as high as the P/E ratio of the bank stocks. Average rates of return do not differ between the two groups. Brazil has fifteen stocks in nonbank and only three in bank. The P/E ratio for nonbank is on average slightly higher than that of bank, but average rates of return do not differ between the two groups.

The results of similar regressions as in tables 5.8–5.10 but now with a dummy added for sector (nonbank = 0, bank = 1) are reported in table 5.11. As can be observed, for both countries and for the P/E ratio as well as for the rate of return equations, the sector dummies have the right (negative) sign, indicating that the industry classification affects a stock's P/E ratio. For Malay-

---

15. We are grateful to Donald Lessard for suggesting this extension.

Table 5.10   Time-Series Summary of Cross-Sectional Regressions of Standardized Price/Earnings Ratio (P/E) against Investability Index (1989–1992)

	MN δ	T δ	MN T δ	MN β_w	T β_w	MN T β_w	MN $\beta_j - \beta_a$	T $\beta_j - \beta_a$	MN T $\beta_j - \beta_a$	MN MV	T MV	MN T MV
Malaysia	1.95	2.94	−0.04									
Philippines	3.92	3.5	1.08									
Thailand	0.35	3.2	0.64									
Greece	1.89	3.7	1									
Jordan	10.13	3.38	0.23									
Brazil	1.72	3.03	0.21									
Mexico	0.63	4.31	0.98									
Malaysia	2.48	1.8	−0.06	2.68	1.37	0.23						
Philippines	−3.54	−3.23	−0.28	3.64	2.85	−0.23						
Thailand	−1.94	−8.34	−1.01	0.81	9.76	1.44						
Greece	8.17	1.95	0.76	−6.43	−1.68	−0.71						
Jordan	0.39	1.07	−0.01	1.16	3.61	0.21						
Brazil	0.58	2.07	0.34	0.01	0.25	−0.24						
Mexico	1.2	2.93	0.38	−0.36	−1.24	0						
Malaysia	3.18	1.59	−0.1				−0.86	−0.32	0.37			
Philippines	0.67	1.74	−0.24				−5.62	−3.07	−1.39			
Thailand	−0.7	−6.04	−0.31				0.86	8.43	1.94			
Greece	15.95	1.71	0.21				13	1.61	−1.02			
Jordan	2.54	2.37	−0.08				0.55	0.75	−0.45			
Brazil	1.03	2.69	0.59				−0.3	−5.6	−1.02			
Mexico	0.87	3.65	0.48				−0.29	−1.14	−0.25			

	1	2	3	4	5	6	7	8	9	10	11	12
Malaysia	-0.04	-0.05	-0.17				-0.7	-2.79	0.31			
Philippines	-2.59	-2.38	0.04				0.03	0.15	-0.77			
Thailand	-0.99	-7.69	-0.47				0.09	4.79	0.55			
Greece	-3.36	-1.47	0.28				3.36	1.82	0.17			
Jordan	3.69	3.89	0.45				-0.53	-4.6	-0.51			
Brazil	-2.49	-2.38	-0.68				0.4	3.33	1.36			
Mexico	1.07	2.25	0				-0.02	-0.15	0.69			
Malaysia	3.05	1.54	-0.08	1.66	0.83	0.37	-0.65	-0.22	0.51			
Philippines	0.28	1.11	0.04	0.81	1.92	-0.75	-5.29	-3.06	-1.22			
Thailand	-1.41	-5.93	-0.58	0.34	4.28	0.41	0.67	6.63	1.11			
Greece	20.83	1.78	0.35	-6.32	-1.67	-1.21	13.39	1.67	-1.06			
Jordan	1.61	1.91	-0.02	3.12	3.07	0.21	1.69	1.56	-0.25			
Brazil	1.04	2.61	0.71	-0.2	-3.5	-0.69	-0.4	-7.26	-1.34			
Mexico	1.22	3.16	0.57	-0.74	-1.54	-0.11	-0.22	-0.67	-0.45			
Malaysia	1.17	1.12	-0.13	2.61	1.35	0.18				-0.32	-1.43	0.4
Philippines	1.13	2.34	0.28	5.67	2.97	0.07				-1.72	-3.4	-0.87
Thailand	-2.05	-8.44	-1.17	0.9	10.34	1.61				0.13	8.45	0.96
Greece	-1.41	-0.45	0.35	-2.16	-0.9	-0.45				2.81	1.76	0.16
Jordan	4.41	3.94	0.54	1.84	4.31	0.34				-0.79	-4.44	-0.57
Brazil	-0.28	-0.99	-0.39	0.06	1.19	-0.12				0.24	8.24	1.67
Mexico	1.23	2.31	0.07	-0.36	-1.37	-0.18				0	0.02	0.64
Malaysia	1.22	0.74	-0.19				-0.95	-0.35	0.34	-0.74	-2.78	0.28
Philippines	1.5	3.16	0.32				-5.69	-3.11	-1.54	-0.31	-3.44	-0.95
Thailand	-0.78	-6.11	-0.4				0.84	7.94	1.58	-0.01	-0.49	0.06
Greece	9.69	1.68	0.02				11.98	1.61	-0.86	2.64	1.79	-0.08
Jordan	2.57	3.43	0.49				0.66	0.88	-0.53	-0.04	-0.29	-0.55

(*continued*)

Table 5.10 (continued)

	MN δ	T δ	MN T δ	MN β$_w$	T β$_w$	MN T β$_w$	MN β$_j$ - β$_a$	T β$_j$ - β$_a$	MN T β$_j$ - β$_a$	MN MV	T MV	MN T MV
Brazil	0.26	0.47	-0.12				-0.22	-2.99	-0.65	0.19	5.51	1.38
Mexico	1.04	2.39	0.09				-0.28	-1	-0.44	-0.12	-0.64	0.65
Malaysia	1.7	1.04	-0.16	1.59	0.82	0.34	-0.69	-0.23	0.51	-0.35	-1.49	0.34
Philippines	2.66	3.09	0.47	2.16	2.56	-0.41	-5.05	-3.01	-1.22	-0.98	-3.31	-0.8
Thailand	-1.66	-5.86	-0.71	0.52	4.29	0.57	0.57	4.7	0.57	0.05	2.48	0.34
Greece	13.53	1.76	0.06	-3.37	-1.25	-0.75	12.7	1.69	-0.84	1.93	1.77	0.11
Jordan	2.59	2.92	0.53	3.59	3.48	0.34	1.8	1.67	-0.35	-0.25	-1.46	-0.55
Brazil	0.44	0.79	0.07	-0.07	-1.37	-0.51	-0.29	-3.9	-0.96	0.16	4.4	1.1
Mexico	1.29	2.47	0.23	-0.73	-1.63	-0.22	-0.23	-0.68	-0.62	-0.05	-0.29	0.67

Note: MN stands for the time-series mean of the cross-sectional regression coefficients. T stands for the *t*-value of the mean of the time-series of coefficients, i.e., mean*sqrt(n)/std. MN T stands for the mean of the *t*-values of the individual cross-sectional regressions. We use stocks with complete observations from 1/86 through 12/92. δ stands for the investability index. β$_w$ are world betas. β$_j$ are the betas against the local index and β$_a$ are the betas from the mimicking portfolios. MV are one-month lagged log market values. For the number of stocks, see table 5.6 on the investability index.

Table 5.11   **Time-Series Summary of Cross-Sectional Regressions of Price/Earnings Ratio (P/E) and Rates of Return against Investability Index and Sector Dummy (1989–1992)**

A. P/E Ratio

	MN δ	T δ	MN β_w	T β_w	MN $\beta_j-\beta_a$	T $\beta_j-\beta_a$	MN MV	T MV	MN SEC	T SEC
Malaysia	11.40	1.21							−19.39	−0.94
Brazil	2.14	0.59							−2.2	−1.53
Malaysia	27.12	1.01	23.03	0.46					−12.43	−0.53
Brazil	10.54	2.34	−1.6	−1.83					−7.58	−2.98
Malaysia	35.20	1.17			−2.22	−0.04			−21.19	−0.89
Brazil	10.69	2.32			−4.25	−8.5			3.01	1.13
Malaysia	−53.37	−2.66					−19.43	−2.77	−31.08	−1.33
Brazil	−11.68	−1.78					3.19	4.2	−2.98	−1.71
Malaysia	33.16	0.93	1.52	0.03	2.27	0.04			−15.5	−0.55
Brazil	10.62	2.25	−3.45	−2.87	−5.10	−8.84			−1.47	−0.42
Malaysia	−17.74	−0.65	19.03	0.39			−9.17	−1.49	−19.5	−0.77
Brazil	2.86	0.60	−1.22	−1.33			2.24	7.05	−9.74	−2.45
Malaysia	−34.04	−1.13			−2.56	−0.04	−20.54	−2.74	−33.94	−1.26
Brazil	6.62	0.96			−3.19	−2.71	1.49	2.93	−3.86	−0.73
Malaysia	−14.42	−0.41	−1.47	−0.03	3.02	0.04	−10.45	−1.55	−23.48	−0.76
Brazil	6.92	1.02	−2.87	−2.39	−3.74	−3.04	−1.59	3.06	−14.2	−2.24

B. Rates of Return

	MN δ	T δ	MN β_w	T β_w	MN $\beta_j-\beta_a$	T $\beta_j-\beta_a$	MN MV	T MV	MN SEC	T SEC
Malaysia	0.03	1.27							0.01	0.47
Brazil	0.02	0.69							−0.00	−0.12
Malaysia	0.03	1.04	0.00	−0.30					0.00	0.46
Brazil	0.02	0.37	−0.03	−1.29					−0.03	−0.58
Malaysia	0.02	1.17			0.00	0.44			0.00	0.38
Brazil	0.05	1.16			−0.03	−1.62			0.05	0.68
Malaysia	0.02	1.01					0.00	−0.81	0.00	0.25
Brazil	0.00	0.04					0.00	0.30	0.01	0.24
Malaysia	0.03	1.04	0.00	0.02	0.00	0.25			0.01	0.41
Brazil	0.04	0.81	−0.03	−1.39	−0.04	−1.73			0.04	0.55
Malaysia	0.02	0.81	0.00	0.23			0.00	0.96	0.00	0.22
Brazil	−0.01	−0.31	−0.02	−0.94			0.00	0.44	−0.03	−0.49
Malaysia	0.02	0.78	0.01	0.40	0.01	0.49	0.00	−0.99	0.00	0.12
Brazil	−0.02	−0.54			0.01	0.41	0.01	0.61	−0.03	−0.43
Malaysia	0.02	0.78	0.01	0.40	0.01	0.49	−0.00	−0.99	0.00	0.12
Brazil	−0.00	−0.10	−0.02	−1.22	−0.01	−0.38	0.00	0.00	−0.05	−0.56

Note: MN stands for the time-series mean of the cross-sectional regression coefficients. T stands for the t-value of the mean of the times-series of coefficients, i.e., mean*sqrt(n)/std. We use stocks with complete observations from 1/86 through 12/92. δ stands for the investability index. β_w are world betas. β_j are the betas against the local index and β_a are the betas from the mimicking portfolios. MV are one-month lagged log market values. SEC stands for the sectoral dummy. For the number of stocks, see table 5.6 on the investability index. Results are similar when using local betas and betas from mimicking portfolios separately rather than taking the difference between them.

sia, however, the dummies are never significant, while for Brazil only three out of eight are significant in the case of the P/E regressions and none for the rates of return regressions. (Note, however, that there are only three stocks in the Brazil bank group.) Introducing the sector dummy does affect the other slope coefficients, however. In particular, for Malaysia the t-statistics for δ become insignificant for almost all specifications. For Brazil, on the other hand, t-statistics often improve. For Malaysia, this raises the possibility that the regressions on the P/E ratio on δ without sector dummy are misspecified because of multicollinearity between δ and sector (i.e., sector-specific factors other than δ determine a stock's P/E ratio in such a way that high δ sectors end up with high P/E ratios and vice versa). As we use no factors other than δ and sector dummy to control for a stock's P/E ratio, we cannot determine conclusively either way whether it is the sector or the level of δ which is driving the relationship between δ and the P/E ratio. In the case of Brazil, there is no evidence of a coincidence between the industry sector of a stock and its δ.

The negative results for the rates of return are consistent with Bekaert (1993). He finds that there is not a significant relationship between ownership restrictions and the integration of an emerging market with world markets. He conjectures that ownership restrictions are not binding or are being circumvented.

5.7   Conclusions

Tests of market integration using the Stehle (1977) model, employing nonlinear, seemingly unrelated regressions (equivalent to the MLE), reject the market integration hypothesis for most and fail to reject segmentation for all. In particular, we find that over this period Brazil, Greece, Korea, Mexico, Pakistan, the Philippines, Taiwan, and Thailand are segmented from international markets.

We have evidence that the degree of investability affects P/E ratios for seven countries in the expected way. When including other explanatory variables, we find this result to be robust for four markets to the inclusion of the two additional explanatory variables, and for two, Jordan and Mexico, when including three additional variables. It is also robust to the standardization of the P/E ratios. When using rates of return, we only find the expected results for Jordan.

Our weak results for the rates of return are likely because we cover time-series as well as cross-section effects. Without any change in access, that is, on a cross-sectional basis, one would expect stocks which are more accessible to have lower return. However, many markets have opened up and as a result stock prices have increased, implying that ex post returns have been high (even though expected returns may have declined). This implies that on a cross-sectional basis one may not find a negative relationship between a stock's return and its investability index. The other possibility, of course, is that the CAPM is not the right model to use.

Our results indicate two possible avenues for improvements: one, we should attempt to keep the degree of access over time constant; and two, to expand the model to test for the importance of the investability indexes in explaining rate of return behavior. This is left for future research.

Appendix A
General Criteria for Inclusion in the IFC Indexes[16]

The IFC selects stocks for inclusion in the indexes on the basis of three criteria: size, liquidity, and industry. The indexes include the largest and most actively traded stocks in each market, with a target index total representing the top 60 percent of total market capitalization at the end of each year and, as a second step, the top 60 percent of total trading value during each year. Size is measured by market capitalization; liquidity is the total value of shares traded during the year.

Only stocks that are listed on one of the major exchanges in the emerging markets are included in the index. The index will not include stocks whose issuing company is headquartered in an emerging market but listed only on foreign markets.

If several stocks meet the liquidity and size criteria, but only one or two are needed, the IFC selects the stocks that represent industries that are not yet well represented in the IFC index.

In a few instances, particularly where multiple classes of stocks are common (e.g., Brazil and Mexico), the IFC may include in the IFC index more than one class of stock for the same company even though they are not necessarily actively traded. The purpose is to give a balanced view of the capitalization of companies that have other classes of stock that are actively traded.

Stock market "float" (i.e., the amount of issued stock held by the general public and generally assumed to be available for trading) is not a consideration in weighing the indexes, due to the difficulty of obtaining accurate information in a timely manner.

---

16. Appendix A and appendix B are copied from the IFC methodology notes.

Appendix B
Criteria Used by the IFC for the Investable Indexes and Restrictions on Foreign Investors in Selected Countries

Criteria Used by the IFC for the Investable Indexes

As a first screen, stocks are included in the investable indexes if they are in the global index and are available for purchase by nonresident investment institutions to some degree; the degree is determined by national laws and by company statutes. Governments and companies impose a variety of restrictions on foreign ownership, which may also differ by sector. In addition, individual firms may restrict foreign ownership of (certain classes of) shares. Several examples are shown here; appendix B summarizes the restrictions in effect at the end of 1992 for some selected markets.

General national limits, such as "foreigners as a group may not own more than 10 percent of any company";

Special class of shares, such as A and B class shares in the Philippines. The two are equivalent except that foreigners may not own A class shares:

Sector restrictions, most commonly used to limit foreign ownership of financial institutions, energy producers, utilities, and the media;

Single foreign holder limitations on general classes of shares, such as Brazil's "no more than 5 percent of the voting classes, nor more than 20 percent of aggregate capital" or Colombia's 10 percent limit per investor. The IFC rule in this regard is to use the aggregate that foreign investors as a whole may acquire;

Example: In Colombia, foreigners may own 100 percent of most companies, although no single foreigner may own more than 10 percent. The investable market capitalization would be considered as 100 percent;

"Foreign board" adjuncts to the main stock exchange, where foreign investors may trade listed stocks among themselves, assuring that trades conducted there will not cause the foreign ownership content to exceed maximum permitted level;

Prohibitions on individual foreign investors while permitting multiple foreign mutual funds, if they meet certain criteria, such as minimum fund size and experience. The IFC rule in this regard is to consider the market as open as it is to authorized investors, using the "aggregate investor" rule noted above for individual stock investability factors;

Company statutes that impose limits that differ from national law in some markets. In those case, the IFC uses the most restrictive limit;

Example: The national limit is 49 percent, but a company's articles of incorporation set a limit of 25 percent. The IFC would use a weight of 25 percent;

National limits on the aggregate permitted foreign investment. For example, Taiwan set a ceiling of US$2.5 billion on foreign inflows when it opened its stock market in January 1991. At the end of 1992, this represented about 2.5 percent of total Taiwan Stock Exchange (TSE) capitalization. In this case, the IFC would apply the relative shares of the available stocks within the market against the aggregate limit.

Example: The national limit in a market is $1 billion, and the investable index in the market consists of two stocks, XYZ Inc. and ABC Corp., which have available market capitalizations of $2 billion and $500 million, respectively. In the absence of the aggregate limit, the investable index would use $2 billion and $500 million as the available market capitalization.

However, these amounts would exceed the limit, and the IFC would apply the relative share approach: two stocks represent 80 percent and 20 percent of the available market capitalization, so the investable index would use $800 million and $200 million as the two stocks' "available" market capitalization.

For the calculation of the various IFC price and rate of return indexes, the investable market capitalization of each stock is used for its weight in the index instead of the stock's total market capitalization.

Example: XYZ, Ltd. has a total market capitalization of $100 million but national law prohibits foreign ownership of more than 49 percent of a company. The IFC global index would use the full $100 million as the stock's market capitalization while the investable index would use only $49 million.

To take concerns regrading illiquidity or relatively small market capitalizations into account, the IFC excludes stocks from the investable index if
1. trading value for the year totals less than $10 million, using total trading value unweighted for foreign access.
2. the investable market capitalization is less than $25 million. An exception occurs when the investable capitalization is small but the trading is large. The IFC will not exclude a stock if the value traded exceeds $100 million for the year, regardless of the stock's investable capitalization.

Example: A stock in Korea has a total capitalization of $240 million and trading totaling $1,300 million for the year. With the 10 percent limit currently in effect in Korea, the investable capitalization is only $24 million. It is clearly an accessible, large, and liquid stock, and foreigners are unlikely to have difficulty in trading it.

In rare cases, the selection screens could produce fewer than five stocks in an investable market, which is insufficient for an index. If that happens, the IFC will select as many stocks as needed to reach the minimum of five stocks, using investable capitalization ranked in decreasing order by size.

Restrictions on Foreign Investors at the End of 1992 in Selected Countries

Argentina   The market is considered generally 100 percent investable; some corporate statute limitations apply.

Brazil   The market is considered generally investable; since May 1991 foreign institutions may own up to 49 percent of voting common stock and 100 percent of nonvoting participating preferred stock. Some corporate statute limitations (e.g., Petrobras common are off-limits) apply.

Chile   Foreign portfolio investment is considered to enter Chile through the 1987 Law of 18657 regarding foreign capital investment funds, which limits aggregate foreign ownership to 25 percent of a listed company's shares.

Colombia   The market is considered 100 percent investable from February 1, 1991.

Greece   The market is generally 100 percent investable.

India   A press note issued by the Ministry of Finance of the government of India on September 14, 1992, announced that foreign institutional investors (FIIs) could henceforth invest in all listed securities in both primary and secondary markets. FIIs are required to register with the Securities and Exchange Board of India before making any investment. The market is effectively considered open from November 1, 1992.

Investments are subject to a ceiling of 24 percent of issued share capital for the total holdings of all registered FIIs and 5 percent for the holding of a single FII in any one company. The ceiling includes the conversion of fully and partly convertible debentures issued by the company.

Indonesia   Until December 1987, the market was closed to foreign investment. In December 1987, the government introduced deregulation measures that allowed foreigners to purchase shares in eight nonjoint venture companies. On September 16, 1989, the minister of finance of the Republic of Indonesia issued Decree Number 1055/KMK.013/1989, which allowed foreigners to purchase up to 49 percent of all companies' listed shares, including foreign joint ventures but excluding banks. The Bank Act, 1992, enacted on October 30, 1992, allowed foreigners to invest in up to 49 percent of the listed shares in three categories of banks—private national, state, and joint foreign. Currently only private national banks are listed.

In a few markets, such as Indonesia, companies do not list all the shares outstanding. For its indexes, the IFC counts only the shares listed at the stock exchange.

Jordan   The market is considered generally 49 percent investable.

Korea   Since January 1, 1992, authorized foreign investors have been allowed to acquire up to 10 percent of the capital of listed companies; some corporate statute limitations apply (e.g., POSCO & KEPCO, 8 percent, and some are permitted up to 25 percent). The 10 percent limit applies separately to common and preferred stock. Under the revised regulations of June 22, 1992, effective in July 1992, companies whose foreign holdings already exceeded 10 percent could apply to Korea's securities and exchange commission to increase their limit to 25 percent. As of March 1993, four companies had received permission: Korea Electronic Parts, Korea Long-Term Credit Bank, Trigem Computer, and Young Chang Akki. The ceiling automatically declines when foreign-held shares are sold to domestic investors.

Malaysia   The limit on foreign ownership of Malaysian stocks is subject to some debate. Bank Negara, the central bank, restricts the ownership of banks and financial institutions by foreigners to 30 percent. However, these limits do not appear to be strictly enforced. Under the 1989 Banking and Financial Institutions Act, the approval of the minister of finance is required before foreign investors can buy or sell shares of a licensed bank or finance company amounting to 5 percent or more. Certain nonbank stocks have different foreign share holding limits for tax and other reasons. These are MISC, Proton, Telekom, Tenaga Nasional, Tai Wah Garments, and Yantzekiang. All other stocks are open to foreign portfolio investment without any limits. However, the approval of the Foreign Investment Committee is required for acquiring 15 percent or more of the voting power of a company by any one foreign interest and for acquiring the assets or interests of a company when they exceed M$5 million, whether by Malaysian or foreign interests. Except for a few specific cases, the IFC uses 100 percent for most stocks and 30 percent for banks and financial institutions.

Mexico
Foreign portfolio investment is permitted in designated classes of shares, and since May 1989 in most other shares through the use of the Nafinsa Trust arrangement. It is now considered generally 100 percent investable, except for banks, where foreign ownership is restricted to 30 percent.

Nigeria
Closed to foreign investment.

Pakistan
The market is considered 100 percent investable from February 22, 1991.

Philippines
National law requires that a minimum of 60 percent of the issued shares of domestic corporations should be owned by Philippine nationals. To ensure compliance, Philippine companies typically issue two classes of stock: A shares, which may be traded only among Philippine nationals, and B shares, which may be traded to either Philippine nationals or foreign investors and which usually amount to 40 percent of the total. Mass media, retail trade, and rural banking companies are closed to foreign investors.

Portugal
The market is considered generally 100 percent investable; some corporate statute limitations apply, particularly regarding shares issued in privatizations.

Taiwan
The market was opened to foreigners on January 1, 1991, though foreign investors must meet high registration requirements and total cash inflows from abroad cannot currently exceed an official ceiling of $2.5 billion. There is a 10 percent limit on aggregate foreign ownership of issued capital. The domestic transportation industry is closed to foreign investors.

Thailand
Various Thai laws restrict foreign share holdings in Thai companies engaged in certain areas of business. The Banking Law restricts foreign ownership in banks to 49 percent. The Alien Business Law, administered by the Ministry of Commerce, restricts foreign ownership of stocks in specified sectors to 49 percent. In addition, other laws provide similar restrictions on foreign ownership. Restrictions are also faced by foreign investors through limits imposed by company by-laws, which range from 15 percent to 65 percent. The Foreign Board was established in 1988 to facilitate trading in shares registered in foreign names.

Turkey
The market is considered 100 percent investable from August 1989.

Venezuela   Nonfinancial stocks are considered generally 100 percent investable from January 1, 1990, but some restricted classes do exist. Bank stocks are currently not available.

Zimbabwe   Effectively closed to foreign investment by virtue of severe exchange controls.

References

Alexander, G., Cheol Eun, and S. Janakiramanan. 1988. International listing and stock returns: Some empirical evidence. *Journal of Financial and Quantitative Analysis* 23 (2): 135–52.

Bailey, Warren, and Julapa Jagtiani. 1992. Time varying premiums for international investment: Some empirical estimates. Cornell University and Syracuse University. Mimeo.

Bekaert, Geert. 1993. Market segmentation and investment barriers in emerging equity markets. In *Portfolio investment in developing countries,* eds. Stijn Claessens and Sudarshan Gooptu. World Bank Discussion Papers, no. 228. Washington, D.C.: The World Bank.

Black, Fischer. 1974. International capital market equilibrium with investment barriers. *Journal of Financial Economics* 1: 337–52.

———. 1978. The ins and outs of foreign investment. *Financial Analyst Journal* 34 (May/June): 1–7.

Buckberg, Elaine. 1993. Emerging stock markets and international asset pricing. In *Portfolio investment in developing countries,* eds. Stijn Claessens and Sudarshan Gooptu. World Bank Discussion Papers, no. 228. Washington, D.C.: The World Bank.

Claessens, Stijn, Susmita Dasgupta, and Jack Glen. 1993. Stock price behavior in emerging stock markets. In *Portfolio investment in developing countries,* eds. Stijn Claessens and Sudarshan Gooptu. World Bank Discussion Paper, no. 228. Washington, D.C.: The World Bank.

Demirguc-Kunt, Asli, and Harry Huizinga. 1992. Barriers to portfolio investment in emerging markets. PRE Working Paper no. 984. The World Bank.

De Santis, Giorgio. 1993. Asset pricing and portfolio diversification: Evidence from emerging financial markets. In *Portfolio investment in developing countries,* eds. Stijn Claessens and Sudarshan Gooptu. World Bank Discussion Papers, no. 228. Washington, D.C.: The World Bank.

Divecha, Arjun, Jaime Drach, and Dan Stefek. 1992. Emerging markets: A quantitative perspective. *Journal of Portfolio Management* 19 (fall): 41–56.

Diwan, Ishac, Vihang Errunza, and Lemma Senbet. 1993a. The pricing of country funds and their role in capital mobilization for emerging economies. PRE Working Paper no. 1058. The World Bank.

———. 1993b. Country funds for emerging economies. In *Portfolio investment in developing countries,* eds. Stijn Claessens and Sudarshan Gooptu. World Bank Discussion Papers, no. 228. Washington, D.C.: The World Bank.

Errunza, Vihang, and Etienne Losq. 1985. International asset pricing under mild segmentation: Theory and test. *Journal of Finance* 40:105–24.

———. 1989. Capital flows, international asset pricing and investors' welfare: a multi-country framework. *Journal of Finance* 44:1025–37.

Errunza, Vihang, Etienne Losq, and Prasad Padmanabhan. 1992. Test of integration, mild segmentation and segmentation hypotheses. *Journal of Banking and Finance* 16:949–72.

Eun, Cheol. 1990. International ownership structure and the cost of capital: A case study of Swiss firms. University of Maryland. Mimeo.

Eun, Cheol S., and S. Janakiramanan. 1986. A model of international asset pricing with a constraint on foreign equity ownership. *Journal of Finance* 41:897–914.

———. 1990. International ownership structure and the firm value. University of Maryland. Mimeo, July, 1–29.

Eun, Cheol, Stijn Claessens, and Kwang Jun. 1993. International trade of assets, pricing externalities and the cost of capital. In *Portfolio investment in developing countries,* eds. Stijn Claessens and Sudarshan Gooptu. World Bank Discussion Papers, no. 228. Washington, D.C.: The World Bank.

Fama, Eugene. 1991. Efficient capital markets: II. *Journal of Finance* 46(5): 1575–1617.

Fama, Eugene, and James Macbeth. 1973. Risk, return and equilibrium: Empirical tests. *Journal of Political Economy* 81:607–36.

Gibbons, Michael. 1980. Econometrics methods for testing a class of financial models—An application of the nonlinear multivariate regression model. Ph.D. diss., University of Chicago.

———. 1982. Multivariate tests of financial models: A new approach. *Journal of Financial Economics* 10:3–27.

Gibbons, Michael R., Stephen A. Ross, and Jay Shanken. 1989. A test of the efficiency of a given portfolio. *Econometrica* 57:1121–52.

Harvey, Campbell R. 1993. Portfolio enhancement using emerging markets and conditioning information. In *Portfolio investment in developing countries,* eds. Stijn Claessens and Sudarshan Gooptu. World Bank Discussion Papers, no. 228. Washington, D.C.: The World Bank.

Hietala, Pekka. 1989. Asset pricing in partially segmented markets: Evidence from the Finnish Market. *Journal of Finance* 44(3): 697–718.

International Finance Corporation. *Emerging markets factbook.* Various years.

Jorion, Philippe, and Eduardo Schwartz. 1986. Integration vs. segmentation in the Canadian stock market. *Journal of Finance* 41:603–14.

Lessard, Donald. 1973. International portfolio diversification: A multivariate analysis for a group of Latin American countries. *Journal of Finance* 28(3):619–33.

———. 1974. World, national and industry factors in equity returns. *Journal of Finance* 29:379–91.

Litzenberger, Robert H., and Krishna Ramaswamy. 1979. The effects of personal taxes and dividends on capital asset prices: Theory and empirical evidence. *Journal of Financial Economics* 7(2): 163–96.

Mankiw, N. Gregory, and A. Shapiro. 1986. Risk and return: consumption versus market beta. *Review of Economics and Statistics.* 68 (August): 452–59.

Mathieson, Donald J., and Liliana Rojas-Suárez. 1993. Liberalization of the capital account: Experiences and issues. IMF Occasional Paper no. 103. Washington, D.C.: International Monetary Fund.

Mittoo, Usha R. 1992. Additional evidence on integration in the Canadian stock market. *Journal of Finance* 47(5): 2035–54.

Reisen, Helmut, and Bernard Fischer. 1993. *Financial opening: Policy issues and experiences in developing countries.* Paris: OECD Development Center.

Stehle, Richard. 1977. An empirical test of the alternative hypotheses of national and international pricing of risky assets. *Journal of Finance* 32:493–502.

Stulz, René M. 1981. On the effects of barriers to international investment. *Journal of Finance* 36:923–34.

Stulz, René M., and Walter Wasserfallen. 1992. Foreign equity restrictions and shareholder wealth maximization: Theory and evidence. NBER Working Paper no. A217. Cambridge, Mass.: National Bureau of Economic Research, November.

Tesar, Linda, and Ingrid Werner. 1993. U.S. Equity investment in emerging stock markets. In *Portfolio investment in developing countries,* eds. Stijn Claessens and Sudarshan Gooptu. World Bank Discussion Papers, no. 228. Washington, D.C.: The World Bank.

World Bank. 1993. *World debt tables, 1993/94.* Washington, D.C.: The World Bank.

Comment   Michael Dooley

This paper attempts to utilize the predictions of a capital asset pricing model to draw inferences about the extent of integration of emerging stock markets with equity markets in industrial countries. The basic idea is straightforward and appealing. If the markets are well integrated, excess returns of individual stocks in the emerging markets should be related to their covariance with the industrial country market portfolio. If the emerging markets are not integrated, excess returns should be related to their covariance with the domestic market portfolio.

One reason to be concerned about the extent of integration is that it might help explain historically large inflows to emerging stock markets since 1989 and the spectacular increases in the market value of these equities. An interesting conjecture is that foreign investors have "finally" recognized that such equities are part of an efficient portfolio. If this is the driving force, we can understand the large inflows in part as a response of international investors to opportunities to improve their risk-return trade-off. Such inflows would be expected even if the expected rate of return in emerging markets were the same as in the world portfolio.

Another possibility is that emerging markets become more attractive for a given level of integration because expected average returns have improved. Such an improvement might be unrelated to diversification but instead be a result of changes in economic policies or the economic environment. In this case the equilibrium excess return on any individual stock would be related to its covariance with the domestic portfolio. In fact, a reasonable interpretation is that recent capital inflows are returns of flight capital. In this case the emerging markets have not become more integrated since residents of the developing countries have always had access to both domestic and international equity

Michael Dooley is professor of economics at the University of California, Santa Cruz, and a research associate of the National Bureau of Economic Research.

markets. The evidence from excess rates of return reported here are consistent with this hypothesis.

The first result reported is that excess returns are better predicted by a model that assumes segmentation of markets. One reason this might be the case is that legal restrictions continue to limit nonresidents' holdings of individual stocks in many emerging markets. In these circumstances it would not be surprising were excess returns to reflect the different legal and effective "access" of nonresidents to individual stocks. To control for this possibility the authors use an "investability index" published by the International Finance Corporation (IFC) that measures the intensity of legal restrictions on emerging market stocks. As the authors point out, this proxy is imperfect and it is available for only a few years. But it seems clear that any test of integration of these markets should attempt to control for legal restrictions on nonresident holdings.

Controlling for access, the authors again test the segmentation hypothesis using the covariance of excess rates of return as the measure of integration. The results are that neither access nor covariance with the world portfolio seems to predict excess returns. In contrast, access does seem to explain ex post price earnings ratios.

This result suggests a fundamental difficulty in testing the capital asset pricing model in these markets. As the authors point out, legal restrictions were liberalized rapidly in many of these markets over the short time period for which measures of access are available. If these liberalizations were unanticipated, which seems quite likely for individual stocks, ex post excess returns are very poor predictors of expected returns. While realizations might be unbiased estimates of expected values, the noise might make it difficult to find the systematic pattern suggested by the capital asset pricing model.

The point is probably more general than the authors suggest. It seems quite implausible that the kinds of movements in stock prices observed in recent years in emerging markets could have been expected. Ex post rates of return on the dollar-denominated Brady bonds issued by governments of these countries have also been very high and in this case there clearly was no change in the access of nonresidents to these securities or the integration of world bond markets. Finally, privatization and other policy changes have generated large and probably unexpected changes in the market valuation of firms in emerging markets. In the context of first-order changes in first moments for returns on all investments in emerging markets, it is not surprising that the relatively subtle implications of a capital asset pricing model for first and second moments are difficult to capture.

Comment   Don Lessard

Claessens and Rhee examine the impact of the opening of emerging markets to inward foreign investment on the pricing of emerging market assets from two perspectives: whether the risk-return relationship for these assets is consistent with some form of a worldwide capital asset pricing model (CAPM), and whether within country, cross-sectional differences in asset prices correspond to differences in measurable barriers to inward investment.

The answer to the first question—whether the ex ante risk return relationship for emerging market equities is consistent with a worldwide CAPM—is definitely not or probably not. For ten of the sixteen markets examined, integration is rejected, and segmentation is not rejected for any of them.

These results are disappointing, but not surprising. The tests employed require long data series from relatively stable risk and pricing structures, and yield mixed results even for major world markets that have been open to foreign investment for some time and whose institutional structures have been relatively stable. Given that most of the countries in Claessens and Rhee's sample significantly altered the rules for inward investment within the sample period, often in conjunction with other policy and institutional changes such as drastic deficit reduction, monetary reform, privatization of major state enterprises, the establishment of vehicles for contractual savings, and the restructuring of external obligations, it would have been a surprise if strong results had been obtained.

Even the finding that segmentation cannot be rejected for any of the markets may reveal little about the relationship between ex ante returns and risk. It could also reflect the fact that returns in these countries have experienced large country-specific and countrywide "surprises" due to changes in objective local prospects, in local perceptions of those prospects, or in world investor perceptions of those prospects or access to those markets. However, since the tests are well specified and conducted with great care, the results demonstrate the limits of this class of tests that rely on return data alone, rather than any shortcoming in their application by Claessens and Rhee.

The second approach, although less technically sophisticated, offers much more promise. It does not rely on returns data alone, but seeks to explain differences in market valuations of specific stocks, and by inference the discount rates imbedded in them, by measurable differences in barriers to inward foreign investment. Price-to-earnings (P/E) ratios, their dependent variable, are not a very good basis for comparison for two reasons. Earnings are not measured uniformly across countries because of differences in accounting practices and rates of inflation. Second, even within countries, firms differ in their

Don Lessard is professor of international management at the Sloan School of Management at the Massachusetts Institute of Technology.

mix of assets in place, which give rise to current earnings, and growth opportunities, which give rise to future earnings.

Claessens and Rhee are careful, though, and make these comparisons only within countries, mitigating the inflation and accounting issues. Most of the within-country variation in investability, as determined by the International Finance Corporation (IFC), is the result of differences in (*a*) the sector represented by the stock, given that many countries are more restrictive with respect to foreign ownership in banking, for example, than in industry at large; or (*b*) the stock's market capitalization, since small cap stocks are deemed to be less investable, presumably because of the fixed cost involved in following a particular company. Claessens and Rhee control for the bank versus industry distinction, and the result that P/E is a positive function of investability appears to hold. Given the size factor, though, the results must be viewed with caution. P/E itself may be correlated with a stock's market capitalization. Perhaps some other control for size that is not correlated with earnings, such as sales, could be employed.

The larger question with respect to emerging markets, which both sets of tests address only obliquely, is the extent to which the boom that many of these markets have experienced in recent years is the result of changes in the prospects of those countries, or the recognition of these prospects or access to these markets by outside investors. While disentangling the two sets of factors would be very difficult, there is promise. The relationship between P/E ratios and sovereign debt prices/yields, for example, would largely separate country prospects from foreign investor awareness or access, since the sovereign debt has always been held primarily by foreign banks, and typically in large enough concentrations so that the fixed costs of following a country cannot have been a major consideration. Awareness might be proxied by the marketing of a major stock issue on world markets, such as the Telmex flotation. Further, the diffusion of these effects across different assets from one country as well as across countries could provide important insights regarding causality.

Both sets of tests, and much of the recent literature on emerging markets, assume on the basis of the magnitude of capital flight from these countries that the binding barriers are on inward rather than outward investment. This assumption seems correct on its face, and I have used it many times, but upon reflection it may be invalid. Clearly, wealthy individual investors from less-developed countries have been able to diversify abroad, but less wealthy individuals who cannot effectively overcome the fixed costs of investing overseas and regulated investors such as pension funds or insurance companies are effectively restricted. For a country such as Chile, where pension funds in aggregate are very large relative to the value of local stocks and bonds, outward restrictions may be binding. Of course, inward or outward restrictions have a similar effect in that they cause local dimensions of risk to be priced, but the specification of the spanning portfolios would differ. While this appears to be primarily a technical matter, it may also reflect a policy bias—that the problem of emerging countries is that they are not sufficiently open to inward foreign investment. The bigger issue in terms of world welfare is the opportunity cost imposed on local savers by restrictions that limit them to home assets that are highly risky on their own, but only weakly correlated with asset returns in the rest of the world. This was the point of my early work on international portfolio diversification for developing countries (Lessard 1973). Merton (1990) has proposed that rate of return swaps on broad market indexes be used to facilitate market integration. This recommendation is especially relevant for emerging markets where concerns over corporate governance and capital flight are paramount.

References

Lessard, Donald R. 1973. International portfolio diversification: A multivariate analysis for a group of Latin American countries. *Journal of Finance* 28 (3): 619–33.

Merton, Robert C. 1990. The financial system and economic performance. *Journal of Financial Services Research* 4:263–300.

6   International Experiences with Securities Transaction Taxes

John Y. Campbell and Kenneth A. Froot

6.1   Introduction

During the past few years securities transaction taxes (STTs) have been debated in a number of countries. In some places, the debate has focused on the effects of changing technology and deregulation for sustaining or removing transaction taxes. In others, shortages of revenues and a change in atmosphere from the 1980s have led to talk of instituting taxes anew. The U.S. government, for example, reviewed a proposal during the 1990 budget negotiations for a broad-based 0.5 percent tax on transactions in stocks, bonds, and exchange-traded derivatives. The Congressional Research Service estimated at the time that such a tax might raise $10 billion in revenue, and this figure has been widely cited in subsequent discussions of STTs. Moreover, in 1993 the Clinton administration proposed a fixed fourteen-cent tax on transactions in futures contracts and options on futures.

Based on this, it seems safe to conclude that STTs are important because of their clear and current policy relevance. However, there is at least one other reason that recent international experiences with transaction taxes are of interest: STTs reveal the nature and scope of powerful underlying changes in international capital markets, and offer a glimpse into a future in which government policy not so much disciplines, but is instead disciplined by, competition in modern capital markets.

In this paper we consider the international experience with STTs. We argue that this experience is in many ways quite varied. There is, for example, an almost bewildering variety of details in their nature, size, and implementation.

John Y. Campbell is the Otto Eckstein Professor of Applied Economics at Harvard University and a research associate of the National Bureau of Economic Research. Kenneth A. Froot is professor of business administration at Harvard Business School and a research associate of the National Bureau of Economic Research.

Transaction tax rates may vary with the type of financial instrument (equities typically being taxed at higher rates than debt instruments or derivatives), with the location of trade (on or off an exchange, at home or abroad), and with the identity of the buyer or seller (domestic or foreign resident, market maker, or general trader). But we also point out a number of similarities across countries. For example, as table 6.1 shows, while many countries currently impose STTs of varying sizes, there is a marked recent trend toward lower taxes.[1] To emphasize the differences and underlying similarities in some detail, we begin by describing the apparently dissimilar experiences of two countries, Sweden and the United Kingdom.

Next we try to provide an overall framework for understanding STTs. We propose two principles that might be used to rationalize transaction tax rates across securities. The first principle is that transactions which give rise to the same pattern of payoffs should pay the same tax. Although this seems appealing on prior grounds, we show that it is conceptually impossible to apply this principle consistently. Accordingly, most actual tax systems rely on a second principle, that transactions which use the same resources should pay the same tax. Different countries tax different types of resources: Sweden, for example, taxes domestic brokerage services (the Swedish resources used in matching buyers and sellers), whereas the United Kingdom taxes registration (the legal transfer of ownership of U.K. equities).

Any tax gives people an incentive to change their behavior to reduce their tax liability. We argue that in the case of STTs, several changes in behavior are relevant. First, investors can change the location of trade, moving transactions off-exchange or abroad. Second, investors can trade substitute securities which generate payoffs similar to those whose transactions are taxed. Third, investors can choose not to trade, accepting a change in the payoffs they receive in order to reduce their STT liability. We discuss the importance of each of these behavioral changes for different STT systems, in particular the Swedish and British systems. We show that offshore trading has been a particularly important response to the Swedish equity STT, while investors have responded to the Swedish fixed-income STT by trading untaxed local substitutes. The British STT cannot be avoided by trading abroad, but it does stimulate trading in untaxed substitute assets and also seems to reduce total trading volume to some degree.

In addition to examining the Swedish and British cases, we look at the econometric evidence on the elasticity of trading volume with respect to changes in transaction taxes. There are a number of estimates of this elasticity in the literature; however, few take into account the margins of substitution that we describe.

---

1. Sweden, Finland, and Taiwan have recently cut or removed altogether their turnover taxes. Several other countries, such as Australia, Japan, and the United Kingdom have recently considered reductions in existing tax rates.

Table 6.1   **Transactions Taxes around the World (through 1993)**

Country	Tax Size 1991	Description	Notes; Changes since 1991
Australia	0.3%	Transaction tax	Additional stamp tax removed in 1991
Austria	0.15%	Transfer tax	May be avoided by trading off exchange
	0.06%	Arrangement fee	May be avoided by trading off exchange
	0.04% - 0.09%	Courtage fee	
Belgium	0.17%	Stamp tax on buys and sells	No tax ex country; maximum of 10,000 Belgian francs
	0.025%	Stock market fee	No tax ex country; maximum of 2,500 Belgian francs
Canada		No taxes	
Denmark		No taxes for nonresidents	
Finland	0.5%	Transaction tax	Waived if both parties foreign, eliminated in 1992
France	0.15%	Trading tax	Tax on trades > 1 million francs, rate is doubled on smaller transactions, may be avoided by trading ex country
Germany	0.125%	Boersmumsatz Steuer	Residents only
	0.06%	Courtage tax (official broker fee)	Tax may be avoided by trading ex country
Hong Kong	0.25%	Stamp duty	
	0.006%	Special levy	May be avoided by trading off market
	0.050%	Exchange levy	May be avoided by trading off market
Italy	0.05%	Stamp duty tax	Tax may be avoided by trading ex country
Japan	0.30%	Sales tax	May be avoided by trading ex country
Malaysia	0.05%	Clearing fee	Maximum $100; may be avoided by trading off exchange
	0.3%	Transfer stamp duty on purchases and sales	Eliminated in 1992
Netherlands		No taxes	
New Zealand	0.0057% plus per trade fee	Transaction levy	May be avoided by trading off exchange; eliminated in 1992
Norway		No taxes	
Singapore	0.1%	Contract stamp duty	May be avoided by trading off exchange
	0.05%	Clearing fee	Maximum S$100, may be avoided by trading off exchange
	0.2%	Transfer stamp duty	Purchases only; eliminated in 1992
Sweden	0.5%	Turnover tax	Tax may be avoided by trading ex country; eliminated in 1991
Switzerland	0.0005%	Exchange fee	Tax may be avoided by trading ex country
	0.01%	State tax	Tax may be avoided by trading ex country
	0.075%	Stamp tax	Tax may be avoided by trading ex country
United States	0.0033%	SEC fee	
United Kingdom	2 pounds	Levy	On trades over £5,000
	0.5%	Stamp duty tax	On purchases only

Source: UBS Phillips and Drew.

We conclude by drawing some lessons for the U.S. debate. Some proponents of an STT favor it on the grounds that it would reduce trading volume, while others seem more interested in the revenue that might be raised by the tax. An STT will disappoint both types of proponent if it causes investors to move trading into offshore markets or untaxed assets. Accordingly we argue that an STT along British lines would be far more workable than a Swedish-style STT. Even a British-style STT, however, would likely lead to major behavioral changes and we argue that the widely cited figure of $10 billion in revenue for a 0.5 percent STT is too optimistic.

6.2   Case Studies

6.2.1   Transaction Taxes in Sweden

Summary of the Swedish Transaction Tax Regime

Sweden's recent experiment with transaction taxes began in January 1984 with a levy of fifty basis points on both the purchase and sale of equities.[2] Support for the tax came from the Labour Party—the tax was approved by Parliament over the objections of the Finance Ministry and business sectors. Labour did not view trading in itself as undesirable; however, it objected to the idea that bright young people were being paid so much for performing what seemed to them essentially unproductive tasks.

Partly as a result of this sentiment, the tax was levied directly on registered Swedish brokerage services. Such services (plus those of a registered Swedish exchange bank) were required for local stock transactions of meaningful size between domestic residents as well as those between domestic and foreign residents. Trades between two foreign principals were taxed only if they involved a security registered in Sweden. No tax was levied on transfers of stock ownership unless a broker was involved. For example, no tax was levied on gifts or inheritances of stock. In addition, private trades involving domestic entities were free of taxation, provided that the trades were small enough and the entity did not trade too frequently.

The initial legislation also included a tax on stock options. The tax was for two hundred basis points (for round-trip transactions), calculated as a percentage of the option premium. In addition, exercise of the option was treated like a transaction in the underlying stock, thereby resulting in an additional levy of one hundred basis points (based upon the exercise price).[3] As the tax was in-

2. The tax was announced on October 24, 1983; that day the Swedish All-Share equity index fell 2.2 percent. See Umlauf (1993).

3. Unlike options, warrants were taxed on the amount of stock they (potentially) represented, and at the same rate as stocks. Conversions from warrants into stock were not taxed. Futures transactions in equity-linked instruments were taxed at the same rate as stock transactions, with the tax applying to the underlying notional amount.

tended to resemble a kind of sales tax, that is, a tax on final consumption of local brokerage services, interdealer trades, which were viewed as "intermediate" and not final trades, were exempted.

Over the following two years, the government came under pressure to raise more revenue from the tax. In July 1986, Parliament acceded, doubling the rates on equity and equity-derivative transactions.[4] Moreover, in early 1987, Parliament broadened the scope of the tax to include interdealer equity trades (at one hundred basis points per round trip, half the rate of the brokerage tax).

Also in early 1987, several large losses in interest-rate futures and options were announced. The largest and most highly criticized of these were the city of Stockholm (which lost SEK [Swedish kronor] 450 million) and the insurance company Folksam (which lost SEK 300 million). Soon thereafter Stig Malm, chairman both of the Swedish Trade Union Council and of Folksam, attacked the money markets "for creating economic instability and excessive wage differentials" (see Lybeck 1991, 162). In September 1987, through the trade union council, Malm proposed a turnover tax to "reduce the overly large and socially worthless activities on the money market" (Lybeck 1991, 156). The government followed up on Malm's initiative, although its official reasoning for a turnover tax on money-market instruments was to create "neutrality" with the stock market's tax. While the government actually worked out a legislative prototype almost immediately, the fixed-income turnover tax did not actually take effect until January 1, 1989.

The tax applied to fixed-income securities, including government debt and associated derivatives, such as interest-rate futures and options. The rates on these instruments varied, but were considerably lower than those on equity, reaching a maximum of only fifteen basis points of the underlying notional or cash amount. For example, the tax rate on a round-trip transaction was three basis points for bonds with maturities exceeding five years, one basis point for one-year bonds, and 0.2 basis points for maturities of less than ninety days.[5]

Beginning in 1989, the political climate began to change. Disappointment with the revenues raised, and concerns that taxes on the money market merely raised the costs of government borrowing, led to an erosion in political support for turnover taxes. The taxes on fixed-income securities were abolished as of April 15, 1990. On January 1, 1991, tax rates on the remaining instruments were cut by one-half. Then on December 1, 1991, all remaining security transaction taxes were completely removed.

---

4. The tax increase was announced on March 11, 1986; that day the Swedish All-Share index declined by 0.8 percent.

5. Intermediate maturities received intermediate rates: four-, three-, and two-year bonds were taxed at 2.6, 2.0, and 1.5 basis points, respectively. For securities with maturities of less than one year, the tax levy increased linearly with the investor's holding period. The tax on fixed-income futures contracts was levied on the notional amount, at a rate equivalent to that on the underlying instrument.

Effects on Volume and Location of Equity Transactions

Several studies have argued that the stock transaction tax had a negative effect on local Swedish trading (see, for example, Umlauf 1993 and Ericsson and Lindgren 1992). Table 6.2 reviews the evidence, showing the location of trading in stocks of about a dozen large Swedish companies.[6] Unfortunately, data prior to 1988 are not available. The data include volume in Stockholm, London, and the United States,[7] and trading in both restricted and unrestricted shares.[8]

Table 6.2 clearly shows a high level of offshore trading in 1988 and 1989, when the stock turnover tax was at its maximum level. For example, only 27 and 23 percent of trading in Ericsson, Sweden's most actively traded company, took place in Stockholm in 1988 and 1989, respectively. Comparable average fractions across all stocks in table 6.2 were 61 and 57 percent of total volume. The fraction of trade in Stockholm continued to decline through 1991, when it reached a low of 52 percent. By 1992 (after taxes had been completely removed), trade in Sweden had increased to 41 percent for Ericsson and to 56 percent for the average stock in table 6.2.[9]

The effect of the tax on local trading volume does not appear to be instantaneous. For example, even though the tax was instituted prior to 1988, the fraction of trading taking place in Stockholm declined from 1988 through 1991, when tax rates were cut. Such lagged trading volume responses are not too surprising in practice, as it is likely that shifts in institutional capacity and expertise—needed inputs in the production of brokerage services—take time.

The tax on equity transactions was avoided in different ways and to different extents by different types of traders. Foreign investors were most able to use non-Swedish brokers for transactions in Swedish stocks. One way to see this behavior in the data is to compare the degree of trading migration in unrestricted versus restricted shares. This sheds some light on the relative behavior of foreign and domestic clienteles since unrestricted shares are disproportionately owned by foreigners and restricted shares are owned exclusively by domestics.

6. We thank Lief Vindevag of the Stockholm Stock Exchange for supplying us with the data used in tables 6.2 and 6.3.

7. Trading in the United States is small, and is predominantly on the NASDAQ (an over-the-counter electronic exchange). This probably reflects liquidity considerations (London and Stockholm are open during the same hours, and therefore help provide liquidity for one another) more than it does the profile of shareholder domiciles.

8. Some Swedish shares carry ownership restrictions, while others do not. Restricted shares can only be owned and voted by Swedish nationals. Transactions taxes apply to trades in both types of shares, as long as a registered Swedish brokerage house is involved.

9. Other authors have found responses of local trading volume to transactions costs, including taxes, at least as large as this. Lindgren and Westlund (1990), for example, estimate the long-run elasticity of trading volume on the Stockholm market with respect to transactions costs to be approximately -1. Jackson and O'Donnell (1985) estimate elasticities in the range of -1 to -1.7 in their study of U.K. stocks.

Table 6.2   Trading of Swedish Stocks inside Sweden (percentage of turnover in
London, New York, and Stockholm taking place in Stockholm)

	1988	1989	1990	1991	1992
Aga	59%	64%	63%	47%	53%
Alfa Laval		71%	41%		
ASEA	50%	39%	36%	34%	56%
Astra	88%	59%	44%	34%	36%
Atlas Copco	51%	40%	26%	44%	44%
Electrolux	43%	32%	46%	41%	45%
Ericsson	27%	23%	26%	28%	41%
Gambro	97%	92%	31%	35%	58%
Pharmacia	39%	33%			
Procordia			78%	68%	55%
Incentive				75%	79%
Saab-Scania	80%	77%	70%		
Sandvik	80%	51%	56%	56%	55%
SCA	84%	84%	88%	76%	73%
SKF	43%	50%	59%	45%	39%
Skandia			75%	57%	72%
Stora		78%	77%	76%	72%
Trelleberg		73%	73%	69%	81%
Volvo	55%	38%	54%	50%	50%
Average	61%	57%	56%	52%	56%

Source: Central Bank of Sweden.

Table 6.3 provides this breakdown, taking those companies from table 6.2 for which there is liquid trade in restricted shares. The table reports the fraction of trade in *unrestricted* shares that took place in Stockholm relative to total trade in New York, London, and Stockholm. The first point to note is that, during the 1988–91 period when the tax was in place, the fraction of trading taking place in Stockholm was much lower for unrestricted shares. For example, during 1988, only 47 percent of trade in unrestricted shares took place in Stockholm (versus 61 percent for all shares—see table 6.2). After the tax was removed, however, trading of unrestricted shares in Stockholm rebounded considerably, rising from 40 percent in 1991 to 50 percent in 1992. This evidence suggests that foreign investors tended to substitute more toward trading abroad than did domestic investors, who substituted more toward not trading at all.

Naturally, domestic investors also had an incentive to evade the tax when they did trade. However, for them it was harder. Domestic investors had to establish an offshore domicile or company if they were to avoid using a Swedish broker for transactions. And they were taxed in the process: a tax equal to three times the round-trip tax on equity applied to funds moved offshore.

Perhaps the clearest way to measure foreign investors' response to the tax is to use data on the trading patterns of specific foreign investors. One such data

Table 6.3   Trading of Swedish Unrestricted Shares inside Sweden (percentage of turnover in London, New York, and Stockholm taking place in Stockholm)

	1988	1989	1990	1991	1992
Aga	30%	34%	46%	34%	42%
Alfa Laval		67%	24%		
ASEA	35%	15%	32%	26%	49%
Astra	77%	33%	24%	18%	30%
Atlas Copco	49%	40%	26%	44%	44%
Electrolux	43%	32%	46%	41%	45%
Ericsson	27%	23%	26%	28%	41%
Gambro	95%	85%	23%	27%	48%
Pharmacia	11%	19%			
Procordia			55%	43%	45%
Incentive				61%	75%
Investor					76%
Saab-Scania	58%	50%	50%		
Sandvik	60%	34%	24%	39%	48%
SCA	71%	65%	73%	61%	68%
SKF	34%	34%	53%	39%	36%
Securitas					16%
Skandia			75%	57%	72%
Stora		68%	66%	61%	68%
Trelleborg		40%	34%	36%	70%
Volvo	25%	27%	34%	26%	31%
Average	47%	42%	42%	40%	50%

Source: Central Bank of Sweden.

base is maintained by Frank Russell Securities, Inc. Russell monitors the transactions costs paid by a group of large U.S. institutional clients.[10] These clients traded large amounts of international equities. It is worth noting that these U.S. institutions found trading in the United States considerably cheaper than in other countries. Figure 6.1 reports average taxes, fees, and agency commissions paid by these institutions when trading in securities from the world's ten largest equity markets. Average direct costs total about thirty basis points in the United States, compared with about seventy-six basis points in Japan and ninety-six basis points in the United Kingdom.

Figure 6.2 depicts average round-trip trading costs paid by large U.S. institutions when trading Swedish equities. The figure shows that during the 1987–92 sample period, commissions remained roughly constant, while taxes paid fell

10. The data base, assembled by Richard Kos and Thomas Morton, analyzes the trades of U.S. institutional clients that are members of Russell's portfolio verification service. Altogether the data include well over two-million transactions, recorded over six years (1987–92), from approximately five thousand actively managed portfolios. Equity securities from over thirty-five counties are represented in the data.

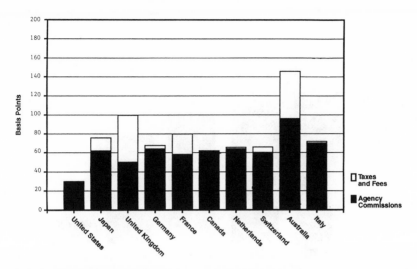

Fig. 6.1   1992 global trading costs, ten largest markets
Source: Frank Russell Securities, Inc.

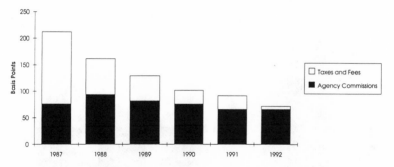

Fig. 6.2   Round-trip trading costs in Swedish Equities for U.S. institutional investors
Source: Frank Russell Securities, Inc.

from 136 basis points in 1987 to only 6 basis points in 1992. During the 1987–90 period there was no change in the statutory tax rate, yet the average round-trip tax payment fell by over 100 basis points. Thus, whereas these U.S. institutions paid 68 percent (136 basis points relative to the statutory rate of 200) of the statutory tax in 1987, they were paying only 13 percent (26/200) of the statutory rate by 1990. U.S. institutions (and their brokers) were increasingly able to evade the tax by eliminating the use of Swedish brokers when trading in Sweden or by exchanging Swedish securities in London or New York.

It appears also that the Swedish tax had only a marginal effect on the volume of trade in Swedish equities by foreign institutions. Figures 6.3A and 6.3B

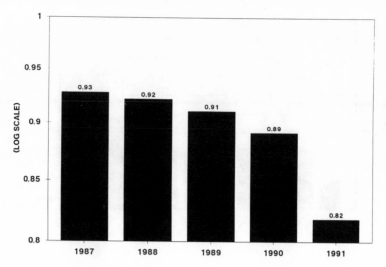

Fig. 6.3A   Ratio of median equity turnover ratios, Stockholm versus the United States

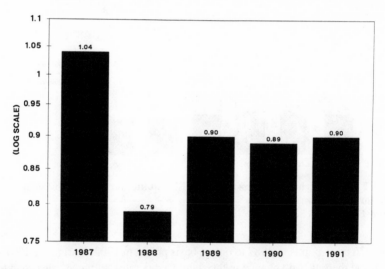

Fig. 6.3B   Ratio of median turnover ratios, average of Stockholm versus that of sixteen other markets

show the Swedish-share turnover rates for Russell's investors relative to U.S.-share turnover and to average total turnover. There is little evidence that total trading volume in Swedish stocks responded strongly to changes in taxation of trades in Stockholm. This lends additional support to the view that international investors easily evaded Swedish turnover taxes.

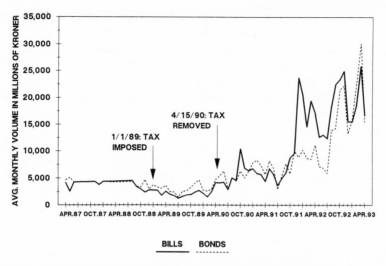

Fig. 6.4   Volume of trade in Swedish money markets, spot market

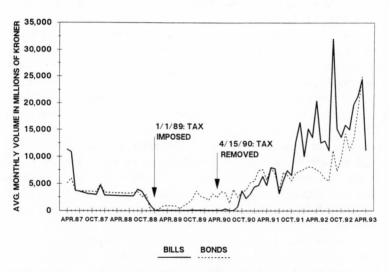

Fig. 6.5   Volume of trade in Swedish money markets, futures market

Effects on Volume and Location of Fixed-Income Transactions

The transaction tax on fixed-income securities had a larger impact on local trading volume than did the tax on stocks. Figures 6.4 and 6.5 show the trading volume in Swedish government bills and bonds and in futures on bills and bonds, respectively.[11]

---

11. We thank Pehr Wissen and the Bank of Sweden for providing the data in figures 6.4 and 6.5.

There are several noteworthy aspects to these data. First, the effect of the tax (proposed in late 1987 and implemented in early 1989) seems to be quite large. During the first week of the tax, bond trading volume fell by about 85 percent from its average during the summer of 1987.[12] Trading in futures on bonds and bills (in figure 6.5) fell by about 98 percent over the same period. Trade in options essentially disappeared. The effects were less dramatic for bills, whose trading fell by only about 20 percent.

Second, much of the volume decline in futures occurred in anticipation of the tax. However, there was also a large decline in volume in January 1989, the month when the tax was instituted. One possible explanation for the anticipatory decline is that low levels of future liquidity raise the current risk of illiquidity. If the risk of low liquidity is high, investors who value liquidity most will prefer to trade securities with lower liquidity risk, thereby reducing current liquidity in futures.

Third, these effects ran in reverse once the tax was removed in April 1990. Trading volume subsequently increased, in both bonds and bills, spot and futures. At the same time, the yield on bonds relative to that on bills fell. This could be explained by the liquidity arguments above and by the high tax rate on bonds relative to bills.

Why does fixed-income volume appear more sensitive than stock-market volume, even with much smaller taxes, and with no viable offshore replacements? The answer would appear to lie in the relative ease with which substitutes for bonds can be created—substitutes which avoid the tax even if they are local. For example, the market for Swedish debentures (which were not subject to the tax) became more active when the tax was imposed. The market for VRNs (variable-rate notes) also grew rapidly.[13] VRNs avoid taxation because they are traded by counterparties, without a broker. Finally, FRAs (forward-rate agreements) quickly took the place of futures markets in bills and bonds.[14] By moving from futures to forwards, transaction taxes could easily be avoided with little change in payoff patterns.[15] Swaps performed a similar service for longer-maturity instruments, serving as a close substitute for futures on bonds.

Because trade in fixed-income securities can move so easily into debentures and forward contracts, the turnover tax raised little revenue, and a good deal less than the authorities expected. Whereas the Finance Ministry initially estimated tax revenues from fixed-income transactions at SEK 1500 million per

12. Lybeck (1991) estimates the elasticity of Swedish money-market trading with respect to the turnover tax to be 3.0.
13. VRNs carry longer maturities, but are priced more like short-maturity bills because their value is reset every three months at par.
14. See Lybeck (1991).
15. Indeed, the substitutability between futures and forwards became quite close; beginning in mid-1989, the FRA market was standardized to the futures-contract expiration dates.

year, the realized revenue averaged only about 50 million per year, reaching only 80 million in 1989.

The fixed-income tax created considerable substitution toward other Swedish instruments, with little migration offshore. If the tax had remained in place, however, offshore migration might also have occurred. There were no barriers to trading SEK-denominated bonds, bills, and associated derivatives in foreign markets. Presumably, offshore migration did not occur because foreign investors are not so active in Swedish money markets, and because it is so easy to create forward contracts for fixed-income instruments. Thus, the reason for the lack of migration in fixed-income trade was not that offshore trading was relatively more costly than it was for stocks, but that there were even less costly local alternatives available.

6.2.2   Transaction Taxes in the United Kingdom

Summary of the U.K. Transaction Tax Regime

The securities transaction tax in the United Kingdom is known as "stamp duty." As the name suggests, stamp duty began as a tax on the transfer of a financial instrument from one owner to another, a transfer which could only be made legally effective by an official stamp applied to the instrument. Thus stamp duty is a tax on the registration of ownership of a financial asset. In 1986 the U.K. government closed certain loopholes in the application of stamp duty by introducing a "stamp duty reserve tax" (SDRT) which substitutes for stamp duty itself and is paid at the same rate.[16] In what follows we use the term "stamp duty" to refer to both stamp duty proper and the SDRT, and we use "taxable" to mean subject to stamp duty (as opposed to other U.K. taxes that are outside the scope of this paper).

Stamp duty applies to transactions in ordinary shares (common stock, in U.S. terminology), and in assets convertible to shares such as convertible unsecured loan stock (convertible bonds, in U.S. terminology) while the conversion option is still exercisable. Futures and options transactions are not taxable, but the exercise of an option is treated as a purchase of ordinary shares at the exercise price and is therefore taxable. Transactions in the shares of investment trusts (closed-end funds, in U.S. terminology) are taxable in the ordinary way, as are the transactions carried out by the managers of investment trusts. Purchases and redemptions of units in unit trusts (open-end funds, in U.S. terminology) are taxed as if they were transactions in the underlying shares held

---

16. For example, the SDRT is payable when investors buy shares and then resell them within the same two-week London Stock Exchange account period, thereby avoiding the need for a transfer of registered ownership. The SDRT is also payable on transactions in "renounceable letters of allotment or acceptance," which are traded in place of shares themselves during the six months after shares are first issued to the public.

by the trust. Transactions in fixed-income securities, such as corporate and government bonds, are not taxable.

Stamp duty applies to both primary and secondary market transactions. When new shares are issued the issuer pays the tax, whereas in secondary market transactions the purchaser pays the tax. Corporate repurchases of shares are also taxable.

There are a few exemptions from stamp duty. Registered charities are exempt, as are market makers registered by the London Stock Exchange when they trade in the securities for which they make a market, and member firms of the London International Futures and Options Exchange (LIFFE) when they trade to hedge equity options positions or to meet delivery obligations following the exercise of equity options.

The rate of stamp duty has varied over the years. In August 1963 the rate was lowered from 2 percent to 1 percent, increasing to 2 percent in May 1974, falling again to 1 percent in April 1984 and to 0.5 percent in October 1986. In its 1990 budget the British government announced its intention to abolish stamp duty altogether when the London Stock Exchange's Taurus system for electronic settlement came on-line. With the collapse of the Taurus development project in the spring of 1993, the future of stamp duty is uncertain.

Effects on Market Institutions and Trading Strategies

To understand the effects of stamp duty, it is important to realize that stamp duty is not a tax on the domestic consumption of transactions services. Accordingly the British system does not make any distinction between domestic and foreign investors.[17] Nor is stamp duty a tax on the domestic production of brokerage services. Indeed, the City of London thrives by providing brokerage services for trading in foreign shares, and these transactions are not subject to stamp duty. Instead, stamp duty is effectively a tax on registration, the transfer of legal ownership of U.K. shares.[18]

Since stamp duty is a tax on registration, investors have an incentive to reduce their consumption of this service by using nominees to hold assets in their name ("street name," in U.S. terminology). An investor could receive assets from the account of another investor using the same nominee without incurring a tax liability.[19] Recognizing the potential for tax avoidance of this type, the British tax authorities distinguish between "custodial nominees," who perform regular custodial functions, and "active nominees," who in addition may trans-

---

17. An exception is that for practical reasons the U.K. tax authorities do not try to collect the SDRT on transactions between foreign investors.

18. Transactions in some non-U.K. shares, mainly South African, Australian, and Irish shares, are settled in the United Kingdom using the London Stock Exchange's Talisman system. Stamp duty is payable at the South African and Australian rates for South African and Australian shares, while the U.K. and Irish tax authorities share stamp duty revenues for purchases of Irish shares through U.K. brokers.

19. Conversely, stamp duty is payable if an investor does not sell shares but simply changes nominees.

fer assets between the accounts of their clients. A typical custodial nominee is a large U.K. clearing bank (commercial bank, in U.S. terminology). Active nominees include domestic clearance services, and depositories that allow claims on assets held in their name to be traded in U.S. stock markets (these claims are known as American depository receipts, or ADRs). Transfers of shares into the name of an active nominee are taxable at three times the ordinary rate, compensating to some extent for the free trading which is possible once the shares are held by the active nominee.

More generally, stamp duty generates an incentive for the creation of bearer instruments, which can be traded without using registration services. To offset this incentive, stamp duty applies at the triple rate on any such creation of bearer instruments. For example, shares in Eurotunnel (the company operating the channel tunnel) were issued in both the United Kingdom and France. In the United Kingdom the shares were registered in the usual way, but in France the shares are bearer instruments. Triple stamp duty is payable when a holder of U.K. registered Eurotunnel shares converts them to French bearer shares.

Of these various devices for economizing on registration services, ADRs are the most commonly used. In the last six months of 1992, total trading volume in U.K. equities and ADRs on the London Stock Exchange amounted to 136.1 billion pounds, of which 10.5 billion pounds were U.K. ADR trading. In addition, there were 13.8 billion pounds of U.K. ADR trading in U.S. markets.[20] Thus trading in U.K. ADRs accounted for 16 percent of the total (U.K. ADR plus U.K. equity) trading in this period.

There are two other important means by which investors can reduce their liability to U.K. stamp duty. First, investors can switch from trading U.K. equities directly to trading U.K. equity derivatives. Futures transactions incur no stamp duty, and options transactions incur duty only when the options are exercised. Furthermore, LIFFE member firms can hedge equity options transactions without paying stamp duty. This gives derivatives a substantial tax advantage for many transactions. The LIFFE reports considerable trading volume in futures on the FTSE 100 index of U.K. equities (2.6 million contracts were traded in 1992, up 52 percent from 1991), in FTSE 100 options (3.1 million options in 1992, up 37 percent from 1991), and in options on individual U.K. equities (4.6 million options in 1992, down 4 percent from 1991).[21]

Second, investors can reduce stamp duty liability by trading less frequently. The magnitude of this effect is hard to estimate. Jackson and O'Donnell (1985) and Ericsson and Lindgren (1992), in econometric studies of U.K. and international equity turnover, respectively, find that the long-run elasticity of turnover with respect to overall transactions costs is in the range of -1 to -1.7. That

---

20. The U.S. figures are calculated as follows. In the last six months of 1992 there were $20.4 billion of trading in U.K. ADRs listed on the New York Stock Exchange, and $3.0 billion of trading in U.K. ADRs listed on the NASDAQ. Converting to sterling at an exchange rate of $1.70 per pound gives 13.8 billion pounds of U.K. ADR trading in U.S. markets.

21. Before March 1992 the equity options were traded on the London Traded Options Market, which has now merged with LIFFE.

is, a 10 percent increase in transactions costs reduces turnover by 10 to 17 percent in the long run. Since U.K. stamp duty appears to account for about half of the total trading costs in U.K. equities, these estimates imply that turnover is less than half of what it might be in the absence of stamp duty. Alternatively, without relying on econometric studies, one might note that in 1992 the ratio of trading volume to market value of domestic equities on the London Stock Exchange was only 62 percent of the corresponding ratio for the New York Stock Exchange (NYSE) and NASDAQ (National Association of Securities Dealers Automated Quotations) combined.[22]

Despite the availability of various means by which investors can substitute away from taxable trading, the stamp duty still has a considerable tax base. Trading volume in U.K. equities on the London Stock Exchange was 216.9 billion pounds during calendar 1992, and stamp duty on U.K. equities raised 830 million pounds in revenue in the fiscal year 1992–93. The revenue raised is somewhat less than the statutory 0.5 percent of trading volume because of the various exemptions. These exemptions do not reduce the liability of foreign investors, and figure 6.6 shows that the investors whose U.K. equity transactions are recorded in the Frank Russell data base pay close to the statutory fifty basis points per round-trip transaction. This is in marked contrast to the Swedish evidence reported earlier.[23]

6.3   Securities Transaction Taxes and Market Responses

By taxing an activity, the government creates an incentive to replace it with a nontaxed substitute. In the case of securities transaction taxes, the availability of alternative securities or trading methods creates many possible means of tax avoidance. Investors, intermediaries, and securities issuers can all attempt to pursue lower-cost trades through a variety of alternatives. Trading may migrate into substitute securities or it may move out of the government's physical tax jurisdiction, or both.

In this section, we examine different means of taxing transactions and the resulting tax incentives for migration and financial innovation. We first look at two rules that countries seem to apply in choosing which transactions to tax and how much to tax them. We argue that regardless of which rule is used, its application will create incentives for participants to avoid the taxes. We then turn to describe various ways in which taxes might change behavior (other than simply inducing investors not to trade): moving transactions to offshore or off-market locations; changing the nature of securities that investors and intermediaries trade; and changing the kinds of securities that issuers are likely to provide.

---

22. These figures come from the 1993 edition of the *London Stock Exchange Fact Book*.

23. Note, however, that the Frank Russell data base does not include transactions in U.K. ADRs or U.K. equity derivatives.

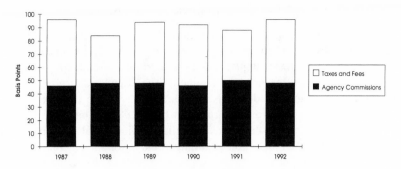

Fig. 6.6   Round-trip trading costs in U.K. equities for U.S. institutional investors
Source: Frank Russell Securities, Inc.

6.3.1   What to Tax and How Much to Tax It?

Any attempt to tax transactions must face questions of what constitutes a transaction and how much to tax different transaction types. While it seems simple enough to define a transaction as the transfer of legal ownership of a financial security, that definition does not go very far toward building a transfer tax program. No actual systems equally tax *all* financial ownership transfers; all exempt (partially or completely) certain types of securities or transfers between certain parties.

The main consequence of such selective taxation is a high degree of complexity in rates and scope. In the British system, for example, transfers of domestic equities and convertible bonds are taxable but transfers of straight bonds are not. In the Japanese system, straight bond transfers are taxable but at a lower rate than convertible bond transfers, which in turn are taxed at a lower rate than equity transfers. In the Swedish system, the statutory tax rate depended on who was trading as well as what was traded; for example, the taxes could be avoided by using offshore brokers for trades in Swedish equities. Moreover, derivative securities are taxed in many different ways: in the British system, futures transactions are untaxed, while options are taxed only upon exercise. In the Japanese and Swedish systems, futures and options are taxed, but at a much lower rate than either bonds or stocks.

One is naturally led to ask whether there are any underlying principles that can be used to determine which asset transfers are taxable and at what rate. Two principles are appealing on a priori grounds, and these seem to underlie at least some features of the systems we see in different countries. A first principle is that *transactions that generate the same payoffs should pay the same tax*. A second principle is that *transactions that use the same resources should pay the same tax*. The first principle emphasizes the outcome from a transaction, while the second emphasizes the resource cost of the transaction.

6.3.2   Taxing Transactions According to Their Payoff Patterns

Despite the a priori appeal of taxing transactions according to the payoffs they generate, this approach rapidly runs into difficulties. The problem arises from what we saw in the examples above—that for any *given* tax regime, behavioral responses will occur to undermine it. The effect of a turnover tax is rarely just to discourage trade. It also encourages a move in the location of taxed services, or a switch to an instrument which is a close, but more lightly taxed, substitute. These problems make it difficult or impossible to implement a system which taxes a transaction according to the payoffs it generates.

To take an example, consider what the presence of derivative securities does to a system that tries to tax payoff patterns. As is well-known, derivatives deliver payoffs which can be replicated through trading the underlying assets (along with short-term borrowing and lending).[24] For example, the payoff pattern obtained by purchasing and holding an option can be replicated by undertaking a dynamic trading strategy in the underlying asset, and, reciprocally, the payoff pattern from buying and holding the underlying asset can be replicated through a dynamic trading strategy in the option. Only the *intensity* of trading separates the two strategies for any given return pattern. Once a transaction tax is imposed, some payoff patterns will likely be cheaper to achieve with derivatives, and others will be cheaper to achieve with the underlying asset. Transaction taxes will generally not be able to equate the tax burdens from trading the two instruments.[25]

To see this, suppose that the system taxes the purchase of shares at rate τ. What should the tax rate on options be? A tax rate of zero would clearly encourage investors to substitute away from trade in the stock. Most investors would prefer to adjust their exposures to the stock through trade in the option.[26]

Alternatively, suppose a positive tax rate is levied on the option's market price. If an investor uses the option to duplicate the return from buying and holding the stock for, say, a year, a larger number of options transactions will be required. For this investor, the option can turn out to be more expensive than the stock for all but the lowest option tax rates. However, for another investor, one who wants the downside protection that options offer, the option will need to be purchased only once; a low option tax rate will make the option less expensive than the stock for this latter investor. A tax on option prices will therefore not satisfy the principle of taxing payoff patterns.

More generally, taxing the market price of a derivative is, in any case, a problematic proposition. After all, it is always possible to redesign a derivative

24. The replication is precise under simplifying assumptions such as those made by the Black-Scholes option-pricing model, and approximate otherwise.

25. The presence of a transaction tax can also make the derivative an imperfect substitute for the underlying asset. In such cases, the replication described above will not be exact.

26. Of course, even in the absence of taxes, transactions have costs (brokerage fees plus the difference between execution price and the middle of the bid/ask spread). Thus there will be some trade in the stock even if options are completely untaxed.

to include more leverage. For example, futures contracts cannot be taxed according to their market price, as they have a price of zero when written.

The last possibility might be to tax options' "deltas"—that is, the notional amount of the stock an investor would currently need to buy to perform the stock-option replication discussed above. This method of taxation would also fail to tax transactions according to payoff patterns. First of all, implementation would be a nightmare: option deltas vary with both the market price and the strike price of the stock, so that tax rates across options would have to differ, and would have to vary over time. Second of all, the previous argument still applies: investors who want the return from buying and holding the stock will need to buy and sell options frequently if they are to achieve the return through options, and will therefore avoid using options; alternatively, those who prefer the payoff pattern of the option will find that the necessary frequent trading in the stock will make options the cheaper alternative for all but the highest option tax rates.

Thus it seems clear that no system of tax rates will enable a government to tax transactions according to their payoff patterns. Such a system does not in any case correspond exactly to any country's system. However, it does appear to have been part of the motivation in Sweden for extending the tax on underlying stocks and government bonds to futures and options.

6.3.3 Taxing Transactions according to Their Resource Costs

An alternative principle of transactions taxation is to equate the transactions tax burden across assets as a fraction of total transactions costs. On this principle, transactions with the same resource costs should be taxed equally.

For example, by some measures derivatives represent low-cost means of purchasing exposure to an underlying asset. Accordingly, this principle would suggest that transactions in derivatives should be lightly taxed compared to "expensive" transactions in cash markets.

This principle can be implemented in several ways. One possibility is to tax transactions costs directly; for example, Japanese brokers' commissions are subject to a 3 percent sales tax. Another approach is to tax the notional amounts invested, but at lower rates for assets with low transactions costs. This might help explain, for example, what was done in Sweden, with different rates on a wide range of instruments handled by Swedish brokers. Also, in Japan futures transactions are taxed at 0.001 percent, while cash transactions are taxed at 0.3 percent for general investors.

The third interpretation of this principle stresses that "resource costs" refers to indirect as well as direct costs. A number of arguments have been made that higher trading volumes stimulate negative externalities. These externalities typically fall into one of two groups: (*a*) excessive volatility of asset prices, higher risk premia, and, therefore, lower levels of investment;[27] and (*b*) excess

---

27. See, for example, Summers and Summers (1989).

or misallocated investment in speculative activities.[28] Either way, one might imagine a tax system which attempts to tax transactions as a way of compensating for the externality and reducing its size.

Such externalities provide a kind of economic rationale for transactions taxes as "sin" taxes. Such arguments were used by the Swedish Trade Union Council in initiating Sweden's discussion of transaction taxes. The tax rates that follow from this application of the resource-cost principle depend on the magnitude of the negative externalities. In Sweden, for example, where the sentiment focused on the negative consequences of excessive speculation, it is perhaps not surprising that tax rates on derivatives were set so high as to practically eliminate trade.

Can governments expect to accomplish their objectives when taxing transactions according to their "costs"? By taxing transaction inputs, such as brokerage or local trading services, taxes can indeed discourage local production of those inputs. That is because, in practice, these inputs are relatively inelastically supplied. In Sweden, for example, there is little question that the equity turnover tax succeeded in hurting local equity brokers and floor traders, at least to the extent that they could not costlessly move their services to offshore markets. However, no one has claimed that Sweden's tax should therefore be judged a success. This suggests that the tax's true objective had never actually been to discourage the allocation of local inputs into trading.

Suppose, instead, that the objective of the tax is to reduce negative externalities (allegedly) associated with trading "too much." In this case it is clearly not enough simply to discourage local investment in inputs. Externalities due to excess volatility or short-termism will not be reduced if total trading remains as its original level merely by moving abroad or into local close substitutes. Thus, a necessary condition for meeting this objective is for the tax to discourage *total* trading volume.[29] In terms of reducing total volume, the U.K. tax might be considered a success relative to the Swedish taxes.

6.3.4   Econometric Evidence on Market Responses to Transactions Taxes

Our case studies have shown that investors respond to transactions taxes by reducing the volume of taxable transactions. There is also some econometric evidence for this behavior.

28. Stiglitz (1989) argues that profit-maximizing investors overinvest in information gathering relative to the social optimum. Froot, Scharfstein, and Stein (1992) show that short-horizon trading can lead researchers to "herd" on some sources of information and to ignore others. Presumably, the costly externalities here are not the misallocation of investor resources, but the potential for corporate resource allocation to be affected by inefficient investment in information. See Froot, Perold, and Stein (1992) for an analytic review of these issues and that of excessive volatility. Schwert and Seguin (1993) provide a broad overview of the literature.

29. It is important to emphasize that reducing total volume is by no means sufficient to ensure the tax's success. For example, lowering total volume does not ensure that excess volatility is reduced (even if it is present to begin with). If the demands of "stabilizing" traders are reduced along with the demands of "destabilizing" or noise traders, then the overall effect on excess volatility of reduction in volume will be ambiguous. See Froot, Perold, and Stein (1992) for an elaboration of and evidence on this argument.

The original work on this topic was done by Jackson and O'Donnell (1985), who studied U.K. trading volume over the period 1964–84. Jackson and O'Donnell estimated an equation of the form

$$v_t = \alpha_0 + \alpha_1 v_{t-1} + X_t \beta + e_t \, ,$$

where v is the log of trading volume and X_t is a vector of explanatory variables including some contemporaneous and some lagged variables. One of the explanatory variables, say, X_{1t}, is a measure of log transactions costs; Jackson and O'Donnell call the coefficient on this variable β_1, the short-run elasticity of trading volume with respect to transactions costs, and they call $\beta_1/(1 - \alpha_1)$ the long-run elasticity of trading volume with respect to transactions costs since this is the effect of a one-time permanent change in transactions costs after trading volume has fully adjusted to its new level.

Jackson and O'Donnell measure trading volume in a rather unusual way. They divide the value of shares traded by the level of the *Financial Times* (FT) all-share stock price index, instead of dividing by the total value of shares outstanding. The latter procedure would give a measure of turnover; Jackson and O'Donnell's procedure approximates turnover only if the number of shares outstanding is fairly constant and if the FT stock price index adequately proxies the price behavior of the market as a whole.

To measure transactions costs, Jackson and O'Donnell assume that other costs equal 0.75 percent for a one-way transaction. They add the one-way stamp duty rate to this to get a total transactions cost, and then take logs.

Jackson and O'Donnell also include a large number of other variables in their X_t vector. They use the log of the total value of shares outstanding, deflated by the consumer price index; the log of expenditure on mergers and acquisitions, deflated by the FT stock price index; the log of net inflows to life assurance and pension funds (the leading institutional investors in the U.K.), again deflated by the FT price index; the change in the log stock price index and the absolute value of this change; and seasonal dummies for the third quarter of every year (to capture low trading volume in the summer) and for the first quarter of 1981 and every subsequent year (to capture capital gains tax effects).

In their preferred specification, Jackson and O'Donnell estimate the coefficient on lagged log trading volume to be 0.55, and the coefficient on log transactions costs to be -0.48. This implies a long-run elasticity of trading volume with respect to transactions costs of -1.65. Starting from an initial transactions tax rate of 2 percent, a reduction to 1 percent is a 0.45 reduction in total log transactions costs, which is estimated to increase trading volume by about 70 percent. Starting from an initial transactions tax rate of 0.5 percent, abolition of the tax is a comparable reduction in total transactions costs with a similar estimated effect on trading volume.

Jackson and O'Donnell also experiment with other specifications and find that the estimated long-run elasticity of trading volume with respect to transactions costs varies from -0.9 to -1.7. In very similar work with Swedish data over the period 1970–88, Lindgren and Westlund (1990) estimate the long-run elasticity to be in the range of -0.85 to -1.35. Ericsson and Lindgren (1992) extend the approach to international panel data. They estimate the long-run elasticity to be in the range of -1.2 to -1.5. Thus all these studies give fairly similar results.

There are some small differences in specification between the Lindgren-Westlund and Ericsson-Lindgren papers and the original Jackson-O'Donnell paper. Lindgren and Westlund use $\log(1 + z)$ in place of $\log(z)$, where z is the merger activity variable and the net inflow to institutions variable. This is to avoid the implication of the Jackson-O'Donnell specification that stock market trading volume would fall to zero if merger activity or net inflow to institutions ceased. Ericsson and Lindgren use a standard measure of turnover as the dependent variable, they drop the merger activity and institutional inflow variables, and they include both market size and interest-rate movements in the vector of regressors. More importantly, they include time and country dummies to pick up fixed country effects and common movements in trading volume across countries.

Although these studies are suggestive, there are several reasons why their results should be treated with some caution. First, the time-series studies tend to begin with equations that include long lags and hence a very large number of regressors, testing down to a more parsimonious final specification. Jackson and O'Donnell, for example, begin by estimating thirty-seven coefficients when they have eighty-three observations! Even their final equation includes nineteen explanatory variables. In this situation it is easy to overfit the data and end up with spuriously significant coefficients.

Second, it is not easy to measure total transactions costs accurately. Transactions costs include not only bid-ask spreads and brokerage commissions, but also the price impact of trading and the effects of capital gains taxes. It is not at all clear that these factors can be proxied adequately by any fixed number.

Third, the effect of transactions costs on trading volume depends on the other margins of substitution that investors have available. This is a point that we have emphasized elsewhere in this paper. If investors can easily switch from taxed and measured trading volume to untaxed, unmeasured trading in offshore markets or substitute assets, then transactions costs should have a large effect on measured trading volume. If investors can only choose between taxed trading on the exchange and holding their assets, then transactions costs should have a much smaller effect. None of the econometric studies adequately capture the variation over time and countries in the alternatives available to investors.

Fourth, many of the other variables included by Jackson and O'Donnell and the other authors are arguably endogenous. The growth rate of stock prices and the absolute value of this growth rate (a measure of volatility) may well respond to changes in transactions costs. The same can be said of merger and acquisition activity. Some of the effects attributed to these variables in the regressions may in fact be due to changing transactions costs.

Last but not least, transactions costs themselves may be endogenous. Our analysis of Sweden shows that the authorities reduced transactions tax rates in response to declining trading volume and disappointing revenue. It is possible that the secular decline in U.K. stamp duty rates from 2 percent in the late 1970s to 0.5 percent today has also occurred because the authorities perceive that investors are increasingly able to substitute away from taxable trading.

For all these reasons we believe that the elasticity of trading volume with respect to exogenous changes in transactions taxes remains uncertain. The estimates of Jackson and O'Donnell and others are plausible values to use in rough calculations, but not more than that.

6.4 Conclusion

Any analysis of a proposed tax change must take account of the behavioral responses that may result from it. The main lesson from the international experience with securities transaction taxes is that these behavioral responses can be quite large, and that they are sensitive to the way an STT is implemented. The important responses seem to be:

1. A reduction in overall trading. The response here was greater for the United Kingdom than for Sweden's equity or fixed-income taxes. While volume in Swedish money markets fell most dramatically, this was not true for total volume in money market securities and their substitutes. The effects on total trading are often difficult to measure because trade moves off the market where it is taxed.

2. A migration of trading into offshore markets for the same securities. Here the response was greater for Swedish equities than it was for U.K. equities or Swedish fixed-incomes. There is no perfect substitute for a share of Volvo, but there are nearly perfect substitutes for Swedish brokerage services to trade Volvo. The result was a steady movement away from the use of local brokerage services to consummate trades. Similar experiences abound: taxes on futures transactions in Tokyo led to the migration of trade to Osaka and Singapore; taxes on stock transactions in Finland (removed as of May 1992) caused a large fraction of local trading to migrate to London; and so on.

3. A migration of trading into local substitute securities. In the United Kingdom local trading of ADRs and in Sweden the trading of forward contracts (versus taxed trade in futures) demonstrate that markets can and will shift toward existing substitutes or create new ones when taxes are imposed. Substitution by the original issuer may also take place. For example, taxation of corporate equity but not debt (as in the United Kingdom) may lead companies to lower capital costs by issuing more debt and less equity, all else equal.

4. A combination of (2) and (3): A migration of trading into offshore markets for substitute securities. ADRs traded in the United States permit untaxed trading of a security closely related to the U.K. ordinary stock.

The importance of these behavioral responses for any specific tax proposal will depend on the available alternatives as well as on the specific tax design.[30] Indeed, alternatives that do not yet exist can be important. The establishment of new instruments or trading environments is particularly likely when the tax base is large in an absolute sense, since then the fixed costs of establishment can be spread over a large number of trades.

All these responses tend to shrink the tax base as tax rates increase, reducing the revenue that might otherwise be expected. A basic principle of public finance is that the shrinkage of the tax base is more severe when a tax is levied on a good or service that is supplied and demanded elastically. In such circumstances sellers greatly reduce supply rather than accept lower prices, and buyers greatly reduce demand rather than pay higher prices; the tax wedge between the seller's price and the buyer's price then greatly reduces the quantity of the good traded and the revenue that can be raised by the tax. This principle can be applied to STTs once one thinks of them as taxes on one or more of the resources that are used as inputs to a transaction. Different countries tax different resources. As we have seen, the Swedish system taxes domestic brokerage (the domestic resources used in matching buyers and sellers), whereas the U.K. system taxes registration (the resources used to make a transfer of ownership legally binding).

The demand for domestic equity brokerage is highly elastic because investors can easily trade abroad and use foreign brokers instead of domestic brokers. Similarly, the demand for domestic fixed-income brokerage is highly elastic because it is easy to create local untaxed substitute assets. Accordingly, the Swedish STTs on equities and particularly fixed-income securities produced disappointingly little revenue for the Swedish government.

The demand for registration appears to be less elastic, at least in the short run.[31] Trading offshore does not by itself remove the need to make a transfer of ownership legally binding, and hence does not shrink the tax base for the U.K. securities transaction tax. To reduce their tax liability, investors in U.K. equities must trade in closely related but not identical securities (ADRs or UK equity derivatives), or must reduce their volume of trading. These alternatives are certainly important, but the U.K. securities transaction tax base remains large enough for the U.K. government to raise about 800 million pounds a year from a 0.5 percent STT on equity transactions.

What are the lessons from international experience for the U.S. debate on securities transaction taxes? Proponents of an STT argue that it would reduce trading volume (and negative externalities that are alleged to be associated with volume), while raising much-needed revenue for the U.S. Treasury. The "externality" argument for an STT requires that investors act to reduce their tax lia-

---

30. Any impact of a tax on parts of the domestic securities industry is likely to be similarly sensitive to the specifics of the tax and feasible responses to it.

31. Long-run elasticities may be a good deal higher. Evidence for this comes from the secular downward trend in U.K. stamp duty rates, which may be attributable to the growing availability of untaxed substitutes.

bility, but specifically by reducing trading volume rather than by moving trading to untaxed assets or jurisdictions.[32] If an STT is to raise much revenue, however, investors must not reduce their tax liability too far. Thus there is some conflict between these two arguments for an STT, but both arguments clearly fail if investors find it easy to trade in untaxed assets or foreign markets.

The first lesson from international experience is therefore that an STT fails when it taxes a transaction input that has close untaxed substitutes. The Swedish equity transaction tax applied only to transactions using Swedish brokerage services, which are highly substitutable with foreign brokerage services. The tax has some effect on domestic trading volume (as measured by transactions in restricted Swedish shares), but did not reduce the volume of trade in London and may even have increased this volume as investors moved trading offshore. The Swedish fixed-income transaction tax was a more dramatic failure; investors did not even have to move offshore because they were able to find untaxed domestic assets that were close substitutes for the taxed assets.

The British stamp duty has clearly been more successful than the Swedish STT, because it taxes registration. This is a necessary input no matter where a transaction is carried out, and so the British tax does not give investors incentives to move trading offshore. In the long run, however, even the British tax is vulnerable to innovation as investors discover that they can avoid stamp duty by trading ADRs or equity derivatives. This is an example of the point emphasized by Kane (1987), that long-run elasticities of substitution tend to be much larger than short-run elasticities. Governments must continually update their tax systems if they are to avoid erosion of the tax base through financial innovation.

How much revenue might the U.S. government raise if it imposed a securities transaction tax of the British type, at the British rate? The U.S. Congressional Budget Office (1990) estimate of $10 billion in annual revenue has been widely cited. One way to get a number of this magnitude is to scale up the U.K. annual revenue by the trading volume in U.S. equities relative to the trading volume in U.K. equities. First, we convert the U.K. annual revenue of 800 million pounds to dollars; using an exchange rate of $1.7 per pound, this is about $1.4 billion. Then we note that U.S. equity trading volume on the NYSE, AMEX (American Stock Exchange), and NASDAQ is almost eight times the U.K. equity trading volume on the London Stock Exchange, implying revenue of about $11 billion. One could get an even higher revenue estimate if one assumed that the U.S. STT would be applied to fixed-income securities, which are not taxed under the British system.

But this revenue estimate ignores the behavioral responses that would surely follow the imposition of a U.S. securities transaction tax. Once an STT is in

32. Note again that a reduction in trading volume is necessary but not sufficient for the externality argument to be valid. Even if an STT reduces trading volume, it might reduce positive-externality transactions more than negative-externality transactions.

place, investors have the incentive to replace taxed transactions with innovative untaxed transactions or simply to reduce the volume of trade. The Swedish experience with a fixed-income STT suggests that substitution makes it hard to raise much revenue in the fixed-income markets. In the equity markets, the econometric studies of Jackson and O'Donnell (1985) and Ericsson and Lindgren (1992) imply that the long-run elasticity of taxable trading volume with respect to transactions costs is in the range of -1 to -1.7; that is, a 10 percent increase in transactions costs reduces taxable trading volume by 10 to 17 percent in the long run. The large U.S. investors whose trades are recorded in the Frank Russell data base pay about thirty basis points for an average U.S. equity trade. A 0.5 percent STT would add fifty basis points to this, reducing taxable trading volume by 62 percent if the elasticity is -1 and by 81 percent if the elasticity is -1.7. The implied tax revenue falls proportionally to $4 billion if the elasticity is -1 and to $2 billion if the elasticity is -1.7.

It is important to note that an STT of given size has a particularly large impact on U.S. markets because U.S. trading costs are presently so low. The investors recorded in the Frank Russell data base pay about fifty basis points, excluding taxes, when they trade U.K. equities; trading costs in other national equity markets are typically even larger. An STT has a much larger proportional impact when other trading costs are thirty basis points (as in the United States) than when other trading costs are fifty basis points or more. The calculations above take account of this effect.

Of course, one may not want to rely too heavily on the econometric methods of Jackson and O'Donnell (1985) and Ericsson and Lindgren (1992). An alternative, simple way to estimate the revenue that could be raised by a U.S. STT is to scale up the revenue raised by the U.K. securities transaction tax by the total capitalization of the U.S. market relative to the U.K. market. U.S. equities listed on the NYSE, NASDAQ, and AMEX together have a total capitalization almost five times bigger than the U.K. equities listed on the London Stock Exchange. This scale factor of five is smaller than the trading volume scale factor of eight because U.S. equities trade more actively, just as one would expect given the low transaction costs in U.S. markets. Scaling up the U.K. transaction tax revenue by a factor of five gives a revenue estimate of only $7 billion.

One other consideration suggests that investors' behavioral responses would severely limit the revenue of a U.S. STT. The sheer size of U.S. financial markets makes it worthwhile for institutions to pay the fixed costs of developing and marketing tax-driven financial innovations. From this perspective it is not surprising that U.S. markets have been particularly innovative in the past, and one should expect similar levels of innovation in the face of new taxes. It is striking that in no country have the investors in the Frank Russell data base paid securities transaction taxes that exceed the other transaction costs in that country's market. Given the low general level of U.S. transaction costs, this leads to a pessimistic assessment of the revenue potential of a U.S. securities transaction tax.

References

Ericsson, Jan, and Ragnar Lindgren. 1992. Transaction taxes and trading volume on stock exchanges: An international comparison. Working Paper no. 39. Stockholm School of Economics, May.

Froot, Kenneth A., David Scharfstein, and Jeremy C. Stein. 1992. Herd on the street: Informational inefficiencies in a model with short-term speculation. *Journal of Finance* 47 (September): 1461–84.

Froot, Kenneth A., André Perold, and Jeremy C. Stein. 1992. Shareholder trading practices and corporate investment horizons. *Journal of Applied Corporate Finance* 5 (summer): 42–58.

Jackson, P. D. and A. T. O'Donnell. 1985. The effects of stamp duty on equity transactions and prices in the U.K. stock exchange. Discussion Paper no. 25. Bank of England, October.

Japan Securities Research Institute. 1991. *Securities market in Japan 1992.* Tokyo, Japan: Japan Securities Research Institute, December.

Kane, Edward J. 1987. Competitive financial regulation: An international perspective. In *Threats to international financial stability,* eds. R. Portes and A. Swoboda. London: Cambridge University Press.

Lindgren, Ragnar, and Anders Westlund. 1990. How did the transaction costs on the Stockholm Stock Exchange influence trading volume and price volatility? *Skandinaviska Enskilda Banken Quarterly Review* 2:30–35.

Lybeck, Johan A. 1991. On political risk: The turnover tax on the Swedish money and bond markets, or how to kill a market without really trying. In *Recent developments in international banking and finance,* ed. S. J. Khory. New York: North-Holland.

Schwert, G. William, and Paul Seguin. 1993. *Securities transaction taxes: An overview of costs, benefits, and unresolved questions.* Chicago: Midamerica Institute, April.

Stiglitz, Joseph E. 1989. Using tax policy to curb speculative short-term trading. *Journal of Financial Services Research* 3:101–15.

Summers, Lawrence H., and Victoria P. Summers. 1989. When financial markets work too well: A cautious case for a securities transactions tax. *Journal of Financial Services Research* 3:261–86.

Umlauf, Steven R. 1993. Transaction taxes and stock market behavior: The Swedish experience. *Journal of Financial Economics* 33 (April): 227–40.

United States Congressional Budget Office. 1990. *Reducing the deficit: Spending and revenue options.* Washington, D.C., February.

Comment   René M. Stulz

Introduction

The paper by Campbell and Froot provides an extremely careful analysis of the impact of security transaction taxes (STTs) on security markets. They show that these taxes have three effects on the trading of securities: (a) they decrease trading in taxed securities; (b) they increase trading in nontaxed substitutes; (c) they increase foreign trading of domestic shares at the expense of domestic

René M. Stulz is the Ralph Kurtz Professor of Finance at The Ohio State University and a research associate of the National Bureau of Economic Research.

trading. An important implication of these three effects for the use of STTs as a source of tax revenue is that they raise less funds than one would expect based on the transaction volume before their imposition. I fully agree with the message of the Campbell and Froot paper. In my discussion, I want to point out some additional implications of STTs which are outside the focus of their paper. In turn, I discuss the implications of STTs for share ownership, stock return volatility, the cost of capital, and the geography of trading. Finally, I talk briefly about the political economy of globalization.

Transaction Taxes and Share Ownership

If trading is cheap, investors can follow the Wall Street Rule—sell when dissatisfied with management—at little cost.[1] This means that they have little incentive to invest resources to monitor management. As trading becomes more expensive, investors become locked into their holdings and can increase the performance of their portfolios through actions designed to improve the performance of management. Since STTs increase the cost of trading, this reasoning implies that they increase the monitoring of management and hence improve corporate performance.

As Campbell and Froot point out, STTs can be avoided by trades in untaxed securities which have highly correlated payoffs with the taxed securities. For instance, a shareholder who wishes to sell his holding of shares of firm X can avoid the transaction tax by engaging in an asset swap whereby he swaps his shares of firm X for shares of some other firm. With such a swap, ownership of the shares is not affected and no explicit security is exchanged, hence no transaction tax is paid. Yet, the investor ends up with a portfolio whose payoffs do not depend on the performance of firm X shares because he pays to the counterparty all the payoffs from his shares of firm X. Hence, for investors who can find ways to alter the return distribution of their portfolios without paying the tax, the tax affects how these investors trade but not how they monitor management.

It is reasonable to think that most of the cost of drawing up a contract to sell a payoff pattern is represented by a fixed cost which does not depend on the magnitude of the payoffs sold. A swap involving ten times more shares of company X for ten times more shares of another firm is not ten times more expensive to set up. Consequently, one would expect that large investors would find it beneficial to use derivatives to alter the return distribution of their portfolios, whereas small investors would not. This is because for a small investor the fixed cost of the derivative transaction would most likely be greater than the tax payment. Hence, for small investors, STTs have a lock-in effect, but it is doubtful that they have as much of a lock-in effect for large investors. This suggests that STTs penalize small investors relative to large investors. Further, if use of the Wall Street Rule by shareholders leads management to pay excess

---

1. See Bhide (1993) for the argument that a low cost of trading increases corporate control costs.

attention to short-run performance measures at the expense of long-run performance, STTs reduce the use of the rule mostly by small shareholders. Typically, those who are concerned about short-termism tend to blame fund managers rather than small shareholders,[2] so it is difficult to believe that STTs do much about short-termism.

One might argue that a well-designed tax would be such that it could not be avoided through sales of payoffs through derivative transactions. This view overlooks the fact that, whereas share transfers are easy to tax, transactions which take place outside of organized exchanges are not. Even if the intent is to tax trades of payoffs instead of trades of securities, it is unclear how well this can be done. Many derivatives have no value when the contract is opened. For example, forward contracts have no value when the parties agree to the forward transaction. Consider an investor who sells the security forward with a contract which has a long maturity. Eventually, the security will be sold as the forward contract is executed. At that time, the transaction tax will have to be paid. The present value of the tax payment is small, though. To make it uneconomical for investors to substitute forward sales for cash market sales, forward contracts will have to be taxed. Effectively, though, the tax authority would have to devise a formula that states that a forward sale is equivalent to some fraction of a cash sale.

Forward contracts are just one example of derivative assets. These contracts are the easiest to analyze. To avoid providing incentives to investors to substitute derivative trades for cash transactions, the tax authority will have to provide complicated formulas that require precise valuation of the derivative trades. There are an infinite number of ways through which payoffs can be sold. This means that markets will always be one step ahead of the tax authorities. In addition though, it seems unlikely that the tax authorities would know how to evaluate each derivative transaction without making valuation mistakes. After all, for most derivative securities, there is no unanimously agreed upon valuation approach.

Security Transaction Taxes and Volatility

It is sometimes suggested that security transaction taxes reduce volatility by decreasing trading. It is true that there is substantial empirical evidence which shows a positive relation between trading and volatility,[3] so that a mechanical application of this relation suggests that a decrease in trading will indeed reduce volatility. The problem is that the behavior modifications induced by the transaction tax themselves change the relation between trading and volatility. The argument I want to make is that STTs may increase volatility for a given volume of trading, so despite their negative effect on trading volume, they may increase volatility.

2. See, for instance, Jacobs (1991).
3. See Karpoff (1987) for a review of the evidence.

Note that STTs reduce liquidity. To see this, suppose that unexpectedly a block of shares for firm X is offered for sale on the exchange. To absorb this block, investors want a price concession, so that the price of the share drops slightly. Investors who are willing to make these trades possible provide liquidity to the markets.[4] They probably do not intend to hold on to these shares for very long, but they are providing an important service. With an STT, investors who provide liquidity want the stock price to fall more than in the absence of an STT before they buy shares, since their profit from doing so is decreased by the STT. Hence, an STT is likely to increase the short-run volatility of share prices.

If the concern is that there is excessive volatility because large groups of investors may trade without regard for fundamentals but simply to anticipate or react to trades by other large groups of investors, the effect of an STT on this excessive volatility is ambiguous.[5] This is because the STT affects the incentives of investors who trade on fundamentals as well as the incentives of those who do not. Short of carefully modeling the behavior of both classes of investors, it is unclear which category reduces its trading the most as the STT is introduced. If investors who trade on fundamentals reduce their trading the most, it is possible for excessive volatility to increase following the imposition of the STT.

The effect of an STT on information acquisition is also ambiguous. The reward for trading on a given piece of information falls with the STT because the cost of trading increases. Hence, one would expect investors to invest less in information collection. At the same time, though, the gain from collecting information to monitor management increases. Because small investors do not monitor management, the STT is likely to decrease information acquisition if it ends up favoring large investors over small investors.

STTs and the Cost of Capital

Suppose now that the STT cannot be avoided through trades in untaxed substitutes. When investors purchase securities, they do so based on their expectation of the return net of trading costs. Consider the case of a tax of 0.5 percent which is expected to be maintained forever. In this case, if investors have a discount rate of 8 percent and expect to hold securities for two years, the unexpected imposition of an STT should decrease stock prices by 3.5 percent and increase the before-tax expected return required by investors to hold shares by 0.25 percent.[6] Hence, the imposition of an STT decreases shareholder wealth and increases the cost of capital of firms. This means that one would

---

4. See Grossman and Miller (1988).
5. See, for instance, Froot, Scharfstein, and Stein (1992) for a model where some investors behave this way.
6. This number equals

$$0.005 + 0.005/(1.08)^2 + 0.005/(1.08)^4 + \ldots = 0.035.$$

expect an STT to decrease investment within a country and hence to have a negative impact on growth.

STTs and the Geography of Trading

Governments can tax and regulate within their borders. In the absence of cross-border restrictions on capital flows, one expects security markets to grow where taxes and regulations are the least onerous. Hence, governments that tax securities trades take the risk of driving away from their countries security markets altogether. Taxes and regulations imposed in the 1960s in the United States played a major role in the creation of the Euromarkets. Taxes and regulations within European countries have played a major role in the growth of trading of European stocks in London. In particular, the Swedish STT shifted trading of Swedish shares to London as discussed by Campbell and Froot.

In the presence of cross-border restrictions on capital flows, there is a role for national stock markets. This is because residents within a country can share risks among themselves more efficiently than they can with outside investors. In addition, when information flows slowly from one place to another, it makes sense for shares to trade where information is generated. Over the past ten years, however, barriers to international investment have fallen dramatically and technological advances have eliminated the informational advantage of proximity. In this setting, it is unclear what role there is for national stock markets.

One plausible scenario is that the Euromarkets will keep growing and will extend more to trading in shares. With this scenario, trading in shares would progressively be concentrated offshore and national markets would become less important, catering mostly to small investors. It is not clear how regulators can make the costs of trading offshore higher without imposing cross-border restrictions which would lead to renewed market segmentation. Hence, it would seem that offshore trading will keep creating pressures for deregulation as long as barriers to international investment keep falling.

STTs and the Political Economy of Globalization

Over the past ten years, markets have become more integrated mostly because of the decrease in barriers to international investment and, to a lesser extent, because of technological advances in communication. Although many seem to believe that globalization is irreversible, the experience of STTs should make us careful about drawing such a sweeping conclusion. In the absence of barriers to international investment, trade in securities takes place where it is most advantageous, which makes it difficult for countries to tax and regulate them. Hence, countries that wish to tax and regulate trade in securities may decide that they can only do so effectively if they limit cross-border flows. As countries place more restrictions on cross-border flows, offshore markets become less liquid and trading flows back to national markets, making it easier for governments to regulate and tax securities trading. This is not the first time in history that barriers to international investment are low.

References

Bhide, Amar. 1993. The hidden cost of stock market liquidity. *Journal of Financial Economics* 34:31–52.

Froot, Kenneth A., David Scharfstein, and Jeremy C. Stein. 1992. Herd on the street: Informational inefficiencies in a model with short-term speculation. *Journal of Finance* 47:1461–84.

Grossman, Sanford J., and Merton H. Miller. 1988. Liquidity and market structure. *Journal of Finance* 43:617–33.

Jacobs, Michael. 1991. *Short-term America.* Boston: Harvard Business School Press.

Karpoff, Jonathan M. 1987. The relation between price changes and trading volume: A survey. *Journal of Financial and Quantitative Analysis* 22:109–26.

7 Price Volatility and Volume Spillovers between the Tokyo and New York Stock Markets

Wen-Ling Lin and Takatoshi Ito

7.1 Introduction

Since the stock market crash of October 1987 there has been substantial interest in research on why stock returns and volatility are propagated across world markets. One possible interpretation for such interdependence of stock returns and volatility is an informational link across markets: news revealed in one country is perceived as informative to fundamentals of stock prices in another country.[1] This view can be attributed to real and financial linkage of economies.[2] Another possible interpretation for this issue is market contagion: stock prices in one country are affected by changes in another country beyond what is conceivable by connections through economic fundamentals. According to this view, overreaction, speculation, and/or noise trading (e.g., DeLong, Shleifer, Summers, and Waldman 1990) are transmissible across borders.

This paper studies the interdependent relationship between the Tokyo and New York stock markets by focusing on interactions of intradaily returns, volatility, and trading volume from October 1985 to December 1991. The principal objective of this paper is to disentangle the two possible interpretations by using three approaches. First, unlike other papers which analyze only price changes and volatility, this paper examines the effect of trading volume on

Wen-Ling Lin is assistant professor of economics at the University of Wisconsin-Madison. Takatoshi Ito is professor of economics at Hitotsubashi University, visiting professor at Harvard University, and a research associate of the National Bureau of Economic Research.

The authors are grateful to Jeffrey Frankel, Allan Kleidon, Bruce Lehmann, George von Furstenberg, Campbell Harvey, and participants at the NBER summer institute and the conference.

1. See, for example, Chan, Chan, and Karolyi (1991); Dravid, Richardson, and Craig (1993); and Lin, Engle, and Ito (1993).

2. An international asset pricing model (e.g., Adler and Dumas 1983 and Solnik 1974) can incorporate correlations between stock returns in different countries.

intermarket dependence in stock returns. Second, unlike several papers which study a causal relationship between price volatility and trading volume using one (domestic) market (usually the New York market), this paper is an international extension of volatility and volume studies. Third, unlike many academic and journalistic papers on the worldwide transmission of the price declines after Black Monday of 1987 in New York, this paper attempts to extend the literature of crashes by encompassing different episodes in the international transmission of large shocks in prices and volume, including the periods before and after Black Monday and the periods of the forming and bursting of the bubble of the Tokyo market.

The focus on trading volume in this paper follows from the view that trading volume is a good proxy for the degree of heterogeneity in investors' opinions and beliefs. (See the model built by Epps and Epps [1976] and Tauchen and Pitts [1983].) Most studies have reported a positive relationship between volatility and trading volume in the (domestic) stock market (see Karpoff 1987 for an excellent survey and Gallant, Rossi, and Tauchen 1992 for the empirical regularities). According to the mixture-of-distribution hypothesis, this positive relation is often attributed to the rate of information which drives both volatility and volume.

Another line of research on the price and volume relationship (in the domestic market) attempts to explain why correlations in stock returns depend on volume and price volatility. Morse (1980) found a positive effect of trading volume on the degree of autocorrelations in domestic stock returns. He interpreted this evidence as traders' revisions of prior beliefs of shocks. (See also Harris and Raviv 1991 for a theoretical model.) By contrast, Campbell, Grossman, and Wang (1993) uncovered a negative effect of trading volume on the autocorrelation of stock returns. They associated this phenomenon with the increased expected returns that compensate for informed traders' accommodation of liquidity traders' sales, which induce higher trading volume.

This paper extends these two views of autocorrelations of stock returns to an international context. In particular, the following two hypotheses for explaining the cause of international transmission of stock returns and volatility will be examined.[3] First, if correlations between international stock returns are caused by international contagion of liquidity traders' sentiments or by resolution of heterogenous interpretations of foreign news, such correlations are likely to be positively influenced by foreign trading volume. We call this the market contagion hypothesis. Second, if correlations between international

3. In this paper, we define correlations of stock returns between the New York and Tokyo markets as the cross-correlation between the daytime returns in one market and the overnight returns in the other market, where the time span of both returns overlaps in real time. By contrast, we define spillovers of stock returns between the two markets as correlations between the daytime returns in one market and the subsequent daytime returns in the other market, where the time span of the two returns does not overlap. A similar definition is also applied to trading volume and price volatility.

stock returns are associated with the informativeness of stock price changes in one market to another market, these correlations are likely to be positively influenced by foreign price volatility, but not by foreign trading volume. For instance, the domestic traders' extraction of a global factor from the observed foreign price change (e.g., King and Wadhwani 1990; and Lin, Engle, and Ito 1993) implies such a relation. The reason is that volatility is a better measure of the rate of information flow than trading volume. We call this the informational efficiency hypothesis. The use of trading volume enables us to assess the two possible channels of international transmission of international stock returns and volatility by examining the causal relation between the correlations of international stock returns, trading volume, and volatility.

To carry out the above analysis, we follow Lin, Engle, and Ito (1993) and Hamao, Masulis, and Ng (1990) in using the intradaily data of stock returns for both markets in order to clearly define the daytime and overnight returns for the two markets. Since the opening time of the Tokyo market is ahead of that of the New York market by either fourteen or thirteen hours, the information contained in the daytime return in one market is a subset of the information contained in the overnight return in the other market. Hence, we can examine the above two hypotheses—informational efficiency versus market contagion—by examining correlations between the daytime return in one market and the overnight returns in another market. Because the two daytime returns are not overlapped in real time, unlike the daily analysis by von Furstenberg and Jeon (1989) and Eun and Shim (1989), our framework is able to identify the origination of shocks so a clean test of how fast news from one market is transmitted to the other can be implemented. Suppose that a piece of news is revealed in the foreign market such as a trade balance or gross national product (GNP) announcement. This news is likely to affect the earnings of domestic export or import firms. According to the informational efficiency hypothesis, the domestic market is efficient in processing the foreign information so that such foreign information is incorporated into the domestic opening price. Lagged spillovers from foreign prices, volatility, or trading volume to their domestic counterparts after the domestic market opens should not arise. In other words, the opening prices should reflect overnight information relevant to the domestic country. If the domestic market is inefficient in the sense that domestic investors overreact or underreact to such information, spillovers are likely to arise, in particular when the domestic investors attempt to revise their prior beliefs about the value of stock returns or the domestic market gropes for the equilibrium price in resolving heterogenous beliefs of traders. The dependence of volatility correlations on the dispersion of expectations about the fundamental value of asset prices is suggested in a two-period, noisy, rational expectations model of Shalen (1993). Tests for no spillovers of return, volatility, or volume (as in Engle, Ito, and Lin 1990; and Lin, Engle, and Ito 1993) provide a rigorous method to test for the informational efficiency hypothesis.

One may argue that the existence of volatility spillover is not necessarily against the informational efficiency hypothesis because an informational link between two markets implies that price innovations in one market can predict the arrival of information in the other market (as predicted by the model of Ross 1989). Similarly, volume spillovers do not necessarily contradict the informational efficiency hypothesis because cross-border trading induces dissemination of information across markets. However, many studies in the literature have reported that cross-border trading is very light (Kleidon and Werner 1993), and that the arrival rate of marketwide information is not correlated due to infrequency policy coordination and competition between Japan and the United States (see Ito, Engle, and Lin 1992 for evidence). We believe that the possibility of either dependence on the arrival of information or cross-border trading exists, but that their effect on the stock prices may be very weak.

The test for volume spillovers is also motivated by the volume behavior on Black Monday, October 19, 1987. On that day, the Standard and Poor's 500 (S&P 500) composite index plunged 22.9 percent, setting off international repercussions. The next day, the Nikkei 225 index declined 16.1 percent and other world stock markets experienced similar sharp price declines. This well-known fact is still fresh in our memories. However, little attention has been paid to the volume behavior during the Crash period. The price declined on Black Monday in New York in heavy trading of 604 million shares, whereas Tokyo, the next day, traded only 618 million shares, which is rather light for the Tokyo market. As shown in figures 7.1 and 7.2, which plot the number of shares traded before and after the crash, the New York volume remained high for several days before and after Black Monday, while there was no such volume surge in Tokyo. This extended lack of volume surge cannot be explained by the trading halts of several individual stocks in Tokyo on the day after Black Monday.[4] This phenomenon motivates us to seek an alternative way to examine the informational efficiency hypothesis by testing for no return, volatility, and volume spillovers when a large foreign price (volume) shock occurs. Since price changes contain information and noise, under either one of the above two possibilities there is an increase in uncertainty in interpreting the effect of foreign price changes on the domestic stock price through connection of fundamental information. Hence, the domestic market may take more time to digest the foreign price changes. Return, volatility, or volume spillovers are likely to appear. We will take a close look at the effect of the Crash of October 19,

4. On October 21, 1987, Nihon Keizai Shimbun reported: "The limit on price changes in a day is as follows: 50 yen for stocks with prices between 100 and 200; 80 yen for stocks with prices between 200 and 500; 100 yen for stocks between 500 and 1,000, etc. . . . Theoretically, if all listed stocks on the Tokyo Stock Exchange were at the bottom of the price change limit, it would be -4059.75 in the Nikkei 225 index, while the actual change on October 20 was $-3,386.48$. On October 20, trading occurred on 753 stocks out of 1,100 listed stocks. Of the 753 stocks, 569 were at the bottom of the price limit" (translated by the authors). In sum, on October 20, many stocks were not traded because of the price change limit. During several weeks after October 20, there was little evidence that the price limit prevented trading from taking place.

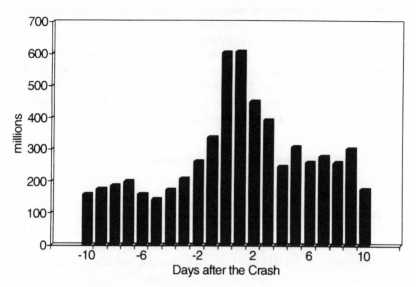

Fig. 7.1   **The number of shares traded on the NYSE during the Crash**

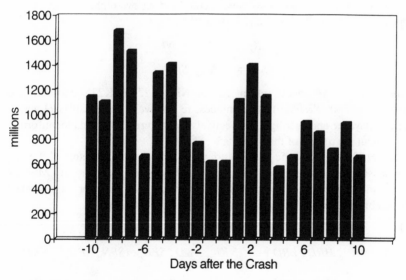

Fig. 7.2   **The number of shares traded on the TSE during the Crash**

1987, on the international transmission of stock returns. In particular, we will use hourly data to examine whether the correlation of stock returns in the United States and Japan increased during the Crash period and whether spillovers of international stock returns, volatility, and volume are likely to prevail when a large foreign price (volume) shock occurs during the other periods.

The rest of this paper is organized as follows: section 7.2 describes the empirical framework; section 7.3 presents an analysis of the correlation of stock returns between the New York and Tokyo markets; section 7.4 reports empirical results for the causal relationship of volatility and trading volume between New York and Tokyo; section 7.5 examines the effect of the Crash on correlations between the New York and Tokyo stock markets; section 7.6 concludes the paper by summarizing our main findings.

7.2 The Model and Econometric Specification

7.2.1 The Return Process

To analyze the international transmission of stock returns and volatility, King and Wadhwani (1990) set out a simple autoregressive and moving average process implied by a time-invariant extraction process; Hamao, Masulis, and Ng (1990) employed the GARCH-in-mean process; and Lin, Engle, and Ito (1993) used a signal extraction (Kalman filter) model with time-varying variances. This paper examines the issue along this line.

Following Lin, Engle, and Ito (1993), a daily (close-to-close) return is divided into a daytime (open-to-close) return and an overnight (close[$t-1$]-to-open) return for both Tokyo and New York:

$$NK_t = NKN_{t-1} + NKD_t$$

$$SP_t = SPN_t + SPD_t,$$

where NK and SP denote returns for the Nikkei 225 (NK225) and Standard and Poor's 500 (S&P500) price indices, respectively, and suffixes D and N denote daytime and overnight, respectively. See figure 7.3 for detailed information about the timing of the markets.[5]

Let HR be the domestic stock return and FR be the foreign return. Allowing for possible autocorrelations from the preceding overnight return, for Monday or postholiday effects through a dummy variable, DM, and for the influence from abroad, we can write the domestic overnight return as[6]

(1) $HRN_t = a_n + b_n HRD_t + c_n DM_t + m_{n,t} FRD_t + e_{n,t}$,

where $(HRN_t, HRD_t, FRD_t) \in \{(NKN_t, NKD_t, SPD_t), (SPN_t, SPD_{t-1}, NKD_t)\}$.

---

5. According to analyses by Stoll and Whaley (1990) and Lin, Engle, and Ito (1993), the 9:15 quotes for the TSE and the 10:00 quotes for the NYSE were chosen to avoid the nonsynchronous trading problem.

6. The Monday dummy for SPN is equal to one for returns from Friday close to Monday open and returns during holidays, and is equal to zero otherwise. The Monday dummy for NKN is equal to one for returns from Friday close to Monday open in the absence of Saturday trading, returns from Saturday close to Monday open in the presence of Saturday trading, and returns during holidays, and is equal to zero otherwise. See Gibbons and Hess (1981) for the evidence on the day-of-week effect.

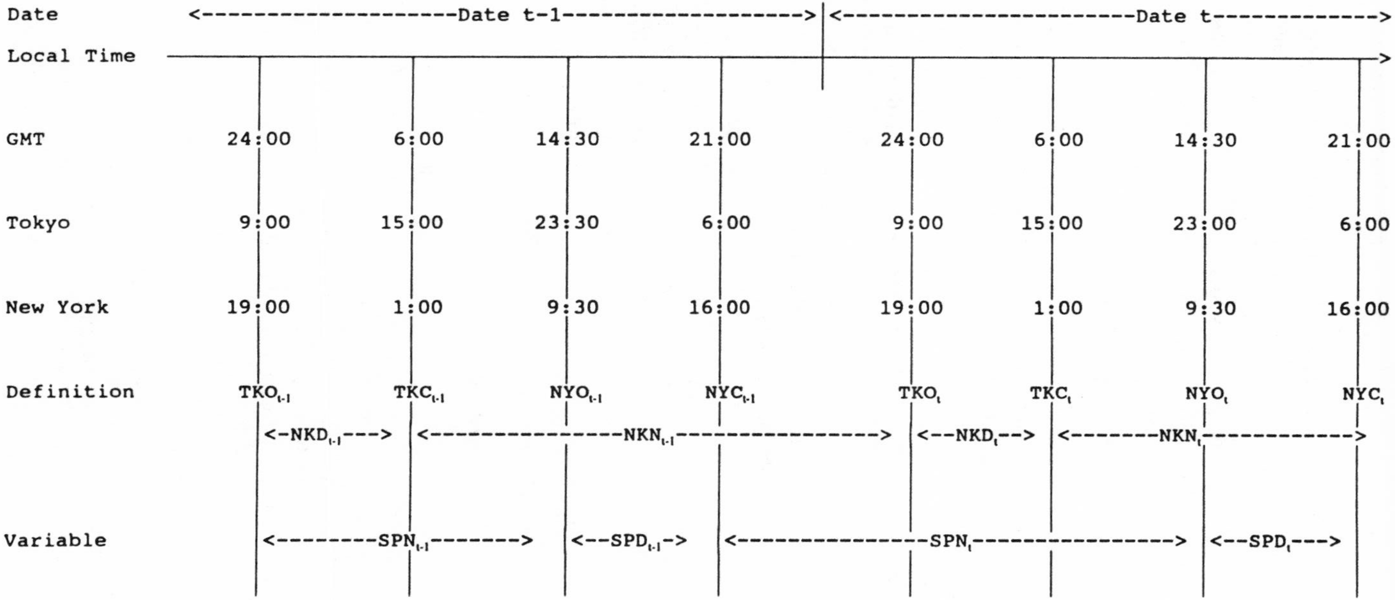

Date   <-------------------Date t-1-------------------> <-----|-----------------Date t----------------->

Local Time

GMT   24:00   6:00   14:30   21:00   24:00   6:00   14:30   21:00

Tokyo   9:00   15:00   23:30   6:00   9:00   15:00   23:00   6:00

New York   19:00   1:00   9:30   16:00   19:00   1:00   9:30   16:00

Definition TKO_{t-1} TKC_{t-1} NYO_{t-1} NYC_{t-1} TKO_t TKC_t NYO_t NYC_t

    <--NKD_{t-1}-->   <-------NKN_{t-1}------->   <--NKD_t-->   <-------NKN_t------->

Variable   <-------SPN_{t-1}------->   <--SPD_{t-1}-->   <-------SPN_t------->   <--SPD_t-->

Fig. 7.3   Timing of the New York and Tokyo stock exchanges

Notes: TKO = opening time in the Tokyo market; TKC = closing time in the Tokyo market; NYO = opening time in the New York market; NYC = closing time in the New York market; NKD = Nikkei 225 daytime (open-to-close) return; NKN = Nikkei 225 overnight (previous close-to-close) return; SPN = S&P 500 daytime (open-to-close) return; SPN = S&P 500 overnight (previous close-to-open) return.

We denote (x_t, y_t) as an element containing any pair of intradaily returns x_t and y_t on the New York Stock Exchange (NYSE) and the Tokyo Stock Exchange (TSE), $\{\}$ as a set of such elements, and E as the mathematical symbol for belonging to. Similar notations are used throughout the paper. The (contemporaneous) effect of foreign information is $m_{n,t} FRD_t$. A shock (news) revealed after the close of the foreign market but before the opening of the domestic market is denoted as $e_{n,t}$. We also assume that the daytime return follows a process similar to that of the overnight return:

$$(2) \qquad HRD_t = a_d + b_d HRD_t + c_d DM_t + m_{d,t} FRD_t + e_{d,t},$$

where $(HRD_t, HRN_t, FRD_t) \in \{(NKD_t, NKN_{t-1}, SPD_{t-1}), (SPD_t, SPN_t, NKD_t)\}$ and $e_{d,t}$ is the unexpected part of the return.[7] Since the information about the foreign market movement has become available to domestic investors at the open, $m_{d,t} FRD_t$ is the spillover effect from the foreign market to the domestic daytime returns. If the market is efficient, foreign news should be fully reflected in the opening price of the domestic market and $m_{d,t}$ will be equal to zero.

As mentioned in the above section, the objective of this analysis is to disentangle the informational efficiency versus market contagion hypotheses for the nature of international correlations of stock returns. Therefore, we allow $m_{n,t}$ to vary with dummy variables for periods of large volume, large shocks, and the sign of price changes in the foreign market.[8] The effect of a big shock using absolute returns as a proxy for volatility incorporates the implication of the informational efficiency hypothesis (such as predicted by the signal extraction model), whereas the effect of foreign trading volume incorporates the implication of the market contagion hypothesis. Specifically, $m_{n,t}$ follows

$$(3) \qquad m_{n,t} = \mu_{n,0} + \mu_{n,1} I\{FRD_t < 0\} + \mu_{n,2} I\{|FRD_t| > \sigma(FRD)\}$$
$$+ \mu_{d,3} I\{FRV_t > \sigma(FRV)\},$$

where $I\{A\}$ is an indicator function whose value is equal to one if statement A is true, $\sigma(X)$ is the sample standard deviation of variable X, and FRV is the foreign trading volume after detrending and removing the day-of-week effect. For simplicity, we denote $I\{FRD_t < 0\}$ as I_n, $I\{|FRD_t| > \sigma(FRD)\}$ as I_b, and $I\{|FRV_t| > \sigma(FRV)\}$ as I_V in tables 7.3 to 7.4. To test for lagged spillovers, we also allow $m_{d,t}$ to vary with the above three dummies. $m_{d,t}$ is specified as

---

7. Note the time difference: Tokyo is ahead of New York by either fourteen hours or thirteen hours (when New York is observing daylight saving time). Hence, the past foreign daytime returns, FRD, on the right-hand-side of equation (1), should be *day t-1*, S&P500 in the Tokyo equation, and *day t*, Nikkei in the New York equation.

8. We also add dummies for a small return shock and a low trading volume to our specification of returns, volatility, and trading volume processes. In almost all cases, we find insignificant results. Therefore, we only report the results for a large return shock and a large trading volume.

(4) $m_{d,t} = \mu_{d,0} + \mu_{d,1} I\{FRD_t < 0\} + \mu_{d,2} I\{|FRD_t| > \sigma(|FRD_t|)\}$

$+ \mu_{d,3} I\{FRV_t > \sigma(FRV)\}.$

If the market is efficient, we expect that $m_{d,t} = 0$.

7.2.2 Volatility and Volume Process

It has long been recognized that the volatility of stock prices is time-varying and clustered (see Bollerslev, Chou, and Kroner 1992 for a survey article). To examine the cross-market dependence on trading volume and volatility, we extend the specification of the GARCH process to account for possible variations in the effect of volatility spillovers across markets and the effect of the foreign trading volume on the domestic conditional variances. The processes of $e_{d,t}$ and $e_{n,t}$ follow

$$e_{n,t}|\Omega(j) \sim N(0, h_{nt})\ j \in \{TKC_t, NYC_t\}$$
$$e_{d,t}|\Omega(j) \sim N(0, h_{d,t})\ j \in \{TKO_t, NYO_t\},$$

where $\Omega(j)$ denotes the information set containing domestic and foreign daytime and overnight stock returns up to time j, and $N(.,.)$ denotes a normal distribution with the first element being the mean and the second element being the variance conditional on $M(j)$. The conditional variance, $h_{d,t}$ or $H_{n,t}$, follows

(5) $h_{k,t} = \omega_k + \alpha_k (e_{k,t-1})^2 + \beta_k h_{k,t-1} + \gamma_n DM_t$

$+ \delta_k (FRV_t)^2 + \rho_{k,t} (r_t)^2$ for $k = n$, and d.

In equation (5), we allow squared changes in shocks from the foreign daytime returns and trading volume (denoted as r_t and FRV_t, respectively) to influence the conditional variances of overnight returns. r_t is the unexpected part of stock returns (i.e., residuals from ordinary least squares [OLS] regression), whereas FRV_t is the foreign trading volume after removal of a trend component and the day-of-week effect. This setup enables us to test for contemporaneous correlations and lagged spillovers of price volatility between the international stock markets as studied by Lin, Engle, and Ito (1993) and Hamao, Masulis, and Ng (1990). A notable difference from the previous studies is that we allow the impact of the squared foreign return shock on the domestic variance to vary. Accounting for the effects of the sign of returns, a large shock, and high volume, we write $\rho_{k,t}$ for $k = n$ and d, as

(6) $\rho_{k,t} = \rho_{k,0} + \rho_{k,1} I\{r_t < 0\} + \rho_{k,2} I\{|r_t| > \sigma(r)\}$
$+ \rho_{k,3} I\{FRV_t > \sigma(FRV)\}.$

The specification of $\rho_{k,t}$ is motivated by the idea of Engle, Ito, and Lin (1990) for intermarket dependence in volatility and of Black (1976) and Christie (1982) for the leverage effect. In particular, when a large shock (due to a large rate of information flow) or large volume (due to the increased heterogeneity in investors' beliefs or sentiments) occurs in the foreign market, it may take more time for the market to resolve heterogenous interpretations or to disseminate information. In this situation, the market is not efficient in digesting new information and lagged spillovers will occur.

It is a well-known stylized fact that trading volume and volatility are positively correlated. Lamoureux and Lastrapes (1990) found that trading volume, a proxy for information arrival time, can affect the conditional variances (contemporaneously). The interpretation of this phenomenon is along the line of the mixture-of-distribution hypothesis—the rate of information flows is a driving force for both volatility and volume. In contrast with the mixture-of-distribution hypothesis, we explore whether the trading volume, a proxy for heterogeneity in foreign investors' beliefs, has explanatory power for the conditional variance of domestic returns.

The number of shares traded is used to measure trading volume, which usually exhibits nonstationarity. Campbell, Grossman, and Wang (1993) argued that a one-year backward moving average of past volume seems to be a better measure of market-making capacity. We use a similar procedure to remove the nonstationarity by obtaining the deviation from the one-hundred-day backward moving average of past volume.[9] Trading volume strongly exhibits the day-of-week effect as reported by Jain and Joh (1988) and Gallant, Rossi, and Tauchen (1992). We also remove the day-of-week and holiday effects from the one-hundred-day backward moving average of past volume. This daily volume variable, after removal of nonstationarity and the day-of-week and holiday effects, is denoted as HRV or FRV. To test our hypothesis of cross-market volume-price relation, we specify the volume process as

$$(7) \quad HRV_t = \sum_i \pi_i HRV_{t-i} + \sum_i \theta_i FRV_{t-i} + \sum_i \phi_i |HRD_{t-i}| + \sum_i \lambda_i |FRD_{t-i}|$$
$$+ \phi^* I\{HRD_{t-1} < 0\}) |HRD_{t-1}| + \lambda^* I\{FRD_t < 0\}) |FRD_t| + v_t,$$

where $(HRV_t, FRV_t, HRD_t, FRD_t) \in \{(NKV_t, SPV_{t-1}, NKD_t, SPD_{t-1}), (SPV_t, NKV_t, SPD_t, NKD_t)\}$. In equation (7), like many studies of the volume and volatility relation (e.g., Jain and Joh 1988), we use the absolute returns as a proxy for the rate of information to examine whether new information increases investors' heterogeneity and increases the incentive to trade. Unlike those studies, we allow both foreign and domestic absolute returns to affect the domestic trading volume. Similarly, a decrease in prices often suppresses

---

9. We denote the deviation of the trading volume from a one-hundred-day backward moving average as $HRMAV$. To remove the day-of-week effect and holiday effect, we obtain HRV from the OLS residuals of the regression of $HRMAV$ on several dummy variables as follows:

$$HRMAV_t = c + d_0 MON_t + d_1 TUE_t + d_2 THR_t + d_3 FRI_t + d_4 SAT_t$$
$$+ b_1 PHR_t + b_2 PSH_t + b_3 CHRS_t + HRV_t,$$

where $MON, TUE, THR, FRI,$ and SAT are the dummy variables for Monday, Tuesday, Thursday, Friday, and Saturday; and $PRH, PSH,$ and $CHRS$ are dummy variables for the day before holidays, the day after holidays, and the Christmas season from December 20 to January 10.

the incentive to trade because of an increase in risk aversion, a short-sale constraint, or other market frictions. We also specify this effect in a cross-market framework.

7.3   Cross-Market Dependence of U.S. and Japanese Stock Returns

7.3.1   Data Summary

The Tokyo Stock Exchange (TSE) and the New York Stock Exchange (NYSE) are the two largest equity markets in the world. We adopt the NK225 and S&P500 as the stock price indices for our analysis.[10] The NYSE opens its trading at 9:30 A.M. and continues trading until 4:00 P.M. The TSE opens at 9:00 A.M. and trades until 11:00 A.M., when it breaks for lunch. Prior to spring 1991, the afternoon session began at 1:00 P.M. and continued until 3:00 P.M. Since the spring of 1991 the afternoon session has started at 12:30 P.M. Tokyo is ahead of New York by either fourteen hours (in the winter) or thirteen hours (in the summer), so these trading hours do not overlap in real time.

Since we use the stock price indices, we need to be concerned about the problem of stale quotes in the opening of the market. As analyzed by Stoll and Whaley (1990), the average time to open a NYSE stock was fifteen minutes during 1982–88. Consequently, the opening index defined only a minute after trading begins may not reflect all the relevant information. Lin, Engle, and Ito (1993) reported a wide range of correlation analyses between S&P500 and NK225 daytime and overnight returns and found that thirty (fifteen) minutes after the official opening of the New York (Tokyo) Stock Exchange is a good proxy for opening quotes which can mitigate the effect of stale quotes or nonsynchronous trading.

To analyze whether interdependence in international stock returns depends on the regimes of bull or bear markets, we divide our sample from October 1985 to December 1991 into four subperiods: the first period runs from October 1, 1985, to September 30, 1987; the second from October 1, 1987, to December 31, 1987; the third from January 1, 1988, to December 31, 1989; and the last from January 1, 1990, to December 31, 1991. The first period was a bull-market period in which the Nikkei index moved from 12685 to 26010; the second was a bear-market period during which the Nikkei index dropped from 26010 to 21564; the third started tranquilly and then turned into a bull market in which the Nikkei index went from 21564 to 38915; and the last was a bear market period for the TSE during which the Nikkei decreased to 22983.

The data summary for these four subperiods is presented in table 7.1. Standard errors adjusted for heteroscedasticity and serial correlations (e.g., Newey

10. The Standard and Poor's 500 (S&P 500) is the equity-value weighted arithmetic mean of 500 stocks selected by Standard and Poor, Inc. The hourly data for the S&P 500 were kindly provided to us by Dr. J. Harold Muherlin. The Nikkei 225 (NK225) is a price-weighted simple average of 225 stock prices selected by Nihon Keizai Shimbun Sha.

Table 7.1   **Data Summary**

A. Nikkei 225

	NKMAV[d]		NKN[e]		NKD[e]	
	Mean[b]	Standard Deviation	Mean	Standard Deviation	Mean	Standard Deviation
Regime 1[a]	0.175	0.531	0.181	0.385	−0.052	0.776
	(0.069)	(0.024)	(0.016)	(0.019)	(0.033)	(0.056)
Regime 2	−0.422	0.507	0.078	0.733	−0.353	2.523
	(0.123)	(0.046)	(0.094)	(0.056)	(0.211)	(0.820)
Regime 3	0.010	0.472	0.150	0.384	−0.037	0.505
	(0.053)	(0.030)	(0.015)	(0.022)	(0.022)	(0.034)
Regime 4	−0.231	0.373	0.050	0.786	−0.157	1.360
	(0.046)	(0.033)	(0.032)	(0.039)	(0.057)	(0.144)
Test[c]	34.556	10.910	13.926	76.627	5.874	31.500
	(0.000)	(0.001)	(0.003)	(0.000)	(0.118)	(0.000)

B. Standard and Poor's 500

	SPMAV[d]		SPN[e]		SPD[e]	
	Mean[b]	Standard Deviation	Mean	Standard Deviation	Mean	Standard Deviation
Regime 1[a]	0.141	0.201	0.026	0.466	0.086	0.795
	(0.020)	(0.015)	(0.021)	(0.027)	(0.034)	(0.037)
Regime 2	0.107	0.363	−0.076	1.831	−0.337	2.888
	(0.090)	(0.073)	(0.140)	(0.383)	(0.388)	(0.988)
Regime 3	−0.036	0.211	0.024	0.446	0.047	0.826
	(0.019)	(0.011)	(0.020)	(0.030)	(0.028)	(0.093)
Regime 4	0.020	0.213	−0.010	0.513	0.043	0.803
	(0.020)	(0.015)	(0.022)	(0.046)	(0.034)	(0.034)
Test[c]	43.335	3.204	2.185	6.422	2.061	1.916
	(0.000)	(0.361)	(0.535)	(0.093)	(0.560)	(0.590)

[a]The number of observations in panel A is 566, 64, 522, and 499; in panel B, 506, 64, 504, and 506.

[b]The sample mean and standard deviations are reported in this table. The standard errors computed from the Newey and West 1987 autocorrelation- and heteroscedasticity-consistent covariance matrix for the sample mean and standard deviations are reported in the parentheses.

[c]Wald test statistics are for the null hypothesis that all coefficients of regimes 1 to 4 for the column are identical.

[d]NKMAV and SPMAV denote the deviation of the log of trading volume from its one-hundred day backward moving average of past volume.

[e]NKN = Nikkei 225 overnight (previous close-to-open) return;
NKD = Nikkei 225 daytime (open-to-close) return;
SPN = S&P 500 overnight (previous close-to-open) return;
SPD = S&P 500 daytime (open-to-close) return.

and West 1987) are reported in parentheses. Panel A of table 7.1 shows the results for the Tokyo overnight and daytime returns, and trading volume after removal of a trend component and the day-of-week and holiday effects. The Tokyo stock returns became more volatile in both the Crash and the fourth periods, while trading volume decreased. The stability test for the null hypothesis of equality of mean returns and their variances is rejected. Panel B of table 7.1 shows the counterparts in the NYSE. The standard deviation of stock returns in the NYSE was higher in the Crash period, and trading volume was lower in the third and fourth regimes. The stability test also shows a rejection of the equality of the variances of stock returns and trading volume across the four regimes.

7.3.2 Cross-Market Dependence

We begin by presenting evidence concerning the time-varying dependence of international stock returns. This dependence of international stock returns may result from traders' extraction of foreign news (e.g., King and Wadhwani 1990); and Lin, Engle, and Ito 1993), which depends on price volatility. A related study by Neumark, Tinsley, and Tosini (1991) assessed the dependence of volatility on correlations of international stock returns by sorting data during several weeks of the Crash period according to high or low volatility periods.[11] Gauging this volatility dependence hypothesis is a first step toward understanding the informational efficiency versus market contagion hypotheses. We use the above four data periods from 1985 to 1991 covering the Crash and the bull and bear periods of the Tokyo stock market to examine whether correlations (spillovers) between international stock returns depend upon the regimes of bull and bear markets and exhibit a structural break, whether correlations increase during the Crash period, and whether the Crash increased the international transmission of stock returns and volatility afterwards.

Table 7.2 shows the estimated regression results for cross-market dependence in stock returns across the New York and Tokyo stock markets. The results are obtained by using the ordinary least square estimation of equations (1) and (2) and by fixing $m_{n,t}$ or $m_{d,t}$ to be a constant. The coefficient m_n measures the impact of the foreign daytime return on the domestic overnight returns (i.e., the contemporaneous correlations of stock returns), while the coefficient m_d measures the impact of the foreign daytime return on the domestic daytime returns (i.e., the lagged spillover effect). The second and third columns in table 7.2 present the results for the impact of the New York daytime returns on the Tokyo daytime and overnight returns, whereas the fourth and fifth columns present the results for the effect of the NK225 daytime return to the S&P500 daytime and overnight returns. White's (1980) heteroscedasticity consistent

---

11. They assert that when volatility is high, the cross-border transaction is likely to be profitable and the correlations of international stocks will increase.

322   Wen-Ling Lin and Takatoshi Ito

Table 7.2   Cross-Market Dependence in Stock Returns

OLS regression:

(1) $HRN_t = a_n + b_n\,HRD_{t-1} + c_n\,DM_t + m_n\,FRD_t + e_{n,t}$,

where $(HRN_t, HRD_{t-1}, FRD_t) \in \{(NKN_t, NKD_t\,SPD_t), (SPN_t, SPD_{t-1}, NKD_t)\}$.

(2) $HRD_t = a_d + b_d\,HRN_t + c_d\,DM_t + m_d\,FRD_t + e_{d,t}$,

where $(HRD_t, HRN_t, FRD_t) \in \{(NKD_t, NKN_{t-1}, SPD_{t-1}), (SPD_t, SPN_t, NKD_t)\}$.

Equation No.	(1)	(2)	(1)	(2)
LHS Variables	NKN	NKD	SPN	SPD
Coefficients	m_n (t-statistic)	m_d (t-statistic)	m_a (t-statistic)	m_d (t-statistic)
Regime 1	0.194	−0.061	0.083	0.020
	(9.955)	(−1.172)	(2.312)	(0.443)
Regime 2	0.085	0.547	0.214	0.109
	(2.376)	(2.764)	(1.987)	(1.456)
Regime 3	0.217	−0.068	0.099	0.037
	(11.103)	(−1.510)	(2.096)	(0.649)
Regime 4	0.388	−0.033	0.156	−0.009
	(9.803)	(−0.307)	(6.323)	(−0.275)
Test[a]	33.296	9.317	3.612	2.285
	(0.000)	(0.025)	(0.307)	(0.515)

Note: LHS variables = left-hand-side variables.

[a]Wald test statistics are for the null hypothesis that all coefficients of regimes 1 to 4 for the column are identical. *P*-values are reported in parentheses.

standard errors are reported in the parentheses. Several conclusions emerge from table 7.2.

First, the first column in table 7.2 shows the coefficient of S&P500 daytime returns (*SPD*) on the regression of NK225 overnight returns (*NKN*). The hours defining *SPD* are a subset of those defining *NKN*, as shown in figure 7.3. Similarly, the third column shows the coefficient of *NKD* on the regression of *SPN*, where the hours of *NKD* are a subset of those of *SPN*. In general, the two contemporaneous effects of the foreign daytime return on the domestic overnight return, coefficient m_n, are statistically significant in all regimes when the lagged effects of the home market and various weekend and holiday effects are controlled. The second and fourth columns, using equation (2), show the estimated coefficients of (lagged) spillovers from SPD_{t-1} to NKD_t and NKD_t to SPD_t. These estimates and Student *t*-statistics show that (lagged) international spillovers are generally insignificant. Combining the results of significant contemporaneous dependence in stock returns but insignificant spillovers, we can assert that any news revealed in the foreign market overnight is completely incorporated into the opening prices of the home market as we allow some minutes to avoid a stale quote problem (see Lin, Engle, and Ito 1993 for further discussion of this issue).

Second, the contemporaneous correlations of international stock returns measured as m_n in equation (1) for regime 2, the Crash period, are smaller than those for other periods, while the coefficients for the lagged spillovers of the Crash period are greater than those of other periods. A comparison of the magnitude of coefficients in regime 2 to those in other regimes suggests that during the Crash period, news revealed in the foreign markets could not be incorporated into the opening price due to the increased uncertainty and breakdown in interpretation of large shocks. Hence, because the Crash period is so different, we will not use it in our subsequent analysis.

Third, a comparison of the magnitudes of the two coefficients for contemporaneous correlations shows both the effect of *SPD* on *NKN* and the effect of *NKD* on *SPN*. The former effect (column 1) is greater than the latter effect (column 3). In addition, the impact of foreign stock returns on domestic overnight stock returns increased in the fourth period but declined in the Crash period. Tests for structural breaks, given these three break points, show a rejection of the null hypothesis of no structural breaks in the Tokyo market, but not in the New York market. Finding a positive and larger coefficient for contemporaneous correlations in international stock returns may not imply the increased integration of the international financial markets. One explanation for this is that the correlation of the stock returns depends on the nature of the shocks. Some shocks affect the stock returns in the same direction but others affect them oppositely. Thus, the sign of the contemporaneous correlations of the international stock returns depends on the combined effects of these two types of shocks. Moreover, the evidence that the impact of *SPD* on *NKN* is larger than that of *NKD* on *SPN* does not imply that New York news is more important for the Tokyo market, because the effect of a third country is ignored in our analysis.[12]

7.3.3   Asymmetric Effects on Cross-Market Correlations and Spillovers

In the above analysis, we have shown that domestic overnight returns are significantly affected by foreign daytime returns. In this section, we extend our previous analysis by examining the following asymmetric effects on the international transmission of stock returns and volatility: (*a*) volatility effect— the cross-market dependence on stock returns (contemporaneous correlations or lagged spillovers) is greater when the volatility increases; (*b*) volume effect—the cross-market dependence on stock returns is greater when international stock return correlations or spillovers are associated with trading volume; (*c*) sign of price changes—a decline in prices, as opposed to an increase, increases the effect of international transmission on stock returns and volatility.

In the context of the international transmission of stock returns, King and Wadhwani (1990); Lin, Engle, and Ito (1993); and Neumark, Tinsley, and Tosini (1991) have highlighted the importance of the increase in correlations of

12. We thank George von Furstenberg for his comments to us about these phenomena.

international stock returns during a period of high volatility. The purpose of examining the first and second effects is to disentangle the informational efficiency hypothesis from the market contagion hypothesis. As for the third effect, Nelson (1991) argued that a decline in prices is associated with higher future price variability. This asymmetry has been attributed to a leverage effect (e.g., Black 1976 and Christie 1982) in which a decline in equity prices decreases the equity to debt ratio and increases the riskiness of the firms. From an international perspective, a leverage effect may increase domestic price volatility and hence increase the international correlation coefficient as investors extract the information from overseas price changes.

In table 7.3, we present the empirical results for various asymmetric effects on cross-market dependence in stock returns, which can be viewed as an extension of correlations of stock returns in the home market (e.g., Antoniewicz 1992; Campbell, Grossman, and Wang 1993; and LeBaron 1992) to an international context. Our interacting variables include dummies for a negative return, a large price shock (i.e., absolute returns greater than one standard deviation of returns in the sample), and large volume. Since the Crash period spans only three months (the number of observations is less than seventy), we report the results only for the other three periods in the following and section 7.4.

These empirical results are not strongly supportive of asymmetric effects on cross-market correlations. A large shock from S&P500 returns significantly increased the influence of S&P500 daytime returns on NK225 overnight returns in regimes 1 and 3, and negative S&P500 daytime returns also increased such an impact in regime 1. However, a large foreign trading volume has no impact on the contemporaneous correlation of stock returns across markets. The results for the asymmetric effect of NK225 daytime returns on the S&P500 returns is also weak. There is no evidence of a significant effect of either Tokyo volume or price volatility on New York stock returns, which can be repeatedly shown across all three regimes.

The aim of the above analysis in tables 7.2 and 7.3 is to shed light on the market contagion and informational efficiency hypotheses. Under the market contagion hypothesis, applying the idea of Campbell, Grossman, and Wang (1993), the informed traders in the home market would be likely to accommodate the sales of uninformed traders who, upon observing a price drop in the foreign market, may become more risk averse. As a result, the expected returns would increase, the current price would drop, and the effect of foreign daytime returns on domestic overnight (daytime) returns would increase (decrease) when the foreign trading volume increased. Under the informational efficiency hypothesis, the foreign price changes are informative to the fundamentals of the domestic stock returns. As a result, a higher rate of information in the foreign market increases (contemporaneous) correlations of stock returns between the home and foreign markets as investors extract this information from the observed foreign price change. Our findings of contemporaneous correlations of stock returns across markets in tables 7.2 and 7.3 dispute the market

Table 7.3   **Asymmetric Effect on Cross-Market Dependence in Stock Returns**

OLS regression:

(3) $HRN_t = a_n + b_n\,HRD_{t-1} + c_n\,DM_t + (\mu_{n,0} + \mu_{n,1}I_n + \mu_{n,2}I_b + \mu_{n,3}I_v)FRD_t + e_{n,t}$,

where $(HRN_t, HRD_{t-1}, FRD_t) \in \{(NKN_t, NKD_t, SPD_t), (SPN_t, SPD_{t-1}, NKD_t)\}$.

(4) $HRD_t = a_d + b_d\,HRN_t + c_d\,DM_t + (\mu_{d,0} + \mu_{d,1}I_n + \mu_{d,2}I_b + \mu_{d,3}I_v)FRD_t + e_{d,t}$,

where $(HRD_t, HRN_t, FRD_t) \in \{(NKD_t, NKN_{t-1}, SPD_{t-1}), (SPD_t, SPN_t, NKD_t)\}$.

A. From SPD to NKN or NKD

Equation No.	(3)			(4)		
LHS Variables	NKN			NKD		
Coefficients	$\mu_{n,1}$ (*t*-statistic)	$\mu_{n,2}$ (*t*-statistic)	$\mu_{n,3}$ (*t*-statistic)	$\mu_{d,1}$ (*t*-statistic)	$\mu_{d,2}$ (*t*-statistic)	$\mu_{d,3}$ (*t*-statistic)
Regime 1	0.125 (2.364)	0.115 (2.439)	0.027 (0.493)	0.037 (0.250)	0.029 (0.287)	0.018 (0.140)
Regime 3	−0.028 (−0.621)	0.096 (2.120)	0.026 (0.693)	−0.050 (−0.703)	0.061 (0.874)	−0.051 (−0.736)
Regime 4	−0.071 (−0.599)	−0.009 (−0.095)	0.145 (1.630)	0.017 (0.056)	0.008 (0.045)	0.166 (0.502)

B. From NKD to SPN or SPD

Equation No.	(3)			(4)		
LHS	SPN			SPD		
Coefficients	$\mu_{n,1}$ (*t*-statistic)	$\mu_{n,2}$ (*t*-statistic)	$\mu_{n,3}$ (*t*-statistic)	$\mu_{d,1}$ (*t*-statistic)	$\mu_{d,2}$ (*t*-statistic)	$\mu_{d,3}$ (*t*-statistic)
Regime 1	0.101 (1.042)	0.028 (0.382)	−0.078 (−1.131)	−0.048 (−0.346)	−0.158 (−1.357)	−0.254 (−2.209)
Regime 3	−0.035 (−0.234)	0.067 (0.731)	0.025 (0.242)	−0.096 (−0.617)	−0.051 (−0.282)	0.170 (0.959)
Regime 4	0.022 (0.306)	−0.012 (−0.255)	−0.022 (−0.416)	0.005 (0.073)	−0.231 (−3.357)	−0.004 (−0.051)

Note: LHS variables = left-hand-side variables.

contagion scenario. Moreover, the findings of no significant spillover from the foreign daytime return to the domestic daytime return are supportive of the informational efficiency hypothesis in that the domestic market can very quickly process the foreign information.

7.4   Evidence on the Volatility and Volume Processes

The cause of correlations and spillovers in volatility and volume across markets is another focus of this paper. In this section, we apply a two-stage GARCH estimation method to specify the processes of time-varying conditional variances: first, we employ an OLS regression for equations (1) and (2) and obtain OLS residuals; second, we fit a GARCH process for conditional variances of unexpected returns. After fitting the GARCH model, we calculate the skewness and the kurtosis of standardized residuals. These statistics are still too large to accept the null hypothesis of a normal distribution. Therefore, we report the robust standard errors as calculated by Bollerslev and Wooldridge (1992). The volume process is estimated by OLS with White's (1980) heteroscedasticity consistent covariance matrix.

7.4.1 The Volatility Process

One line of research on intermarket dependence of financial markets examines volatility correlations and spillovers across markets. For instance, Engle, Ito, and Lin (1990) and Ito, Engle, and Lin (1992) investigated this issue for the foreign exchange markets. Chan, Chan, and Karolyi (1991) examined intermarket dependence across the stock index and the stock index future markets. Since volatility is related to the rate of information flows (e.g., Ross 1989), the intermarket dependence between the volatility of each market can be attributed to the dissemination of information flow across the two markets. Volatility is also partly related to the dispersion of prior beliefs (e.g., Shalen 1993). As predicted by Shalen's (1993) model, an increase in the dispersion of beliefs may induce volatility correlations (spillovers). In this section, the test for no volatility spillovers is used to gauge the second hypothesis by examining how fast the market gropes for the equilibrium price and resolves heterogenous beliefs.

Following the procedure described in the beginning of section 7.4, we report the empirical results in table 7.4. A large shock or a large volume dummy interacting with the square of foreign price volatility does not have explanatory power for the domestic price volatility. Furthermore, we found that there is no causal relation between lagged foreign trading volume and domestic conditional variances. Overall, our results are consistent with Lin, Engle, and Ito (1993), who showed a lack of volatility correlation or spillover effects. These findings suggest that the domestic market may adjust to foreign information very quickly in resolving domestic investors' dispersion of beliefs about foreign information. Hence, there are no volatility spillovers. Some attention may be given to the asymmetric effect of the sign of the foreign price change on the volatility spillovers.

7.4.2 Volume Processes

Why might trading volume be correlated across markets? Several possible factors may contribute to this phenomenon. The first is cross-market trading. Chowdhry and Nanda (1991) developed a theoretical framework to explain the practice of multimarket trading. They showed that when a security trades at multiple locations simultaneously, an informed trader has several ways to exploit his private information. As the proportion of liquidity trading by large

Table 7.4   **Cross-Market Dependence in Volatility of Stock Returns**

Model:

$$e_{n,t}|\Omega(j) \sim N(0, h_{n,t}) \quad j \in \{TKC_t, NYC_t\}$$

(5) $\quad h_{n,t} = \omega_n + \alpha_n (e_{n,t-1})^2 + \beta_n h_{n,t-1} + \gamma_n DM_t + \delta_n (FRV_t)^2 +$
$\quad\quad (\rho_{n,0} + \rho_{n,1}I_n + \rho_{n,2}I_b + \rho_{n,3}I_v) (r_t)^2$

or

$$e_{d,t}|\Omega(j) \sim N(0, h_{d,t}) \quad j \in \{TKO_t, NYO_t\}$$

(6) $\quad h_{d,t} = \omega_d + \alpha_d (e_{d,t-1})^2 + \beta_d h_{d,t-1} + \gamma_d DM_t + \delta_d (FRV_t)^2 +$
$\quad\quad (\rho_{d,0} + \rho_{d,1}I_n + \rho_{d,2}I_b + \rho_{d,3}I_v) (r_t)^2,$

where $\Omega(j)$ denotes the information set containing domestic and foreign daytime and overnight stock returns up to time j, $e_{n,t}$ or $e_{d,t}$ denotes the OLS residuals from the last regression, r_t is the most recent foreign unexpected returns (OLS residuals), and FRV_t is the foreign trading volume after removal of the day-of-week and holiday effects and nonstationarity.

A. NKN

LHS Variables (equation)	NKN (5)				
Coefficients	$\rho_{n,0}$ (*t*-statistic)	$\rho_{n,1}$ (*t*-statistic)	$\rho_{n,2}$ (*t*-statistic)	$\rho_{n,3}$ (*t*-statistic)	δ_n (*t*-statistic)
Regime 1	−0.021	0.011	0.023	−0.002	−0.006
	(−1.418)	(1.300)	(1.662)	(−0.274)	(−0.138)
Regime 3	−0.033	0.026	0.015	−0.003	0.135
	(−0.505)	(5.007)	(0.227)	(−0.523)	(1.469)
Regime 4	−0.049	0.048	0.007	−0.006	−0.040
	(−1.247)	(2.249)	(0.211)	(0.354)	(−0.415)

B. NKD

LHS Variables (equation)	NKD (6)				
Coefficients	$\rho_{d,0}$ (*t*-statistic)	$\rho_{d,1}$ (*t*-statistic)	$\rho_{d,2}$ (*t*-statistic)	$\rho_{d,3}$ (*t*-statistic)	δ_d (*t*-statistic)
Regime 1	0.115	0.027	−0.101	0.014	0.002
	(1.082)	(0.938)	(−0.976)	(0.327)	(0.011)
Regime 3	0.064	0.035	−0.088	−0.010	0.344
	(0.413)	(3.315)	(−0.566)	(−0.847)	(1.555)
Regime 4	−0.200	0.013	0.087	0.035	1.146
	(−2.393)	(0.482)	(1.386)	(1.376)	(1.735)

C. SPN

LHS Variables (equation)	SPN (5)				
Coefficients	$\rho_{n,0}$ (*t*-statistic)	$\rho_{n,1}$ (*t*-statistic)	$\rho_{n,2}$ (*t*-statistic)	$\rho_{n,3}$ (*t*-statistic)	δ_n (*t*-statistic)
Regime 1	0.011	0.011	−0.005	0.022	−0.036
	(0.213)	(0.623)	(−0.101)	(1.139)	(−1.778)
Regime 3	−0.145	0.033	0.137	−0.074	0.019
	(−3.132)	(1.301)	(3.069)	(−3.820)	(1.117)
Regime 4	0.016	0.013	0.004	−0.022	0.013
	(0.488)	(1.067)	(0.129)	(−1.897)	(0.396)

Table 7.4   (continued)

D. SPD

LHS Variables (equation)	SPD (6)				
Coefficients	$\rho_{d,0}$ (*t*-statistic)	$\rho_{d,1}$ (*t*-statistic)	$\rho_{d,2}$ (*t*-statistic)	$\rho_{d,3}$ (*t*-statistic)	δ_d (*t*-statistic)
Regime 1	−0.247	−0.061	0.261	0.094	0.025
	(−4.954)	(−6.032)	(5.461)	(4.387)	(1.315)
Regime 3	0.702	−0.136	−0.554	0.018	0.035
	(1.756)	(−0.955)	(−1.538)	(0.182)	(0.369)
Regime 4	0.027	0.052	−0.041	−0.010	0.029
	(0.398)	(2.581)	(−0.587)	(−0.475)	(0.418)

Note: LHS variables = left-hand-side variables.

traders who can split their trades across markets increases, the correlation between volume in different markets will increase. A second factor is an increase in the dispersion of beliefs about the information revealed in other markets.

Table 7.5 reports the estimated processes for trading volume and shows that trading volume in one market cannot significantly Granger cause trading volume in the other markets. The behavior of trading volume across markets has not received great attention in the literature. French and Poterba (1990) showed that cross-border trading accounts for less than 1 percent of trading in the Tokyo and New York markets. Kleidon and Werner (1993) also show limited cross-border trading for the London and New York markets. Due to the limited cross-border trading, it is not surprising that there is no significant evidence of intermarket dependence on the trading volume (except in the case of the Tokyo stock market in the fourth period).

We also test whether absolute returns, used as a proxy for the arrival rate of information, will affect trading volume across markets. By evaluating Wald statistics having a chi-squared distribution with six degrees of freedom, we find that the null hypothesis of no effect of foreign absolute returns on domestic trading volume cannot be rejected except for the effect of *SPD* on *NKV* in the first period. This result suggests that foreign information may not change domestic investors' incentive to trade. This result, along with the result of no evidence of cross-market interdependence in trading volume, suggests that the dissemination of foreign information does not increase the heterogeneity in domestic investors' beliefs about foreign news nor increase incentives to trade. These results also suggest that the market may be efficient in processing foreign news and that opening prices incorporate such overnight news.

We also examine the asymmetric effects on trading volume and report the results on the left side of table 7.5. Literature has documented that volume becomes lower when returns fall than when returns rise. Studies attribute this

Table 7.5   **Cross-market Dependence in Trading Volume**

Model:

(7) $\text{HRV}_t = \Sigma_i \pi_i\, \text{HRV}_{t-i} + \Sigma_i \phi_i\, \text{FRV}_{t-i} + \Sigma_i \phi_i |\text{HRD}_{t-i}| + \Sigma_i \lambda_i |\text{FRD}_{t-i}|$
$\qquad\qquad + \phi^* \, \text{I}\{\text{HRD}_{t-i}<0\})|\text{HRD}_{t-i}| + \lambda^* \text{I}\{\text{FRD}_t<0\})|\text{FRD}_t| + v_t,$

where $(\text{HRV}_t, \text{FRV}_t, \text{HRD}_t, \text{FRD}_t) \in \{(\text{NKV}_t, \text{SPV}_{t-1}, \text{NKD}_t, \text{SPD}_{t-1}), (\text{SPV}_t, \text{NKV}_t, \text{SPD}_t, \text{NKD}_t)\}.$

A. NKV

| | HRV = NKV   FRV = SPV | | | | |
| | Causality | Test[a] | | Asymmetric Effect[b] | |
Coefficients	$\theta_i, i = 0,5$ (p-value)	$\phi_i, i = 1,5$ (p-value)	$\lambda_i, i = 0,5$ (p-value)	ϕ^* (t-statistic)	λ^* (t-statistic)
Regime 1	4.268 (0.640)	11.510 (0.042)	24.807 (0.000)	−0.136 (−4.257)	−0.119 (−4.185)
Regime 3	3.155 (0.789)	1.534 (0.909)	6.585 (0.361)	−0.253 (−5.462)	−0.061 (−2.060)
Regime 4	21.863 (0.001)	10.199 (0.070)	10.378 (0.110)	−0.029 (−1.105)	−0.029 (−1.743)

B. SPV

| | HRV = SPV   FRV = NKV | | | | |
| | Causality | Test[a] | | Asymmetric Effect[b] | |
Coefficients	$\theta_i, i = 0,5$ (p-value)	$\phi_i, i = 1,5$ (p-value)	$\lambda_i, i = 0,5$ (p-value)	ϕ^* (t-statistic)	λ^* (t-statistic)
Regime 1	6.554 (0.364)	33.539 (0.000)	7.789 (0.254)	−0.061 (−3.367)	−0.035 (−1.657)
Regime 3	4.271 (0.640)	38.071 (0.000)	6.975 (0.323)	−0.008 (−0.290)	0.043 (1.396)
Regime 4	10.530 (0.104)	11.303 (0.046)	7.693 (0.261)	−0.049 (−2.598)	0.008 (0.550)

[a]The causality test is a Wald test using White's (1980) heteroscedasticity-consistent covariance matrix, which is distributed as a chi-squared distribution with the degree of freedom of 5 or 6. P-values are reported in the regression.
[b]The estimated coefficients and corresponding t-statistics are in parentheses.

phenomenon to the cost of short selling, borrowing, or an increase in risk aversion (see the survey by Karpoff 1987). The results reported in the middle part of table 7.5 show evidence of the asymmetric effect of returns on trading volume not only in the domestic market, but also across markets.[13]

13. We also test for the asymmetric effect of a large lagged return shock and a large lagged trading volume on the current trading volume. We find insignificant results. Therefore, the results are not reported.

7.5   Return Spillovers during the Crash Period

The stock market crash of October 19, 1987, has inspired several studies of its causes, although consensus has not yet been reached. Roll (1989) suggested downward revised expectations for worldwide economic activity, while Seyhun (1990) argued for the overreaction of uninformed traders by using positive feedback strategies. Evidence of the abnormally higher autocorrelations of high frequency (cash) stock index returns is also reported in Harris (1989) and Kleidon (1992). Harris suggested that this was due to nonsynchronous trading, whereas Kleidon (1992) argued that it was caused by stale quotes attributable to the physical limitations in the processing of automated orders on the NYSE during the crash period.

In section 7.3.2, we found that there is a significant increase in return spillovers from *SPD* to *NKD*. Hence, we further investigate how fast such spillovers can die out. In contrast to the analysis of correlations in domestic (cash and future) stock returns by Harris (1989) and Kleidon (1992), this analysis is an examination of cross correlations of New York and Tokyo stock returns during the Crash period. Table 7.6 reports an OLS regression, similar to equation (2), for hourly stock returns. The standard errors are also adjusted for heteroscedasticity. We found a significant spillover effect of *SPD* on NK225 hourly returns. The significant impact of *SPD* on hourly NK225 returns appears during all business hours in the Tokyo market except for the lunch break, while the impact of *NKD* on S&P500 hourly stock returns is significant only from 1 P.M. to 2 P.M. Since we did not observe abnormal trading volume in Tokyo during the Crash period, we conjecture that the Crash was informative to Tokyo traders but they were skeptical about the causes of the Crash. Thus, uncertainties about the cause of the Crash may have led to a lag adjustment of this information and a significant return spillover.

7.6   Conclusion

The world scope of the stock market crash in October 1987 raised concerns about how financial disturbances transmit from one market to another. In this paper, we extend the previous work in this area (e.g., King and Wadhwani 1990; Lin, Engle, and Ito 1993; and Hamao, Masulis, and Ng 1990) by accounting for the interactions of trading volume, returns, and volatility across markets. Trading volume is used because it can serve as a proxy for the degree of heterogeneity in investors' beliefs. We approach this issue by using a simple regression model with a GARCH process and by considering the asymmetric effects of the sign and magnitude of stock returns and the magnitude of trading volume.

Using this framework, we test whether the transmission of international financial disturbances is due to liquidity traders' sentiments or to the informativeness of stock returns. On one hand, if the transmission of international fi-

Table 7.6   **Returns Spillovers during the Crash Period—Hourly Analysis**

A. Spillovers from SPD to NKD

NK225[a] Hourly Returns	9:15–10	10–11	11–13:15	13:15–14	14–15
SPD	0.088[b]	0.113	0.039	0.082	0.163
	(2.844)	(2.231)	(0.845)	(3.024)	(2.792)

B. Spillovers from NKD to S&P500 Hourly Stock Returns

S&P500[a] Hourly Returns	10–11	11–12	12–13	13–14	14–15	16–16:30
NKD	0.055[b]	−0.020	−0.028	0.108	0.012	0.053
	(0.463)	(0.359)	(−0.774)	(2.289)	(0.191)	(1.002)

[a]The first row lists the time span for hourly stock returns of dependent variables, and the first column lists the exogenous variable.

[b]The estimated coefficients and corresponding t-statistics (calculated using White's [1980] heteroscedasticity-consistent covariance matrix) are in parentheses.

nancial disturbances results from the first source, as the model of Campbell, Grossman, and Wang (1993) predicts, the impact of foreign daytime returns on domestic overnight (daytime) returns is likely to increase (decrease) when the volume is higher. On the other hand, if the transmission results from the second source, the correlation will increase with the volatility of shocks as domestic investors extract the foreign information, as described by King and Wadhwani (1990) and Lin, Engle, and Ito (1993).

Our general finding is supportive of the second hypothesis for the transmission of shocks from the New York market to the Tokyo market. We uncovered evidence that the regression coefficient of the S&P500 daytime returns on the NK225 overnight returns increases when a large shock occurs. In addition, we found no evidence on volume, volatility, or return spillovers for the four regimes except the Crash period, so opening prices, after allowing some time for clearing stale quotes, reflect all world news revealed overnight. Thus, both markets adjust to foreign information efficiently.

References

Adler, Michael, and Bernard Dumas. 1983. International portfolio choice and corporation finance: A synthesis. *Journal of Finance* 38:925–84.

Antoniewicz, Rochelle. 1992. An empirical analysis of stock returns and volume. Ph.D. diss., University of Wisconsin, Madison.

Black, Fischer. 1976. Studies of stock market volatility changes. Proceedings of the American Statistical Association, Business and Economic Statistics Section, 177–81.

Bollerslev, Tim, Ray Y. Chou, and Kenneth F. Kroner. 1992. ARCH modeling in finance: A review of the theory and empirical evidence. *Journal of Econometrics* 52:5–60.

Bollerslev, Tim, and Jeffrey Wooldridge. 1992. Quasi maximum likelihood estimation of dynamic models with time varying covariances. *Econometric Reviews* 11:143–72.

Campbell, John Y., Sanford J. Grossman, and Jiang Wang. 1993. Trading volume and serial correlation in stock returns. *Quarterly Journal of Economics* 108:905–39.

Chan, Kalok, K. C. Chan, and G. Andrew Karolyi. 1992. Intraday volatility in the stock index and stock index futures markets. *Review of Financial Studies* 4:657–84.

Chowdhry, Bhagwan, and Vikram Nanda. 1991. Multimarket trading and market liquidity. *The Review of Financial Studies* 4:453–511.

Christie, Andrew A. 1982. The stochastic behavior of common stock variances: Value, leverage and interest rate effects. *Journal of Financial Economics* 10:407–32.

DeLong, J. Bradford, Andrei Shleifer, Lawrence Summers, and Robert J. Waldman. 1990. Noise trader risk in financial markets. *Journal of Political Economy* 98:703–38.

Dravid, A., Matthew Richardson, and Andrew Craig. 1993. Explaining overnight variation in Japanese stock returns: The information content of derivative securities. Working paper, Wharton School, University of Pennsylvania.

Engle, Robert F., Takatoshi Ito, and Wen-Ling Lin. 1990. Meteor showers or heat waves? Heteroskedasticity intra-daily volatility in the foreign exchange market. *Econometrica* 58:525–42.

Epps, Thomas W., and Mary L. Epps. 1976. The stochastic dependence of security price changes and transaction volumes: Implications for the mixture-of-distributions hypotheses. *Econometrica* 44:305–21.

Eun, Cheol S., and Sangdal Shim. 1989. International transmission of stock market movements. *Journal of Financial and Quantitative Analysis* 24:241–56.

French, Kenneth R., and James M. Poterba. 1990. Japanese and U.S. cross-border common stock investment. *Journal of the Japanese and International Economy* 4:476–93.

Gallant, A. Ronald, Peter E. Rossi, and George Tauchen. 1992. Stock prices and volume. *Review of Financial Studies* 5:199–242.

Gibbons, Michael and P. Hess. 1981. Day of the week effect and asset returns. *Journal of Business* 54:579–96.

Hamao, Yasushi, Ronald W. Masulis, and Victor Ng. 1990. Correlations in price changes and volatility across international stock markets. *Review of Financial Studies* 3:281–308.

Harris, Lawrence. 1989. The October 1987 S&P 500 stock-futures basis. *Journal of Finance* 45:77–99.

Harris, Milton, and Arthur Raviv. 1991. Differences of opinion make a race horse. *Review of Financial Studies*. Forthcoming.

Ito, Takatoshi, Robert F. Engle, and Wen-Ling Lin. 1992. Where does the meteor shower come from? The role of stochastic policy coordination. *Journal of International Economics* 32:221–40.

Jain, Prem J., and Gunho Joh. 1988. The dependence between hourly prices and trading volume. *Journal of Financial and Quantitative Analysis* 23:269–83.

Karpoff, Jonathan M. 1987. The relation between price changes and trading volume: A survey. *Journal of Financial and Quantitative Analysis* 22:109–26.

King, Mervyn, and Sushil Wadhwani. 1990. Transmission of volatility between stock markets. *Review of Financial Studies* 3:5–33.

Kleidon, Allan W. 1992. Arbitrage, nontrading, and stale prices: October 1987. *Journal of Business* 65:483–507.

Kleidon, Allan W., and Ingrid M. Werner. 1993. Round-the-clock trading: Evidence from U.K. cross-listed securities. NBER Working Paper no. 4410. Cambridge, Mass.: National Bureau of Economic Research.

Lamoureux, Christopher G., and William D. Lastrapes. 1990. Heteroskedasticity in stock return data: Volume versus GARCH effects. *Journal of Finance* 46:221–29.

LeBaron, Blake. 1992. Some relations between volatility and serial correlation in stock market returns. *Journal of Business* 65:199–220.

Lin, Wen-Ling, Robert F. Engle, and Takatoshi Ito. 1993. Do bulls and bears move across borders? International transmission of stock returns and volatility. Unpublished working paper.

Morse, Dale. 1980. Asymmetric information in securities markets and trading volume. *Journal of Financial and Quantitative Analysis* 55:1129–48.

Nelson, Daniel B. 1991. Conditional heteroskedasticity in asset returns: A new approach. *Econometrica* 54:347–70.

Neumark, David, Peter A. Tinsley, and Suzanne Tosini. 1991. After-hours stock prices and post-crash hangovers. *Journal of Finance* 46:159–78.

Newey, Whitney K., and Kenneth D. West. 1987. A simple positive semi-definite heteroskedasticity and autocorrelation consistent covariance matrix. *Econometrica* 55:703–8.

Roll, Richard. 1989. Price volatility, international market links, and their implications for regulatory policies. *Journal of Financial Services Research* 3:211–46.

Ross, Stephen A. 1989. Information and volatility: The no-arbitrage martingale approach to timing and resolution irrelevancy. *Journal of Finance* 45:1–17.

Seyhun, Nejat N. 1990. Overreaction or fundamentals: Some lessons from insiders' response to the market crash of 1987. *Journal of Finance* 45:1368–88.

Shalen, Catherine T. 1993. Volume, volatility, and the dispersion of beliefs. *Review of Financial Studies* 6:405–34.

Shiller, Robert J., F. Kon-ya, and Y. Tsutsui. 1991. Investor behavior in the October 1987 stock market crash: The case of Japan. *Journal of the Japanese and International Economies* 5:1–13.

Solnik, Bruno. 1974. An equilibrium model of the international capital market. *Journal of Economic Theory* 8:500–24.

Stoll, Hans R., and Robert E. Whaley. 1990. Stock market structure and volatility. *Review of Financial Studies* 25:37–71.

Tauchen, George E., and Mark Pitts. 1983. The price variability-volume relationship on speculative markets. *Econometrica* 51:485–505.

von Furstenberg, George, and Bang N. Jeon. 1989. International stock price movements: Links and messages. *Brookings Papers on Economic Activity* 1:125–67.

White, Halbert. 1980. A heteroskedasticity-consistent covariance matrix and a direct test for heteroskedasticity. *Econometrica* 48:421–48.

Comment   Allan W. Kleidon

The paper by Wen-Ling Lin and Takatoshi Ito (henceforth LI) falls in the general category of market microstructure, which includes the structure of markets, the causes of transaction-to-transaction price movements, and the way in

Allan W. Kleidon is vice-president of Cornerstone Research and lecturer in finance at the Graduate School of Business, Stanford University.

which information from diverse individuals is aggregated into market prices. The paper makes two main contributions. First, it adds to the growing literature that exploits the potential information in the market behavior of assets that are traded in different international markets, but that are identical or at least very similar. LI examine the behavior of broad market indices in Japan and the United States, namely, the Nikkei 225 index from the Tokyo Stock Exchange and the S&P 500 index from the New York Stock Exchange (NYSE).

Second, LI provide detailed statistics on price and volume in these markets, including mutual statistical dependencies. Overnight and daytime returns for several time periods are examined, as are some intraday (hourly) returns during the Crash of October 1987. In general the statistical analysis is thorough and reliable, although the robustness of large sample test statistics for the current application is a potential issue.

My main concerns relate to the interpretation of results. To illustrate, much of the paper tests ostensibly alternate theories of market microstructure: the "market contagion" and the "informational efficiency" hypotheses. The conclusion reached (section 7.3.3) is that the data support the informational efficiency hypothesis but not the market contagion hypothesis. For several reasons, I do not believe that the results currently support such strong conclusions. The use of data from different countries raises questions about the extent of integration across markets and the possible effects of different types of market structure. The main issue, however, is the importance of precision in empirical inferences drawn from ostensibly competing hypotheses.

Integration of Japanese and U.S. Markets

One theme of the paper is to examine the degree and causes of correlations across these markets. While minute attention is placed on some analysis—for example, hourly returns around the 1987 Crash—the paper does not attempt a broader perspective on the level of integration. It seems clear from a comparison of price paths for Japanese versus U.S. stocks that there are key differences in behavior across the markets over the period examined, which indicates either imperfect integration or imperfect comparability. For example, Japanese price movements are closely linked to Japanese land prices, which contain idiosyncratic elements. Stone and Ziemba (1993) conclude that there is little evidence of a bubble in Japan's essential land or stock markets, despite the dramatic declines in both these markets in the early 1990s that are not observed in U.S. returns.

Frankel, in his introduction to this volume, comments that it is surprising "that the authors find no evidence that volatility in Tokyo is associated with volatility in New York, as they have found in earlier work on the foreign exchange market." The foreign exchange market is one of the most highly integrated international markets, which may explain at least some of the differences.

Effects of Market Structures

Even in the foreign exchange market, however, there are clear differences in the behaviors of quotes that are generated simultaneously by traders physically located in different countries (see, e.g., Bollerslev and Domowitz 1993 and Hsieh and Kleidon 1992). This is particularly evident around the "open" and "close" of trading. Kleidon and Werner (1993) document differences in the behavior of prices for cross-listed securities on the London and New York exchanges when New York opens and London closes. LI's overnight and daytime return series, which are defined around open and close of trade, may be influenced by market peculiarities. Although the authors control for nontrading at open, more attention may be warranted.

Precision in Empirical Inferences

Great care must be exercised in drawing inferences from market microstructure theories. It is not clear that the empirical inferences drawn in this paper are precise. Consider the clearest statement in the paper concerning the alternate models examined (section 7.3.3):

The aim of the above analysis in tables 7.2 and 7.3 is to shed light on the market contagion and informational efficiency hypotheses. Under the market contagion hypothesis, applying the idea of Campbell, Grossman, and Wang (1993), the informed traders in the home market would be likely to accommodate the sales of uninformed traders who, upon observing a price drop in the foreign market, may become more risk averse. As a result, the expected returns would increase, the current price would drop, and the effect of foreign daytime returns on domestic overnight (daytime) returns would increase (decrease) when the foreign trading volume increased. Under the informational efficiency hypothesis, the foreign price changes are informative to the fundamentals of the domestic stock returns. As a result, a higher rate of information in the foreign market increases (contemporaneous) correlations of stock returns between the home and foreign markets as investors extract this information from the observed foreign price change. Our findings of contemporaneous correlations of stock returns across markets in tables 7.2 and 7.3 dispute the market contagion scenario. Moreover, the findings of no significant spillover from the foreign daytime return to the domestic daytime return are supportive of the informational efficiency hypothesis in that the domestic market can very quickly process the foreign information.

This is a key part of LI's analysis, yet the inference seems fragile at best. The following attempts to lay out the paper's logic in seven steps and to suggest plausible alternative inferences.

1. *Campbell, Grossman, and Wang* [henceforth CGW] *(1993) imply that uninformed domestic traders may become more risk averse when they observe a price drop in the foreign market, leading them to sell to domestic informed*

traders. CGW distinguish between price changes due to public information and price changes due to a change in the risk aversion of uninformed investors that leads them to change their holdings. If uninformed traders seek to sell stocks, then risk averse informed investors will require compensation for increasing their holdings. CGW assume that volume provides information about the cause of price changes. Public information results in price changes with low volume and no changes in required return for the marginal holder, while increased risk aversion of uninformed investors leads to high volume (as they sell stocks) and high future expected returns (to compensate the marginal risk averse traders who now hold a larger portfolio of risky stock). The second scenario provides a source of negative serial correlation in returns (lower returns now, higher returns next period). The empirical implication is that price changes with high volume indicate a source of negative serial correlation (or lower positive serial correlation). CGW document evidence consistent with their model.

CGW do not address foreign versus domestic trading. Theoretical questions arise concerning the possible effects on their model if informed traders can respond in the overseas market to price changes there. LI note a relative absence of cross-market trading (section 7.4.2), so let us assume that traders are restricted to their domestic markets. The argument as stated in LI makes no distinctions based on the cause of the overseas price change, which presumably may be due to public information, to information available to the informed, or to noninformation-based events (such as the actions of uninformed overseas investors).

In any case, unless the domestically informed knew perfectly the cause of the overseas price decline, most models would suggest that a rational domestic response would be a domestic decline. Certainly LI do not rule out overseas price changes based on information, but assume an additional effect, namely, increased risk aversion by the domestic uninformed, leading to a sell-off to domestic informed traders. The link between overseas price declines and domestic uninformed risk aversion is outside CGW, and is simply assumed in LI.

2. *This causes expected returns to increase and the price to drop.* As noted above, the domestic price may fall even absent the assumption of increased risk aversion by the uninformed. The argument here seems to be that such a domestic response would be exacerbated. Note that foreign daytime returns occur when the domestic market is closed, that is, during the domestic overnight. Hence the enhanced domestic price drop will be observed at the start of trading in the next domestic daytime trading period, so that the overnight return will be lower and the following daytime return higher than otherwise expected.

3. *Consequently the effect of foreign daytime returns on domestic overnight (daytime) returns increases (decreases) when the foreign trading volume increases.* LI posit a contemporaneous correlation between foreign daytime and domestic overnight returns that is higher when volume increases. The key question, What volume is implied by the theory?

The answer must be *domestic* volume, since the point of CGW is the accommodation of (domestic) uniformed traders whose risk aversion changes, and LI do not assume cross-market trading. However, LI explicitly look at the effect of *foreign* volume: "[T]he effect of foreign trading volume incorporates the implication of the market contagion hypothesis" (section 7.2.1). Table 7.3 examines foreign but not domestic volume. The story in CGW begins with the increase in uninformed traders' risk aversion, which LI identify with an overseas price decline irrespective of its cause. The increase in risk aversion then induces high domestic volume as traders rebalance their portfolios. Without something to tie the paper's market contagion story to foreign volume, the current results do not seem to shed light on the issue. Moreover, the relevant test should look at domestic volume, as in CGW.

4. *The findings of contemporaneous correlations of stock returns across markets in tables 7.2 and 7.3 dispute the market contagion scenario.* This conclusion seems unrelated to the argument. The paper is silent about the causes of the overseas decline, which seem irrelevant for the assumed increase in risk aversion of *uninformed* traders. There is nothing in the market contagion scenario as argued from CGW that prohibits a contemporaneous correlation between overseas daytime returns and domestic overnight returns. Indeed, I would generally expect that information-based models would imply a contemporaneous correlation between foreign and domestic returns, irrespective of any incremental effects of increased risk aversion for domestic uninformed traders.

5. *Under the informational efficiency hypothesis, the foreign price changes are informative regarding contemporaneous domestic returns.* The paper explicitly accepts such contemporaneous correlation, but informational efficiency and the stated market contagion scenario of CGW are not mutually exclusive.

6. *Hence a higher rate of information in the foreign market increases contemporaneous correlations between foreign and domestic returns.* However the "empirical results are not strongly supportive" (section 7.3.3), with a possible exception of New York to Tokyo.

7. *No significant spillover from foreign daytime return to the domestic daytime return supports informational efficiency.* This conclusion seems too strong since the market contagion alternative being considered is explicitly stated to imply that there will be a lower correlation than otherwise between foreign daytime and domestic daytime returns (see [3] above). Conceivably the observed results in LI could be due to an interaction between, on the one hand, domestic inefficiency that causes positive correlation between domestic overnight and domestic daytime returns, and, on the other hand, market contagion that induces some negative correlation between domestic overnight and domestic daytime returns.

Conclusions

The paper by Lin and Ito provides valuable information concerning empirical regularities linking Japan's Nikkei 225 index and the U.S. S&P 500 index. Nevertheless, much work remains before these empirical results are tied to rigorous tests of market microstructure theories.

References

Bollerslev, T., and I. Domowitz. 1993. Trading patterns and prices in the interbank foreign exchange market. *Journal of Finance* 48:1421–43.

Campbell, J. Y., S. J. Grossman, and J. Wang. 1993. Trading volume and serial correlation in stock returns. *Quarterly Journal of Economics*, November, 905–39.

Frankel, J. A. 1993. The internationalization of equity markets. NBER Working Paper no. 4590. Cambridge, Mass.: National Bureau of Economic Research.

Hsieh, D. A., and A. W. Kleidon. 1992. Determinants of bid-ask spreads: Evidence from foreign exchange markets. Stanford University, Graduate School of Business. Mimeo.

Kleidon, A. W., and I. M. Werner. 1993. Round-the-clock trading: Evidence from U.K. cross-listed securities. NBER Working Paper no. 4410. Cambridge, Mass.: National Bureau of Economic Research.

Stone, D., and W. T. Ziemba. 1993. Land and stock prices in Japan. *Journal of Economic Perspectives* 7:149–65.

Comment   George M. von Furstenberg

Lin and Ito offer careful estimates of correlations of one stock-price index change with another, recorded in the daily sequence of trading in the United States and Japan. Their time-varying estimates are conditioned by aspects of these changes, such as direction and relative size, by changes in foreign trading volume, and by "unexpected" returns in foreign and domestic markets. Surprises are inferred from ordinary least squares (OLS) residuals of equations that use stock-market data alone. The thrust of this comment is that the substantive composition of the news, its rate of capture in markets over any twenty-four-hour period, and the time allowed for disentangling the news are crucial to the question of what correlations to expect.

In particular, increasing positive correlations of rates of return between successive stock markets cannot provide conclusive evidence of globalization. Rather, globalization could be perfect even while these correlations are zero or negative. If stock prices are formed efficiently, and with the same functional regard for news about changing fundamentals everywhere, both the Tokyo and New York markets would apply the same pricing function, making them en-

George M. von Furstenberg is the Rudy Professor of Economics at Indiana University.

tirely integrated and global. Even then coefficients on *daytime* returns in one market, in the preferred regression for the *overnight* returns in the market trading next, may differ by location of markets. The reasons can easily be misinterpreted.

For instance, if one market's intraday trading span can capture less information than that of another or if one market has more time to figure out the heterogeneous content of the news that may have given rise to intraday stock-price movements in the prior market, symmetry should not be expected. Conversely, statistical evidence of asymmetry between New York to Tokyo (on the next date) versus Tokyo to New York (on the same date) should not necessarily be attributed to national differences in acuity: the critical issue is whether there was good reason for successive markets to react differently to what may have been heard equally well by all.

Reasons for Asymmetry

Every country's major market contains stock-price reaction to news of local origin and significance that adds noise to the signals which foreign markets are trying to pick up. Now assume that variance levels of country-specific noise are about the same in each market, but the amount, that is, the total variance, of global signal content captured is proportional to the daytime length of operation of a particular market, as in a diffusion process. Then the signal-to-noise ratio of, say, the Frankfurt market, open for only two hours per day during much of the period October 1985 through 1991 analyzed by the authors, would be less than a third of that of the New York market, open for six and one-half and then seven hours a day. German investors would rationally expect that much less predictive power of the German for the U.S. market than vice versa, and so would investors elsewhere. Indeed, all investors should rather look to the London market, which overlaps and straddles trading hours in Frankfurt, for whatever advance information there may be on the overnight returns to be expected in New York by the time it opens.

Lin and Ito refer instead only to the five-and-three-quarter-hour-wide span covered by the legs of "daytime" trading in the Tokyo market as measured. They ignore the six hours of trading available in the London market just before the start of "daytime" trading in New York, which they set at 10 A.M. local time. U.S. "overnight" returns are thus left statistically uninformed of anything that transpired (*a*) after the New York close on the previous date and before 9:15 A.M. Tokyo time on the same date, a time distance of three and one-quarter hours, and (*b*) after the Tokyo close and 10:00 A.M. New York time on the same date, a time distance of nine hours. Segment *b,* covering the active time in the Middle East and Europe, is not only much longer but also much more information intensive than segment *a,* which contains prime time in the Pacific and along its rim for what business news there is before a time (9:15 A.M.) soon after the Tokyo open.

As trading moves from New York across the international date line to Tokyo, the next overnight returns, registered in Tokyo, will be uninstructed by the same major segment b, since they are statistically informed of only the prior daytime returns in New York. Continuing in chronological order on from Tokyo back to New York, both on the next date, will again find overnight returns in New York missing the major information segment b, but for the first time on the next date. Overnight returns in New York on one date followed by overnight returns in Tokyo on the next date will have the same observation on (b) missing. By contrast, overnight returns in Tokyo followed by overnight returns in New York on a single date are affected by different observations on (b) that are asynchronous and quite possibly serially uncorrelated.

The fact that Tokyo's close is almost three times as far removed in time from New York's soon-after-open as vice versa can give rise to yet more asymmetries in first and second moments. If news arrives in a heterogeneous glob whose composition can only gradually be disentangled, the expected *precision* of a market's reaction will rise with the length of time available for news analysis. As I emphasized already in my paper with Jeon (von Furstenberg and Jeon 1989, 136), news that affects one market can be redistributive as well as corroborative and anything in between, and still be entirely global in the way it affects, or on balance fails to affect, prices in another stock market. Redistributive news affects two countries in opposite directions either because their economies, like those of oil-exporting and oil-importing countries, are different, or because their major industries compete, like two grain-exporting countries, each standing to gain from crop failures in the other. Instead of being good for one and bad for another or vice versa, corroborative news affects countries' welfare in the same direction on account of common exposure and impact. Most global news has some redistributive as well as corroborative components, thereby differentiating the expected stock-price reactions by country.

Why time distance matters can best be shown by proceeding in a manner analogous to that of Goodfriend (1992). He showed how news that may arise from one of two initially indistinguishable causes or any combination thereof gets decoded, and thus affects markets, in two successive stages. Assume, therefore, that news originating during daytime trading in both the Tokyo and New York markets arrives as a glob that moves these markets for reasons not instantly ascertainable. What is known, for the sake of simple illustration, is that there is a 75 percent prior probability that such news will be perfectly corroborative, calling for matching percentage price changes in both markets. On the other hand, there is a 25 percent probability that the news is perfectly redistributive, calling for exactly opposite percentage changes in price. Thus any news on foreign stock prices will be met predictably by a 50 percent response in the next market, as long as the news glob remains unidentified.

If the New York market is up 1 percent in daytime trading, the Tokyo overnight rate of return on the next date should be 0.5 percent, since $0.75(1) + 0.25(-1) = 0.5$. If "Tokyo" has too little time to disentangle the "New York" news, meaning any market-relevant news that transpired during the hours of daytime trading in New York earlier, its movements would follow those of New York rather closely. Now consider the processing of news originating during Tokyo daytime trading that lifted its index by 1 percent. While the average reaction of "New York" to "Tokyo" on a single date would again be a 0.5 percent rise, investors transacting in New York will have had much more time to disentangle news from the Tokyo market. Furthermore, they will have received important help from the analytical power concentrated in London's financial community before they must act. Assuming, therefore, that what is behind Tokyo's 1 percent rise has been discovered by 10 A.M. New York time, overnight returns in New York will be +1 percent three-quarters of the time and −1 percent one-quarter of the time.

The implied rise in the standard error of the coefficient of 0.5 that would be estimated on Tokyo's daytime rate of return in the New York market does not indicate that news gets fuzzier or the conditional reaction to news less predictable as the time interval that has elapsed from the news event to (thirty minutes after) the next market's opening increases. Rather, it implies that there has been more time to figure out the substantive content of the news. Less statistically predictable reaction to a foreign stock-price index change thus may be due to a more precise reaction to each of the different types of events that could have caused it. Markets that are efficient in identifying the content of specific news events are the enemy of Pavlovian correlations, and not their friend as frequently implied.

Developing Heterogeneity of Beliefs and Its Stock-Price Effects

A number of authors have linked trading volume with heterogeneity of beliefs. Lin and Ito note, however, that the link of volume change (the deviation of current volume from a backward moving average of one hundred daily observations on number of shares traded in their study) to stock-price index change within or across countries is less certain. To provide insight into the latter relation, consider two investors who, after a period of steadiness, are confronted with what could be a permanent change in noisy fundamentals. Once fully recognized, this change may be such as to imply a large decline in stock prices under the universal pricing function. If one allowed the two investors to trade in each other's market, they could be assigned to different countries, but there will be no such elaboration here.

Instead, the investors differ in only one respect, the strength of their prior beliefs in the endurance of the old and previously well established fundamentals. Investor i may also fear being misled by noise more than missing out on news. He would then be much more willing to discount evidence of something new because he is most concerned about avoiding the Type I error that would be committed by rejecting the old null when it remains true. Investor j, on the other hand, will take more risks of being misled by noise for fear of missing out on news. Seeking to avoid Type II errors, she seeks quickly to grasp any change in fundamentals that might have occurred. Thus either investors i and j

view the world differently, one thinking that permanent changes in fundamentals are much rarer than the other, or the types of errors that most concern them are different for reasons that may have to do with differences in tastes, responsibilities, or social circumstances. Investor i may be called a slow learner and investor j a fast learner, without impugning the rationality of either.

Using the information-theoretic design of Taylor (1975) as interpreted in von Furstenberg 1990, the precision which investor i attributes to his prior beliefs can be represented by the inverse of the variance assigned to the mean of the old fundamentals, $w_i \equiv s_0^{-2}$. A low variance means that the investor has had the time and experience to pin down the enduring fundamentals supporting the status quo. In that case it will take a great deal of evidence to convince him of new fundamentals should the status quo ever change. When a covert change in fundamentals occurs that, if recognized, would call for the stock-price index to change by dF, this change has to be inferred from the unfolding $0 \rightarrow t$ data points by all investors. Simplifying by assuming a commonly known, time-invariant level of the variance of data on the new fundamentals, s^2, the inverse of the variance of the mean of the first t observations, if accumulated under the new regime, is $z(t) \equiv t/s^2$. Then the heterogeneity of beliefs about the present state of fundamentals, $x(t)$, that would be expected by an inactive (nontrading) observer with private knowledge of dF is

(1) $$E[x_i(t) - x_j(t)] = [w_i/(w_i+z(t)) - w_j/(w_j+z(t))] \, dF.$$

Assume now that $w_j = \alpha w_i$ and $\alpha < 1$, meaning, the precision which investor i attributes to his beliefs in the persistence of the status quo ante is greater than j's precision. Substituting for w_j and maximizing the expected gap between these beliefs with respect to $z(t)$, heterogeneity of beliefs turns out to be greatest when $z(t) = \alpha^{0.5}w_i$, or $t = \alpha^{0.5}(s/s_0)^2$. For example, if $(s/s_0) = 4$ and $\alpha = 0.25$, it would take eight trading periods or observations on the new fundamentals for the maximum heterogeneity of beliefs to be reached about such fundamentals.

Slow learners eventually catch up with fast learners in gaining a complete and correct understanding of the new fundamentals. Yet the distance between the beliefs of slow and fast learners, starting out from a common position, widens for a time after any permanent, but not immediately clear, shock to fundamentals, and then declines.

The greater the difference in the speed of learning or the smaller α, the faster convergence of beliefs sets in. For $\alpha \ll 1$, the gap between beliefs widens and reaches a maximum soon after the first occurrence of noisy data generated under the new fundamentals. Because the total amount of learning that causes the market-weighted average of $x_i(t)$ and $x_j(t)$, and hence current stock price levels, to change, is always greatest right after the unobserved change in fundamentals and then steadily declines, stock prices fall at a decreasing rate from the initial to the lower equilibrium. Volume, however, being tied to heterogeneity of beliefs, peaks in the *intermediate* stages of the learning process. If the peak comes early so that the rise is steep and short and the decline long, a positive correlation between volume and the size of the absolute price change could predominate. Conversely, if the peak is reached much later because α is not far below 1, there may be zero or negative correlation. The reason is that prices change by decreasing absolute amounts throughout while volume builds in the initial phases of learning about the new fundamentals.

Conclusion

The theory of information extraction can suggest alternative possibilities, but it cannot predict the sign and size of correlations actually found between the New York and Tokyo stock exchanges. For instance, increased globalization need not produce higher positive correlations or greater symmetry in the response of successive national stock-market rates of return to innovations. Perhaps equally counterintuitive, more precise processing of information may *reduce* the predictability of response from market to market. Hence the outcome of empirical work cannot be left to speak for itself or it will surely be misinterpreted. Instead, observed correlations or the lack thereof can only be appreciated against a background of conditional predictions derived from theory under alternative assumptions and specifications.

References

Goodfriend, Marvin. 1992. Information-aggregation bias. *American Economic Review* 82, no. 3 (June): 508–19.

Taylor, John B. 1975. Monetary policy during a transition to rational expectations. *Journal of Political Economy* 83, no. 5 (October):1009–21.

von Furstenberg, George M. 1990. Neither gullible nor unteachable be: Signal extraction and the optimal speed of learning from uncertain news. In *Acting under uncertainty: Multidisciplinary conceptions.* ed. G. M. von Furstenberg, 301–24. Boston: Kluwer.

von Furstenberg, George M., and Bang Nam Jeon. 1989. International stock price movements: Links and messages. *Brookings Papers on Economic Activity* 1:125–67.

8   What Moves the Discount on Country Equity Funds?

Gikas Hardouvelis, Rafael La Porta, and
Thierry A. Wizman

8.1   Introduction

Country funds are publicly traded investment companies (closed-end funds) that trade on the open market and, unlike domestic-equity funds, hold and manage portfolios concentrating in the equity markets of particular *foreign* countries. Throughout the late 1980s and into the 1990s, country funds were the fastest growing segment of the public fund universe, and a minor sensation on Wall Street. In December 1984 only four U.S.-listed country funds existed. By December 1992, forty-one funds traded in New York, each specializing in one of twenty-six countries, and altogether representing $4.3 billion in market value of equity.[1]

Figure 8.1 illustrates the recent growth in the number of U.S.-based country funds by charting the dollar volume of initial public offerings (IPOs) by fund and by year from 1981 to 1992. The rise in country fund IPOs parallels the growth in capitalization and liquidity in foreign stock markets. As of 1993, there were some forty foreign equity markets in the world, and non-U.S. equity

Gikas Hardouvelis is professor of finance in the School of Business at Rutgers University. Rafael La Porta is a lecturer in economics at Harvard University. Thierry A. Wizman is an investment officer and senior economist at Strategic Investment Partners, Inc. At the time this paper was written, he was an economist at the Federal Reserve Bank of New York.

The authors wish to thank the Federal Reserve Bank of New York for research support, and Maria Varvatsoulis and Stuart Schweidel for research assistance. Special thanks go to Andrei Shleifer, Robert Vishny, and Judy Chevalier. Jeffrey Frankel, Vihang Errunza, Rob Neal, Michael Boldin, David Laster, Peter Gray, and participants at the conference provided helpful comments. The views expressed in this article, however, are the authors' own and do not reflect the views of the Federal Reserve Bank of New York or the Federal Reserve System and its staff.

1. The precursors to the modern publicly traded country funds were the internationally diversified investment trusts first formed in Great Britain in the 1860s. They originally invested in foreign government bonds, and eventually diversified into foreign industrial bonds, land mortgages, and American railroad debentures. Foreign equity funds in the United States have a history dating back to 1951–52 with the Israel Development Corporation and the Canadian Fund. During the 1980s, the London and Hong Kong stock exchanges also emerged as centers for country fund trading.

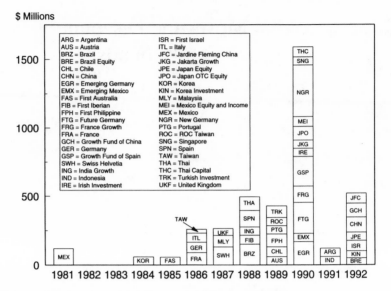

Fig. 8.1   Initial public offerings of country funds: 1981–92
Source: Moody's Financial Handbook.

market capitalization was twice as great as U.S. capitalization. The country funds allow U.S.-based investors to participate in the expansion of foreign markets by providing a managed and diversified portfolio at a minimal transaction cost, and without the use of foreign currencies to make settlements.[2]

Country funds have exhibited periods of high returns as well as high volatility. Like most publicly traded funds, country funds typically trade at substantial discounts to the underlying value of the portfolio they hold (the fund's net asset value or NAV). The discount, however, is not constant, and varies substantially over time. Anecdotal evidence suggests that the unusual volatility in country fund prices can be attributed to volatility in the discounts. Consider the changes in the discount/premium of the Mexico Fund from 1986 to 1993, shown in figure 8.2A. The fund typically traded at a discount in the range of 0 percent to 40 percent. The discount varies substantially from week to week, occasionally turning into a premium. Variation in the Mexico Fund's discount is typical of many country funds and cannot be easily attributed to identifiable news events.

In addition to high volatility, some country funds have also experienced crashlike episodes unrelated to the state of the foreign stock market. Figure 8.2B shows the behavior in the discount of the Germany Fund. This country fund was subject to especially volatile swings in the winter of 1989–90 as the

2. Recent work on international investment has stressed the role of foreign and emerging markets in effective diversification (Divecha, Drach, and Stefek 1992). Diwan and Galindez (1991) and Diwan, Errunza, and Senbet (1992) discuss the role of country funds from the host country's perspective.

Percent

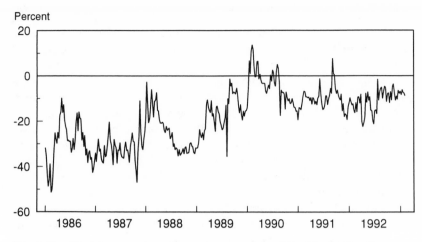

Fig. 8.2A   Weekly percentage discount or premium of the Mexico Fund

Percent

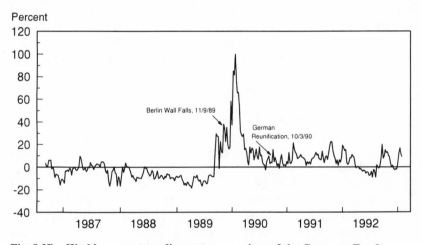

Fig. 8.2B   Weekly percentage discount or premium of the Germany Fund

premium rose to 100 percent after the fall of the Berlin Wall. Popular accounts of the episode attributed it to speculation on the part of investors waiting to "cash in" on new investment opportunities in Germany. What made the behavior doubly impressive was that it seemed to carry a cross-border contagion. Between November 9 and January 26, the Austria (AUS), the First Iberian (FIB), the Italy (ITL), the Swiss (Helvetia) (SWH), and the far-flung Malaysia (MLY), Thai (THA), and Taiwan (TAW) funds experienced dramatic but short-lived increases (decreases) in the premium (discount).[3] Figure 8.2B suggests

3. The rise (fall) in the premiums (discounts) between November 3, 1989 and January 26, 1990 were as follows: AUS: 77 percent, FIB: 54 percent, SWH: 21 percent ITL: 29 percent, MLY: 55 percent, THA: 60 percent, TAW: 27 percent.

that the events of 1989 have not yet dissipated for the Germany Fund. Whereas the fund traded at a discount of between 20 percent and 0 percent prior to November 1989, on a typical day following October 3, 1990, the fund traded at a premium.

Discounts contradict the value-additivity principle of efficient and frictionless capital markets. However, as Rozeff (1991) notes, truly frictionless markets do not exist. In efficient and frictionless markets, investment companies would not arise because they could not offer diversification services at a lower cost than zero, and no benefit could accrue to professional managers. Therefore, because the funds exist, they should be expected to trade at prices different than the NAV. Intriguing issues, of course, relate to the *source* of the frictions and inefficiencies that give rise to the existence, persistence, and time-variation in discounts (Brauer 1992).

The behavior of country fund discounts may reflect items that preclude costless cross-border transactions: official and unofficial barriers to capital movements, transaction costs, time mismatch in trading hours, or risk arising from the time required to complete a full arbitrage transaction. Barriers to capital movements, for example, could potentially explain the variability of the discount: in a segmented market, the price of a U.S.-based country fund is determined by the diversification needs of U.S. investors, whereas the NAV of the fund is determined by the diversification needs of the investors in the fund's host country. Put differently, the relevant (priced) systematic risks of the fund and its net assets are based on different benchmark portfolios in segmented markets. Weekly changes in the gap between price and net asset value could be generated by time variation in the difference between these risk measures.

Alternatively, discounts may be caused not by market frictions but rather by the mechanism of public trading. This explanation emphasizes the role of irrational investors, called "noise traders" or "ordinary investors," who interact in the market with rational investors (DeLong et al. 1990; Shiller 1984; Zweig 1973). Lee, Shleifer, and Thaler (1991) evaluate empirically this explanation of the behavior of fund discounts using data on domestic-equity funds. An important feature of this model is the variation in the demand of noise traders caused by shifts in "sentiment" or by "misperceptions" of fundamental value. DeLong et al., for example, characterize sentiment as the excess of investor return expectations over the mathematical expectations. While variation in sentiment potentially explains variation in country fund discounts, DeLong et al. add structure to their model by introducing the idea of noise-trader *risk*. If variation in investor sentiment or misperceptions on individual assets vary systematically, then assets subject to sentiment will be riskier and underpriced, on average, relative to fundamentals.

The first aim of the present paper is to characterize some empirical regularities of *country fund* prices. Owing to the recent emergence of country funds, relatively little empirical work has been conducted on their pricing; much of the evidence remains anecdotal. In contrast, there is a large body of empirical literature on the behavior of prices of domestic-equity funds. A second aim is to examine whether the sentiment model is consistent with closed-end fund pricing.[4] Accordingly, the paper relies on the noise-trader model to motivate and guide the empirical relationships that we examine using the country funds. The empirical regularities we uncover present a challenge to asset pricing models that assume investor rationality and market efficiency, but this challenge is left to future research.

Country funds have a number of distinct advantages over domestic-equity funds in determining the validity of models based on investor sentiment. First, country fund discounts are better suited to detect movements in sentiment than domestic-equity fund discounts. As noted by Chopra, Lee, Shleifer, and Thaler (1993), the discounts of domestic-equity funds may not fully capture swings in sentiment because the same U.S. investor sentiment affects both the price of the fund and its underlying assets, so that swings in investor sentiment leave the discount largely intact. U.S.-based country funds, on the other hand, may not suffer from this problem; while their prices would be subject to U.S. investor sentiment, prices of their underlying assets (which determine the NAV) will be determined largely on foreign equity markets, which, presumably, are not subject to U.S. investor sentiment. Variation in the discounts of the country funds would, therefore, reflect any *differences* in sentiment between U.S. and foreign-based investors, resulting in both more volatility in discounts and greater statistical power.

Second, compared with domestic-equity closed-end funds, the comovement of country fund discounts provides a stronger indication of common variation in sentiment than of common variation in fundamentals. The underlying assets of domestic-equity funds are U.S. stocks, and thus a large component of their prices or NAVs is due to common variation in U.S. fundamentals. On the other hand, the underlying assets of different country funds are equities of different countries, and thus common cross-country variation in fundamentals represents a much smaller fraction of the total variation in country fund discounts. Finding a strong common component in discounts across country funds is, therefore, more likely to be the result of common variation in U.S. investor sentiment than the result of common cross-country variation in fundamentals.

Finally, compared with domestic-equity funds, country funds enable us to analyze a richer array of factors that may potentially drive the movement of investor sentiment and misperceptions over time. Such factors can be changes in foreign exchange rates, host country stock prices, world stock prices, and U.S. stock prices.

The rest of the paper is organized as follows: Section 8.2 reviews the stylized facts regarding the pricing of publicly traded funds. The same section extends the model of DeLong et al. in a multiasset context. The predictions of

---

4. In this regard, the work presented in Bodurtha, Kim, and Lee (1993) is in the same spirit and has results similar to ours.

the model subsequently serve as a heuristic guide for our empirical work. Section 8.3 discusses our data and its sources and provides some additional institutional facts about country funds. Section 8.4 focuses on the time-series behavior of country fund prices. Section 8.5 explores the determinants of the returns on country funds. In particular, the section examines the response of the fund returns and discounts to financial variables such as foreign stock market returns, exchange rates, and U.S. stock returns. Section 8.6 summarizes our main conclusions.

8.2   The Closed-End Fund Puzzle and the Noise-Trader Model

8.2.1   The Puzzle

Unlike an open-end mutual fund, the shares of a publicly traded fund cannot be redeemed at net asset value and thus the link between the market value of the fund shares and the market value of the fund's NAV is tenuous. The "closed-end fund puzzle" refers to the finding that publicly traded funds always trade either at a discount or at a premium to their respective NAVs. The empirical literature finds that discounts are the norm.[5]

The existence and persistence of discounts seem to contradict the value-additive principle of frictionless efficient capital markets. Moreover, no generally accepted explanation for the existence of premia and discounts exists. Explanations of this puzzle consistent with market efficiency and frictionless capital markets emphasize that the fund's net asset value may be mismeasured. For example, the reported NAV does not correctly account for management fees, illiquid "letter stock" in the portfolios, or the implicit capital-gains tax liability on unrealized price appreciation (see Boudreaux 1973 and Roenfelt and Tuttle 1973). However, the above sources of NAV mismeasurement can only partially explain the existence of persistent discounts on domestic-equity funds (Malkiel 1977; Lee, Shleifer, and Thaler 1991). Moreover, anecdotal evidence and academic research suggest that the mismeasurement hypotheses are unable to explain the variation in discounts across funds.[6]

In light of the problems in explaining the discounts, both generally and for country funds, Brauer (1992) stresses that further insights might be derived from research into the behavior of discounts through *time*. In this regard, Lee, Shleifer, and Thaler summarize four stylized facts concerning the time-series properties of domestic-equity closed-end funds, which cannot be explained by the mismeasurement hypothesis.[7] Lee, Shleifer, and Thaler assert that any the-

5. Lee, Shleifer, and Thaler (1991), for example, examine a sample of twenty primarily domestic-equity stock funds and find that on average, the value-weighted discount on a portfolio of these funds trades at 10 percent less than the NAV over the period 1965–85.

6. Ammer (1990), for example, finds that the organizational expenses of British closed-end funds fail to play a role in the time-series or cross-sectional variation in discounts.

7. The stylized facts are as follows. First, new funds are typically priced at a premium reflecting underwriting and organizational costs. Subsequent to the IPO, funds tend to underperform relative to other IPOs and returns on the net asset value (Peavey 1990 and Weiss 1989). Six months follow-

ory purporting to explain the existence of discounts must also be consistent with the stylized facts. However, the standard explanations cannot, separately or together, explain the ancillary pieces of the puzzle represented by the stylized facts. Lee, Shleifer, and Thaler demonstrate that the noise-trader model of DeLong et al. is not only consistent with the stylized facts, but implies them as well. Using a sample of primarily domestic-equity funds, Lee, Shleifer, and Thaler test those implications of the model which had not been derived or tested in the context of other theories of discounts.

8.2.2   A Model of Investor Sentiment

We now present a general multiasset version of a model with both rational (informed) investors and noise traders in order to motivate the implications of the sentiment model for country fund data. The economy contains one riskless asset, which earns a gross rate of return $1 + r$, and K risky assets, which we interpret as equities. The risky assets are in *fixed* supply which we denote by the K-dimensional vector ι. The number of shares of each risky asset is normalized to equal one, so that ι is a vector of ones. We let P_t and D_t denote the K-dimensional vectors of the prices and dividends paid on the K risky assets, respectively. The jth element of P_t and D_t represents the price and dividend of the j_{th} asset, respectively. As in DeLong et al. (1990) and Shiller (1984), we postulate the existence of two representative agents: a rational (informed) investor and an ordinary investor (noise trader). Informed investors are present in the market in measure $1 - \mu$; noise traders are present in measure μ.

The informed agent chooses his portfolio to maximize his perceived expected utility given his own beliefs about the mean of the normally distributed with-dividend price vector $(P_{t+1} + D_{t+1})$:

$$(1) \qquad \lambda_t^I = \Omega_t^{-1}[E_t(P_{t+1} + D_{t+1}) - (1 + r)P_t]/\gamma.$$

Here λ_t^I is a K-dimensional vector representing the demand for shares by the informed investor, while Ω is the variance-covariance matrix of $(P_{t+1} + D_{t+1})$, and γ is the coefficient of absolute risk aversion. The jth element in λ_t^I represents the number of shares of risky asset j demanded by the representative informed agent.

Whereas informed agents respond only to expected returns optimally forecast, noise traders respond to another factor denoted by ρ_t. ρ_t is assumed to enter the demand of noise traders in linear fashion and represents either an over- or underreaction to news about fundamentals or represents a "fad." For

---

ing the IPO, the average fund trades at a significant discount. Second, Brauer (1984) and Brickley and Schallheim (1985) show that when funds announce plans to open-end or liquidate (and distribute the proceeds to shareholders) the discounts move toward zero and positive returns accrue to fund shareholders. Third, fund prices appear to be excessively volatile: the variance of fund returns exceeds the variance of returns on the underlying assets (Sharpe and Sosin 1975). Finally, portfolios of funds with large discounts subsequently generate excess risk-adjusted returns (Thompson 1978), and abnormal profits can be generated using the information content of publicly disclosed discounts (Richards, Fraser, and Groth 1980; Anderson 1986).

now, we adopt DeLong et al.'s (1990) assumption that ρ_t captures the noise trader's misperception of the expected with-dividend price vector of the risky assets. Specifically, the demand of the noise trader is given by

$$(2) \qquad \lambda_t^N = \Omega_t^{-1} [E_t(P_{t+1} + D_{t+1}) + \rho_t - (1 + r) P_t]/\gamma.$$

That is, if the rational expectation of $P_{t+1} + D_{t+1}$ is given by $_t(P_{t+1} + D_{t+1})$, then the noise trader's expectation is given by $_t(P_{t+1} + D_{t+1}) + \rho_t$. The two investors' problems are similar except for the term ρ in (2). When the noise trader is "bullish" on risky asset j, the jth element of the vector ρ is large, and he will nominally demand more shares of that asset than the rational investor. The demand functions reflect a crucial assumption made by DeLong et al.: that investors' horizons are short, so that they care only about their wealth, one period hence.[8]

Market clearing requires: $(1 - \mu)\lambda_t^I + \mu\lambda_t^N = \iota$. Substituting the demand functions into the equilibrium condition yields required excess returns:

$$(3) \qquad E_t(R_{t+1}) = E_t(P_{t+1} + D_{t+1}) - (1 + r)P_t = \gamma\Omega_t\iota - \mu\rho_t.$$

Equation (3) suggests that equilibrium returns are relatively high when noise traders are bearish. In other words, ordinary investors systematically "mistime" the market. The limit of (3) as the measure of noise traders, μ, goes to zero is the ordinary efficient markets model.

To derive useful closed-form solutions, we assume that both dividends and sentiment follow first-order autoregressive processes. Thus, for any asset j, $j = 1, \ldots, K$, that earns dividends or is subject to sentiment:

$$(4) \qquad d_{j,t+1} = \phi_j d_{j,t} + v_{j,t+1}; \ v_{j,t+1} = z_{t+1}^d + \varepsilon_{j,t+1}^d$$

$$(5) \qquad \rho_{j,t+1} = \Psi_j \rho_{j,t} + u_{j,t+1}; \ u_{j,t+1} = z_{t+1}^\rho + \varepsilon_{j,t+1}^\rho.$$

The disturbance terms, v and u, are assumed to be normally distributed, white noise processes. Each error term contains two components. The systematic component, denoted by z^d for fundamentals, and by z^ρ for sentiment, is a white noise, normally distributed shock common to all assets. z^d and z^ρ may be contemporaneously correlated. The idiosyncratic terms, denoted by ε^d for fundamentals and by ε^ρ for sentiment, are white noise, normally distributed errors that are contemporaneously uncorrelated across assets and between sentiment and fundamentals. Equations (4) and (5) embody DeLong et al.'s assumption that noise traders' sentiment is stochastic and cannot be perfectly forecasted by rational investors. Closed-form steady-state solutions for prices and expected returns on any risky asset j are given by

---

8. The demands of the two representative agents can be derived as the first-order condition of a problem in which each agent maximizes the expected value of an exponential utility function in next-period wealth and where asset prices are normally distributed (DeLong et al. 1990).

$$(6) \qquad p_{j,t} = \frac{\beta \phi_j}{1 - \beta \phi_j} d_{j,t} + \frac{\beta}{1 - \beta \Psi_j} \mu \rho_{j,t} - \frac{\gamma}{1 - \beta \phi_j} \left(\frac{\sigma_{v_j,W}}{r} \right)$$
$$- \frac{\gamma \beta}{1 - \beta \psi_j} \left(\frac{\sigma_{u_j,W}}{r} \right)$$

$$(7) \quad E_t(R_{j,t+1}) = \gamma \sigma_{R_j,W} - \mu \rho_{j,t} = \frac{\gamma \beta \phi_j}{1 - \beta \phi_j} \sigma_{v_j,W} + \frac{\gamma \beta \psi_j}{1 - \beta \psi_j} \sigma_{u_j,W} - \mu \rho_{j,t},$$

where the σ terms represent the steady-state covariances of the error terms from (4) and (5) with aggregate wealth W, where $W = \sum_{k=1}^{K}(p_k + d_k)$; and $\beta = (1 + r)^{-1}$.

If variation in sentiment for asset j is not idiosyncratic, but instead reflects systematic variation in noise trader sentiment which affects other assets, or is positively correlated with innovations in fundamentals, then the covariance term $\sigma_{u_j,W}$ in (6) and (7) will be positive. By raising systematic risk, variation in noise trader sentiment lowers the price of the risky asset j, and correspondingly raises the expected return. Note that the expected return on asset j will be higher even if noise traders are neither *currently* bullish nor bearish ($\rho_{j,t} = 0$), because the systematic risk attached to noise trader activity in asset j remains.

The second term in (6) captures the "price pressure" effect of sentiment. As soon as fundamental (or nonfundamental) news gives rise to an increase in sentiment, the price of the stock will jump to reflect not only what rational investors think the announcement means for future dividends but also what they think the announcement means for current and future demand by ordinary investors. From (7), the model has the property that any variables dated t or earlier which are known to reflect current noise trader sentiment will also help predict returns.

8.2.3 Fund Discounts and the Noise Trader Model

A crucial assumption needed to apply the sentiment model to the pricing of publicly traded funds is that publicly traded funds and their underlying assets are not subject to the same variation in noise trader sentiment. One way to rationalize this is to assume that the fund and its underlying assets have different investor clienteles, and that one clientele is subject to swings in sentiment and misperceptions while the other is not. In the context of the model presented above, we can think of assets not subject to noise trader sentiment as falling within a nontrivial subset of all risky assets, call it K', where $K' \subset K$. Now consider a risky asset $j' \in K'$, whose dividend stream is identical to the dividend stream of another risky asset $j \in K - K'$, but, being in K' is not subject to sentiment. Assuming that the fund itself is subject to noise trader sentiment, but the underlying assets are not, we can think of asset j as a stylized publicly traded fund, and asset j' as the fund's underlying portfolio. From (6) and (7) we derive the price of j' as

$$(8) \qquad p'_{j,t} = \frac{\beta\phi_j}{1 - \beta\phi_j} d_{j,t} - \frac{\gamma}{1 - \beta\phi_j} (\frac{\sigma_{v_{j,w}}}{r}).$$

Subtracting $p'_{j,t}$ from $p_{j,t}$ yields an expression for the discount:

$$(9) \qquad p'_{j,t} - p_{j,t} = \frac{\gamma\beta}{1 - \beta\psi_j} (\frac{\sigma_{u_{j,w}}}{r}) - \frac{\beta}{1 - \beta\psi_j} \mu\rho_{j,t}.$$

Taking the unconditional mean we are able to express the average discount:

$$(10) \qquad \overline{p'_j - p_j} = \frac{\gamma\beta}{1 - \beta\psi_j} (\frac{\sigma_{v_{j,w}}}{r}).$$

Equations (9) and (10) embody an "answer" to the closed-end fund puzzle: discounts will vary inversely with sentiment. Assuming that the underlying assets of the fund are not subject to the same variation in sentiment, the discount on the fund will shrink when noise traders are bullish on the fund. If the innovation in noise trader sentiment covaries positively with the innovation in total wealth, the covariance terms in equations (9) and (10) will be positive. Thus, discounts on the fund may prevail even when noise traders are neither currently bearish nor bullish. In section 8.4.1, below, we examine the average discount of country funds.

Because sentiment is not directly observable, the sentiment model per se does not generally establish any readily testable implications. However, in the context of publicly traded fund pricing, the difference between the price of a fund and its NAV can serve as this proxy. Equation (9) suggests that the sentiment attached to each fund j will be perfectly correlated with its discount. Under the hypothesis that sentiment is attached only to the price of the fund, any testable implication that applies to the level of sentiment equally applies to the discount. With this in mind, one implication can be derived from rearranging (9) and substituting into (7).

$$(11) \qquad E_t(R_{j,t+1}) = \gamma\sigma_{R_j w} - \gamma \frac{\sigma_{u_j w}}{r} + \frac{1 - \beta\psi_j}{\beta} (p'_{j,t} - p_{j,t}).$$

The expected return on the fund is a function of its discount. The relationship is positive, so long as ψ_j is less than one, that is, as long as sentiment is mean-reverting. If sentiment for a fund drives the discount, then the discount will predict future risk-adjusted returns. These issues are examined in sections 8.4.2 and 8.4.3, below

The difference in the unconditional variance of the fund and the net asset returns is given by

$$\text{Var}(R_j) - \text{Var}(R'_j) = \left[\frac{\beta}{1 - \beta\psi_j}\right]^2 \sigma^2_{u_j} + \left[\frac{1}{1 - \beta\psi_j}\right]\left[\frac{\beta}{1 - \psi_j}\right]\sigma_{u_j v_j}.$$

The model predicts that the fund will exhibit more variability than the underlying assets so long as the shock to fundamentals does not covary excessively negatively with the shock to investor sentiment. We look at this in section 8.4.4.

From (6), the innovation in wealth is given as a weighted average of the innovations to fundamentals and sentiment:

$$(12) \qquad W_t - E_{t-1} W_t = [(P_t + D_t) - E_{t-1}(P_t + D_t)] \, \iota =$$
$$\sum_{k \in K} \frac{1}{1 - \beta \, \phi_k} v_{k,t} + \sum_{k \in K'} \frac{\beta}{1 - \beta \psi_k} u_{k,t}.$$

Using (12), we can express the covariance term in (9) as

$$(13) \qquad \sigma_{u_j, W} = \left(\sum_{k \in K} \frac{1}{1 - \beta \phi_k} \sigma_{z^d, z^p} \right) + \left(\sum_{k \in K'} \frac{\beta}{1 - \beta \psi_k} \sigma^2_{z^p} \right)$$
$$+ \left(\frac{1}{1 - \beta \phi_j} \right)^2 \sigma^2 \varepsilon^d_j + \left(\frac{\beta}{1 - \beta \psi_j} \right)^2 \sigma^2 \varepsilon^p_j.$$

For the sentiment attached to any risky asset, or fund, j to covary appreciably with wealth when K is large, one of two conditions must be imposed on the behavior of noise traders. Specifically, either some component of the innovation in noise trader sentiment on fund j covaries with the systematic variation in fundamentals, so that the first term in (13) is nontrivial; or the set of assets subject to common variation in noise trader sentiment, $K - K'$, is large relative to K, so that the second term in equation (13) is nontrivial. Since publicly traded funds make up a small portion of all risky assets, for the second condition to hold, the systematic component in the innovation in sentiment must also be present in other risky assets besides being present in the funds. These two conditions lead to testable implications. First, the innovations in the discounts on funds will be correlated with innovations in the systematic component of fundamentals. Second, the innovations in the discounts of country funds will share a common component across the funds. Third, there will be other risky assets, besides the funds, whose prices rise independently of fundamentals when discounts on the funds narrow. A natural candidate for such an asset is one whose clientele is the same as the funds. We examine these issues in sections 8.4.5 and 8.5.1.

A specification for the innovations in fund discounts can be derived using the difference in returns between the fund and the net assets:

$$(14) \qquad R_{j,t+1} - R'_{j,t+1} = (\sigma_{R_j, W} - \sigma_{R'_j, W}) - \mu \rho_{j,t} + \frac{\beta}{1 - \beta \psi_j} u_{j,t+1}.$$

Equation (14) says that the difference in realized returns between the fund and the net assets is due to shocks to investor sentiment. Equation (14) is a useful analytic tool in the context of the model because it implies that any variables which help to explain (are correlated with) the contemporaneous difference between the return on the fund and its assets, *after controlling for the predictive power of the discount,* will be variables correlated with either idiosyncratic or systematic variation in noise-trader misperceptions. Empirical versions of equation (14) are examined in section 8.5.2.

8.3   Sample Data and Variable Definitions

8.3.1   The Sample

The country funds used in our empirical work consist of the thirty-five single-country publicly traded funds which were covered in *Barron's* publicly traded funds column from January 1985 through January 1993, inclusive, and for which at least nine months of price data exist within that period. Table 8.1 provides the names of the country funds along with the date of their respective IPOs. Table 8.2 presents some summary statistics on the sample of country funds, and compares them with similar statistics for a sample of publicly traded domestic-equity funds, as well as a random sample of firms with market capitalizations comparable to that of the country funds. The sample of domestic-equity funds is taken from the list of "general equity funds" in *Barron's*. It includes the oldest and most well known domestic-equity funds. The samples of operating firms are random samples drawn from the third and fourth market-capitalization quintiles of firms in *Standard & Poor's Industrial Compustat* Tape (the first quintile being the smallest firms).

The market capitalization of the country funds is on average smaller than that of the domestic-equity funds. This reflects, possibly, the older average age of the domestic-equity funds. Institutional ownership, measured as the fraction of shares owned by institutions, is smaller for the domestic-equity funds than for the country funds. However, both types of funds have much lower institutional ownership than operating firms with comparable levels of market capitalization. A common explanation for the lower participation of institutions in publicly traded funds is that institutional portfolio managers would rather not have to worry about justifying why they hold another managed fund and thus incur two management fees, one implicit and the other explicit. Table 8.2 suggests that individual investors are the clientele of country funds.

One difference between country funds and domestic-equity funds is that country funds may invest in stock markets which otherwise restrict international investment.[9] A government contemplating opening its markets to U.S. investors may choose to admit a U.S.-based country fund as a means of limiting

---

9. Another difference between country funds and domestic-equity funds is that a host government may withhold taxes upon distributions to country fund shareholders. With reciprocal agreements between the host government and the U.S. government, the U.S. shareholder will include the withheld taxes as a foreign tax credit against U.S. taxes. In the absence of reciprocal agreements, however, the shareholder may be doubly taxed. The latter may have the effect of depressing the fund's price below its NAV in the presence of cross-border investment restrictions.

Table 8.1   **Sample of Closed-End Country Funds (dates of initial public offerings and dates of initial time-series observations)**

Country Fund (CODE)	Date of Initial Public Offering (IPO)	Date of Initial Time-Series Observations
Austria (AUS)	9-21-89	10-6-89
Brazil (BRZ)	3-31-88	4-15-88
Brazil Equity (BRE)	4-3-92	4-10-92
Chile (CHL)	9-26-89	10-20-89
Emerging Germany (EMG)	3-29-90	4-20-90
Emerging Mexico (EMX)	10-2-90	10-12-90
First Australia (FAS)	12-12-85	1-3-86
First Iberian (FIB)	4-3-88	4-22-88
First Philippine (FPH)	11-8-89	12-1-89
France Growth (FRG)	5-10-90	7-27-90
Future Germany (FTG)	2-27-90	3-9-90
Germany (GER)	7-18-86	8-22-86
Growth Fund of Spain (GSP)	2-14-90	3-9-90
Helvetia (Swiss) (SWH)	8-19-87	8-28-87
India Growth (ING)	8-12-88	8-26-88
Indonesia (IND)	3-1-90	3-16-90
Irish Investment (IRE)	3-3-90	4-13-90
Italy (ITL)	2-26-86	4-4-86
Jakarta Growth (JKG)	4-16-90	4-20-90
Japan OTC (JPO)	3-14-90	3-30-90
Korea (KOR)	8-22-84	1-4-85
Korean Investment (KIN)	2-18-92	3-13-92
Malaysia (MLY)	5-8-87	6-5-87
Mexico Equity and Income (MEI)	8-14-90	9-7-90
Mexico (MEX)	6-3-81	1-3-86
New Germany (NGR)	1-24-90	2-9-90
Portugal (PTG)	11-1-89	11-17-89
ROC Taiwan (ROC)	5-19-89	5-19-89
Singapore (SNG)	7-24-90	8-3-90
Spain (SPN)	6-21-88	7-15-88
Taiwan (TAW)	12-23-86	2-13-87
Thai (THA)	2-17-88	2-26-88
Thai Capital (THC)	5-22-90	6-8-90
Turkish Investment (TRK)	12-5-89	12-15-89
United Kingdom (UKF)	8-6-87	8-7-87

Source: IPO dates are from Moody's Financial Manual.

such an opening to professional managers buying a fixed amount of shares. Typically, a fund is admitted prior to, or instead of, the introduction of American depository receipts (ADRs) or a full opening. Table 8.2 shows that country funds investing in unrestricted foreign markets tend to have smaller institutional ownership than funds investing in countries that restrict international

Table 8.2   **Market Capitalization and Institutional Holdings of Country Funds**[a]

	Number of Firms/Funds in Sample	Average Market Capitalization ($ million)	Average Number of Institutional Owners	Average Percentage of Shares Held by Institutions
Country funds	35	110.92	18	14
Unrestricted	21	87.13	16	11
Restricted	14	146.6	21	18
Domestic funds	19	402.4	23	6
Third quintile *Compustat* firms	40	57.13	22	25
Fourth quintile *Compustat* firms	43	236.13	60	40

Source: Data on market capitalization and institutional holdings is from *Standard & Poor's Stock Guide* for December 1992.

[a]Summary statistics for the sample of thirty-five country funds are compared to a sample of domestic equity funds and to a sample of operating firms whose average capitalization is comparable to the country funds. The sample of domestic equity funds is taken from the list of "general equity funds" in *Barron's*. The samples of operating firms are random samples drawn from the third and fourth quintiles in *Standard & Poor's Industrial Compustat* Tape, on the basis of total market capitalization (first quintile being the smallest firms). See the text for a description of the classification of country funds into the *unrestricted* and *restricted* samples.

investment in their respective equity markets.[10] Apparently, an institution can justify investing in particular foreign markets, and incurring an additional management fee, if the country fund is the only avenue by which such diversification is possible.

8.3.2   Variable Definitions

Weekly data on price and reported NAV of the funds was collected from *Barron's* and the funds themselves.[11] With the exception of the India Growth Fund (ING), which is excluded from the regressions in the empirical sections below, a complete time series of NAVs was obtained for each of the thirty-five funds. *Barron's* reports either the Friday or Thursday closing price in New York. The funds compute their reported NAVs by translating the local currency price of the assets at the local market close into U.S. dollars. The translation to dollars, however, is not uniform as some funds use the exchange rate at the local market close, whereas others use an afternoon fix in New York. Since foreign markets close on a given day prior to the close in New York, prices and NAVs will be only approximately synchronous. Constructed financial returns

10. Our classifications, "restricted" and "unrestricted," are based on the classification given in the International Finance Corporation's *Emerging Markets Handbook*. The IFC classifies countries into five categories according to their degree of openness: "free," "relatively free," "authorized investors," "special classes of shares," and "closed." We placed all countries represented in our sample which are not classified as emerging markets in the "unrestricted" category, along with those classified as "free" by the IFC. All others were placed in the restricted category.

11. The integrity of the data was ensured by checking all outliers and missing observations against the data bases kept at the offices of the fund managers or administrators.

were adjusted for splits and in-kind distributions using the data in *Standard and Poor's Dividend Record.*[12] Table 8.3 provides a description of the variables used in the later empirical analysis.

We compute funds i's "discount" as the natural logarithm of the ratio of the fund's net asset value per share (NAV) to its share price (FND). Specifically,

$$DISC_{i,t} = \ln(NAV_{i,t}/FND_{i,t}).$$

The continuously compounded return on the fund itself, $RFND_{i,t+1}$, and on the net assets of the fund, $RNAV_{i,t+1}$, are defined as follows:

$$RFND_{i,t+1} = \ln\!\left(\frac{FND_{i,t+1} + DST_{i,t+1}}{FND_{i,t}}\right),$$

$$RNAV_{i,t+1} = \ln\!\left(\frac{NAV_{i,t+1} + DST_{i,t+1}}{NAV_{i,t}}\right),$$

where $FND_{i,t+1}$ and $NAV_{i,t+1}$ are the price and the net asset value (per share) of the ith fund at the end of week $t + 1$; and $DST_{i,t+1}$ is the distribution during week $t + 1$, assumed to take place at the end of the week. Cumulative returns for horizons of four and thirteen weeks are defined by adding the individual weekly returns over the relevant horizons.

Observe that if the dividend distribution is zero or very small, the change in the discount, $\Delta DISC_{i,t+1} = DISC_{i,t+1} - DISC_{i,t}$, reflects the difference between the continuously compounded weekly return on net assets, $RNAV$, and the continuously compounded weekly return on the fund itself, $RFND$: $\Delta DISC_{i,t+1} = RNAV_{i,t+1} - RFND_{i,t+1}$.

8.4   The Time-Series Behavior of the Discount

This section investigates the time-series behavior of the discount or premium on country funds. We begin with an examination of the average discount over the full sample, as well as its behavior during the first six months after the initial public offering of the fund. We continue with standard nonstationarity tests of country fund discounts, which lead us to examine the predictive power

12. Pursuant to the Investment Company Act, the funds make two kinds of distributions: an income distribution based on portfolio earnings net of expenses, and a capital gains distribution based on realized portfolio appreciation. The shareholder is taxed on capital gains distributions at his relevant capital gains tax rate. Income distributions are taxed at the regular income tax rate. Whereas the Internal Revenue Code requires the funds to distribute at least 98 percent of their income in order to avoid an excise tax, the funds may choose to retain capital gains. Most funds elect to make capital gains distributions, rather than retain them, because corporate tax rates on capital gains exceed individual rates. If the fund does choose to retain portfolio capital gains and pay taxes on them, the taxpaying shareholder can earn a tax credit equal to the proportionate amount of the share of federal taxes paid by the fund on the shareholder's behalf and then increase the year-end cost basis of the shares by the retained amount. This is because the shareholder is deemed to have reinvested the amount retained by the fund net of tax (see Fredman and Scott 1991).

Table 8.3   **Variable Definitions and Construction**

$FND_{i,t}$

Dollar price of country fund i at the end of week t. All prices are recorded at Friday's market close in New York with the following exceptions: the Brazil (BRZ), Brazil Equity (BRE), Emerging Mexico (EMX), Mexico Equity and Income (MEI), Mexico (MEX), Singapore (SNG), and Taiwan (TAW) fund prices are recorded at Thursday's market close; the India Growth Fund (ING) prices are recorded at the Wednesday close. If the reporting day is a New York holiday, the previous day's New York closing prices are used.

$NAV_{i,t}$

Dollar net asset value of fund i at the end of week t. The NAV is computed by the fund itself using the local-currency prices of the underlying assets recorded at Friday's local market close and the Friday afternoon fix for exchange rates in New York with the following exceptions: the BRZ, BER, EMX, MEI, MEX, SNG, and TAW funds construct the NAV using prices at Thursday's local market close, and Thursday afternoon's New York exchange rate. The ING fund uses Wednesday's prices and exchange rates. If the reporting day is a New York holiday, the previous day's local closing prices and exchange rates are used.

$REX_{i,t+1}$

$\ln(EX_{i,t+1}/EX_{i,t})$, the continuously compounded weekly dollar return on holding a unit of the currency of the country represented by fund $_i$. $EX_{i,t}$ represents the exchange rate at 3:00 P.M. in New York (expressed in dollars per foreign currency unit) at the end of week t, where the day marking the end of the week matches the day on which $FND_{i,t}$ and $NAV_{i,t}$ are recorded. *Source:* Federal Reserve Bank of New York for the currencies of Australia, Austria, France, Germany, Ireland, Italy, Japan, Spain, Switzerland, and the United Kingdom (all bids). Remaining exchange rates come from Banque de Generale through Data Resources (DRI), and reflect the middle of the bid-ask spread.

$RFST_{i,t+1}$

$\ln(FST_{i,t+1}/FST_{i,t})$, the weekly return (excluding dividends) on the host country's aggregate stock market in local currency units. $FST_{i,t}$ is the host country's aggregate stock market price index in local currency at the end of week t, matching the day that FND and NAV are recorded. *Source:* Morgan Stanley Capital International (MSCI) through DRI.

$RSP_{i,t+1}$

$\ln(SP500_{t+1}/SP500_t)$, the weekly return on the Standard and Poor's 500 (excluding dividends), computed separately for each fund to match the same calendar horizon as RFND and RNAV. *Source:* DRI.

$RSML_{i,t+1}$

$\ln(R2000_{t+1}/R2000_t)$, the weekly return on the Russell-2000 index of small capitalization stocks (excluding dividends), computed separately for each fund to match the same calendar horizon as RFND and RNAV. *Source:* DRI.

$RWRD_{i,t+1}$

$\ln(WORLD_{t+1}/WORLD_t)$, the weekly return on the world stock market in dollars (excluding dividends), computed separately for each fund to match the same calendar horizon as RFND and RNAV. *Source:* MSCI through DRI.

of the discounts. Finally, we present evidence that, consistent with the predictions of the noise-trading model, a large fraction of the variation in individual country fund discounts is common across the funds.

8.4.1 Average Discounts and Aftermarket Performance of Country Funds

The first column of Table 8.4 presents the cross-sectional average of time-series means of the discount of all thirty-five funds over the sample period.

Table 8.4   Post-Offering Price Performance and Average Premium/Discount(−) of Country Funds[a]

	Average Premium/ Discount	Mean Underwriter's Premium	Mean Premium at First Observation	Mean Premium at:						Average Premium/ Discount (not including weeks 0 to + 24)
				+4	+8	+12	+16	+20	+24	
Country funds (35)	−0.031 (0.025)	0.0755	0.142 (0.049)	0.061 (0.053)	0.031 (0.049)	−0.002 (0.038)	−0.044 (0.037)	−0.061 (0.036)	−0.070 (0.045)	−0.056 (0.022)
Unrestricted (21)	−0.067 (0.019)	0.0767	0.074 (0.034)	−0.019 (0.037)	−0.023 (0.041)	−0.047 (0.035)	−0.098 (0.031)	−0.117 (0.022)	−0.139 (0.021)	−0.091 (0.019)
Restricted (14)	0.020 (0.048)	0.0737	0.244 (0.106)	0.180 (0.113)	0.112 (0.055)	0.112 (0.057)	0.081 (0.055)	0.058 (0.044)	0.068 (0.047)	−0.007 (0.044)

[a]The table reports the cross-sectional means and standard errors of the premium/discount on the first date for which the fund reports a net asset value and at subsequent four-week intervals. In all but two cases (MEX and KOR) the first NAV observation date corresponds to the first sample observation reported in table 8.1. The first NAV observation date usually follows the IPO by two to three weeks. The table applies the convention that premia are denoted as positive while discounts are denoted as negative. See the text for a description of the classification of *unrestricted* and *restricted* funds.

Although the average discount is not significantly different from zero, separating the funds into those pertaining to countries with *restricted* and *unrestricted* equity markets reveals a difference between the two groups. The average discount on funds whose host markets are unrestricted is almost 7 percent and significantly different from zero (t-statistic $= 3.53$), while the average discount on funds associated with restricted host markets is not significant. This evidence is consistent with theoretical models illustrating that international investment barriers can cause prices of assets of equal risk to differ across countries. All else equal, a binding restriction will raise the price-NAV ratio above the level prevailing in the absence of such restrictions (Errunza and Losq 1985; Eun and Janakiramanan 1986).[13]

Table 8.4 also examines the *aftermarket performance* of the country funds relative to their underlying assets. One prediction of the noise-trading model is that a new fund will be issued only when sentiment for the fund is high. After an IPO, the fund's organizers invest the proceeds, net of underwriting fees, in accordance with the fund's investment objective. Because the amount of the offering exceeds the proceeds which constitute the initial NAV of the fund, the fund is issued at a premium. This premium is a derivative of the underwriting fees and start-up costs. A successful offering implies that some investors are willing to pay a premium for the cash that the fund is holding after the offering. The fact that some investors are willing to pay a premium can also be taken as evidence of bullish noise trader sentiment for a country. Naturally, organizers will try to time issuance to coincide with this bullishness. If the noise-trading story is true and sentiment is mean-reverting, following an IPO the original high premium ought to deteriorate. A deterioration would occur even if, with cross-border restrictions, the average discount is small or if on average a premium prevails. Table 8.4 confirms these predictions.

Table 8.4 shows that country funds are issued with an underwriter's premium of about 7.5 percent. Market premia appear to be larger, however. Our first NAV data are available on average about two weeks after the IPO. They show that funds associated with restricted markets trade, at that time, at premia of almost 25 percent whereas funds associated with unrestricted markets trade at a premium of roughly 7.4 percent. Following the first price-NAV observation, the premia begin to erode. After twenty-four weeks, the premium on restricted funds falls to 6.8 percent from the original 24.4 percent, and the premium on unrestricted funds becomes -13.9 percent (a discount) from the original 7.4 percent. Recall that the change in the premium can be approximately interpreted as the difference between the cumulative returns on the fund and on the NAV. Accordingly, investors who buy an *unrestricted* country's fund in the

---

13. Bonser-Neal, Brauer, Neal, and Wheatley (1990) demonstrate that a relation exists for all but one of the five countries examined, between announcements of changes in investment restrictions and changes in discounts and premia. Bonser-Neal et al. confirm, however, that changes in cross-border restrictions are unable to account for much, if not all, of the time-variation in discounts and premia.

immediate aftermarket and sell it twenty-four weeks later experience a negative return of 21.3 percent relative to the NAV, while holders of a *restricted* country's fund experience a loss of 17.6 percent relative to the NAV. Assuming cross-sectional independence, both of these average cumulative returns are significantly different from zero. Moreover, a nonparametric U-test does not reject the hypothesis that the average twenty-four-week returns are the same across the two groups of funds.[14] Finally, the last column of table 8.4 shows that if the first twenty-four weeks are omitted from each fund's time series, the average discount for the full sample is almost 6 percent and significant, while the average discount for the unrestricted sample is 9 percent and also significant. The evidence presented in table 8.4 suggests that after taking account of the effects of cross-border restrictions, the aftermarket performance of country funds adheres to the stylized facts derived for the domestic equity funds: in the long run a discount prevails.

8.4.2   Stationarity Tests[15]

If all publicly traded funds are ultimately liquidated, discounts are in the long run stationary. Over short time intervals, however, discounts could be nonstationary. Discount stationarity is relevant in the context of the noise-trader model because the discount reflects the sentiment attached to a particular country fund. If sentiment is mean-reverting, and variation in sentiment drives the discount, then discounts should also be mean-reverting. Alternatively, if under cross-border segmentation, variation in discounts is driven by changes in the ratio of the domestic price of risk to the foreign price of risk, then the price of a fund might have no inherent tendency to revert to the market price of the underlying assets, and the discount could be nonstationary.

To test the hypothesis of nonstationarity, we employ Stock and Watson's (1988) unit root test twice, for the model with and without a time trend. We also perform the test using either one or eight autoregressive lags. Table 8.5 presents the results. The hypothesis of nonstationarity is rejected for most of the country funds. When the number of autoregressive lags is one, the hypothesis is rejected at the 10 percent level for twenty-three funds in the model with a time trend, and for twenty-three funds in the model without a time trend.

---

14. Weiss (1989) examines aftermarket prices of both domestic- and foreign-equity fund IPOs. Although she finds that the mean premium for a sample of foreign stock funds (country funds and internationally diversified funds) is significantly negative (-11.42 percent) six months following an IPO, unlike the domestic-equity funds examined, the cumulative returns on the international funds over six months are not statistically different from zero. Because Weiss evaluates an earlier period (1985–87), her sample of fifteen foreign funds is relatively small, and this may explain her negative results. Peavey (1990) examines IPOs and aftermarket performance of publicly traded funds between 1986 and 1987, including five country funds. His tests make no reference to fund returns relative to NAV returns, yet he finds that T-bill- and market-adjusted returns are significantly negative in the aftermarket.

15. The tests in this section, as well as the regressions and tests in the rest of the paper, exclude the India Growth Fund (ING). We were unable to obtain an unbroken time series of NAVs for this fund.

Table 8.5   **Tests of the Nonstationarity of Country Fund Discounts[a]**

		Stock-Watson Test Statistic			
		Autoregressive Corrections = 1		Autoregressive Corrections = 8	
Fund	Time-Series Observations	Time-Trend Filtered	Not Time-Trend Filtered	Time-Trend Filtered	Not Time-Trend Filtered
AUS	174	−2.37	−2.39	−2.70	−2.93**
BRZ	251	−3.25*	−2.05	−2.04	−1.19
BRE	43	−3.05	−2.21	−2.43	−1.94
CHL	172	−2.50	−2.70*	−1.59	−2.08
EMG	146	−4.48***	−4.01***	−3.35*	−2.55
EMX	121	−4.47***	−2.97**	−3.55**	−2.33
FAS	370	−4.37***	−4.28***	−4.00***	−3.72***
FIB	250	−2.70	−2.54	−2.43	−2.36
FPH	167	−2.71	−3.00**	−4.36***	−4.66***
FRG	132	−5.19***	−3.97***	−2.22	−1.55
FTG	152	−4.46***	−4.22***	−3.85**	−3.49***
GER	337	−3.54**	−3.25**	−3.14*	−2.93**
GSP	152	−3.35*	−3.19**	−2.77	−2.38
SWH	284	−4.40***	−3.59***	−3.56**	−3.00**
ING	323	—	—	—	—
IND	151	−3.88**	−2.93**	−3.29*	−2.02
IRE	147	−4.25***	−3.31**	−3.00	−1.82
ITL	357	−4.10***	−3.61***	−4.09***	−3.49***
JKG	145	−3.33*	−2.36	−3.72**	−1.95
JPO	148	−2.76	−2.20	−3.72**	−2.41
KOR	422	−2.69	−2.43	−3.04	−2.74*
KIN	47	−1.43	−1.81	−2.22	−2.77*
MLY	296	−3.00	−3.02**	−3.43**	−3.42**
MEI	126	−4.27***	−2.64*	−3.97***	−2.33
MEX	370	−4.97***	−3.87***	−3.70**	−2.54
NGR	156	−4.82***	−5.12***	−2.72	−2.87**
PTG	168	−2.84	−2.93**	−3.26*	−3.44***
ROC	194	−3.53**	−3.07**	−4.42***	−3.60***
SNG	131	−4.24***	−2.07	−2.99	−2.24
SPN	238	−1.82	−1.73	−2.40	−2.30
TAW	312	−3.43**	−3.42**	−4.21***	−3.73***
THA	258	−3.39*	−2.58*	−3.28*	−2.27
THC	139	−4.18***	−4.22***	−3.22*	−3.22**
TRK	164	−3.22*	−1.55	−2.15	−1.23
UKF	287	−7.22***	−4.49***	−3.80**	2.66*
Number significant at the 10% level		23/34 68%	23/34 68%	20/34 59%	16/34 47%

[a]The table reports the results from applying Stock and Watson's (1988) unit-root test (for a univariate time-series) to the country fund discount data. The test requires first transforming each fund's discount by taking first differences. The first-differenced series are then passed through two separate filters. The first filter removes autoregressive dependence of order 1 or 8 (the "autocorrelation

Table 8.5   (continued)

correction") as well as a time trend. The second filter makes the autocorrelation correction of order
1 or 8 but does *not* remove the time trend. Each filtered series $F\Delta DISC_{i,t}$ is then regressed on the
lagged value of the discount:

$$F\Delta DISC_{i,t} = -b_i DISC_{i,t-1} + e_{i,t}.$$

The table reports (for each fund) the test statistics associated with the null hypothesis that b_i is less
than or equal to zero (a unit root). The test statistics are distributed under the null according to the
empirical distributions given in Stock and Watson 1988.
*Test statistic is significant at the 10 percent level. **Test statistic is significant at the 5 percent
level. ***Test statistic is significant at the 1 percent level.

When the number of autoregressive lags is eight, the hypothesis is rejected for
twenty funds in the model with a time trend, and for sixteen funds in the model
without. Assuming independence across the funds, and using the normal approximation to the binomial distribution, one can compute the probability that
the above results were generated under the null hypothesis that all fund discounts are nonstationary. In all four cases, rejections occur at the 1 percent
significance level.

In some funds, the hypothesis of nonstationarity is not rejected. In these
exceptional cases, however, changes in the ratio of foreign to domestic price
of risk in the context of cross-border investment restrictions are unlikely to be
responsible for the failure to reject nonstationarity. Examination of table 8.5
reveals no special pattern across the restricted and unrestricted funds. The
Emerging Mexico (EMG, First Philippine (FPH), Indonesia (IND), Mexico
(MEX), Mexico Income and Equity (MEI), Taiwan (TAW), ROC Taiwan
(ROC), Thai (THA), and Thai Capital (THC) funds generally reject nonstationarity of discounts even though they are associated with restricted capital
markets. Meanwhile, the Austria (AUS), Japan OTC (JPO), Singapore (SNG),
and Spain (SPN) funds fail to reject nonstationarity even though they invest in
largely unrestricted markets.

The median first-order autoregressive coefficient across the thirty-five discounts of the country funds is 0.887, implying that an innovation in the discount has a half-life of roughly five weeks. Similarly, the average correlation
between consecutive weekly discounts is approximately 0.854, implying that
the first-order autoregressive process can explain about 73 percent of discount
variation. The correlation at four weeks is 0.57 ($R^2 = 0.32$), and is substantially
less than the one-month correlation (0.85) found by Pontiff (1991) using Lee,
Shleifer, and Thaler's domestic-equity fund data.

8.4.3   Do Fund Returns Vary Excessively?

Sharpe and Sosin (1975), using quarterly data from 1966 to 1973 on eight
domestic funds, find that the unconditional variance of the median fund's return is 36 percent greater than the variance of its net asset value return. Pontiff

(1991), using Lee, Shleifer, and Thaler's data set, finds that return volatility is 73 percent greater than the volatility of the fund's assets. The relative variance of returns on the funds is important because it addresses the issue of excess volatility that noise traders, through the mechanism of public trading, may induce in the prices of traded assets. The fund's return is excessively volatile if $\text{Var}(RFND) > \text{Var}(RNAV)$, or $\text{Var}(\Delta DISC) - 2\text{Cov}(\Delta DISC, RNAV) > 0$. Following Pontiff (1991), to reduce skewness we computed the log variance ratio on each of the thirty-five country funds as the natural log of the ratio of the variance of the fund's return to the variance of the return on its assets. This ratio will be zero if the variance of a fund's return is equal to the variance of the NAV return. For our sample of funds we found the mean log variance to be 1.17 (standard error = 0.57). The median ratio is 1.135, implying that for the median fund (UKF), the variance of its return is more than three times greater than the variance of its net asset return. It is unlikely that a variance ratio of this magnitude could be attributable to bias in the variance estimates deriving from bid-ask spread bias.

8.4.4 The Predictive Power of Discounts

Mean reversion in the discounts, as demonstrated above, implies that the discount of a given country fund can predict a subsequent change in the discount. Moreover, since the change in a discount reflects (approximately) the difference between the returns on the fund and its assets, a larger premium predicts either (a) a smaller subsequent cumulative return on the fund, or (b) a larger cumulative return on the fund's assets, or (c) both a smaller return on the fund and a larger return on the NAV. In the context of the noise-trader model, the first case occurs when sentiment affects only the *price* of the fund, and the fund premium is perfectly positively correlated with that sentiment. In the second case, sentiment affects only the underlying assets, and the premium on the fund price is perfectly negatively correlated with that sentiment. In the third case, both the fund and the underlying assets are subject to sentiment, and the discount is a noisy measure of both sentiment on the fund and sentiment on the underlying assets. Thus, although from the level of the discount we can infer only the differential in sentiment between the country-fund and foreign-market clienteles, the power of the discount in predicting fund returns (relative to its predictive power for the NAV returns) can be taken as an indication of the extent to which sentiment affects only the fund price.

The empirical literature on domestic-equity funds upholds that deep discounts are indicative of positive risk-adjusted returns.[16] Although this empirical relation is well established for domestic-equity funds and has become pop-

---

16. Thompson (1978), using a sample of twenty-three (primarily NYSE) domestic-equity funds traded between 1940 and 1975, demonstrates that risk-adjusted returns on portfolios of discounted fund shares outperformed the market. Richards, Fraser, and Groth (1980) and Anderson (1986), using a sample of diversified and specialized domestic-equity funds, derive optimal trading rules for earning excess rates of return.

ularized (Malkiel 1990), to our knowledge no one has examined these empirical relations for country funds.[17] To examine the predictive power of country fund discounts we ran regressions of the form

(15)
$$\sum_{n=1}^{N} RFND_{t+n} = \alpha_i^f + \beta_i^f DISC_{i,t} + e_{i,t}^f$$

$$\sum_{n=1}^{N} RNAV_{t+n} = \alpha_i^a + \beta_i^a DISC_{i,t} + e_{i,t}^a,$$

where the α_i and β_i are fund-specific intercepts and slope coefficients and N denotes the cumulative return horizon. In table 8.6, we report the estimates of β_i^f and β_i^a, as well as the adjusted R^2, for regressions using cumulative return horizons of one, four, and thirteen weeks. Panel A in table 8.6 shows that an increase in the discount is generally associated with a subsequent increase in the fund's return. As the return horizon increases from one week to thirteen weeks, the reversal in the fund price becomes progressively stronger, generating a larger regression coefficient between the cumulative return on the fund and the discount. Evidently, bid-ask bias or other measurement errors cannot account for the price reversal.[18] The average adjusted R^2s of the regressions are 0.053 for the one-week return horizon, 0.106 for the four-week horizon, and 0.179 for the thirteen-week horizon. The strong predictability of fund returns supports the hypothesis that sentiment is a component of the price of the fund.

High discounts are less successful at predicting low NAV returns. Few regression coefficients are negative and significant in panel B of table 8.6 and the R^2s are much lower, on average, than in panel A. The average adjusted R^2s are 0.007, 0.031, and 0.084 for the one-, four-, and thirteen-week horizons, respectively. Nonetheless, most regression coefficients in panel B are negative, and for five funds (AUS, IND, JKG, ROC, TAW) the regression coefficients are generally negative and significant. Occasionally, therefore, discounts contain some information about future net asset value returns, implying that a small component of the discount reflects the sentiment of foreign investors which affects the price of the underlying assets. That is, the price of the fund captures fundamental information not captured by the NAV.

8.4.5   Is There a Common Component in Country Fund Discounts?

So far, we have analyzed individual country funds in isolation. We now examine comovement in country fund discounts. The noise-trader model sug-

---

17. Some commentators have argued that a country fund with a large premium may reflect the underpricing of the underlying assets due to unwarranted bearishness by the local investors. For example, see the discussion in Fredman and Scott (1991) concerning the views of Jon Woronoff in the *International Fund Monitor,* June 1990.

18. For the equations describing the thirteen-week cumulative returns on the country funds, we find that the coefficient on the discount is positive and significant at the 10 percent level or less for twenty-seven (79 percent) of the country funds. Using the normal approximation to the binomial distribution, and assuming cross-sectional independence, this result is associated with a p-value of less than 1 percent under the null hypothesis that no positive association exists between discounts and future returns on the fund.

Table 8.6   **The Predictive Power of Country Fund Discounts**[a]

A. Cumulative Return on the Fund Is Regressed on the Discount

Fund	Return Horizon = 1 week		Return Horizon = 4 weeks		Return Horizon = 13 weeks	
	β_i^f	Adjusted R^2	β_i^f	Adjusted R^2	β_i^f	Adjusted R^2
AUS	0.033	0.00	0.063	−0.00	0.173	0.01
BRZ	0.027	0.01	0.033	0.00	0.104	0.01
BRE	0.249**	0.10	0.849***	0.41	0.823***	0.14
CHL	0.129***	0.06	0.340***	0.12	0.934***	0.27
EGR	0.289***	0.10	0.711***	0.20	0.938***	0.23
EMX	0.303***	0.09	0.592***	0.11	1.432**	0.16
FAS	0.117***	0.04	0.272**	0.06	0.517**	0.08
FIB	0.057***	0.02	0.214**	0.07	0.405*	0.10
FPH	0.076***	0.04	0.237**	0.13	0.828***	0.47
FRG	0.584***	0.28	1.055***	0.40	1.140***	0.36
FTG	0.330***	0.13	0.853***	0.26	1.107***	0.34
GER	0.064*	0.01	0.170	0.03	0.400*	0.06
GSP	0.225***	0.08	0.578***	0.12	1.084***	0.16
SWH	0.129***	0.05	0.283***	0.07	0.655***	0.16
ING	—	—	—	—	—	—
IND	0.100*	0.03	0.160	0.03	0.004	−0.01
IRE	0.251***	0.16	0.558***	0.23	1.067***	0.29
ITL	0.079***	0.03	0.242***	0.07	0.570***	0.16
JKG	0.065*	0.01	0.167*	0.04	0.422*	0.09
JPO	0.014	−0.01	0.088	0.00	0.701***	0.25
KOR	0.026*	0.01	0.090*	0.02	0.297**	0.34
KIN	0.012	−0.02	0.030	−0.02	0.043	0.07
MLY	0.077**	0.03	0.288***	0.10	0.940***	−0.02
MEI	0.298***	0.14	0.713***	0.25	1.323***	0.34
MEX	0.077***	0.02	0.184**	0.03	0.416*	0.33
NGR	0.168***	0.11	0.497***	0.28	0.737***	0.05
PTG	0.081**	0.03	0.231**	0.07	0.595***	0.43
ROC	0.057*	0.01	0.136	0.02	0.530**	0.20
SNG	0.139***	0.07	0.366***	0.16	0.778***	0.10
SPN	0.022	0.00	0.079	0.02	0.400**	0.35
TAW	0.006	−0.00	0.027	−0.00	0.179	0.12
THA	0.061***	0.02	0.149**	0.14	0.305	0.03
THC	0.192***	0.06	0.615***	0.04	1.727***	0.05
TRK	0.029	0.00	0.036	−0.00	0.025	0.36
UKF	0.247***	0.10	0.512***	0.15	1.091***	−0.01
AVG	0.135	0.05	0.336	0.11	0.667	0.18

Table 8.6 (continued)

B. Cumulative Return on the Net Asset Value Is Regressed on the Discount

Fund	Return Horizon = 1 week		Return Horizon = 4 weeks		Return Horizon = 13 weeks	
	β_i^a	Adjusted R^2	β_i^a	Adjusted R^2	β_i^a	Adjusted R^2
AUS	−0.060***	0.06	−0.204***	0.18	−0.444***	0.30
BRZ	−0.026	0.00	−0.086	0.01	−0.137	0.01
BRE	−0.002	−0.02	0.222	0.01	0.109	−0.03
CHL	0.016	−0.00	0.054	0.00	0.409**	0.10
EGR	−0.078	0.01	−0.036	−0.01	−0.128	0.00
EMX	0.030	−0.00	0.080	−0.00	0.680	0.05
FAS	−0.037	0.01	−0.072	0.00	−0.147	0.01
FIB	0.005	−0.00	0.009	−0.00	−0.047	0.00
FPH	−0.001	−0.01	−0.006	−0.01	0.080	0.01
FRG	0.039	−0.00	0.222*	0.05	0.248**	0.02
FTG	−0.027	−0.00	−0.007	−0.01	−0.025	−0.01
GER	−0.022	0.01	−0.052	0.01	−0.071	0.01
GSP	0.020	−0.01	0.074	−0.00	0.183	0.00
SWH	−0.016	−0.00	−0.031	−0.00	−0.054	−0.00
ING	—	—	—	—	—	—
IND	−0.046**	0.04	−0.202***	0.14	−0.727***	0.37
IRE	−0.006	−0.01	0.026	−0.01	0.214	0.02
ITL	−0.017	0.00	−0.043	0.01	−0.137*	0.03
JKG	−0.031	0.02	−0.109***	0.08	−0.234*	0.08
JPO	−0.054*	0.03	−0.171**	0.08	−0.189	0.03
KOR	−0.009	0.00	−0.020	0.00	−0.054	0.01
KIN	−0.063	0.02	−0.293**	0.19	−1.090***	0.82
MLY	0.001	−0.00	0.082*	0.03	0.363**	0.21
MEI	0.054*	0.02	0.162*	0.04	0.507	0.09
MEX	−0.016	−0.00	−0.063	0.00	−0.094	−0.00
NGR	−0.028	0.00	−0.059	0.01	−0.054	−0.00
PTG	−0.013	−0.00	−0.057	0.02	−0.159	0.04
ROC	−0.053**	0.02	−0.178**	0.05	−0.437	0.09
SNG	0.002	−0.01	0.037	−0.00	0.104	0.00
SPN	−0.004	−0.00	−0.013	−0.00	−0.020	−0.00
TAW	−0.044***	0.06	−0.171***	0.18	−0.440***	0.35
THA	−0.016	0.00	−0.035	0.00	0.602	0.08
THC	−0.050	0.00	−0.004	−0.01	−0.147	0.02
TRK	−0.034	0.00	−0.111	0.02	−0.386	0.09
UKF	0.003	−0.00	0.003	−0.00	0.387	0.07
AVG	−0.017	0.01	−0.031	0.03	−0.039	0.08

[a]Results from the following regressions are presented:
Panel A:

$$\sum_{n=1}^{N} RFND_{i,t+n} = \alpha_i^f + \beta_i^f DISC_{i,t} + e_{i,t}$$

(*continued*)

Table 8.6   (continued)

Panel B:

$$\sum_{n=1}^{N} RNAV_{i,t+n} = \alpha_i^f + \beta_i^f DISC_{i,t} + e_{i,t},$$

where $RFND_i$ and $RNAV_i$ are the returns on fund $_i$ and on the net assets of fund $_i$, respectively, $DISC_{i,t}$ is the discount on the ith country fund at the end of week t. α_i and β_i are fund-specific parameters. The regressions are generated for cumulative return horizons of one, four, and thirteen weeks ($N = 1, 4, 13$). Test statistics are based on standard errors corrected for conditional hetero-scedasticity ($N = 1$) and for autocorrelation of order $N-1$ ($N = 4, 13$) using the methods in White 1980 and Newey and West 1987, respectively.
*indicates significance at the 10 percent level. **indicates significance at the 5 percent level. ***indicates significance at the 1 percent level.

gests that persistent discounts across country funds imply that fund discounts may be subject to a common (systematic) source of risk. If U.S. investors act on general bullish and bearish sentiment which affects all country funds, their behavior is likely to affect country fund prices systematically, resulting in a common component across the fund discounts.[19]

To capture a possible common component across the fund discounts, we estimate a parametric version of the "single index" models discussed by Sargent and Sims (1977). Estimation of the unobserved component model provides a succinct test of the presence of a common component across funds as well as a convenient tool for analysis. The empirical model is as follows. Each discount $DISC_{i,t}$ is hypothesized to move contemporaneously with an unobserved scalar ("index"), Z_t, which is common to all funds, and an idiosyncratic component $\varepsilon_{i,t}$. Both the unobserved index and the idiosyncratic component of each fund's discount are modeled as having linear stochastic structures. In addition, Z_t is assumed only to enter each fund's discount contemporaneously. The formulation is

$$DISC_{i,t} = B_i Z_t + u_{i,t};$$

(16)

$$\alpha(L)Z_t = e_t; \delta_i(L) u_{i,t} = v_{i,t}; i = 1, \ldots, K,$$

where $\alpha(L)$ and $\delta(L)$ are polynomials in the lag operator L, e_t and v_t are white noise errors, and K represents the number of assets. The main identifying assumption of the model expresses the notion that comovements in the multiple discounts arise from a single source Z_t. This is formalized by assuming that the terms $u_{i,t}$, $i = 1, \ldots, K$, and the term Z are mutually uncorrelated at all leads and lags.

Because estimation of the model requires exactly overlapping time-series of

19. Lee, Shleifer, and Thaler (1991) examine the comovements in discounts by computing the pairwise correlations across ten funds using monthly data over a period of twenty years. They conclude that correlations are high enough to suggest that the discounts of different domestic funds move together.

fund discounts, we choose the estimation period in order to balance the need for a long weekly time series and the need to include many and diverse funds. We restricted the sample to include the nine oldest funds (MEX, FAS, GER, SWH, ITL, KOR, MLY, TAW, and UKF) over the period January 1988 to January 1993. We estimate the model by first casting it into a (vector) state-space form and then applying the Kalman filter to evaluate the likelihood function.[20] To simplify estimation, we further assume that $\alpha(L)$ and $\delta(L)$ represent first-order polynomials. In addition, we normalize the variance of the innovation in the common factor, v_t, to equal 1.[21]

The results from estimating the unobserved components model are given in table 8.7, panel A. Several features are worth noting. First, seven of the nine slope coefficients, B_i, that relate the common factor to the discount of each country fund, are significant, while two are marginally significant. Furthermore, the estimate of the autoregressive coefficient of the common component, α, is 0.96 (standard error = 0.03). This implies a level of persistence of the common component (half-life = seventeen weeks) considerably greater than the persistence of the idiosyncratic components implied by the estimates of the δ, whose median value is 0.78 (half-life = three weeks). A likelihood ratio test of the hypothesis that there is no common factor, that is, that the B_i and α are all jointly zero, strongly rejects: $\chi^2(10) = 131.4$; p-value = 0.00. Based on the estimates of the slope coefficients (B_i), the estimates of the autoregressive parameters (α and δ_i), and the estimates of the variances of the idiosyncratic errors, we computed for each of the nine funds the fraction of the unconditional variance of the discount attributable to the common factor. We found that on average, the variance in the common factor accounts for roughly 20 percent of the variance in the discounts (last column, panel A).

Inspection of the errors generated by the model estimated above reveals serial correlation in the residuals. In other words, specifying AR(1) processes for the common and idiosyncratic components is not general enough to fully capture the dynamic behavior of discounts. Checking the robustness of our results to a higher-order dynamic specification could be done, in principle, by allowing more lags in the factor dynamics. However, this turns out to be computationally costly. Instead, we applied the Kalman filter to prewhitened dis-

---

20. The Kalman filter is a well-known way to compute the Gaussian likelihood function. The filter recursively constructs minimum mean-square-error estimates of the unobserved state vector, given observations of the measurable variables. This has two parts: the transition equation and the measurement equations. The transition equation describes the evolution of the unobserved state variables, Z_t and $u_{i,t}$, and their respective lags. The measurement equation relates the observed variables to the state variable.

21. A specification test for the model was also conducted (Sargent and Sims 1977). Specifically, we test the restriction that all comovements in the series arise from a single source against the alternative that they have an unrestricted covariance matrix. The test examines the implication that the spectral density matrix of the vector $DISC_t$, constructed by arranging the fund discounts into a $Kx1$ vector, has a factor structure. We perform the test by partitioning the cross-spectrum into five equally spaced frequency bands. The χ^2 statistic has 275 degrees of freedom and equals 130.65 with a p-value of 0.99. This provides little evidence against the restrictions.

Table 8.7 **Estimation of an Unobserved Components Model of Country Fund Discounts**[a]

A. The estimate of α, the autoregressive parameter for the common factor Z_t, was estimated to be 0.96 (standard error 0.031). The parameters pertaining to the individual funds were estimated as follows:

Fund	Parameter B_i	Parameter δ_i	Contribution of Variance of Z to Variance of $DISC_i$
FAS	0.0082**	0.67	0.186
GER	0.0161**	0.74	0.411
SWH	0.0081**	0.57	0.286
ITL	0.0098**	0.78	0.218
KOR	0.0059*	0.98	0.077
MLY	0.0120**	0.85	0.263
MEX	0.0080**	0.81	0.120
TAW	0.0069*	0.95	0.056
UKF	0.0048**	0.64	0.136
AVG	0.0088	0.78	0.195

B.

Fund	Parameter B_i	Parameter $\sigma(v_i)$	Contribution of Variance of Z to Variance of $A_i(L)DISC_i$
FAS	0.027***	0.056	0.155
GER	0.047***	0.072	0.298
SWH	0.028***	0.045	0.274
ITL	0.024***	0.063	0.129
KOR	0.019**	0.075	0.061
MLY	0.033***	0.070	0.185
MEX	0.025***	0.076	0.101
TAW	0.026**	0.102	0.061
UKF	0.024***	0.039	0.272
AVG	0.028	0.066	0.171

[a]Results from estimating the following models are presented:

Panel A:

$$DISC_{i,t} = B_i Z_t + u_{i,t} \, ; Z_t = \alpha Z_{t-1} + e_t \, ; u_{i,t} = \delta_i u_{i,t-1} + v_{i,t} \, ; i = 1,...,K$$

Panel B:

$$A_i(L) \, DISC_{i,t} = B_i Z_t + u_{i,t} \, ; Z_t = e_t \, ; u_{i,t} = v_{i,t} \, ; i = 1,...,K$$

where e_t and $v_{i,t}$ are normally distributed white noise errors, Z represents the common component in discount variation, $u_{i,t}$ is the idiosyncratic component of the discount of country fund, i, L is the lag operator, and α and δ_i are autoregressive parameters to be estimated. Each of the two models is estimated with nine country funds ($K = 9$) using weekly discount data over the period January 1988 through January 1993. The models are estimated by casting them in a vector state-space form and applying the Kalman filter to evaluate the likelihood functions. In the second model

Table 8.7   (continued)

(panel B), the discounts for the funds are each filtered through $(A_i(L)$, a polynomial in L, to "pre-whiten" the data. The choice of A_i for $i = 1,...,K$, is described in the text. In each case, the variance of e_i is normalized to 1, while $\sigma(v_i)$, the standard error of v_i, is an estimable parameter.

*indicates significance at the 10 percent level. **indicates significance at the 5 percent level.
***indicates significance at the 1 percent level.

counts for the nine country funds under consideration and tested for a common component in the *innovation* in the country fund discounts. Formally, we replaced $DISC_{i,t}$ in the formulation above, with $A_i(L)DISC_{i,t}$ (for $i = 1, \ldots, K$) and forced the Z_t and $u_{i,t}$ to be white noise. $A_i(L)$ is a polynomial in the lag operator which "whitens" the discounts.[22]

Results from estimating the model using the prewhitened data are in panel B of table 8.7. The estimates of the B_i, the exposure of the fund discounts to the common innovation, are now highly significant for all nine funds. The likelihood ratio test of the hypothesis that there is no common disturbance strongly rejects $(\chi^2(9) = 140.6; p\text{-value} = 0.00)$, and simple diagnostic tests on the errors generated by the model reveal no evidence of serial correlation. The average estimate of the contribution of the common factor to the variances of the country fund discounts remains roughly 17 percent. Overall, the results presented in table 8.7 provide strong evidence of common variation across the fund discounts.

Further insight into the results can be gained by examining the behavior of the unobservable common factor during the sample period. A plot of Z_t, generated from the first model, is presented in figure 8.3. Because the variance of the innovation in Z_t is normalized to 1, the reader should focus on relative changes instead of the level. The most noticeable feature of the common factor is its behavior in late 1989, which coincides with the fall of the Berlin Wall.[23] Although the noise-trader model does not explicitly specify any one source of investor misperception or sentiment, Shiller (1984) discusses one characterization of sentiment as a change in investors' attitude toward future returns, which may occur as an arbitrary social reaction to some widely noted events. In the introduction, we noted that the fall of the Berlin Wall might qualify as such an event. The analysis of this subsection seems to confirm that the event was associated with an innovation in the unobserved common component in the discount across the country funds. Compared with the sentiment model, initial public offerings of country funds shown in figure 8.1 peaked in 1990.[24]

22. To prewhiten the discount data, autoregressions of orders one through twelve were run. The order of the process was selected so that it minimized the maximum deviation from the cumulative spectrum of a white noise process.

23. Excluding the Germany Fund from the above procedures does not lead to a significant change in the test results or in the series plotted in figure 8.3.

24. During the 1980s, offerings of domestic-equity funds peaked in 1986 and 1987, prior to the stock market crash.

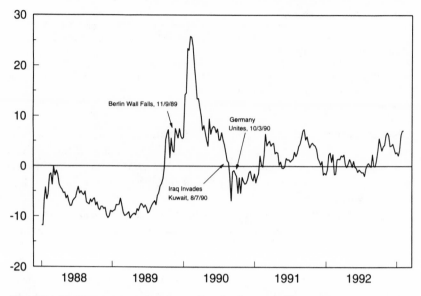

Fig. 8.3   Common component in country fund premia/discounts

8.5   Sources of Variation in Country Fund Discounts

Although widely noted events may account for some large coherent swings in sentiment, casual observation suggests that they cannot account for all of the variation in the discounts of country funds. In this section we examine the response of fund prices to specific aggregate financial variables such as the exchange rate, the index of the host country's stock prices, an index of world stock prices, and indices of stock prices for large- and small-capitalization U.S. firms. Our aim is to explore potential sources of the variation in fund discounts that we documented in earlier sections, and to examine whether or not the noise-trader model can accommodate some of the evidence we uncover. In order to shed some light on the ability of models with rational agents and investment restrictions to explain the time-variation in discounts, we also perform the empirical analysis separately for funds whose host countries restrict international investment from funds whose host countries allow free capital movements. We also examine the differences between host countries with developed stock markets and those with emerging stock markets and between Asian, European, and Latin American funds.

8.5.1   Specification

For each country fund i we estimate basic regression equations of the form

$$(17) \qquad \sum_{n=1}^{N} RET_{i,t+n} = \beta_0 + \beta_1 DISC_{i,t} + \sum_{j=2}^{J} \beta_j (\sum_{n=1}^{N} X_{j,t+n}) + e_{i,t+n},$$

where *RET* denotes alternatively the weekly return on the country fund, *RFND*, the weekly return on the NAV, *RNAV*, and the excess return on the country fund, *RFND* − *RNAV*. *DISC* is the country fund discount, and is observed at the beginning of the holding period prior to the realization of the cumulative return $\sum RET$. Hence, the equation is an extension of the earlier forecasting equations of section 8.4. The X_js are weekly returns of different financial variables observed simultaneously with the dependent variable. *N* denotes the holding period horizon in weeks. As before, we show results for $N =$ one, four, and thirteen weeks.

When the dependent variable is *RFND* − *RNAV*, the above equation becomes the empirical counterpart of equation (14) of the sentiment model. In this framework, *DISC* captures the level of sentiment in the beginning of the holding period, while the remaining independent variables capture the influence of innovations in sentiment during the holding period. Being financial rates of return, the X_j variables are nearly serially uncorrelated and thus may readily capture *innovations* in sentiment.

The first financial variable that we use as an explanatory variable in the regression is fund-specific and represents the cumulative return on a broad index of stocks from fund *i*'s host country, *RFST*. *RFST* is included to capture the component of returns that are attributed to *local currency* variation in the host country's stock market. The second variable, *REX*, is the weekly dollar return on holding the foreign country's currency. Changes in the value of the dollar relative to the foreign currency result in an unambiguous change in the dollar value of the fundamental. While small exchange rate movements that are perceived by the market as temporary may not affect the fund price and thus may move the discount/premium, large changes in the dollar value of foreign currency ought to move the price of the fund sufficiently in order to leave the discount/premium unaffected. Nonetheless, casual observation of the events of September 1992 suggest otherwise. This month saw an appreciation of the dollar as speculators bet against certain weak European currencies in anticipation of the withdrawals from the *ERM*, which did occur. The resultant appreciation of the dollar was associated with significant drops in the premia of the European country funds: as the NAV (translated to dollars) fell, the price of the funds generally did not.

Our earlier empirical analysis showed that country fund discounts shared a common component. We now include three explanatory variables that are common to all country funds in order to capture some of this common variation. The first of these variables, *RWRD*, is the dollar return on a world stock market index. The next variable, *RSP*, is the dollar return on an index of large U.S. stocks. The last variable *RSML* − *RSP*, represents the excess return on an index of small-capitalization U.S. stocks over the return on the large stocks. Under Lee, Shleifer, and Thaler's (1991) assertion that noise trader sentiment is associated with individual investors, and thus largely affects small-cap stocks, an index of large U.S. stocks is more apt to capture variation in U.S.

fundamentals, while the excess return on small caps will capture variation in noise trader sentiment. Detailed definitions of all variables are given in table 8.3.

8.5.2 Results

Table 8.8A presents the main results. In order to abstract from unnecessary details, the table presents only summary results for all funds from stacked regressions. The stacked regressions restrict the slope coefficients to be the same across funds but allow individual fund intercepts. In addition to the multivariate regression described above, table 8.8A also provides results from univariate regressions in which the cumulative returns $\Sigma RFND$, $\Sigma RNAV$, and $\Sigma RFND - \Sigma RNAV$ are separately regressed on each of the independent variables. Panel A of table 8.8A reports the results for the one-week holding-period horizon, panel B the four-week horizon, and panel C the thirteen-week horizon.[25]

The fund discount has strong explanatory power for fund returns ($\Sigma RFND$) in both the multivariate and univariate regressions. As already noted in the earlier sections, high discounts are associated with positive future returns on the fund but negative future returns on the net assets. As a result, the association with excess fund returns, $\Sigma RFND - \Sigma RNAV$, is even stronger. Observe also that as the holding period horizon increases, the absolute size of the β_1 coefficients also increases. There is strong reversion of the fund price toward the NAV, as well as a smaller but statistically significant reversion of the NAV toward the fund price. A relative fall of the fund price—that is, an increase in the discount—by 100 basis points is followed by an increase in the fund price and a decrease in the NAV. The multivariate regression shows that after thirteen weeks the fund price has increased by 37.5 basis points and the NAV has fallen by 6.4 basis points, thus 44 of the original 100-basis-points gap have been eliminated.

Turning to the response of country fund prices to local stock returns, $\Sigma RFST$, country fund returns themselves have significantly lower betas than do the NAV returns. The average local market beta for the NAV return (fund return) is 0.608 (0.428) for the one-week return horizon and 0.718 (0.600) for the thirteen-week horizon.[26] These observed differences between the fund and

---

25. The Newey-West t-statistics of panels B and C treat the stacked data as a single time-series, that is, they do not recognize the break in the stacked data between two separate funds. This fact is likely to bias the reported t-statistics slightly downward.

26. It is interesting to note that the beta of the underlying assets (NAV) with the local market is significantly less than one in the multivariate regressions that control for exchange-rate changes. This potentially reflects one of two things. First, the foreign equity holdings of the funds may indeed be less "risky" than the foreign market. By holding a disproportionate amount of small firms, the fund reduces its exposure to a foreign market index that may be dominated by two or three large firms (Mexico is well-known example). Second, a country fund is never 100 percent fully invested in the foreign-equity market it represents, especially if the fund is new and still holds a large portion of the IPO proceeds as cash. In general, the fund's NAV may represent nonequity assets such as local and dollar-denominated time deposits and repurchase agreements, tax refunds, interest receivable, and currency options.

Table 8.8A Country Fund Return-Generating Equations[a]

A. Cumulative Return Horizon Is One Week ($N = 1$)

Multivariate Regression—Slope Coefficients and t-statistics

Dependent Variable	DISC	$\Sigma RFST$	ΣREX	$\Sigma RWRD$	ΣRSP	$\Sigma RSML - \Sigma RSP$	Adjusted R^2	Number of Observations
$\Sigma RFND$	0.059	0.428	0.088	0.500	0.377	0.285	0.26	6469
	(10.1)	(21.3)	(1.96)	(10.5)	(7.26)	(5.48)		
$\Sigma RNAV$	−0.009	0.608	0.621	0.153	−0.017	0.070	0.63	6469
	(−2.89)	(24.9)	(13.0)	(6.42)	(−0.75)	(2.51)		
$\Sigma RFND - \Sigma RNAV$	0.069	−0.180	−0.533	0.344	0.394	0.215	0.11	6469
	(10.6)	(−6.44)	(−8.53)	(6.99)	(7.22)	(3.79)		

Univariate Regressions—Slope Coefficients, t-statistics, and Adjusted R^2

Dependent Variable	DISC	$\Sigma RFST$	ΣREX	$\Sigma RWRD$	ΣRSP	$\Sigma RSML$
$\Sigma RFND$	0.053	0.537	0.019	1.092	0.969	0.941
	(8.93)	(24.5)	(0.35)	(24.6)	(20.2)	(23.1)
	[0.02]	[0.16]	[0.00]	[0.14]	[0.11]	[0.13]
$\Sigma RNAV$	−0.021	0.611	0.491	0.608	0.380	0.429
	(−5.35)	(23.5)	(11.0)	(21.3)	(12.1)	(13.4)
	[0.01]	[0.54]	[0.05]	[0.11]	[0.04]	[0.07]
$\Sigma RFND - \Sigma RNAV$	0.074	−0.074	−0.472	0.484	0.590	0.511
	(12.23)	(−2.57)	(−8.66)	(11.3)	(13.1)	(12.4)
	[0.04]	[0.00]	[0.02]	[0.03]	[0.04]	[0.04]

(continued)

Table 8.8A (continued)

B. Cumulative Return Horizon Is Four Weeks ($N = 4$)

Multivariate Regression—Slope Coefficients and t-statistics

Dependent Variable	DISC	$\Sigma RFST$	ΣREX	$\Sigma RWRD$	ΣRSP	$\Sigma RSML - \Sigma RSP$	Adjusted R^2	Number of Observations
$\Sigma RFND$	0.155	0.557	0.470	0.584	0.118	0.347	0.46	6367
	(10.9)	(23.9)	(10.5)	(11.7)	(2.19)	(8.01)		
$\Sigma RNAV$	−0.028	0.697	0.700	0.111	0.020	0.031	0.77	6367
	(−3.46)	(50.0)	(18.8)	(4.49)	(0.85)	(1.36)		
$\Sigma RFND - \Sigma RNAV$	0.183	−0.140	−0.230	0.473	0.097	0.316	0.19	6367
	(11.8)	(−5.68)	(−4.13)	(9.12)	(1.76)	(6.99)		

Univariate Regressions—Slope Coefficients, t-statistics, and Adjusted R^2

Dependent Variable	DISC	$\Sigma RFST$	ΣREX	$\Sigma RWRD$	ΣRSP	$\Sigma RSML$
$\Sigma RFND$	0.143	0.649	0.164	1.331	1.244	0.913
	(8.03)	(24.2)	(2.38)	(21.6)	(18.2)	(19.7)
	[0.04]	[0.31]	[0.00]	[0.24]	[0.20]	[0.21]
$\Sigma RNAV$	−0.064	0.675	0.419	0.745	0.656	0.488
	(−4.42)	(37.2)	(5.40)	(14.0)	(11.0)	(11.4)
	[0.01]	[0.66]	[0.03]	[0.14]	[0.11]	[0.12]
$\Sigma RFND - \Sigma RNAV$	0.208	−0.027	−0.255	0.586	0.588	0.425
	(13.8)	(−1.04)	(−4.73)	(13.4)	(13.1)	(13.3)
	[0.12]	[0.00]	[0.01]	[0.07]	[0.07]	[0.07]

C. Cumulative Return Horizon Is Thirteen Weeks ($N = 13$)

Multivariate Regression—Slope Coefficients and t-statistics

Dependent Variable	DISC	$\Sigma RFST$	ΣREX	$\Sigma RWRD$	ΣRSP	$\Sigma RSML - \Sigma RSP$	Adjusted R^2	Number of Observations
$\Sigma RFND$	0.375	0.600	0.645	0.487	0.193	0.187	0.59	6061
	(11.2)	(15.8)	(9.16)	(5.34)	(2.14)	(3.05)		
$\Sigma RNAV$	−0.064	0.718	0.751	0.050	0.089	−0.010	0.82	6061
	(−3.28)	(29.1)	(20.9)	(1.26)	(1.94)	(−0.30)		
$\Sigma RFND - \Sigma RNAV$	0.439	−0.120	−0.106	0.437	0.104	0.196	0.36	6061
	(12.0)	(−3.73)	(−1.31)	(4.61)	(1.10)	(3.35)		

Univariate Regressions—Slope Coefficients, t-statistics, and Adjusted R^2

Dependent Variable	DISC	$\Sigma RFST$	ΣREX	$\Sigma RWRD$	ΣRSP	$\Sigma RSML$
$\Sigma RFND$	0.396	0.640	0.056	1.633	1.556	0.878
	(7.60)	(16.7)	(0.55)	(17.3)	(17.3)	(16.0)
	[0.09]	[0.36]	[0.00]	[0.32]	[0.32]	[0.29]
$\Sigma RNAV$	−0.132	0.644	0.319	0.828	0.855	0.482
	(−3.16)	(30.0)	(3.48)	(9.18)	(8.44)	(9.31)
	[0.02]	[0.64]	[0.03]	[0.14]	[0.17]	[0.15]
$\Sigma RFND - \Sigma RNAV$	0.528	−0.004	−0.263	0.805	0.701	0.397
	(14.5)	(−0.11)	(−5.66)	(11.3)	(9.85)	(10.1)
	[0.30]	[0.00]	[0.02]	[0.14]	[0.12]	[0.11]

(continued)

Table 8.8A   (continued)

[a]Results from multivariate and univariate regressions are presented. The multivariate regression is of the form

$$\sum_{n=1}^{N} RET_{i,t+n} = \beta_1 DISC_{i,t} + \beta_2 \sum_{n=1}^{N} RFST_{i,t+n} + \beta_3 \sum_{n=1}^{N} REX_{i,t+n} + \beta_4 \sum_{n=1}^{N} RWRD_{t+n} + \beta_5 \sum_{n=1}^{N} RSP_{t+n}$$

$$+ \beta_6 \sum_{n=1}^{N} (RSML_{t+n} - RSP_{t+n}) + e_{i,t+n},$$

where RET represents the de-meaned return on either the fund itself ($RFND$), the NAV of fund i ($RNAV_i$), or the difference ($RFND_i - RNAV_i$). The regressions are estimated for cumulative return horizons of one, four, and thirteen weeks ($N = 1,4,13$) and are presented in panels A, B, and C, respectively. The equations are estimated by stacking the country funds returns data so as to restrict the slope coefficients on the independent variables to be the same across funds. Numbers in parentheses are t-statistics corrected for conditional heteroscedasticity (panel A) autocorrelation of order N-1 (panels B and C) using the methods in White 1980 and Newey and West 1987, respectively. In the univariate regressions, the numbers in square brackets are the adjusted R^2s.

the NAV are significant at each horizon although the magnitude of the difference decreases with the return horizon. Country fund prices are apparently sticky with respect to movements in the host country's stock market.

A similar stickiness is observed in the response of country fund prices to the exchange rate. In the one-week horizon, fund prices show practically no reaction to changes in the exchange rate, when at the same time the NAV shows a strong response: the fund return has a beta with *REX* of 0.088, while the NAV has a beta of 0.621.[27] The difference between the fund beta and the NAV beta weakens at longer holding horizons. As the horizon increases, the fund price becomes statistically indistinguishable from the response of the NAV to ΣREX.

Consistent with both the excess volatility of fund returns and the existence of a strong common component among fund discounts, table 8.8.A shows that the fund returns are excessively sensitive to all three financial returns that are common across the different country funds. In the multivariate regressions, fund returns have significantly higher betas with respect to the world stock index return (*RWRD*) than NAV returns at every holding-period horizon.[28] In the univariate regression, we find that the beta of the fund with respect to the world index is significantly larger than the beta of the NAV with the world index. The difference is not affected by the return horizon. Thus, if the world index is the appropriate benchmark for measuring wealth, the result suggests that the country funds are systematically riskier than the underlying assets.

Excess sensitivity is also present in the response to U.S. stock returns.[29] For the one-week holding-period return, fund return betas with respect to *RSP,* the large-firm return index, are positive and statistically significant after controlling for the return on the foreign (host country's) market (*RFST*) and the world index (*RWRD*). By comparison, the NAV return displays absolutely no exposure to *RSP.* Not surprisingly, the difference between the fund the NAV returns, *RFND − RNAV,* has a significant positive beta with *RSP.* However, the difference between the exposures of the fund and the NAV to *RSP* is marginally statistically significant only at the one-week horizon (*t*-statistic = 7.22). At the four- and thirteen-week horizons, the difference is not significant. By contrast, and more interesting perhaps, fund return betas with respect to *RSML − RSP,* the excess return on small U.S. firms, are significantly higher than the corresponding NAV betas at *every* holding period horizon, after controlling for the effects of the other financial variables.

27. The exchange rate, of course, is a component of the NAV computation (see section 8.3).

28. That the NAV retains exposure to both the world index and the U.S. index, after controlling for the local market return, may reflect the choice of fund managers to invest in firms which are export-oriented and more highly linked to the world and U.S. economies than the firms represented in the host country's stock market in general.

29. This result may be implicit in Bailey and Lim 1992. They find that country fund price volatility is higher during New York trading hours than during host-country trading hours.

8.5.3   Is the Noise-Trader Interpretation Reasonable?

Table 8.8A suggests that country fund prices overreact to U.S. and world financial returns, but underreact to price innovations in the stock markets of the host countries and to currency revaluations. Can the noise-trader story accommodate these observations? Although the model does not explicitly specify the origin or source of investor sentiment and misperceptions, Shiller (1984) discusses two characterizations of sentiment which may be relevant for the pricing of country funds. In the first characterization, investors' misperceptions of returns are the result of an overreaction (or underreaction) to news about fundamentals. In this case, news about future dividends, for example, elicits an unwarranted change in the difference between noise traders' perception of future dividends on an asset and the corresponding perception of rational investors. In the context of publicly traded fund pricing, positive domestic news that increases the level of the broad U.S. market and positive "world" news that raises the level of the world market would unduly raise the fund price and decrease the discount of country funds.[30] Conversely, investors may not make immediate effective use of all available information, and thus underreact to innovations in the host country's stock market and to innovations in the exchange rate.

An alternative characterization of sentiment is given by Shiller as follows: sentiment may be the result of "fluctuations in attitudes which occur widely in the population and often appear without any apparent logical reason." In this case, variations in discounts on the country funds would reflect widespread changes in noise trader sentiment unrelated to changes in fundamentals. A possible implication of this view is that the same investor sentiment that affects discounts on country funds must affect other assets as well which have little to do with the country funds. Recall from the theoretical discussion that if variation in sentiment in country funds is not correlated with fundamentals, then the same component of sentiment must appear across a wide range of assets. Although the theory does not specify which assets will be affected by the same widespread innovation in sentiment, a natural candidate for such assets is small capitalization stocks since individuals, who are more likely to trade on sentiment and to misperceive fundamental value, specialize in both smaller stocks and publicly traded funds (Lee, Shleifer, and Thaler 1991).

The results in table 8.8A suggests that both interpretations of the noise-trader model may have some validity. The strong link between changes in the discount and the financial variables *RFST, REX, RWRD,* and *RSP* suggests that

30. Evidence of such a phenomenon is found in Roll (1992), which shows that international stock correlations for firms within a given industry are "too low." That country fund prices may overreact to innovations in the world index, controlling for innovations in the domestic (U.S.) index may be evidence that country fund investors have some sophistication in that they react (albeit excessively) to extranational events. Alternatively, country fund investor clienteles may include Japanese individuals who overreact to fundamental innovations in their own country, which is given much weight in the value-weighted world stock market index.

investors overreact to fundamental revaluations that are closer to home and underreact to those with which they are less familiar, supporting the first interpretation. Moreover, the explanatory power of excess small firm returns persist even when we control for variables such as *RWRD* and *RSP*. This provides substantial support for the second interpretation of the noise-trading hypothesis, assuming that the excess return of small firms captures a sentiment factor independent of fundamentals.

8.5.4   Two Extensions: The Influence of the Japanese Market and the Asymmetric Effect of News

The growth in country funds listed in New York has reflected more than just U.S. investor demand. Just as the funds may be easy sells to American individuals, they may also appeal to Japanese individuals seeking to invest abroad. On February 19, 1990, near the market peak as measured by premia paid, market observers estimated that Japanese investors owned as much as 80 percent of the Spain and Germany funds. Some sources reported that major Japanese retail brokers were the buyers as prices rose and that they then sold the shares to their clients near the market top on the (irrational) enthusiasm generated by the events in Europe. The resultant sharp drop in the country fund premia, while reflecting the invariable dissipation of ordinary-investor sentiment as modeled above, may have been accelerated by Japanese individuals selling country fund shares in New York in order to meet margin calls on their portfolios as the Japanese equity market fell in the spring of 1990. Alternatively, as part of the general "panic" on the Tokyo market between January and April 1990, Japanese individuals may have dumped international-linked assets, such as country funds, first. The fall in the prices of the funds held predominantly by the Japanese generally exceeded the fall in the Japan Nikkei index.[31]

The events described in the financial press raise two interesting issues. First, is there any validity to the idea that prices of New York–traded funds representing Latin American, European, and Asian stocks can ostensibly diverge from fundamental value on the basis of developments in *Japanese* equity markets? Second, to what extent is investors' overreaction documented in table 8.8A asymmetric, in the sense that negative news about world or U.S. fundamentals has a stronger "panic" effect on country fund prices, while positive news or noise elicits a positive, albeit smaller, overreaction?

To examine the first issue, we modified the behavioral excess return equation estimated in table 8.8A to include the current and one-to-four lagged returns of the Japanese stock market. We also divided the time series of country fund returns into two subperiods: one part pertaining to the period of supposedly

31. To see how the popular press covered these events, see Tatiana Pouschine, "How Do You Say 'Manipulation' in Japanese," *Forbes,* 19 February 1990; Nikhil Hutheesing, "What Did In Those Country Funds," *Forbes,* 28 May 1990; Deborah Hargreaves, "Korea Fund Comes at Difficult Time," *Financial Times,* 24 April 1990; and "The Spain Fund Saga," *Barron's,* 25 September 1989.

heavy Japanese involvement, that is August 1989 to July 1990, and a second part pertaining to all other weeks. The regression was estimated separately for each of the thirteen funds which spanned the period of heavy Japanese involvement.[32] In general, our results were unimpressive. We found little evidence that events in the Japanese stock market had an additional effect on country fund excess returns either for the whole sample or for the period of heavy Japanese involvement. Moreover, including the current and lag values of Japanese market returns in the regression did not affect the relationship between the other financial variables (*DISC, RFST, REX, RWRD, RSP, RSML* − *RSP*) and the excess country fund returns (*RFND* − *RNAV*).

To examine asymmetries, we experimented with regressions of the form

$$\sum_{n=1}^{N} (RFND_{i,t+n} - RNAV_{i,t+n}) = \beta_0 + \beta_1 \, DISC_{i,t} + \sum_{j=2}^{J} \beta_j^{PS} \left(\sum_{n=1}^{N} X_{j,t+n}\right)^{PS}$$

$$+ \sum_{j=2}^{J} \beta_j^{NG} \left(\sum_{n=1}^{N} X_{j,t+n}\right)^{NG} + e_{i,t+n}.$$

The variable $(\sum X_{j,t+n})^{PS}$ takes on the value of $\sum X_{j,t+n}$ when $\sum X_{j,t+n}$ is *positive* and takes on the value "0" if $\sum X_{j,t+n}$ is otherwise. Conversely, $(\sum X_{j,t+n})^{NG}$ takes on the value of $\sum X_{j,t+n}$ if $\sum X_{j,t+n}$ is *negative* and takes on the value "0" if $\sum X_{j,t+n}$ is otherwise. If the excess return on country funds responds in an asymmetric fashion to innovation in the financial variable X_j, the coefficients β_j^{PS} and β_j^{NG} will differ.

Although we found little evidence of an asymmetric response of the funds' excess returns with regard to the local stock market (*RFST*) or exchange rate (*REX*) in both univariate and multivariate regressions, we did find evidence of asymmetry in the response to other financial variables. Table 8.8B presents the results of one multivariate specification where we allowed for asymmetric effects of *RWRD, RSP,* and *RSML* − *RSP,* for return horizons of one, four, and thirteen weeks. Two results stand out. First, at the one-week return horizon, but not at the four- or thirteen-week horizon, we find a significant asymmetric response of country fund excess returns to the excess small firm return (*RSML* − *RSP*). The oversensitivity to *RSML* − *RSP* exists exclusively in a down market. That is, when negative sentiment unrelated to fundamentals affects individual investors, it (negatively) affects their demand for country funds to a larger extent than positive sentiment would. Second, using the four- and thirteen-week holding period returns, we found evidence of a significant asymmetric exposure of fund excess returns to world stock returns (*RWRD*). Specifically, the excess country fund returns are more greatly exposed to negative world stock returns than they are to positive world stock returns. That the asymmetry is strongest at long horizons suggests that investors overreact much

---

32. The funds are: BRZ, FAS, FIB, GER, SWH, ITL, KOR, MLY, MEX, SPN, TAW, THA, UKF.

Table 8.8B   Country Fund Return-Generating Equations: Tests of Asymmetric Response to Financial Variables[a]

Return Horizon				Slope Coefficients and t-statistics								Test of No Asymmetries	
				$\Sigma RWRD$		ΣRSP		$\Sigma RSML - \Sigma RSP$					
	DISC	$\Sigma RFST$	ΣREX	(+)	(−)	(+)	(−)	(+)	(−)	Adjusted R^2	(p-value)	Observations
1 week	−0.070	−0.184	−0.532	0.279	0.372	0.472	0.350	−0.141	0.573	0.12	0.00	6469
($N = 1$)	(−10.8)	(−6.58)	(−8.48)	(3.29)	(4.74)	(4.78)	(3.94)	(−1.55)	(5.10)			
4 weeks	−0.183	−0.141	−0.224	0.366	0.592	0.085	0.087	0.240	0.365	0.19	0.08	6367
($N = 4$)	(−11.8)	(−5.71)	(−4.00)	(4.99)	(6.50)	(1.19)	(0.89)	(3.16)	(4.20)			
13 weeks	−0.442	−0.102	−0.122	0.248	0.639	−0.023	0.124	0.182	0.222	0.37	0.00	6061
($N = 13$)	(−12.1)	(−1.24)	(−3.78)	(2.08)	(4.62)	(−0.19)	(0.99)	(1.73)	(2.18)			

[a]Results from estimating multivariate regressions of the following form are presented:

$$
(\sum_{n=1}^{N} RFND_{i,t+n} - \sum_{n=1}^{N} RNAV_{i,t+n}) = \beta_0 + \beta_1 DISC_{i,t} + \beta_2 \sum_{n=1}^{N} RFST_{i,t+n} + \beta_3 \sum_{n=1}^{N} REX_{i,t+n} + \beta_4^{PS} (\sum_{n=1}^{N} RWRD_{t+n})^{PS}
$$

$$
+ \beta_4^{NG} (\sum_{n=1}^{N'} RWRD_{t+n})^{PS}) + \beta_4^{NG} (\sum_{n=1}^{N} RWRD_{t+n})^{NG} + \beta_5^{NG} (\sum_{n=1}^{N} RSP_{t+n})^{NG} + \beta_6^{NG} (\sum_{n=1}^{N} (RSML_{t+n} - RSP_{t+n}))^{NG} + e_{i,t+n}.
$$

$$
+ \beta_5^{PS} (\sum_{n=1}^{N'} RSP_{t+n})^{PS} + \beta_6^{PS} (\sum_{n=1}^{N'} (RSML_{t+n} - RSP_{t+n}))^{PS}
$$

Results for cumulative return horizons of one, four, and thirteen weeks ($N = 1, 4, 13$) are presented. The equations are estimated by stacking the country funds returns data so as to restrict the slope coefficients on the independent variables to be the same across funds. Numbers in parentheses are t-statistics corrected for conditional heteroscedasticity (for $N = 1$) and autocorrelation of order $N-1$ (for $N = 4, 13$) using the methods in White 1980 and Newey and West 1987, respectively. The second to last column reports the p-value associated with the null hypothesis that the excess country fund returns display no asymmetries with respect to the financial variables, $\Sigma RWRD$, ΣRSP, and ($\Sigma RSML - \Sigma RSML$).

more strongly, over time, to negative news about world fundamentals than they do to positive news about world fundamentals.

8.5.5   The Time-Varying Risk Hypothesis and Market Segmentation

It is conceivable that the explanatory variables in the regressions in table 8.8A capture the influence of time-varying risk premia in a model with market segmentation. If markets are segmented, innovations in the ratio of the domestic price of risk to the foreign market price of risk can affect the discounts. Such variation can result from changes in the volatility of domestic relative to foreign stock returns. All else constant, an increase in the *domestic* price of risk will reduce the price of the fund (and increase the discount), and at the same time reduce the domestic market price index. An increase in the *foreign* price of risk will reduce the NAV (and lower the discount) while lowering the foreign market price index. Compared to the fund price, the effect of segmentation would be to make the NAV more highly correlated with the local market index (*RFST*), and less correlated with the domestic market indices (*RSP, RSML*). Moreover, because the discount would reflect the ratio of the domestic price of risk to the foreign market price of risk, the discount would help predict the excess return on a fund.

The hypothesis of time-varying risk (as an explanation of time-varying fund discounts) can be tested without the need to model risk explicitly. To do this, we divided our sample of funds according to whether their host equity markets are restricted or unrestricted. In each group of funds, we regressed the excess fund return (*RFND − RNAV*) on the earlier set of explanatory variables. If market segmentation plays a role in the results in table 8.8A then *RFND − RNAV* will be more sensitive to foreign stock returns and less sensitive to U.S. (and world) stock returns for funds whose host countries restrict capital movements. Table 8.9 contains the results of these regressions as well as tests of coefficient differences along the two groups of funds. In the one-week return horizon the differences between the betas on the U.S. market indices (*RSP* and *RSML − RSP*) are not statistically significant (p-values = 0.99 and 0.63). Interestingly, the exposure of *RFND − RNAV* of the restricted funds to the local market stock index (*RFST*) is significantly *smaller* than the exposure of the unrestricted funds to the same variable (p-value = 0.07). At the four-week return horizon, the differences in domestic market betas remain statistically insignificant, while the foreign market beta of the *restricted* funds remains significantly *lower* than that of the unrestricted funds. At the thirteen-week horizon, none of the observed betas differ significantly across the two groups. Thus, the overall results show no strong evidence that market segmentation plays a role in the time-variation in discounts. Consequently, models of time-varying risk premia may have a difficult time explaining the variability of excess fund returns. Explicitly modeling the time-variation in the ratio of the foreign to domestic price of risk is left to future research.

Table 8.9 Country Fund Return-Generating Equations: Results for Restricted and Unrestricted Markets[a]

A. Cumulative Return Horizon Is One Week ($N = 1$)

Market Status (number of funds)	Slope Coefficients and t-statistics						Adjusted R^2	Observations
	$DISC$	$\Sigma RFST$	ΣREX	$\Sigma RWRD$	ΣRSP	$\Sigma RSML - \Sigma RSP$		
Restricted (13)	0.069 (8.38)	−0.113 (−4.07)	0.188 (1.13)	0.482 (6.19)	0.395 (4.57)	0.345 (3.86)	0.12	2238
Unrestricted (21)	0.069 (7.65)	−0.244 (−5.03)	−0.601 (−9.37)	0.311 (4.86)	0.394 (5.68)	0.160 (2.17)	0.12	4231
Test of subsample differences (p-value)	0.75	0.07	0.00	0.03	0.99	0.63	—	—

B. Cumulative Return Horizon Is Four Weeks ($N = 4$)

Market Status (number of funds)	Slope Coefficients and t-statistics						Adjusted R^2	Observations
	$DISC$	$\Sigma RFST$	ΣREX	$\Sigma RWRD$	ΣRSP	$\Sigma RSML - \Sigma RSP$		
Restricted (13)	0.182 (9.61)	−0.074 (−2.19)	0.159 (0.93)	0.532 (6.19)	0.180 (1.92)	0.351 (4.68)	0.22	2199
Unrestricted (21)	0.183 (8.48)	−0.196 (−5.60)	−0.290 (−4.90)	0.482 (7.36)	0.064 (0.94)	0.277 (4.94)	0.18	4168
Test of subsample differences (p-value)	0.96	0.01	0.01	0.64	0.31	0.43	—	—

(continued)

Table 8.9 (continued)

C. Cumulative Return Horizon Is Thirteen Weeks ($N = 13$)

Market Status (number of funds)	Slope Coefficients and t-statistics						Adjusted R^2	Observations
	$DISC$	$\Sigma RFST$	ΣREX	$\Sigma RWRD$	ΣRSP	$\Sigma RSML - \Sigma RSP$		
Restricted (13)	0.482 (10.5)	−0.098 (−2.34)	0.243 (1.08)	0.555 (3.39)	0.083 (0.45)	0.236 (2.08)	0.43	2082
Unrestricted (21)	0.409 (8.13)	−0.151 (−3.08)	−0.157 (−1.73)	0.414 (3.60)	0.127 (1.15)	0.138 (1.90)	0.33	3079
Test of subsample differences (p-value)	0.29	0.41	0.10	0.46	0.81	0.46	—	—

[a] Results from multivariate regressions of the following form are presented:

$$\left(\sum_{n=1}^{N} RFND_{i,t+n} - \sum_{n=1}^{N} RNAV_{i,t+n} \right) = \beta_0 + \beta_1 DISC_{i,t} + \beta_2 \sum_{n=1}^{N} RFST_{i,t+n} + \beta_3 \sum_{n=1}^{N} REX_{i,t+n} + \beta_4 \sum_{n=1}^{N} RWRD_{t+n} + \beta_5 \sum_{n=1}^{N} RSP_{t+n}$$

$$+ \beta_6 \sum_{n=1}^{N} (RSML_{t+n} - RSP_{t+n}) + e_{i,t+n}.$$

The sample of country funds is divided into two groups, each representing funds investing in restricted and unrestricted equity markets, respectively. The regressions are estimated for cumulative return horizons of one, four, and thirteen weeks ($N = 1,4,13$) and are presented in panels A, B, and C, respectively. The equations are estimated by stacking the country funds returns data so as to restrict the slope coefficients on the independent variables to be the same across country funds within each group. Numbers in parentheses are t-statistics corrected for conditional heteroscedasticity (panel A) and autocorrelation of order N-1 (panels B and C) using the methods in White (1980) and Newey and West (1987), respectively. The last line in each panel reports the p-values associated with the null hypothesis that the coefficients are equal across the two groups of funds. See the text for a description of the classification into *restricted* and *unrestricted* funds.

8.5.6   Emerging Equity Markets Versus Developed Equity Markets

In the last few years, a number of foreign stock markets have become increasingly liquid and have emerged as vehicles for international investment. The International Finance Corporation classifies the stock markets of the following countries represented in our sample of country funds as "emerging markets": Portugal, Turkey, Mexico, Brazil, Chile, the Philippines, India, Indonesia, Malaysia, Korea, Thailand, and Taiwan. Because these markets are new to U.S. investors, information about fundamentals affecting asset prices in these countries may be harder (or costlier) to collect and interpret. As a result, the country fund price may be sticky with respect to developments in the emerging markets which affect fundamentals. Conversely, U.S. investors might place undue reliance on information on U.S. fundamentals as a substitute for fundamentals in the foreign market. To test for differences between emerging and developed markets, we divided our sample of funds according to whether the host market is developed or emerging, and for each group regressed the excess fund return $RFND - RNAV$ on the financial variables in multivariate regressions.

Table 8.10 contains the results of these regressions along with tests of coefficient differences along the emerging and developed funds. The results for return horizons of one, four, and thirteen weeks are presented in panels A, B, and C, respectively. In the one-, four-, and thirteen-week horizons, the betas of excess returns $(RFND - RNAV)$ of the emerging-market funds are generally more highly exposed to U.S. and world risk than are the excess returns of the developed-market funds. However, these differences are far from statistically significant. There is weak evidence, on the other hand, that the excess sensitivity of emerging-market funds to the excess return on small-cap U.S. firms is greater than the corresponding exposure of the developed markets (p-values = 0.1 in panel A, 0.05 in panel B). Speculative bullishness by individuals for small firms may coincide with small investor sentiment for small countries.

8.5.7   Regional Differences and Trading Hours Mismatch

As noted in our data section, the period over which the fund return is computed does not exactly overlap with the period over which the NAV return is computed. This mismatch arises because the local currency net asset value of the country funds is computed on the basis of the market prices prevailing at the close of stock trading in the host country. The fund's price in dollars, however, is computed on the basis of the last market transaction closest to the close of trading on the New York or American stock exchanges. Thus, fund prices and NAVs are only approximately synchronous.

Nonsynchronous returns data may introduce biases in the return-generating equations estimated above, especially for the one-week horizon returns. For example, suppose that the U.S. and foreign fundamentals are correlated, and a country fund's price observations are matched with the weekly close of the *U.S.* market, while its NAV is matched with the weekly close of the *local* mar-

Table 8.10   Country Fund Return-Generating Equations: Results for Emerging and Developed Equity Markets[a]

A. Cumulative Return Horizon Is One Week ($N = 1$)

Market Status (number of funds)	Slope Coefficients and t-statistics						Adjusted R^2	Observations
	DISC	$\Sigma RFST$	ΣREX	$\Sigma RWRD$	ΣRSP	$\Sigma RSML - \Sigma RSP$		
Emerging (18)	0.064 (7.97)	−0.167 (−5.06)	−0.337 (−2.51)	0.415 (5.83)	0.393 (4.72)	0.310 (3.52)	0.10	3120
Developed (16)	0.079 (7.17)	−0.222 (−5.19)	−0.661 (−10.6)	0.343 (4.94)	0.372 (5.36)	0.141 (2.00)	0.14	3349
Test of subsample differences (p-value)	0.27	0.31	0.03	0.47	0.84	0.13	—	—

B. Cumulative Return Horizon Is Four Weeks ($N = 4$)

Market Status (number of funds)	Slope Coefficients and t-statistics						Adjusted R^2	Observations
	DISC	$\Sigma RFST$	ΣREX	$\Sigma RWRD$	ΣRSP	$\Sigma RSML - \Sigma RSP$		
Emerging (13)	0.161 (8.94)	−0.152 (−5.82)	−0.121 (−1.29)	0.542 (7.18)	0.159 (1.86)	0.366 (5.44)	0.20	3066
Developed (21)	0.227 (7.92)	−0.059 (−0.90)	−0.353 (−5.85)	0.408 (5.34)	0.007 (0.10)	0.187 (3.20)	0.19	3301
Test of subsample differences (p-value)	0.05	0.18	0.04	0.21	0.16	0.05	—	—

C. Cumulative Return Horizon Is Thirteen Weeks ($N = 13$)

Market Status (number of funds)	Slope Coefficients and t-statistics						Adjusted R^2	Observations
	DISC	$\Sigma RFST$	ΣREX	$\Sigma RWRD$	ΣRSP	$\Sigma RSML - \Sigma RSP$		
Emerging	0.385	−0.159	−0.177	0.473	0.184	0.274	0.37	2904
(18)	(8.85)	(−4.58)	(−1.57)	(3.09)	(1.15)	(2.98)		
Developed	0.538	−0.038	−0.004	0.292	0.026	0.127	0.37	3157
(16)	(8.30)	(−0.51)	(−0.06)	(2.60)	(0.23)	(1.87)		
Test of subsample differences (p-value)	0.05	0.02	0.19	0.33	0.42	0.20	—	—

[a]Results from estimating multivariate regressions of the following form are presented:

$$\left(\sum_{n=1}^{N} RFND_{i,t+n} - \sum_{n=1}^{N} RNAV_{i,t+n} \right) = \beta_0 + \beta_1\, DISC_{i,t} + \beta_2 \sum_{n=1}^{N} RFST_{i,t+n} + \beta_3 \sum_{n=1}^{N} REX_{i,t+n} + \beta_4 \sum_{n=1}^{N} RWRD_{i,t+n} + \beta_5 \sum_{n=1}^{N} RSP_{t+n}$$

$$+ \beta_6 \sum_{n=1}^{N} (RSML_{t+n} - RSP_{t+n}) + e_{i,t+n}.$$

The sample of country funds is divided into two groups, each representing either funds investing in emerging markets or funds investing in developed markets. The regressions are estimated for cumulative return horizons of one, four, and thirteen weeks ($N = 1,4,13$) and are presented in panels A, B, and C, respectively. The equations are estimated by stacking the country funds returns data so as to restrict the slope coefficients on the independent variables to be the same across country funds within each group. Numbers in parentheses are t-statistics corrected for conditional heteroscedasticity (panel A) and autocorrelation of order N-1 (panels B and C) using the methods in White (1980) and Newey and West (1987), respectively. The last line in each panel reports the p-values associated with the null hypothesis that the coefficients are equal across the two groups of funds. See the text for a description of the classification of funds into the *emerging* and *developed* samples.

ket. Then both the correlation of the fund's return with the foreign market and the correlation of the NAV return with the U.S. market will be biased downward. As a result, the excess return on the fund may display an excess negative correlation with the foreign market and an excess positive correlation with the U.S. market, even if both fund and NAV reflect fundamental information. These biases will be least severe for funds whose host countries have trading hours most synchronous with the U.S. markets, and most severe for funds investing in countries whose trading hours are least synchronous.

To examine whether nonsynchronous data can explain part of the correlations observed in table 8.8A, we partitioned our sample into three groups based on the geographical region: East Asian (including Australia) funds, European (including Turkey) funds, and Latin American funds. The Latin American funds' NAV data are the most synchronous with the actual price data from New York trading. The East Asian funds are the least synchronous. For each geographic group, we regressed the one-week excess fund return, $RFND - RNAV$, on the explanatory variables. If nonsynchronous trading accounts for part of the results in table 8.8A, then the $RFND - RNAV$ of the East Asian funds will have the greatest (positive) exposure to U.S. stock returns, and the greatest (negative) exposure to local stock returns. Excess returns on Latin American would have the least exposure to both U.S. and local stock returns.

Table 8.11 contains the results of the regressions for the one-week holding-period horizon (where biases would be most important). The European funds have greater exposure to the local market stock returns ($RFST$) than either the Asian or Latin American funds. These differences are statistically significant in each case. Meanwhile, there is no significant difference between the betas of the Asian and Latin American funds with respect to the foreign stock returns. The excess returns of the Latin American funds have *more* exposure to the U.S. return indices (RSP and $RSML - RSP$) than do the Asian or European funds, even though the Latin funds suffer less from nonsynchronous price/NAV observations. This difference is statistically significant for the beta with the large U.S. firm index, RSP, although insignificant for $RSP - RSML$. Thus, the findings in table 8.11 do not support the hypothesis that nonsynchronous data play a role in the findings of table 8.8A.

8.6 Conclusion

This paper examined the weekly price behavior of thirty-five country funds that traded on the New York and American stock exchanges between 1985 and 1993. The aim was to characterize some basic empirical regularities of country fund prices and to examine the extent to which the noise-trader model of asset prices is consistent with the regularities.

Unlike domestic-equity funds, not all country funds trade at an average discount. However, controlling for the effect of cross-border restrictions, we find

Table 8.11   Country Fund Return-Generating Equations: Results for East Asian, European, and Latin American Funds[a]

Region (number of funds)	Slope Coefficients and t-statistics						Adjusted R^2	Observations
	DISC	$\sum RFST$	$\sum REX$	$\sum RWRD$	$\sum RSP$	$\sum RSML - \sum RSP$		
East Asian Funds	0.068	−0.157	−0.438	0.460	0.358	0.238	0.11	2406
(13)	(8.08)	(−5.25)	(−5.77)	(5.77)	(4.34)	(2.54)		
European	0.073	−0.278	−0.670	0.425	0.317	0.176	0.14	3097
(15)	(6.94)	(−7.23)	(−11.0)	(5.88)	(4.29)	(2.39)		
Latin American	0.064	−0.139	−0.327	0.139	0.648	0.301	0.08	966
(6)	(3.62)	(−2.00)	(−1.97)	(1.07)	(3.49)	(1.75)		

[a]Results from estimating multivariate regressions of the following form are presented:

$$\left(\sum_{n=1}^{N} RFND_{i,t+n} - \sum_{n=1}^{N} RNAV_{i,t+n}\right) = \beta_0 + \beta_1 DISC_{i,t} + \beta_2 \sum_{n=1}^{N} RFST_{i,t+n} + \beta_3 \sum_{n=1}^{N} REX_{i,t+n} + \beta_4 \sum_{n=1}^{N} RWRD_{i,t+n} + \beta_5 \sum_{n=1}^{N} RSP_{t+n}$$

$$+ \beta_6 \sum_{n=1}^{N'} (RSML_{t+n} - RSP_{t+n}) + e_{i,t+n}.$$

The sample of country funds is divided into three groups representing funds investing in the Far East, Europe, and Latin America, respectively. Regressions are estimated for cumulative return horizons of one week ($N = 1$). The equations are estimated by stacking the country funds returns data so as to restrict the slope coefficients on the independent variables to be the same across country funds within each group. Numbers in parentheses are t-statistics corrected for conditional heteroscedasticity using the method in White (1980).

that country funds adhere to the stylized facts established for domestic-equity funds: in the long run, discounts prevail for funds whose host countries allow free cross-border capital movements. Like their domestic-equity counterparts, country funds are typically issued at a premium, and this premium erodes by about 20 percent over the twenty-four weeks that follow the IPO. The deterioration in the premium is the same for funds invested in restricted markets and those invested in unrestricted markets.

The noise-trading model of DeLong et al. (1990) can easily explain the previous evidence. The average discount for funds invested in countries with no restrictions on capital movements is attributable to noise-trader risk, which depresses fund prices relative to the NAVs. The premium at the initiation of a country fund is explained by the ability of fund organizers to time the issuance of country funds to coincide with positive investor sentiment. The subsequent decline in the premium is explained by mean-reversion in investor sentiment.

Discounts vary substantially over time and contribute to a variance in country fund returns which is generally three times greater than the variance of the return on the underlying assets. However, discounts are largely stationary, implying either that the NAV captures information about fundamental value not captured in the fund price (that is, the fund is mispriced); the fund price contains information about the fundamental value not captured in the market value of the underlying assets; or both the fund price and the NAV carry fundamental information not captured by the other. Regressions of fund returns and NAV returns on discounts suggest that the discount has significant predictive power for the fund return, but little predictive power for the NAV return. This asymmetry suggests that mean-reverting sentiment is an important component of the price of the country funds but not in the market value of the underlying assets, so that it is the fund which is primarily mispriced. This is consistent with the idea that compared to the investor clienteles of country funds' underlying assets (presumably foreign institutions and individuals), U.S. individuals, the investor clientele of country funds, are prone to trade on sentiment and to misperceive fundamental value.

Estimation of an unobserved components model on the discounts of the nine oldest funds reveals a common component which is strongly persistent. This common and persistent behavior is consistent with the structure imposed on the noise-trader model by DeLong et al. (1990), which requires that variation in sentiment be systematic if it is to be priced in equilibrium. The common component we estimate accounts for roughly 20 percent of the variance of weekly country fund discounts. Examination of the estimated common component reveals that systematic variation in sentiment may be driven in part by widely noted world events such as the fall of the Berlin Wall in 1990. In the aftermath of this event, country fund IPOs peaked.

To capture the source of part of the variation in discounts over time, we ran regressions of the fund return, the NAV return, and their difference—the excess fund return—on returns of a number of aggregate financial variables. We find that fund prices are "sticky," that is, they do not move as much as their respective NAVs with respect to movements in the host country's aggregate stock market. Similarly, fund prices, which are quoted in dollars, are sticky with respect to exchange-rate revaluations, although this is largely a short-horizon phenomenon. On the other hand, fund prices are overly sensitive to movements in world stock returns and to U.S. stock returns as captured by the Standard and Poor's 500. The oversensitivity to the world stock market index is present for all holding-period horizons that we examine. Hence, if discounts reflect the sentiment and misperceptions of the country funds' investor clientele, then this sentiment is partly driven by "world" fundamentals.

The excess return on U.S. small firms, which are predominantly traded by individual investors, is also a significant factor in explaining contemporaneous country fund excess returns. Country fund prices are overly sensitive to the small-firm/large-firm return differential. This result is robust to the inclusion of other financial variables correlated with fund discounts, and is also robust to the return horizon. The finding upholds Lee, Shleifer, and Thaler's (1991) idea that sentiment, if it is systematic, will affect assets with little fundamental similarity to country funds except that they share the same investor clientele, namely individual U.S. investors.

A model of rational traders could potentially explain the above correlations if the model were enriched by introducing sufficient frictions. However, we provide evidence which casts doubt on the ability of rational models in the context of market imperfections to explain variation in country fund discounts. First, apart from the evidence on the *average* discounts, we find no evidence that the discounts of funds whose host countries restrict cross-border equity investments behave differently from the discounts of funds that invest in unrestricted markets. Moreover, we also find little evidence in favor of market frictions caused by informational factors, or by nonsynchronous data. For example, the excess returns of funds invested in emerging markets, where information about fundamentals may be harder or costlier to obtain, do not exhibit a higher correlation with the U.S. market than the excess returns of country funds in developed markets. Similarly, the excess returns of funds whose price and NAV data suffer from the most time-mismatch do not generally exhibit higher correlations with the U.S. market. Overall, the facts we uncover present a challenge to asset-pricing models based on fully rational international investors.

References

Ammer, John M. 1990. Expenses, yields, and excess returns: New evidence on closed-end fund discounts from the UK. Financial Markets Group Discussion Paper no. 108. London School of Economics.

Anderson, Seth Copeland. 1986. Closed-end funds versus market efficiency. *Journal of Portfolio Management,* fall, 63–65.

Bailey, Warren, and Joseph Lim. 1992. Evaluating the diversification benefits of the new country funds. *Journal of Portfolio Management,* spring, 74–80.

Barker, David. 1991. Cross-sectional variation in closed-end fund discounts. University of Chicago. Manuscript.

Bodurtha, James N., Dong-Soo Kim, and Charles M. C. Lee. 1993. Closed-end country funds and U.S. market sentiment. Working paper, University of Michigan.

Bonser-Neal, Catherine, Greggory Brauer, Robert Neal, and Simon Wheatley. 1990. International investment restrictions and closed-end country fund prices. *Journal of Finance* 45:523–47.

Boudreaux, Kenneth. 1973. Discounts and premiums on closed-end mutual funds: A study in valuation. *Journal of Finance,* May, 515–22.

Brauer, Greggory A. 1984. "Open-ending" closed-end funds. *Journal of Financial Economics* 13 (December): 491–508.

———. 1988. Closed-end fund shares' abnormal returns and the information contents of discounts and premiums. *Journal of Finance* 43 (1): 113–27.

———. 1992. Closed-end mutual funds. In *The new Palgrave dictionary of money and finance,* eds. Peter Newman, Murray Milgate, and John Eatwell. London: Macmillan.

Brickley, J. A., and J. S. Schallheim. 1985. Lifting the lid on closed-end investment companies: A case of abnormal returns. *Journal of Quantitative and Financial Analysis* 20:107–18.

Chopra, Navin, Charles M. C. Lee, Andrei Shleifer, and Richard Thaler. 1993. Yes, discounts on closed-end funds are a sentiment index. *Journal of Finance* 48 (June): 801–8.

DeLong, J. Bradford, Andrei Shleifer, Lawrence H. Summers, and Robert Waldmann. 1990. Noise trader risk in financial markets. *Journal of Political Economy* 98(4): 703–38.

Divecha, Arjun B., Jaime Drach, and Dan Stefek. 1992. Emerging markets: A quantitative perspective. *Journal of Portfolio Management,* fall, 41–51.

Diwan, Ishac, and Santiago Galindez. 1991. Country funds. Debt and International Finance Division of the World Bank, Washington, D.C. Manuscript.

Diwan, Ishac, Vihang Errunza, and Lemma Senbet. 1992. The pricing of country funds and their role in capital mobilization for emerging economies. Working Paper no. 1058. Debt and International Finance Division of the World Bank, December.

Errunza, Vihang, and Etienne Losq. 1985. International asset pricing under mild segmentation: Theory and tests. *Journal of Finance* 40 (March): 105–24.

Eun, Cheol, and S. Janakiramanan. 1986. A model of international asset pricing under mild segmentation: Theory and tests. *Journal of Finance* 41:897–914.

Fredman, Albert J., and George C. Scott. 1991. *Investing in closed-end funds: Finding value and building wealth.* New York: New York Institute of Finance, Simon and Schuster.

Harvey A. C. 1981. *Time series models.* Oxford: Phillip Allan.

Jorion, Philippe, and Eduardo Schwartz. 1986. Integration vs. segmentation in the Canadian stock market. *Journal of Finance* 41(3): 603–15.

Lee, Charles M. C., Andrei Shleifer, and Richard Thaler. 1991. Investor sentiment and the closed-end fund puzzle. *Journal of Finance* 46(1): 75–109.

Malkiel, Burton G. 1977. The valuation of closed-end investment company shares. *Journal of Finance* 32(3): 847–60.

———. 1990. *A random walk down Wall Street.* New York: Norton.

Newey, W., and K. West. 1987. A simple positive-definite heteroskedasticity and autocorrelation consistent covariance matrix. *Econometrica* 55:703–8.

Peavey, J. W. 1990. Returns on initial offerings of closed-end funds. *Review of Financial Studies* 3:695–708.

Pontiff, Jeffrey. 1991. Closed-end fund premia and returns: Implications for financial market equilibrium. William E. Simon Graduate School of Business Administration, University of Rochester. Manuscript.

Richards, R. Malcolm, Don R. Fraser, and John C. Groth. 1980. Winning strategies for closed-end funds. *Journal of Portfolio Management,* fall, 50–55.

Roenfelt, Rodney L., and Donald Tuttle. 1973. An examination of the discounts and premiums of closed-end investment companies. *Journal of Business Research* 1:129–40.

Roll, Richard. 1992. Industrial structure and the competitive behavior of international stock market indexes. *Journal of Finance* 47 (March): 3–41.

Rozeff, M. S. 1991. Closed-end fund discounts and premiums. In *Pacific Basin Capital Markets Research.* Vol. 2:503–22.

Sargent, Thomas J., and Christopher A. Sims. 1977. Business cycle modelling without pretending to have too much a-priori economic theory. In *New methods in business cycle research,* eds. C. Sims et al. Minneapolis: Federal Reserve Bank of Minneapolis.

Sharpe, William F., and Howard B. Sosin. 1975. Closed-end investment companies in the United States: Risk and return. In *European finance association 1974 proceedings,* ed. B. Jacquilat. Amsterdam: North Holland.

Shiller, Robert. 1984. Stock prices and social dynamics. *Brookings Papers on Economic Activity* 2:457–98.

Stock, James, and Mark Watson. 1988. Testing for common trends. *Journal of the American Statistical Association* 83 (404): 1097–1107.

Thompson, Rex. 1978. The information content of discounts and premiums on closed-end fund shares. *Journal of Financial Economics* 6:151–86.

Weiss, Kathleen. 1989. The post-offering price performance of closed-end funds. *Financial Management,* autumn, 57–67.

White, Halbert. 1980. A heteroskedasticity-consistent covariance matrix estimator and direct test for heteroskedasticity. *Econometrica* 48:817–38.

Zweig, Martin E. 1973. An investor expectations stock price predictive model using closed-end fund premiums. *Journal of Finance* 28:67–87.

Comment   Vihang Errunza

The paper investigates the behavior of country fund (CF) premium/discounts. After analyzing some basic empirical regularities, the authors test various hypotheses based on noise-trading literature. (See, for example, DeLong et al. 1990 and Lee, Shleifer, and Thaler 1991.) They conclude that the data are consistent with the models of investor sentiment.

In general, the topic is interesting and timely. On balance the empirical tests are conducted with care. To avoid duplication, I do not discuss the issues related to data (e.g., dividend/capital gains distributions), and insights regarding

Vihang Errunza is professor of finance and international business at McGill University.

discounts on closed-end funds covered by my codiscussant Rob Neal. I focus on the equilibrium determinants of country fund premium/discounts.

The authors seem to suggest that stationary discounts imply noise trading whereas nonstationarity implies market segmentation (section 8.4.4). I do not understand this line of reasoning since market segmentation is consistent with stationarity. Further, 40 to 60 percent of discounts (table 8.5) are nonstationary. Thus, one cannot dismiss the importance of market segmentation. In essence, given the results, a more complete understanding of premium/discounts should include explanations other than noise trading.

There are three approaches that provide insights regarding country fund premia. The traditional literature (e.g., Malkiel 1977 and Brauer 1984) suggests fees, illiquid stocks, and taxes as explanations of the discounts on U.S. closed-end funds. Similarly, as argued by the authors, noise-trading models suggest that systematic variations in (individual) investor sentiment would render CFs riskier and underpriced relative to fundamentals, thus leading to discounts on CFs. Of course, this requires that funds and underlying assets are not equally subject to the same variation in noise trader sentiment. Finally, equilibrium models of international asset pricing under barriers to capital flows (e.g., Stulz 1981 and Errunza and Losq 1989) suggest that unrestricted domestic securities will be priced by global risk, and that restricted foreign securities will be priced by global and national risks. Further, if foreign assets can be fully spanned by domestic assets, the national risk premium will disappear. The integrating impact of CFs leads to the conclusion that there will be no premium/discount on CFs. The models implicitly assume perfect cross-border arbitrage.

Thus, the available models deliver discounts or zero premium/discounts on CFs. The reality is, however, quite different. For example, some CFs have fluctuated between substantial premiums and discounts over time (e.g., Malaysia Fund), whereas others have traded consistently at high premiums (e.g., Korea Fund). Moreover, the authors report consistent premiums for the restricted sample (table 8.4). Thus an appropriate model must explain average premiums or discounts for a fund, it must explain the average premium/discount across funds at a given time, and it must explain time-series behavior of premium/discounts.

Diwan, Errunza, and Senbet (1993) develop a new equilibrium international asset pricing model (IAPM) that incorporates barriers to capital flows, imperfect substitution between the CF and its underlying assets, imperfect arbitrage, and investor sentiment. The model suggests that in equilibrium, the premium/discount will depend on the degree of access to the originating market, the degree of spanning of foreign assets within the host (U.S.) market, the degree of substitution between the fund and its underlying assets, and the common global country fund premia.[1] In empirical tests, the authors use the return on

---

1. The Errunza (1991) model, although it does not explicitly consider investor sentiment, delivers similar results.

the world market portfolio (R_w), Standard and Poor's 500, and Russell 2000 to capture commonality among funds, whereas Diwan, Errunza, and Senbet [1993] use the value-weighted average premium/discount on U.S.-traded country funds to proxy the common factor. The similarity between the authors' common factor (figure 8.3) and the value-weighted average premium/discounts on U.S.-traded country funds (reported as figure 3 in part I of Diwan, Errunza, and Senbet [1993]) is striking. Further, the time-series and cross-sectional test results of Diwan, Errunza, and Senbet (1993) are consistent with the predictions of the IAPM.

Finally, CFs from perfectly integrated markets (e.g., United Kingdom) should be priced similarly to U.S. closed-end funds. In other words, traditional factors and noise trading should explain their discount behavior. However, the available evidence suggests that most markets are not fully integrated. In a mildly segmented world market structure, the CF premiums/discounts will be determined by the factors suggested by IAPMs, traditional literature, and investor sentiment. In summary, the paper is very interesting but it could benefit from the theoretical insights of IAPMs.

References

Brauer, G. 1984. Open-ending closed-end funds. *Journal of Financial Economics* 13:491–508.

DeLong, J., A. Shleifer, L. Summers, and R. Waldmann. 1990. Noise trader risk in financial markets. *Journal of Political Economy* 98(4): 703–38.

Diwan, I., V. Errunza, and L. Senbet. 1993 Country funds: Theory and evidence. World Bank. Mimeo.

Errunza, V. 1991. Pricing of national index funds. *Review of Quantitative Finance and Accounting* 1(1): 91–100.

Errunza, V., and E. Losq. 1989. Capital flow controls, international asset pricing and investor's welfare: A multi-country framework. *Journal of Finance* 44:1025–37.

Lee, C., A. Shleifer, and R. Thaler. 1991. Investor sentiment and the closed-end fund puzzle. *Journal of Finance* 46(1): 75–109.

Malkiel, B. 1977. The valuation of closed-end investment company shares. *Journal of Finance* 32:847–59.

Stulz, R. 1981. On the effects of barriers to international investment. *Journal of Finance* 36:923–34.

Comment   Robert Neal

Closed-end country funds are interesting for two reasons. First, they provide a convenient channel for international funds to be invested in a specific country. This channel can be valuable to countries attempting to attract capital and to

Robert Neal is assistant professor of finance at the University of Washington.

investors attempting to reduce risk (Diwan, Errunza, and Senbet 1993). Second, closed-end funds are now the subject of spirited debate. A recent paper by Lee, Shleifer, and Thaler (1991) has prompted researchers to look outside the conventional model of investor behavior and consider whether investor sentiment can influence returns. Regardless of one's prior beliefs regarding the role of investor sentiment, we can all agree that careful analysis of new data helps our understanding of these issues. Herein lies the key contribution of the paper by Hardouvelis, La Porta, and Wizman. The paper seeks to explain the time-series behavior of country fund returns by using economic factors, as well as proxies for market sentiment. Their approach focuses on the forecast power of discounts and thus should be more convincing to a skeptical reader.

Overall, the paper makes a solid contribution to our understanding of country fund returns. Where the paper falls short, it is due to the large scope of the analysis. The paper provides a model of fund discounts, discusses the stylized facts of country funds, and seeks to resolve the country fund discount puzzle. Given this range of issues, the paper is remarkably thorough. My comments fall into four areas: the noise-trader model, the dividend adjustment process, the cross-correlations between price changes and net asset value changes, and the interpretation of the regression results. Most of my criticisms are already addressed in the paper but I still feel there is room for improvement.

Let me first focus on their model. The paper presents a model of noise-trader risk and country fund discounts. The model can be summarized in the following two relations:

1. $E(\text{Fund Return}_i) = a_i + b_i \text{Cov(sentiment innovations, wealth)} + c_i$ sentiment, and

2. $\text{Discount}_i = b_i\text{Cov(sentiment innovations, wealth)} + c_i$ sentiment.

In this notation, a_i is determined by the fundamentals of the fund. Since the fundamental return can be represented by the NAV return, subtracting the a_i from both sides of (1) will yield (2).

In this model, it is necessary to assume that investor sentiment is not perfectly forecastable, cannot be diversified away, and has a stronger effect on fund returns than the average stock. Given these assumptions, investor sentiment can affect fund returns. This holds even if the expected value of the sentiment is zero, as long as the covariance between sentiment innovations and wealth is nonzero. While this framework has an intuitive appeal, it is subject to several criticisms. First, it associates the entire discount movement to investor sentiment innovations. There is no role for nonsentiment factors such as those considered by Malkiel (1977), Brauer (1984), or by Bonser-Neal, Brauer, Neal, and Wheatley (1990). Second, it is possible that country fund sentiment is a proxy for some unspecified time varying risk premium. Neal and Wheatley (1993) show that this is unlikely for domestic funds, but do not extend the analysis to country funds. Third, if markets are segmented to some degree, it is not obvious that the a_i will drop out for country funds. Under segmentation, the valuation based on the fundamentals may differ for domestic and foreign investors.

A second issue is that the adjustment for dividends can be improved. The paper provides two ways to calculate the change in the premium.

$(R_{fund} - R_{nav}) = \ln[(\text{Fund Price}_t + \text{Dividend}_t)/\text{Fund Price}_{t-1}] - \ln[(NAV_t + \text{Dividend}_t)/NAV_{t-1}]$ and

$DISC_t = \ln(\text{Fund Price})_t /NAV_t.$

These two approaches will produce different values for the changes when pre-counts (or premiums) are large and the dividend payout is large. For example, suppose the price of a fund is $30, the NAV is $20, and the dividend is $5. Before the dividend, the fund has a 50 percent premium. Suppose that the premium is unaffected by the dividend, so the ex-dividend price is $22.50. This implies that the fund return will be negative while the NAV return is zero. Moreover, the adjustment process for large discount or premium funds should probably focus on the announcement date, and not the ex-date. As a practical matter, I doubt that these adjustments would have a large effect on their findings except, perhaps, for the Taiwan Fund, which traded at large premiums and paid large dividends.

A third issue is that some of their results may be influenced by the relatively large cross-correlations between a fund's price and the NAV. For example, in Bonser-Neal, Brauer, Neal, and Wheatley (1990), the average cross-correlation for country funds between the change in price at time t and the change in NAV at time $t - 1$ is .24. Similarly, the average between the change in price$_t$ and the change in NAV$_{t+1}$ is .29. If these cross-correlations result from nonsynchronous trading or delayed reporting, then the predictive power of discounts to explain subsequent fund returns may be overstated. I doubt that this would have much effect on the regressions in table 8.6 and tables 8.7 through 8.11, which are based on thirteen-week intervals. However, the cross-correlations certainly have the potential to influence the regressions based on one- and four-week intervals. A related point is that the regressions that are based on the four- and thirteen-week intervals use overlapping data. As Kim and Nelson (1990) have shown, the use of overlapping data can make the regression R^2 an unreliable measure.

The fourth issue is the author's interpretation of table 8.8A. This table contains the main regression result in the paper: fund returns are regressed against home country returns, the change in exchange rates, the Standard and Poor's 500 return, the world return, U.S. small firm returns, and the lagged discount. Similar regressions are presented using the NAV returns and the difference between fund returns and NAV returns. My interpretation of these regressions is that after controlling for fundamentals, there is evidence that discounts have forecast power, and this is consistent with the noise-trader model. Their interpretation is much stronger. In their view, each of these "fundamental" factors reflect innovations in investor sentiment, and significant t-statistics for these factors therefore provide additional support for their noise-trader model. As indicated above, however, if markets are segmented, then their conclusion may be unwarranted.

A related issue is that I found the regression in table 8.8B to be unconvincing. This regression is similar to that in table 8.8A, except that it allows for an asymmetric response to the independent variables. The motivation for this section is that Japanese investors, who supposedly drove up the price of country funds in 1989–90, faced a liquidity constraint when the Japanese market fell in 1990. Hence the performance of funds may differ between up and down markets. They find little evidence of a Japanese effect, but do report an asymmetric effect from the return to the world portfolio. They conclude that small investors overreact more strongly to negative news than to positive news. While this is an interesting result, the link to the existing theory is not obvious, and there is also the possibility that fund managers changed their portfolios in response to anticipated changes in the market.

Finally, it is possible that the forecast power of discounts may reflect common changes in the relative price of risk. If markets are segmented then discounts should be proportional to the ratio of the domestic price of risk to the foreign price of risk. Changes in the domestic price of risk will therefore affect all country fund discounts and could induce a common time-series variation in discounts. It would be interesting to include proxies for the domestic price of risk as another variable in table 8.8A regressions. Alternatively, for countries with multiple country funds (Germany, Taiwan, etc.), it would be interesting to see whether funds from the same country behave similarly.

In summary, this paper provides a comprehensive analysis of closed-end country funds. The paper provides many interesting results, including evidence that lagged discounts have predictive power for future fund returns. While the authors' interpret their results as offering strong support for the investor sentiment story, I suggest a more cautious interpretation. I am also concerned that noise-trader models can rationalize almost any behavior. However, I have yet to see a convincing model of discounts that is based on rationality. The least implausible model I have seen is the costly arbitrage model by Pontiff (1993).

References

Bonser-Neal, C., G. Brauer, R. Neal, and S. Wheatley. 1990. International investment restrictions and closed-end country fund prices. *Journal of Finance* 45:523–47.
Brauer, G. 1984. Open-ending closed-end funds. *Journal of Financial Economics* 13:491–507.
Diwan, I., V. Errunza, and L. Senbet. 1993. The pricing of country funds and their role in capital mobilization for emerging economies. Working paper, McGill University.
Lee, C., A. Shleifer, and R. Thaler. 1991. Investor sentiment and the closed-end fund puzzle. *Journal of Finance* 46:75–109.

Kim, M., and C. Nelson. 1990. Predictable stock returns: Reality or statistical illusion? Working paper, University of Washington.

Malkiel, B. 1977. The valuation of closed-end investment company shares. *Journal of Finance* 32:847–60.

Neal, R., and S. Wheatley. 1993. Closed-end fund discounts and the predictability of small firm returns. Working paper, University of Chicago.

Pontiff, J. 1993. Costly arbitage and closed-end fund discounts. Working paper, University of Washington.

Contributors

Geert Bekaert
Graduate School of Business
Stanford University
Stanford, CA 94305

John Y. Campbell
Department of Economics
Littauer Center
Harvard University
Cambridge, MA 02138

Stijn Claessens
World Bank
1818 H Street, NW
Washington, DC 20433

Michael Dooley
Department of Economics
University of California, Santa Cruz
Crown College, Room 226
Santa Cruz, CA 95064

Bernard Dumas
Department of Finance
HEC School of Management
78351 Jouy-en-Josas Cedex
France

Charles M. Engel
Department of Economics
University of Washington
Seattle, WA 98195

Vihang Errunza
Faculty of Management
McGill University
1001 Sherbrooke Street West
Montreal, Quebec H3A 1G5
Canada

Wayne Ferson
Department of Finance DJ-10
University of Washington
Seattle, WA 98195

Jeffrey A. Frankel
Department of Economics
549 Evans Hall #3880
University of California
Berkeley, CA 94720

Kenneth A. Froot
Graduate School of Business
Harvard University
Soldiers Field Road
Boston, MA 02163

Gikas Hardouvelis
Department of Finance
Rutgers University
Avenue D and Rockefeller Road
New Brunswick, NJ 08903

Campbell R. Harvey
Fuqua School of Business
Duke University
Durham, NC 27708

Takatoshi Ito
NBER
1050 Massachusetts Avenue
Cambridge, MA 02138

Philippe Jorion
Graduate School of Management
University of California
Irvine, CA 92717

Allan W. Kleidon
Cornerstone Research
1000 El Camino Real
Menlo Park, CA 94025

Rafael La Porta
Department of Economics
Harvard University
Cambridge, MA 02138

Bruce N. Lehmann
1415 Robinson Building Complex
Graduate School of International
    Relations and Pacific Studies
University of California at San Diego
La Jolla, CA 92093

Don Lessard
Sloan School of Management
MIT
50 Memorial Drive
Cambridge, MA 02142

Richard Levich
Stern School of Business
New York University
44 West 4th Street
New York, NY 10012

Wen-Ling Lin
Department of Economics
University of Wisconsin-Madison
1180 Observatory Drive
Madison, WI 53706

Richard K. Lyons
Haas School of Business
350 Barrows Hall
University of California, Berkeley
Berkeley, CA 94720

Robert Neal
University of Washington
School of Business
DJ-10
Seattle WA 98195

Moon-Whoan Rhee
Department of Finance
School of Business and Economics
Towson State University
Towson, MD 21204

G. William Schwert
Simon School of Business
University of Rochester
Rochester, NY 14627

René M. Stulz
College of Business
Ohio State University
1775 College Road
Columbus, OH 43210

Linda L. Tesar
Department of Economics
University of California
Santa Barbara, CA 93106

George M. von Furstenberg
Department of Economics
Indiana University
Bloomington, IN 47405

Ingrid M. Werner
Graduate School of Business
Stanford University
Stanford, CA 94305

Thierry A. Wizman
Strategic Investment Partners, Inc.
1001 19th St. N., 16th floor
Arlington, VA 22209

Author Index

Adler, Michael, 4n4, 6, 8, 25, 26, 63, 143, 216, 309n2
Ammer, John M., 350n6
Anderson, Seth Copeland, 350–51n7, 366n16
Ando, Albert, 83
Antoniewicz, Rochelle, 324
Auerbach, Alan J., 83

Backus, D. K., 24n3
Bailey, Warren, 234, 244, 248, 381n29
Bansal, R., 25, 63
Baring Securities, 223n5, 224n8, 225n10
Barro, R. J., 24n1
Basu, Sanjoy, 60, 62
Baxter, Marianne, 24n3, 174
Bekaert, Geert, 177, 178n1, 179, 181t, 183, 233, 234n3
Bhide, Amar, 304n1
Black, Fischer, 60, 234, 317, 324
Bodurtha, James N., 349n4
Bollerslev, T., 4, 157, 317, 326, 335
Bonser-Neal, Catherine, 16n22, 362n13, 400, 401
Boudreaux, Kenneth, 350
Brainard, William, 9n12
Brauer, Greggory A., 16n22, 348, 350, 362n13, 398, 400, 401
Brickley, J. A., 350–51n7
Buckberg, Elaine, 233

Cai, J., 182
Campbell, John Y., 15, 54, 154, 176, 177, 310, 318, 324, 331, 335

Canova, F., 24n3
Chan, K. C., 309n1, 326
Chan, Kalok, 309n1, 326
Chan, Louis K. C., 60, 62
Chen, Nai-Fu, 54
Choi, Frederick D. S., 226n12
Chopra, Navin, 349
Chou, Ray Y., 317
Chowdhry, Bhagwan, 326
Christie, Andrew A., 317, 324
Christopherson, Jon A., 61
Claessens, Stijn, 13n19, 235, 248n10
Clare, Andrew, 149n2
Cooper, I. A., 208
Craig, Andrew, 309n1
Crucini, M. J., 24n3
Cumby, R., 179

Dasgupta, Susmita, 235
DeLong, J. Bradford, 54, 309, 348, 351, 352, 394, 397
de Macedo, Jorge, 4n4
Demirguc-Kunt, Asli, 243n9
de Santis, Giorgio, 233
Divecha, Arjun, 233, 346n2
Diwan, Ishac, 233, 248n12, 346n2, 398, 399, 400
Domowitz, I., 335
Dornbusch, R., 4n4
Drach, Jaime, 233, 346n2
Dravid, A., 309n1
Dumas, Bernard, 4n4, 5, 6, 8, 10n14, 23,

Subject Index

Stock options: transactions tax in Sweden, 280–81; U.K. transaction tax on, 289

Stock prices: economic indicators to explain returns, 23–24; information in opening index, 319; leading indicators as forecast of returns, 44–48; returns related to, 5–6

STTs. *See* Securities transactions taxes (STTs)

Summers ketchup critique, 5–6

Taxation. *See* Derivatives tax; Equities tax; Money-market instruments tax; Option deltas tax; Revenues; Securities transactions taxes (STTs)

Timing: of New York and Tokyo stock exchanges, 15, 314–17, 319; of release of economic indicator information, 41; return spillovers in October 1987 Crash, 330–31; of trading in international markets, 339–40, 389, 392–93

Trading volume: cross-market correlation, 326, 328–29, 336–37; cross-market dependence, 317–19; lagged spillover from foreign markets, 312; relation to heterogeneity of beliefs, 342–43; relation to U.S. equity flows and turnover, 200–205; test for spillover, 312–13

Valuation ratios: country level, 61–62, 92, 93–94; cross-country differences, 140–41. *See also* Dividend-to-price ratios; Price-to-book value ratios; Price-to-earnings ratio